EAST ASIA
AT THE CENTER

EAST ASIA
AT THE CENTER

FOUR THOUSAND YEARS
OF ENGAGEMENT WITH THE WORLD

WARREN I. COHEN

COLUMBIA UNIVERSITY PRESS   NEW YORK

Columbia University Press

Publishers Since 1893

New York   Chichester, West Sussex

copyright © 2000 Columbia University Press

All rights reserved

Library of Congress Cataloging-in-Publication Data

Cohen, Warren I.

East Asia at the center : four thousand years of engagement with

the world / Warren I Cohen.

p. cm.

Includes bibliographical references and index.

ISBN 978-0-231-10108-0 (cloth)
ISBN 978-0-231-10109-7 (paper)

1. East Asia — Relations — Foreign countries. 2. Asia, Southeastern — Relations —
Foreign countries.   I. Title: Four thousand years of engagement with the world.

II. Title.

DS511 .C786 2000

303.4'8259 — dc21   00–031615

IN MEMORY OF DOAK BARNETT AND PAUL KREISBERG

friends who'll never read this

And

FOR NANCY

who must read them all—or so it is written in the Ketubah

CONTENTS

Maps   xi
Tables   xii
Preface   xiii
Acknowledgments   xvii

ONE

The Emergence of an International System in East Asia   1
   In the Beginning There Was China   1
   Other Rooms, Other Voices   17
   Empire of the Han, Challenge of the Xiongnu   19
   The Diffusion of Power   41
      China   41
      Korea   48
      Japan   51
      Southeast Asia   54
   Conclusion   59

TWO

Shadows Over Tang Splendor   62
   The Sui   62
   The Years of Tang Ascendance   66
   Korea, Japan, and Southeast Asia   82
   Conclusion   87

THREE

East Asia Uncentered   89
   Late Tang   90
   The Tibetan Factor   92
   The Demise of the Tang Dynasty   94
   Northeast Asia   97
   Southeast Asia   101
   The Song reunify China   106
   Koryo   114

Japan   118

Southeast Asia in Turmoil   121

Conclusion   126

FOUR

The Mongol Ascendancy   128

Chinggis Khan and his sons   128

Khubilai Khan and the Chinese   132

Asian Resistance to Khubilai as Universal Ruler   141

The last days of the Yuan   147

Conclusion   148

FIVE

The Resurgence of Chinese Power and the Coming of Islam   150

Rise of the Ming   150

Koreans, Japanese, and Ryukyu Islanders   166

Southeast Asia and the Spread of Islam   173

Ming China on the Eve of the Portuguese intrusion   179

Conclusion   181

SIX

Europe and Japan Disrupt the East Asian International Order   183

Arrival of the Portuguese   183

The Ming Under Siege   189

The Rise of Japanese Power   194

Other Europeans: The Arrival of the Dutch and
the English   200

Southeast Asia: Magnet for the West   204

Last Days of the Ming   211

Conclusion   213

SEVEN

The Great Qing Empire   216

Rebuilding of the "Chinese" empire   216

Japan and Korea   227

Southeast Asia in flux   232

The Approach of the British empire   239

Conclusion   243

EIGHT

Triumph of the West   245
    The British Are Coming   245
    The Yanks Are Coming   258
    France's Quest for Glory   265
    Russia as a Pacific Power   267
    And Then There Were the Dutch   268
    Conclusion   271

NINE

The Ascendance of Japan   273
    Restoration and Self-strengthening in China   273
    The Meiji Restoration   280
    Japan Ascendant   285
    The United States as an East Asian Power   291
    The Boxer War   295
    In the Light of the Rising Sun   299
    Conclusion   302

TEN

Challenge to the West   303
    Development of the Japanese Empire   304
    The Rise of Chinese Nationalism   310
    Nationalism Elsewhere in East Asia   318
    Washington and Moscow Look to East Asia   322
    Nationalist Revolution in China   328
    Crisis in Manchuria   334

ELEVEN

War and Decolonization, 1932–1949   338
    In the beginning It Was Manchuria   338
    China Imperiled   341
    War comes to Asia   344
    Japan's Greater East Asia Co-Prosperity Sphere   351
    The War Ends in East Asia   358
    Decolonization in Southeast Asia   362
    Conclusion   367

TWELVE

The Cold War in East Asia   370

   The Occupation of Japan   372

   Revolution in China   376

   War in Korea   383

   Southeast Asia and the Cold War   390

   China, Taiwan, and the United States   404

   Conclusion   413

THIRTEEN

The Resurgence of East Asian Economic Power   415

   Japan as # 1   415

   Little Dragons   424

   Southeast Asia   435

   China Joins the World Market Economy   441

   The Japan That Can Say No   444

   Conclusion   447

FOURTEEN

On the Eve of the 21st Century   449

   Disaster at Tiananmen   449

   Democracy Comes to Taiwan   454

   The Korean Peninsula: Democracy and Nuclear Weapons   459

   Red Star Over Hong Kong   465

   Crisis in Southeast Asia   468

   Conclusion   474

Closing Thoughts   477

   Notes   485

   Further Reading   495

   Index   503

MAPS

1. Ancient Civilizations, c. 1000 BCE   6

2. Warring States, c 225 BCE   14

3. Central Asia, c 100 BCE   23

4. Three Kingdoms: China c. 250 BCE   42

5. Three Kingdoms: Korea, c. 450 CE   49

6. Southeast Asia c. 450 CE   56

7. Tang Empire, c 750   80

8. Southeast Asia, c 900   104

9. China, c 975   109

10. China, c 1150   113

11, Mainland Southeast Asia, c 1150   124

12. Mongol Empire, c. 1280   138

13. Ming China and Asia, c 1400   156

14. Ming Empire and Voyages of Zheng He, c. 1450   162

15. Japan, Korea, Ryukyu Islands, c. 1450   172

16. Southeast Asia, c. 1450   176

17. East Asia, c. 1600   188

18. Pressures on Ming China: 16th Century   193

19. Dutch in East Asia, c. 1650   203

20. Qing Empire, c. 1800   224

21. Treaty Ports, c. 1842   254

22. Western Colonies in East Asia, c. 1880   270

23. Japanese Empire, c. 1931   336

24. Japan Dominates East Asia, c. 1943   354

25. Stages of Korean War, 1950–1953   388

26. Cold War in Asia, c. 1960   407

27. Taiwan, Taiwan Strait   458

TABLES

1.1. Some Notable Dates of the Ancient World: 3500–1000 BCE   1

1.2. Some Notable Dates of the Ancient World: 600–200 BCE   15

1.3. Some Major Figures of the Ancient World   30

1.4. Some Notable Dates of the Ancient World: 200 BCE–200 CE   34

1.5. Some Notable Dates of the Ancient World: 200–600 CE   47

2.1. Some Notable Dates of the Sui and Early Tang Years   71

2.2. Some Major Figures of the Seventh and Eighth Centuries   77

3.1. Some Notable Dates of the Ninth to Twelfth Centuries   90

3.2. Some Major Figures of the Ninth to Twelfth Centuries   121

4.1. Some Notable Dates of the 13th and 14th Centuries   131

4.2. Some Major Figures of the 13th and 14th Centuries   141

5.1. Some Notable Figures of the 15th Century   165

5.2. Some Notable Dates of the Late 14th and 15th Centuries   178

6.1. Some Major Figures of the 16th and 17th Centuries   197

6.2. Some Notable Dates of the 16th and 17th Centuries   209

7.1. Some Notable Figures of the Late 17th and 18th Centuries   226

7.2. Some Notable Dates of the Late 17th and 18th Centuries   241

8.1. Some Notable Events in the Years 1800–1866   257

8.2. Some Notable Figures of the Period 1800–1866   265

9.1. Some Notable Figures of the Years 1867–1905   285

9.2. Some Major Events in the Period 1867–1905   294

10.1. Some Major Figures of the Period 1915–1931   315

10.2. Some Notable Events of the Period 1905–1931   333

11.1. Some Notable Events of the Period 1932–1949   350

12.1. Some Notable Events of the Period 1947–1953   382

12.2. Some Notable Events of the Period 1954–1969   403

12.3. Some Notable Events of the Period 1972–1975   413

I was on my way to Kenya several years ago when a friend, the late Paul Kreisberg, urged me to read Philip Snow's *Star Raft*. Snow tells the tale of the Chinese eunuch Zheng He's extraordinary voyages early in the 15th century, many years before those of Vasco da Gama and Christopher Columbus. Crossing the Indian Ocean, Zheng He's fleet called at ports in East Africa, where, it appeared, the Chinese had been trading for centuries. On my own voyage, wandering north from Mombassa along the coast of Kenya, I came across the remains of a 13th century Swahili village where, to my astonishment, I found Chinese coins and shards of Chinese pottery recently uncovered by archeologists. As a historian of 20th century American foreign policy whose most daring previous feats had been forays into 18th and 19th century Chinese-American relations and the world of art historians, I realized it was time to broaden my education. With the encouragement of my editor, Kate Wittenberg, I decided to study the international relations of East Asia since they began. What follows is a taste of what I've learned, traveling through the history of that region.

Some readers may be as surprised as I was to find that Shang dynasty rulers, c. 1500 BCE, maintained a zoo containing exotic animals—a rhinoceros, for example— obtained from other parts of Asia. Most will be intrigued by evidence of the changes in "Chinese" identity, the changes in what it meant to be Chinese, as the original "Chinese" conquered or were conquered by their neighbors—and enlarged their gene pool.

I discovered that by the 7th century BCE, during the Zhou dynasty, the Chinese had already developed a sophisticated collective security system and that contacts between Han China and the West, seaborne as well as across the famed Silk Road, began approximately 2,000 years ago. Perhaps most striking for students of China will be the persistent record of Chinese imperialism, of Chinese efforts to expand and to dominate their neighbors whenever they had sufficient power—and sometimes when they didn't.

Contact with alien societies had a major impact on China. Lovers of Chinese food will learn that it was undistinguished before being seasoned by spices from India and, much later, the introduction of the chili pepper from the Americas. Indian influence on Chinese culture, especially art and religion, as well as cuisine, was enormous.

The cosmopolitan nature of Tang China was extraordinary: merchants from all over Eurasia and north Africa could be found in the major cities— Arabs, Christians, Jews, and Persians mixed with the local people. In later years, Armenians dominated the region's trade with the West.

Of course, China was never the whole story of events in East Asia. I was astonished to discover that Tibet had been a major power from the seventh through ninth centuries CE, frequently invading China and decimating Chinese armies. I had never realized how dependent Japan had been on Korea for its early development, how much of Japanese culture derived from Korea—or that Japanese military involvement on the Korean peninsula had occurred as early as the fourth century CE. I knew about the Mongol conquest of China, but not that Khubilai Khan's mother was a Christian.

Americans and Europeans are familiar with the narrative of Western imperialism in Asia. They are less likely to know that Egyptian and Ottoman Turkish fleets came to the defense of their Muslim brethren, helping them to fight the Portuguese in India and the Dutch in Sumatra. They probably will be less surprised to learn that wherever the Muslims and Christians gained control of societies in Southeast Asia, the status of women was diminished. The key role played by the Americas in the early years of contact between Europe and Asia was to supply the silver, shipped on galleons from Acapulco to Manila, that fueled the worldwide economic expansion of the late 16th century. The story of the U.S. involvement in East Asia has been the subject of most of my previous work, but I was not aware that the U.S.S. Constitution had shelled the city of Danang in Vietnam in 1846. I knew of American sympathy for the Korean victims of Japanese imperialism: I did not know that a Korean Youth Army School had been established in Nebraska in 1909. I suspect every reader will discover something new and interesting in the pages that follow.

I am not so arrogant as to believe that I have mastered the history of all the countries of East Asia and their relations with each other and the rest of the world since the beginning of time. Specialists on every country of the region and every period I have covered doubtless will be appalled at the brevity of my treatment of issues on which they have written countless monographs. Some will be troubled by the lack of detail in a landscape painted with so broad a brush, by my apparent lack of appreciation of the subtle distinctions they have portrayed so painstakingly. To them, I apologize. I can only thank them for those monographs without which my task would have been impossible. I trust they will find my work useful in their teaching.

The reader should be warned that many of the issues I discuss are the focus of debates among historians. I refer to some of these in my notes. Usually, however, I choose my course without burdening the narrative with reference to possible alternatives. Several of my previous writings have been historiographic. This book is not. Much as I would like specialists to read it, on this occasion they are not my primary audience.

My wife, Nancy Bernkopf Tucker, and my friend, Akira Iriye, insist that I also owe specialists an explanation for my idiosyncratic conceptualizations and methodology. Most scholars referring to "East Asia," a relatively recent construct, limit themselves to the countries of the northeast, to China, Japan, and Korea. Southeast Asia, for no compelling reason, is perceived as a separate entity. I am aware that parts of Southeast Asia are linked more closely to the Indian subcontinent than to China and the northeast generally, but some—most obviously Vietnam—are not. As I studied events in the region, I concluded that the separation created more problems than it solved, that important parts of the story involve relations between north and south. And so, stretching myself geographically as well as chronologically, I chose to conceive of East Asia most broadly, to include the south.

Less easily justified is my central conceit that contemporary modes of analyzing international relations cast light on the interactions of ancient political entities. Having begun my study of world affairs with Hans Kohn and Karl Deutsch more than forty years ago, I am not unaware of the range of theories of nationalism or of the fact that scholars consider the nation-state to be of modern origin. I am deliberately applying the vocabulary of modern world affairs to relations among the peoples of early Asia as a means of rendering the past less exotic. I realize that some of my colleagues may object, but I believe the understanding gained outweighs the theoretical precision lost. Mankind's means of communication, items of trade, and weapons of choice have changed radically over the centuries, but few would deny that the quest for wealth and power is universal chronologically as well as spatially. I chose to underline that reality by using language familiar to students of contemporary affairs.

Finally, although Iriye has taught me much about the importance of cultural relations and of non-state actors in international relations, I must concede that I have written primarily about states. To the extent that I have transcended this limitation—and readers will find frequent reference to cultural relations—it is doubtless because I knew he would be looking over my shoulder.

I hope readers will share my delight in discovering the extensive involvement of the peoples of East Asia in world affairs even before the beginning of recorded history. For some of them contact with the outside world has been constant for at least 4,000 years. For most of that time, their civilization and the sophistication of their management of foreign affairs surpassed that of the strangers who came in quest of their treasures. More recently, for a few hundred years, some fell victim to the superior discipline and technology of others, but the twentieth century has marked the recovery of their independence and their standing in the world community. Today, China and Japan claim a place among the world's great powers. Many other states of East Asia experienced extraordinary growth late in the twentieth century, only to be set back by the financial crisis that swept the region in the late 1990s. Until then, the twenty-first century had promised to be Asia's century. It may yet be.

Warren I. Cohen
June 2000

ACKNOWLEDGMENTS

The late Paul Kreisberg, scholar and diplomat, insisted—as he was wont to do—that I read *Star Raft*. I enjoyed the book and the thoughts it inspired, most obviously those resulting in this volume. Most sensible people suspected I was out of my mind to undertake the project. Paul Cohen and Carol Gluck were willing to indulge me, as was Kate Wittenberg. Mary Brown Bullock, then director of the Asia Program at the Woodrow Wilson Center, encouraged me constantly. So did the late A. Doak Barnett.

Getting other scholars to contribute the time and effort to read the manuscript, or parts thereof, proved astonishingly difficult. No one considered himself or herself competent to judge it in its entirety, perhaps an indication that we have become overspecialized. I was fortunate, however, to get some help. Nancy Bernkopf Tucker, my wife, took occasional leave from her scholarly and policy-related activities to read my chapters and demand improvements. My colleague at the University of Maryland, Baltimore County, Ka-Che Yip, also read and commented gently on the entire manuscript. Akira Iriye, exposed by his idiosyncratic criticism despite the anonymity of a reader's report to the press, was helpful as always. He has taught me a great deal—although not nearly as much as he'd hoped—in the years we've worked together. Another friend, Alan Karras, provided extensive suggestions as to how I might make this book useful to teachers of world history. Two anonymous readers provided aid and comfort. One of these, obviously a specialist on early Chinese and Central Asian history caught errors in the first six chapters of the book. The other, a student of Southeast Asia, relieved my anxiety about what I had written about the area of his or her expertise. Finally, I am indebted to Jim Millward who, as he eagerly awaited the arrival of his latest offspring, found time to savage my first seven chapters. He will not accept any complaints about the last seven.

My remaining expression of gratitude must be to the University of Maryland, Baltimore County (UMBC), the institution that has provided the time and research support essential for this and all my other projects since 1993. Despite its awkward name, UMBC has attracted superb scholars, students, and administrators and I am delighted to be a part of it.

Warren I. Cohen
March 2000

EAST ASIA
AT THE CENTER

ONE

The Emergence of an International System
in East Asia

In the Beginning There Was China

The origin of the state in East Asia remains shrouded in the mists of pre-history, but archeologists continue to find bits and pieces, potsherds, tex-tiles, and bones, promising that someday we will be able to explain this and other ancient mysteries, to penetrate the fog of the distant past. For now we must be content to estimate that in the course of several thousand years before the so-called Christian Era, somewhere around 2000 BCE, people liv-ing in what is now east central China did create something akin to a state. Mesopotamia, Egypt, and South Asia had developed urban civilizations earlier, probably hundreds of years earlier. The Chinese state appears to have evolved independently, although before very long, perhaps three thousand or so years ago, contact with peoples far to the west is evidenced by the import of a variant bronze technology, the so-called "lost wax" method of casting. Recent discoveries in western China of the burial sites of Caucasians dating from around 1200 BCE suggest the possibility of other cross-cultural influences early in the history of the Chinese people.[1]

TABLE I.I. Some Notable Dates of the Ancient World: 3500–1000 BCE
(Dates are approximate. Events in bold face are referred to in text)

First year of Jewish calendar	3760 BCE
Sumarian civilization in Mesopotamia (modern Iraq)	3500 BCE
Pyramids and Sphinx built at Giza, Egypt	2700–2500 BCE
Indus Valley civilization in India	2500–1500 BCE
Xia Dynasty in north China	2000–1450 BCE
Hammurabi of Babylon provides first legal system	1792–1750 BCE
Peak power of Nubian kingdom of Kush (Sudan)	1700–1500 BCE
Shang Dynasty in north China	1450–1122 BCE
Moses leads Israelites out of Egypt	1225–1200 BCE
Destruction of Troy	1184 BCE

Zhou Dynasty in north China	1122–221 BCE
David becomes king of all Israel	1000 BCE

Perhaps most striking to the modern reader, however, is the relative speed with which an international system developed in East Asia, foreshadowing much of what is known of the practice of international relations. Theoretical works written by Chinese more than two thousand years ago are still studied today in military academies in the United States as well as China. Critical concerns that have challenged policymakers throughout the ages—the role of morality in foreign policy, the balance of power, questions of when to use force and when to appease, and of appropriate military strategy when force is the option chosen—were debated by Chinese analysts throughout much of the Zhou Dynasty (c.1122–221 BCE). *Realpolitik* and *Machtpolitik* as concepts of international politics may evoke images of amoral Germanic statesmen, of Otto von Bismarck and Henry Kissinger, but the Chinese were practicing—and criticizing—them while Central Europe was still populated with neolithic scavengers.

The path to an understanding of the emergent international system leads through more than a thousand years of Chinese history. From archeological evidence we know something of the material culture, even the religious practices of the ancient peoples of Central Asia, Japan, Korea, and Southeast Asia, but the earliest indications of statecraft are to be found in China. The Chinese call these formative years, 2000–221 BCE, the *Sandai* or Three Dynasties (Xia, Shang, Zhou) era. For most of these years there are at least traces of records of the contacts between the Chinese and their neighbors, including the nomadic peoples of Inner Asia and especially the relations of the first "Chinese" to those ultimately absorbed into the Chinese state. It should never be forgotten that the early Chinese did not expand into empty space, but rather by force into territories already occupied by peoples of similar race and language. Like all the world's empires, the Chinese Empire was based on conquest, the subjugation of militarily inferior peoples whom the Chinese portrayed as subhuman to justify their own conduct.

Archeologists and students of ancient Chinese history, examining objects such as pottery, stone tools, bronze, and oracle bone inscriptions,[2] have concluded that several similar but discrete neolithic cultures, including the Xia, Shang and Zhou, existed simultaneously in north China in the second millennium BCE. The Xia were the first to organize a political entity that might be called a state. Leaders of that entity had a conception of boundaries and distinguished between those who accepted their rule and the "others." Members of the Xia state identified themselves as the Hua-Xia (flowers of summer) and disdained those who did not, who were different, whether living among them or outside the borders of their state. With creation of the state came the conception of the defense of its people and its boundaries, necessitating military power.[3]

The Xia had external relations with culturally similar people such as those who lived under Shang and Zhou rule. They also encountered dissimilar peoples, some speakers of Indo-European languages to their west, some of nomadic stock. These contacts were often warlike, involving the expansion and contraction of Xia influence, sometimes peaceful, such as the exchange of goods, intermarriage, and diplomacy. But at the dawn of the twenty-first century, despite extraordinary archeological work by scholars of the People's Republic of China, we still know little about the details.

In mid-fifteenth century BCE, with the defeat of the Xia by their eastern neighbors, the Shang, the record improves. The recent recovery of thousands of Shang oracle bones provides precious insights into foreign relations, as well as into the Shang view of the world in which they lived. It is apparent, for example, that during the nearly five centuries in which they dominated north China, Shang rulers perceived of a world order in which their territory was at the center, ringed by subordinate states.

By the time of the emergence of the Shang state, the people of north China had evolved a settled agrarian style of life in which most lived clustered around a local leader. Inscriptions on oracle bones and bronzes indicate that they had developed a written language, recognizable to modern scholars as Chinese. A highly sophisticated indigenous art, most notably painted pottery and bronzes, had emerged from local neolithic cultures. Shang bronzes, cast by a unique piece mold method, were the most complex technologically that the ancient world had ever seen, far surpassing bronze age works of contemporary Mesopotamia—and incomparably imaginative.

The state was a monarchy imposed on a shifting federation of autonomous groups whose loyalty depended on the leadership ability of the king—or shared lineage with him. The king was central and the composition of the state varied in accordance with his ability to attract and hold allies. The state was also a theocracy, in which the king was the main diviner. One historian, David Keightley, has described Shang China as a "politico-religious force field" whose authority fluctuated over areas and time.[4] At the head of both the political and religious orders stood the king.

In brief, more than 3,000 years ago, just as Cretan civilization was spreading across the Aegean to Greece, a people were creating the institutions of a state in China, defining themselves and their borders, and attributing differences to, "objectifying," those who were not members of their state. Those who lived beyond the frontier were understood to be culturally different, "barbarians." The state was perceived as encompassing all of the civilized world and its king proclaimed supremacy over all of that world *and* exclusive access to the supreme divinity. Here was the foundation of the later Chinese conception of the relationship between the emperor and the ruler of the heavens.

Groups drawn into the Shang state, such as the Zhou who eventually destroyed the Shang dynasty, accepted the king's claim to universal dominion. As subjects are wont to do, some offered tribute, sending gifts to their ruler. Conceivably this practice evolved into the elaborate tributary system of a later time. Such gifts had symbolic value, attesting to the monarch's overlordship—and may have had economic value as well. Some peoples to the east and south were absorbed through cultural expansion, mixing with the Shang until they were indistinguishable. Others, who resisted assimilation into Chinese civilization, tended to move beyond the frontiers, or opposed Shang rule by force. Oracle bone inscriptions offer evidence of extensive military campaigns, but also suggest that diplomacy and intermarriage were frequent instruments of external relations. Defense of the state was the king's responsibility in the most literal way: he was expected to lead his followers and his allies into battle.

Archeologists have also found evidence of trade between the area controlled by the Shang and other peoples to the south, both coastal and interior. The clay used by potters, the copper and tin used in making bronze implements, the cowrie shells that may have been a form of currency, gold and precious jewels found in ornaments, were all imported. The art historian Sherman Lee has determined that a Shang bronze currently at the Asian Art Museum in San Francisco was modeled after an Indian rhinoceros, supporting reports that the Shang maintained a royal zoo containing exotic animals obtained from other regions of Asia.[5]

The emergence of the Shang state and the exercise of its power forced people on the periphery to organize for their defense. Oracle bones record frequent border skirmishes with the Qing to the west and several major battles with a people called the Guifang, probably nomads to the north. But when the Shang dynasty fell, the attack came from within, from the Zhou, who were members of the Shang state, but sufficiently marginal to constitute a separate core of power by the eleventh century BCE. Less sophisticated than the Shang in civilized refinements, the Zhou expanded aggressively alongside the Shang, formed important alliances with political entities surrounding the Shang, and defeated them in battle at mid-century, approximately 150 years after Achilles and Agamemnon sacked Troy. Building on Shang accomplishments, the Zhou dynasty ruled China, at least nominally, for the next 800 years. Population estimates are necessarily crude, but it is likely that the Xia controlled lands in which the people numbered in the hundreds of thousands, that millions came under Shang dominion, and that by the end of the Zhou dynasty in 221 BCE, China's population was in the vicinity of fifty to sixty million.

Students of ancient China consider the early or Western Zhou dynasty to be the wellspring of Chinese civilization. Notions of the central kingdom and the universal state had appeared perhaps as early as the Xia era, and certainly under the Shang; but they were articulated most explicitly by the Zhou, who claimed that China was the *only* state, that its authority extended to all under heaven. Certainly they were aware of others beyond their rule, but such independent status was deemed temporary. Central to the universe was the Zhou state whose management was supervised by heaven. The Zhou developed the concept of the mandate of heaven, of a contractual arrangement between the ruler and the heavenly power, allowing the king to rule only so long as he served the people well. They did so to legitimize their rule, to explain why they had seized power from the Shang.

The Zhou had long been a Shang tributary. They succeeded in overthrowing their powerful overlords by winning allies among groups all around the periphery of the state. Once in control, they adopted Shang material and political culture, winning Shang collaboration as well. The Zhou organized a central bureaucratic administration and maintained a royal army to cope with unrest at home or major barbarian raids on the frontier. On the periphery, relatives and allies of the king were awarded control of local people, becoming feudal lords. Their dominion was over

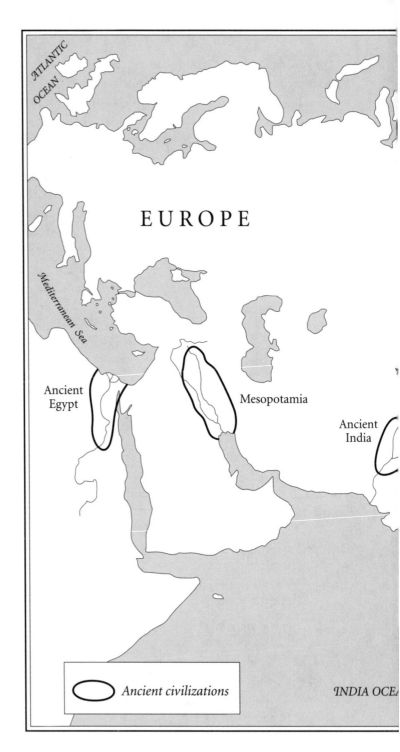

MAP I.   ANCIENT CIVILIZATIONS, C. 1000 BCE
(After Fairbank and Reischauer, *East Asia: The Great Transformation*, pp. 10–11).

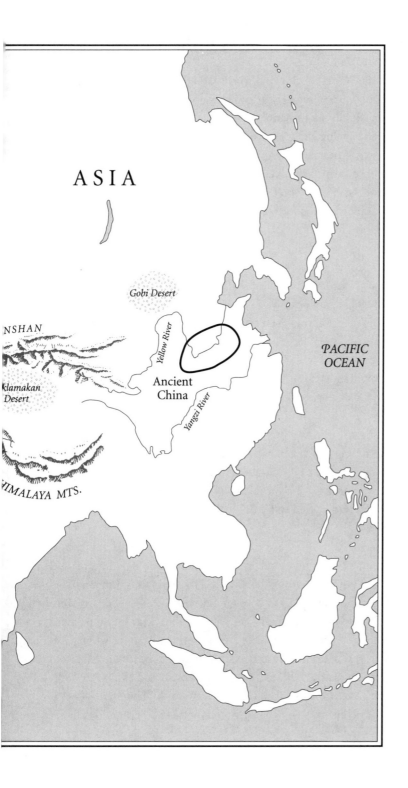

a specific population rather than a territory and they were frequently sent with their people into new areas as military colonists. Initially weak, the feudal lords gradually increased their power at the expense of the center, ultimately reducing the Zhou king to but nominal suzerainty.

The Zhou were markedly aggressive and expanded the area of Chinese civilization enormously. Neighboring peoples were conquered and assimilated into the central kingdom. A newly conquered territory would quickly be occupied by a garrison that likely composed the entire populace; led by a Zhou feudal lord, an entire feudal realm moved and became a military colony, overwhelming but not obliterating the local culture, absorbing local collaborators into the political elite. Whether the means of expansion was military or diplomatic, achieved by force or intermarriage, barbarians had the option of assimilation. The success of pacification in the border lands was linked to cultural fusion, to Zhou willingness to accept and integrate local culture and elites rather than impose the Shang-Zhou hybrid found at the center.

After approximately three hundred years of extending its power, the Zhou dynasty overreached itself. As it pressed eastward toward the coastal regions, unassimilated Rong barbarians rose in the west, feudal lords embellished their own powers rather than support the king, and both capital and king fell to the barbarians in 770 BCE. The surviving heir to the throne fled east to a new capital in the vicinity of modern Luoyang and the dynasty survived for more than five additional centuries. Real power, however, had passed to feudal realms that became de facto independent states.

Clearly, the early or Western Zhou, like the Shang and Xia before them, had been deeply involved in foreign affairs. They fought and formed alliances with foreign peoples, seized foreign lands, intermarried with foreigners, and learned from foreign cultures. Indo-Europeans were among the tribute bearers at the Zhou court c. 1000 BCE. Many of these foreigners were absorbed into China, becoming Chinese, but they also had an impact on what it meant to be Chinese. As Chinese rule extended over other peoples, as the Chinese had contact with and assimilated foreigners, China's culture as well as Chinese geography changed.

By the eighth century BCE, other incipient states had come into being on territory claimed by the Zhou—and on its borders. In the later or Eastern Zhou period (c. 770–221), a multistate system began to develop in the region. The first three hundred years are known to the Chinese as the Spring and Autumn period, followed by the age known, for reasons that quickly become obvious, as that of the Warring States.

As Zhou power ebbed, the relative peace the Chinese and their neighbors had enjoyed since the overthrow of the Shang disappeared, remaining but a glorified memory to men and women made desperate by avaricious rulers and increasing disorder. To Chinese intellectuals like the great Confucius (c. 551–479), the days of the early Zhou were a golden age somehow to be recaptured.

Deprived of their base of power in the west, the Zhou kings became dependent upon feudal lords, remaining rulers in name only. Regional leaders arrogated power to themselves and governed their own fiefdoms. The pattern was similar to feudalism as it later developed in Europe. The master of each locality organized the territory he controlled as though it were a state entirely separate from all others. But by the eighth century BCE the tradition of a unified China was firmly rooted and most, certainly the more powerful of the king's erstwhile vassals, aspired to establish a new dynasty in place of the Zhou. More than five hundred years passed before the leader of the Qin state succeeded. Throughout the Spring and Autumn period—and for long afterward—no state was strong enough to conquer all others. No ruler dared claim the mandate of heaven.

At the outset of the Spring and Autumn era, the struggles were primarily diplomatic. Diplomacy was an art much studied and much written about. Military encounters were governed by elaborate rules of chivalry. They required gamesmanship rather than warfare. Concerning themselves little with the lot of the common people, lords great and small maneuvered among themselves, jousting for advantage. Alliances were made and unmade as several states demonstrated might sufficient to disrupt the existing order without any state being able to dominate the empire. But by the fifth century warfare had intensified, diplomacy had fallen by the wayside, and demagogues were appealing for popular support in their need for infantry.

Central to the political disequilibrium of the period was the rapid rise of the state of Chu, the major power in the Yangzi River valley. In less than three centuries Chu conquered and absorbed *forty-two* other states. Considered semi-barbarian by Chinese of the central plain, the expansion of Chu culture was, according to the Chinese historian Li Xueqin, a major event of Eastern Zhou times, changing the ethnic mix of those considered Chinese.[6] Chu efforts to unite all of China were stopped only late in the seventh century by a coalition of northern states led by Jin. Confronted by a stalemate, the northern states agreed to accept Chu into the structure of Chinese states, but Chu persisted in its attacks and attempts to absorb the territory of its neighbors.

One response to Chu aggressiveness is particularly fascinating: the creation by the Chinese of the institution of the "Hegemon" to direct their embryonic international system. In 681 BCE a conference was convened by Duke Huan of Qi, a leading state in the northeast, out of which came the first recorded collective security arrangement, joining all of the eastern and central states. The obligations mutually undertaken were sanctified by the authority of the Zhou king. A few years later Duke Huan was named hegemon, or director of collective security for the member states. The system survived him and relative peace lasted approximately 200 years, but the league was never as central to the international system after his death. Leadership shifted from Qi to Jin and then the institution disappeared at the onset of the Warring States period toward the end of the fifth century.

Another interesting phenomenon of the Spring and Autumn era was the rise of a class of intellectuals, political theorists who aspired to be advisers on national security to the various feudal lords. Guan Zhong, architect of the Hegemon system, was one of the most successful. Confucius, who never attained the post he sought, is doubtless the best remembered of the breed. His contemporary, Sun Wu (Sun Zi), the military strategist from the state of Qi, continues to be studied in military academies all over the world.

Confucius came to manhood as the existing order was disintegrating. He was eager to find the ear of a powerful ruler, to advise him on how to reestablish order with justice in his own state and in all of the civilized world. He was persuaded that the Zhou had devised an international system that had functioned satisfactorily, assuring the wellbeing of the people. Much of his teaching was designed to restore that order. Peace and security were his highest priorities. To achieve peace and security, no subterfuge was denied to diplomatists. Repelled by the warfare around him, Confucius nonetheless accepted the idea that force might be necessary to punish unruly or disloyal feudal lords or barbarians who stirred trouble within the state or on its frontiers. For him, as for national security intellectuals over the next two thousand years or so, the ends justified the means.

Sun's guide to military strategy, *Sun Zi's Art of War (Sun Zi Bing Fa)*,[7] was written about 500 BCE. Although it often has been perceived as a text on how to gain victory without going to war, the political scientist Iain Johnston has argued persuasively that Sun always assumed the centrality of military power in achieving state security; that his stratagems were designed to gain a position of overwhelming superiority before attacking.[8] Like Confucius, Sun opposed the aggressive use of force for expansionist purposes—he feared the drain on the resources of the state—but he had little use for diplomacy or static defense. He did not consider virtuous conduct a high priority in warfare. The wise leader, with absolute flexibility as to means, first maneuvered as necessary to ensure victory, and then went to war. Confucian discomfort with violence as an instrument of state power may have dominated Chinese rhetoric, but Sun's approach prevailed in practice.

Before the Spring and Autumn period exploded into that of the Warring States, Chinese contacts with non-Chinese peoples—beyond the Chu, Qin, and Yue who pressed on their periphery—increased. Horse nomadism had appeared by the eighth century, if not before, and the Chinese began to trade for horses. Collisions and trade with the Xiongnu, fierce Turkic-speaking nomads of the north and west, began in the lifetime of Confucius. The Xiongnu craved Chinese grain, wine, and silks. The Chinese wanted horses. When both sides were satisfied with the terms of trade, they exchanged goods in peace. When either side was dissatisfied, conflict ensued. The pattern continued for centuries.

These contacts with nomadic cultures beyond the pale affected Chinese culture in many different ways. Chinese art was influenced by an animal style that originated in Siberia and probably reached China via the Xiongnu or other Inner Asian peoples. The "lost-wax" technique of bronze casting, inferior to Shang technology, came to China from the West. Glass beads came from Egypt. The historian H. G. Creel has noted that Chinese silk was one of the principal commodities in the foreign trade of the Roman Empire.[9] Clearly the universe in which the Chinese functioned was expanding beyond their earlier conceptions. The need to reinvent their place in the world was increasing, but from early in the fifth century to late in the second, the Chinese were too busy fighting each other. The Zhou peace had collapsed completely.

Historians estimate that during the Spring and Autumn era, 170 distinct political entities existed in China. Only seven of these survived to the advent of the Warring States period—seven large states that owed their size and presumably their wealth and power to the absorption of the smaller states around them. These states were all "Chinese," although some doubtless had "barbarian" antecedents. Their people spoke and wrote mutually intelligible languages and shared most elements of Chinese culture. But they considered themselves to be independent states and preserved their separateness with military fortifications and customs restrictions. Each had its own army, led by professional generals. Each had professional diplomats, trained in the art of intrigue, making and breaking alliances. Together they controlled virtually all of north China.

The political order that existed throughout the years of nominal rule by the Eastern Zhou was a multistate system that grew increasingly apparent as Zhou power evaporated. Treaties were signed and violated, embassies and hostages were exchanged, and a nascent system of international law came into existence. But the idea of a universal kingdom, that there could be only one ruler under heaven, persisted nonetheless. As the larger states devoured the smaller, their lords dared to call themselves kings and each imagined himself the man who would reunify China, the founder of a new dynasty. Gradually Qin, the most westerly of the states, a people with probable Rong barbarian roots, emerged as the most powerful. In 256 BCE Qin destroyed the remnants of Zhou rule and the other states were faced with the likelihood of destruction unless they united in opposition to Qin aggression. For thirty-odd years they rarely stood together, usually appeased and cooperated with Qin, until one after another they were conquered. Qin succeeded in reunifying China in 221 BCE under the rule of the man who called himself *Qinshi Huangdi*, the Qin Emperor.

As Qin moved toward dominating China, the Xiongnu began to press on the frontier of several Chinese states. Reserving the bulk of their infantry to fight among themselves, the Chinese attempted to contain Xiongnu expansion by building walls to keep them out. These were the walls later connected by Qinshi Huangdi as the first Great Wall of China, a boundary drawn between China and the nomads. But as yet the Xiongnu were an unorganized force, more of a nuisance than a threat to the security of any of the Chinese contenders for hegemony.

Throughout the incessant warfare of the age, the common people suffered terribly. They fought and died, had their land overrun, their crops robbed, their families ravaged. It was a cruel world in which brute force and cunning prevailed over virtue and decency. Sun Wu would not have been surprised. It was the kind of world Thomas Hobbes envisioned when he wrote *The Leviathan* many centuries later. Then and ever after, confronted with such conditions, some people have found solace in other-worldliness, seeing the will of Heaven at work. Others ought more temporal explanations for human suffering, and still others devised plans and arguments for reducing human misery.

Confucius had longed to restore a golden age of peace that he imagined his world had once enjoyed under the Zhou. For three centuries after his death, conditions deteriorated and the search for peace, for order, became more urgent. Two themes gained centrality in the writings of Chinese intellectuals during the Warring States era and variations on these themes have dominated the discourse of analysts of international relations for thousands of years afterward. One argument, for which the classic exponent was Mozi (c.480–390), a contemporary of Socrates, focused on the need for a balance of power to protect small and weak states against potential aggressors. The other, expounded by Mencius (c.371–289), a contemporary of Aristotle, and perhaps even earlier by Laozi (c. 6th century BCE), was universalist, seeking a unified world state, specifically the unification of the known world under one Chinese government.[10]

Mozi perceived the universe as pluralistic and accepted the multistate system of his time. His objective was to protect the weaker states by preserving the system. Part of his approach, unsuccessful when he used it—and forever after—was to argue the disutility of aggression. He insisted that the victors as well as the vanquished paid too high a price in warfare. The cost of war, even when won, was enormous in terms of human suffering and the impact on the economies of the states involved. War was not only disruptive of the world order; it also had destructive effects on those who chose to wage it. These were not arguments likely to appeal to the men who dreamt of unifying the entire world under their rule—or even to lesser men who saw an opportunity to seize a piece of land, whether to increase their wealth, their power, or their security.

Mozi also had advice for the rulers of smaller states on how to survive in a hostile, anarchic world. He concentrated on developing defensive schemes and emerged as a military strategist as well as a philosopher and political theorist. But all his brilliance was to no avail as the warring states warred on until only the Qin survived.

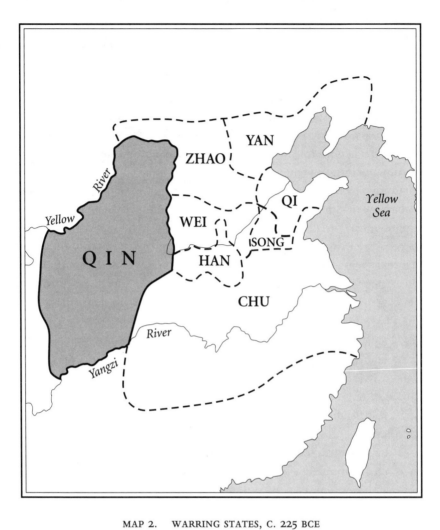

MAP 2.   WARRING STATES, C. 225 BCE

After Twitchett and Loewe, *Cambridge History of China I: Ch'in and Han Empires,* p. 390

Laozi and Mencius sought respite in universal kingship. A good king would bring small states under his benign protection. Attracted by his kindness and his righteousness, weak states would flock to him. Mencius rejected the concept of a balance of power as it was known in the days when Duke Huan served as Hegemon. Competing alliances would inevitably provoke war. China—the world—needed a virtuous king to unify the known world and bring peace.

Other Chinese intellectuals in the declining days of the Eastern Zhou debated whether moral influence would suffice or power would dictate the outcome of world affairs. If one argued that the world was a murderous place in which force determined outcomes, another argued that aggression bred retaliation and that only moral force could bring peace. Clearly they anticipated the concerns of modern international relations theorists. But also resonant with readers today would be the work of another breed of ancient Chinese analysts whose sole concern was the enhancement of state power. Shang Yang (4th century BCE), the great Lord Shang, devised strategies for acquiring the wealth and power necessary to achieve control in the anarchic Chinese world. It was his advice that ultimately led to Qin hegemony in the third century BCE.

TABLE I.2. Some Notable Dates of the Ancient World: 600–200 BCE
(Dates are approximate. Events in boldface are referred to in text)

Mayan civilization in Mexico	600 BCE
Cyrus the Great founds Persian empire	538 BCE
Parthenon in Athens consecrated	438 BCE
Peloponnesian Wars	431–404 BCE
Choson kingdoms in north Korea	**400–108 BCE**
Alexander the Great invades India	327 BCE
Kingdom of Parthia founded	
(in modern Iran and Afghanistan)	249 BCE
China unified under Qinshi Huangdi	**221 BCE**
Hannibal crosses the Alps	218 BCE
Rise of the Xiongnu led by Modun	**209 BCE**
Han Empire in China	**206 BCE–220 CE**

The Qin had been viewed with contempt by the Chinese states of the central plain because of their suspect ethnicity. Living on the western frontier of Chinese civilization, among the Rong barbarians, they had developed a distinct culture. But as Qin troops marched through the rest of China, they adopted many of the ways of the conquered people, becoming more "Chinese" at the same time that their political dominance of China changed what it meant to be Chinese.

Qin success is usually attributed to the reforms of Shang Yang, especially those which weakened hereditary landholders and increased the power and efficiency of the central government. Shang's ideas had been rejected by the ruler of his native state, but the Qin had a reputation for receptivity to outside talent and he won a place for himself as adviser to the Qin ruler. The Qin state also had a geographic advantage over the plains states, based as it was on the rocky prominences of modern Shaanxi and Sichuan. It was simply easier to sweep down from the hills across the plain than it was to fight one's way up into the centers of Qin strength.

The Qin conquest was complete in 221 BCE and all of the Chinese culture area, all of the states that had viewed themselves as Chinese, were unified. The Qin king now ruled the entire Chinese world, the entire "civilized" world. To reign over "all," however, it was not enough to be a king (wang). Assigned the task of finding a grander title, advisers to the Qin ruler pronounced him First August Emperor, Qinshi Huangdi. The emperor then proceeded to eliminate feudalism, replacing the feudal system of the Eastern Zhou, not unlike that which later evolved in medieval Europe, with a centralized bureaucracy that governed through commanderies established over the length and breadth of the land.

Qinshi Huangdi and his principal advisers conceived of the sociopolitical order as all-embracing, controlling all activity. They standardized weights and measures, coinage, script—and attempted to standardize thought. Dissident thought and argument was prohibited. Books other than those approved by the emperor were burned. Dissenters were executed. The Qin people would be as one.

But Qinshi Huangdi was not content to rule over all of China. He was aware that there were other peoples beyond the frontiers and he pressed northward against the Xiongnu and even more aggressively to the south. Qin China seized parts of modern Inner Mongolia and Gansu to the north, most of Guangdong and Guangxi, and part of Fujian to the south. In addition to placing military outposts in these outlying regions, colonists were sent, often involuntarily. The Yue people, related to the Vietnamese, were driven further south, resisting assimilation every step of the way.

In 209, only a year after the First August Emperor's death, the great Maodun rose to organize a powerful Xiongnu confederation. Once united the Xiongnu not only resisted assimilation into China, but also constituted a major threat to China's security—a threat that waxed and waned for centuries, until nomadic horsemen overran China.

Pressed by the Xiongnu to the north, resisted fiercely in the south by the Yue, the Qin empire survived its first ruler by only a few years. Weakened by excessive military expansion, the regime could not suppress internal rebellions and fell to rebels in 206 BCE. Out of the rebel forces emerged the founder of the Han Dynasty.

There are two points about China's place in the world to be noted at the end of the third century BCE. First, the affairs of the Chinese people had ceased to be a model for international relations theory. China now existed as a single state and external affairs, whether war, diplomacy, trade, or cultural interaction, meant contact with alien cultures—to be found in Korea, Japan, Southeast Asia, India, Central Asia, and along the Mediterranean, as well as among the nomads of the north. Second, a large, centrally controlled and militarily effective China now loomed as one of the great powers of the ancient world, along with Rome, India, and the Parthians who dominated Inner Asia. For the peoples of East Asia, and for travelers from afar, China was the force to be reckoned with, the state to which tribute would be paid or against which resistance had to be organized. The power of Han China dictated the international system of the region.

Other Rooms, Other Voices

Elsewhere in East Asia people had roamed for thousands of years before the Christian Era. Although most lived happily ignorant of the existence of the Chinese Empire, Koreans, like the Vietnamese to the south, felt the pressure of the eastward Chinese drive. They were among the "barbarians" the Chinese colonized, especially during the era of the Warring States. The state of Yen, with its capital near modern Beijing, pushed into southern Manchuria driving the indigenous people before it. In the third century BCE, as Qin crushed its rivals, Chinese crossed the Yalu and set up the state of Choson as a haven for refugees. When the Qin collapsed toward the end of the century, still more Chinese fled to the Korean peninsula. Similarly the rise of the Xiongnu pushed the Koreans southward and eastward. As with billiard balls, those bumped down the peninsula bumped those who preceded them, some of whom crossed over to the Japanese isles.

By the fourth century BCE the Koreans had access to bronze weapons, some from China, some from Inner Asia, but their level of political organization remained the stone age village. The Korean historian Ki-baik Lee suggests that several such villages, or "walled-town states" had combined to form a "confederated kingdom."[11] Their material culture indicated Siberian as well as Chinese influence. Bronze casting, for example, was marked by use of Scythian-Siberian rather than Chinese technology. Similarly Korean combware, the earliest known pottery on the peninsula, appears to derive from Siberian styles, probably via Mongolia. Not until the Yen invasion c. 300 BCE were the Koreans subjected to the overwhelming force of Chinese culture. Again like the Vietnamese, however, they resisted assimilation, maintaining a continuous sense of themselves as not Chinese.

Of Japan in the years of the Zhou and the Qin, little is known. The earliest identifiable culture, the Jomon, produced a unique art with no evidence of continental influence. On the other hand, rice and the knowledge with which to construct an agricultural economy seems to have come across the East China Sea as early as the fifth century BCE. About two hundred years later, a more complex Yayoi culture emerged—with much stronger mainland influence. The earliest stimulus to change came from immigrants driven off the continent by the advancing Chinese empire. These were followed by Koreans who crossed the Tsushima Strait to Kyushu, fleeing pressures generated by the Chinese, but bringing with them elements of Chinese culture as well as their own. These migrations, too, were an important part of the international relations of East Asia on the eve of the Han Empire. Leading to the formation of Yayoi "kingdoms" in Japan, bringing an awareness of China, they set the stage for diplomatic relations between Japan and China.

Southeast Asia in pre-Han days arguably included much of China south of the Yangzi where many of the people were more closely related to the Thai and Vietnamese than to the Chinese. They resisted Chinese encroachment, resisted assimilation, and sometimes fled. By the end of the third century BCE, Chinese troops occupied much of the coastline.

Although island Southeast Asia lacked coherent settlement in pre-Han days, some of the peoples of the mainland had entered the bronze age and developed agricultural economies several hundred years before—certainly by the fifth century BCE. The region in the vicinity of the modern Thai-Cambodian border appears to have been the most highly developed politically. The bronze Dong-san drums found in much of mainland Southeast Asia probably originated in Yunnan or Vietnam and owed nothing to Chinese techniques, which they almost certainly antedated. Their dispersion through the region is evidence of trade mechanisms and routes that had been developed before the Han—patterns for which China was irrelevant, although Malay sailors were frequenting coastal China by the third century.

Those parts of Southeast Asia contiguous with China could not resist its influence, and were continuously forced to react to Chinese pressures. At its steadily expanding borders, China behaved as any imperialist power would: exploiting weaker people and seizing their territory. Island Southeast Asia, however, was beyond the ken of Chinese leaders and few Chinese traveled to the farther reaches of the mainland. Trade was not yet an important means of cross cultural contact as the first Han emperor ascended to the throne in 206 BCE. In brief, Southeast Asians experienced the Chinese as aggressors or, more likely, not at all.

Empire of the Han, Challenge of the Xiongnu

Bereft of the forceful leadership of the First Emperor, the Qin teetered under the pressure of rebellion—the inevitable result of imperial overreach and the oppression and exploitation of their people. As Qinshi Huangdi lay in an enormous tomb near modern Xi'an, accompanied by thousands of terra-cotta warriors, the empire collapsed, ceasing to exist by the end of the year 206 BCE. Soon the unity achieved by the Qin was threatened by the reemergence on Chinese soil of multiple kingdoms, perhaps as many as twenty, several with antecedents in the Warring States era. After several years of battling among these, the two most successful "kings" agreed to divide the country between them. One of them,

Liu Bang, a man of peasant origins, in due course violated the agreement and succeeded in destroying his rival. Undisputed as master of China, in 202 he took the title of emperor. Having previously declared himself King of Han, he became Han Gaodi, founder of the Han empire.

The Han empire might fairly be said to comprise two dynasties, the Former Han (206 BCE–9 CE) and the Later Han 25–220, divided by the reign of Wang Mang, long written off by Chinese scholars as a usurper. The fifth emperor, who took the dynastic name of Han Wudi, ruled a united China for more than fifty years, from 141–87 BCE. Wudi was one of the greatest imperialists of all time, building an empire larger than that of Rome at its mightiest. Under his leadership an aggressive China struck out in all directions, ultimately seizing control of parts of Korea, Mongolia, and Vietnam—and much of Central Asia. China was manifestly the regional hegemon, a position of dominance the Chinese came to see as their birthright.

At the outset, however, the brilliant future of the Han was by no means assured. Han Gaodi's empire was relatively weak. He was fortunate to prevent the breakup of China into the loose confederacy espoused by his rivals and to reaffirm the principle of a single imperial entity. But even after he prevailed in the civil strife that followed the collapse of the Qin, the territorial integrity of China was threatened. To the north the Xiongnu had united under the leadership of Maodun and Gaodi's regime lacked the strength to defend its people against nomadic raids. To the south, in modern Fujian, Guangdong, and Guangxi, areas claimed by the Qin rejected Gaodi's rule. He was forced to acknowledge the independence of the king of Donghai in Fujian. The man who controlled Guangdong and Guangxi proclaimed the kingdom of Nanyue and Gaodi lacked the resources to stop him. External enemies would have to be appeased. Separatism on the periphery required at least temporary acquiescence. The first task was to consolidate power in China's heartland—and that took about sixty years.

Qinshi Huangdi had been relatively successful in containing the nomadic Xiongnu. But led by Maodun, who came to power just before the collapse of the Qin, the Xiongnu succeeded in penetrating and circumventing the "Great Wall." Given the military technology of the day, Chinese troops were no match for the speed and maneuverability of Maodun's cavalry. Xiongnu raids for grain and cloth, badly needed products of sedentary Chinese society, were incessant.

Han Gaodi, having demonstrated his prowess on the battlefield against all other challengers following the collapse of the Qin, decided to attack the Xiongnu and put an end to their depredations. The results were disastrous, very nearly costing him his life. Complicating efforts by the Han to cope with the Xiongnu threat was the uncertain loyalty of Han border forces. Ambitious generals occasionally defected to the Xiongnu, choosing a share of the spoils over possible defeat and death at the hands of the Xiongnu or their own vindictive superiors. There was little sense of being Han Chinese, of the need to defend the motherland against the foreign invader. A military solution to the problem was beyond reach.

Initially, appeasement of the Xiongnu was the only option available. The Xiongnu state was offered recognition as an equal. Concession after concession was granted, allowing the nomads increasingly favorable access to Chinese goods until it became clear that China was a de facto tributary of the Xiongnu. Gifts of food, wine, and silk in increasing quantities were sent to Maodun and finally a woman of the Han imperial family, designated a princess, was given to him in marriage. All of these gestures won Maodun's agreement not to invade Han territory, but he and his heirs frequently demanded more. In 177 BCE the Xiongnu launched a major invasion. Peace was purchased by opening border markets, but proved no more lasting than before. There were annual raids, and major attacks in 166 and 160, all of which indicated the failure of the Chinese to meet the expectations of the militant horsemen. Traditionally, Chinese historians have blamed the constant friction on nomad greed. The anthropologist Thomas Barfield has argued that Xiongnu leaders depended on the distribution of Chinese goods to hold the support of their followers. He contended that they established a "deliberately predatory policy" and cultivated a "particularly violent reputation" to maximize their bargaining position with Han China.[12] Others, more sympathetic to the Xiongnu, have criticized Chinese efforts to cheat and manipulate their less sophisticated neighbors, insisting that when the nomads were allowed to obtain the commodities they needed, peace was possible.[13]

Han Wudi ascended to the throne in 141 BCE at a time of relative equilibrium in Han-Xiongnu relations. Chinese defenses had held since approximately 160. By mid-century all of the major independent Chinese kingdoms had been eliminated and their populations brought under control of central government commanderies, adding to the security of the borders. Initially, Wudi maintained the appeasement policy of his predecessors which, backed by growing Chinese power, had achieved stability on the frontier. Among his advisers, however, a disinclination to continue paying tribute to the Xiongnu was emerging: the price of peace was too high. Perceiving that the balance of power was tilting in China's favor, the emperor decided to take the offensive.

One problem of which Han strategists were very much aware was the extent of Xiongnu dominance of Central Asia, of the area the Chinese called the Western Regions. Control of the caravan routes carrying goods to Southwest Asia and of the oasis states along the way gave the Xiongnu access to valuable resources, human and materiel. In 139 BCE, Zhang Qian set out from the court on a journey to the Far West to seek alliances for the Han, to attempt to win away supporters vital to the Xiongnu and to find a source of desperately needed war horses. His efforts failed. Captured along the way by the Xiongnu, he spent ten years as their prisoner, but upon his eventual return to China he provided Wudi with valuable intelligence. Zhang undertook a second mission to the West in 115. On the basis of the information he provided about trade opportunities and the potential for finding allies among the states of the Western Regions, Wudi concluded that China's destiny lay in westward expansion. The deployment of Han troops to the northwest and the colonization of areas in the vicinity of modern Dunhuang—where remnants of ancient walls and forts still stand—was critical to the success of the campaign against the Xiongnu and evidence of Wudi's ambitions.

The operations against the Xiongnu began in 134 BCE with a trap designed to capture their leader. The trap failed and was followed by a series of battles costly to both sides. In 129, fullscale war began. Gradually Wudi's forces drove the Xiongnu out of their grazing areas in China's Yellow River heartland toward a region north of the Gobi Desert. For the next fifty years, the Han and the Xiongnu struggled for control of the West, for the wealth of the caravan routes and the support of the oasis city-states. The Han military expeditions advanced further and further to the West, reaching Sogdiana and Ferghana, in the vicinity of modern Uzbekistan and Tajikistan, making contact with the Persian empire.

What gifts of silk and gold and marriageable princesses did not accomplish was achieved by the conquest of Ferghana in 101 BCE. When Ferghana rejected Chinese demands for horses, the emperor and his advisers recognized that the credibility of the empire was at stake and committed the resources necessary for a military victory—which came

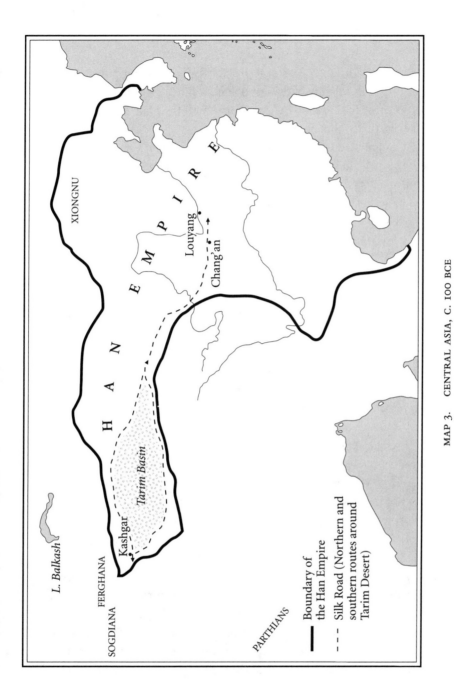

MAP 3.   CENTRAL ASIA, C. 100 BCE

After Fairbank and Reischauer, *East Asia*, p. 100.

despite the extraordinary logistical problems of projecting power so far from the heartland. Many of the lesser states of the region benefited from the demonstration and chose to pay homage to the Han. Xiongnu influence was virtually eliminated.

The Xiongnu had fallen on hard times as a result of the successful challenge by Han Wudi. They lost control of cultivated land as well as grazing land. Subject peoples, sensing Xiongnu decline, perhaps assuming Chinese support, revolted. Sources of revenue were lost as was access to iron weapons. Tensions among the Xiongnu, submerged by the charismatic Maodun, less successfully by subsequent leaders, surfaced anew in the face of adversity. By 70 BCE rivalry between two brothers divided the Xiongnu into two separate kingdoms, one in Inner Mongolia and one in Outer Mongolia. The kingdom in Inner Mongolia soon became an ally of the Han, a relationship which survived to the end of the Former Han dynasty.

The decline of the Xiongnu was demonstrated dramatically in 51 BCE when Hu-han-yeh, the leader of Inner Mongolia, appeared at the Han court to pay homage to the emperor. His son remained at the court as a hostage to his good behavior. In return, the Chinese protected him from his brother and other enemies and sent provisions of food and silk for his people. Hu-han-yeh requested a Han princess in marriage but settled for a lady-in-waiting. She and her offspring are believed to have helped the Xiongnu court continue its pro-Han policies for the remainder of the century. A Han-Xiongnu military alliance was signed c. 43 BCE with the Xiongnu of Inner Mongolia serving as China's first line of defense against their northern brethren. Throughout the last years of the Former Han, the Xiongnu of Outer Mongolia chose not to challenge Chinese power.

The relationship between the Han and their Xiongnu allies served the security ends of both regimes. For the Xiongnu, access to Chinese goods was of enormous importance, compensation for their role as mercenaries of the empire and the nominal homage they paid to the Han emperor. The nomads were not interested in becoming Chinese nor did the Han press sinicization upon them. Nonetheless, at the principal points of contact, some nomads accepted elements of Chinese culture—and some Chinese became more like the Xiongnu. The most useful paradigm is probably that of the "Middle Ground," developed by Richard White in his study of early contacts between the Indians of North American and European traders.[14] On the frontiers a culture emerged that was neither Chinese nor Xiongnu, but a melding of both, evidence of mutual accommodation.

It was during these years that the Chinese developed practices for managing foreign affairs traditionally referred to as the tributary system, a system of enormous *political* importance to Chinese ruling elites and of great *economic* importance to those regimes that accepted tributary status. Under the system, non-Chinese—"barbarian"—states accepted a nominally subordinate place in the Chinese imperial order. They demonstrated this subordination by sending missions to the Chinese court and paying homage to the Chinese ruler to whom they presented acceptable gifts. Usually they left hostages, presumably members of their ruling families. In return they received gifts from the emperor, often more valuable than those they had submitted, and opportunities for private trade.

Obviously, the greater the Chinese need for the submission of the tributary state-the greater its potential threat to Chinese security or importance as an ally-the greater the value of the goods sent back with the tribute mission. The system appears to have been expensive for the Chinese, but the symbolic submission of the barbarian state was more palatable politically than outright appeasement and less problematic than endless warfare on the periphery. To the barbarians, ritual submission was a price they grudgingly paid in exchange for Chinese bribes and access to trade. Yu Ying-shih, the leading authority on Han foreign relations, argues that the tribute system was a net loss to China at the state level, although individual Chinese profited.[15]

The various states of the Western Regions, of Central Asia, were drawn into the tribute system as part of the Han crusade against the Xiongnu. But in the course of sending troops westward, Chinese officials and entrepreneurs recognized the magnificent commercial potential of links to the area. They found some Chinese goods already available and a great hunger for more. The Han conquest of Ferghana brought a flurry of envoys from the west bearing tribute for the emperor in 101 BCE, but the states of the Western Region remained wary of Xiongnu retribution until Hu-han-yeh, too, paid homage to the Han emperor. After 53 BCE the system was greatly strengthened and remained effective until the end of the Former Han.

The trade dividend derived from Han expansion to the west brought the Chinese into contact with India, Parthia, and Rome. Chinese silks reached Rome via India and over the Silk Road from the Han capital at Chang'an across the Tarim Basin through Samarkand to Iran, Iraq, and Syria, the eastern reaches of the Roman Empire. Most of the Chinese products that reached Egypt and other Mediterranean countries passed through Parthian and Indian middlemen. The bulk of the products of the Roman Empire and the Western Regions found in Han China were luxury goods, used by the court to enhance its prestige, but of little consequence for its subject people.

The Han ruling class was well aware that a world existed beyond the control of the Chinese empire; that the emperor did not rule all under heaven. The emperors and their advisers understood that some neighbors could be subjugated and absorbed, that the character of the relationship to others would depend upon the extent of Chinese power at a given moment, and that still others would remain distant, touching China rarely, perhaps only indirectly. To enhance the legitimacy of the dynasty, all peoples might be declared part of the tributary order, but little was expected of those outside the reach of Chinese power. The critical areas were those recently conquered, presumably pacified, and those in the hands of peoples only nominally friendly, whose allegiance to China depended on the local power balance. Toward these areas the Han looked anxiously, eager to see tribute missions testifying to their loyalty, ever fearful of desertion. They knew that the sinocentric regional order they desired depended on variables over which they had limited influence and they recognized the existence of peoples who might fail to appreciate the superiority of Chinese culture and Chinese rule. And they did not hesitate to use military power whenever they met resistance.[16]

The Koreans and China's southern neighbors benefited but temporarily from Han preoccupation with the Xiongnu. As Han power grew in the reign of Wudi, China's outward thrust could not be contained. Large parts of Korea, modern southeast and southwest China, and Vietnam fell under the occupation of Han troops.

Although Chinese influence in Korea was longstanding, dating back hundreds, perhaps thousands, of years, the Koreans had maintained a separate identity. In the Warring States era and again during the last years of the Qin, Chinese emigrated to the Yalu region to escape the tribulations of warfare at home. Early in the second century BCE, after a failed revolt against the Han, more Chinese fled to Korea, to the vicinity of the ancient kingdom of Choson at P'yongyang. In 195 BCE they seized control of the kingdom and established their leader Wei Man (Wiman) as king. For nearly seventy years Choson remained on the periphery of Han concerns, dominating most of the rest of Korea and brokering contact with China.

By 128 BCE, Wudi would tolerate Korean independence no longer, but a Han offensive was thrown back by the Koreans. Over the next two decades, as the Xiongnu threat subsided, the Chinese brought more and more pressure to bear, finally overcoming—but not ending—Korean resistance by 109 BCE. On Korean territory the Chinese established four commanderies or occupation districts, one of which was abandoned in 81 BCE as an economy measure, two of which eventually surrendered in the face of Korean resistance and the growing power of the Korean kingdom of Koguryo. The fourth, Luolang, located in the northwest, around modern P'yongyang, lasted until 313 CE when the Chinese were finally driven out by Koguryo forces.

Luolang functioned as a Chinese enclave in Korea, in which the Chinese lived the good life imperialists have enjoyed throughout history while exploiting indigenous peoples. It became a center of high Chinese culture, little of which seems to have affected the native population. The extraordinary quality of objects, particularly lacquers, found in Luolang era tombs indicates just how splendidly Chinese officials, merchants, and scholars managed their expatriate existence. Luxury items imported from Sichuan and from parts of the Roman Empire have been found in Luolang. It is perhaps not surprising that some wealthy Chinese, seeking to live the good Chinese life away from the tax collectors of the central government, chose to retire there. And before the colony reverted to Korean control, it became a staging post between Japan and Han China, foreshadowing a role Korea would play through much of its subsequent history.[17]

While one set of Han armies was marching into Korea, others moved south-toward the east coast and modern Guangdong and Hainan Island, into Guangxi and Vietnam, southwest into Yunnan, toward India. China's motives for the attacks varied, as the rationalizations for imperialism often do. Nanyue was invaded and the city of Guangzhou seized in 111 BCE in response to the murder of a Chinese-born queen. Doubtless some other provocation would have been found in due course. Nine commanderies were established to maintain order in the south—although efforts to subdue Fujian were abandoned because of the difficult terrain and fierce local resistance. Elsewhere in the south Han advances were limited by tropical diseases, Southeast Asia's best protection against Chinese aggression. Forays into Yunnan appear to have been driven by economic interests, by the quest for a passage that would permit direct trade with India, cutting out the tenacious Parthian middlemen who dominated the southern and southwestern trade routes out of Central Asia. In most of the south, as in Korea, the local people resisted assimilation-although they could not be unaffected by various aspects of Chinese culture, ranging from Confucianism to the iron technology that provided the Han with a military advantage over its neighbors.

The cost of Han imperialism was enormous and, perhaps inevitably, a debate emerged among the emperor's advisers and public intellectuals that will seem only too familiar to modern readers. Was the empire expending too much of its resources on military and foreign affairs? Could it afford further expansion? Was an aggressive foreign policy in China's interests? Who was benefiting from Chinese imperialism at whose expense? These kinds of issues, disagreements over the proper distribution of social and economic resources, are perennials, but Wudi's policies spawned not only critics but also the world's first recorded public debate on foreign policy, the *Yantie lun* or Salt and Iron debate of 81 BCE, a few years after the end of his reign.[18]

The salt and iron monopolies were the most important sources of revenue for the Han government. The state, unfriendly to private enterprise, to nongovernmental repositories of wealth and power—which thrived nonetheless—controlled these two industries and used their huge proceeds to maintain its armed forces, initially for frontier defense but ultimately to underwrite expansion. The foreign policy debate of the last century BCE focused on the use of those funds and included a challenge to the state monopoly. Opposition to government policy came primarily from Confucian scholars who were profoundly troubled by the constant resort to force in foreign affairs and by what they perceived as the misuse of state funds, the senseless loss of life among the Chinese people, and the waste of labor. In the traditional Confucian-Mencian discourse, the would-be reformers argued that if the emperor and his ministers were more virtuous, military means would not be necessary to win the submission of the Xiongnu or other barbarians. Military expansion, they contended, had weakened China rather than assuring its security. They were troubled by the accumulation of great wealth by those who profited from foreign trade and the ostentatious displays of luxury by the newly rich and by the court. Distinguishing between the court and the state, these critics contended that expansion and the import of barbarian goods served the interests of a privileged few and not the interests of the Chinese people. They were critical of what they perceived as extravagant entertainments at the capital, designed to impress foreigners.

The Han government rejected these claims and charges. Han administrators demonized the Xiongnu, insisting they were not responsive to virtue, but only to overwhelming military power. Frontier defense required a large and aggressive army which, in turn, required the revenues of the salt and iron industries. Border posts and expeditions to protect caravans merely facilitated the movement of local products, ultimately enriching the entire empire, benefiting all of the Chinese people. With a few minor concessions, such as the termination of peripheral commanderies, one in Korea in 82 BCE and the one on Hainan island in 46 BCE, the government prevailed. Discontent with government policy persisted, however, and the continuing debate over foreign policy was reflected even in Han tomb decoration.[19] Retrenchment from the expansiveness of Han Wudi proved necessary as the cost of empire began to exceed the capacity of the government to maintain it, even before Wudi's death.

On the other hand, with the submission of the southern Xiongnu in 51 BCE, the Chinese enjoyed unprecedented peace on their northern border. For much of the century the country enjoyed an economic boom, as promised by the government. One historian refers to an "explosive" development of commerce as an upwardly mobile population clamored for consumer goods, especially luxury objects that provided material evidence of success.[20] Explosive trade, wealthy merchants, and what Thorstein Veblen 2,000 years later would label "conspicuous consumption" added up to a Confucian scholar's nightmare.

Han administrators also found that foreign adventures once embarked upon were not so simple to terminate. Moreover, the men who thought they were determining policy in the capital had not anticipated the extent to which their gallant generals might expend lives and treasure on the frontier, involving the empire in affairs in which it had little if any interest. Critics insisted that the government stop rewarding army officers for winning battles in distant lands, seizing unwanted territory, and increasing China's commitments, but the state of communications limited the court's control of its advancing forces. And if an alliance was signed, how could the Han refrain from honoring it simply because its minor ally provoked a scrape in which China had no stake? What would happen to China's credibility with other, more valuable allies if it failed to honor its commitment? If China sent a princess to wed a foreign leader, to demonstrate the sincerity of its friendship, could it stand by idly if she were endangered? The contentious city states of the Western Region provided a constant series of headaches for Chinese policymakers.

TABLE 1.3.　Some Major Figures of the Ancient World
(Dates are often approximate. Names in boldface are discussed in text))

Hammurabi of Babylon	1810–1750 BCE
Tutankahamen of Egypt	1400–1352 BCE
Cyrus the Great of Persia	585–529 BCE
Buddha (Siddhartha Gautama)	563–483 BCE
Confucius	**551–479** BCE
Pericles of Athens	495–429 BCE
Mozi	**470–391** BCE
Socrates	469–399 BCE
Plato	428–348 BCE
Aristotle	384–322 BCE
Mencius	**371–289** BCE
Alexander the Great of Macedon	356–323 BCE
Asoka of India	265–238 BCE
Qingshi Huangdi	**260–210** BCE
Hannibal of Carthage	247–183 BCE
Judah Maccabee	190–162 BCE
Han Wudi	**170–87** BCE
Julius Caesar	102–44 BCE
Jesus of Nazareth	6 BCE–30 CE
Caligula	12–41 CE
Marcus Aurielius	121–180 CE
Cao Cao	**180–230** CE
St. Augustine	354–430 CE
Attila the Hun	406–453 CE

The remaining years of the Former Han dynasty were marked by consolidation and retrenchment, a defensive rather than an offensive posture. Mounting opposition to the costs of empire, complaints about maldistribution of wealth, and the absence of any plausible threat after the submission of the southern Xiongnu undermined the expansionists. The central government attempted to rein in its more adventurous military officers, refusing them rewards and rejecting opportunities to engage potential enemies. Occasional battles could not be avoided, but it was clear that the court accepted these challenges reluctantly. Overtures for new alliances, as from Sogdiana in Central Asia, were rejected, and relations with Kashmir terminated. Instead of costly and logistically problematic expeditions into increasingly more distant lands, China moved toward the establishment of colonies along its new and extended frontiers. One product of the attempt to reconcile political and economic policy was the development of agricultural garrisons which could provide for frontier defense and feed themselves. Remains of some of these are still visible today in China's Far West.

Increasing Chinese diffidence in Central Asia was indicated by the decision not to seize the opportunity provided by the defeat of a major adversary in 36 BCE. A Xiongnu leader had aligned his forces with those of Sogdiana and together they were trying to dominate the region, interfering with Han operations there, murdering Han diplomats who sought to negotiate with them. Leading a force of primarily local, non-Chinese troops, a young Han officer attacked and defeated the Xiongnu-Sogdian raiders, killing their leader. Han Wudi would have lavished rewards on his officers and exploited the occasion to strengthen his outposts in Central Asia. His successors were more than content to be rid of the irritant, unwilling to capitalize on the achievement. Fearful of encouraging other would-be heroes, the emperor's men had scant praise and few gifts for the victor.

Another indicator of the changed climate of opinion among Han policymakers was their ambivalent response to provocations by Yunnanese locals who resisted assimilation. Although troops were sent from time to time in an effort to keep open trade routes to India, the court was divided. Again the issue was whether it was appropriate to spend Chinese treasure and Chinese lives in a region so remote from the Han heartland. Were the interests served worth the cost? Increasingly, as Han officials and intellectuals imagined the borders of their society, they were disinclined to include lands to the west that had been forced to submit to the empire by Wudi's armies.

In the last years of the Former Han, one powerful leader, Wang Mang, persisted in the vision of a greater Chinese empire. Wang, nephew of the empress dowager Wang Zhengjun, was named regent—a post held previously by several of his uncles—in 8 BCE. The emperor Chengdi (r. 33–7 BCE), Zhengjun's son, was weak and uninterested in governing. The Wang family filled the vacancy. Forced out of office by a new emperor in 7 BCE, Wang returned in 2 BCE. In the midst of a succession crisis a few years later, he assumed the title of acting emperor. In 9 CE he brushed aside the Han and proclaimed himself emperor of a new dynasty over which he reigned for fifteen years until his defeat and death in 23 CE opened the way for a Han restoration, the years of the Later Han. Although Wang is dismissed by most Chinese historians as an inept and murderous usurper, at least one modern historian has argued persuasively that Wang demonstrated "impressive mastery" of foreign affairs.[21] It was the flooding of the Yellow River that undermined his efforts at home, leading to peasant rebellion and his ignominious end.

As the Western world entered the Christian era, the Chinese under the rule of the Former Han, Wang Mang, or the Later Han, faced familiar problems of frontier defense and the restlessness of unassimilated peoples within their borders. The Xiongnu stirred again, despite a powerful pro-Chinese faction led by a half-Chinese princess. In 9 CE they broke the peace that had lasted more than a half century. Wang Mang responded by mobilizing his forces, demonstrating that China had the will and the might to resist armed intrusion, and then negotiated an agreement that successfully precluded major Xiongnu attacks for the remainder of his reign. Dissatisfaction with Chinese suzerainty in the Western Regions was also chronic, but Wang Mang yielded nothing. In 13 CE Karashahr killed the Chinese protector-general assigned to the area and in 16 CE ambushed a punitive expedition, but Wang Mang's forces succeeded in reasserting Chinese control. Similarly, Chinese troops seized territory in the vicinity of Kokonor, overcoming the Qiang state there.

In the northeast, more trouble was brewing for the Chinese empire as the aggressive Korean tribesmen of Koguryo, centered on the upper reaches of the Yalu in Manchuria, challenged the Chinese occupation of northwestern and central Korea. Wang Mang had attempted to enlist Koguryo against the Xiongnu, the traditional Chinese policy of using barbarians against barbarians, but Koguryo attacked China instead. Chinese tactics, including the murder of the Koguryo leader, succeeded and in 12 CE China reestablished its hegemony over much of Korea.

As civil war wracked China in the last years of Wang Mang's reign, his achievements in foreign affairs inevitably unraveled as well. Beyond the core of Chinese speaking peoples—and even at the edges of that entity—only Chinese power could hold the loyalty of the empire's subjects. The Xiongnu and other nomadic peoples of the northern frontiers were not voluntary tributaries of China; nor were the Koreans, the various peoples of the Western Regions, the Vietnamese, or the hostile tribes of Fujian, Guanxi, Guangdong, and Yunnan. When the Xiongnu had been stronger, the Chinese had brought *them* tribute. The others were willing enough to leave the Chinese alone, eager only to be free of Chinese administrators and their enforcers. When internal strife weakened China, distracted Chinese imperialists, non-Chinese—and some Chinese—went their own ways, asserted their independence and, in some instances, tried to recoup earlier losses. It was this struggle for dominance with those who had freed themselves of Chinese oppression and exploitation that marked the early years of the Later Han.

The founding emperor of the Later Han, Guang Wudi (r. 25–57) necessarily focused his attention on internal affairs, on consolidation of his power at home. His preoccupation with domestic affairs assured continued slippage on the frontiers of the empire. Unable and unwilling to confront a renewed challenge by the Xiongnu, he attempted to appease them. His policy failed. The Xiongnu persisted in raiding Chinese settlements, driving off Chinese farmers. Before long they had moved into territory long considered Chinese. The Han empire was contracting.

When several states of the Western Regions proposed reestablishment of the Chinese protectorate to defend them against Yarkand, the area's dominant power of the moment, Guang Wudi refused. Presumably he was deterred by the high cost of foreign adventure and frontier garrisons. Several leaders of the Western Regions promptly submitted to the Xiongnu, seeking the protection China would not provide. On the other hand, when the Vietnamese rebelled against the flow of Chinese immigrants into their land, an able Chinese general crushed the rising and followed his military success with the forced sinicization of the people of north Vietnam. Had the general required additional support from the capital, the outcome might well have been different.

Fortune favored the emperor. Once again (c. 50 CE) the Xiongnu divided regionally into northern and southern factions, spurring diplomatic and military action by China. Each of the Xiongnu factions was interested in enlisting Chinese support against the other. Once again the Chinese chose to join forces with the southern Xiongnu, who ultimately surrendered to the Han, accepting tributary status to their ultimate gain. Efforts to send back Chinese who had fled from regions under Xiongnu control failed, however, and the presumably friendly southern Xiongnu continued to exist as an independent state within China's borders. Guang Wudi's generals called for an attack on the northern Xiongnu, to eliminate the persistent threat, but he refused, perfectly content to hold a strong defensive position buffered by the southerners who remained in a state of tension with their brethren to the north. His generals feared a Xiongnu reconciliation; he did not, confident of his policy of divide and conquer. In the long run they were right, but not before Guang Wudi went peacefully to his grave.

Although the Xiongnu long constituted the greatest threat to the Chinese empire, there were other "barbarians" who gave the Han grief. Among these were the Wuhuan and the Xianbi, both of whom operated in the north, occasionally allied or subordinate to the Xiongnu, occasionally at war with them. With both of these, Guang Wudi's appeasement policy was successful, at least in his lifetime. The Wuhuan gladly entered the tribute system in 49 CE and in the same year, a major Xianbi leader accepted a Chinese bribe.

In Guang Wudi's reign, the dynasty was firmly established and he, for one, would have considered his foreign policy a success. He left his people enjoying peace with the Xiongnu threat in particular greatly reduced. He had minimized the empire's commitments in Central Asia and his armies had kept hostile forces in the region at bay. The Vietnamese had been taught a lesson and the difficulties posed by other obstreperous tributaries were relatively minor. Direct trade links with India had been established. His generals were not altogether happy, but they gave him less trouble than his in-laws. It was not a bad record.

TABLE I.4.   Some Notable Dates of the Ancient World: 200 BCE–200 CE
(Dates are approximate. Events in boldface are referred to in text)

Yayoi Culture in Japan	**200 BCE–250 CE**
Maccabean revolt against Romans	167 BCE
Carthage destroyed by Romans	146 BCE

Iron and salt debates in China	**81** BCE
Julius Caesar murdered	44 BCE
Chinese establish control over Korea	**12** CE
Pontius Pilot orders crucifixion of Jesus	30 CE
Romans invade Britain	43 CE
Japanese missions to Han China	**57** and **107** CE
Buddhism reaches China	58 CE
Jews revolt; Romans destroy Jerusalem	66–70 CE
Chinese establish direct trade links with India	**75** CE
Mesoamerican city of Teotihuacan (Mexico) built	100 CE
Rome declares war on Parthia	113 CE
Hadrian's Wall built across Britain	122–127 CE

The remaining years of the Later Han were marked by increased contact with the outside world, not all of it friendly. Trade relations spread from Japan to the east and westward across Central Asia all the way to Rome. The impact on Chinese culture was profound, from the adaptation of Mediterranean lead glazes on Chinese ceramics to what some scholars have called the Indianization of China through the influence of Buddhism. The recurring theme in China's foreign relations, however, was struggle with its immediate neighbors, the "barbarians" who surrounded them, the Xiongnu, the Qiang (often called Tibetans or proto-Tibetans), the Wuhuan, Xianbi, and Man.

The extent of trade relations and the volume of the trade itself depended largely on China's relative power at any given time. Han troops paved the way for merchants as they marched north, south, east, and west. And the merchants, as they developed ties to the economies of distant cities, facilitated expansion. Indeed they sometimes served as the advance agents of empire. The relationship between the tributary system and trade was equally important. Many peoples that accepted tributary status did so in anticipation of using tribute missions as vehicles for trade. Similarly, extensive private trade was conducted by Chinese envoys traveling to the outer reaches of the empire, especially to the Western Regions. When Chinese power was in decline or when the court sought greater economies in foreign relations, the tributary system, a financial liability to the state, shrank, Chinese troops were less evident on the periphery, and Chinese merchants went forth less boldly.

Silk was, of course, the Chinese product most treasured abroad. The frontier nomads, the Indians, the various peoples of Central Asia, and inhabitants of the Roman Empire all found ways to obtain Chinese silk. Much of the trade ran over the fabled Silk Road, through the Gansu corridor, around the Tarim Basin, into what is now Xinjiang, and on to India, Syria, and Rome itself. It was an extraordinarily hazardous journey, over mountains and through the terrible Taklamakan Desert. The northernmost route, north of the Tianshan mountains, was the least desolate, but its semi-pastoral terrain harbored nomadic bandits. South of the mountains ran a double track, a necklace of oases populated by Indo-Europeans, on either side of the nearly dry Tarim River. Merchants who survived sandstorms and lack of water often fell victim to bandits, but they drove their camel caravans on because of the enormous profits to be made.

For many years the Parthians served as middlemen between China and both India and the Roman Empire, but before the end of the first century CE, the Han established direct, official trade with India. Even before, some of India's trade with Rome was in Chinese silk. And at the oases along the Silk Road, Chinese and assorted foreign merchants mingled—a critical point of contact between cultures that brought new religious and philosophical visions as well as exotic goods such as Baltic amber, Red Sea pearls, and grape wine from Central Asia back to the Chinese heartland.

Some international trade was seaborne, often carried by boat to and from intermediate points in Southeast Asia. Sumatra, Malaya, Burma, Ceylon, and India moved goods across the waters to and from China and Chinese vessels plied the same waters. Much of China's trade with Rome in the days of the Later Han went by sea via India as both sides tried to cut out the Parthians and the tariffs they imposed. Indeed the Chinese perceived Rome to be a maritime country. The modern city of Guangzhou (Canton) was the port of entry for most goods coming from the south by sea. Chinese and Korean mariners sailed the waters between their countries, competing with overland carriers in the movement of goods. And, of course, all contact with the Japanese islands was by sea—although often via Korea. Japanese missions to the Han in 57 and 107 CE, for example, are believed to have come through Korea.

Clearly trade brought the Chinese into contact with much of the rest of Eurasia. The Han, like most Confucian-influenced dynasties, did not encourage such activity. Indeed, merchants were forced to overcome a variety of government obstructions and taxes. But then, as so often in the years to follow, the ingenuity of the merchants prevailed.

Foremost among the foreign ideas to reach China in the years of the Later Han was Buddhism, which entered through the trade routes, most obviously along the Silk Road from Central Asia. Buddhist monks from India and Ceylon sailed to Vietnam and then walked into China. By the time of Guang Wudi's death Buddhist influence had reached east central China and a Buddhist monastery could be found in the capital by the end of the first century CE.

Initially Buddhist teaching and religious activity was wholly foreign dominated. Indian texts were translated into Chinese by Parthians, Sogdians, Khotanese, Iranians, and assorted Central Asian barbarians as well as Indians. The best known of these was a Parthian monk who reached Luoyang in 148 and taught there for twenty years. Buddhism, especially Mahayana Buddhism with its bodhisattvas, intrigued Chinese intellectuals and the court aristocracy. It was exotic, interesting, and it seemed to fill a need not met by traditional Confucian, Daoist, and animist beliefs. Monasticism appealed to the Chinese. Entering the country peacefully, posing no apparent threat to the authority of the state, Buddhist teachers encountered no resistance. Indeed, foreign monks were in great demand in the capital and in 166 Buddhism was formally introduced at court. The emperor included the Buddha among the recipients of his religious sacrifices. Mid-second century appears to have been a time of great interest in things foreign and a time when the court amused itself by imitating fashions from India and Parthia, from the "west." But Buddhism was very much more than a fad. It was becoming a major element in Chinese intellectual and religious life as it gradually permeated mass culture.

As new ideas and products flowed into China, old problems persisted. An empire the size of the Han would almost always have problems of frontier defense. When the Xiongnu were united, China's borders were never secure. When the raids came, as they did almost inevitably, the debate over China's response settled into a familiar pattern. Could barbarians be used against barbarians? Could China divide the Xiongnu and play one faction off another? Were there other nearby barbarians who could be induced to assist in the suppression of the nomads? Could China launch an offensive against the Xiongnu? Would it be a better use of Chinese resources to concentrate on a static defense of critical areas? And if the Xiongnu were momentarily weak or divided, some other peoples at some other point on the frontier would covet Chinese territory or wealth, whether it be grain or silk or iron tools. There could be no rest for the leaders of a hegemonic empire.

A little more than a decade after his death, the Chinese court reversed Guang Wudi's decision to leave the Western Regions outside the empire's defensive perimeter. His policy had been questioned at the time and the rise of northern Xiongnu influence in the area strengthened those who argued for a more expansive policy. In 73 CE a Han offensive began, but despite success in driving a wedge between the Xiongnu and the remaining peoples of the area it took sixteen years for China to regain its dominance in Central Asia. A number of oases states resisted the reassertion of Chinese authority. The principal Chinese administrator, the Protector General of the Western Regions, and his forces were massacred in 75 CE by troops from Kucha and Karashahr in the Tarim Basin.

Once again the court debated the wisdom of offensive campaigns. The Xiongnu had not been particularly aggressive. Indeed they had been weakened by battles with the Xianbi and had pulled back far from the frontier with China. Several of the emperor's advisers argued that it would a waste of imperial resources to chase after them, a mistake to send Chinese troops so far from home. They contended that the potential benefits were not worth the cost. The emperor rejected their advice. Joined by the southern Xiongnu, the Han launched a massive offensive and crushed the northern Xiongnu. For more than half a century, China enjoyed the dominance it regained in Central Asia. Indeed in 97 CE its victorious generals marched to the Caspian Sea and, searching for the Mediterranean, may have had a scouting party reach the Persian Gulf.

But into the vacuum created by the defeat of the northern Xiongnu rode the Wuhuan and Xianbi. And while the Han were pursuing the northern Xiongnu, the southern Xiongnu resumed tormenting them. But the next major problem came in Korea, where the kingdom of Koguryo, having progressed in the organization of its resources, attacked Han bases in 106, driving the Chinese westward. In 132 the Chinese regained some of the lost territory, but they knew they now had another formidable antagonist.

When the Xiongnu attacked Dunhuang, along the Silk Road, in 119, Chinese strategists saw another challenge to their influence in the Western Regions. This time advocates of a new campaign were overruled. Instead, the prevailing argument called for merely reinforcing bases such as Dunhuang and tightening Chinese control of roads and mountain passes. This static defense proved sufficient until mid-century—and it allowed the Han to reserve forces for confrontation with the Xianbi closer to home.

The Xianbi, like the Wuhuan, had little contact with China before the Han dynasty. They ranged across modern Inner Mongolia, separated from the Chinese by the Xiongnu and the Wuhuan, who more often than not were allied with and subordinate to the Xiongnu. Relations between the Chinese and the Xianbi began in 49 CE when Guang Wudi bribed a Xianbi leader and won Xianbi support against the Xiongnu and Wuhuan. It was another classic example of the Chinese practice of yi yi zhi yi, the use of barbarians to control barbarians. The Xianbi agreed to join the tributary system, but their price was very high. One historian estimates that Han gifts to the Xianbi were twice the value of the tribute the Xianbi delivered to the Han court.[22] Nonetheless, before the century was over, the Xianbi had resumed raiding well-stocked Chinese frontier communities every winter, seizing the grain, cloth, and iron implements nomadic peoples could not produce for themselves.

In 110 the Chinese offered the Xianbi better trading opportunities, but the terms proved unsatisfactory and both the demands and the raids continued. By mid-century, the Xianbi had created a powerful nomadic confederation, cast off all pretense to tributary status, and posed a major threat to China's northern border. Aided by Han defectors and possessed of iron weapons despite Chinese efforts to ban their sale, they attacked with impunity. After many years of passive response and failed efforts at appeasement, in 177 the Han, supported by the Xiongnu, mobilized a large expedition to send against them. In 180, following the death of the principal Xianbi leader, the confederation crumbled and the Chinese had a brief respite on that edge of their frontier.

Again, the critical point is that the men responsible for China's security could never rest. Somewhere in the empire or on its fringes, there was almost always trouble. In addition to the Xiongnu, Xianbi, Wuhuan, and various peoples of the Western Regions, there were, closer to the heartland, the Qiang of the northwest and the Man of the south who became increasingly difficult toward the close of the second century CE.[23] Chinese troops were almost constantly on the march, trying to preserve the empire by intimidating nomadic raiders, pacifying buffer states, and suppressing peoples in the provinces who resisted assimilation.

The assumption that all conquered peoples would welcome the blessings of Chinese civilization was a delusion that came early and is not likely ever to disappear entirely. Beginning with the Yellow Turban rebellion in 184, the Han dynasty began to come apart. The death of the Emperor Lingdi in 189 triggered a great struggle for power involving regional governors, the empress, various family members, and the court eunuchs. Amidst turmoil within the borders of the empire and around the periphery, the warlord Cao Cao eventually emerged as the dominant figure and in 220 the last Han emperor was forced to abdicate in favor of Cao Cao's son.[24] The empire shattered and China ceased to exist as a single entity for more than three hundred years until reunited by the Sui in 589. In the interim a succession of competing kingdoms ranged over the territory of the once mighty Han empire and other polities rose to challenge China's preeminence in East Asia.

For most of the roughly four hundred years of the Han Dynasty, Former and Later, and the Wang Mang Interregnum as well, China was the paramount power in East Asia. Obviously, the Han had little influence on Japan or the islands of Southeast Asia. Much of continental Southeast Asia was beyond China's reach. Parts of Inner Mongolia, Korea, and Manchuria were under Han control, but other parts remained in the hands of fiercely independent people who occasionally yielded to superior Han forces, but were quick to reassert themselves at the first opportunity. Nomadic cavalry, especially that of the Xiongnu and Xianbi, provided nearly constant grief for the Chinese, but during this era their peoples were unwilling to surrender their way of life, to leave the steppe, to settle down long enough to supplant China in the region. China's strength waxed and waned over these centuries, but the relative sense of oneness of the Chinese people preserved China's dominance.

China's strategists practiced all the tricks of their trade and debated all of the central issues of international relations. They argued among themselves about when to appease and when to fight, about the value of various parts of the empire and the cost of maintaining it, about the usefulness or trustworthiness of this or that barbarian. They created an ingenious but expensive tributary system that greatly enhanced the status of the throne and proved to be a reasonably successful means of holding alien forces in China's orbit. They built and sustained Chinese power for four hundred years, despite weak emperors and court intrigues, but the rot within the empire ultimately undermined their efforts and the unity of China.

Also of great significance during the centuries in which the Han ruled was the greatly expanded scope of China's foreign affairs. The international relations of East Asia ceased to be primarily war and diplomacy involving various parts of China and the Xiongnu. Han contacts spread across the length and breadth of East Asia, including the islands. They reached by land and by sea to India and Ceylon. And as a harbinger of the distant future they reached across Central Asia and the Indian Ocean to the Mediterranean, to the great civilizations of Egypt and Rome, as well as those of India and Parthia. Han China's international contacts, through diplomacy, trade, and warfare, touched every part of the then civilized world. Not least were the cultural connections that brought fresh ideas from India and the West to China-and vice versa. Of the cultural transfers that occurred in these years, the most enduring was Buddhism, which spread in its various forms to much of Central Asia and East Asia, as well as to China itself. East Asian culture was never the same.

The Diffusion of Power

China

The great and much feared Cao Cao was able to pass control of the Han capital to his son, who renamed the dynasty Wei, but he did not succeed in subduing two other pretenders to the succession. Three kingdoms, Wei, Shu Han (home of the legendary hero Zhuge Liang), and Wu, vied for dominance over the Chinese empire, but for a half century no one of them could succeed. The struggle between Cao Cao and his rivals provided the basis for the single most popular Chinese novel, the fourteenth-century *Sanguozhi yanyi* or *Romance of the Three Kingdoms*.

China's disunity of necessity shrank its role in world affairs. There was still cultural exchange, trade, war, and diplomacy, but a divided China could not regain its empire, let alone transcend the heights achieved by the Han. Nonetheless, weak neighbors in Vietnam, Yunnan, Manchuria, and Korea learned not to trifle with the Chinese. Strong neighbors, such as the Xianbi and Qiang, however, soon moved across the northern and

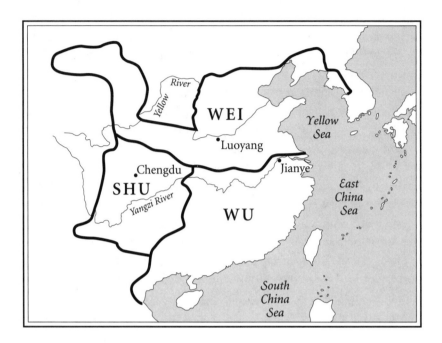

MAP 4.   THREE KINGDOMS: CHINA, C. 250 CE
After Dun J. Li, *The Ageless Chinese*, p. 133.

western frontiers. The Xiongnu, allowed by the Later Han to live within China's borders, shook off their vassalage and reasserted themselves. In the course of the fifth century, the north China plain, the Chinese heartland, was lost to these long-time adversaries. Only south of the Yangzi, with a capital located at the modern city of Nanjing, did a largely Chinese political entity survive. But the Chinese were not able to reunify their country. Ultimately, toward the end of the sixth century, that task was accomplished by sinicized "barbarians" from the north.

Although Wei was unable to prevail over its Chinese competitors for many years, it reacted sharply to raids by the Korean kingdom of Koguryo and crushed the pretensions of those who proclaimed the kingdom of Yen in southern Manchuria. In a seven-year campaign that began in 238, Wei troops extended Chinese control over Korea. Similarly, Shu Han forces subdued the restive tribes of the southwest and Wu drove further into Vietnam. But the Three Kingdoms fought each other continuously and in 263, Wei finally conquered Shu Han. A few years later, a usurper seized the Wei throne and declared himself first emperor of the Jin Dynasty, Jin Wudi. In 280 he succeeded where the Wei had failed: he defeated the Wu and reunited China, however briefly. Although the Jin Dynasty lasted, at least nominally, until 317, it began to fragment with Jin Wudi's death in 290. The restoration would have to wait three hundred more years. Indeed, the worst was yet to come.

Of the several "barbarian" peoples, primarily nomadic, who gave the Chinese grief in the fourth century, the Xiongnu, Xianbi, and Qiang were the most prominent. As early as 281, the Xianbi began edging into north China. Further west, the Qiang moved across the frontier in 296. The history of China in the fourth century is that of a people constantly beset by nomadic raiders, many gradually abandoning their lands north of the Yangzi and fleeing south. In 311 the capital at Luoyang was sacked by a Xiongnu war party and in 316 the Xiongnu destroyed the kingdom of Jin. Some Chinese fled to the Gansu corridor; but most went south in one of the largest mass migrations in world history. They established a new capital at the site of modern Nanjing for a regime called the Eastern Jin in 317. Fighting between the "barbarians" controlling north China and the "Chinese" of the south continued until the late sixth century with the Yangzi holding as a dividing line for most of that period.

The indigenous peoples of south China were none too pleased by the influx of immigrants from the north and tensions between them were frequent. By sheer weight of numbers the Chinese from the north forced the pace of sinicization of the south. The newly arrived northerners monopolized the principal government positions, but were preoccupied initially with recovering their homeland. Wisely, they did not interfere with the holdings of the local elites and were able to mute their hostility. The only major uprising was a peasant rebellion in 400, which they managed to survive. On the other hand, the northerners were never able to muster support in the south sufficient to enable them to mount a successful expedition across the Yangzi.

In North China, various groups of nomads vied for power, each controlling a chunk of territory for a relatively brief period, establishing ephemeral kingdoms and dynasties. At mid-century, a Qiang army marched in from the west, slowly overcoming all resistance, and by 376 the Qiang were in control of all of North China. Their leader, Fu Jian, determined to do more than rape and pillage, set up a civil authority modeled after that of the Chinese, relying heavily on Chinese advisers. He won

Chinese support for his efforts and in due course came to think of himself as the founder of a new Qin dynasty that would reunify China and restore the empire to the heights of splendor achieved under the Han. But the million man army he led southward was repelled by the Eastern Jin in an epic battle in 383. His regime in the North collapsed soon afterward.

The regime in the South appears to have reached the peak of its power early in the fifth century under the leadership of the usurper Liu Yue, but the dynasty he founded fell to a succession of military men a generation later. Liu led the most successful southern foray into the North, seizing Luoyang and Chang'an in 417, but with his home base insecure, he was forced to surrender both cities. Another modicum of stability was achieved by Xiao Yan, the "Martial Emperor" in 502, whose reign lasted almost to mid-century when his capital was overrun by "barbarians" from the North. The last of the southern states was established in 557, surviving until the Sui conquest and reunification of China in 589.

In the North it was the Northern Wei dynasty (386–535), ruled by Turkic-speaking former nomads (Tuoba or Tabghach), that provided the most interesting regime between the fall of the Han and the founding of the Sui dynasties. Although its efforts to conquer the South failed, it had succeeded in eliminating its competitor states in the North and checking the rise of new nomadic forces in Manchuria and Mongolia. In the middle of the fifth century, its troops had reopened some of the caravan routes in Central Asia. Now dominant over the Chinese with whom they shared the North China plain, many of the Tuoba stopped resisting assimilation and willingly adopted Chinese culture. On the one hand they taught the Chinese the military tactics that had facilitated nomadic dominance. On the other, they learned language and philosophy from the Chinese and found some of the comforts of sedentary Chinese life to their liking.

The Northern Wei emperor Xiao Wendi (r.471–99) liked the amalgam of Chinese and nomadic culture that he found and encouraged his officials to marry Chinese women—and took several Chinese wives himself. Perhaps best known for his successful land reform, facilitated by the distribution of land abandoned by Chinese who fled south, he is also remembered for mandating Chinese dress at court and Chinese as the official language. Over time he insisted upon the sinicization of surnames and required the study of the Confucian classics. In 493 he moved his capital south to Luoyang, the last capital of the Han, a further symbol of his aspiration to rule as a Chinese emperor.

Not all of Xiao Wendi's followers were pleased by his deviations from their native culture. His son and heir apparent resisted and was executed. The emperor's reliance on Confucian scholars for advice further alienated Tuoba elites, but the opposition was intimidated and contained throughout his life and for a quarter of a century afterward. In 524, several military men, leaders of the institution least receptive to forced sinicization, revolted. Out of the resulting strife came several lesser and competing states, all largely sinicized, but headed by families skeptical about continuing the process. All of these states were, however, sufficiently Chinese, sufficiently well-versed in the appropriate rites, to be considered by the South suitable partners in diplomatic discourse. Ambassadors were frequently exchanged.

In 577 the North was reunified by a state calling itself the Northern Zhou. A few years later, one of its generals usurped the throne, a prelude to his march south and the reunification of China in 589. Yang Qian, founding emperor of the Sui, is believed to have been of Xianbi origin, and was married into the Xianbi aristocracy of the North, but he claimed to be Chinese. He was obviously sinicized enough to gain the support or at least acquiescence of Chinese North and South and to restore the glory of the Chinese empire.

Of course, if Yang Qian and all of the erstwhile Tuoba, Xianbi, Xiongnu, and Qiang of North China were now Chinese, the definition of what it meant to be Chinese was demonstrably more elastic than in an earlier time when a "barbarian" was a "barbarian." If they dressed like Chinese, walked like Chinese, talked like Chinese, then they had to *be* Chinese.

In the nearly four hundred years during which "barbarians" and their descendants ruled North China, the international relations of the region were reminiscent of the Warring States era. Across China in both epochs there were usually several states, usually at war with one another, less than identical ethnically, and clearly functioning independently. All became one people under the overwhelming power of first the Qin and the Han, and in 589 the Sui. But these latter years, labeled the Six Dynasties period by Chinese historians, were different in the absence of anything that might be called an international *system*. No institution comparable to the hegemon emerged. On the contrary, with the exception of the diplomatic gestures of the late sixth century, the competitiveness of the various political entities that comprised China approximated the anarchic system imagined by later day proponents of realist theory.

But the most striking difference between the years of the Six Dynasties and any preceding period in Chinese history was the extraordinary influence of an utterly foreign system of thought, the Buddhist religion, Indian in origin. There could be no more impressive evidence of East Asia's involvement with South and Central Asia than the way in which Buddhism swept into China, winning over large numbers of Chinese and most nomadic peoples before being carried on to Korea and through Korea to Japan. And in Southeast Asia, a variant form won millions of additional believers. John King Fairbank once argued that Buddhism "constituted a far more serious challenge to Chinese civilization than the mere conquest of the land by 'barbarian' invaders."[25]

It is never easy to understand why a new belief system is attractive to a given people at a given time. Clearly, for Chinese who had seen their land overrun by nomads, who had been driven from their homes, who witnessed massacres and the destruction of great cities, customary beliefs and habits were inadequate. Confucian explanations about the lack of virtue on the part of their leaders brought little solace. Maldistribution of wealth, long a problem in Chinese society, could not be assuaged by familiar political and religious practices. Buddhism brought the promise of personal salvation. At a time when the suffering of the average Chinese peasant was great and there seemed no respite from the everyday misery of existence, Buddhism brought hope of a future and better world. In brief, it would be reasonable to assume that the Chinese people turned to Buddhism for solace that could not be found in traditional Chinese civilization. Buddhism could be seen as Karl Marx would later describe religion generally, as the opiate of the masses.

The problem with this explanation of Buddhism as balm for the afflicted masses is that is was not they who were initially attracted to it. Among Chinese, it was the rich and the aristocracy who had been attracted during the years of the Later Han and who remained the principal adherents of Buddhism until the eighth or even ninth century—a much happier time when Buddhism demonstrated mass appeal. Equally difficult to fit into the Marxist equation is the fact that Buddhism was even more attractive to the victorious nomad warriors of the North. The "barbarians" of the Northern Wei became the great patrons of Buddhism in China in the fourth century, more than a hundred years before it became popular in the South. It was the Wei who patronized the great Buddhist sculpture at Longmen, near Luoyang—two of the finest examples of which can be found can be found in museums in New York and Kansas City.[26]

Again, Chinese civilization survived the Buddhist intrusion, but it was a very different Chinese civilization than the one Confucius or Han Wudi had known. The study of Buddhist scriptures affected Chinese learning and ultimately Chinese literature. Buddhist monasteries and temples popped up everywhere, sometimes so rich and powerful as to challenge existing centers of economic and political power. Chinese art was changed irrevocably, both in terms of medium and subject. Sculpture, never before important, was given enormous impetus by the demand for statues of the Buddha and the various bodhisattvas. One boddhisattva evolved into Guanyin, the Goddess of Mercy, arguably the most worshipped figure in Chinese history before—and since—Mao Zedong. The Buddhist scriptures provided subject matter for painters as well as calligraphers. And who can imagine Chinese architecture without the Buddhist reliquaries known as pagodas? Finally, Buddhism provided an engine for cultural exchange. Thousands of Buddhist missionaries entered China from Central, South, and Southeast Asia, bringing information about their homelands and the roads they traveled-and the objects to be found there. Similarly, thousands of Chinese made the pilgrimage to the homeland of the Buddha where they studied and brought knowledge of China. Chinese troops may not have ranged as far and as successfully as they did under the Han, but China was by no means cut off from the rest of Asia during these centuries of travail.

TABLE 1.5.   Some Notable Dates of the Ancient World 200–600 CE
(Dates are approximate. Events in boldface are referred to in text)

Three Kingdoms era in China	**220–264** CE
Yamato Kingdom in Japan	**250–587** CE
Goths sack Athens, Sparta, and Corinth	268 CE
Partition of Roman Empire	285 CE
Korean Three Kingdoms (Koguryo, Paekche, Silla)	**313–668** CE
Six Dynasties in China	**317–589**
Constantine the Great reunites Roman Empire	324 CE
The Visgoths invade Italy	401 CE
The Franks under the Merovingians	431–751 CE

Attila leads the Huns through Europe	445–453 CE
The Vandals sack Rome	455 CE

Korea

But the story of the international relations of East Asia in these years is much more than the story of China. Certainly as interesting and complex were developments in and near Korea, which experienced its own era of Three Kingdoms, and which rose to challenge China for dominance in Northeast Asia. Despite the increasing influence of Chinese culture on the peoples of the Korean peninsula and their relatives on the Manchurian side of the Yalu, they resisted Chinese political influence, cooperating with China only when they were attempting to destroy each other. All three kingdoms—Koguryo, Paekche, and Silla—were aggressive and expansionist. Koguryo in particular was hostile to China and its skilled horsemen posed a serious challenge to Chinese defenses.

Koguryo had emerged as a political entity in the upper reaches of the Yalu River during the days of the Later Han, the first of the Korean kingdoms to acquire a metal culture. Another Korean people, the Puyo, also emerged in Manchuria and were perceived by the Chinese as a threat comparable to that of the Xianbi and Koguryo. In fact, Puyo sought ties to China, hoping to enlist China against Koguryo and the Xianbi. Han records indicate that Puyo sent emissaries to China almost every year beginning mid-first century CE. When Wei dynasty forces defeated Koguryo c. 245, Puyo provided assistance to the Chinese. Puyo managed to maintain a separate identity but was overrun by the Xianbi and Paekche in 346 and ultimately absorbed by Koguryo.

Early in the fourth century, Koguryo took advantage of China's internal strife and drove the Chinese out of Korea, ending four hundred years of Chinese domination. Given China's size and proximity, it was inevitable that China would remain a shadow over Korean affairs for all time, but China never regained the degree of control it had enjoyed under the Han. Nonetheless, the Chinese retained sufficient strength to thwart Koguryo's initial efforts to become the major power in the region.

The kingdom of Paekche emerged on the Korean peninsula in the third century CE and quickly established an alliance with the Wa people of Japan. Soon Koguryo was being squeezed by the Xianbi coming out

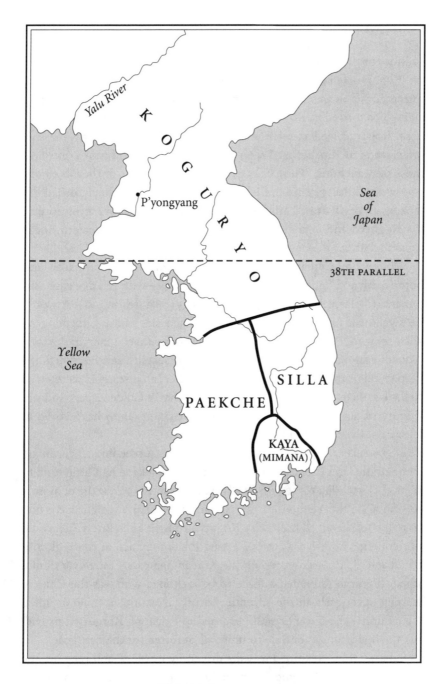

MAP 5.   THREE KINGDOMS: KOREA, C. 450 CE

After Fairbank and Reischauer, *East Asia*, p. 407.

of Mongolia and Paekche pushing up the peninsula. In 342 and again in 371 Koguryo fell under those pressures. Enter the kingdom of Silla, formed c.350 on the east coast. Threatened by Paekche and its Japanese allies, Silla looked to Koguryo for support. With Silla engaging the Japanese, Koguryo leaders were able to regroup their forces for a massive offensive in all directions. They occupied Liaodong and took control of most of Manchuria. They drove Paekche's forces out of their territory and invaded Paechke itself. Before they were finished, they crushed the Japanese army that had attacked Silla. At the outset of the fifth century, the Koguryo and Silla alliance was dominant, but southwestern Korea remained under the control of Paekche and its Japanese ally.

While China remained divided, Koguryo maintained contacts with both North and South, manipulating the Chinese with relative ease. But pursuing a classic balance of power strategy, Silla, fearing that it would be swallowed by its powerful ally, switched sides in 435, forming an alliance with Paekche that endured for more than a hundred years. Nonetheless, in 475, Koguryo attacked and defeated Paekche, which fell despite aid from both Silla and China. One Korean historian has referred to the last quarter of the fifth century as Koguryo's Golden Age.[27] Indeed, Koguryo's days of primacy in Northeast Asia appear to have lasted at least until the middle of the sixth century.

In 551 Silla and Paekche attacked Koguryo, succeeding in regaining some of the land Paekche had lost in 475. But Paekche had little time to rejoice. In 555, Silla turned on its ally, seeking access across the peninsula to China via the Yellow Sea. As any armchair analyst might have predicted, Paekche allied itself with Koguryo to fight Silla. But if Silla could not conquer Koguryo as the two vied for dominance in the region, it could and did drive Koguryo off the Korean peninsula. However diminished, Koguryo remained a force to be reckoned with—as the Chinese learned again early in the seventh century. Not until 668 did a united China under the Tang Dynasty succeed in defeating Korguryo, providing the opportunity for Silla to unite all of Korea for the first time.

To a world accustomed to wars driven by ideology and religion, the constant bloodshed up and down the Korean peninsula and in Manchuria where Koguryo was centered may seem meaningless. But of course none of the peoples involved thought of themselves as Koreans. All could see the virtue of increasing their holdings by taking from others. All recognized the value of defending what they had from any who came to take it from them. The emergence of kingdoms in this era certainly gave the ruling class in each of them a sense of identity and a stake in the survival of the regime. It ceased to be a Hobbesian world of everyman against all others, but it was very much the anarchic world of the realist theorists. The only restraint was the superior power of an adversary.

There seems to be little to distinguish one Korean regime from another except geography and the sequence in which they learned to make weapons and organize their society. All adopted Chinese style bureaucracy. Buddhism traveled from China to Koguryo and on down the peninsula—and ultimately across the sea to Japan. All sought to learn from China, to trade with China, and to resist Chinese efforts to control them. In the end, sameness facilitated unification, but as in China, it required conquest to accomplish it.

Japan

The final actor in the Northeast Asian drama was Japan. While Six Dynasties sprawled over China and Three Kingdoms vied over Korea, the Japanese began to cohere as a people. It is evident that Japan became a major player in the balance of power in Korea and as such could have an impact on Chinese ambitions.

Japan's earliest connections with the continent were, of course, prehistoric, and primarily with China and Korea. Much of the contact with China had come through Korea and some very likely through the Ryukyu Islands. Archeological evidence suggests that the southernmost Japanese isle, Kyushu, had encountered Korea as early as 3000 BCE. Indeed, rice cultivation and metallurgy, both introduced from the continent, provided the foundation of the Yayoi culture that developed about the same time as the Han empire. Most students of ancient Japan believe that the Yayoi culture was a fusion of the earlier Jomon (cord pottery)[28] civilization, little affected by continental influences, and that brought by Korean refugees from Chinese aggression during the Qin and Han dynasties.

Relying on Chinese records and archeological discoveries in Japan, historians estimate that by the time of the Later Han dynasty, there were at least thirty small states across the Japanese islands, many of these with formal diplomatic relations with China. Chinese influence was evident in wheel-thrown pottery and in bronze and iron implements, probably brought over by Koreans. Han urban culture, presumably flowing from the Han commanderies in northwest Korea, reached the Japanese islands. In the first century CE, trade between China and Japan increased, continuing the transfer of technology from the continent. The Japanese—or people of Wa—were considered by the Chinese to be tributary peoples. For Japanese leaders, official recognition of their rule by the Han enhanced their stature among their followers. According to Chinese records, the third century Wei Dynasty, at the request of a Queen Himiko of Wa, served as a mediator in Japanese politics.

The rapid changes in Japan during the Yayoi period would not likely have occurred had the islands not become involved in foreign affairs. Jomon culture appears to have been stagnant and it was the flow of immigrants from the mainland, new technologies brought by them or obtained through trade that brought about the transformation. There is even evidence of Japanese contacts with the islands of the South Seas—the discovery of sea shells peculiar to those waters in Yayoi burial urns. Participation in the international relations of East Asia was the ingredient essential to Yayoi development.

In the last half of the third century, one of the Japanese states, Yamato, unified Japan. It evolved much as the Zhou Dynasty had, partly by force of arms, partly by diplomacy—the incorporation of its competing clans into the central administration. Its power, both material and intellectual, derived from continental imports and it was therefore eager for continued intercourse with the Asian mainland. China, however, was disintegrating and formal contact between Japan and China was lost for more than a century. It was to Korea that the Yamato state looked to meet its need for iron and the modern technology of the day. It was also to Korea that the Yamato elite looked for the pleasure of luxury goods and urban culture. The huge tombs (*Kofun*) they built appear to have been a version of those built in Koguryo and by the fourth century they were being filled with objects imported from Korea.

Given its needs and desires—and the likelihood that the ethnic differences that divide Japanese and Koreans today did not exist in the fourth century—Yamato did not hesitate to involve itself politically and militarily, as well as economically and intellectually, in the affairs of the Korean peninsula. The small Kaya (Mimana to the Japanese) federation in the vicinity of modern Pusan looked to the warriors of the Japanese islands for protection. Yamato troops were stationed there and the Yamato court perceived Kaya as its colony-and its vital foothold on the mainland.

The rise of Koguryo in the fourth century had important ramifications for Japan. When Koguryo wiped out the Chinese commanderies in northwest Korea early in the century, many of the Chinese who lived there eventually made their way to Japan, adding to the existing ethnic mix and bringing their skills and elements of their culture. When Koguryo threatened Paekche, Paekche looked to Japan for assistance. When Silla arose late in the century and threatened Kaya, Japan attacked. Aligned with Paekche, Japan defeated Silla in 391, but in 399, Silla turned to Koguryo for assistance and together they drove the Japanese back, although they retained a foothold in Kaya until mid-sixth century. Japan's ties to Paekche remained strong because of Paekche's need for a counterweight to the Koguryo-Silla alliance and Japan's need for access to Korean supplies of iron and apprehensions about Silla's intentions.

The Yamato state appears to have reached its peak of power and prosperity in the fifth century when, with the help of Paekche, it reestablished direct ties with South China. Chinese records list thirteen tribute missions from Japan between 413 and 502, ten of them between 421 and 478. The Yamato elite once again had assured access to Chinese luxuries, especially silk. But it was also clear that it recognized the advanced state of Chinese learning and institutions and that its missions were also designed to study China, to discover the sources of Chinese wealth and power, to be adopted for the advancement of Japan. Much was gained by these journeys to China; nonetheless Korea remained the principal conduit for the Chinese culture that reached Japan. Korean artists taught the Japanese how to glaze pottery. Immigrant technicians from Korea increased rice production. Paekche sent teachers who introduced the Chinese writing system to Japan. And not least, Buddhism reached Japan through Korea, influencing Japanese art and architecture as well as religion.

Military and political gains were less striking. The Japanese did learn mounted warfare from the Koreans, but they and their allies in Paekche could not overcome the Koguryo-Silla alliance. While Japan and Paekche courted South China, Koguryo and Silla found friends in North China. Japanese military aid sustained Paekche when it was attacked by Koguryo in 455, but could not save it in 478; nor did an appeal for Chinese help bring an adequate response. Neither military nor political setbacks, however, appear to have staunched the flow of goods, technology, and technicians to Japan.

And this pattern continued all through the life of the Yamato state.

Political and military affairs in Korea were not striking successes. Even Paekche relieved Japan of part of its Kaya protectorate in 512. Still uneasy about Silla, Yamato chose not to alienate Paekche by rejecting its "request." An army mobilized for operations in Korea in 527 was needed first to quell domestic unrest. It reached Korea eventually, stayed briefly without seeing action, and left when Kaya chose accommodation with Silla—which swallowed the erstwhile Japanese protectorate in several stages before the end of the century.

Japanese military involvement in Korean affairs continued, but there were no major invasions for many years. In 540, the Yamato leaders, already divided by a succession crisis, had one of those classic foreign policy debates. Should troops be sent once more against Silla? Recent sorties had been unsuccessful. There was little reason to believe an expedition would be more fortunate in 540. The limits of Yamato military power had been surpassed. Restlessness in various parts of the state was noted and the conclusion reached that troops would not be sent. The government would concentrate on domestic affairs, strengthening its control and improving the welfare of the people. Yamato interests in Korea would be managed diplomatically with support from Paekche. Military aid was sent to Paekche in 552 in exchange for teachers—of Buddhism and Confucianism—and technicians, but there were also diplomatic exchanges with Silla and Koguryo as well.

The shifting Yamato focus toward the home isles did not prevent civil war in 587—and the Yamato clan was defeated by the Soga clan-on the eve of the Sui reunification of China. And while the Soga reformed Japanese government to their own tastes, Japan became a less significant participant in the international relations of Northeast Asia, where a reunified China in all its glory was confronted by an aggressive Koguryo.

Southeast Asia

There is not yet a great deal of evidence to document Southeast Asia's involvement in world affairs in these early years. Only the Vietnamese kept records, Chinese penetration was limited, and archeological sources require further analysis. Coherent, stable political entities do not seem to have existed in the islands or on the mainland outside of the territory of modern Thailand and Vietnam before the seventh century CE. But there is enough information to indicate that the region was enormously important for international trade, primarily between India and China, but also involving East Africa, the Persian Gulf, and the Roman Empire. There is abundant evidence of the Chinese role in North Vietnam and of Indian influence in Borneo, Java, and Bali as well as the mainland. Malay sailors appear to have been central in the carrying trade, familiar along the China coast and also the coast of East Africa where they established a community on Malagasy that has endured to this day.

Vietnam is probably the most fascinating arena for the student of the region's foreign affairs in the days of the Later Han and during the chaotic years of China's disunion, before the coming to power of the Sui. Han troops seeking to secure trade routes to India and to pacify the unruly peoples of southern China and its frontier pushed into Vietnam during the glory days of the Former Han. Vietnamese rulers, bowing to *force majeure*, accepted tributary status within the empire. When the Former Han came under the control of Wang Mang, many Han leaders sought refuge in Vietnam. Northern Vietnam, beset by Chinese troops, awash in Chinese settlers, lost much of its original culture, becoming increasingly sinicized by the third century CE. It also developed a stable political regime in collaboration with Chinese administrators. Nonetheless, whenever China's grip loosened, as in the sixth century, the Vietnamese were quick to reassert their political independence—although some of those rebelling against China's control were themselves descendants of earlier Chinese immigrants.

But it is Vietnam's role in the coastal trade between India and China that stands out in this era. From the time that trade began through to the middle of the fourth century, merchant vessels hugged the coasts in both directions. Cargoes were usually unloaded at either the Bay of Bengal or the Gulf of Thailand side of the Malay peninsula for land transit and then restowed on board craft at the far coast to continue the voyage. Facilitating this commerce was the great entrepot that emerged in the first century CE on the southern coast of Vietnam, near modern Ho Chi Minh City (Saigon). The Chinese called it Funan. It appears to have been a small state with its capital in what is now Cambodia and a seaport on the Mekong, in Vietnam.

Kenneth Hall suggests that Funan's success was based on its ability to produce surplus food with which to feed the seamen and merchants who sought a congenial harbor at which to anchor until the monsoon winds shifted and allowed them to continue their voyages.[29] Depending upon

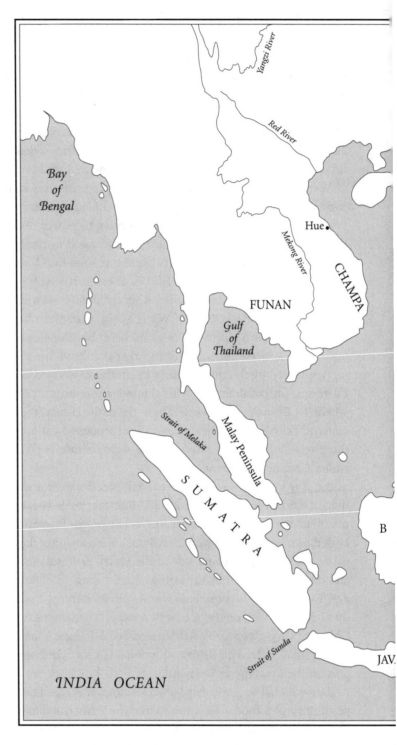

MAP 6.   SOUTHEAST ASIA, C. 450 CE

After maps in D.H. Hall, *History of Southeast Asia*, before p. 1 in 4th ed.

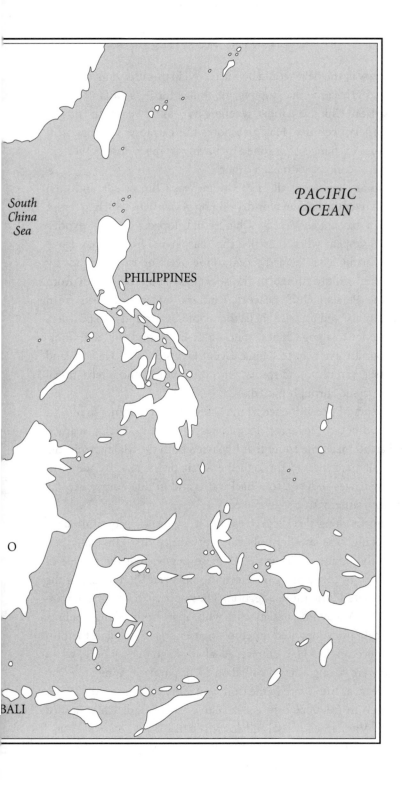

the time of arrival, the delay could be measured in months. Funan served them well and it became the stopover of choice for Persian Gulf sailors as well those from China and India, reaching its peak in wealth and power early in the fourth century. Hall also notes the extraordinary opportunity for cultural exchange occasioned by having so many foreign visitors in Funan and in contact with each other.

The essential element in all of this trade was Chinese silk and men came from all over the known world, bringing goods with which to tempt the Chinese in exchange. Wealthy Chinese developed a taste for exotica that did not disappear when they fled the "barbarian" hordes that drove them from North China. Denied access to the overland caravan trade by the North, they simply turned to the sea. Glass and stone beads from India and the Persian Gulf, peacock feathers, horns and tusks from unknown animals, and tortoise shells that could be ground into powders restoring potency to aging Chinese men—a desire second only to immortality—all found their way to China. Eventually goods native to island Southeast Asia, camphor and spices, won the favor of the international traders who passed through Funan.

Funan's years of preeminence in the international commerce of East Asia were numbered, however. In mid-fourth century, Malay seamen developed an all maritime route that bypassed both the Malay peninsula and Funan, slipping instead through the Strait of Melaka. By the sixth century, Funan was reduced to a backwater and in due course Melaka took its place as the entrepot of choice.

Further north along the Vietnamese coast, in the vicinity of modern Hue or Da Nang, was another political entity called first Linyi and then Champa by the Chinese. From the Chinese perspective the people of Champa existed to torment them. From the sinicized Vietnamese of the north, they elicited little more affection. They appear to have been maritime nomads of Malay-Polynesian stock who, apart from fishing, trading, and occasional piracy, devoted much of their energy to raiding the borders of the once mighty Han empire. As always and everywhere, when the Chinese were strong, they intruded on Champa space. When the Chinese were weak, as they were in the third and fourth centuries, the Cham raids increased in frequency. In 446 a rejuvenated South China joined forces with its Vietnamese vassal and destroyed the Cham center at Hue.[30]

By the end of the sixth century, a reunited China stood ready to dominate East Asia once more. At the same time, trade networks across

Southeast Asia, especially on the islands were exploding. Political entities were coalescing. Indian influence, following trade and Buddhist missionaries, was growing rapidly in Southeast Asia. The stage was set for one of the great cosmopolitan eras of world history.

Conclusion

Diplomacy, trade, cultural transfer, and warfare—the stuff that students of international relations write about—has been the story of human existence. Neolithic men and women negotiated arrangements with each other, exchanged goods and services, influenced each other's ideas about art and religion, and fought each other when they were not satisfied with the results. Perhaps it all began as Hobbes suggested, man against man, total anarchy. And then came families, clans, tribes, villages, towns, cities, and countries—constantly engaged in diplomacy, trade, cultural transfer, and warfare, always aware of others who, whether they became friends or enemies, were different. So it was with East Asia in ancient times.

The first political grouping worthy of being called a state emerged on the North China plain about four thousand years ago. The people who lived there gradually assumed an identity we call Chinese. They expanded by absorbing their neighbors, sometimes by peaceful assimilation, sometimes by conquest. Among them the principal differences seem to have been geographic, specific points of origin, east or west, north or south of ground zero. The Shang pushed aside the Xia and, in due course, the Zhou swallowed the Shang.

As the Zhou polity weakened, it spawned several smaller states, frequently at odds with each other and with new political entities emerging on their periphery. Of necessity, the art of statecraft evolved, ultimately engaging the finest minds in the country, including Confucius and Mencius, Laozi and Mozi. An extraordinary interstate system was created, an institutionalized balance of power, guided by a "hegemon." Eventually, however, diplomacy failed, the system collapsed, and the age of the Warring States ravaged the land, ending only when the overwhelming power of the Qin brought unification in 221 BCE.

As a unified state, China quickly became, under the Han, one of the world's great powers, conquering an empire that surpassed that of its Roman contemporary. Having stopped warring on each other, the Chinese struck out against their neighbors, challenging or being challenged by the Koreans and Vietnamese, as well as the various peoples of Inner Asia, of whom the Xiongnu were the most formidable. Under Han Wudi (r. 141–87 BCE), Chinese imperialism dominated East Asia and established a standard to which would-be imperialists might aspire forever after.

The growth of the empire facilitated trade and cultural exchange with virtually all of the known world. Chinese silks were treasured throughout Asia and across Inner Asia to the Mediterranean, eventually in Rome itself. Ceramics from the Mediterranean, pearls from the Red Sea, amber from the Baltic, were prized in China and Buddhism entered the land, foreshadowing the striking influence India was to have on Chinese culture. In ideas as well as material goods, the Han empire facilitated cultural transfer, not least the spread of the Chinese writing system and Confucianism in East Asia.

And then there was the tributary system, variations on which can be found in much subsequent Chinese history. In its most obvious form, a foreign ruler paid homage to the Chinese emperor by sending an embassy or appearing himself at the Chinese court. Once there he would present gifts to the emperor and very likely leave a hostage or hostages, perhaps even his son. In return the Chinese would lavish gifts upon him, more often than not of a value in excess of those received, and permit private trade. The tributary system was at once a formula for diplomatic intercourse, a symbol of peace and friendship between unequal sovereign states—a nonaggression pact or even alliance, and a vehicle for trade relations. The Chinese received acknowledgment of their superiority, at least nominal, and assurances of the vassal states' good behavior. The tribute bearers obtained insurance against Chinese aggression, the possibility of protection against other enemies, access to Chinese goods, and a significant profit through the exchange of presents itself. It was a system the Chinese found useful when they lacked the will or the power to crush or occupy another state. But it was an expensive system and there always those at court who argued it was cheaper to fight or even ignore a given group of foreigners—and times when the critics won the debate. The existence of the tributary system should not be allowed to conceal the fact that the Chinese were masterful practitioners of *Realpolitik*.

The principal challenge to Chinese power during the Han dynasty and in the three and a half centuries that followed was provided by the nomads of Inner Asia, especially the Xiongnu and the Xianbi. Military

technology throughout these years provided nothing for Chinese arse-
nals that would enable them to cope with horse cavalry. China prevailed
over the nomads when the latter were divided, preferably when they
fought among themselves. On the occasions when the nomads formed
great confederations or the Chinese were themselves divided, the
Xiongnu, Xianbi, or others could not be contained and China would suffer frequent raids at best and death, destruction, and defeat at worst.
Appeasement, enmeshing some of the nomad leaders in the tributary system, was at times successful, but extended periods of peace were few.
Total, final, Chinese dominance over the horsemen of Inner Asia was
many centuries away.

Elsewhere in East Asia, groups of people came together much as the
Chinese had, slowly forming larger and larger political entities and
becoming involved as active participants in the international relations of
the region. Of these the Koreans were the first and most important; by
the fourth century CE they were able to beat back Chinese aggression
and they generally held their own for some long time thereafter. Awak-
ened by Korean refugees from struggles on the Korean peninsula, the
peoples of the Japanese isles also created a coherent regime under the
direction of the Yamato clan. Troops from Japan fought on the Korean
peninsula, forming alliances, controlling territory, working closely with
one Korean kingdom against others, becoming a force to be reckoned
with. In Southeast Asia, Vietnam and Champa were already major players, the former in its constant struggle against Chinese imperialism and
the latter as the critical entrepot for the India-China trade. By the end of
the sixth century it was evident that Chinese diplomatists were facing a
much more complex world, with cultural and economic challenges, as
well as military and political ones, on a scale they had never before
known.

TWO

Shadows Over Tang Splendor

The early years of the Tang Dynasty (618–907) were certainly among the most glorious in Chinese history and probably were also the years in which China had the greatest influence on the rest of East Asia. Physically, the empire expanded aggressively, imposing Chinese culture forcibly on peoples to the north, south, east, and west. Other peoples, who either resisted Chinese imperialism successfully or were beyond the reach of Chinese power, nonetheless voluntarily studied and adopted Chinese practices, political as well as cultural. China was admired and envied as well as feared. It was also an era in which many travelers from the West—Arabs, Christians, Jews, and Persians—made the pilgrimage to China, primarily in search of opportunities for profit. Large numbers of foreigners resided in the port city of Guangzhou (Canton) and in the Tang capital of Chang'an, arguably the most magnificent city of the seventh and eighth century world.

But the historian looking back to the those years sees shadows on China's periphery and potent dangers at the heart of the Chinese polity. China's extensive frontier regions were rarely secure. In the territory China claimed for itself remained peoples resistant to Chinese rule. Beyond its presumed borders were always restless peoples with ambitions of their own. The Turkic peoples to the north and west continued to pose a potential threat. Koguryo to the northeast was a formidable foe, at least as aggressive as the Chinese themselves. To the west, the Tibetan empire arose to challenge Chinese hegemony. Further west, Arab forces were marching into Central Asia, posing a new threat to China's pretensions there. And at home a huge standing army, its commanders perceiving that their interests were not identical to those of the court, ultimately constituted the gravest threat of all.

The Sui

First came the unification of China under the Sui Dynasty. Yang Jian, or Sui Wendi, as he was later known, gained control of the North in 581 and conquered the South in a struggle that lasted from 587 to 589. China was once again a unified empire with power resting in the hands of sinicized Tuoba military aristocrats, many of mixed blood, many at least as comfortable speaking a Turkic language as they were conversing in Chinese. Culture wars continued in the North between those who adopted Chinese ways and those who preferred nomadic traditions, but the latter had little influence at court. The addition of the relatively small Chinese population from the South tipped the scales further. In 589, there was one China, in which the Chinese language and customs prevailed, but the racial stock of the "Chinese" people had changed significantly since the days of the Han.

Wendi brought China a degree of stability it had not known for centuries. Seeking to transfer power from warlords to the court, he laid the groundwork for a professional bureaucracy, based on merit as demonstrated by examination, to replace government by the military aristocracy. He used Buddhism to fashion a state ideology intended to strengthen the ties that bound the empire. Indicative of China's increasing cultural diversity and contact with the rest of the world was the man Wendi chose to lead his Buddhist campaign—a Chinese-born Iranian whose family had migrated to China via Vietnam. Wendi began construction of the Grand Canal, facilitating the movement of troops as well as goods north and south. And, of course, he accrued to himself more power than any of his immediate predecessors had enjoyed—perhaps any since Han Wudi.

As a northerner, Wendi was most troubled by threats to Chinese security posed by the steppe nomads, the "Turks" beyond the Great Wall. He was determined to occupy all of Manchuria and much of northern Korea—an extension of Chinese imperialism justified by the need to create ever larger buffers between China and its potential enemies. In 598, allied with Silla in southern Korea, he sent his troops against the Turks and Koguryo, who were supported by Paekche—and he failed. In a series of battles that Koreans celebrate as one of their greatest acts of resistance to Chinese aggression, Wendi's forces were thrown back. For some long time, the power balance in Northeast Asia—Koguryo, Paekche, and the nomads of Manchuria versus China and Silla—tilted against China.

To the south, the situation was considerably more fluid. Most Chinese were concentrated along the Yangzi. The local peoples of most of modern Fujian, Guangdong, Guangxi, Guizhou, Yunnan, and vicinity were decidedly unfriendly, but they lacked the apparatus of government and the military power with which to stand up to a great power. They resisted bravely—then and from time to time in the centuries that followed—but Wendi's men slaughtered and enslaved them, and forcibly converted them to Chinese ways. The Vietnamese had reasserted their independence, but they, too, fell victim to the overwhelming force of China's armies and were reconquered in 602. The Cham realized they had no chance to defeat China and sent tribute in 595, but Wendi and his advisers, believing Champa to be a land of great wealth, attacked anyway. Chinese troops won easily, found little of value to bring home, and were decimated by disease on the way back. Thereafter, the court decided to leave Champa alone and settle for tribute. Although some Chinese military operations in the south might be rationalized as essential to the security of the state, those against Champa were motivated by nothing more than the desire to relieve another people of its treasure. Chinese imperialism, like that of other great powers throughout history, had more than one face, more than one motive.

Wendi's son and successor, Yangdi, inherited his father's taste for empire-building and his obsession with destroying Koguryo, which proved to be his undoing. He ascended to the throne in 604 and by 609 was devoting his attention almost exclusively to foreign affairs, to the displeasure of many of the Confucian scholars who attempted to advise him.

As in the Iron and Salt debates nearly seven hundred years earlier they indicated their suspicion of economic growth that seemed to benefit the court more than the people—or themselves. They stressed the disadvantages, particularly the high cost of foreign military adventures. Even Pei Zhu, a geographer who served as Yangdi's principal national security adviser and is often blamed for China's foreign misadventures, stressed peaceful means, the winning over of non-Chinese by demonstrations of China's wealth and international prestige—although he conceded the need to garrison key towns to force and maintain the submission of the local people. But events reinforced Yangdi's penchant for military solutions.

The key to China's security in the seventh century was continued division among the Turks, and Yangdi proved no less adept than his father in exploiting the fissures. In 605, when the Khitan—a people whose territory in Manchuria bordered that of Koguryo, China, and the Eastern Turks—raided China, Yangdi persuaded the Turks to send 20,000 horsemen under the command of a Chinese general to retaliate. Efforts to use the Turks against Koguryo, on the other hand, were unsuccessful and the Chinese lived in constant fear of a Koguryo alliance with the Turks, each a credible threat by itself. But Pei Zhu managed to keep the Eastern Turks in the tributary system and to keep them pacified for a decade. In the West, the primary direction of their expansion, the Chinese responded to a request for help by the Turkic Tu Yuehun, under attack from a steppe rival, by joining in the attack and seizing the lands of the Tu Yuehun—an unfriendly act to be sure, but another example of Chinese *Realpolitik* in practice.

In Japan the government recognized the fact that China had been reunified and was attempting to reestablish its hegemonic position in Asia. Japan's interests on the Korean peninsula and its future security seemed more likely to be affected by the Chinese than by any of the Korean kingdoms. In 607, the Japanese sent a major diplomatic mission to the Sui, eager to gather intelligence and to assure Yangdi of their respect. The mission inadvertently offended the Sui emperor by presenting a letter in which the Japanese emperor appeared to claim for himself equality with Yangdi, but diplomatic ties were strengthened nonetheless by the exchange of emissaries the following year.

Yangdi's interest in expansion does not appear to have encompassed Japan, but he did demonstrate interest in other islands in the East China Sea. In 610 he sent an expedition to pacify an island or islands in the region. As Arthur Wright has explained, there is some confusion in the historical record as to just where the expedition went and whether it was successful. Japanese scholars believe the Chinese went to Taiwan; others believe they sought control of *all* of the islands of the region. Again some records indicate that the expedition was a tremendous success; others contend that it failed miserably. All that can be said with confidence is that the Sui attempted to expand their empire into the East China Sea, but whatever the initial results of their effort, they left no enduring presence.[1]

Shortly after the Japanese diplomatic effort a new regional power, the Tibetans, sent embassies to China in 608 and 609. Tibetan origins are still unclear, but it is readily apparent that in the seventh century Tibet emerged as a prominent challenger to China's pretensions in the West. At stake was nothing less than control of Central Asia and the caravan routes to the Middle East. During Yangdi's reign, the Tibetans were consolidating their power, testing their strength against lesser rivals. Contacts with the Chinese were correct and unthreatening, allowing Yangdi to concentrate on his personal *bête noir*, Koguryo.

Preparations for an offensive against Koguryo commenced in 610 and in 612 China launched a massive invasion with an army of one million men supported by naval forces that struck simultaneously. Despite initial successes on the battlefield, Yangdi's forces failed to reach the capital of Koguryo, suffered heavy losses, and ultimately were forced to withdraw. Undeterred, Yangdi tried again in 613 only to have his campaign interrupted by rebellion at home. As the war-weary country seethed with unrest, Yangdi attacked again in 614—but on the verge of success was unable to force the king of Koguryo to appear at the Chinese court to pay homage. Plans for still another campaign had to be set aside as civil strife left the emperor no choice but to abandon his vision of conquest and attempt to preserve his dynasty. His armies had more than enough to do to suppressing uprisings all over China.

Yangdi's militant imperialism, a recurring theme in Chinese history, usually triggered by indications of Chinese military superiority and dreams of emulating Han Wudi, met with considerable success, but ultimately foundered on his campaigns against Koguryo. Like his father before him and other emperors to follow, he found Korean independence intolerable, a potential threat to Chinese security. His efforts to force Koguryo into submission exhausted his treasury and alienated his own people. In 615 he was further embarrassed by a narrow escape from an Eastern Turk force that besieged his summer palace and in 618 he was murdered by a trusted aide. The brief history of the dynasty that had reunited China was over.

The Years of Tang Ascendance

The beneficiary of Sui Yangdi's excesses, as well as of Sui success in unifying China and revitalizing its administrative apparatus, was a powerful general, Li Yuan, who had joined the rebellion against his emperor. When the dust of battle had cleared, it was Li, Duke of Tang, who reestablished order and the authority of the central government. And, of course, it was Li who founded the Tang Dynasty and reigned as Tang Gaozu.

Once again, the immediate task of China's leaders was to consolidate their power at home. Most of them, like Gaozu, were men whose bloodlines traced the course of China's history since the fall of the Han—Chinese only if one understood that to be Chinese in the seventh century allowed for one or more Xianbi or Turkic ancestors. Gaozu and his supporters were remarkably successful. The institutions they created, economic as well as military and political, survived for centuries, until the end of imperial China. Their successors found these institutions sufficiently flexible to serve them well under radically different circumstances—and Koreans, Vietnamese, and Japanese studied them and found them enormously useful in organizing their own societies.

Gaozu's China was less powerful than that of the Sui Dynasty. The aggressive foreign policy of his predecessors was not an option. His contemporary in Koguryo, recognizing Gaozu's less threatening posture, desperately in need of peace in order to rebuild his own war-ravaged country, sent a tributary mission, declaring his fealty to the new Chinese emperor. The Eastern Turks and the Tibetans, however, posed serious challenges to China's security. The Turks raided at will and a major invasion was a constant possibility. Gaozu had little choice but to try to appease, to respect their strength and to buy peace. Contemptuous of the Chinese, the Turks took the bribes and continued to harass them and to act obstreperously even in the Chinese capital, where they murdered a leader of the rival Western Turks. In 626 the long-feared invasion came and Gaozu bought them off again. His hold on China was not yet sufficiently secure to risk committing the forces necessary to stop the Turks. He played for time, bolstering his defenses all the while, but time ran out on his reign. Similarly, the court recognized the increasing aggressiveness of the Tibetans further west, but China lacked the means to deliver a preemptive blow. In 623 the Tibetans moved across the frontier into Gansu.

Gaozu's son, Taizong, ascended to the throne in 627, and was quickly warned against an aggressive foreign policy. Although Chinese society was stable and the place of the dynasty seemed secure, officials who recalled the disastrous results of Sui imperialism urged the new emperor to concentrate on domestic affairs. In particular they feared the economic consequences of major military operations. Taizong abided by their instructions for several years, appeasing the Turks, while patiently noting the excellent harvests and the growing reserves in the treasury. For the moment he relied on diplomacy, dividing China's enemies, manipulating them, occasionally offering a Chinese royal bride as a small price for peace. And in due course China was prosperous again, its people well-fed and responsive to his rule. By 630, he was ready to act.

Once again a Chinese emperor dreamt of surpassing the Han empire. Once again China mobilized its forces and sent its mighty armies forth to conquer its neighbors. The first target was of necessity the Eastern Turks and Taizong's men, having first stirred unrest among them, smashed them quickly, absorbing many of their horsemen into their own ranks. As the Chinese military regained control of the northern frontier, Taizong accepted advice to allow many of the Eastern Turks to remain on Chinese soil in hope of eliminating their threat through assimilation. If Taizong and his relatives were now "Chinese," why not the Eastern Turks as well?

Defeat of the Eastern Turks, however, provided an opportunity for the Western Turks, already masters of Central Asia from Gansu westward to Persia and from Kashmir north to Mongolia, to flow eastward. Their defeat was also essential to Taizong's objective of seizing control of Central Asia—and the lucrative caravan routes—for China. Once again, Chinese diplomatists did what they could to sow dissent among the Turks, exploited the resulting divisions, used Turks against Turks, and weakened the influence of the Western Turks over the oasis kingdoms. Stalled for several years, Chinese offensives in the 640s forced the submission of one kingdom after another. The historian Howard Wechsler contends that "the [Chinese] conquest of Karashahr [644] and Kucha [648] was a mortal blow to the Indo-European culture and civilization of central Asia."[2]

Taizong's ministers persisted in their arguments against expanding so far to the west, against direct Chinese control of the oasis kingdoms, but he ignored them. They worried about the cost—the threat to China's economy—and about the dangers of imperial overreach. Taizong pointed to China's growing prosperity, to reopened trade routes, and the elimination of tolls once exacted by those who had previously controlled passage across Central Asia. Indeed, his armies were strong enough by his estimate to put down the Tibetans and various nomadic tribes to the northwest and prepare for revenge against Koguryo without easing the campaigns in Central Asia.

The westward movement of Chinese forces carried them into the Tibetan borderlands in the mid-630s. Tibetan society had come together by the beginning of the century and Tibetan power and concomitant appetites had grown. Nonetheless, the Tibetans were prepared to play, at least nominally, by Chinese rules. They sent emissaries bearing tribute to the Chinese court and asked for the frequently proffered Chinese princess in a marriage alliance. Someone at the court apparently thought them presumptuous and the request was denied. Rejection outraged the Tibetan emperor and in 638 the Tibetans attacked, seizing a Chinese border town in Sichuan and threatening a major invasion if their demands were not met. They quickly defeated Chinese troops sent to dislodge them and began to stir rebellion among local tribes previously subjugated by the Chinese. A second Chinese effort was more successful, but the Tibetans had focused Taizong's attention on their aspirations. He recognized his earlier mistake, indicated a willingness to enter into a marriage alliance, and negotiations were resumed. In 640 the Chinese received impressive tribute in the form of gold and jewels from Tibet and a few months later the Tibetan emperor had a Chinese princess for his bride. Good relations between Tibet and China lasted for the remainder of Taizong's reign. Indeed, in 648 the Tibetans helped the Chinese in a punitive expedition against a minor Indian kingdom.

Only the Chinese failure to conquer Koguryo remained as an irritant to Taizong, as an obstacle to his vision of creating the greatest empire China had ever known. Koguryo had used the years of peace well, building massive fortifications to shore up its defenses against another Chinese invasion. Once confident they could fend off the Chinese, Koguryo's leaders attacked Silla, attempting to regain territory Silla had seized while Koguryo was fighting for its survival against the Sui. Silla called for help from China and Taizong, furious at Koguryo arrogance, decided the moment had come for China's revenge. Once again his ministers opposed what they perceived as costly and unnecessary military adventurism. Once again he ignored their warnings, insisting that Koguryo had to be brought to heel before it allied with other forces potentially hostile to China such as Japan or nomadic tribes in Manchuria. He would not risk a Koguryo victory over Silla that might result in a united Korea, a long-term threat to Chinese security.

The mighty Tang armies failed disastrously in 645 as Koguryo's defenses held. Undeterred, Taizong sent another massive force against Koguryo in 647. On this occasion, Tang troops prevailed in a great battle, inflicting heavy casualties on the defenders, but they were unable to deliver the decisive blow. Koguryo still stood. Taizong's ambition had not been realized. As he prepared for still a third expedition against Koguryo, death intervened. His accomplishments in the two decades of his reign were extraordinary; the empire was enormous; but victory over Koguryo had eluded him.

Taizong is most likely to be remembered for his conquests, for his aggressive foreign policy, for his contribution to the tradition of Chinese imperialism. But students of Tang history will also note the peaceful expansion of China's contacts with the rest of the world during his days on the throne. China's power and wealth attracted people from all over Asia, the Middle East, and Africa. Trade and cultural exchange increased rapidly, especially in the port city of Guangzhou and in the capital at Chang'an. Large numbers of Arabs, Indians, and Persians could be found in both cities. By sea to Guangzhou also came the Cham, Khmers, Javanese, and Sinhagalese. Overland to Chang'an flocked all manner of Turks, Uighurs, Tokharians, and Sogdians, representatives of much of Central Asia. And they lived among the Chinese, intermarried or fornicated with the Chinese, enlarging their genetic pool as well as influencing their conception of art and music, food, clothing, and religion. The Chinese delighted in the exotic and many of the tribute bearers and traders brought animals, drugs, and dyes unknown to China. Edward Schafer, in a wonderfully entertaining book on Tang culture, goes so far as to argue that Chinese food before the seventh century was relatively uninteresting, becoming the great cuisine we know today as a result of Indian influence during the Tang Dynasty.[3]

Taizong is generally assumed to have been a Confucian, but his tolerance of and interest in other belief systems was remarkable. As soon as he succeeded his father, he ended the latter's efforts to suppress the spread of Buddhism. Xuan Zang, a famous Buddhist monk who spent fifteen years traveling around India, became the emperor's confidant, feeding his curiosity about Indian culture, geography, politics, and produce— as well as religion. Taizong had many of the Buddhist tracts the monk brought back from India translated into Chinese so they could be more readily accessible to his people. Similarly, he welcomed a Nestorian monk from Central Asia who taught him about Christianity—and had the Christian texts translated. And the Taoists, often disconcerted by the introduction of alien religions, also found his favor. Religious persecution was unknown in China during Taizong's reign.

TABLE 2.1. Some Notable Dates of the Sui and Early Tang Years
(Dates are approximate. Events in boldface are referred to in text)

Plague decimates Europe	542–594
Sui Dynasty	**581–618**
Horiuji Temple built in Nara, Japan	585–607
Rise of Tibetan Empire	**600–700**
First Japanese diplomatic mission to China	**607**
Tang Dynasty	**618–907**
Muhammed captures Mecca	628
Fujiwaras seize power in Japan	**645**
Muslim fleet defeats Byzantine fleet in Lycia	655
Tang fleet destroys Japanese fleet near Korea	**660**
Tibetans dominate Central Asia	**670–692**
Reign of Empress Wu	**690–705**
Arab armies capture Bukhara and Samarkand	711–712
Franks defeat Moors in Battle of Tours	732
Arabs defeat Chinese at Talas	**751**
An Lushan Rebellion	**755–763**
Buddhists build Borobudur in Java	**800**

Of all the cultures with which China came in contact, that of India appears to have been the most influential, especially with the spread of Buddhism. There was considerable traffic between the two countries, in trade as well as religion. Pepper, introduced to China by Persian sailors, appears to have originated in India. Chinese art, specifically sculpture, was greatly influenced not merely by Buddhism imported from India, which provided the dominant motifs of the day, but also by Indian styles.

Other foreign influences on Chinese culture were equally apparent. Tang figurines differed from those of the Han by their inclusion of non-Chinese subjects. Many seemed caricatures of Westerners, heavily bearded and endowed with the enormous noses by which the Chinese distinguish Caucasians from themselves. Music and dance were strongly influenced by Central Asia. And the Chinese transmitted much of what they learned from Central Asians and South Asians to the rest of East Asia, as Koreans, Japanese, and Vietnamese came to China to discover the sources of its wealth and power.

These days of Tang glory continued throughout the seventh century and well into the eighth. Indeed the Tang dynasty reached the peak of its power and prestige during the reign of Taizong's son, Gaozong, who fulfilled his father's dream of building the greatest empire in Chinese history. With the help of Silla, he even succeeded in defeating Koguryo, long a burr under the saddle of Chinese emperors. But the great triumphs and the expansion of the empire were transitory. As Gibbon taught us in his study of Rome, empires rise and empires fall—as if they were bound by some Newtonian law. As China conquered one neighbor and extended its defenses to a distant region, another neighbor rose to torment the giant. As there have been limits to the power of all other political entities known to man, so there were limits to Chinese power. Before Gaozong died and the Empress Wu came out from behind the throne to rule in her own right, territories he and his ancestors had won at great cost in lives and treasure were once again in hostile hands.

As the Chinese exulted in their accomplishments under Taizong's leadership, there was ample recognition accorded from afar. The Sassanid Persians, defeated by invading Arabs, fled in large numbers to China. Indeed, the pretender to the Persian throne set up a court in exile at Chang'an. Aware of China's splendor, mindful of Chinese power, the mighty Arabs of West Asia sent an embassy to Chang'an in 651. But closer to home there were early indications of trouble.

Heartened by news of Taizong's death, the Western Turks reunited and soon regained control of the Tarim basin and much of their erstwhile empire across Central Asia to Persia. To the northeast, Koguryo was on the march again, equally ready to challenge the new emperor. Koguryo's objective seems to have been the defeat of Silla and the unification of Korea under its leadership. The strategists of Koguryo even deluded themselves into thinking they might gain China's support in their quest.

Gaozong quickly rallied his forces and sent them against the Western Turks. At the same time his diplomacy, modeled after the traditional tactic of divide-and-rule employed so well by his father, succeeded. By 657 Chinese troops and their local allies had fractured the Turk empire. At least nominally, China reigned supreme once more from Persia to the coastal waters of the Pacific. In reality, local rebellions were a constant drain on Chinese resources.

Koguryo proved tougher. Perceiving Korguryo to be the greater threat, Gaozong chose to join forces with Silla. Paekche, fearful of Silla, sided with Koguryo. The Japanese, initially on the sidelines, grew fearful of the Tang-Silla alliance. Paekche had been Japan's historic friend on the Korean peninsula, but apprehension about the extension of Tang power across the Korean peninsula, ultimately to threaten Japan directly, probably drove Japan's decision to intervene. Japanese leaders may not yet have conceived of the simile of Korea as a dagger pointed at the heart of Japan, but they had the general idea. In 660 a large Japanese fleet attempted to interdict Tang naval operations against Paekche—with disastrous results, most notably the loss of 400 vessels and the destruction of Paekche. Nonetheless, Koguryo staved off Tang and Silla forces until 668 when a combined Chinese and Silla force invaded from the south. Northern Korea and western Korea fell under Chinese control. But if Gaozong assumed Silla would be next, giving him the control of the peninsula so feared by the Japanese, he was to be greatly mistaken. Although Silla accepted Chinese overlordship, it proved to be a very independent and ungrateful vassal, pushing the Chinese out of Paekche and parts of Koguryo. Unification of the Korean peninsula was a goal Silla shared with China, but to Silla's leaders it would be a Korea under their control.

Of course, the Chinese had little time to enjoy their triumph over Koguryo or to indulge themselves in bringing Silla to heel. In the West, the Tibetan empire rapidly became a major threat not only to imperialist China's colonies and protectorates, but also to what the court perceived to be part of the Chinese heartland. In 662, a Chinese army, exhausted by its successful campaigns against the Western Turks, was confronted by a combined Tibetan and Turkic force in the vicinity of Kashgar. It chose not to fight and apparently traded military equipment for assurance of safe passage. Over the next several years, while the Chinese were fighting in Korea, the Tibetans were eliminating Xianbi and Western Turk rivals on China's western frontiers. By 670 they were ready to take on the Chinese and launched a massive attack on China's dependencies in the Tarim Basin region (in modern Xinjiang). Gaozong and his advisers had little choice but to abandon plans for the conquest of Korea and respond to the threat from Tibet.

Forced to withdraw from their forward positions, the Chinese staged a counteroffensive in the Kokonor region, east of the Tarim Basin. They succeeded in surprising the Tibetans in their initial encounter. Chinese reinforcements, however, were overwhelmed by superior numbers of Tibetan troops and driven back. Gaozong's commanders were fortunate to escape with their lives, but at great cost to the empire. All of his gains in the Tarim Basin were swept away and control of the caravan routes that carried goods from China across the Eurasian continent was lost. 670 marked the beginning of Tibetan domination of Central Asia.

Gaozong did not live to see China regain control of the Tarim Basin region, but what Chinese armies could not accomplish, the local oasis kingdoms did from time to time, throwing off Tibetan rule and calling for Chinese help. But Chinese expeditions against the Tibetans in 678 failed to dislodge them or to contain their advances into Sichuan and Gansu. On the other hand, the Tibetan advance was halted by a succession crisis and the Chinese gained respite, rendered all the more vital by Gaozong's death and their own succession problems.

As Gaozong's consort maneuvered to retain her power, ultimately becoming, as the Empress Wu, China's first female ruler, China's woes were compounded by rebellion among the Eastern Turks. They were suppressed before the emperor's death, but again only at great cost to victor as well as to vanquished. For all Gaozong's accomplishments, he left a China in crisis, its defenses and its treasury strained, its people weary of battle—and its empire held together only by the extraordinary machinations of a very shrewd woman.

Wu Zhao, who had been one of Taizong's concubines, captured the affection and admiration of Gaozong and became his empress. She had considerable influence on Gaozong's policies and appears to have had a particular interest in foreign policy. She contributed greatly to the cosmopolitan nature of Tang society by her receptiveness to foreign merchants and the trade they stimulated. She was also probably the architect of the successful Tang policy toward Korea in the 660s and retained Silla's respect throughout the years of her reign, 690–705. China was able to establish its authority in parts of Manchuria earlier controlled by Koguryo. The Korean front proved manageable, relatively quiescent in the last years of the seventh century and the first half of the eighth. For a woman strong enough and clever enough to seize and maintain power without even the pretext of a male on the throne, international politics presented a relatively modest challenge.

In 687, before Wu Zhao had begun to rule in her own name—and before she changed the dynasty name to Zhou—the Tibetans stirred again, invading Kucha in the far west. Her initial inclination to mount a campaign against them was overcome by the advice of her ministers who noted that China's weaknesses both north and west suggested limited prospects for success against the Tibetans. She was also reminded that domestic problems, including the succession to Gaozong, were not quite resolved. It was not an auspicious moment to take the offensive. She waited two years, grew impatient, and attacked Tibet in 689. Chinese troops were defeated by the Tibetans and proved unable to drive them out of Kucha or the Tarim Basin generally, but were able to prevent further advances. For several years they pursued a policy of containment until in 692, the balance shifted in their favor. Unable to expand further, the Tibetans imploded, and thus divided, fell to the next Chinese offensive. The Chinese regained control of the fortified cities of the Tarim Basin and for a few years Tibet ceased to be a major threat.[4]

Once again the perennial debate divided the court: was the empire worth the cost? Throughout the history of international relations foreign and domestic policy advisers have been pitted against each other in the struggle over the use and abuse of finite resources. Should available funds be used for the army or for agriculture, to build distant defenses or improve the infrastructure of the heartland? Did the benefits of war accrue to all or just a few? More spears and horses for the army or more rice and vegetables for the masses? Could the country afford both? Sometimes, of course, outside pressures, real or imagined, decide the issue. With both the Koreans and the Tibetans looking inward for the moment, advocates of emphasis on internal affairs might have prevailed. But their opponents, as is so often the case, found a new foreign threat. The Turks were on the march again.

First, in 695, it was the Northern Turks, reunited under a new leader, that had to be bought off. Then it was the Western Turks, allied now with the Tibetans. And within a year the Eastern Turks had reunited and resumed their raids on Chinese territory. In 696, the Tibetans, supported by the Western Turks, defeated Chinese defenders in a battle less than 200 miles from Chang'an. If the Empress did not have enough to occupy her military strategists, the Khitan peoples of Manchuria, tired of being mistreated by the Chinese, rebelled; they defeated Chinese forces in the vicinity of modern Beijing. The western and northern frontiers were under siege.

Temperamentally, the empress was attracted to arguments favoring a militant response against all of her foreign tormentors, but she fought off her instincts. She understood that as powerful as China was, it could not afford to do battle on so many fronts. Her advisers suggested more promising approaches, less expensive, less dangerous. She chose to focus her military response against the Khitans while appeasing the Eastern Turks and exploiting divisions between various Turks and Tibetans. And it worked. Her forces repelled the Khitan with help from the Eastern Turks. The Eastern Turks extended their power from Manchuria westward all the way to the Yili Valley, harassed the Chinese constantly, but at a level they could endure—at least until 705. The Tibetans fragmented again and were defeated by Chinese troops in 699. By 702 they had resumed tribute payments to the Tang court. Later Chinese historians might call Wu Zhao a usurper, but they had little cause to criticize her foreign policy.

Nonetheless, Chinese interests in the west were far from secure. The Turks and Tibetans were as eager to control the lucrative caravan routes as were the Chinese. The outposts guarding the routes, stretching thousands of miles across western China and Central Asia, would always be vulnerable. There would be rare moments, to be sure, when Chinese power was so overwhelming or potential adversaries so divided that the defenders could sleep easily. More often, however, given the limitations of the communications and transportation systems of the time, some local force would be confident of its superiority on the ground—and attack. The forced settlement of Chinese peasants, slaves, and criminals at the garrisons and oases along the way improved the odds slightly, but did not suffice to make a safe bet of China's imperialist gamble.

Anger at the machinations of her lovers undermined Wu Zhao's popularity in the early years of the eighth century and she was forced to abdicate in 705. China lacked stable leadership for several years. Chinese forces were hurt by the Eastern Turks in 705 and then by the Turgesh branch of the Western Turks in the vicinity of Kucha in 708 and 709. In both cases, China's leaders opted for appeasement, biding their time until the correlation of forces had shifted in their favor. Similarly, extended negotiations ending in a marriage alliance pacified the Tibetans for much of this time. And then in 712, the Chinese were blessed with another great ruler, Xuanzong, who restored the Tang and led them to heights reminiscent of the days of Taizong.

TABLE 2.2.   Some Major Figures of the Seventh and Eighth Centuries (Dates are often approximate. Names in boldface are referred to in text)

Muhammed	570–632
Taizong	**600–649**
Empress Wu	**626–705**
Yang Guifei	**715–756**
Charlemagne	742–814
Harun ar-Rashid of Baghdad	766–809

In the same year that Xuanzong began his reign in Chang'an, Arab forces driving across Central Asia captured Samarkand, having seized Bukhara the year before. Sogdiana was theirs and Ferghana was clearly next. Another powerful competitor had arrived on the scene. Xuanzong hesitated only briefly. He had every intention of pursuing an aggressive foreign policy and throwing back all challenges to China's hegemony over East and Central Asia. As he strengthened his defenses, the Tibetans betrayed his trust and attacked at Lanzhou, in Gansu. The Chinese won a decisive victory, but Xuanzong's troubles with Tibet were just beginning. Successful campaigns against the Turks in 721 and 722 similarly failed to provide a long-term solution to their raids.

Except for the Tibetans, most of China's adversaries did not try to seize and hold territory. They relied on cavalry raids to obtain the cattle, grain, and horses they wanted. Chang'an could not respond in a timely and effective manner to this form of opposition. It was not a new problem, but rather one sedentary Chinese society had confronted against nomadic horsemen for centuries. Xuanzong and his advisers were not the first Chinese to attempt to overcome the problems of frontier defense. Their immediate predecessors had experimented with the creation of large permanent armies on the frontier under the direction of military governors. In a variant of Han agricultural garrisons, the troops farmed to provide their own supplies. These became professional armies and a source of great power to their commanders, a potential danger accepted as a not unreasonable price for the protection they offered. There were nearly 500,000 of these troops by mid-century and they were proving to be very expensive—but they were effective against the nomadic raiders and the Tibetans.

To the northeast, Chinese military operations might be considered defensive. Xuanzong doubtless would have liked control of all of Mongolia, Manchuria, and Korea. Had there been fewer problems in Central Asia, and especially with the Tibetan empire, he might have behaved more aggressively toward the Khitan, the new state of Parhae, or Silla. He appears, however, to have found the wealth of Central Asia and the trade routes that ran across it more attractive, and to have been willing to settle for what was already China's domain in the east. Silla, for its part, was reasonably content to avoid confrontation with China; the Khitan and Parhae were not.

In 714 Tang armies regained control of southern Manchuria and won promises of allegiance from the Khitan rulers. Given the impressive Chinese garrisons in the region the Khitan found it expedient to remain passive until 730 when they rebelled again, quite possibly because of continued abuse by the Chinese occupying force and its hangers-on. The first round ended in a Chinese victory with Khitan rebel forces fleeing to the mountains of Inner Mongolia. Reorganized in 733 they came out of the hills to defeat a Chinese force sent to destroy them. Peace was restored in 735 but it did not last, probably could not last given the inability of the Chinese to demonstrate their power lightly. The Khitan rose again in 736, won a number of battles over the next several years, only to be subdued again in 740. Few in Chang'an had any illusions as to how long they would remain pacified and a large number of troops were deployed to the region for nominally defensive purposes.

Parhae was a new state established in Manchuria by a former Koguryo general early in the eighth century. Adopting a Tang-style centralized administration, Parhae quickly gained control of much of what had been Koguryo's territory and generated wealth and power sufficient to cause unease both in China and in Silla. China established diplomatic relations with it and looked to Silla for support should Parhae become as aggressive as Koguryo had been. In 732, Chinese fears were realized when Parhae launched a successful naval raid against a city on the Shandong peninsula. Chinese retaliation had little impact and Silla, presumably no less apprehensive about China's intentions, provided little support. At mid-century Parhae was thriving, greatly influenced by Chinese culture, participating in the tributary system, but very much an independent power of whose peaceful intentions China could not be assured. The Tang had little choice but to treat Parhae with respect and to maintain defensive forces wherever Parhae might strike.

But for Xuanzong, the principal obstacle to his visions proved to be the Tibetan Empire. Tibet was the emerging great power in Central Asia and as such constituted a clear threat to Chinese pretensions to hegemony over the region. China's task was the same as that any hegemonic power faces when confronted with a rising new power: either coopt the new power into the existing interstate system that favors the hegemon, work out a plan for sharing influence and wealth, or subdue it. All three approaches had been tried before Xuanzong's reign without enduring success. Xuanzong also tried all three, but when he could, he preferred to push the Tibetans aside. The Tibetans had many successes against Chinese troops, but on the whole, they came out second best. Badly defeated by a Chinese army—led by a general of Korean origin—in 747 and pressed from the west by the Arabs, the Tibetans reached their "military nadir" in 750.[5]

The Tibetans, to be sure, were provocative. In 714 they conducted a series of raids across the Yellow River, falling back in the face of well-prepared Tang defenders. They offered Xuanzong peace, but addressed the Chinese as equals, perceived by the Chinese as an insult—and their offer was rejected. In 715 they allied briefly with the Arabs to defeat Ferghana and again the Chinese drove them out. The Tibetans were not willing to accept the status quo and the Chinese preferred combat to the voluntary surrender of any of their interests in Central Asia.

Xuanzong did not eschew diplomacy. Troubled by Tibetan inroads in the region of the Pamirs and Hindu Kush, he sent emissaries to the various potentates of the region to remind them of their obligations to the Tang. As the Chinese shut them out of the southern trade routes, in 717 the Tibetans sent troops to join Arabs and Turgesh forces attacking Chinese protectorates on the northern edge of the Tarim Basin. The Chinese defenders, none of whom were ethnic Chinese, drove them off. The Tibetans tried raids across the Yellow River again, with no more luck

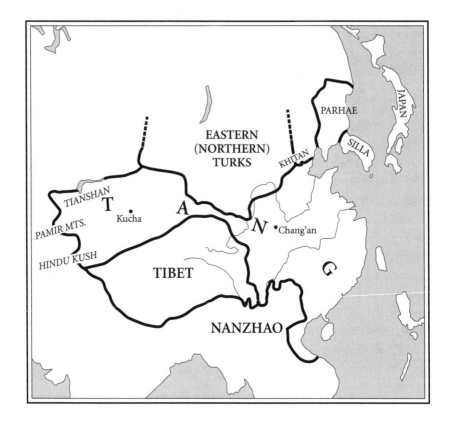

MAP 7.   TANG EMPIRE, C. 750.
After Fairbank and Reischauer, *East Asia*, p. 156.

than before. Several small Central Asian states aligned with Tibet considered it expedient to defect to the Chinese side.

The 720s were not good years for the Tibetans. Xuanzong went on
the offensive, despite arguments of his ministers to the contrary. *He*
would not put a price tag on the security of the empire. In 722 Chinese
forces smashed the Tibetans, gaining four or five years of quiet on the
western frontier. When the Tibetans launched new raids in 726 and 727,
Chinese troops pursued and defeated them. And again in 728, Tang forces
repelled Tibetan raids on China's frontiers. Finally, in 729 Tibetan armies
won a major battle against the Chinese, but before they could relish their
victory, most of their army was needed to defend against the Arabs to
their west. Tibetan leaders recognized the need for peace with China to

cope with the Arab threat. Once again they asked Xuanzong for peace and this time, mindful of his inability to win a total, final victory over them and of the criticism of his military budget, he accepted.

The Chinese-Tibetan detente lasted approximately seven years. Some of the Tang frontier generals became involved in court politics in the mid-730s and their views provided Xuanzong with a useful counter to the more pacific views of his civilian advisers. He was displeased by Tibetan troop movements around Central Asia. He and the generals feared a possible Tibetan-Turgesh alliance, although ostensibly aimed at the Arabs, would be used ultimately to challenge Chinese influence in the region. The militarists won the debate at court and China launched a preemptive attack on Tibet in 737. Preoccupied with the Arabs, the Tibetans were caught by surprise and the attack succeeded in weakening their forces and ability to fight on two fronts. Skirmishes continued for years, escalating in 740, and ending in the crushing defeat of the Tibetans in 747. It would take them a decade to recover.

Central Asia now belonged to the Chinese and the Arabs as these two empires moved relentlessly toward each other. In 751 their troops met near Samarkand in a ferocious battle won by the Arabs when key Turkic troops supporting the Chinese defected to the Arab side. The tide had begun to run against the Tang.

At home the central government's authority declined, its finances shaken by the breakdown of the tax system. Factional struggles wracked the court and the aging Xuanzong began to lose his grip on power. Infatuated with the beautiful courtesan Yang Guifei, he devoted his energies to pleasing her. His generals were only too eager to manage the affairs of state. In particular, the military governors in the frontier commands acted increasingly like feudal lords. Indeed, some revealed more interest in political than in military matters and China began to suffer serious military setbacks. In the same year the Arabs defeated Chinese troops in the west, the Khitan decimated a Chinese army in the north. In the southwest, in the vicinity of modern Yunnan, a new, ethnically Thai state, Nanzhao, emerged and battered Chinese forces stationed nearby. As the military situation deteriorated and the emperor's grasp of reality slipped, one of his commanders, An Lushan, of mixed Soghdian and Turkic ancestry, rebelled in December 755 and marched from the north through Luoyang and on to Chang'an, capturing both cities easily. Xuanzong and

Yang Guifei—who had adopted An Lushan and was rumored to be his lover—fled to Sichuan. There the emperor was forced to have her executed and, before his ordeal was over, to abdicate. One of the most brilliant eras in Chinese history, indeed in world history, had come to an end.

Korea, Japan, and Southeast Asia

Tang influence was, of course, enormous on those parts of East Asia that were under direct Chinese control, as, from time to time, were parts of Korea and northern Vietnam. In most instances, conquered peoples were forced to accept various elements of Chinese civilization. Indeed, the Chinese expectation was that these people would eventually be assimilated, surrendering their indigenous culture. Although forced assimilation often met stiff resistance, many of China's victims perceived value in China's methods of political organization, bureaucratic administration, philosophy, religion, and art. At least as interesting is the fact that some *potential* victims, such as the Japanese, concluded there was much to be gained from adopting elements of Chinese culture.

The obvious point is that the culture of the dominant power in a given region at a given time will hold great attraction for neighbors who envy its wealth and power. Edward Sapir, an early-twentieth-century American anthropologist, argued that a conquering culture is superior to that of its victim. Few scholars would agree with Sapir today. Nonetheless, as Koreans, Japanese, and Vietnamese witnessed Tang greatness, they sought to find its sources and to incorporate them into their own cultures. None wanted to become Chinese—anymore than the Chinese would later wish to become "Western," but they wanted take from the Chinese that which would allow them to become wealthy and powerful while remaining Korean, Japanese, and Vietnamese—a process repeated by peoples around the world as disparate cultures appear dominant.

Tang efforts to assimilate the Koreans conquered in Koguryo and Paekche in the seventh century failed. The Chinese set up puppet regimes in both states, refused to return to its erstwhile ally Silla territory Silla had lost earlier to Koguryo, and encouraged hostility to Silla in the territories controlled by Tang troops and administrators. Silla prevailed in 671, however, and drove the Chinese off the Korean peninsula back to the Liaodong peninsula in Manchuria. But despite the persistent tension between one or another Korean entity and China, Koreans both in Silla and in Parhae, successor state to Koguryo, consciously modeled their regimes after the Tang.

Although Silla traded widely and had contacts with merchants throughout Asia, including Arabs who came by sea, the bulk of its trade was with China. Silla eagerly participated in the tributary system through which Chinese officials attempted to control international commerce, keeping it in their hands rather than those of the merchant class disparaged by Confucian intellectuals. All involved, however, understood and ultimately sanctioned large volumes of private trade, mostly in luxury goods, that accompanied diplomatic missions.

And in a pattern familiar to modern readers, Silla sent thousands of students to China. Most studied Confucianism, but some also studied the natural sciences in which China was the acknowledged leader in seventh- and eighth-century Asia. Another handful studied art. Monks traveled around China studying various forms of Buddhism that had taken root there. The Sokkuram grotto, a major monument of Silla art, was modeled after the cave temples of China. Those who returned to Silla brought with them books and techniques that facilitated and accelerated the spread of Chinese culture. By 682 Silla had created a national Confucian college to train its young people in the Confucian classics. As in China, Confucian scholarship became popular among upper-class Koreans.

Equally important was the movement toward a Chinese-style bureaucratic government. The king viewed sinicization as a means of strengthening his power against an aristocracy that sought to circumscribe it. The establishment of an examination system was designed to make learning rather than class status the criterion for selecting officials. It was, of course, the upper classes that could devote the time and money to obtain the Confucian learning necessary to excel in the examinations. Still, qualified officials, even if largely upper class, were preferable to the aristocracy by birth that continued to dominate Silla society.

Parhae, although considered a Korean state, and ruled primarily by Koreans, was populated largely by the Malgal tribes of Manchuria. The ethnic difference between the ruling elite and the majority was apparently a source of social instability. Chinese culture was more appealing to the Koreans than to their subjects. Once it had fought off both China and Silla, and gained acceptance by China, Parhae followed Silla's lead. It, too, sent students and monks to China, engaged in extensive trade, and conducted a vigorous campaign to introduce Chinese culture. Like Silla, Parhae adopted a Chinese form of bureaucratic administration, the better to rule the Malgal.

None of this appreciation of Chinese civilization prevented Parhae from taking advantage of China's distress during the An Lushan rebellion to expand into territory claimed by the Tang. To protect itself against the Chinese, it established ties with some of the Turkic nomads who harassed China's northern frontiers. Geography dictated less contact with the maritime world, but archeological findings indicate that Japan was a Parhae trading partner, as well as a potential political ally.

In this story of the expansion of the Chinese culture area, Korea was enormously important, not only for what occurred throughout Korea, but also for the role played by Koreans in carrying their own and Chinese culture to Japan. Although Japan had direct contacts with China, many of the teachers and craftsmen who brought Chinese learning and techniques to Japan were Korean refugees either from Tang armies or wars among Korean states. Others may have been captives or slaves taken by the Japanese on the various occasions in which they intervened in the affairs of the peninsula. As Tang forces overran Koguryo and Paekche in the 660s, a substantial number of educated and skilled Koreans migrated to Japan where they were well received by the emperor and his advisers. The defenses the Japanese subsequently built late in the seventh century, when they feared invasion by Tang troops, were based on Korean techniques and are believed to have been designed by immigrants from Paekche.

The Japanese had resumed sending embassies to China early in the seventh century and continued to send them until early in the ninth. The embassies included monks and students, artists and craftsmen, many of whom remained in China for years, absorbing local customs and knowledge. Buddhism imported from China, often through Korea, was most successful in Japan, where it revolutionized architecture, sculpture, calligraphy and painting. Study of the Confucian classics became central to the Japanese educational system. But Japanese leaders looked to China for more than art, more than philosophy, religion or science. Like the Koreans, they sought to master the sources of Chinese wealth and power, to match the splendor of the Tang.

In 645, a coup d'état placed power in the hands of a clan that came to be known as the Fujiwara and led to the enthronement of the Emperor

Kotoku. Using information they had collected over several decades, the emperor's advisers immediately began a series of reforms designed to allow him to rule in the Chinese manner. They began with an edict adopting the Chinese system of land tenure and taxation and followed—after the unpleasantness of Japan's whipping by the Tang in Korea in the 660s and a succession crisis at home—with law codes and administrative reforms modeled after their Tang equivalents. These changes were all intended to reduce the power of the great provincial landholders and concentrate it in the central government, at least nominally in the hands of the emperor. The court also attempted to use Buddhism, along with the indigenous Shinto religious practices, to augment the spiritual legitimacy of the emperor's rule—as the emperor's advisers believed had been done in China and Korea.

If imitation is indeed the sincerest form of flattery, Japan's first permanent capital, built by the Fujiwaras at Nara, would have pleased the Tang rulers. It appears to have followed closely the plan of the Tang capital at Chang'an.[6] Nara today contains the best examples of Tang architecture to be found in East Asia and its treasure houses contain the finest surviving examples of Tang art.

Japan's voluntary absorption of so many elements of Chinese civilization reflects the unquestionable attraction of Tang culture, the threat Japanese leaders perceived in the growth of Chinese power, and the desire of Japan's ruling class to enhance its own power. They accepted Chinese ideas and material culture, more often than not through Korean filters, in an urgent effort to offset the temporal power of their continental neighbor and to enjoy the authority and quality of life available to the Tang court. Chinese influence was probably greatest in Japan from roughly 650–750, when the magnificence of the Tang was most evident.

The Japanese may have been less important players in the international system of East Asia than the Chinese or Koreans during these years of Tang splendor, but they were obviously participants. Diplomatically they were engaged with China and Korea. Militarily, they intervened on the Korean peninsula and fought both Chinese and various Korean forces. The defenses they prepared against invasion from the continent were also evidence of their international security concerns. Economically, trade with China and Korea was extensive and critical for Japan's technological advancement, but there is also evidence of trade with countries as far away as Persia—although it may not have been direct. Culturally, the traffic seems to have been one way. Although many Japanese traveled abroad, there are no indications of Japanese culture being exported, overwhelming evidence of Korean, Chinese—and even Indian—culture being imported. The movement of Buddhism from India through China to Korea and on to Japan is a fascinating story in its own right. And in 752, when the Great Buddha of Todaiji in modern Kyoto was dedicated, Buddhists came from all over Asia for the ceremony, from Champa and India as well as China and Korea. Japan was in no way isolated from the main currents of continental affairs.

Of Southeast Asia generally, there remains little to be said of the seventh and early eighth centuries. Vietnam, of course, was an established polity, the most developed part of which struggled under Chinese occupation. Champa survived the rapaciousness of Chinese invaders, kept a hand in the coastal trade—and probably a considerable involvement in piracy. The Thai people were among those who established Nanzhao in the vicinity of modern Yunnan in mid eighth century and forced the Chinese to accept their independence. The Khmers were beginning to organize Cambodia, but Angkor was still a half century away. Mainland Malays had yet to create a coherent political entity, but they too were deeply involved in coastal trade—and piracy. Chinese culture did not spread much beyond northern Vietnam. Indian culture, Buddhism and Hinduism in particular, was having a major impact further south, especially in those areas adjacent to India and those along the maritime trade routes between India and China.

Island Southeast Asia was just beginning to develop coherent political entities in Sumatra and Java, where Indian influence was important. Profits from coastal trade led to the formation of one political grouping near Palembang in southeastern Sumatra in the seventh century out of which emerged the kingdom of Srivijaya. Maritime traffic was the source of Srivijaya's strength and it became the principal entrepot for the India-China run and the dominant force in the region for centuries to come. Buddhism took root there, supported by the rulers, who served as patrons for monks from all over Asia. Aware of the glories of the Tang court, Srivijaya's ruler sent emissaries to Chang'an several times in the early eighth century, signaling his intention to be a participant in the East Asian international system. Perhaps a few decades behind Srivijaya, the kingdom of Majapahit arose in Java, where Buddhists and Hindus vied for control in the eighth and ninth centuries. Java, too, was a participant in the burgeoning trade of the region, but as a political force, it could not yet compete with the Sumatrans—nor gain the attention of the Tang.

As trade increased between East Asia on the one hand, South Asia, the Middle East, and the Mediterranean on the other, Southeast Asia increased in importance. This was especially true in those years, all too frequent, when the struggle for control of Central Asia made overland traffic dangerous and expensive. Various coastal areas of Southeast Asia, mainland and island, offered havens from the seas, resting places between monsoons, and eventually products of their own. Strong maritime powers like Srivijaya could also offer protection from pirates, for a fee of course, but at a price that might well be attractive compared to the cost of overland travel. And the merchants and sailors that stopped along the way planted seeds of their own cultures as well. Most were South Asians rather than Chinese and thus it was Indian culture that had the greatest impact, Indians who facilitated culture transfer.

Conclusion

The seventh century and the first half of the eighth unquestionably constituted a period in which China dominated East Asia, much of Central Asia, and part of Southeast Asia—especially if one includes as Southeast Asia those parts of modern China south of the Yangzi that Tang armies brought into the empire. Tang culture was magnificent, renowned for its art, literature, music, and science all over Asia and those parts of Africa and Europe involved in international affairs. China was a magnet, drawing merchants, pilgrims, and products from much of the world. The splendor of Chang'an was unsurpassed.

Elements of Chinese civilization, itself Turkic influenced, spread everywhere, most obviously to Korea, Japan, and Vietnam. But the cultural transference was not unidirectional. The Chinese learned from others, as with Buddhism, transmuted it to suit their own needs, and passed it on, perhaps in forms barely recognizable to the originators. Central Asian music became popular in China as its troops returned from the wars there and as peoples of Central Asia moved in and out of the Chinese heartland. Edwin Cranston, a student of Japanese culture, contends that "the oasis culture of central Asia was in fact the fountainhead of much of the subsequent music of East Asia."[7] Persian lutes, Vietnamese mouth organs, dances from various parts of Asia became popular in Tang China and were passed on to Korea and Japan. In painting the Chinese learned something about shading from India and, early in the eighth century, according to Sherman Lee,[8] produced the first landscape painting, the beginnings of landscape painting for its own sake—an art form that became exceptionally popular throughout East Asia. Chinese ceramics became highly prized in the Middle East. Tang era Yue ware, porcelains with green-toned glazes, have been found in Egypt and Iraq, as well as India and Japan, and influenced porcelain production everywhere. The heyday of the Tang was an era of extraordinary culture exchange—and China was at the center of it, both giving *and* receiving.

Obviously there was much cultural, economic, political, and military movement outside of China at this time. Koreans, Japanese, Tibetans, various Mongol and Turkic peoples, Southeast Asians—especially Malays—Indians, Persians, and Arabs were interacting with the Chinese and sometimes with each other. Sometimes their activities were threatening, often they were enriching, but all added to the complex mosaic that constituted the international system of East Asia.

The Tang faced two classic problems of international relations. First, great and rich as China was, it was an attractive source of plunder to its neighbors. Its colonies and protectorates, particularly those along the Silk Roads, were perceived by others to be the source of Chinese wealth and power. These were constantly raided and sometimes conquered by forces hostile to China. Tang China could never be secure. Its borders were too extensive to defend at a time when the limits of military technology favored the hit-and-run raider. Chinese defenders invariably were spread too thin.

The second classic dilemma was the question of how much of the empire's resources could be committed to defense. How much defense could China afford? More significantly, as it turned out, was the question of whether, if the government created a powerful military, it could prevent that military from becoming the ultimate authority in the empire. The answer proved to be "no," as An Lushan demonstrated.

CHAPTER THREE

East Asia Uncentered

As rebellion swept through China, frontier garrisons were recalled to defend the dynasty, abandoning key positions intended to contain the Tibetans and other potential enemies. A power vacuum appeared in northwest and Central Asia, which was quickly filled by the Tibetans, Uyghur Turks, and others. The Chinese empire collapsed and nearly a thousand years passed before Chinese political influence in Central Asia again reached the heights enjoyed during the heyday of the Tang. Although Chinese cultural influence in East Asia continued to increase in Korea, Japan, and northern Vietnam, by the end of the eighth century, Chinese military power was greatly diminished relative to that of its antagonists and Chang'an lost the centrality it had enjoyed in the region.

The Tang dynasty survived rebellions and invasions until early in the tenth century. Its demise appeared to presage the end of the Chinese empire as it had been known to the Han and regained by the Tang. China itself fragmented once again and a student of China's past might have seen parallels with the decline of the Zhou—an end, conceivably permanent, to China's unity. But before the century had ended, a new dynasty, the Song, emerged to reunify the country and revive its cultural glory. The Song, however, never had the means to regain the empire, wisely choosing to avoid the lethal temptations of imperialism. Outside pressures on the Song were relentless, the territory under Song control shrank, and before the end of the thirteenth century, China and much of the rest of Asia, had fallen completely under the control of Khubilai Khan and the Mongols.

Korea, Japan, and the several Southeast Asian political entities were not adversely affected by the decline of the regional hegemon. Spared a threat from China, Korea and especially Japan focused on domestic affairs, developing their own unique cultures. Vietnam struggled, with mixed results, to regain its independence from its Chinese overlord. The Thai state of Nanzhao prospered, as did a newly evolved Cambodian kingdom at Angkor. Other peoples began to cohere on the mainland of Southeast Asia, while on the islands major powers grew in Sumatra and Java. The obvious point is that in the five centuries between the An

Lushan rebellion that undermined the Tang and the conquests of the Mongols, political and military power in East Asia were greatly dispersed.

TABLE 3.1.   Some Notable Dates of the Ninth to Twelfth Centuries
(Dates are approximate. Events in boldface are referred to in text)

Arabs sack Rome	846
Hindus build Prambanan in Java	**856–910**
Kingdom of Ghana at zenith	900–1000
Koryo Dynasty in Korea	**918–1392**
Northern Song Dynasty in China	**960–1126**
Michinaga rules Japan	**995–1028**
Leif Ericson founds Vinland in Newfoundland	1000
Cola fleet from India destroys Srivijaya	**1025**
Norman conquest of England	1066
Crusades in Holy Land	1095–1291
Suryavarman II builds Angkor Wat	**1115–1150**
Southern Song	**1127–1289**
Minamoto Yoritomo triumphs in Japan	**1185**
Richard the Lion Hearted leads Third Crusade	1189

Late Tang

Xuanzong's infatuation with Yang Guifei not only distracted him from the affairs of state, but also gave her family enormous influence at the court. The political machinations at Chang'an ultimately affected policy, military as well as economic and political.

China suffered three important defeats in 751, omens of what lay ahead. In the far west, a Chinese army that had been remarkably successful for a decade was defeated by the Arabs, marking the limits of Chinese expansion in the region, the ebbing of the Chinese tide. In the northeast, An Lushan, having defeated the Khitan and their allies in a war he provoked in 750, launched another offensive, overreached himself and lost most of his men. In the southwest, Nanzhao had resisted exploitation by neighboring Chinese officials and launched successful punitive expeditions against the offenders. An attempt to force Nanzhao into submission resulted in the third disaster for Tang forces. Expectations of using Nanzhao as a buffer against Tibet evaporated when Nanzhao opted to ally with the Tibetans against China. It was not a very good year.

An Lushan recovered from his defeat and raised a new army, but his plan to avenge himself against the Khitan was aborted by the defection of one of his generals and his growing concern about loss of influence at the capital. In November 755, he led his forces southward against the court. After a successful opening attack, they were beaten back by imperial troops late in 757. An was assassinated in 757, but rebel forces stayed in the field, often victorious, until the final government offensive in the fall of 762, and the death of the last rebel leader in January 763. After seven years of civil war, the Tang had prevailed and the dynasty lived on—thanks largely to the aid of Uyghur mercenaries.

The Uyghurs were a Turkic people, centered in the northern reaches of modern Xinjiang. Once subjects of the Eastern Turks, they had rebelled and facilitated the Tang victory over their former rulers. By mid-eighth century they had become the dominant force on the steppe, engaged in agriculture as well as traditional nomadic pursuits. Coveting no Chinese territory, eager for trade, the Uyghurs had no interests in conflict with China—so long as China did not threaten their lands and permitted trade on reasonable terms. Tang willingness to court the Uyghurs paid off handsomely during the rebellion. Uyghur mercenaries played a critical role in the liberation of Chang'an from rebel occupation in 757 and again in the decisive assault on the rebels in 762. An uneasy alliance between the Uyghurs and the Chinese lasted until mid-ninth century.

Another indication of the importance of Uyghur support was the unpredictability of imperial troops, some of whom changed sides, others of whom pillaged and raped between battles with the rebels. In 758 they failed to defend Guangzhou, which was taken over by Muslims resident there—probably Indians as well as Arabs—and sacked. The most grievous incidents occurred in the winter of 760–761 when resentment against wealthy foreign merchants led to the massacre of thousands of them by government forces who followed suppression of revolt along the Yangzi with a looting spree. There were, however, countless other instances in which forces nominally loyal to the Tang inflicted misery upon ordinary people who were unfortunate enough to cross their paths. Tang leaders exercised little control over their forces.

And if presumably friendly forces could exploit the chaos, enemies of long standing, like the Tibetans, were only too eager to seize the opportunity to move across unguarded or thinly garrisoned frontiers. Xuanzong had taken advantage of internal turmoil among the Tibetans to drive them back. Now the situation was reversed and the Tibetans would provide the Chinese with no respite for the next century. Quickly in 756 the Tibetans took back territory in what had once been their northeast, overwhelming Chinese forts there. Once again they expanded into northwest China and eastern Central Asia, eventually occupying much of modern Gansu and Ningxia. Late in 763, *after* the An Lushan rebellion had ended, the Tibetans moved into modern Shaanxi province, then attacked and systematically looted Chang'an, which they held for two weeks before withdrawing. They left no doubt in the minds of China's leaders that they were aware of the shift in the balance of power in East and Central Asia. Year after year they struck, undermining China's recovery, forcing the diversion of men and treasure from badly needed reconstruction to defense. Not until 783 did China succeed in gaining a truce with Tibet— and that at great cost to a desperate Chinese regime, which was forced to concede all the territory Tibet had taken since 756.

The Tang were desperate in 783 because of a new spate of rebellions that forced the emperor to flee Chang'an and threatened to result in the fragmentation of China. Chinese forces were not able to fight both Tibetans and rebels and were fortunate that the Tibetans, exhausted by their own military adventurism, were willing to grant them peace on the western front. For Dezong, the Tang emperor, the more pressing threat was the insubordination of several provincial leaders, four of whom signed a mutual defense pact against the central government. An effort to bring the provinces to heel by force failed and some of the provincial leaders declared themselves kings of the territories over which they ruled de facto. Dezong never succeeded in regaining control of provincial China and fell back on the defense of the capital against foreign invaders. China in the closing days of the eighth century bore resemblance to the Zhou era when the emperor ruled little more than the capital of a country which was only nominally united.

The Tibetan Factor

Promised Chinese acceptance of its territorial gains and with an expectation of being recognized as an equal, Tibet accepted a truce with China in

783, entered into negotiations for a peace treaty, and helped the Tang put down a rebellion that had been abetted by the Uyghurs—not always the loyal allies the Chinese desired. But the Tibetans were angered by what they perceived to be a Chinese failure to comply with the terms of the truce. The peace treaty was never concluded and the Tibetans resumed their raids on Chinese territory. Moving their forces in a northeasterly direction just beyond the Great Wall, they appeared to be seeking control of China's entire land frontier.

A desperate Tang emperor acceded to the advice of his ministers to seek a classic grand alliance, a regional pact that would include every major state bordering on Tibet. Together they would do what China could not do alone: contain Tibet. The Uyghurs were most important, their cavalry probably essential to holding the northern front. Nanzhao and Hindustan were to worry Tibet from the south and the Arabs were to attack from the west. The Uyghurs readily entered the fray. Hindustan did not. Indeed, it may never have been approached. Nanzhao clung to its Tibetan overlord, perceiving China to be the greater threat to its security. The Arabs, on the other hand, attacked, whether in collusion with China or not. For the next several years Tibet was locked in combat with Arab armies in Central Asia. There is no evidence of formal alliances among the several powers involved, but Tibetan pressure on China was unquestionably relieved.

The principal tension in the late 780s seems to have been between the Uyghurs and the Tibetans, each seeking to control Eurasian trade routes and to extort as much as they could from passing merchants and officials. Chinese forces were not without influence in Central Asia; nor were they major contenders for dominance. In the early 790s, Tibet finally captured Khotan and began an extended period in which it controlled the southern routes. At the same time, however, Uyghur offensives pushed Tibet back in the northeast. A effort by Tibet to get its vassal Nanzhao to provide troops in the north failed in 794. Indeed, Nanzhao defected from its alliance with Tibet—with considerable encouragement from China.

Although Tibet was still a powerful force in Central Asia, it had been weakened in the east. And even its hold on Central Asia was relatively shaky in the seesaw battles with the Uyghurs and Arabs. In 801 it lost a major battle to a combined Chinese-Nanzhao force—although most of the troops captured by the victors were reported to be Arabs and soldiers from Samarkand under Tibetan command. It was not until the 820s, after frequent military engagements, that Tibet finally concluded peace agreements with both the Uyghurs in 822 and the Chinese in 823. By the standards of Sino-Tibetan relations, it became a long peace that endured for more than twenty years.

Of the major powers of the eighth and ninth centuries, the Uyghurs were the first to be destroyed. In 840 the Kirghiz peoples, of mixed Mongolian and Turkic origin, charged across the Uyghur empire and smashed it. Most of the Uyghur peoples migrated to the northern rim of the Tarim Basin, where they established a sedentary Uyghur kingdom. Others fled into China and Tibet, never again to enjoy a political entity of their own or a position of influence in Asian affairs. The Tibetans were only slightly more fortunate. In the 840s the Tibetan leader was assassinated; his generals disputed the succession, and the central government lost control of its forces. As Tibetans fought among themselves, their Central Asian protectorates regained their autonomy and the Chinese surged into the territories disputed between them. In 866 the Tibetan empire collapsed. A truncated Tibetan state survived, only to become the plaything of the great powers that struggled for dominance over Central Asia in the centuries to come.

The Demise of the Tang Dynasty

The Tang had a brief revival early in the ninth century when Tang Xianzong reasserted the power of the central government, bringing most of the separatist provinces under Chang'an's control. The existing balance of power in Asia was favorable to China and Xianzong exploited opportunities to strengthen the dynasty and reclaim parts of the empire, especially some previously lost to the Tibetans. Peace with the Tibetans brought additional time to heal internal wounds and shore up defenses and the later collapse of both Uyghur and Tibetan empires eliminated the principal threats to Chinese security. The Kirghiz, once having crushed the Uyghurs, preferred trade to war with China.

By mid-century, however, Nanzhao was at best a restive ally. When a large-scale rebellion broke out in Vietnam, Nanzhao chose to align itself with the Vietnamese against their Chinese overlords. Tang forces attempting to suppress the Vietnamese independence movement were attacked by Nanzhao troops and beaten badly in the late 850s and early

860s. A massive Tang offensive reimposed Chinese imperialism in northern Vietnam in 868, but at enormous cost to the people of China. Nanzhao remained a problem until 875. Expenditures required to defend the empire, however truncated, exhausted the treasury and required unacceptable levels of taxation in manpower and materiel. As non-Chinese peoples within the borders of the Tang state perceived weakness, they, too, became rebellious and trouble spread along the Yangzi and along the southern frontier. The penultimate blow to the dynasty came in the form of a major internal rebellion that began in 875 and lasted nearly ten years.

Efforts to rejuvenate the dynasty in the 870s failed miserably as banditry and rebellion festered, aggravated by famine and misgovernment, as well as the diversion of scarce resources to the military. Funds that might have been used to ameliorate living conditions in rural China were spent on defenses against possible naval attacks from Silla or Japan. The discontented grew bolder as their numbers increased, joining forces, creating small armies of hundreds, even thousands, of men, and launching large-scale attacks on provincial cities. Efforts to restore order were ultimately successful, but not before one army, fleeing government troops in the north, marched all the way to Guangzhou in 879. Unable to negotiate satisfactory surrender terms, the rebel leader, Huang Chao, ordered his men to attack the city, where they killed the military governor and thousands of the city's inhabitants, including large numbers of foreign merchants from all the maritime trading countries of South and Southeast Asia, Persia, and the Arab world.

As the dynasty struggled, its own military commanders often proved unwilling to risk their lives or those of their men in confrontation with bandit forces. Many sought to position themselves so as to take advantage of what they perceived as the imminent fall of the central government, of the Tang. By 880, Huang's forces, greatly augmented by defecting imperial troops, marched back across the Yangzi and ultimately captured the capital, where he clearly intended to establish his own dynasty. Chang'an was probably the world's most splendid city when he arrived, but his men ignored his efforts to establish discipline and quickly defiled it, looting, burning, raping, and murdering their way through it. Huang occupied Chang'an for more than two years while the powerless emperor, Xizong, waited in exile in Sichuan. The inability of the Tang leaders to overcome Huang's forces with their own led them to call in foreign troops, specifically those of the Shatuo, the easternmost branch of the western Turks, many of whom had come to live within the Great Wall.

Shatuo warriors had fought against Tibet for much of the eighth century, allied with the Uyghurs or the Chinese. Late in the century, they shifted sides, aiding the Tibetans against the Chinese. For most of the ninth century, despite occasional skirmishes, they were at peace with China, with many of them moving into northern Shaanxi. In 882 they rode to the rescue of the Tang, driving Huang from the capital. In 884, aided by local warlords, the Shatuo finally caught up with and destroyed Huang and his army in Shandong. Banditry persisted, but the rebellion that nearly overthrew the Tang had ended.

Xizong returned to a ravaged Chang'an in 885, but the imperial treasury was empty, the military governors had no intention of surrendering the power they had acquired, and civil strife continued. Within months, the emperor was forced to flee again as the Shatuo forces that had saved the dynasty in 884 now marched on the capital. Disagreements among the military leaders allowed him to survive and return to Chang'an early in 888, but he died shortly thereafter. The dynasty tottered, was saved again by the Shatuo in 895, and continued with little if any authority until the last emperor was murdered in 904 by Zhu Wen, a powerful warlord and former bandit who gradually moved to establish his own dynasty in 907.

The interplay of foreign and domestic affairs that eventually brought an end to the glories of the Tang contained echoes of the fall of the Han empire, perhaps of a dirge heard eventually in all great empires. But the collapse of the Tang dynasty was no more inevitable than any other major historical event. The traditional Chinese assumptions of the cyclical nature of dynastic rule need not be accepted as the political equivalent of Newton's laws of gravity. Within the nearly three hundred years of Tang rule, there were several occasions when the empire or the dynasty seemed on the brink of destruction, only to be spared by fortuitous events or skillful leadership or both. Even in the ninth century, the process was not one of steady decline.

The Tang were unquestionably guilty of imperial overreach and at times paid a not inappropriate price for their aggression against their neighbors. On the other hand, several of their neighbors, most notably the Tibetans, were no less ruthless in their determination to create great empires, often at Chinese expense. Similarly, the movement of Arab forces eastward across Eurasia had little to do with decisions made in

Chang'an. Claims that Chinese military actions were often defensive are not wholly without merit. Simply stated, China had formidable enemies, not all of its own making, and their existence demanded enormous sums for defense, required a large standing army. By the middle of the eighth century, China had ceased to be the hegemon of East and Central Asia. External pressures, developing at times over which Chang'an had no control, drained resources, and resulted in the transfer of power from the court to the frontier military commanders. Nonetheless, the Tang survived the devastating An Lushan rebellion and had some very good years in the ninth century. It had an outside chance to survive the horrors of the banditry and Huang Chao's depredations late in the ninth century—had the emperor not died at the age of 27 and had the dominant warlord of the moment believed his interests were best served by preservation of the dynasty. In the event, the Tang were not so lucky—and today one must travel to Nara, Japan, to see Tang-age temples, to get a sense of the splendor of Chang'an during the height of Tang glory.

Northeast Asia

Silla's "Golden Age" corresponded roughly to that of the Tang, ending not long after the An Lushan rebellion undermined Tang rule in China. Relations between Silla and China were always uneasy, despite Silla's wholesale borrowing of Chinese institutions and culture, despite Silla's annual tribute embassies to Chang'an. China, even as it faced more serious threats from Tibet, maintained defenses against a possible naval attack by Silla. The leaders of Silla constantly anticipated an attack by Tang forces. Had the two countries been able to eliminate these anxieties, they might have been able to use their resources more efficiently. Unfortunately, they never were able to devise the necessary confidence-building measures, although in 735 China did recognize Silla's control of all territory south of the Taedong River. Of course, the Tang did not relinquish its claim to the Korean peninsula between the Taedong and Yalu rivers.

In the eighth century, Buddhism, imported from India as well as China, proved exceptionally popular in Silla. Korean aristocrats, unattracted by Confucian meritocracy, preferring to retain their dominance by birth, patronized Buddhist monasteries and financed pilgrimages. The monasteries became producers and repositories of some of the finest Buddhist art the world would ever see. The court, seeking to undermine the influence of the hereditary aristocracy, the "Bone Ranks" by which the Korean elite defined themselves, encouraged Confucianism, but succeeded in establishing an examination system for administrative office only in 788. Thereafter there was a dramatic increase in the number of Koreans going to China to study the Confucian classics, but Silla society was already beginning to disintegrate and the aristocracy never lost its hold on government.

Excluded from public office, ordinary Koreans found an outlet in trade. They traded primarily with China, but also maintained an extensive commerce with Japan. Indeed, while the Koreans established merchant settlements in Shandong and Jiangsu, the Japanese set up special offices on Tsushima to manage contacts with Silla. In addition, Arab merchants found their way up the coast to do business with their Korean counterparts. By the middle of the ninth century, private trading operations were flourishing in Silla and Korean sailors and traffickers dominated the triangular trade with China and Japan. Of course, with so much valuable merchandise moving across the East China Sea outside the tributary system, without government protection, piracy proved irresistible to many poor fisherfolk in the region and became a major problem.

To the rescue sailed Zhang Boha, a Korean who had served in the Tang military and subsequently developed extensive maritime interests. Zhang created his own private army and coast guard, received an official appointment from the king of Silla, and cleared the sea lanes of pirates. Not quite coincidentally, he also became the dominant figure in the waterborne trade of the region. Ki-baik Lee calls him the "master of the Yellow Sea."[1]

Zhang also evidenced an interest in the governance of Silla and used his power base to intervene in affairs of the capital, where he became a kingmaker in 839. But his political activities—and lack of social standing—assured him of powerful enemies among the aristocracy and he was assassinated in 846.

The Silla regime, racked by rivalries between the court and the aristocracy and between aristocratic factions, plagued by banditry and other evidence of unrest among exploited peasants, had been in trouble since the late eighth century. In 780, the king, the last direct descendent of the founder of the dynasty, was killed. Rivalry for the throne became rampant. Over the next century and a half, Silla had twenty different kings, most of whom were eventually murdered by other aspirants or their agents. The central government lost control over most of the country while local elites created private armies and fortified their estates. By the beginning of the tenth century, Silla existed in name only.

Domestic rather than foreign affairs destroyed the Silla dynasty in Korea. Nonetheless, the end came as rival power brokers set up their own states on Korean soil, beginning with Later Paekche in 892 and Later Koguryo in 901. The new states had their own armies, developed their own trade patterns, and intimidated each other and Silla as best they could. In 918, the newly anointed king of Later Koguryo renamed his domain Koryo and developed close ties to Silla. In 935, the king of Silla submitted to Koryo and a year later the troops of Koryo destroyed Later Paekche. Parhae, the remnant of old Koguryo, reached the peak of its power early in the ninth century when it expanded into Siberia. It continued to exist until 926 when it was overrun by the Khitan. The Koguryo elite fled to the Korean peninsula, abandoning its indigenous subjects, and submitted to Koryo rule. The destruction of Parhae ended Korean control of any part of Manchuria, but all Korea was now under one umbrella and the Koryo dynasty presided over a unified country for four centuries.

If Silla was relatively secure compared to Tang China, Japan was even more so. Worries about an invasion from Silla or China faded in the eighth century and the only major foreign adventure contemplated was a Japanese attack on Silla, planned for but abandoned in 765. That did not mean, however, that imperial forces lacked employment. The court, which moved from Nara to Heian (modern Kyoto) in 784, was pained by the opposition to Japanese settlement and rule by the Ainu, an aboriginal people with whom they coexisted uneasily in northern Honshu, the main Japanese island. The Ainu were not interested in the blessings of Japanese civilization and resented the movement of its frontier into their lands. After a number of unsuccessful sorties against the Ainu, the court sent in a major force to do the job in 789—only to have it routed by the local people. It took several more major campaigns, an enormous amount of treasure, and fourteen more years to subdue the Ainu, who remain a mistreated minority in Japan to this day. And then the Japanese military rested and gradually atrophied. In the ninth century, it ceased to be a significant drain on government resources—although other court extravagances precluded any risk of fiscal surplus.

Of course the decline of military activity did not mean an end to Japan's involvement in the international affairs of East Asia. In the eighth century, many large missions, including hundreds of students as well as diplomats, monks, craftsmen, and merchants continued to travel to China, but because of tensions with Silla they sailed directly across the open sea rather than the traditional routes via Korea or Korean coastal waters. The frequency of such missions declined, however, partly because of the danger of the voyage, partly because of the disorder in China after mid-century. There was no mission between 781 and 803 or between 805 and 838, the last official visit to the Tang court. A proposal for renewed diplomatic contact in 894 was never implemented. As the Tang dynasty collapsed, there seemed little reason to embark on so hazardous a trip.

The ninth century remained, however, a period of great cultural borrowing from China, of continued enthusiasm for all aspects of Chinese culture. Private contact with the continent, both cultural and commercial, never ceased. In addition to the luxury goods Japanese leaders imported from China, Buddhism, in a variety of versions, proved to be an extraordinarily important mainland export. Indeed, before the end of the eighth century, the Buddhist church in Japan had become the major rival of state power. As the court attempted to tighten its control throughout the country, church control of vast tracts of land denied the state revenue and monks meddled in court affairs, one allegedly becoming the empress's lover in mid-century. In 784 the capital was moved from Nara to Heian (modern Kyoto) to escape the influence of the great Nara monasteries. Nonetheless, Buddhism remained attractive to the ruling class as the principal vehicle of higher learning in Japan and monks continued to be sent to China to study.

Early in the ninth century, two new Buddhist sects were founded in Japan by monks returning from China—in particular by two men of extraordinary leadership ability. One, Saicho, founded the Tendai sect upon his return in 805 and the other, Kukai, founded the Shingon sect when he arrived home in 806. Tendai was based on a Chinese school that had reacted against the metaphysical complexity of most Indian Buddhism. Shingon was based on Indian Buddhism, but a late form very popular in Tibet. Both men and their followers won support in Heian and contributed to the broadening appeal of esoteric Buddhism in ninth-century Japan. Neither challenged native Shintoism nor sought political power.

The principal political tensions in late Nara and early Heian Japan were between emperors who wanted actual power and the Fujiawara family that dominated government administration, monopolizing the posts of chancellor or regent, and many lesser positions. Foreign affairs was not an issue: the importance of Chinese learning was accepted by all contenders. Although there was less reliance on Chinese models of government or taste at Heian, nativism did not appear to roil the waters. During the reign of the Emperor Kammu (781–806), the throne reached its peak of power and prestige and again from roughly 810–840, Fujiwara influence was limited. At all times the person of the emperor was accorded divine or at least mystic powers and there was no attempt to replace the dynasty. By the end of the ninth century, however, the Fujiwara had created the post of dictator (*kampaku*) and had usurped imperial power. The Fujiawara were probably also responsible for pushing Confucian values on a resistant people. The ruling class in Japan, like its model in China, and perhaps ruling classes everywhere at all times, had a fondness for those elements of Confucian thought that placed duty to the state above individual rights.

Without foreign interference, requiring nothing from foreign cultures, the eternal struggle for power continued in Japan. Throughout the tenth century, the Fujiawara governed Japan, accruing power at the expense of the emperors. But others aspired to greater wealth and power, including several regional military leaders who challenged the authority of the central government unsuccessfully in mid-century. But the great landholders could not be controlled forever, especially as their armies waxed while those of the Court waned. The threat of the warrior clans was just beyond the horizon.

Southeast Asia

Chinese control of Vietnam always depended on force. Whenever the Vietnamese sensed weakness or whenever Chinese imperialism became unbearable for them, they rebelled. The Tang, like the Sui before them, had been able to establish their authority over northern Vietnam, or Annam. In 622 the Tang had declared the region a protectorate and managed to keep the region quiet for a century. A revolt in 722, possibly with Cham and Khmer support, failed. In 791, the Vietnamese rose again—and held off the Chinese for several years—but the Chinese eventually overpowered them. The Vietnamese were simply too few. They were no match for the overwhelming force China could usually bring to bear. But they consistently rejected assimilation and made life as difficult and insecure as possible for the occupying armies and officials. Other predators in the region also raided Vietnam. An invasion fleet from island Southeast Asia, probably from Java, attacked in 767 and was driven off by the Chinese. Nanzhao, probably more interested in harassing Chinese troops than in controlling Vietnam, launched an attack in the mid-ninth century, with varying degrees of success. The Chinese prided themselves on their ability to endure suffering (*chiku*), but the Vietnamese had more than their share in this era. At last in 907 the Tang dynasty disintegrated and the Vietnamese gained de facto control of their own affairs, while submitting to a series of Chinese overlords. In 938, a major Chinese effort to force renewed submission was defeated. The Vietnamese were independent in name as well as fact—and remained so for several centuries despite continuing Chinese efforts to restore them to China's empire. Although their culture was thoroughly sinicized, the Vietnamese reached out to other trading partners, seeking links to the rest of Southeast Asia rather than risk Chinese economic exploitation.

Afflicted as they were with China as a neighbor, angered as they must have been by Thai raids from Nanzhao, by Cham and Malay piracy, the Vietnamese may not have noticed the rise of a new threat in Cambodia, where the Khmer people were creating a coherent political community in the eighth century and where Jayavarman II emerged to found a great civilization at Angkor in the ninth. Archeological finds have indicated that the Cambodian region, long known to the Chinese as Zhenla, engaged in trade that brought objects from the Mediterranean, including Rome itself, Iran, and, of course, India and China, probably as early as the days of the Later Han Dynasty.

Much is known of the magnificent art—especially sculpture of Angkor—but little of its political affairs, domestic or foreign. Art historical evidence reveals that the primary influence on Khmer culture at the time was Indian, both Buddhist and Hindu, stemming from maritime contacts, much of it filtered through Java. Indeed, Jayavaraman II may have come across from Java, although he was presumably of Khmer stock. His successors enlarged upon his imperial pretensions, creating an empire that by the tenth century was pressing against the frontiers of China, dominating the northern part of the Malay peninsula, reaching the Indian Ocean to its west and threatening Champa and Vietnam to the east.

Java itself was under strong Indian influence, again both Buddhist and Hindu. A Hindu king, dominant in the first half of the eighth century was overshadowed by a Buddhist monarch by the end of the century. In the eighth and ninth centuries, two competing lines of kings, one Buddhist, one Hindu, vied for control of a central Javan polity located at Mataram. At the end of the eighth century the Buddhists built the extraordinary Great Stupa of Borobudur on the plain outside of modern Yogyakarta. This huge monument is composed of seemingly endless terraces, the walls of which are covered with approximately three miles of bas-reliefs illustrating Buddhist texts. When the Hindus became dominant in the mid-ninth century, they expelled the Buddhist royalty and then began their own incomparable monument, the temple complex at Prambanan, dedicated to Siva and completed early in the tenth century.

Shortly after the creation of Prambanan, the center of power in Java moved eastward, establishing a new capital near modern Surabaya. Java turned increasingly to international trade, especially in spices, as a source of wealth. The people of Java were apparently able to produce and stockpile large quantities of rice which they exchanged for spices and other products of the smaller islands along the archipelago.[2] The availability of spices attracted merchants from India, Sri Lanka, mainland Southeast Asia, and China. Conceivably Arabs and Persians also found their way there. Unfortunately, Java became a competitor of Srivijaya, the powerful Sumatran kingdom, resulting in frequent conflict. A Javanese attack on Srivijaya in 992 failed. A retaliatory attack by Srivijaya in 1016 spelled disaster for Java for almost a decade.

Although it constructed no temples or monuments to compare with Borobudur or Prambanan, Srivijaya was clearly the dominant force in Indonesia and coastal Southeast Asia as well for most of the period from the late seventh century until early in the eleventh century. Its navy, composed largely of coopted pirates, ruled the sea lanes between India and China, providing for peaceful transit of the straits of Melaka and Sunda, as well as transshipping goods from all over the region. The wealth thus acquired did not pass unnoticed. The famous Chinese Buddhist pilgrim, Yizing, spent several years there in the late seventh cen-

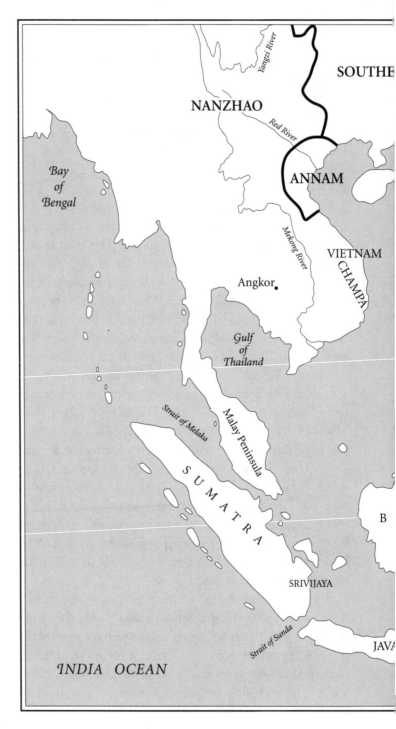

MAP 8. SOUTHEAST ASIA, C. 900.

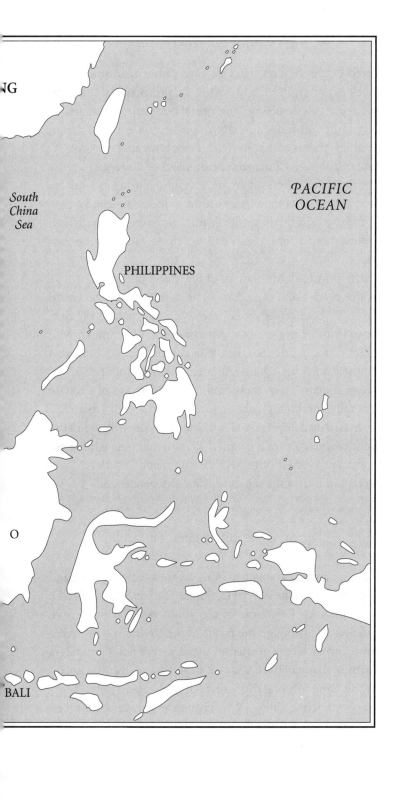

tury and reported extensively on what he saw. Other maritime states, from India as well as Java, noticed and envied the prosperity of the great international entrepot at Palembang. The rise of competitors was nearly as certain as that of the sun and sailors from all over Asia, especially from China, appeared in the islands. Srivijaya's sophisticated diplomacy, including tribute missions to China and the building of Buddhist temples in India, apparently staved off third-party intervention during its conflicts with Java. But in 1025, a Cola fleet from southern India launched a devastating attack from which Srivijaya never fully recovered. It remained an important political entity for several centuries more, but did not regain its earlier primacy.

There is little reason to doubt that all of the states of Southeast Asia were aware of the glories of Tang China. The merchants of the world who passed through these states spread the word and several of them sent tribute missions to Chang'an. But other than the Vietnamese, who were under direct Chinese rule, Southeast Asians did not see Chang'an as the center of their universe. Chinese influence was minor at best, significantly less than Indian. They knew little of the blessings of Chinese civilization, generally combining ancient local customs with what they borrowed from Indian Buddhism and Hinduism. With the collapse of the Tang, China became even less of a magnet. The Vietnamese, who could not escape the shadow of their huge neighbor, remained sinicized to an enormous degree, but even they regained their independence.

The Song Reunify China

From 907 to 960, China was an imagined state, an entity remembered and honored in its absence. As in the days of Confucius, the once great empire had disintegrated into ten kingdoms in the south and five successive "dynasties" in the north. Although the rulers of the southern states were for the most part Chinese, in the north they usually were not—reminders of the foreign armies that had been allowed to stay to protect the northern frontiers of the Tang. Among the leaders of these many states, however, the vision of reunifying China, of receiving the mandate of heaven and becoming emperor of all China, was ever present.

Throughout these years the various states that once had constituted

China treated each other like foreign lands and conducted war and diplomacy accordingly. Before long a loose balance of power developed among them, something like, but not as formal as, the hegemon system that had evolved in the Spring and Autumn period more than a thousand years before. This balance was complemented by the relationships they cultivated with non-Chinese states as each sought both to protect itself from and gain advantage over the others. Of their non-Chinese neighbors, the Khitan state of Liao was the most powerful. It dominated Manchuria, Mongolia, and a slice of north China, including Peking. Abandoning pretense to Chinese superiority, one of the northern dynasties accepted Liao as its overlord and the others were relieved to be treated as equals. None demanded tribute from the Khitan; several became tributaries of the Liao instead. These were years when existence depended on military power and shrewd diplomacy. Given their awareness of their vulnerability, the leaders of the various Chinese states avoided giving gratuitous offense through arrogant claims and pursued realistic foreign policies.

Eventually, as in the days of the ancient Zhou, the balance among the several Chinese states was upset by the emergence of one powerful state against which the others failed to unite. In 960, Zhao Kuangyin, a northern general, seized power in the Later Zhou dynasty and created the first stable government of the century in North China. Over the next sixteen years he subdued most of the southern states and established the Song dynasty. At the time of his death as Song Taizong in 976, only two of these states and the territory controlled by the Liao remained beyond the control of the new dynasty.

One of the holdout states, Wu Yue, centered on the port of Hangzhou in modern Zhejiang province, was notable for the trade and diplomacy with which it sustained itself. Its leaders formed marriage alliances with some of their neighbors, sent tribute missions to the northern dynasties, and maintained the fiction of submission to the distant north as a means of protecting itself from threats closer at hand. Wu Yue conducted extensive trade, both international and with other Chinese states. It also maintained relations with the Khitan, Japan, and Korea. With the latter two, Buddhist monks were exchanged in addition to formal embassies and considerable commercial activity. But as Song troops headed south, not even Wu Yue's demonstrated diplomatic skills could uphold the balance of power. In 976 it was forced to join in the attack on the one state that stood between it and the Song, aware that with the elimination of that buffer, its own days of existence were numbered. One year later, in 978, the state of Wu Yue was dissolved and absorbed by Song China.

It took yet one more year for the Song to eliminate the last independent Chinese state in the northwest and a unified—albeit somewhat abbreviated—China emerged to claim its place at the center of East Asia. Unfortunately for the Chinese, they lacked the strength to resume their role as hegemon. Much of the Tang empire was out of reach. They could not reestablish their presence in Central Asia; nor did they have the means to reconquer Vietnam. The Song emperors and their advisers generally recognized their relative weakness. Although they never openly conceded China's loss of primacy, with few exceptions they pursued a very cautious foreign policy, choosing appeasement over combat. The principal exception to their overall pragmatism and prudence was their determination to regain control of Peking and the surrounding area held by the Khitan.

Treating the Khitans as equals, let alone superiors, did not come easily to the Song. Unlike most of the other nomadic or semi-nomadic peoples who lived inside the Great Wall, the Khitan resisted sinicization. They discouraged intermarriage with the Chinese and treated Chinese contemptuously. These were truly "barbarians" who could not be allowed to remain on Chinese territory. In the 980s the Song made several sorties across the border into Liao with ambiguous results. In 986, however, the Chinese pinpricks angered the Khitan leaders who struck back in force and inflicted a massive defeat on the Song warriors. It was time to reconsider.

The emperor called a meeting of his national security advisers in 989 to discuss ways to manage barbarian affairs. The basic conflict in the discussions was between those who insisted on what the historian Tao Jing-shen calls the "myth of Chinese superiority"[3] and those who called attention to Song military weakness, the power of the Khitan, and the overall cost of trying to extend or even defend China's borders by military means. The problem was exacerbated by the emperor's unwillingness to risk the Tang error of creating large standing armies that resisted central control. Most of his advisers told him what he probably wanted to hear: that attacks against the barbarians were not always successful, but they were always expensive. Accepting the fact of Khitan military superiority—but certainly not cultural superiority—and bribing them to leave China alone

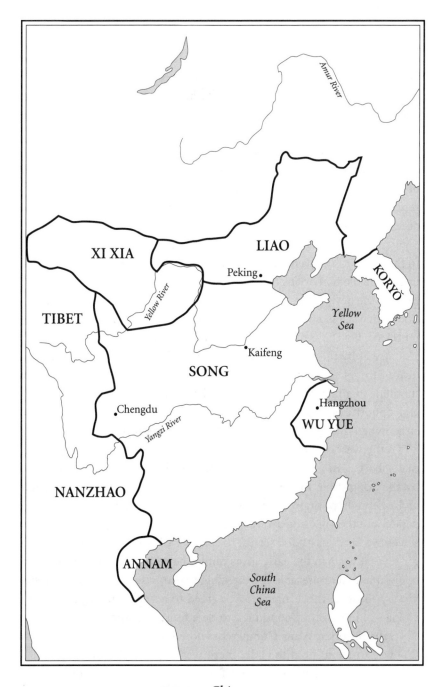

MAP 9.   China, c. 975.

After Fairbank and Reischauer, *East Asia*, p. 199.

would cost a fraction of what it would cost to send his troops into the field. There were other officials, of course, who were appalled at the humiliation of paying tribute to barbarians. These and perhaps others warned of the unpredictability of barbarians and called for a war to annihilate the Khitan, a final solution.

It took another twenty years of relatively minor skirmishing and evidence of Khitan strength before the Song concluded they could handle the barbarians best with kindness, that is to say annual payments of tribute in return for secure borders. In 1004, the Khitan attacked and once again defeated the Chinese decisively. In the treaty that ended the conflict the Song renounced their claim to Peking and the region around it and agreed to the terms of the payment in silk and silver demanded by the Liao. The unpredictable barbarians to whom the Song grudgingly conceded equality kept the peace for more than a hundred years—although they chose a time when the Chinese were under attack by others in 1042 to extort better terms. On the other hand, when the peace agreement was broken in 1118, it was by the Chinese who, finding the Liao distracted by a life and death struggle for survival against the invading Jurchens, chose that moment to attack them. It was clear that Chinese policy was pragmatic and opportunistic: grovel when necessary before superior power and strike when the correlation of forces proves more favorable.

To the west of the Liao, in the vicinity of the Gansu corridor, another major barbarian force, the Tanguts, troubled China. Initially impressed by the Song drive for reunification, the Tangut leaders offered tribute and accepted a position of inferiority in the Chinese universe. As the years passed and they became aware of China's weakness, they declared themselves the Xia dynasty and set out to conquer China. The two sides fought for several years in the early 1040s until it became clear that the Tanguts could make life miserable for the Chinese but could not win a decisive victory. In 1044, the Tanguts, too, agreed to accept annual tribute from China—although they continued to be a nuisance if not a threat.

As the historian Wang Gungwu has noted, when all the Chinese could do "was to try to hold the line, there was obviously no Chinese world order."[4] The Vietnamese, like the Tangut, observed the rhetoric and ritual of the tribute system, but went their own way. The Koreans paid their tribute to the Liao, the de facto dominant power in East Asia at the time. No state in the vicinity of China took seriously its pretensions to superiority—nor could Chinese leaders themselves, however comforting the language of superiority may have been in their internal discourse.

And yet, despite these obvious tribulations, Song China in the eleventh century was arguably the most prosperous, and most cultured, state in the world. Unable to intimidate their neighbors, the Chinese were nonetheless able to defend themselves. They spent heavily on their military, but used it sparingly. Appeasement worked well for them. The key to their success was foreign trade. Despite their inability to control the caravan routes across Central Asia, they had little trouble sending their silks overland and importing luxury goods by the same route. But even more impressive was the great range of Song shipping. The Tang had encouraged seaborne trade and found it highly profitable. The Song followed suit. The result was a dramatic increase in maritime trade with Southeast Asia, India, and Persia, as well as Japan and Korea. Chinese junks traveled as far as the Red Sea and the Persian Gulf. East Africa, Egypt, and the eastern shore of the Mediterranean also had access to Song porcelains. This commerce provided revenue for the government, horses for the army, and all manner of exotica for wealthy Chinese. Indeed, China's favorable balance of trade with the Khitan and Tangut peoples recouped much of the silver it paid out in tribute. The success of Song mercantile policy went a long way toward assuaging the humiliation of eroding the tribute system and losing China's place at the center of the universe.

This cultural renaissance and commercial success continued through the twelfth and well into the thirteenth century as well. Unfortunately, an unstable balance of power in East Asia encouraged opportunism and led the Song into a series of disastrous military adventures early in the twelfth century. As a result, the Chinese lost control of North China and were forced to abandon their capital at Kaifeng, regrouping in the south where the court established itself at Hangzhou. The southward relocation of China provided further stimulation of foreign trade, most obviously with South and Southeast Asia.

Military affairs began reasonably enough with successful Chinese attacks on the Tibetans between 1102 and 1105. The Tibetans invited Chinese aggression by fighting among themselves. The Chinese did not resist temptation. The court enjoyed its successes in the field and the Emperor Huizong, a great patron of the arts, presided over a capital known for its glamour and luxury. On the other hand, Song leaders seem to have enjoyed themselves a little too much, dropping their guard, and suffering a punishing attack by the Tanguts in 1115. Ultimately of greater consequence was their misreading of the significance of the rise of the Jurchen people of northeast Manchuria.

In 1114, the Jurchens rebelled against the Liao and began to drive south. When the Song court realized that Liao was in distress, that it could not crush the rebellion, it saw an opportunity to regain the border prefectures around Peking. Allying with the Jurchens, who had designated themselves the Jin, the Chinese attacked Liao in 1118. It took about four years for the allies to finish off Liao, at which time they sat down to divide the spoils. The Chinese contribution to the defeat of the Liao had been minimal, mere pinpricks compared to the overwhelming Jin offensives, but they nonetheless had grandiose expectations about the territorial rewards to which they were entitled. They were outraged when the Jin offered them a few, but not all of the prefectures in the vicinity of Peking. Their arrogant demands offended the Jin and the alliance collapsed in 1125.

Recognizing Chinese hostility, the Jin decided to continue their march southward, driving the Chinese in flight before them. Quickly they overran ineffectual Chinese opposition and in 1126 captured the Song capital at Kaifeng and the emperor. Chinese resistance stiffened as the Jin chased them across the Yangzi and eventually the overextended Jin gave up the chase, leaving the Song in control of south China. Eventually a new capital was established at Hangzhou and a regime called by historians the Southern Song survived in south China and parts of central China from 1127 to 1279. Once secure in the South, Chinese leaders debated the next course of action: counterattack in hope of regaining control of all China as urged by the military and the intellectuals—or accept Jin control of the North and concentrate on developing the South as advocated by most landowners and politicians. Efforts to regain control of the North failed and in 1141 the advocates of peace prevailed: a treaty was signed between the Jin and the Southern Song. Under its terms, China became a tributary of the Jin empire, forced to pay annual tribute and denied the right to defend its northern border. Other states that had previously sent tribute to the Chinese noted China's weakness and subordination to the Jin— and stopped their payments.

Border skirmishes between China and the Jin recurred and major battles were fought in the 1160s and early in the thirteenth century. In the first of these a Jin effort to complete the conquest of China failed and in

MAP 10.   CHINA, C. 1150.
After Fairbank and Reischauer, *East Asia*, p. 210.

the second a Song effort to drive the Jin from North China also failed. In each case, the attacking side paid a heavy penalty for its failure, a reduction in tribute payments in the first instance and a further loss of territory in the second. The Chinese had the brief satisfaction in 1232 of destroying the Jin in tandem with the Mongols, but in a few years it became apparent that they had once again underestimated a collaborator in their eagerness to destroy an enemy. Once again they had joined forces with an outside power stronger than their neighboring enemy, only to find themselves with a much more threatening adversary at their gates. Their strategy was understandable, but short-sighted.

On the other hand, the fragment of China controlled by the Southern Song took Chinese civilization to new heights of glory in the twelfth century. It was "economically and culturally one of the greatest periods in all Chinese history," according to John Fairbank.[5] The Song incorporated the coastal areas of South China, long resistant to Chinese rule. Private maritime trade boomed and great commercial cities began to appear in Guangzhou, Fujian, Jiangsu, and Zhejiang, which became China's principal points of contact with foreigners. Perhaps the most fascinating development was the emergence of the Chinese as an oceangoing people. Chinese merchants flooded the trade routes to both Northeast and Southeast Asia. Whereas earlier foreign trade had been dominated by Persians, Arabs, and Jews, many resident in Chinese ports, the Chinese began to emigrate and to create permanent settlements abroad, especially in Southeast Asia. As in earlier Song times, military shortcomings, China's inability to dominate its neighbors by force, did not preclude the good life for urban Chinese. Landscape painting and porcelain manufacture reached new heights of beauty, with porcelains probably the most popular export item. The court and the merchants and landowners who supported it readily eschewed the blessings of empire and reveled in the wealth created by international trade. For them, at least, it was a wonderful time to be Chinese.

Koryo

The Koryo Dynasty that ruled Korea from 918 to 1392, the last 134 years under Mongol control, never enjoyed the relative tranquillity of Silla's Golden Age. The collapse of Tang China, the subsequent fragmentation of China, and the military weakness of the Song relieved the threat of a

Chinese invasion, but the rise in succession of Khitan, Jurchen, and Mongol forces posed a constant challenge to Korean security. And by the thirteenth century, piracy ravaged Korean coastal areas, adding to the misery of the Korean people.

Of course, not all of Korea's troubles with foreign powers were unprovoked. T'aejo, the founder of the dynasty, aspired to regain the territory in Manchuria once ruled by Koguryo. He and many of his followers did not intend to be contained on the Korean peninsula. They found, however, that the Khitan controlled much of the territory they coveted and in 926 the Khitan destroyed Parhae, gaining a common border with Koryo Korea. Aiming toward the conquest of North China, the Khitan were eager to secure the Korean border and made diplomatic overtures that were rejected brusquely by the Koryo court. The Koreans preferred ties to the various Northern Chinese dynasties and to the Song when they united China, sending tribute missions to each. Beginning in the mid-tenth century, Koryo began its drive to the Yalu, contemptuous of the Khitan and unafraid to provoke them.

Koryo objectives virtually assured conflict with the Khitan. The Khitan, however, were focused on China, especially after its unification in 960. They found themselves confronted by potential enemies on two fronts and they did not intend to be dragged into war on both simultaneously. For years Khitan strategists tested the ties between Song China and Koryo and concluded they were not likely to come to each other's defense. In 993, they sent troops across the Yalu into Korea. In this instance, diplomacy saved the day for Koryo. Well aware that the Khitan perceived Song China to be their principal rival, the Koreans agreed to switch sides in exchange for the withdrawal of Khitan troops and Khitan acceptance of Koryo rule of all territory below the Yalu. In 994 they shifted their allegiance and paid homage to the Khitan. Briefly, Korea seemed to hold the balance of power on continental Northeast Asia.

Allegiance to the Khitan did not mean that Koryo had surrendered its goal of retaking territory on the far side of the Yalu. Having gained control of the lands up to the Yalu, Koryo began a military buildup whose purpose seemed quite clear to Khitan leaders. An interlude of internal conflict in Korea provided the opportunity for a preemptive strike, blunting the offensive capability of Koryo forces. The Khitan withdrew their forces in return for a promise that the Korean king would pay homage at their court—a promise the Koreans never kept. Khitan raids kept the

Koreans off balance for several more years, but a major invasion in 1018 failed. On this occasion, Koryo destroyed the invading army and won an enduring peace with the Khitan, without any territorial gains across the Yalu.

For a brief period in the middle of the eleventh century, Koryo existed without allegiance to any superior power. When the question of resuming diplomatic relations with Song China was raised in 1058, Korean leaders decided not to, unable to see any benefit. It was not that they rejected Chinese culture—and they certainly did not reject trade with Song China—but they were enjoying a sense of independence, of being a free agent in the international politics of East Asia.

Unfortunately, by this time the Jurchen were stirring across the Yalu, which may explain why Koryo was not more responsive to Song diplomatic overtures. Unlike the Khitan, the Jurchen had been attracted to Chinese civilization, at least as they had observed it in Korea. But Koryo had driven the Jurchen out of northwestern Korea at the end of the tenth century and there could be no assurance that the Jurchen would not strike back. In fact, an uneasy peace persisted between the Jurchen and Koryo throughout the eleventh century, until early in the twelfth century. Serious fighting broke out in 1104, apparently precipitated by a Jurchen raid. The Koreans were hurt badly, but succeeded in driving the invaders out by 1107. A year later Koryo launched an attack on the Jurchen who retaliated by invading the Korean peninsula, from which they withdrew soon after. It is difficult to determine who provoked whom in these confrontations or to be certain of the scale of battle or even who won. It does seem clear that the Jurchen and Koreans were not getting on well together.

Perhaps fortunately for Koryo, the Jurchen had greater ambitions than retaking any part of Koryo territory. In 1115 they founded the state of Jin and by 1117 Jin controlled most of southern Manchuria. The Jurchen goal was to replace Khitan power in Manchuria and North China, a task that they accomplished in 1125 with minor help from Song China. When the Jin proceeded to march through China and capture Kaifeng, the world as the Koreans understood it changed radically. The Chinese could hardly pretend to universal rule, nor could the Koreans perceive of themselves as part of a Chinese world order. In 1127, as the Song were fleeing across the Yangzi into South China, the Jin made the Koreans an offer they could not refuse: become a Jin tributary or face an invasion by the very forces that had eliminated Chinese power north of the Yangzi. Without shedding tributary status with the Song, the Koreans accepted the Jin offer—and wisely chose not to provide the Song with the military assistance they requested.

Afterward, there was relatively little tension between the Jin and Koryo. The Jin remained focused on their southern border with the Song. The Koreans were peripheral to the main military theater of East Asia. They could no longer imagine themselves as the state that controlled the balance of power in the region. Nor could they imagine fulfilling their irredentist vision of regaining territory in southern Manchuria. For the foreseeable future Korea would remain a minor power, restricted to the peninsula, relying on diplomacy to survive. On the other hand, the absence of tension between Korea and the Jin allowed Koreans to concentrate on their internal development—without gratifying results. For the last quarter of the twelfth century, the relative absence of external threat allowed for incessant civil war.

In particular the years of the Koryo dynasty manifested little economic progress. The merchants who had played an important role in international trade in the ninth century gradually lost influence. The nation's wealth was concentrated in the capital, siphoned off by the court and those who fed on it. Slavery and other forms of unfree labor were widespread. On the other hand, Korean artisans were producing extraordinary celadon porcelains, of a quality and beauty unsurpassed anywhere in the world. The art collector, marveling at the skill of Koryo era ceramicists, might easily imagine Koreans of that day to be enjoying a tranquil period of high culture. The reality was a people brutally exploited by their rulers, a backward economy, a polity under almost constant external pressure, sliding into civil strife when foreign invaders ceased to threaten.

Whatever respite from war the Korean people enjoyed at the close of the twelfth century ended in the thirteenth with the rise of Mongol power across the Eurasian continent. Mongol horsemen charged across the Yalu in 1231 and quickly forced the Koryo court to submit to their authority. When the Mongols withdrew to continue their onslaught against China and parts west, the court moved the capital to a point of relative safety—an act the Mongols perceived as rebellious. Again and again the Mongols rode into Korea, easily overcoming what little opposition they encountered. In 1254 they reportedly took nearly 207,000 male captives, but the court held out for four more years. In 1258, the Koryo ruler was forced to surrender and become completely subservient to the Mongols.

The Mongols allowed the Koryo dynasty to continue to hold the throne, but they annexed the northern part of the peninsula to their own empire, forced the Korean rulers to marry Mongol princesses and often to live in Peking rather than in Korea. Mongol officials took over direct responsibility for running the Korean government from approximately 1259 to 1392. It was they who propped up the regime as the coastal areas came under attack from the "Japanese" pirates, many of them Chinese and Koreans, who wreaked havoc across the East China Sea in the thirteenth and fourteenth centuries. For Korea, as for China and much of the rest of Asia, the age of Mongol dominance was underway.

Japan

Japan, too, would know the wrath of Khubilai Khan before the end of the thirteenth century. But for several hundred years before the Mongols turned toward Japan, the Japanese had little political contact with the continent. They had no diplomatic relations with either Song China or Koryo Korea after 918, none with the Khitan or Jurchen regimes. They continued to enjoy relief from outside pressure and to see little benefit to be derived from involvement in the turmoil of the rest of the region. Turmoil, they managed aplenty without foreign assistance. All too often it seems to be a law of world affairs that when a state is spared external enemies, its people find sufficient differences among themselves to justify civil war. Hence the frequent resort to foreign wars, to rally the people around the flag, as a means of transcending internal divisions.

Fujiawara power peaked under the leadership of Michinaga, who dominated the court from 996 to 1027. But Michinaga's ability to maintain order in the capital, rife with arson and robbery, depended on the support of warriors of the Minamoto and Taira clans. His influence in the provinces also was limited by the lack of military forces under central control and even greater dependence on the whim and will of local landholders and the troops loyal to them. Gradually it became apparent to the provincial gentry, especially those of the Minamoto and Taira, that the Fujiwara needed them more than they needed the Fujiwara. After

Michinaga, Fujiwara power ebbed, although members of the clan continued to serve as regents until late in the twelfth century.

In the latter half of the eleventh century and early in the twelfth, influence in the capital was exercised, more often than not, by previously abdicated emperors, operating behind the throne. This peculiar Japanese practice is called "Cloister Government," referring to rule by a man who surrendered the throne, usually to a minor he could control, became at least nominally a Buddhist monk, but in fact ran the government as the "Cloistered Emperor," free of ritual responsibilities. By the end of the eleventh century, the Fujiwara had lost most of the major offices, replaced by the Minamoto and courtiers whose loyalties were to the imperial house rather than to the Fujiwara.

By this time the country was rife with bandits, "barbarian tribes" were roiling the hills and valleys of the northwest, landholders deploying private armies were fighting among themselves, the great monasteries were stirring trouble in the capital, and the central government could do nothing to ameliorate conditions. Gradually the maintenance of local order, if there was to be any, fell to the private local armies and a feudal regime emerged. The historian Peter Duus notes that in this period "Japan never faced the threat of outside invasion . . . it was *internal* disorder that prompted the search for new means of maintaining local order."[6]

To this challenge, the Minamoto family, followed eventually by the Taira, responded readily. Year after year they fought bitter battles against various renegade clans, slowly gaining experience and strength. Although the Minamoto led the forces of order in the late eleventh century, one Minamoto leader offended the court and led a rebellion that had to be put down by a Taira general in 1108. Ingratiating themselves with the court, seizing every opportunity to drive a wedge between the court and the Minamoto, the Taira gained primacy. By mid-century, Taira Kiyomori had emerged as the clan leader and he ultimately became the dominant figure in Japanese political affairs, the virtual ruler of Japan for approximately twenty years, his position obtained and secured by military power and legitimized by the positions at the court he took for himself and his relatives.

But the Minamoto were not to be denied. In 1160, collaborating with the Fujiawara, they attempted a coup, the famed Heiji Rising memorialized in an extraordinary scroll painting, the *Heiji Monogatari* (Tales of the Heiji War), now in the collection of the Museum of Fine Arts, Boston. On this occasion, Kiyomori outmaneuvered them and their leaders were killed. In 1180, the Minamoto rose again, beginning a five-year national struggle known as the Gempei War, subject of the great military romance, the *Heike Monogatari* (Tales of the House of Taira), known to every Japanese schoolchild. This time, the Minamoto prevailed and their leader, Yoritomo, is credited with creating the Kamakura *bakufu*, the foundation of the Japanese feudal system. As the dominant military force in the country, he claimed to be the emperor's protector, but in fact he set up a rival administration, a military autocracy, headquartered in the east, closer to modern Tokyo than to Kyoto, where he presided as Shogun. Over the next century, the government Yoritomo established proved to be strong and efficient, crushing the most serious threat to its survival, a revolt led by a former emperor in 1221—and order returned to Japan.

Throughout these years when Japanese leaders were preoccupied with internal affairs and diplomatic relations with the continent seemed unimportant, Japan retained close economic and cultural ties to China. Although trade with Korea continued, China was Japan's most important trading partner. An important international trading community existed in Kyushu and shipping traffic between Song China and Japan never dropped below forty or fifty vessels annually. Most of the trade was in private hands and imports to Japan appear to have consisted of luxury goods—silks, perfumes, porcelains—and Chinese copper coins. Huge quantities of the coins entered the country and facilitated the monetization of the economy. So much coinage flowed out of the country that Song authorities made several unsuccessful efforts to prohibit their export and to reduce the number of Japanese ships coming to China.

In return, the Japanese sent the magnificent swords for which their artisans were justly famous, gold, mercury, and lacquerware. Exchanges of works of art clearly resulted in the influence of Chinese painters on their Japanese counterparts and, arguably of the Japanese on continental artists as well. Trade was continued after Yoritomo established himself in Kamakura, with much of the profit going to his allies.

Two other notable forms of contact with the continent continued in this era. One, frequently noted, was the Chinese export of Buddhist priests to teach in Japan and the pilgrimages of Japanese monks to study in China. The other was piracy, a species of international relations that most states might prefer to do without. Early in the eleventh century, the Japanese had been troubled by pirates operating out of Korea. By the end of the twelfth century the major piracy problem in East Asia was the *wako*, so-called Japanese pirates, many of them Chinese, who ravaged the coastal regions of China and Korea. At one point the Japanese feared pirate raids would provoke an attack from Koryo, but they were unable to stop the raids which persisted well into the thirteenth century, continuing to abrade relations with Koryo.

TABLE 3.2. Some Major Figures of the Ninth to Twelfth Centuries
(Dates are approximate. Names in boldface are referred to in text)

Jayavarman II of Angkor	775–850
Alfred the Great, king of England	849–899
Fujiwara Michinaga	966–1027
Canute the Great, king of England, Denmark, and Norway	980–1035
Airlangga of Java	985–1049
William the Conquer, first Norman king of England	1027–1087
Surayavarman II of Angkor	1075–1150
Taira Kiyomori	1118–1181
Minamoto Yoritomo	1147–1199
Richard the Lion Hearted, king of England	1157–1199

Southeast Asia in Turmoil

In the several hundred years preceding the Mongol onslaught on East Asia, the island polities on Sumatra and Java declined in importance, largely the result of military defeats, but also due to the emergence of China as a major trading competitor and to the rise of other forces on the continent. Srivijaya had crushed the Javanese in 1016 and hardly a decade later was ravaged by the Cola. The archipelago never ceased to be a critical part of the trade of East Asia, but its return to primacy was delayed by the approach of the Mongols and the refugees that fled them, disrupting much of the region.

On the mainland, the Vietnamese, Cham, and Khmer people fought each other when they could and were confronted by a new force as Pagan emerged as a power in Burma. The twelfth century was marked by nearly constant warfare and in the thirteenth all but Champa retreated on the international stage and turned inward to lick their wounds. Before the century had ended, the Mongols appeared, driving the Tai people before them. Nonetheless, the period encompassed by the late tenth century to the early thirteenth was marked by the increased involvement of continental Southeast Asia in international affairs, especially trade.

Srivijaya never recovered its hegemony over the trade routes between East Asia and South Asia. Chinese shipping had expanded greatly under the Song and greatly reduced the importance of Malay merchantmen. This was especially true during the twelfth century when the Chinese under the Southern Song pushed into the Indian Ocean, sailing directly to the Malabar coast. Mainland competitors continued to challenge the Sumatrans, especially the Tai in the thirteenth century. But perhaps the severest blow was the more rapid resurrection of Java.

On Java, the emergence of one of the island's great kings, Airlangga, in the 1020s facilitated East Java's dominance of the international spice trade. He suppressed his local rivals and then shrewdly bought peace with Srivijaya through a marriage alliance. With order prevailing, Java's ports emerged as major maritime trading centers. China's participation was essential to Java's success, given the striking surge in Chinese activity. Although pepper was more expensive in Java than in the vicinity of the Sundra Strait, Chinese merchants preferred the relative security from piracy that Java offered. They brought enormous quantities of fine porcelains to Java from whence they were transshipped to markets in India, West Africa, and the Middle East—and on to the Mediterranean. Java, like most of Southeast Asia, nonetheless remained more indebted to Indian cultural influences than to Chinese.

On the continent, increased involvement in international trade was apparent almost everywhere. The Vietnamese discovered the benefits of selling abroad in the tenth century and moved quickly to make foreign trade the center of their economy before the end of the eleventh. They had a little trouble settling down after freeing themselves from Chinese domination early in the tenth century. It seems to be another law of nature that when a people win their freedom from foreign control, they are compelled to turn on each other. An attempt to establish a monarchy in the tenth century failed, but early in the eleventh an alliance of aristocrats and Buddhist monks succeeded in moving the capital to Hanoi and establishing the Ly Dynasty. The first emperor of Dai Viet was Ly Phat Ma (r. 1028–54), a historical figure still held in great reverence by the Vietnamese people. He had ocean-going junks built that permitted his country to become a major participant in regional trade.

Ly Phat Ma's popularity was increased by his decision to change the laws of the realm, eradicating all trace of the Chinese-imposed legal system. In 1044 he further ingratiated himself with his people by leading a successful naval attack on Champa and using the treasure looted there to finance his government—allowing him to lower taxes, a measure rarely greeted with anything but joy. He also used the proceeds of the raid to provide accommodations for foreign merchants and to develop internal markets, further stimuli to trade.

Things were going so well in mid-century that the next emperor of Dai Viet developed grandiose intentions of expanding his empire, not sparing territory claimed by Song China. Steadily increasing their military power, in 1059 the Vietnamese began a series of raids on the Chinese border. The Song, working with the vengeful Cham, counterattacked in 1072, giving the Vietnamese a lesson on their limits. As the Song prepared their forces for the coup de grace, however, they were disrupted by a Vietnamese preemptive strike. When the attack was launched in 1076, the Vietnamese were able to keep the Chinese at bay. Finally, the two sides conceded the futility of further warfare and negotiated a border settlement that stood the test of time—more or less.

Peace with China enabled the Vietnamese to turn their attention to the Khmer threat from the south. Invasions ordered by the Angkor regime in the twelfth century were resisted successfully, but at considerable cost to the Ly Dynasty. Weakened by its foreign wars, it was forced to confront constant civil war throughout the century and on into the thirteenth century when a new Tran Dynasty was established in 1225. It had hardly asserted its authority over the country when the Mongols appeared.

Champa, long an important maritime entity fared poorly during these years. The Vietnamese sacked their capital twice. The Khmer, at the peak of their power in the twelfth and early thirteenth centuries, occupied Cham territory, an indignity for which the Cham sacking of Angkor in 1177 provided insufficient compensation. When the Mongols approached, the Cham wisely chose to unite with Vietnam against them, buying themselves two more centuries of existence.

Even Angkor found a way to participate in the expanding international

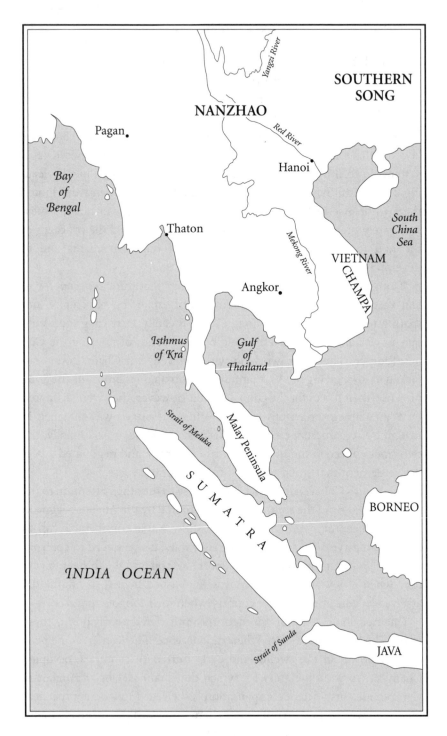

MAP II.   MAINLAND SOUTHEAST ASIA, C. 1150.

trade as it forced its way toward the Isthmus of Kra and into present day Thailand. In particular it developed trade with southern India and maintained its ties to Java. Early in the twelfth century, the Khmer were led by the great Suryavarman, builder of the magnificent temple complex at Angkor Wat. He not only dominated the Cham, but he also went after the Vietnamese, launching an unsuccessful invasion. More sensibly, he chose a diplomatic approach to Song China. Early in the thirteenth century, one of his successors, Jayavarman VII, actually ruled Champa as a province of Angkor for nearly twenty years. For the most part the Khmer were the aggressors rather than the aggressed upon, facing little in the way of external threat until the Tai peoples of southwest China began to move deeper into Southeast Asia in advance of the Mongols.

Still another center of power, Pagan, arose in Southeast Asia during the eleventh century. Several cities had emerged in the Irawaddy Basin in modern Burma and had established trade and cultural relations with India and Ceylon. Pagan had considerable success in its efforts to unite them under the leadership of its rulers. One of these, Anawrahta (r. 1044–77), extended his control into the Malay peninsula without significant opposition from the Khmer and conquered Thaton, home of the Mon people in 1057. The last years of the century constituted the great age of temple building in Pagan and also the era in which Pagan served as the center of the region's trade. Early in the twelfth century, the king of Pagan sent at least two missions to China, the first official links between the two. Although Pagan was frequently involved in clashes with other peoples within Burma, it, too, faced no danger from abroad until the Tai moved against them late in the twelfth century.

The Tai peoples appear to have ranged over parts of what is now southwestern China and to have played a marginal role in the state of Nanzhao as it maintained its independence from China in the eighth and ninth centuries. Their presence in the upper reaches of the Mekong valley was apparent by the eleventh century and Tai warriors are believed to have fought in Vietnamese, Khmer, and Pagan armies by the twelfth century. As the Mongols rearranged the correlation of forces in Asia, the Tai were driven toward the lowlands where they became rivals of the existing political entities. When the Mongols destroyed Nanzhao in mid-thirteenth century, there was no way back for the Tai and their presence constituted a serious problem for both the Khmer and Burmese people.

Clearly, Southeast Asia was teeming with activity in the age of the Song dynasty. The island states were temporarily peripheral, but on the continent the Vietnamese, Khmer, Burmese, and Tai were thriving. They—and the oft beset-upon Cham—were all engaged in international trade—with each other, with India, Ceylon, China, and the Arab, Jewish, and Persian merchants who found their way to Asia. They were active politically and militarily, primarily engaged in empire-building efforts. And their involvement in the affairs of the world was reflected and recorded in their art and architecture, especially in the obvious influence of Indian and Chinese art forms.

Conclusion

As the Tang dynasty disintegrated, Chinese dominance over East Asia ended. China ceased to be a threat to its neighbors, fragmented briefly, and even after it was reunited suffered constant indignities at the hands of its neighbors, ultimately losing control of North China and surviving as a much smaller state south of the Yangzi. Paradoxically, Song China, especially the Southern Song, increased its participation in international trade, sending ships and merchants across the southern seas. It was also an age of great cultural expansion, as military weakness did not prevent Chinese artists from reaching new heights of brilliance in painting and the manufacture of porcelains. Chinese porcelains were in demand as far as the Mediterranean and evidence of their import and influence is found today in West Africa and much of the Middle East, as well as many points along the way. Chinese law, literature, and philosophy continued to attract intellectuals and officials in Japan, Korea, and Vietnam. Obviously, the territorial extent of empire is not the only—and probably not the best—measure of a state's importance in the world.

In Northeast Asia, the Khitan state of Liao and the Jurchen state of Jin undermined Chinese hegemony, ultimately ruling vast areas of China. Neither became a major participant in world trade or provided a lasting cultural contribution to the region. Neither Liao nor Jin was able to project influence beyond the region it was able to control militarily. Elsewhere, the Koreans failed to use the absence of Chinese pressures wisely and failed under the Koryo Dynasty in their efforts to regain territories once held by Kogoryo. Commerce with the outside world grew, but its benefits do not seem to have contributed much to the development of state or society. When external enemies did not appear on the horizon, the Koreans fought among themselves. On the other hand, like the Song, the Koryo dynasty was noted for its exquisite porcelains, although they had yet to be recognized as widely as those of the Song.

Japan, too, enjoyed respite from foreign threat, traded constantly with the mainland, thrived under the Fujiwara, and then allowed itself the luxury of domestic disorder. Eventually, two great warrior clans, the Taira and the Minamoto, in succession brought relative peace to the country—except when they were fighting each other. By the end of the twelfth century, the Minamoto had created the Kamakura *bakufu*, an apparatus with which they were able to govern a feudal society successfully and to control the court at Kyoto. When the Mongols came, the Japanese were ready.

Southeast Asia spawned several major political entities during the last years of the Tang and the life of the Song. The Vietnamese shook off Chinese control early in the tenth century. Angkor and Pagan emerged in Cambodia and Burma to direct the intellectual and material resources of the region. In addition to their empire building, they joined Champa as trading states. On the Indonesian archipelago, great states grew in Java and Sumatra. The Javanese state was crushed early in the eleventh century by its Sumatran rival, in turn destroyed by the Cola a few years later. Nonetheless, Java and Sumatra were central to the international trade of East Asia, both for their geographic position athwart the seaborne routes of communication and their control of the spice trade.

By the thirteenth century, the involvement of East Asia in world trade had grown extensively and all of the states of the region, north and south, were engaged in it. Political activity had increased greatly, especially in Southeast Asia where new forces continued to cohere. The point, of course, is that China was no longer at the center.

FOUR

The Mongol Ascendancy

Chinggis Khan and His Sons

It all began with Chinggis. Born around 1165, named Temujin, he survived a difficult childhood, married well and rose gradually through the ranks of the Mongol tribes abutting North China, then under the control of the Jurchen Jin Dynasty. By all accounts a charismatic personality, in 1206 he succeeded in uniting virtually all Mongol clans and tribes under his leadership, assuming the title of Chinggis Khan. Like all the other nomadic peoples who rode across the steppes, the Mongols needed goods that could be provided only by sedentary societies. Like the Xiongnu and others before them, they did not hesitate to resort to force when denied what they considered reasonable opportunities or terms of trade. Chinggis may have developed a larger vision, a perceived mission to create a great Mongol empire.

His first target was the Xixia, who controlled the territory west of the Jin, northwest of the Southern Song, coterminous with modern Gansu. They had created a Chinese style state and shed most of the seminomadic qualities they had evidenced in the tenth century. Mongol attacks began in 1205, intensified under the command of Chinggis, and led to a major invasion in 1209. Dominated by the Mongols after 1209, the Xixia ceased to exist as a political entity after 1227.

Tensions between the Mongols and the Jin likely began with the usual nomadic dissatisfaction with conditions of trade. Chinggis sent his horsemen into North China in a series of raids that began in 1211 and resulted in destruction of the Jin capital in 1213. Jin efforts to win Song assistance failed and they were fortunate to survive this first Mongol onslaught. Chinggis, once his troops had plundered the countryside, was appeased by extravagant gifts from the Jin court and returned home, although some of his forces remained a threatening presence until 1215. The Mongolian historian Sechin Jagchid argues that at this time Chinggis was not after territory, but was quite satisfied with the booty he and his men obtained.[1] Whatever the reason, the conquest of Jin China was postponed.

In 1217, Chinggis turned his attention westward, sweeping across the ancient caravan routes and conquering everything in his path. The great oasis cities of Bukhara and Samarkand were looted and, by 1221, Mongol forces had charged through all of Central Asia and modern Afghanistan and had reached the Crimea, spreading terror everywhere along the way. Their success is readily explained by superb horsemanship, exceptional military organization, brilliant tactics, and sheer ruthlessness. On the eve of the gunpowder revolution in military tactics, their offensive power was unequaled anywhere in the world. And, dependent as they were upon plunder, the consumption of one region's treasure required them to move on to the next.

Chinggis and his lieutenants were also fast learners. Initially stymied by well-provisioned and heavily defended walled cities, they mastered the art of siege, utilizing skills found among Chinese captives and turn-coats. They found the Uyghurs eager to collaborate, Muslim financiers and traders in Central Asia quite willing to serve them, and Turkic peoples throughout Central Asia anxious to enlist on their side—all choosing submission over its quite horrible alternatives. Indeed, a critical element in the success of the Mongol conquest and the creation of the Mongol empire was the willingness to rely on non-Mongols to manage most nonmilitary affairs.

While the Mongols were slashing their way westward, the Jin and the Song, whose lone chance for survival was a joint defense effort, drifted into a suicidal war with each other. Having failed miserably in their own efforts to defeat the Jin, to regain control of North China, Song leaders were heartened by Mongol pressures. They did not imagine a Mongol threat to themselves, assuming that, like most previous invaders from the steppes, the Mongols would stay north of the Yangzi. The Song not only refused to aid the Jin, but perceiving Jin distress, added to it by refusing to pay the annual tribute required by the last treaty between the two courts.

The Jin, having bought off Chinggis, desperately needed compensatory revenues and demanded the required tribute from the Song, to no avail. Although very much aware that war was the likely result of continued refusal, the Song maintained their disastrous course. Song leaders apparently deluded themselves into believing that a "proto-nationalist appeal" to Chinese living under Jin rule in North China would induce defections to their side.[2] There had not been significant numbers of defections in the past and there were not to be enough on this occasion. Punitive attacks by the Jin overran Song defenses. Fortunately for the Song, Mongol pressures forced the Jin to keep the bulk of their armed forces in the north and they did not capitalize on their initial successes. In 1224, an unrepentant Song court rejected Jin overtures for peace negotiations.

In the meantime the Koreans had bought an uneasy peace with the Mongols. Recognizing rising Mongol power, the Koreans shrewdly came to their aid against the Khitan in 1218, sharing a victory over the latter in 1219. But their erstwhile allies demanded large-scale financial assistance— tribute—far in excess of any amount the Koryo court was prepared to offer. Tensions rose quickly, but Chinggis's preoccupation with the West spared the Koreans during his lifetime.

The end came for Chinggis in 1227, probably the result of wounds suffered in battle. The reins of power were passed to his son, Ogodei, who picked them up quickly and continued his father's drive to conquer the known world. By the time of Ogodei's death in 1241, much of Eastern Europe had been overrun and the Mongols were at the Danube, preparing to move against a disunited and poorly defended Western Europe, against the lands of the pope and the Holy Roman Emperor.

Although the Mongol offensive in the West continued, East Asia simultaneously came under increased pressure soon after the death of Chinggis. The ability of the Mongols to maintain the offensive on several broad fronts can only be explained by their success in recruiting and training men whose lands they rode through, especially the Turkic peoples of Central Asia. Chinggis is believed to have assembled only about 130,000 horsemen in 1227, a decidedly small force by Chinese standards. Even superior organization and tactics would not have sufficed for conquest on the Mongol scale without augmenting those numbers.

The first recorded Mongol raids on Song China came in 1228. The Song had been responsive to Chinggis's diplomatic overtures earlier in the decade, but this did not immunize them from attack permanently. Nonetheless, Song policymakers underestimated the Mongol threat and persisted in focusing on their revanchist goals in North China. The target of their strategic planning was the Jin. By 1225, the Mongols had driven the Jin out of their capital, forcing them to flee south of the Yellow River and regroup around a new capital at Kaifeng. But the Mongols had surprising difficulty finishing off the Jin, perhaps because they were fighting on so many different fronts at the same time. In 1233, they again sought an alliance with the Song, to which the Song were immediately responsive, throwing their forces across the Yangzi against the Jin. Jin appeals for Song help were brushed aside. The Song court had deluded itself into believing that it could destroy the Jin dynasty with Mongol assistance and then push the Mongols out of North China. There was no shortage of advisers to warn the emperor about the extent of Mongol power and the likely result of turning on them, but the emperor could not be dissuaded from his fantasy of ruling all of China. In 1234, as the Jin fell, the Song marched in, ultimately provoking a war with the Mongols.

Again, the Chinese benefited temporarily from other campaigns that distracted the Mongol leaders. To the West Mongol forces conquered Persia and Iraq in 1231. In 1237 they crossed the Volga River in Russia, taking Moscow and Kiev in 1238. And they did not stop there, proceeding into Poland, Hungary, and Bohemia in 1241. Even in East Asia the Mongols had other priorities. With the defeat of the Jin, they turned on Koryo, conceivably to secure their rear before the coming showdown with the Song. The first invasion came earlier, in 1231, and for the next thirty years the Mongols continued to pound the Koreans in response to any sign of resistance.

The Song, however, used the respite poorly. As their forces moved into North China, they mistreated Chinese who had endured Jin rule and might have been sympathetic to the Song. Thus alienated, many northern Chinese saw no reason to risk their lives resisting the Mongols. Indeed, key Chinese military men ultimately defected to the Mongols, facilitating their eventual victory.

It was mid-century, after the death of Ogodei had resulted in a reprieve for Western Europe, after the succession had been resolved, before the Mongols focused anew on China. Now there was no Jin buffer to shield the Song. In 1253 the Mongols, led by Chinggis's grandson Khubilai, completed their capture of Nanzhao, driving the Tai people into Southeast Asia and placing their forces on China's southwestern flank. In 1260, after the death of his brother, two years after the Mongols had destroyed the Abbasid Caliphate headquartered in Baghdad, Khubilai was elected Great Khan.

TABLE 4.1.   Some Notable Dates of the 13th and 14th Centuries
(Dates are approximate. Events in boldface are referred to in text)

Chinggis unites Mongols	**1206**
King John accepts Magna Carta	1215

Mongols reach Crimea	1221
Pope Gregory IX orders Inquisition	1233
Mongols take Moscow and Kiev	1238
Mongols reach Danube	1241
John of Plano Carpini travels to China seeking alliance against Islam and conversion of Mongols	1245–47
Inquisition begins use of torture	1252
Khubilai elected Great Khan	1260
Rise of Aztecs in Mexico	1267
Yuan Dynasty proclaimed	1271
Japanese, aided by kamikaze, repel Mongols	1274 and 1281
Last remnants of Song destroyed	1279
Aztec Empire	1325–1521
Black Death kills one third of Chinese, European, and Muslim populations	1347–1351 (and after)
Collapse of Yuan Dynasty	1368

Khubilai Khan and the Chinese

The great Mongol empire covered too vast an area to be controlled by a central administration in an age when communication depended upon horseborne messengers. The Great Khan, nominally ruler of all, in fact delegated or surrendered authority to three lesser khans, who governed respectively the Khanate of Chaghadai (approximating Afghanistan and Turkestan), the Khanate of Persia (Georgia, Iran, and Iraq), and the Khanate of Kipchak (Russia, Ukraine, parts of Central Asia). The Great Khan reserved East Asia for his own preserve, including China, Korea, Mongolia, and as much of Burma and Vietnam as his forces could reach. The result was a de facto confederation and, perhaps inevitably, a degree of rivalry among Mongol leaders.

When his father died, Khubilai and his mother, a Nestorian Christian of extraordinary ability,[3] were both granted lands in North China in 1236. Although he remained in Mongolia, Khubilai slowly became engaged in the administration of his territory and developed an interest in Chinese culture. His knowledge of the Chinese language was rudimentary at best, but he was nonetheless able to study Buddhism and Confucianism with

Chinese advisers in the 1240s. It is worth noting that he had no difficulty recruiting Chinese intellectuals to serve him, perhaps because the people of North China were long removed from Chinese rule and may not have thought of themselves as part of a Chinese nation. On the other hand, throughout history, there has rarely been a shortage of men and women whose lust for power and its perquisites enabled them to serve despised rulers, whether alien or native. Regardless of what motivated his advisers, the essential point is that of all of the Mongol empire, Khubilai knew China best.

His elder brother, Mongke, became Great Khan in 1251 and awarded him additional lands in North China. As the power of his immediate family grew, Khubilai's personal strength was enhanced by the revenues he extracted from his holdings in China and by the Chinese troops that he mobilized there. He became more deeply involved in Chinese affairs—to the detriment of his reputation within the Mongol nobility.

When Mongke tired of Song pinpricks, Khubilai was an obvious choice to send into action against them. The Mongols had controlled most of North China since the defeat of the Jin, but had failed to prevent the Song from retaking some of the territory they had lost to the Jin. Preparations to put an end to Chinese arrogance began. Mongke's advisers warned against a frontal attack on Song strongholds, having learned that attacks on walled cities could be costly. Instead they decided to open a front on the southwestern flank of South China. In 1252, Mongke ordered Khubilai to attack Nanzhao, which he proceeded to do after a year of elaborate preparations. His forces won handily, destroyed Nanzhao's army, won the surrender of the capital and the submission of the ruling family. His generals pacified the southwest region and even won the nominal submission of the North Vietnamese. And Khubilai, having served his brother well, returned to North China, where he was granted substantially more land.

Unfortunately, relations between the brothers frayed in the mid-1250s. Khubilai, enjoying his successes, built himself a splendid Chinese-style capital at the edge of the steppes. Increasingly, he seemed to be living a life at variance with Mongol traditions, growing fond of the sedentary life of his subjects, becoming like the effete Chinese. Both his successes and his approach to life aroused resentment in Mongke's court. Criticism of Khubilai mounted among the Mongol leaders, some of whom, perceiving a potential threat to Mongke's rule, became apprehensive of his growing power. Mongke's hostility became apparent in 1257 when he sent officials to audit Khubilai's tax accounts and to intimidate Khubilai's followers. Wisely, Khubilai humbled himself and succeeded in effecting a reconciliation in 1258. They needed each other for the planned assault on the Song.

1258 was the year in which Mongke ordered the full-scale invasion of Song China. He led one of the four attacking armies himself, quickly took Chengdu in Sichuan, and headed for Chongqing. Khubilai was directed to march south, and to cross the Yangzi in the vicinity of the modern city of Wuchang. The Mongol strategy was to divide the south, denying the coastal cities access to central and southwestern China. While Mongke's advisers apparently believed the isolated eastern cities would submit soon thereafter, his forces stalled outside of Chongqing, unable to overcome unexpectedly stiff Chinese resistance and heavy spring rains. In August 1259, in the midst of the struggle, he died, ending the southwestern campaign. The ensuing succession crisis probably spared the Song dynasty, allowing it twenty more years of existence.

Advised of his elder brother's death, Khubilai delayed returning to Mongolia to participate in the selection of the new Great Khan. First he sent his men across the Yangzi, establishing a foothold in southern China but unable to capture his objective against determined Song resistance. The Song offered to accept the Yangzi as a border, conceding the lands the Mongols had taken north of it, and promised tribute as well, but appeasement failed. But before Khubilai could consider a new offensive, he learned that one of his younger brothers, Arigh Boke, was challenging his control of North China, and putting forth his own claim to supremacy. Quickly he led most of his forces back toward his capital to meet the threat. Shortly after his return, a rump assemblage elected him Great Khan. Not to be outdone, his brother had himself selected as Great Khan. There could be only one.

The power struggle within the Mongol leadership effectively ended the Mongol threat to Europe and halted their advance everywhere. The khan of Persia, a supporter of Khubilai, was forced to defend himself against the khan of Kipchak (the Golden Horde), who supported Arig Boke. The Mamluks of Egypt had already seized the opportunity to hand Mongol forces their first major defeat in the Middle East. As Khubilai repositioned his forces to met the threat from his brother's armies to the northwest, Song troops attacked his rear guard and drove the Mongols back across the Yangzi, reclaiming the territory Khubilai had won in 1259. The tide seemed to be shifting.

In 1260, Khubilai, on the defensive, offered the Song limited self-rule in exchange for Song acceptance of Khubilai as ruler of all China, as the Son of Heaven. The Song response was to detain Khubilai's envoy and resume raids against North China. For all of their commercial and cultural achievements, Song leaders showed incredibly poor judgment in their national security policy. Although the moment seemed propitious and the degree of autonomy they might have enjoyed under Khubilai's court is problematic, challenging the Mongols was to bring misery for the people of South China and extinction for the dynasty.

For the moment, however, and for several years to come, the Mongols in general and Khubilai in particular had more pressing problems. The overriding issue was the determination of the contest to decide which brother was to be Great Khan. Although Arigh Boke seemed to have the initial advantage in terms of the extent of his support, Khubilai's strategists ultimately prevailed. Their basic plan was to deny Argh Boke's forces access to essential resources, like food and cloth, by driving him deeper into the steppes and away from the areas in which nomads usually met such needs. Khubilai's armies drove their adversaries westward and northward, out of China and ultimately out of Mongolia as well. By 1262, supported by friends among the Uyghurs, Khubilai was able to prevent his brother from finding provisions in Uyghur territory. Gansu and the region around modern Peking was also beyond the reach of Arigh Boke's men. Briefly, Arigh Boke held critical parts of Central Asia, successfully investing his candidate to lead the Chaghadai Khanate, but he was ultimately betrayed. Key defections among his supporters left him no choice but to surrender to his elder brother in 1264. He died two years later, cause of death unknown, foul play not inconceivable.

Khubilai had defeated the primary challenge to his leadership of the Mongol empire and reigned unchallenged as Great Khan. The khans of Persia, Kipchak, and Chagadai all paid homage to him, but he had little influence over them. Each administered his own territory much as he pleased. Khubilai unquestionably had the largest domain under Mongol control, ruled by far the most people, but he never had the power that his grandfather Chinggis had enjoyed—or that of Chinggis's first two heirs, Ogodei and Mongke. Indeed, provocations from Chaghadai plagued the Great Khan for the last third of the thirteenth century.

But it was toward Song China that Khubilai now turned his attention. An uprising in North China in 1262, centered in Shandong, had troubled him deeply. The rebellion had been led by a trusted Chinese general, son-in-law of one of his closest Chinese advisers—who was also implicated. In due course the rebels were crushed, but Khubilai appears to have reached two conclusions. First, he could not allow himself to be dependent upon Chinese in his inner circle. Increasingly he relied on non-Chinese, on Uyghurs, Tibetans, and others of Central or Western Asian origin. Second, Song China had to be subjugated, lest it serve as a beacon to Northern Chinese restive under Mongol rule. Nor was Khubilai unaware of the riches of the South which he hungered to bring under his control.

Diplomatic overtures to the Song continued to be to no avail. The skirmishes of the early 1260s led to a major confrontation in Sichuan in 1265. The Mongols won the ensuing land and sea battle, capturing more than a hundred Song ships. The turning point in the war was a five-year battle over two towns on the northern border of modern Hebei, magnificently described by the historian Morris Rossabi in his biography of Khubilai.[4]

The principal Mongol target, Xiangyang, on the banks of the Han River, was heavily fortified and supplied by boat. The Mongols would have to win control of the river and they would have to devise artillery powerful enough to breach the walls of the castle.

The Song, to their credit, resisted fiercely. Their resistance was facilitated by the Mongol horsemen's relative lack of experience in urban and naval warfare, and by the southerners' propensity, greater than that of northerners, to see themselves as Chinese fighting barbarian hordes. But not all southerners remained loyal to the Song. Khubilai deliberately set out to encourage defections and had striking success in gaining intelligence about Song plans, Song strengths and weaknesses. A Song Chinese defector was instrumental in the creation of the Mongol navy. He and another Chinese were among Khubilai's most successful generals. They, along with Mongol and Uyghur commanders, directed the ultimate Mongol success—with crucial aid from two Middle Eastern Muslim engineers who designed the artillery, the catapults, with which they were finally able to penetrate the walls at Xiangyang. And Rossabi notes that the Mongol ships that won control of the river had been built by Koreans and Jurchens. Khubilai knew how to mobilize the international resources of his empire, especially the leadership skills of men found throughout its length and breadth.

It was 1273 by the time the siege of Xiangyang succeeded and the Song capital of Hangzhou was the Mongols's next target. Slowly, inexorably, led by a Turk general, they drove southward, crossing the Yangzi at Hankou. Song troops suffered many casualties, many deserted, and increasing numbers defected to the Mongols. Efforts by the Song court to appease the Mongols failed. It was too late to offer tribute. Only unconditional surrender was acceptable and this came in January 1276. Still, a small group of loyalists fled further south, first to Fuzhou, then by sea to Quanzhou, and on to Guangzhou. It was March 1279 before the last remnants of the Song dynasty were destroyed at sea by Mongol naval forces. The Mongol success was facilitated by an Arab merchant who had gained control of the region's shipping and chose to side with the Mongols rather than his Song benefactors. At last, Khubilai ruled all of China. And for the first time since the fall of the Tang Dynasty, all of China was united—albeit under alien rule.

It had long been apparent that Khubilai intended to reign over China in the style of a traditional Chinese emperor. In 1271 he adopted a Chinese dynastic name and the Yuan Dynasty officially began. Of course the Mongols had realized many years before that the Chinese could not be assimilated, could not be integrated into Mongol society, could not be governed as Mongols. There were just too many of them and most were steeped in a very different culture, arguably more suitable to the environment in which they lived. On the other hand, few Mongols were interested in being sinicized. It is difficult to imagine two less compatible cultures. Mongols and Chinese spoke distinctly different languages, dressed differently, preferred different food and drink, and enjoyed strikingly different forms of recreation. Mongol leaders before and after Khubilai concluded that their Chinese subjects were most readily governed by a bureaucratic state, much like the one they had lived under since the Tang. The Mongols, for their part, would strengthen their resistance to sinization through contact with the extensive non-Chinese lands and numerous non-Chinese peoples of their empire. Even Khubilai kept his summer capital outside the Great Wall, in Mongolia.

The obvious point that Khubilai could never escape was that the Yuan Dynasty was a conquest dynasty that remained in power, especially in the South, by the judicious—and occasionally brutal—display of force.

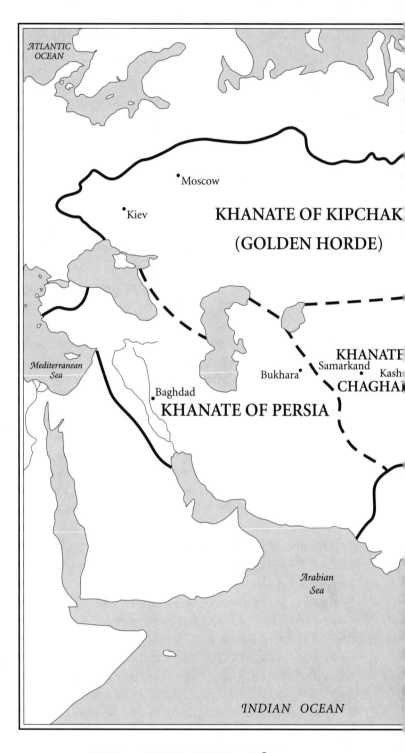

MAP 12.   MONGOL EMPIRE, C. 1280.

After Dun J. Li, *Ageless Chinese*, p. 252; see also Fairbank and Reischauer, *East Asia*, pp. 268–69 and Morris Rossabi, *Khubilai Khan*, p. III.

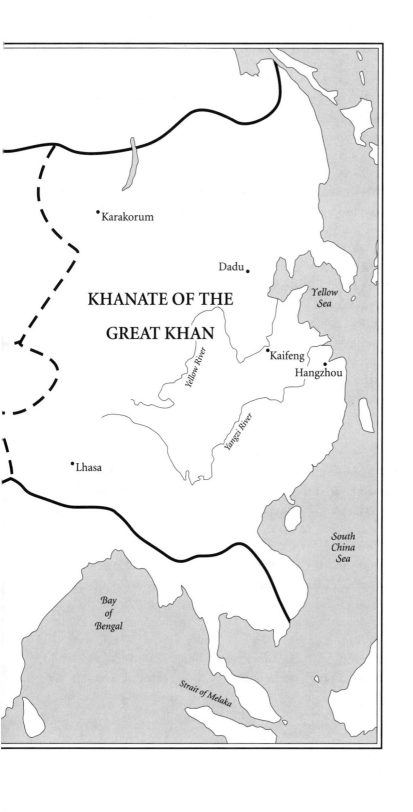

Karakorum

Dadu

KHANATE OF THE

GREAT KHAN

Yellow
Sea

Yellow River

Kaifeng
Hangzhou

Yangzi River

Lhasa

South
China
Sea

Bay
of
Bengal

Strait of Melaka

The contempt most Mongols retained for the Chinese was matched, perhaps exceeded, by continued Chinese disdain for their "barbaric" conquerors. Khubilai's efforts to woo the Confucian literati won collaborators, particularly in the North, but never their respect or admiration. To them he would always be a man who preferred the hunt and falconry to painting and poetry.

The political consequences of the persistent "otherness" of Mongols and Chinese are most easily seen in Khubilai's refusal to resume the examination system for choosing officials. The Mongols had discontinued the examinations when they took control of the North in 1234 and again when the South came under their control in 1274. To resume the examinations would be equivalent to handing the administration of the country back to the Chinese. Instead, the Mongols gave preference to Mongols and their non-Chinese collaborators, mostly from Central and West Asia—men with little knowledge of the Confucian classics. Among Chinese they gave preference to Northerners over Southerners, but few Chinese officials reached the upper echelons of the Yuan regime. In effect, China had an international civil service.[5] It was not a system designed to win the hearts and minds of Chinese intellectuals and office seekers.

China, in the years of Khubilai's reign, was an unusually cosmopolitan society, a fact that the Chinese accepted grudgingly if at all. The Mongol empire had proved tolerant of all religions and patronized Islam in Persia and Nestorian Christianity in Central Asia, as well as Buddhism in China. The Mongols were attracted especially to a Tibetan strain of Buddhism, drawn to it by the alleged magical powers of the lamas, and encouraged its spread in China and Mongolia. Song neo-Confucians were appalled by much of this religiosity and particularly contemptuous of Tibetan (Tantric) Buddhism, which they perceived as anti-intellectual.

But it was not only alien religions that penetrated China. Khubilai's conception of his role as Son of Heaven implied universal rule, as it had for many emperors of China before him. Khubilai's universe, the world of the thirteenth century, was not limited, however, to China. He presumed to be lord of all of Asia and as much of Europe as he could imagine. Muslims from Central Asia and the Middle East were welcome to travel freely through his domains and to reside and trade in his cities. Europeans were equally welcome. The Great Khan received Franciscan friars sent by the Pope and the king of France, and—if his story is to be believed—Marco Polo, who claimed to have spent many years in Khubilai's service.

Khubilai's government encouraged trade and developed commercial contacts with much of the known world. Muslims, primarily of Central Asian origin, dominated foreign trade, importing camels and horses, carpets, medicines and spices, often from the lands of their origin. In return they shipped ceramics, specially designed by Chinese artisans for Muslim taste, as well as the more familiar exports of textiles, lacquerware, and ginger. Equally as significant was the rise of Muslims to dominance in the financial administration of the empire. Jews and Christians, from the Middle East, North Africa, and Europe also appeared in the port cities, attracted by the commercial opportunities, their efforts facilitated by the magnificent transportation system provided by the Mongols, including roads, canals, and merchant shipping. The extent of the empire and the security it provided enabled merchants to travel by land or by sea, integrating China into the international economic system of the day, a system that was very much the product of Mongol triumphs.

TABLE 4.2.   Some Major Figures of the Thirteenth and Fourteenth Centuries
(Dates are approximate. Names in boldface are referred to in text)

Chinggis Khan	**1165–1227**
Khubilai Khan	**1215–1294**
Thomas Aquinas	1225–1274
Kertanagara of Java	**1240–1292**
Dante Alighieri	1265–1321
Tamerlane (Timur the Lame)	**1336–1405**
Geoffrey Chaucer	1340–1400

Asian Resistance to Khubilai as Universal Ruler

Koryo was the first of the states on the periphery of East Asia to confront Mongol power. After thirty years of resisting Mongol invasion, a military coup in 1258 resulted in the Korean crown prince's submission by his appearance at the Mongol court in 1259. Khubilai was pleased by the wisdom thus demonstrated and gave the Koryo prince his daughter's hand in marriage. He further demonstrated his satisfaction with Koryo's subservience by protecting it from attacks by the Jurchens in the 1260s. By 1270 all Korean resistance had ended.

The Mongols annexed northern Korea and administered it and Cheju Island directly. They chose indirect rule for the rest of the country, governing through the Koryo court and bureaucracy. Each successive crown prince made his visit of submission to the Mongol court at Peking and married a Mongol princess. By the end of the century the Koryo ruling family had become thoroughly Mongolized, taking Mongol names, speaking the Mongol language, dressing as Mongol nobility—becoming in effect, an extension of the Mongol court.

The comfortable niche the Koryo nobility found for itself within the Mongol empire brought little relief to the ordinary Koreans upon whom the burden of enormous Mongol tribute requirements fell. In addition to produce and treasure, the Mongols demanded thousands of Korean artisans and women every year and these were duly rounded up and sent off to Peking. From 1264 to 1294 Korea sent thirty-six tribute missions to Khubilai's court. Worst of all was the involuntary participation in the Mongol expeditions against Japan in 1274 and again in 1281. The Koreans had no choice but to build nearly a thousand ships for the invading fleet, provide thousands of men, and the bulk of the provisions for Khubilai's folly.

Despite all of the misery inflicted on the Korean people by the Mongols, one Korean historian has noted a few benefits his countrymen derived from absorption into Khubilai's empire.[6] From China they learned to grow cotton, to make gunpowder, and to appreciate the blessing of neo-Confucian thought. Of perhaps comparable value was the contact with Muslim culture provided by the Mongols. From Persians and Arabs the Koreans acquired advanced mathematical and medical knowledge, new artistic techniques, and a more accurate calendar. And Arab traders found their way to Korean ports, incorporating Korea in the international economic system of the thirteenth century. Another scholar has suggested that the Mongol invasions forced Koreans to the point of national consciousness, moving them beyond their historic loyalties to one or another of the three Korea kingdoms.[7] Few would deny, however, that the price the Koreans paid for these gains was very high.

The Japanese were far more fortunate although they, too, paid heavily as they resisted Khubilai's efforts to subject them to his will. For the first half of the thirteenth century, Japan had confronted serious internal divisions that might have left them vulnerable to invasion, but by the time the Mongols attacked, the Kamakura bakufu had created a strong stable government and it was ready.

Yoritomo's death in 1199, preceded by his elimination of his brothers and other potential rivals, left the bakufu in the hands of his wife's family, the Hojo. They managed superbly. The major challenge to their rule came in 1221 when the retired emperor Go-Toba raised an army and attempted to reassert the authority of the court. His forces were crushed and thereafter the court accepted Hojo direction. The 1240s also proved to be a period of political tensions and once again the Hojo prevailed, destroying a rival family in 1247.

International affairs had not engaged the bakufu deeply. Japan was, to be sure, an active participant in East Asian trade and cultural exchange. Contact with Korea was constant, but both cultural and trade ties were most extensive with Song China. Chinese Buddhist priests had great influence on Japanese thought, as did Japanese priests who studied in China. Many ships, mostly Chinese, crossed the sea between China and Japan and Chinese merchants were resident in Japan. These linkages with Korea and China provided the Japanese with extensive information about the Mongols, although these sources were hardly unbiased. The trade continued throughout the years of the Yuan dynasty, pausing only during those periods when the Mongols were preoccupied with invasions.

There had been a brief war scare in 1227 when the Koreans were angered by Japanese pirate attacks. The bakufu strengthened defenses against a possible Korean attack and attempted to remove the provocation by cracking down on piracy. But the Koreans had more than they could handle as the Mongols swept down upon them from the north. The crisis passed and the Hojo concentrated on solidifying their grip on their country and domestic affairs generally.

In 1266, after the Koryo court had submitted to Khubilai and as his forces battled the Song, he attempted a diplomatic approach to Japan. He began with a letter in which he indicated that his intentions were peaceful, but that as the Son of Heaven, he expected the Japanese to accept tributary status within his empire. The Koryo king, not a completely independent actor, also wrote to urge the Japanese court to respond favorably to Khubilai's message, contending that he sought prestige rather than territory. The court was prepared to acquiesce, disinclined to provoke Khubilai needlessly. The warriors of the bakufu, however, would have none of it. Bluntly, they rejected tributary status and Khubilai's pretensions.

Khubilai simultaneously continued diplomatic overtures and prepared to attack Japan. Bakufu spies in Korea reported the military buildup while pro-Song Chinese warned against accommodation with the Mongols. Again in 1271 the court was interested in finding a peaceful solution, but the bakufu would yield nothing. In 1274 a joint Mongol-Korean force easily overran two small Japanese islands in the waters separating Japan from Korea. When they went ashore on a beach in northern Kyushu, however, they ran into determined resistance. The Japanese were doubtless a match for Mongol courage and ferocity. Whether they could have prevailed against superior Mongol armaments and experience is questionable, but a storm arose to threaten the attacking fleet and it suffered heavy losses as it withdrew. With this assist from the weather, Japan had resisted successfully a force widely perceived as irresistible.

Khubilai resumed his diplomatic offensive, sending two envoys to negotiate with the Japanese. The bakufu executed the Mongol envoys. Rather than seek an agreement with the Mongols, the bakufu toyed with the idea of a preemptive strike at Korean ports where the Mongols were preparing to try again. Ultimately, the Hojo leader decided against the attack on Korea, but when Khubilai sent yet another envoy in 1279, he too was executed by the bakufu. Clearly diplomacy was not a skill the Japanese had cultivated—or in which the bakufu showed much interest.

Once again the Mongols prepared to attack. This time Khubilai sent across nearly a thousand Korean ships and the recently acquired Song navy. He sent five times as many men, approximately 150,000—Mongols to be sure, Koreans, and North Chinese, but largely erstwhile Southern Song troops. The Japanese were waiting for them with reinforced defenses when they battled their way on shore. Day after day the swords clanged and the arrows flew and men died. Again the Japanese proved their mettle and would not give way. Again a storm arose to wreak havoc with the mainland fleet and to cripple the attackers. Again they fled, but only a fraction of Khubilai's fleet and army survived. Twice aided, perhaps saved by storms, the Japanese could hardly be faulted for believing the gods were on their side.

Khubilai did not give up easily. In 1283 he commenced preparations for a third attack on Japan. Although he probably gave up the idea by 1286, the force he began to assemble and train remained in being until he died in 1294. With Khubilai's death, the Japanese would be relieved of the Mongol threat. The news of his death, however, did not bring immediate relief to the Japanese military, which remained on alert until 1312.

Southeast Asia provided little balm for Khubilai's wounded ego. As with Japan, his primary interest seems to have been in gaining the nominal submission of the kings of various polities of the region. Especially after the costly failures in Japan, his leadership and stature at home, even his continued rule, were in question. He apparently felt vulnerable. He needed—or thought he needed—foreign triumphs, external validation of his claim to be the Son of Heaven. The Vietnamese, at least those in the North, had played the game in the early years of Mongol ascendancy and had sent tribute missions to Peking as late as 1279. Most of these were in fact trade missions, staffed by merchants, but there was no indication of Mongol dissatisfaction. The rest of the region proved to be more recalcitrant.

Each local potentate was offered the opportunity to subordinate himself to Khubilai. When he refused, the Mongols attacked. The king of Pagan was enraged by the suggestion of Mongol envoys that he bow to the Great Khan—and he had them executed. The first major battle between the Burmese and the Mongols was won by the Mongols in 1279, but they were unable to conquer the diminutive state of Pagan until 1287. The tribute exacted was never worth the cost of victory. In this campaign, as in most others in the region, Mongol soldiers fared poorly in tropical heat and rains and found the jungles poor terrain for the cavalry maneuvers that had served them so well elsewhere in Asia and Europe.

Little Champa sent an occasional tribute mission but refused to submit and found an unlikely ally in Vietnam when Mongol forces attempted to cross Vietnamese territory enroute to Champa in 1281. In 1284 four columns of Mongol troops attacked Vietnam from different directions and each was smashed by the Vietnamese, often using guerrilla tactics for which the Mongols were ill prepared. The final Mongol attack in 1287 was also thrown back, supply ships sunk and fleeing soldiers decimated. Curiously, but perhaps wisely, at this point, both Champa and Vietnam decided to resume tribute missions rather than risk the cost of yet another invasion.

Angkor was beyond Khubilai's reach, but the Tai people who had fled the Mongols' approach and conquest of Nanzhao had established their control over the upper Mekong and were determined to resist further encroachment. By the time of Khubilai's death they had established a capital at Chiengmai from which they harassed Mongol forces that entered the region. Although they kept the Mongols out, the Tai proved receptive to the peaceful migration of Chinese artisans and merchants who ultimately played an important role in the creation of the state of Ayutthaya.

Island Southeast Asia did not escape Khubilai's attention. The first contact appears to have been initiated by the Sumatrans who sent envoys to Khubilai's court after he proclaimed the Yuan dynasty. Their goal appears to have been to gain his designation of their ports as special entrepots for China's trade with South and Southeast Asia. Sumatran activity triggered aggressive expansion by Kertanagara, ruler of Majapahit in eastern Java. By 1286 he had gained control of the straits and dominated the shipping of the region. In 1289 Khubilai sent envoys to Majapahit demanding tribute. Kertanagara, aware of Mongol failures in Japan and Vietnam, was contemptuous. He disfigured the envoys and shipped them back to Khubilai. Khubilai, unable to come to terms with the lessons of his failures, sent a vast armada, at least a thousand vessels, to punish Kertanagara. By the time they arrived, Kertanagara had been murdered by a rival who was engaged in a struggle for power with Kertanagara's son-in-law. The son-in-law cleverly allied himself with the Mongols to defeat the murderer—and then turned around and drove the Mongols out of Java. In 1293, on the eve of Khubilai's death, the Javanese and the Mongol dynasty ended their conflict and restored commercial relations. There was not much glory in it for the Mongols.

Korea, Japan, and the various Southeast Asian states never posed a threat to Khubilai's imperial rule. In Central Asia, on the other hand, opposition to Khubilai's pretensions was constant, allowing him little opportunity to relax his guard. Several of his cousins, also grandchildren of Chinggis Khan, continued to honor more traditional Mongol values, remaining discomforted by Khubilai's apparent sinicization. They never accepted his claim to be the Great Khan, never recognized his authority over Central Asia. The principal challenge came from his cousin Khaidu who revolted against Khubilai in 1268 and became de facto ruler of the Khanate of Chaghadai. Unable to suppress Khaidu, unwilling to test support for his own claims among other members of the Mongol nobility, Khubilai was forced to accept Khaidu's control of Central Asia as the price of secure passage for the overland trade between China and India, the Middle East, and Europe.

In 1277, Khubilai's forces succeeded in blunting Khaidu's effort to seize control of the Mongolian heartland, but the rest of Central Asia was lost. By 1279, financial difficulties resulting from constant warfare, especially the costly efforts against Japan and Southeast Asia, left Khubilai on the defensive. He suffered defeat after defeat in the northwest, although he never lost Mongolia. But he could never rest, until the end of his days, forced always to be on alert for Khaidu's next foray. Having adopted the ways of a monarch in a sedentary society, he, like so many of his Chinese predecessors, had to endure the unpredictable thrusts of the steppe nomads.

The Last Days of the Yuan

In 1294 Khubilai died. His dynasty survived for another three quarters of a century, but most of his heirs were not worthy of his throne. The grandson who succeeded him was able enough to maintain stability, but when he died in 1307, the struggle for power within the Mongol nobility proved disastrous. For the next twenty-six years, the average reign of an emperor was less than four years—and they all died young. As the Mongols fought among themselves, rebellions broke out among their subjects. Although one man managed to hold on to the throne from 1333, when he was named emperor at the age of thirteen, to 1368, when he left Peking for Mongolia, he could not contain the intramural strife among Mongols, or cope with the natural disasters that struck China—or with the rebels who eventually drove the Mongols out of China.

Most devastating to mid-century China and much of the world with which it had contact was bubonic plague, the Black Death. It appears to have begun in the vicinity of the Gobi desert in the 1320s and than spread throughout China, killing approximately 35 *million* people, nearly a third of the population. In the second half of the century, following the trade routes, the disease spread west to India, the Middle East, and Europe, with comparable results.

But no East Asian polity threatened Mongol hegemony in the fourteenth century. Mongol distractions initially increased Koryo's burdens as the Koreans were forced to lend assistance to the Mongols against rebel forces, some of whom established themselves temporarily in northern Korea. Although the Mongols lost control of the peninsula by 1356, the Koreans did not pursue their historic goals in Manchuria until after the collapse of the Yuan dynasty. Across the sea, the Japanese watched warily, keeping their distance And however hostile Southeast Asian regimes may have been toward their would-be Mongol conquerors, none chose to move against them.

Only other Mongol princes in Central Asia launched attacks on Khubilai's legacy—and they were as divided among themselves as were the Mongols in Peking. The Tibetans, ruled by the Mongols as an autonomous province within the empire, revolted in mid-century and successfully reasserted their independence. For the next several hundred years they seemed happy enough to be free of China and never again behaved as aggressively as they had in the heyday of their empire. Even the Europeans who arrived at the Mongol court all came in peace, as merchants, teachers, and priests.

Within China, however, the challenge to the Yuan dynasty grew rapidly in mid-century. Rebel bands, mostly hungry men, but including some hostile to Mongol domination, overran much of southern China, encountering minimal opposition. The Mongols continued to fight among themselves, although more sensitive to challenges to their rule over North China. But in 1368, Zhu Yuanzhang, a one-time Buddhist monk who emerged as most successful of the rebel leaders, led his troops north against Peking. The Mongol court abandoned the city and fled to Mongolia. Mongol ascendancy over East Asia had ended.

Conclusion

The thirteenth century, which began with Chinggis Khan sweeping across Asia into Europe, constituted an extraordinary period—an era in which one people, the Mongols, dominated the Eurasian continent from the East China Sea to the Danube, the largest empire the world has ever known. These were years in which contacts between East Asia and the rest of the world expanded rapidly as a result of the transportation network built by the Mongols and the relative security of the overland routes they controlled. The movement of people, goods, and ideas led to increased awareness of East Asia among Arabs, Europeans, and Persians—and of these peoples of the West to those of East Asia. It led to the exchange of knowledge—and disease—as well as material culture. More than ever before, East Asia was connected to the rest of the known world.

For more than a century, well into the fourteenth century, some polities, most notably China, Korea, and Tibet, were submerged in the Mongol empire. Most Chinese, Koreans, and Tibetans, however, retained their historic cultures—their pre-Mongol cultures and identities. Indeed, in Korea and in South China, resistance to Mongol invasions and subjugation appear to have fostered proto-nationalist sentiments. And then, before the end of the fourteenth century, the Mongols went home, leaving their former subjects free to suffer under indigenous despots.

FIVE

The Resurgence of Chinese Power and the Coming of Islam

Rise of the Ming

China, over the last twenty to thirty years of the Yuan dynasty, once again hosted an interstate system within its borders, briefly analogous to that which existed during the Warring States era or the tenth-century interlude between the Tang and Song dynasties. Mongol forces, confined largely to the north, broke up into factions with various warlords vying for control of the emperor. Southern and central China were garrisoned by Chinese troops, usually under Mongol or other non-Chinese commanders. None of these forces were effective against the rebellions that swept the south. By mid-fourteenth century, in addition to the Yuan, there were eight other "states" occupying Chinese soil, five essentially provincial and three larger ones, poised in an uneasy balance of power.

Zhu Yuanzhang controlled the least imposing of the three larger states, including parts of modern Jiangsu, Jiejiang, and Anhui. Nonetheless, in 1360 he decided to gamble and attacked the ostensibly stronger state of Han. The war lasted three years, Zhu won, and destroyed the balance of power in central China. Once his army had absorbed the men and resources of Han, no force in the South could resist it. The failure of the other states, especially Wu, the most powerful of them, to come to the aid of Han doomed them. An effective system of collective security might not have deterred Zhu's aggression, but it might have defeated him. It did not exist and soon only the Mongols stood between him and control of all China.

In 1367 Zhu's forces invaded the North China plain, driving the Mongols before them. By mid-1368 Zhu was in Peking and the Mongol armies had been swept out of China, retreating to their ancestral homeland in Mongolia. Unfortunately for the Chinese, the Mongols had suffered relatively few casualties as they fled and their return sorties across the border would plague the dynasty for most of its existence. But Zhu had little reason to think about future danger as he triumphantly declared himself the Hungwu emperor of China, founder of the Ming dynasty.

The founding emperor's principal goals appear to have been to establish himself as unquestioned autocrat of all of China and to gain universal recognition of China's centrality and superiority over all other states and peoples. Toward the first end he soon eliminated the position of prime minister and chose to rule directly, accepting advice only from his Grand Secretariat—which functioned as a cabinet. In foreign affairs he rejected the international system which had existed before the Mongol empire, a system in which China had diplomatic relations with the various states of East Asia—and other parts of Asia—on a basis of rough equality, sometimes even accepting the fact of Chinese military inferiority. Hungwu perceived no militarily superior force outside of China and considered none but the Mongols to be a threat. The idea that another people might claim equality on cultural, economic, or political grounds he found inconceivable. Once the world had been informed of his accession to the throne, he demanded tributary relations with all of the states along China's established trade routes, including Japan, Korea, the Ryukyu (Liuqiu in Chinese) Islands, Tibet, and most of Southeast Asia.

The foremost Western student of the tribute system, John King Fairbank, has explained that it was intended to create a Confucian world order, an extension to the rest of the world of the Chinese social order.[1] Most obviously, it meant that all states that accepted membership acknowledged their inferiority relative to China. Each was equal to every other state, but all were inferior to China—as their representatives would demonstrate with the ritual series of kneelings and prostrations, the "kowtow," required when in the presence of the Chinese emperor, the Son of Heaven.

But the tribute system provided far more than an opportunity for various rulers or their envoys to degrade themselves—or the Chinese might have encountered far more resistance. It allowed for the exchange of envoys essential to the conduct of diplomatic relations. It served to facilitate and regulate trade. By accepting investiture by the Chinese emperor and agreeing to accept the Chinese calendar using the reign of the Chinese ruler rather than his own for dating purposes, a foreign king anticipated Chinese protection against his foreign enemies, noninterference in his internal affairs, a profit on his trade activities, and perhaps a subsidy to fill his coffers. The Chinese often paid dearly for foreign tolerance of their pretensions.

Of course not all states bought into the tribute system, at least not until they concluded the cost of staying out was unaffordable. Koryo played a dangerous game of straddle, trying to buy off the Ming with tribute missions while maintaining diplomatic relations with the Mongols in Karakorum. The Ming response was to imprison all Korean envoys between 1375 and 1377. In 1377 the king of Koryo adopted the Ming calendar and begged to be invested by the Chinese emperor. He sent eighteen tribute missions to Hungwu's capital at Nanjing between 1379 and 1385, several of which the Chinese rejected as inadequate. Finally, in 1385 Hungwu relented and agreed to invest him.

The Japanese infuriated the Ming by failing to stop piracy along the China coast. Hungwu sent three missions to Japan to no avail. The Japanese did send tribute missions, but these failed to meet ritual requirements and appeared to be commercial ventures sent by someone other than the ruler of Japan. Hungwu sent an angry denunciation to the shogun in 1380. The shogun's reply showed contempt for Hungwu's claim to rule over all under heaven. He rejected the idea that the world was ruled by only one man or belonged to one man. Hungwu was never able to bring the Japanese into his system and severed official relations. He was less successful in his efforts to cut off trade between China and Japan. And the "Japanese" pirates, many of them Chinese, continued to plague China long after he was gone.

The states of Southeast Asia were quick to recognize the benefits of accepting tributary status and virtually all sent missions to Nanjing. The Vietnamese and the Cham responded immediately and the Cambodian and Thai rulers followed hard on their heels. In the 1370s the various states of the Indonesian archipelago and the Malay peninsula all submitted tribute to the Ming emperor. Representatives of other states eager to continue their participation in Chinese trade, including some from India and the Eastern Mediterranean, also knelt and prostrated themselves shamelessly before Hungwu.

As has been so often the case in Chinese history, the stubborn peoples of the borderlands gave the Ming the most trouble and had to be met with force. Tibetan resistance was overcome in 1379 at enormous expense to China. The Mongols threw back a Chinese offensive in 1372, mounted sporadic and unsuccessful raids for the next fifteen years, were beaten back by superior Chinese firearms, and finally routed by another major Ming effort in 1388. For the remainder of Hungwu's reign, the Mongols did not pose a significant threat to China. His successors were not so fortunate. In the southwest the Ming were able to suppress resistance in Sichuan, but had considerably greater difficulty coping with the Shan people of Yunnan, who defeated a large Chinese expeditionary force in 1388. A year later the Chinese returned and managed to pacify the region. Yunnan was flooded with Chinese settlers who enabled the Ming to incorporate it for the first time into the Chinese empire. Tibet and Mongolia, however subdued, remained outside the empire.

A fascinating complication in China's problems with Yunnan and the larger international arena of the late fourteenth century was provided by the Japanese, almost certainly without the involvement of the bakufu. Early in the 1380s, a Chinese military officer responsible for overseeing the affairs of the port of Ningbo was charged with misappropriating Japanese goods intended as tribute for the court. He was banished to Japan, but he reappeared at the head of a troop of Japanese warriors, apparently intending to revenge himself on the court. Somehow the Ming co-opted the Japanese and shipped them off to Yunnan where they fought alongside the Chinese against the Shan. A few years later, in 1395, the emperor, troubled by too frequent incidents caused by fierce and obstreperous Japanese warriors arriving on alleged tribute vessels, concluded that there was a plot to use Japanese to overthrow him. His response was to attempt to restrict foreign relations further, to minimize Chinese contacts with the outside world, especially with Japan.

When Hungwu died, he was succeeded initially by a teenage grandson whose major foreign affairs initiative was the importation of war horses from Korea. The young man never had a chance against an ambitious and resourceful uncle, Hungwu's fourth son, who swept out of the north, devastating all before him, and usurped the throne in 1403. Styling himself the Yongle emperor, he reigned until 1424, focusing his energies on frontier defense and the expansion of Chinese hegemony in East Asia. He was a warrior who delighted in combat and died leading a campaign against the Mongols, only a few years after he returned the capital to Peking, the original base of his power. China under his leadership reached new heights of fame and glory throughout Asia and elsewhere in the civilized world, but the cost of his expansive international activities strained the country's finances, leaving his successors without the means to emulate him.

Yongle's approach to foreign affairs, apparently based upon close study of Chinese military classics,[2] was to take the strategic offensive, to take advantage of China's greater military strength to destroy threats to the national security, to take territory from weaker neighbors, and to demonstrate Chinese power as far away as the east coast of Africa and the Persian Gulf. Throughout his reign—and for some long time thereafter—the Mongols, against whom he had honed his martial skills, remained the principal challenge to China's tranquillity. Yongle did not ignore the potential value of diplomacy or of trade in managing the Mongols, but he and his advisers were convinced that any lasting resolution of the threat would require the use of force. To this end he led five major campaigns into Mongolia, as well as engaging Mongol forces in countless skirmishes along the frontier.

The key to Chinese hopes in the fifteenth century, as in years past, was the disunity of the various Mongol tribes, and the use of one group of Mongols against another. When Yongle ascended to the throne, the Mongols were again divided into eastern and western elements, mutually antagonistic but unwilling to serve as Chinese surrogates. Both found raids into North China profitable. In 1409, responding to such a raid, a Ming punitive expedition pursuing eastern Mongol horsemen was defeated. Yongle then raised an expeditionary force of more than 100,000 men, succeeded in buying off the western Mongols and, hauling cannon to the battlefield, prevailed over the eastern Mongols. Victory came relatively easily, but accomplished little. The main force of the eastern Mongols escaped to fight another day and the western Mongols seized the opportunity to expand eastward, into the area vacated by the vanquished. The Mongol threat had not diminished.

Perceiving the danger posed by the western Mongols, Yongle led a second expedition in 1414 and handed them a severe defeat—at a high cost in Chinese lives and treasure. The results mirrored those of 1410. This time the eastern Mongols took advantage of the distress of their bloodied relatives and expanded westward. Soon their horsemen were riding into the North China plain, burning and pillaging as before. In 1422 Yongle mobilized a force of 235,000 men, driving the eastern Mongols into Outer Mongolia. Frustrated by his inability to subdue them, he led a fourth expedition in 1423 which failed to make contact with his enemy and a fifth in 1424 during which he died suddenly. His aggressive tactics against the Mongols had done nothing to ensure China's security. The Mongol threat had not diminished. China's economy had been weakened and Yongle's successors were inevitably forced back to a more passive defense.

Curiously, despite Yongle's campaigns against the Mongols, both eastern and western Mongols sent tribute missions to Peking during most of his reign. The easterners stopped sometime after his first major campaign, but those of the west sent missions almost every year beginning in 1408. Obviously, both sides perceived substantial benefit in continuing the charade, the pretense of Mongol submission to the Ming emperor. Individual Mongol missions sometimes contained as many as three thousand members, many if not most merchants, some from Central Asian states. They came for the exchange of "gifts," the opportunity to trade, and the delight of being China's guests for the duration of their embassy. The Chinese were probably fortunate to break even in these exchanges, considering the cost of hosting hordes of foreign visitors, but for the court there was the additional compensation of the ritual submission, adding to the luster of the throne.

Far to the west was another threat of which the Chinese were at best vaguely aware. There, in Central Asia, the great Timur (Tamerlane) had built an empire extending westward to include Persia, Mesopotamia, and part of Ottoman Turkey. He was disdainful of Chinese efforts to open relations and executed the envoys sent by the Ming. Striving to match the achievements of Chinggis Khan, he defeated Mongol rivals including the Golden Horde in Russia, invaded India, and was preparing to conquer China when he died in 1405 at the outset of the campaign. Yongle might have enjoyed the challenge, but Central Asia was one arena in which he operated with relative restraint.

Yongle sent envoys to the various Central Asian oasis states and gained the warmest response from Uyghurs eager for an alternative to Mongol domination. The Uyghurs happily entered the tribute system, developing mutually profitable trade relations and winning Ming military protection. Chinese troops aided them against the Mongols, but China did not establish any permanent bases in the region. After Timur's death, his son and successor exchanged embassies with the Ming but would not accept tributary status. Yongle seemed perfectly content to allow the relationship to focus on trade and by 1418 was willing to write to the Timurid ruler as a political equal. Of course, when the Timurid empire sent an extraordinarily lavish mission to Peking in 1420, its leaders were forced to behave as would any bearers of tribute to the Ming emperor. Hok-lam Chan, a leading student of Ming history, noted that "whatever concessions the emperor was willing to make in correspondence with the Timurid ruler, at the Chinese court there was no compromise with the pretense of the

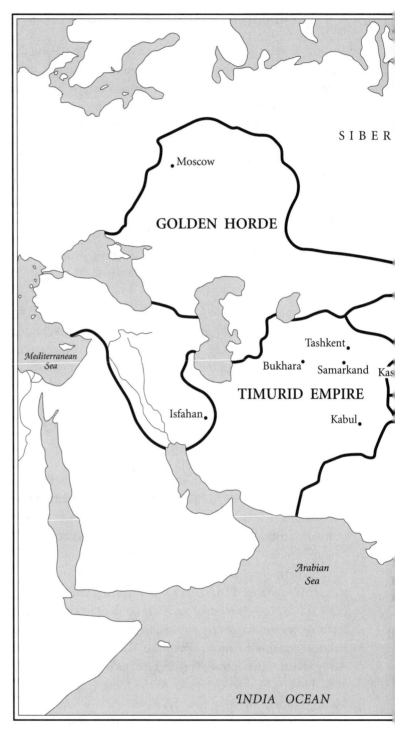

MAP 13.   MING CHINA AND ASIA, C. 1400
After *China and Inner Asia from 1368 to the Present*, pp. 48–49.

OIRAT AND
EASTERN MONGOLS

Karakorum•

MANCHURIA

KOREA

Peking•

Yellow
Sea

Turfan• •Hami
UIGHURISTAN

Xi'an•

Yellow River

Nanjing•

HULISTAN

MING •EMPIRE

hotan•

TIBET

Chengdu•

Yangzi River

•Lhasa

Guangzhou•

South
China
Sea

DIA

Bay
of
Bengal

Strait of Melaka

CEYLON

ruler-vassal relationship."[3] At home the Chinese emperor's claim to universal overlordship could not be brought into question.

On several earlier occasions, Chinese officials accompanied Timurid embassies on their return from China and collected information about the various Central Asian states between Nanjing and the Timurid capital at Samarkand. The intelligence thus gathered assisted the court in developing relations with these states, largely for the purpose of expanding trade. The rulers of the Central Asian states were eager to strengthen commercial ties to China and readily accepted tributary status. The Chinese court never questioned the sincerity of homage paid to the emperor by the thousands of Central Asian merchants who accompanied the many tribute missions—more than a hundred such missions arrived in Nanjing and Peking during Yongle's reign alone. Although the seemingly constant flow of vassals kowtowing to the emperor unquestionably enhanced his prestige among his people, economic interests motivated the Chinese as well as their visitors from afar.

Yongle's approach to Vietnam was markedly less prudent. His father had promised the people of Annam (northern Vietnam) that China would not interfere in their internal affairs if Annam accepted tributary status. The Vietnamese promptly accepted and all was well until Yongle ascended to the throne and ignored Hongwu's commitment. Problems in relations between the two countries during Yongle's reign began almost accidentally as he unwittingly invested a usurper as emperor of Annam in 1403. When the Chinese realized their mistake, they demanded the restoration of their original vassal. Negotiating under pressure, the Vietnamese accepted Chinese demands, but then intercepted and massacred a Ming force escorting the returning emperor. Yongle was not the sort of man to allow a tiny vassal state to abuse him, especially when Vietnamese actions against another vassal state, Champa, and their failure to respect the borders the Ming claimed in Guangxi and Yunnan, had already tried him sorely. It was clearly time to put an end to Vietnamese arrogance and incorporate Annam into the Chinese empire.

In 1407 Yongle sent a large army into Annam and crushed the Vietnamese opposition. Annam was now part of China and Ming officials arrived determined to sinicize the people. Although the Vietnamese had long been influenced by Chinese civilization, they had retained their own language and elements of their indigenous culture. Efforts to make them "Chinese" were not welcomed and provoked widespread anti-Chinese feelings, resulting in a powerful resistance movement. One resistance leader proclaimed the state of Dai Viet (Great Vietnam) and harassed Ming forces until he was captured in 1409. A second resistance leader, Le Loi, relying largely on guerrilla tactics, gradually denied the Chinese freedom of movement in the countryside. By 1427, he had seized control of the entire country save the city of Hanoi—from which the Chinese could not safely travel. A Ming army sent to relieve the besieged city was defeated enroute and the Chinese were forced to surrender and withdraw from Annam. Despite great effort and enormous expense, the mighty Ming empire had to concede its inability to subdue the Vietnamese people. Le Loi proclaimed himself king and shrewdly sent a tribute mission to Peking. Equally as wisely, the Chinese court recognized him and accepted at face value his professed willingness to accept Chinese overlordship. Yongle, however, died before China's ignominious retreat. His preoccupation with the Mongols doubtless contributed to Vietnamese successes, as well as costing him his life.

China's northeast frontier was probably the least troublesome area during the glorious days of Yongle's rule. The Jurchen chieftains, more often than not, were content to acknowledge a tributary relationship. Yongle recognized the need to keep them friendly while he chased the Mongols and he was generous in the terms of trade accorded them. With China's acquiescence if not active assistance, the Jurchens became the dominant force in Manchuria, as Korean influence in the region continued to recede. And the Jurchens, at least superficially, accepted sincization. There was no overt resistance to the spread of Chinese culture. The Jurchens enjoyed the products they obtained from China and profited from the sale of furs, horses, and ginseng. At no time did either the Ming court or the Jurchen leaders find it advantageous to resort to force.

The Koreans, less happily, also refrained from provoking Yongle. The Yi dynasty rulers feared the Ming more than any of their other neighbors and began sending regular tribute embassies to Nanjing on the eve of his ascension. But Yongle's demands were great. Not only did he require annual tribute in gold and silver, but he also wanted—and obtained—large numbers of virgins for his harem and of horses and oxen for his army. This was one tributary relationship that was unquestionably profitable for the Chinese—and extraordinarily one-sided. Stoically, the Koreans bore the humiliation and economic burden of their vassalage. Only the Yi kings could claim any benefit: the legitimacy of the dynasty was bolstered by Ming recognition of their rule. For ordinary Koreans, the relationship had no redeeming features.

Even the haughty Japanese briefly pretended to submit to the tributary system. Hongwu's decision to deny Japanese access to Chinese goods and markets was not easily enforced, but the bakufu and its supporters experienced a decline in trade revenues nonetheless. The shogun Yoshimitsu took the initiative and sent a mission in 1399 that was well received by the Ming court. In 1403 Yongle was delighted to receive a letter in which Yoshimitsu styled himself "your subject, the King of Japan." Yoshimitsu doubtless did not perceive himself to be anyone's subject and he most assuredly was not king of Japan, but the lust for commercial profit was great. Yongle allowed the resumption of trade, albeit limited, and the Japanese came in droves, quickly surpassing the prescribed limits. Despite the obvious benefits for both countries, Yoshimitsu's successor rejected tributary status and broke off official relations with the Ming. The Chinese ignored Japan's diplomatic transgression—if indeed they noticed—and Sino-Japanese trade continued to flourish.

Yongle's greatest international forays had little to do with immediate threats to Chinese security or with his efforts to enlarge the territory of his empire. On six occasions between 1405 and 1421, he dispatched spectacular naval expeditions into the Indian Ocean, at least two of which are known to have reached the eastern coast of Africa and two of which reached the Persian Gulf. In other words, nearly a century before Columbus discovered America, before Vasco da Gama found his way around Cape Hope to India, the Chinese admiral Zheng He was criss-crossing the Indian Ocean with enormous fleets, the first of which consisted of 62 major junks or galleons, more than 200 additional auxiliary vessels, and largely Fujianese crews of nearly 28,000 men.

Yongle's purpose in assembling these armadas is uncertain. No document exists in which he spells out his objectives. Unquestionably this naval demonstration revealed to all of coastal Asia the power and the glory of Ming China. It reminded existing tributaries of the virtue of remaining on good terms with the Son of Heaven. The arrival of the fleet and the exquisite gifts it carried for local rulers suggested to those outside the tribute system the opportunities for profit that they were missing and the danger they might face by refusing nominal submission. On several occasions, the Chinese ships were challenged and crushed those who dared stand in their way. In 1407, on its return voyage, the first expedition ran into a powerful pirate fleet that controlled the Strait of Melaka and defeated it easily. Local potentates whose commerce had been ravaged by the pirates or who had been forced to bribe them as the price of passage took note. The third expedition stopped at Ceylon on its way home where the Sinhalese made the mistake of attempting to rob the ships of their treasure. Again the Chinese prevailed, captured the King of Ceylon, and brought him back to Nanjing to submit to Yongle. The fourth expedition stopped at Semudera where Chinese forces seized a usurper at the Sumatran port and carried him back to Nanjing for execution. To all of coastal Asia, the power and reach of the Ming emperor was evident.

A second result—and probable purpose—of the naval expeditions was the transport of tribute envoys from Africa and the maritime regions of West, South, and Southeast Asia and the treasure and exotica they conveyed to the court. Missions from Hormuz in modern Iran and Malindi, Mogadishu, and Brava on the Somali coast of Africa traveled to China with four of the return voyages. Bengal sent eleven tribute missions. The King of Melaka personally went to China to pay tribute on four separate occasions. After the fourth expedition, eighteen states between Southeast Asia and the east coast of Africa sent tribute missions to Nanjing, an event that Hok-Lam Chan calls "the zenith of the emperor's influence abroad."[4] Soon Nanjing was awash in exotic animals—lions and leopards, ostriches and giraffes, zebras and rhinos and dromedary camels—as well as gold, silver, spices, and slaves, all to the greater glory of Yongle.

A seventh and final fleet sailed in 1431, after Yongle's death, but China's day as the great naval power of Asia was over. None but Yongle had the vision and few outside the court had benefited from the effort. Not even Yongle's regime capitalized on the trade opportunities Zheng He had generated. Although thousands of Chinese merchants settled along the maritime trade routes, no Ming government recognized the potential wealth to be tapped. Contemptuous of merchants, no Confucian scholar would advise the court to support their ventures. The fact that Zheng He was a eunuch—and a Muslim from Yunnan—did not commend him or his efforts to the Confucian intellectuals who saw the court eunuchs as the principal obstacle to their own power. And of course, the voyages and the fleet itself were expensive at a time when the primary threat to the national security came overland, from the Mongols. Without Yongle's sponsorship, the Chinese navy disintegrated and China yielded control of the seas to other powers—to China's ultimate disadvantage.

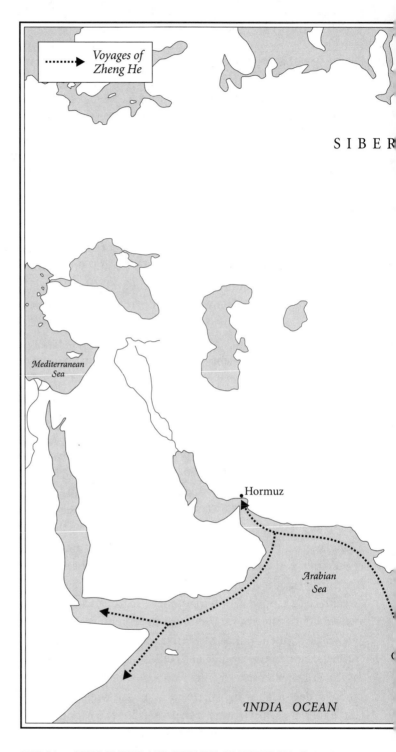

SIBER

Mediterranean
Sea

Hormuz

Arabian
Sea

INDIA OCEAN

MAP 14.   MING EMPIRE AND VOYAGES OF ZHENG HE, C. 1450.

After Fairbank and Reischauer, *East Asia*, p. 318 and Dun J. Li,

Ageless Chinese, p. 285.

There is no question that the emperor perceived China's involvement in the international trading system of the early fifteenth century in primarily political terms. The enormous number of tribute missions from much of the known world greatly enhanced his stature at home. Encountering Chinese military power, naval as well as land forces, some of China's neighbors were probably awed and hoped through tribute missions to stave off Chinese invasions or to buy China's protection.

On the other hand, it is a mistake to undervalue the economic benefits of the trade. No one doubts that most states that accepted tributary status did so in order to gain access to Chinese goods and markets. What is equally clear is that many Chinese—and not just the court—profited from the many foreign merchants masquerading as tribute missions. The court's willingness to countenance sham missions speaks to this point, but far more important is the booming private trade that developed without government interference. Yongle may have kept the giraffes, but exotic spices and other consumer goods generated their own markets and stimulated demand among urban Chinese. Thousands of Chinese merchants left home to seek the source of marketable products and settled in the port cities of Southeast Asia to engage in highly profitable trade. They went without government approval or protection but benefited as much as they suffered from official disinterest. The Ming drew most of its revenue from the land tax and gave as little thought to taxing trade as it did to protecting it. The absence of government protection was doubtless a price most merchants paid happily in exchange for the opportunity to engage in largely unregulated trade and to gain untaxed income.

In the years that followed Yongle's reign, the Chinese diaspora continued, but the court was forced to retreat from much of his extravagant vision. His successor sent Zheng He on one last voyage, despite advice to the contrary, but never followed up. It was the last hour of Chinese naval primacy. On virtually all fronts the Ming were forced to retreat, most obviously from Vietnam in 1427. Worst of all, the nation may well have been less secure rather than more as a result of Yongle's efforts. The Mongol threat remained and indeed increased. Further restructuring of the Great Wall defense forced the Chinese to surrender their hold on all territory beyond the Wall. Decline in the extent of their superiority over the Mongols forced the Ming to shift to the strategic defensive. They may well have retained their contempt for the barbarian nomads, but they were forced to recognize the shifting power balance and were pragmatic enough to adapt their security policy to the new reality. Later Ming emperors probably dreamt Yongle's dreams, but a shrinking treasury and constant danger on the northern frontiers precluded future thrusts for glory.

Under Yongle's leadership, the Chinese did what they always did when they were the strongest power in the region: they intimidated their neighbors as best they could. They chased the Mongols all the way to Outer Mongolia, divided the Tibetans, humiliated the Koreans, and invaded Vietnam, annexing Annam. With Zheng He's fleets they gave notice to all who opposed them of China's might and the consequences of opposing the Ming.. The quest for a Sino-centric world order stirred Yongle's imagination. In brief, China behaved as unchallenged great powers usually do. And when Ming power waned, China's neighbors pushed back and the Chinese sensibly retreated—most of the time.

TABLE 5.I.   Some Notable Figures of the Fifteenth Century
(Dates are sometimes approximate. Names in boldface are mentioned in text)

Ashikaga Yoshimitsu	**1358–1408**
Yongle	**1360–1424**
Henry IV, king of England	1367–1413
Jan Hus	1369–1415
Iskandar Shah (Paramesvara)	**1370–1424**
Zheng He	**1371–1433**
Cosimo de' Medici	1389–1464
Joan of Arc	1412–1431
Torquemada, the Grand Inquisitor	1420–1498
Sesshu	**1420–1506**
Christopher Columbus	1451–1506
Leonardo da Vinci	1452–1519

The resurgence of Mongol power in the late 1430s and 1440s constituted a serious challenge to Chinese security. Once again a powerful leader united Eastern and Western Mongols across China's northern frontier and encroached on Chinese territory. The new Mongol leader, Esen, appears to have had far more limited objectives than had Chinggis or even Khubilai. His principal interest was in obtaining grain and cloth for his people on the most advantageous terms possible. Throughout the

1440s he continued to participate in the tributary system, sending frequent large missions whose primary function was trade. But as Ming military power deteriorated—in part because the army was being used for
corvee labor and was ill-trained and ill-equipped for war—the Mongols
were able to dictate the size of their missions and the terms of trade,
nominally the exchange of gifts. The large number of nomadic warriors
who arrived in China brought the war horses the Chinese wanted, but
demanded in return tea, wheat, and silk in amounts the Chinese considered excessive. Moreover, at great cost, the Chinese were forced to
house and feed their visitors. Under duress the Chinese were in fact paying tribute to the tribute bearers, appeasing them to prevent a conflict
they could not be certain of winning.

In 1449 the Ming court decided to reduce its burden by lowering the
value of the gifts bestowed on the Mongol tribute missions, in effect unilaterally reducing the price they paid for Mongolian horses. Outraged,
Esen mobilized his forces for a large-scale invasion of China. Anticipating the attack the young emperor marched north to meet him. Esen easily defeated the Ming force and destroyed it, capturing the emperor in
the course of battle. Soon afterward he led his horsemen against Peking,
apparently planning to install a puppet emperor and drain Ming treasure
for himself and his people. Peking, however, was well-fortified, defended
by cannon, and Esen had second thoughts. Whatever hopes he may have
had of overrunning North China with a united Mongol force faded
quickly when his principal ally resumed tributary relations with the Ming.
The ensuing divisions and warfare among the Mongols relieved the pressure on China. By 1450, Esen was petitioning for resumption of tributary
relations and he released the emperor as an expression of good will. A
new, mutually satisfactory equilibrium was reached between Mongols
and Chinese, providing the Chinese with a modicum of security at a price
they could afford.

Koreans, Japanese and Ryukyu Islanders

The Koreans, of course, had been caught in the middle of the Ming-Yuan
conflict. They hedged their bets as long as they could and, although
divided among themselves, opted for the winning side. But despite the
pro-Ming stance of the king of Koryo, in 1388 Hongwu proclaimed his

intent to establish a commandery in the northeast, encompassing territory claimed by Koryo. Men who thought the decision to align Koryo with the Ming had been mistaken came to the fore and demanded that Koryo defend its territorial claims, presumably with Mongol support. The army was duly mobilized and prepared to attack Ming forces on the Liaodong peninsula. It was at this point that Yi Song-gye seized power and in 1392, it was he who proclaimed the establishment of the Yi dynasty, with himself as King T'aejo.

King T'aejo's ultimate concern was the survival of his dynasty and it is clear, in retrospect, that he did something right: the Yi dynasty lasted 518 years, a record unmatched by any Chinese dynasty. Domestically, he carried out a radical land reform that facilitated the creation of a strong central bureaucracy. He directed a rigorous sinicization of the country, strengthening the examination system and promoting Confucianism despite his own Buddhist antecedents. He found the Chinese concept of the Mandate of Heaven useful in claiming legitimacy for his rule.

In foreign affairs, T'aejo saw no alternative to alignment with the Ming and was quick to volunteer to participate as a vassal in the tributary system. The Koreans sent three regular embassies every year. Ming demands proved troublesome, however, both in terms of the total value of the gifts they expected and their insistence on the repatriation of Chinese who had fled from Manchuria to Korea. Grudgingly, minimally, the Koreans acquiesced and their responses proved sufficient to satisfy their Chinese overlords. Trade and cultural exchanges flourished. One obvious example was the influence of the great Ming porcelain producers on Korean potters, who in turn greatly influenced later Japanese ceramicists.

At the same time T'aejo, who had earlier distinguished himself fighting the Jurchens, succeeded in pushing the borders of his kingdom northward, at the expense of the nomadic peoples of the region, until he controlled all of the territory south of the Yalu and Tumen rivers. Into these contested regions he sent immigrants from the south, overwhelming the remaining locals with their numbers, absorbing the territory into Korea much as the Chinese expanded their territory from its prehistoric origins in North China. His grandson Sejong, who reigned from 1418 to 1450, secured the border from further nomadic incursions. Both managed the Jurchens in the traditional way, opening markets where they could exchange horses and furs for food and cloth.

Stressing Confucian philosophy, filling offices with Confucian scholars, the early Yi rulers absorbed the classic Confucian disdain for trade. Nonetheless, considerable private trade accompanied tribute missions to China. Japanese traders stopped off regularly at Korean ports on their tribute missions to China. An early effort to stop trade with Japan stimulated piracy and smuggling and eventually the Yi court concluded that allowing trade was a more cost effective way of stopping such illegal and dangerous activity. Opening three ports to the Japanese resulted in a flood of shipping, subsequently limited to fifty per year in a Japanese-Korean accord of 1443. Fifteenth-century Korea was drawn ever so reluctantly into the international economic system, largely by merchants from the Ryukyu Islands (off the southwest coast of Japan), who sent a "tribute" vessel annually, bearing goods from all over Southeast Asia and India. Little of this exotica reached ordinary Koreans, but the existence of a market for such products suggests that Korean elites had developed cosmopolitan tastes.

In Japan, the Kamakura bakufu outlasted Khubilai by little more than a generation, collapsing in 1333 in the course of an effort to prevent a challenge from men who sought to reestablish the power of the emperor and his court. Loyalty to the bakufu among its supporters had worn thin and several provincial military leaders, some attracted to the imperial cause, others out to advance their own fortunes, shifted sides. In the end one of these, Ashikaga Takauji, pushed aside the emperor and other challengers—and had himself declared shogun in 1338. The Ashikaga shogunate, headquartered in Kyoto rather than Kamakura, lasted until 1573.

The Ashikaga shoguns never enjoyed power or control over Japan equal to that of the early Kamakura bakufu. The legal and institutional structure of the central government survived only nominally. Actual authority was decidedly decentralized. Various local lords had been accruing power for themselves ever since the Mongol invasions and the Ashikaga shoguns depended on their voluntary compliance and support. Centralized authority all but disappeared in the wake of the Onin War, a succession struggle that lasted eleven years, from 1467 to 1477. The century that followed was one of almost constant internal strife, analogous to the "Warring States" era in Zhou China.

Despite the apparently grim circumstances of Japan's domestic affairs, the Ashikaga period was one of greatly expanded international activity, especially in economic and cultural affairs. Even during the period of greatest tensions between Japan and Yuan China, trade continued as merchants of both countries ignored restrictions. Similarly, Japanese Zen priests did not allow hostilities to interfere with their studies in China. In 1290, a few years after the last Mongol invasion, the Japanese government authorized the resumption of trade with the continent. Of greater consequence were the lessons the Japanese drew from their encounter with the Mongol fleets. Shipbuilding in Japan accelerated rapidly and the Japanese gained valuable experience at sea. Japanese leaders also seemed to comprehend that they could not isolate their country from the vicissitudes of the continent, that they would have to keep informed of events there, and that it would be wisest to play a more active role in the international system of the region.

The inherently weak Ashikaga bakufu faced two potentially dangerous diplomatic problems. In 1366 the Koreans demanded that Japan suppress the pirates who had become the scourge of Korean coastal waters. The shogun wished to be responsive, but he had little control over foreign affairs, generally managed by an office in Kyushu where the court's influence was greater than his. In 1368 the first Ming envoy arrived, insisting that Japan accept tributary status and pay homage to China, hegemon of East Asia. Initially, the Japanese were unwilling to accept an inferior role. The Chinese also demanded an end to pirate raids, but piracy continued to be a serious problem throughout the Ashikaga era, with more and more Chinese becoming *wako*, or "Japanese" pirates. Not much could be done until foreign policy became the prerogative of the central government.

An important breakthrough occurred in 1372 when a bakufu supporter conquered Kyushu, enhancing the shogun's role in foreign relations generally and trade in particular. The bakufu was able to rein in the *wako* a little and established direct relations with the Korean court. Before the end of the century and until about 1419, trade with Korea boomed, providing profits for the Ashikaga and for Japanese from all over the country who succeeded in sharing in the action. The Zen temples were especially active, seeking funds for building and expansion. Trade with Korea tapered off gradually after 1419 as the Koreans tried to regulate the volume and the Japanese found other buyers and sellers. Japanese-Korean transactions fell sharply between 1450 and 1510, in part because of Korean reactions to violence committed by retired *wako* who had settled permanently in Korean ports.

While the trade flourished, it was enormously important to Japan and its place in the regional economic system. In addition to selling the swords and other metal work, screens, and crafts for which the Japanese were renowned, they transshipped many items from Southeast Asia. From Korea, the Japanese obtained tiger and boar skins, honey, ginseng, and Buddhist scriptures, some of which was resold abroad. The Japanese scholar Kawazoe Shoji has noted that Hakata (modern Fukuoka), in Kyushu, became an international city in the fifteenth century with ships and merchants from all over Southeast Asia, China, Korea, and the Ryukyus to be found there.[5]

Relations with China, of course, had to be Japan's principal concern. China was the dominant power in the region. China was an aggressive power, determined to assert its primacy. As in Mongol times, so in the days of the Ming, China constituted a threat to the security of Japan. Moreover, trade with Ming China was enormously important to Japan's cultural and economic life. Arguably it was equally important politically because the bakufu profited enormously, especially from its monopoly over the import of Chinese coins which were the medium of exchange in regional trade—and ultimately in Japan as well.

Trade missions in the guise of tribute bearers began to flow from Japan to Ming China as early as 1371. Some were efforts by the court to assert itself in foreign affairs. Some were sent by the bakufu to the same end. And still others were sent by men interested only in profit. None satisfied the Ming insistence on Japan accepting its place as a tributary state. It was the third Ashikaga shogun, Yoshimitsu, who decided to meet Chinese requirements and ultimately accepted investiture as the "King of Japan," a subject of the Ming emperor.

Yoshimitsu knew that he was departing from Japanese tradition, that his enemies would use his appeasement of the Chinese against him and his heirs, but the benefits of his nominal subordination to the Ming were too great to be dismissed. He perceived his action as reducing the threat of a Chinese attack and as strengthening his hold on power. First, he was demonstrating his control of foreign affairs, shouldering the imperial court aside. Secondly, he was increasing trade opportunities for himself and his supporters, a valuable source of revenue in a decentralized political system in which local lords kept tax proceeds for themselves.

Although Yoshimitsu found acceptance of tributary status in the Chinese-dominated East Asian international system palatable, his son and successor did not. In 1411, he repudiated his father's agreement with the Ming court. Conceivably he was staking out a bargaining position to obtain better terms. This appears to have been the Chinese perception, for the Ming response was to liberalize the terms of trade, allowing the Japanese to send an additional mission, three instead of two, every ten years. The tribute vessels resumed their voyages in 1432, often in larger numbers than authorized. Neither the Japanese nor Chinese authorities succeeded in controlling the trade, much of which fell into private hands, but for the remainder of the fifteenth century and well into the sixteenth, both countries retained the pretense that the voyages were official tribute missions signifying Japan's acquiescence in China's claim to hegemony.

The substance of the trade is striking in two aspects. One was the extraordinary flow of Chinese coins, perhaps hundreds of millions, to Japan. The other was the cultural value of Japanese imports. In the absence of minting by the bakufu, Chinese coins became not only the medium for international currency exchange, but also for the growing mercantile economy of Japan. Most other goods from China were luxury items, most obviously silk, but also Chinese arts and crafts—exquisite Ming porcelains, landscape paintings, decorative furnishings, and writing materials—and Buddhist scriptures. Much of the trade and diplomacy between Japan and China was managed by Zen monks and their monasteries acquired magnificent collections of Chinese art, Song and Yuan as well as Ming dynasty. Wealthy provincial warrior families also collected art during the fifteenth century, not unlike their counterparts in Renaissance Italy. One such family sent the great painter (and Zen monk) Sesshu (1420–1506) to China to study Chinese monochromes. It was an era of great interest in Chinese culture in which the Zen Buddhist monks played the role of cultural brokers. The Chinese, on the other hand, showed little interest in Japan and Japanese exports of gold, pearls, mercury, sulfur, scrolls, and screens seem to have been little appreciated. On the other hand, Japanese swords were in great demand, commanded excellent prices—and their import became a source of concern to the Chinese government which failed in its efforts to keep them out.

The years of the Ashikaga shoguns constituted an era in which Japan became a major player in the international relations of East Asia, despite the weakness of the bakufu. For nearly all of the fifteenth century and much of the sixteenth, Japan maintained its niche in the Chinese tributary system. It had diplomatic relations with Korea, both under the Koryo and Yi dynasties. Its ships, sailors, merchants, and warriors sailed the seas—the Sea of Japan, the Yellow Sea, the East China Sea, and the South

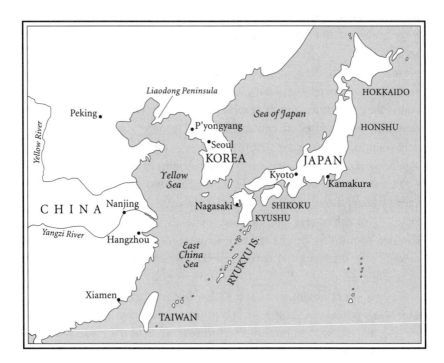

MAP 15. JAPAN, KOREA, RYUKYU ISLANDS, COAST OF CHINA, TAIWAN, C. 1450.

China Sea—and could be found in all the trading ports of the region. Japan had become an important maritime presence. And Japanese gains from these contacts, cultural, economic, and political, are indisputable. Not least, of course, was the import of "Champa" rice, an insect- and drought-resistant strain from Southeast Asia that probably doubled Japanese rice production. But as the Ashikaga grew weaker, the persistent problem of piracy became a renewed source of tension in the region.

The late fourteenth and fifteenth centuries also marked the high point of the Ryukyus Islands as an entrepot in East Asian trade. In particular, the islands' merchants played a critical role as intermediaries between Southeast Asia and Northeast Asia, exchanging the products of Japan and Korea for those of the various island and mainland states, especially Java, Sumatra, and Siam. In 1372 the king of the Ryukyus began sending tribute to the Ming court and included in the goods he sent items originating in Japan and Southeast Asia. Although the islanders are ethnically closer to the Japanese, Chinese cultural influence was great in this period as students from the islands went to China to study and Chinese immigrants settled in the Ryukyus, many in order to evade Ming prohibitions on foreign travel. The greatest levels of prosperity in the Ryukyus may be attributable to Ming efforts to restrain trade along the Chinese coast. The Ryukyu islanders were able to enjoy exceptional prosperity—until the arrival of the Europeans in the sixteenth century.

Southeast Asia and the Spread of Islam

The principal currents affecting mainland Southeast Asia arose from persistent Chinese pressures on the region. The Tai peoples, driven out of what is now southwest China by the Yuan, in turn overran the Mon and Khmer peoples and late in the thirteenth century established political entities at Sukothai and Chiengmai. In mid-fourteenth century the powerful Tai state of Ayutthaya emerged. By the beginning of the fifteenth century Ayutthaya had established itself as a maritime entrepot, undermining whatever residual attraction Angkor may have had for merchants. Abandoning Angkor, the Khmer moved to Phnom Penh where they felt less threatened by the Tai and where they had a chance of attracting foreign vessels. Chinese merchants and artisans flocked to Ayutthaya, however, intermarried with the Tai and helped them build a strong state. They beat back Ming invaders in 1404 and again in 1405. Unwilling to test their chances against a concerted Chinese effort, the Tai chose to accept tributary status. It was a small price to pay to avoid the fate of their Vietnamese neighbors.

The Vietnamese, in addition to being overcome and occupied by Ming armies and paying an enormous price to liberate themselves from the Chinese aggressors, had to endure subsequent raids from a Tai entity that emerged in Laos and from their longstanding rivals in Champa. In due course they eliminated both late in the fifteenth century. The ancient coastal state of Champa had lost its trade revenues to piracy and was reduced to plundering Khmer and Vietnamese settlements for survival. The Khmer lacked the strength to defend themselves; the Vietnamese did not. The disappearance of the Cham state gave Vietnam control of its coastline and of any maritime activity that might appear. The Vietnamese of that era, however, do not appear to have valued international trade to the extent the Cham had.

Offshore, another great empire, Majapahit, had emerged on Java. At its peak it claimed (but did not exercise) hegemony over all of modern Indonesia, New Guinea, and the southernmost of the Philippine Islands. Its founder was Vijaya, son-in-law of the mighty Kertanagara, who had led the resistance to Khubilai late in the thirteenth century. Vijaya avenged his father-in-law's murder in 1293, used the Mongols to destroy his enemies, and then drove them out. Clever enough to outmaneuver the Mongols once, he also was sufficiently wise not to try it again. After his power was established at Majapahit, he quickly made his peace with the Mongols and reestablished trade relations with China. The fourteenth century was Majapahit's time of glory as the archipelago not only became central to the commerce of East Asia and the Indian Ocean, but acquired markets in Western Europe as well.

Majapahit's rise to eminence derived from the spice trade which in turn stemmed from Java's surplus rice. From the east the Maluku Islanders sailed to Java to exchange their spices for rice. From the north and west came merchants from China, India, and the Southeast Asian mainland to exchange whatever they had—silk, copper cash, gold, ceramics—for pepper and other spices. Kenneth Hall notes that as Western Europeans began to consume more meat at this time, they developed a taste and need for Asian spices.[6] Much of the European spice trade was in Venetian hands, as merchants like the family of Marco Polo established trade links with East Asia.

As the Ming seized power in China, Majapahit's rivals on Sumatra and elsewhere in the region perceived opportunities to deal directly with the Chinese. In the first years of the fifteenth century, Ming embassies to the islands had found north Sumatran pepper sources. As the Chinese came to understand the value of the trade passing through the Strait of Melaka and recognized Majapahit's inability to control piracy, they determined to provide naval security themselves, a task they undertook without objection from Majapahit. The Javanese knew when and how to accommodate themselves to superior force. In 1405 Zheng He mopped up a major nest of Chinese pirates at Palembang in Sumatra, reducing the cost of doing business in the strait significantly. He offered the ruler of Melaka Chinese protection, which Melaka enjoyed until the Ming lost interest in the 1430s.

By the 1430s, Majapahit was in decline and its influence even in Java was greatly diminished. A truncated version survived in eastern Java until the early sixteenth century when the rulers fled to nearby Bali. By this time north Sumatran ports were exporting huge quantities of pepper directly to China. In addition, the Malibar coast of India took a large share of the European market, transshipping Indonesian pepper as well as exporting its own. Eastern Java was still involved in the spice trade, but was decidedly less important than it had been in the fourteenth century.

One of the great beneficiaries of Chinese naval power in the early years of the fifteenth century was the city-state of Melaka, near the south-western tip of the Malay peninsula, on the Strait of Melaka. Founded c. 1402 by Paramesvara, a man with links to both Sumatran and Javanese royalty, it gained notoriety as a refuge for pirates and a market for their prizes. Safe passage through the strait soon required a stop at Melaka and payment of a fee to Paramesvara—protection money, a form of insurance against being plundered. The shipping that entered the harbor also found Melaka a superb place to exchange goods and the city rapidly became the principal entrepot of Southeast Asia.

Perceiving threats from Majapahit and the Tai who were extending their power down the Malay peninsula, Paramesvara looked to the more distant Chinese as a counterweight. He responded quickly to Ming overtures, sent a tribute mission to China in 1405 and was invested as king of Melaka by the Ming emperor. Visits by Zheng He's fleets left little doubt in the region that Melaka had become a Chinese protectorate. Taking no chances, Paramesvara personally led tribute missions to Peking on two or three occasions.

Melaka's wealth derived from access to the suppliers of spices and to Western markets. From the ports of north Java, Melaka obtained the spices—cloves, nutmeg, and mace—produced by the Maluku Islanders. From the west came the Gujerati and Tamil merchants who dominated the Indian Ocean trade. All, including the Chinese, stopped at Melaka, to the greater glory of Paramesvara and the enrichment of his people. Long-distance voyages from the Persian Gulf to China and back had given way to shorter, segmented voyages as early as the tenth century. Melaka now took its place as an essential stop-over, becoming in the process one of the world's leading port cities. And, of course, it was the quest for the wealth derived from the spice trade that drove the Portuguese and other Europeans to circumnavigate Africa and find their way to Melaka— where they disrupted the existing balance of power. Indeed, the discovery of the Americas and all that meant for the history of the world was stimulated by the search for a direct route to the spices of Southeast Asia.

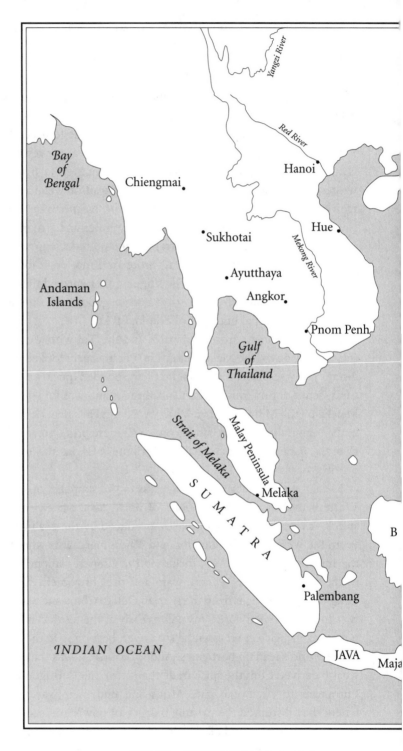

MAP 16.   SOUTHEAST ASIA, C. 1450.

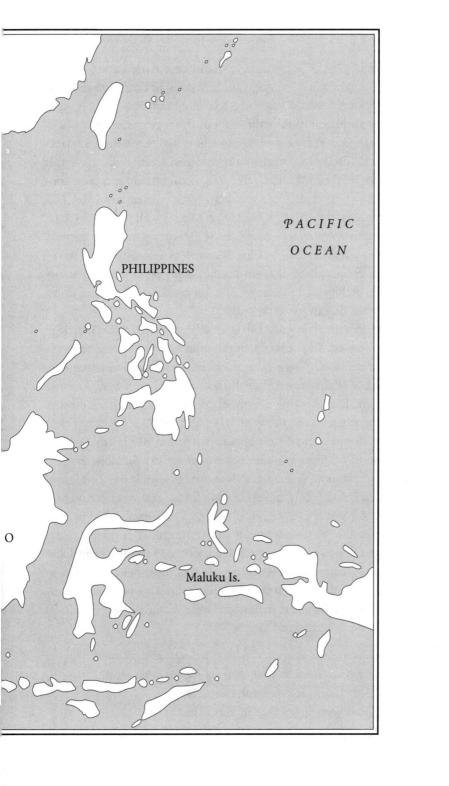

In retrospect, a major watershed in the international history of East Asia occurred c. 1414 when Paramesvara converted to Islam and changed his name to Iskandar Shah. Islam was certainly not new to East Asia. Arab Muslims had been trading throughout the region since the origin of the faith in the seventh century. Tang China had many resident Muslim merchants. Much of Central Asia had turned to Islam by the ninth century. Then, in the 1290s, the ruler of a small Sumatran polity converted and turned his capital into a major center of Islamic studies. Following the trade routes through Southeast Asia, as well as Central Asia, Islam attracted converts everywhere. Zheng He, commander of the great Chinese fleets, was himself a Muslim. Paramesvara's conversion, however, resulted in the spread of Islam up the Malay peninsula and across the Indonesian archipelago, where Muslim religious beliefs became dominant and remain dominant to this day.

Iskandar Shah's discovery of Allah is usually attributed to his marriage to a Muslim woman. Conceivably, admiration for or fear of Zheng He influenced his decision. There were many excellent political arguments for the spread of Islam in the fifteenth century. Kenneth Hall suggests that the Muslim faith became a symbol of autonomy and resentment against the arrogance of the rulers of Majapahit.[7] D. G. E. Hall refers to the assurance Melaka immediately obtained of powerful allies in the Muslim world and of Islam as a "political weapon against Buddhist Siam."[8] But it is also worth noting that Islam was changing and the rise of mysticism in the faith is as likely an explanation for its greater attractiveness in the region. Whatever the reason, Islam was firmly established in maritime Southeast Asia by the end of the fifteenth century and remained a strong enough force to survive the challenge of the Portuguese and Spanish conquerors of the sixteenth century. It was most deeply rooted in those parts of the Indonesian archipelago most directly involved in international trade where believers maintained links with the great centers of the faith at Cairo, Medina, and Mecca.

TABLE 5.2.   Some Notable Dates of the Late Fourteenth
and Fifteenth Centuries
(Events in boldface are mentioned in text)

Era of Majapahit preeminence in Java	1300–1430
Ashikaga Shogunate	1338–1573

Rise of Ayutthaya (modern Thailand)	1350
Aztecs build city of Tenochtitlan	1364
Establishment of Ming Dynasty	**1368**
Great Schism begins in Catholic Church	1378
Establishment of Yi Dynasty in Korea	**1392**
Timur conquers Delhi	1398
City-state of Melaka founded	**1402**
Yoshimitsu accepts tributary status for Japan	**1403**
Yongle annexes Annam (Vietnam)	**1407**
Paramesvara of Melaka converts to Islam	**1414**
Vietnamese free themselves from Chinese rule	**1427**
Joan of Arc burned at the stake	1431
Inca rule established in Peru	1438
Onin War in Japan	**1467–1477**
Columbus sails to New World	1492
Vasco da Gama rounds Cape of Good Hope, reaches India	1497–1498

Ming China on the Eve of the Portuguese Intrusion

The Ming had little respite from the usual frontier problems throughout the last half of the fifteenth century and they also were forced to cope with unrest, even revolts, among many of the peoples China had assimilated forcibly. The court, seated in Peking, focused primarily on fighting Mongols, who were closest at hand, but explosions in the south and west further strained Ming resources and patience.

The Mongol, Jurchen, Uyghur, and Tibetan peoples on China's periphery interacted with the Chinese regularly as nominal tributaries of the Ming. The pattern of contact was one with which the student of China's past contacts with Inner Asians will be familiar. The various peoples of the borderlands did not consider themselves Chinese or Chinese subjects. The Chinese did not consider the border peoples Chinese, assumed their inferiority, and expected them to accept subordinate status. Each side attempted to extract maximum gain from the relationship. The frontier peoples pushed as hard as they could for additional trading privileges and better terms of trade. When they were thwarted or persuaded that they were being cheated, they attacked. Raids were especially likely to be launched by Mongol and Jurchen nomads, but the Uyghurs and Tibetans were far from docile.

Ming offensives—or perhaps more fairly defined as active defensive operations—against divided Mongols were successful in the 1470s, but the threat never disappeared. Joint Chinese and Korean operations against the Jurchens likewise met with success in eastern Manchuria. As is usual in international relations, these victories were not permanent. The Ming never gained more than nominal control of any of the territories they seized from the nomads. The greatest relief to the Chinese came not from their own efforts, but from the conversion of the western Mongols to Islam and their subsequent loss of interest in East Asia in general and China in particular. Of course, as the Mongols focused their attention on Central and West Asia, they left the Chinese little room to maneuver in Turkestan. On the other hand, some Mongols cooperated with the Chinese against unruly peoples in Turfan (in western Xinjiang, then Moghulistan) during a decade of unrest in the 1490s. The sinologist Frederick Mote has argued that the Chinese relationship continued to matter to some of the Central Asian potentates; that alliance with China might serve their purposes against their neighbors.[9]

The major explosion in the south came earlier, in 1464, when the Yao people of Guangxi could no longer tolerate Chinese oppression. Their revolt not only drove the Chinese out of the wilds of their home region but also spilled over into the modern coastal cities. The Miao people also rose in desperate hope of regaining their freedom from the Chinese. At the turn of the century, the Li of Hainan also fought to resist dominance by China. All of these risings ultimately failed when confronted with the overwhelming power of the Ming and the migration of Han Chinese to the south and southwest. But they were an unwelcome reminder that sinicization was not universally attractive, that there were peoples within the empire who would brave death to preserve their indigenous culture.

And then in 1517, out of the West, came the Portuguese—and the Chinese very slowly, too slowly, came to recognize that a major new force had entered the East Asian international system. Having overrun the Chinese protectorate at Melaka, the Portuguese now prepared to challenge the region's hegemonic power. After several years of negotiations between Ming officials in Peking and those in Guangzhou who had the Portuguese on their hands, the Portuguese embassy succeeded in obtaining permission to head north and ultimately were promised an audience with the emperor. But the emperor died and all foreign embassies in Peking were sent away. The moment of reckoning had been deferred.

Conclusion

The years from the establishment of the Ming dynasty late in the fourteenth century through much of the fifteenth century unquestionably constituted an age of Chinese ascendancy, largely the result of the aggressive foreign policies of the early Ming emperors and their successful reassertion of the tribute system. The most dramatic episodes of the era were unquestionably the great naval expeditions of Zheng He. Chinese power was apparent throughout maritime Southeast Asia and across the Indian Ocean to the Persian Gulf and the east coast of Africa. The demonstration was not lost on the Arab, European, Indian, Malay, and Persian merchants resident in many of the ports along Zheng He's route. And alerted by other means, the Japanese and Koreans demonstrated that they were not oblivious to the message.

But we have learned from human experience that no people's hegemony lasts forever. Although we would be wise to discount cyclical theories of the rise and fall of nations, it is nonetheless obvious that they rise and they fall, however unpredictable the timing and the circumstances. The Ming were no exception. The price of maintaining an empire is high and great empires eventually feel the strain. Subjugated people strain at their leashes and bringing them to heel places a burden on the imperial power. Ming China's resources were stretched also to meet the needs of frontier defense, primarily against the Mongols.

In addition to wiser policymakers and perhaps better luck on the battlefield, an empire like the Ming needed additional sources of revenue to maintain or even expand its influence. Perhaps the greatest failing of the Ming emperors was their inability to comprehend the importance of seapower and the trade that Chinese naval strength could open up and protect. Trade was considered an integral part of the tribute system and as such was perceived as an imperial prerogative: "Thus all foreign trade was in eunuch hands, managed in the name of the emperor's private concerns, and nominally not subject to policy planning by the court."[10] Although considerable private trade—in which the personal interests of numerous officials was involved—circumvented the forms established by the Ministry of Rites for the tribute system—little of the profit was available to the state. Virtually none of it entered the state's as opposed to the emperor's budgetary planning. And of course maritime trade embargoes imposed as a response to piracy and smuggling underscored the Peking regime's ignorance of the potential value of foreign commerce.

The key to power in East Asia on the eve of the sixteenth century was control of the spice trade. The Javanese had a geographic advantage over the rest of the world and worked well with Chinese naval power in the days of Zheng He. When the Chinese abdicated control of the sea lanes over which the spice trade flowed from Southeast Asia to China, India, and Europe, the city-state of Melaka came to the fore. But Melaka, too, depended on Chinese protection. Without a powerful patron, it could retain its place only so long as the merchants of the world and the governments who profited from their activities were satisfied with their share of the profits. The Portuguese were not. Control of the spice trade in the sixteenth century was China's to maintain or throw away as it chose. The Ming walked away—and into the vacuum poured the surging Europeans, led by Portugal.

SIX

Europe and Japan Disrupt
the East Asian International Order

Arrival of the Portuguese

Every European and American schoolchild learned at some time that Columbus "discovered" America in 1492, a bonanza for the Europeans, a curse for those peoples whose ancestors had discovered the Western hemisphere thousands of years earlier. Six years later, Vasco da Gama arrived at Calicut, on the southwest coast of the Indian subcontinent, after a long voyage from Lisbon around the Cape of Good Hope and, with the help of an Indian navigator, across the western Indian Ocean. For most of the people of Asia, South and East, the arrival of the Portuguese was no blessing.

We have a surer sense of what made the Portuguese voyages and successes possible than we do of the impulses that drove them to Asian coastal areas. Advances in naval architecture and seamanship, especially navigational skills, were essential to long cruises out of sight of land, across the turbulent Atlantic, and around the dangerous Cape. Developments in naval gunnery changed the nature of warfare at sea in European waters, resulting in heavily armed sailing ships against whose firepower the fleets of the Indian Ocean could not easily defend themselves. As for motive, behind the willingness of the Portuguese court to contemplate the establishment of an Asian empire, the lust for wealth was certainly an enormous consideration. The Portuguese sought direct access to the spices, silks, and other riches of the Orient. They were eager to find sources of precious metals to replace the gold and silver the spice trade was draining from Europe. But the imperialist impulse is usually more complicated: not all men or women live or risk their lives for wealth alone. Some seek adventure, dominance over others, or glory—and these were provided in great abundance by empire building. Yet others are motivated by ideology, most obviously religion, and men of the sort who marched to the Holy Land in the crusades of the Middle Ages were eager to root out Islam in Asia, to bring Christ to the various pagans of South, Southeast, and East Asia. And, some were "New Christians," Jews forced to convert by the Inquisition, seeking safety in lands free of the cross, where they might escape their persecutors. Of course, more than a single motive might be found in many of the Portuguese who planted their flag in various parts of the region.

Portuguese dominance did not come overnight—and was never complete. They began their efforts with a two-day bombardment of Calicut, a none too subtle announcement of their arrival and of their intentions. Initially surprised and intimidated by the guns of the European vessels, the Muslim merchants of the Indian Ocean and their protectors were willing to fight to maintain free trade, to deny the Portuguese efforts to control the sea lanes and the long-distance trade. As late as 1508 a combined Egyptian-Indian fleet repulsed a Portuguese squadron. A year later, however, the Portuguese returned and crushed the opposing naval forces in a great battle at Diu on the Malibar coast of western India. The superior numbers of the Egyptian and Indian ships could not surmount the mastery of the Portuguese gunners. In 1510, the Portuguese seized nearby Goa, which became the headquarters for their Asian operations—and remained in their hands until 1962. The foundations of the empire were in place. The sixteenth century was the era of Portuguese glory in Asia—although they never were as successful at imposing their will in Southeast or East Asia as they were along the Indian Ocean littoral.

At first, the Portuguese profits came from a form of piracy, the extortion of fees from shipping between Asia and Africa or the Middle East by requiring cartazes or licenses to proceed in peace. When they captured Melaka in 1511 they attempted to extend their control to shipping between the Indonesian archipelago and India. But Melaka depended on Javanese rice and the nearby kingdom of Aceh, on Sumatra, was far less pliant than the Indians had been. Bolstering its own navy with aid from the Ottoman Turks, eager to assist their fellow Muslims, as well as guns captured from the Portuguese, Aceh denied Portugal a monopoly over the archipelago and challenged its efforts to block trade with Red Sea ports. Gujerati merchants from northwest India outmaneuvered the Portuguese enroute to Southeast Asia and the Middle East. Ultimately, the Portuguese found that working with Asian merchants in exchange for a share of intra-Asian trade was less risky and more lucrative. In the last half of the sixteenth century and well into the seventeenth, the Portuguese dominated trade in the China Sea, the principal beneficiaries of Ming regulations prohibiting trade between Chinese and Japanese. They were only too happy to provide the fulcrum in the triangular trade that ensued: Chinese merchants in Guangzhou sold to Portuguese in Macao who sold to Japanese in Nagasaki—and Japanese goods and specie returned to the mainland along the same route. The Portuguese middlemen did extraordinarily well.

Efforts by the Portuguese to approach China as they had approached the Malibar coast were easily repelled by Chinese forces. China had abandoned its role as the great naval power of Asia, but its armed junks had no difficulty defending home waters. The Portuguese were perceived as just one more batch of pirates and they functioned primarily as pirates and smugglers for nearly half a century. Diplomatic efforts from 1517 to 1522 came to naught, but Portuguese traders and adventurers kept foraging along China's coast. In 1557, the Chinese, perhaps hoping to localize their activities and make surveillance and control possible, allowed them to establish a trading post at Macao, near Guangzhou. The Portuguese were still there 450 years later. By 1582, when Matteo Ricci, a Jesuit missionary, reached Macao, it was a town with about 10,000 residents, four to five hundred of whom were Portuguese and many of the rest their Indian, Japanese, or Chinese mates and racially mixed children.[1] There were also several hundred black African slaves and a smattering of Chinese and Japanese merchants.

The Portuguese involvement in Japan began more haphazardly. Although they had encountered Japanese traders and pirates in Southeast Asia and along the China coast, the Portuguese had shown no interest in Japan. Very likely the Japanese reputation for being fierce warriors no less ruthless than the Portuguese inhibited their appetites. But in 1543 a shipwreck deposited Portuguese sailors and merchants on Japan's shores. They found the Japanese more open, more receptive to foreign trade and ideas than the Chinese. Japanese silver exports were already affecting the world's economy. Over the next few years, Portuguese drifted in and out of ports on the Japanese island of Kyushu, developing contacts with Chinese and Japanese merchants and the Japanese daimyo of the region, who controlled most overseas trade, benefited from its profits, and were eager for more.

In 1549, Francis Xavier, a Spanish Jesuit priest arrived and received a warm welcome, reflecting Japanese interest in foreign ideas to be sure, but also stimulating hopes that the missionaries would be followed by trade. The next thirty-five to forty years were good years for the Church in Japan—and for the Portuguese whose profits in Japan the Jesuits facilitated—and shared. Japanese converts to Christianity came quickly and in significant numbers. By 1553 one of the earliest converts arrived in Lisbon where he was admitted to the Jesuit order. In 1580, to protect his lands from his rivals and in hope of gaining Portuguese support, one Kyushu daimyo ceded the city of Nagasaki to the Jesuits. By this time, there were approximately 150,000 Christians in Japan, almost all in Kyushu, many the products of mass baptisms that accompanied the conversion of their lords. The connection between receptivity to Christianity and trade was evidenced by the expulsion of missionaries from ports where the merchants did not follow. It should also be noted that the Jesuits, inadequately funded by the Church or by Lisbon, supported their activity by trade, including assurance of a fixed share of the annual cargoes of Chinese silk from Macao. They were eager middlemen between the daimyo and the merchants. And profits soared in the late 1560s when the Ming lifted restrictions on maritime trade, except for Japanese merchants. The Portuguese were the obvious beneficiaries.

The central government of Japan was not as comfortable with missionary activity and appalled when the Jesuits took over administrative control of Nagasaki, creating an alien entity in Kyushu. Toyotomi Hideyoshi, the most powerful military leader in Japan and de facto ruler of the country, was troubled by the questionable loyalty of daimyo who had become Christians and developed close ties to the Portuguese. In 1587 he pushed aside the Kyushu daimyo and took direct control of foreign relations. He ordered the priests out of the country and prohibited the propagation of Christianity. But he allowed the merchants to remain in Japan because only the Portuguese could provide Japan with the European, Indian, and Chinese goods it sought. Indeed, initially he did not enforce his anti-Christian decrees for fear of losing that trade and the wealth the Christians brought.

By the end of the sixteenth century, Portuguese influence had spread across Japanese society, affecting Japanese ideas about art, clothing, food, medicine, science, and warfare. A sizable Luso-Japanese community had come into being in Nagasaki. Japan was changing—and Hideyoshi was not alone in his discomfort with the spread of Christianity and other foreign habits. Shinto and Buddhist institutions were threatened and conservatives, unsettled by the changes the Westerners had wrought, were eager to enforce restrictions on the foreign penetration of their society.

But the Portuguese in Japan were not the only Western threat the Japanese perceived. In 1565 the Spanish secured a foothold in the Philippine Islands. The Portuguese mariner Ferdinand Magellan had been the first European to drop anchor among the islands—and he found the inhabitants decidedly unfriendly. Having succeeded in his mission to find a passage to the Pacific through or around the Americas, he landed in the Philippines in 1521 and was killed in an encounter with the local people. Spain, despite its nearly constant involvement in European wars and its rapidly growing empire in America, found occasion to spar with Portugal over the islands. The Treaty of Sargasso in 1529 left the Philippines in Portugal's sphere, but the Portuguese were overextended and never occupied any of the islands.

To the Spanish, the absence of the Portuguese was an invitation. They were eager for direct access to the spice trade, to challenge Lisbon's dominance. Their king, Charles I, when he was not at war with France, was eagerly fighting Turks, determined to see Christendom triumph over Islam. In 1532 he ordered the colonization of the Philippines, but his agents were too busy in America. When New Spain (Mexico) sent an expedition ten years later, it was driven off by the native peoples and its leader ultimately fell into Portuguese hands. It took another quarter of a century and the reign of Philip II before the Spanish were able to establish a foothold in the Philippines. Manila came under their control in 1571, the same year they won a great battle against the Turks at Lepanto (Corinth).

Manila quickly became an enormously important trade emporium, attracting merchants from all over East Asia, especially from China. It was the center of the "galleon trade" in which Chinese merchants brought their silks, cottons, and ceramics to exchange for silver the Spanish merchants brought from Acapulco. The Spanish also introduced Mexican tobacco in the 1570s, the use of which spread rapidly. But it was the supply of American silver, added to that of the Japanese, that fueled the extraordinary commercial expansion of the era. By 1588, the year the Spanish Armada was destroyed by England, the Chinese were sending sixteen junks a year to Manila.

But Philip wanted more than wealth. He wanted to eliminate Protestantism in Europe and Islam wherever it had spread, including Manila. He took missionary work in the Philippines very seriously. It appears to have been his highest priority. The Spanish Franciscans proselytizing in the

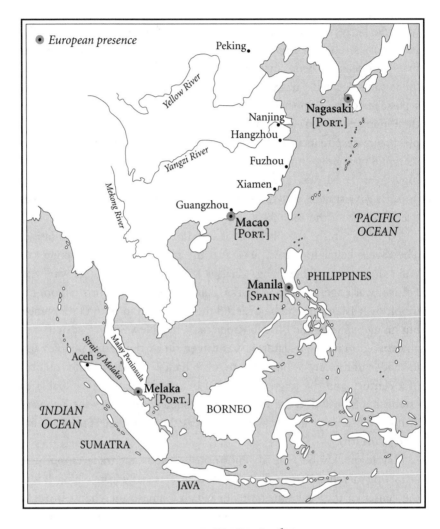

MAP 17.   EAST ASIA, C. 1600.

Philippines reached still further, slipping into Japan where Hideyoshi was already deeply suspicious of their competitors, the Portuguese Jesuits. Jesuits and Franciscans each tried to poison Hideyoshi's mind against the other. Spanish merchants in Manila were also interested in challenging the Portuguese in Japan, but were more easily restrained by officials who feared Hideyoshi's wrath. Indeed, in 1592, he had demanded that Spain recognize his authority over the Philippines and ordered an expedition to attack Manila. A shortage of transport for Japanese troops, an incompetent commander, and the requirements of his Korean campaign spared the Philippines, but the wreck of a Manila galleon on Japanese shores in 1596 led Hideyoshi to conclude that Spain was using the missionaries as advance agents of a plan to invade Japan. He responded to the perceived threat by ordering the crucifixion of 26 Christians, including Portuguese Jesuits, Spanish Franciscans, and Japanese converts. The intensity of the Spanish sense of mission had put all Christians in Japan at risk.

Europeans had been present in East Asia for centuries, primarily as traders, occasionally as missionaries as well. Most had come overland, through Central Asia, but others had arrived by sea, on Arab, Indian, or Persian vessels. All had come in peace, adapting to local customs that they were powerless to change. The arrival of the Portuguese in the sixteenth century heralded a radical change in the nature of the contacts between Europeans and Asians. The Europeans exhibited a ruthlessness to which many Asians responded inadequately, especially to Portuguese efforts to dominate trade and to Portuguese and Spanish determination to root out Islam. Initially, the Europeans benefited from superior military technology, revealed most obviously in naval warfare, but also from the disorganization and relative docility of the peoples of South Asia. The Europeans were not sufficiently powerful to dominate East Asia, but they established important footholds at Melaka, Macao, Nagasaki, and Manila.

The establishment of European-controlled emporia in East Asia also signaled a striking expansion of world trade. The goods of Europe, the Middle East, and Africa were available to Asians as never before—and the volume of Asian goods to markets elsewhere in the world soared. And now, the Americas, connected to East Asia by the Manila galleons, also contributed to the explosion of commercial activity, a new market for Chinese silks and porcelains as well as a source of silver. The integration of East Asia into the international economy accelerated.

The Ming Under Siege

The Chinese were well aware of the arrival of the Portuguese and Spanish, but the Europeans were the least of their problems. The greatest danger to the regime, as in the past, remained the nomadic peoples of the steppes. The sixteenth century was a period of intense conflict between China and the Mongols, in which Chinese forces generally fared poorly. But there were other troubles in Central Asia as well, and before the century ended a new threat came in the form of Hideyoshi's challenge to Ming hegemony over East Asia. Given the pressures they faced elsewhere, it is not difficult to understand why the Chinese perceived the Europeans to be hardly more than fleas to be brushed off the dragon's tail.

The Portuguese had forced themselves on the consciousness of the Ming when they captured Melaka in 1511. As a Chinese tributary, Melaka had reason to expect a Chinese effort to drive out the Portuguese, but the Ming evidenced no need to act to preserve their credibility as protectors of those who submitted to them. Over the next decade, Portuguese overtures received minimal responses from Chinese officials and in 1522 they were forbidden to trade at Guangzhou. Persistent minor Portuguese provocations along the southern coast of China were met by coastal defense forces and local officials, and finally the Portuguese maximized their position by gaining access to and control of Macao in 1557.

The Jiaqing emperor, who reigned over Ming China from 1522 to 1566, had strong views on foreign policy issues. He was convinced that there could be no accommodation with the Mongols; that they understood nothing but the use of force. At a time of declining Chinese power to resist Mongol encroachments, his approach was a recipe for constant conflict— and frequent defeat. On the other hand, his attitude toward the Mongols led him to pursue less aggressive policies elsewhere. In Central Asia the Sultan of Turfan had been pressing eastward against Chinese interests and a settlement between Turfan and the previous Ming emperor had broken down in 1521. It took Jiaqing a few years to recognize the disutility of diluting his efforts against the Mongols by fighting in Central Asia, but by the late 1520s appeasement of the Sultan became an acceptable alternative. Similarly, in 1537 when a faction at court revived the Ming obsession with invading Vietnam, the emperor refused.

The other point on which the Jiaqing emperor had firm convictions was overseas trade, to which he remained adamantly opposed to the end of his days. Even the trade usually veiled by tribute missions declined sharply while he ruled. Beyond traditional Confucian indifference to commerce, the emperor perceived foreign traders as a security threat and imagined he could protect China's coastal regions more easily by denying them access to Chinese ports—and keeping his people ashore. All ships found in Chinese waters could be presumed to be pirates and dealt with accordingly. Fortunately for China's role in world trade, imaginative merchants and shrewd officials consistently circumvented restrictions. The Portuguese dug in at Macao. The Japanese and others found officials at Ningbo receptive. Many Chinese merchants set up operations off shore, settling in Japan and throughout Southeast Asia, from which places they facilitated the movement of goods in and out of China. By mid-century trade had increased enormously, as had smuggling and piracy. Efforts to persuade the emperor to change policy failed and the court even ordered fishing boats to remain in port. The trade ban remained in place until his death, just in time for the beginning of Chinese trade with the Americas via the Philippines, thanks in part to the many Chinese merchants who settled in Manila.

Leading the demand for access to maritime commercial opportunities were Fujianese merchants. It was their governor who won an end to the ban in 1567 and it was in Fujian, near modern Xiamen, that a port was opened, allowing the local people legal opportunities to go to sea. Many of them migrated to the various emporia burgeoning in Southeast Asia, flooding the region with Fujianese communities. By the late 1570s, Guangzhou had emerged as a major port and most foreign shipping passed by Macao and anchored in the Pearl River. There Chinese authorities managed the foreigners as best they could, coercing them to play by Chinese rules under threat of denying them needed supplies. Southeast China was now openly a part of the world trading system.

Among the Chinese who left their shores for the Philippines were a number of pirates who found a congenial home there. The early Spanish arrivals, in addition to contending with unfriendly natives, had to cope with pirates who also resented the arrival of the European ships. When the Ming sent a squadron of ships in pursuit of the pirates, the local Spanish commander was delighted and a brief courtship ensued. The Chinese were eager to have Spanish help in halting the raids on their coastal shipping and the Spanish were interested in trade and missionary opportunities in China. A Spanish mission to China was welcomed warmly, but when the pirates escaped from the Philippines and reestablished themselves elsewhere, the Chinese lost interest in the relationship. The Spanish in Manila, with the vengefulness of spurned suitors, recommended that Spain invade China. Philip was preoccupied fighting Protestants and

Muslims closer to home and the Manila Spaniards ultimately gave vent to their anger, fear, and suspicion by massacring more than 20,000 Chinese residents of the city and its environs in 1603.

With responsibility for maritime problems—and Europeans—largely delegated to local officials in the South, the court focused on a myriad of border threats. The Mongols doubtless would have posed problems for China regardless of Ming policy, as suggested by traditional tensions between nomadic and sedentary societies. But once again, the tensions were exacerbated by the Chinese refusal to trade. To the extent that the Mongols sought weapons or iron with which to make them, Chinese policy could hardly be faulted. But often the Mongols wanted food; sometimes they desperately needed food—and the Chinese turned them away, with predictable results. There were Mongol risings at Datung in 1533 and again in 1545. Throughout the 1540s there were major Mongol raids on China's northern frontier. And then in 1550, driven by famine, the Mongols smashed through China's Great Wall defenses and attacked Peking. Year after year they attacked and only once, in 1560, could the Chinese claim victory, but Jiaqing was unyielding. After his death, his successors, recognizing China's weakness, saw no alternative to appeasement. Rejecting the advice of military leaders to strike preemptively, they chose to allow the Mongols to trade again and to send tribute missions to Peking. The area around Peking remained secure for more than a decade, although splinter groups from the collapsing Mongol federation continued to provoke minor clashes in the far west.

Pacification of the Mongols in the late 1560s and early 1570s brought but temporary relief. The Southwest border regions became increasingly troublesome in the last decades of the sixteenth century as the Burmese challenged Chinese territorial claims and the Miao peoples rebelled against Chinese authority. Ming troops drove the Burmese back twice in the early 1580s, once marching deep into Burma, but a few years later the Burmese struck again. Before the Chinese could restore their control, the Japanese invasion of Korea demanded the court's attention.

In 1592, Hideyoshi suddenly sent an army of 150,000–200,000 men into Korea, announcing his intention to conquer China. Caught by surprise, neither the Ming nor their Korean tributary responded adequately. Japanese troops raced up the peninsula, took Seoul and Pyongyang, and reached the Yalu in little more than two months. They destroyed a small Ming force sent to prevent them from crossing into China. It was obvi-

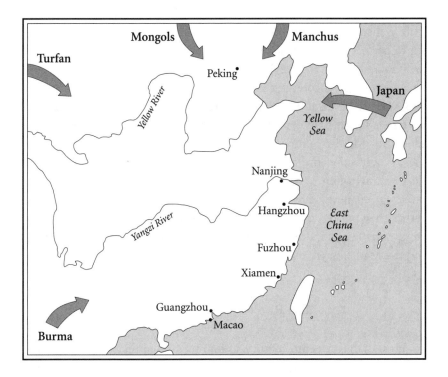

MAP 18.   PRESSURES ON MING CHINA: 16TH CENTURY.
After Jonathan Spence, *Search for Modern China*, p. 19.

ous that the Chinese would have to send a much larger force if they were
to liberate Korea and they mobilized a massive army that crossed the
Yalu in 1593. They intended to throw the Japanese out of Korea and then
move on to an invasion of the Japanese home islands. Neither Hideyoshi
nor the Ming emperor and his advisers appear to have recognized the
magnitude of the tasks upon which they had embarked. Clearly neither
of the two countries could contemplate the other dominating East Asia
in the seventeenth century.

The Chinese expeditionary force succeeded in driving the Japanese
back down the Korean peninsula, but could not break their hold on the
southeastern city of Pusan. Negotiations between China and Japan began
in 1593, but a diplomatic settlement could not be reached. The historian
Ray Huang argues that although the Japanese were willing to end the

war, the principal obstacle was their inability to reach an agreement among themselves as to the terms.[2] In 1596, the Ming negotiators, failing to perceive the collapse of the old order, offered to allow Hideyoshi to become a vassal of the Chinese emperor on condition that he promise never to attack Korea again. Outraged, he sent another 150,000 troops into Korea. This time Korean guerrilla fighters and a resurgent Korean navy saved their own country. Hideyoshi's death brought an end to the adventure and the Ming limped home.

The only good the Ming reaped from the encounter with Japan in Korea came when Ming veterans, assisted by a small remnant of the invading Japanese army, marched down to southern China where together they put down the long-festering Miao rebellion. But Ming military power was approaching its nadir, the treasury was nearly empty, and the Manchus were knocking at the door.

The Rise of Japanese Power

For most of the sixteenth century, as for more than hundred years before, Japan as a country threatened no one. The state was in chaos as the Ashikaga shogunate lost its hold on power and rival daimyo coalitions battled up and down the land. But this was also an era in which Japan was very much a part of world affairs. Japanese pirates roamed the seas and terrorized the continental coast from Southeast Asia to Korea and Japanese trading ships covered the same waters and occasionally found their way to India. The country was open and receptive to new ideas, even to the Portuguese missionaries who arrived in mid-century.

At approximately the same time as the Europeans reached Japan, some of the more prominent daimyo evidenced visions of extending their authority to the entire country. There was obviously an historical basis for the concept of a unified political entity and the city of Kyoto, with the remaining trappings of the imperial court, was a constant reminder of what had been—and could be again. Oda Nobunaga, a relatively minor daimyo, was the man who cleared the way for unification by his military and political prowess. His rise is usually dated to 1560 when he defeated a powerful neighbor and began to weld together an imposing cluster of daimyo allies. His ambitions seemed clear when he secured control of Kyoto and no doubt remained after he deposed the last Ashi-kaga shogun in 1573. Throughout the 1570s Nobunaga and his allies fought other daimyo for control of central Japan. He was also determined to eliminate the military power that a number of Buddhist temples, most notably Enryakuji, had acquired. Indeed, his intense hostility to the Bud-dhist establishment in Japan led him to support the spread of Christian-ity, greatly facilitating the task of the Portuguese missionaries. From the Europeans he acquired firearms and in 1575 he revolutionized warfare in Japan by using his musketeers to smash the charge of sword-wielding samurai cavalry. By 1582, with the unification of Japan in sight, he pro-claimed his intent to conquer China, presumably to unite all under heaven under the rule of Oda Nobunaga. But later that year, he was mur-dered by one of his vassals.

It was, of course, Hideyoshi, who completed the task of unifying the country. A man of humble origins, he had distinguished himself as a war-rior, winning recognition as one of Nobunaga's best generals. Learning of Nobunaga's death, he rushed to fill the vacancy at the top, crushing his rivals and succeeding in holding together most of the coalition Nobunaga had built. He spent the rest of the decade enlarging the coali-tion and routing those who dared oppose him. In 1586 he led an army of 250,000 men into Kyushu, gaining control of the westernmost of the Japanese home islands. By 1590 his allies had eliminated the remaining opposition: Japan was united for the first time in over a hundred years.

Hideyoshi continued to demonstrate his political astuteness by hold-ing the winning combination of daimyo together. He never had suffi-cient power to risk a regrouping of his allies against him. He never tried to make himself shogun. Nonetheless, he acted as ruler of Japan, issuing decrees, minting coins, and controlling foreign relations. Although his loyal daimyo controlled their own lands, Hideyoshi ordered a survey of all the land of Japan. He had, according to Peter Duus, "greater effective political authority than any single person had wielded in centuries, per-haps since the formation of the Japanese state."[3] Naming himself Impe-rial Regent and associating closely with the imperial court appears to have been his most obvious attempt to gain legitimacy for his rule.

The antagonism Hideyoshi manifested toward Christianity does not appear to have had a religious basis. On the contrary, he perceived the Catholic priests in Nagasaki, like the Buddhists in Kyoto and elsewhere, to be seeking and exercising worldly as well as spiritual power. They were a political threat. Moreover, daimyos who converted to Catholicism might have greater loyalty to each other than to him. Last, but by no means least, he was apprehensive about the missionaries' ties to potentially hostile foreign powers. Hideyoshi had limited understanding of the outside world and seems to have viewed it as an extension of Japan: more scheming daimyos and rich lands to be bought under his control.

Hideyoshi was contemptuous of Korea, China, and what little of the rest of the world he comprehended. In 1590 the king of Korea congratulated him on his success in pacifying all of Japan. Hideyoshi replied by asking safe passage through Korea for the troops he intended to use to conquer China. The Korean failure to respond brought the invasion of 1592, an extraordinary feat of military mobilization, but involving considerably fewer men than he had thought necessary to conquer Kyushu. And China's refusal to concede victory to him, to send him tribute, brought the enraged response of the invasion of 1597. In this context the Ryukyu islanders' pretensions to independence were swept away, as one of Hideyoshi's vassals was granted control of the islands and their trade.

Unquestionably, Hideyoshi was a ruthless megalomaniac, a would-be Chinggis Khan or Timur. In the few years of his rule he unified his country and wrought extraordinary misery on the continent. The Koreans suffered terribly from the Japanese invasions of the 1590s and Ming China never recovered from the cost of blunting his attacks. The Portuguese in Japan and the Spanish in the Philippines had reason to fear him. Hideyoshi had demonstrated that Japan was not a nation to be trifled with; that Japan was a contender for the role of hegemon in East Asia.

But in 1598 Hideyoshi was dead. His plan to install his son as his successor fell victim to the ambitions of the most powerful of his vassals, Tokugawa Ieyasu. By 1600, Ieyasu had defeated all rival claimants to Hideyoshi's role and in 1603 had himself named shogun by the emperor. The new shogun had a more limited vision of how his power would be applied. It did not include conquest of the continent or any other foreign adventure. He was content to solidify his power at home, to increase his wealth, and to create a system that would ensure his ability to retain power in a Tokugawa family dynasty. With Hideyoshi's death, Japan ceased to be a threat to the security of the region.

TABLE 6.1.   Some Major Figures of the Sixteenth
and Seventeenth Centuries
(Dates are approximate. Names in boldface are mentioned in text)

Montezuma	1466–1520
Erasmus	1466–1536
Michelangelo Buonarotti	1475–1564
Martin Luther	1483–1546
Suleiman the Magnificent	1494–1566
Jiaqing	**1500–1566**
Philip II of Spain	**1527–1598**
Elizabeth I of England and Ireland	1533–1603
Nobunaga	**1534–1582**
Hideyoshi	**1536–1598**
Akbar the Great	1542–1605
Tokugawa Ieyasu	**1542–1616**
Admiral Yi Sun-sin	**1545–1598**
Matteo Ricci	**1552–1610**
William Shakespeare	1564–1616
Miles Standish	1584–1656
Cardinal Richelieu	1585–1642
Rene Descartes	1596–1650
Oliver Cromwell	1599–1658

Although he passed on the title of shogun to his son in 1605, Ieyasu continued to control the bakufu until his death in 1616. He succeeded in building a stable confederation of daimyo subordinate to the Tokugawa. The
bakufu and the daimyo shared local administration, but Ieyasu and his
heirs, intent upon maintaining the loyalty of the daimyo, were careful not
to interfere in the internal affairs of the domains. Like Nobunaga and
Hideyoshi, Ieyasu recognized the potential profit from foreign trade and
did what he could to promote it and attract it to his capital at Edo. To this
end he was willing to accept Portuguese and Spanish missionary activity.

The Spanish proved to be a great disappointment to the Tokugawa.
It soon became apparent that they were far more interested in proselytizing than in trading. The bakufu was willing to tolerate missionaries if

the merchants followed close behind. But if the priests did nothing to stimulate commerce, the Tokugawa had little use for them, especially after the Japanese encountered Dutch and English traders who brought their goods and left their gods at home. The expansion of the Spanish occupation of the Philippines and attempts by Spanish mariners to chart Japanese waters appeared ominous to Ieyasu and his son. They were aware of how the priests and the conquistadors had collaborated in the winning of Spain's empire in the Americas.

Ieyasu was also troubled by the large number of Christians allied with Hideyoshi's son, who constituted the principal domestic threat to the consolidation of Tokugawa rule. There were Christians among his own men and he was appalled to discover that some of them were plotting against him. It seemed clear that Christianity offered men an alternative loyalty; that Christians could not be trusted to be loyal to the shogun. In 1606 he began issuing anti-Christian edicts, although several years passed before persecutions began.

A few years later, Japanese-Portuguese relations were hurt by an incident unrelated to missionary activity. A Japanese ship involved in trade with Cambodia was delayed in Macao. Several unruly Japanese seamen were shot and killed by Portuguese authorities attempting to subdue them. Another was apparently executed in prison. When the ship returned to Japan, Ieyasu was angered by the crew's version of how they had been treated and decided to teach the Portuguese to be more sensitive to Japanese power. He ordered the seizure of the annual trade vessel from Macao. The ship's captain, confronted by overwhelming force, tried to sail away, but adverse wind conditions precluded escape and he chose to destroy his ship. Swallowing their pride as well as their losses, the Portuguese succeeded in negotiating a resumption of trade.

The arrival of Dutch and British traders early in the seventeenth century left the Portuguese and Spanish—and Christianity—expendable. The Japanese could be assured of access to European, Indian, and Southeast Asia goods without having to tolerate subversive missionary activity. In 1600 a Dutch ship reached Japan and Ieyasu met his first Protestants, including the vessel's English navigator, Will Adams, who remained in Ieyasu's entourage as an adviser on European affairs. By 1609, the Dutch had set up a trading station at Hirado, an island off Kyushu, where they were joined by English traders in 1613. Anti-Christian activity by the bakufu increased. Churches were closed and some Christians were

ordered to turn against the church. Executions began. In 1614, Ieyasu tried
to deport all missionaries. Some escaped; others slipped back in. In 1617,
Ieyasu's son began executing missionaries and their converts—who were
offered the opportunity to deny Christ—or die. Spanish ships were
banned from Japan in 1624, by which time the English, however, had lost
interest in Japan. Still the Portuguese lingered on.

The disastrous conclusion to the Christian movement in early modern Japan came in the late 1630s. A peasant uprising in Kyushu, led by a
Christian convert, was perceived as a Christian rebellion. Local forces
had difficulty suppressing the rebellion and 20,000 families took refuge
in a castle where they succeeded in holding out for weeks against an
army estimated at 100,000. A Dutch warship, firing from offshore, assisted
in the eventual defeat of the rebels, nearly all of whom were killed. Targets of Catholic hostility themselves, the Dutch had little reason to
oppose the Japanese government's determination to liquidate the last
traces of Portuguese and Spanish missionary success. A year later, in 1639,
Portuguese shipping was banned. By 1640 the Dutch were the only Europeans allowed to trade in Japan. All members of a Portuguese embassy
that arrived in 1640 to negotiate the resumption of trade were executed.
Japanese intentions were clear.

By mid-century, the threat of subversion by Christians, foreign or
domestic, had evaporated. Europe posed no threat. The British had found
their operations in Japan unprofitable and retreated to Southeast Asia and
India. The Portuguese and Spanish had found the Japanese too formidable a military power to be trifled with—and both had their hands full with
Dutch and English attacks at various points of their empires, in the New
World as well as the Old. The Dutch had been restricted to Deshima
where they were easily managed and content to make money. They, too,
respected Japanese power—and preferred to harass the Portuguese. Trade
with China continued, most of it direct, some through the Japanese-con-
trolled Ryukyus. The Japanese were obtaining all the Chinese silk they
wanted and reducing the hemorrhaging of specie. Harassed by the
Manchus, the Ming in their death throes posed no danger to Japan. And
the Koreans, still recovering from Hideyoshi's invasions, were grateful to
restrict their contacts with Japan to peaceful trade through Tsushima. All
was quiet and the Tokugawa were content.

The Koreans, of course, had paid the highest price for Hideyoshi's
attempt to rearrange the East Asian international system. Japan had

become Korea's bete noir, the scourge of Korea. First it was Japanese pirates terrorizing coastal communities and then it was disagreeable Japanese resident in Korean ports. And then came attacks, culminating in Hideyoshi's massive invasions.

The immediate legacy of the Japanese march up and down the Korean peninsula was devastation, from which the country did not recover quickly. The "liberating" Ming armies also ravished the land. But the Koreans also came out of the horrors of the 1590s with national heroes and a source of national pride. They understood that it was their own efforts, their own guerrilla fighters, and the brilliance of Admiral Yi Sun-sin, whose ironclad "turtle boats" had defeated the Japanese at sea, decimating Japanese shipping, that had saved them from possible annexation by Japan.

Hatred of Japan endured, but Korea established cordial relations with Tokugawa Japan in 1606. One long-standing grievance was the loss of Korean potters and their techniques to the invaders. One Korean historian has argued that "Japan benefited in particular from the abduction of skilled Korean potters as prisoners of war, who then became the instruments of great advance in the ceramic art of that country"—a charge that Sherman Lee, the great American art historian, has substantiated in part.[4]

Although the Chinese had negotiated peace with Japan without Korean participation, the Korean court saw no alternative to remaining a Ming tributary. Loyalty to the Ming augered poorly as the power of Jurchen (Manchu) tribesmen in Manchuria increased and the Ming began to fall back. Nonetheless, the Koreans managed to stay out of the growing strife on the continent until 1627. In that year, and again in 1636 after the Manchus had proclaimed the Qing dynasty, Korean loyalty to the Ming provoked invasions. But when it was clear that the Manchus had prevailed over the Ming, the Koreans had little trouble accepting Qing dominance: it was unquestionably more benign than their experience with the Japanese.

Other Europeans: The Arrival of the Dutch and the English

After more than a decade of discontent, insurrection, and Spanish efforts to repress the peoples of the Netherlands, the northernmost provinces united in the Union of Utrecht and declared independence from Spain in

1579. With English assistance, the Dutch waged the Eighty Years War against Spain, finally winning recognition of their independence in the Treaty of Westphalia in 1648. Philip II's determination to eliminate Protestantism proved very costly to Spain. Not least were the losses incurred by the destruction of a Spanish fleet at Cadiz in 1587 and the defeat of the Great Armada Philip sent against England in 1588.

In 1580, Philip sent his forces into Portugal, where they were victorious. Before the year was out, he acceded to the throne of Portugal. Portugal and its empire thus became fair game for the Dutch in their struggle against Spain. The Dutch onslaught against the Portuguese in Asia did not begin until the late 1590s, after they had honed their maritime skills by expanding their trade into the Mediterranean and the South Atlantic. By 1596 they were ready for the next step: to break into the Indonesian spice trade. Portugal, of course, was the principal obstacle.

Initially, Dutch merchantmen, financed by competing investors, headed for anywhere in South or Southeast Asia where pepper and spices might be found and where the Portuguese were not already dug in. One such entrepreneur set up shop in Sumatra in 1596 and many rivals set out over the next several years. In 1601, a year after the first Dutch vessel reached Japanese shores, fourteen Dutch fleets set sail in hope of making fortunes for their backers in the spice trade. But at the same time, the Dutch government and the merchants who were its backbone decided to create the East India Company (the Dutch version of which was abbreviated as VOC), a corporate entity which would have a monopoly on Dutch trade in Asia—and the power to make treaties of peace and alliance, wage "defensive" war, and build fortresses. C. R. Boxer has called it a "state within a state."[5]

At first, the Dutch operated primarily offshore, obtaining the products they sought and other valuables by plundering Portuguese and Chinese shipping. In 1602, a combined Anglo-Dutch squadron captured the annual Portuguese ship that carried goods for the Japanese market between Goa and Melaka. In 1603 the Dutch seized a Portuguese vessel leaving Macao with the previous year's profits from the Macao-Nagasaki run. Not long afterward they caught the annual "Great Ship" headed for Nagasaki from Macao. It was a profitable business, but a bit unpredictable, as piracy usually is.

The Dutch recognized the importance of Melaka as an emporium for the spice trade and decided that control of the city was highly desirable.

They attacked in 1603 and pressed on into 1604, but the Portuguese, supported by a strong Japanese contingent, drove them off. It was the first encounter the Dutch had had with Japanese military prowess, for which they henceforth had a healthy respect. Although they tried several times, more than three decades passed before the Dutch were strong enough to take Melaka.

Unable to drive the Portuguese out of the key transit point, the Dutch went after the source of the spices in the Maluku Islands. In 1605 they succeeded in wresting control of the islands from Portugal, with the collaboration of the local Muslims eager to be rid of the Catholics and their priests. It was an early example of the technique many Asian peoples used to get rid of European conquerors—to ally themselves with one set of Europeans against another in hope of ameliorating their condition. Holding the islands proved more difficult for the Dutch. They lost control of several to Spanish forces from the Philippines in 1606 and had to fight off English intruders from 1618 to 1620—until VOC directors in Europe decided it was cheaper to give the English a share than to continue military operations against them. From 1620 to 1623, the Dutch and English cooperated once again to harass Portuguese shipping out of Goa.

By 1608 the VOC had massed formidable power in Asia. It claimed to have forty ships and more than 5,000 men stationed there, mostly on the Indonesian archipelago. No European force could compete with the Dutch in island Southeast Asia. And they had learned enough about Asia to realize they could not confront China or Japan directly. In 1618 they decided to base their operations in Batavia, on Java, and in the decade that followed they began to function largely as legitimate traders, major participants in the international commerce of the region rather than mere marauders. In 1624 they established a trading station on Taiwan, ultimately driving out the Spanish who had gotten there before them and the various Chinese and Japanese pirates who operated out of the island's many coves. Dutch delight in military operations at sea never vanished, however. In 1622 a Dutch fleet attacked and destroyed a flotilla of eighty Chinese vessels. Unable to drive the Portuguese out of Goa, they blockaded the harbor every year between 1636 and 1645, wreaking havoc on any Portuguese vessels that sailed out to challenge them. It was clear that Portuguese naval power in Asia had been trumped. And to prove it, the Dutch finally captured Melaka in 1641.

After 1639, the Dutch were the only Europeans with direct access to

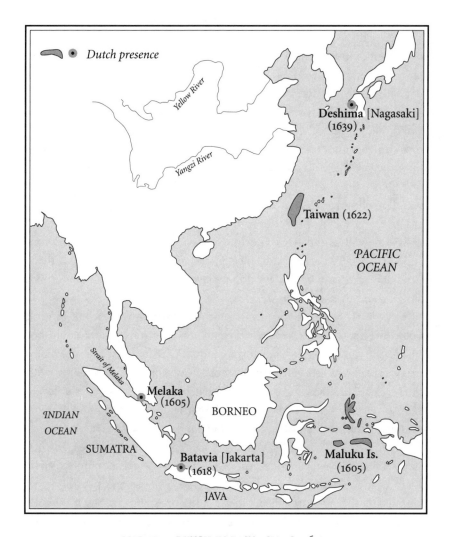

Dutch presence

Yellow River

Yangzi River

Deshima [Nagasaki]
(1639)

Taiwan (1622)

PACIFIC
OCEAN

Strait of Melaka

Melaka
(1605)

INDIAN
OCEAN

BORNEO

SUMATRA

Batavia [Jakarta]
(1618)

Maluku Is.
(1605)

JAVA

MAP 19.   DUTCH IN EAST ASIA, C. 1650.

trade with Japan. From Zeelandia on Taiwan, the Dutch developed a valuable trade with coastal China and provided a safe haven for Chinese settlers fleeing unrest. Control of Batavia, Melaka, and most of the Malukus
put them well ahead of all competitors, European or Asian, by mid-century. The founders of VOC had been eager to destroy Spanish power in
Asia and some of their early operations seemed like an anti-Catholic crusade. But they never gave up the search for profit and it was apparent that
trade always took precedence. In any event, the Portuguese had regained

their independence from Spain in 1640, and Spain was preoccupied with both the Thirty Years' War in Europe and the Catalan revolt at home. Moreover, by mid-century English Protestants were looming as a greater threat to Dutch imperial aspirations than Iberian Catholics.

The English had actually organized their East India Company in 1600, before the creation of the VOC. The great English mariner, Francis Drake, had circumnavigated the globe between 1577 and 1580, stopping from time to time to harass Spanish and Portuguese shipping and coastal settlements. Anchoring in the Malukus he found the local sultan eager for English aid against the Portuguese. After he and his colleagues succeeded in eliminating the threat of the Spanish navy in the battles of 1587 and 1588, a number of his countrymen set off on privateering adventures in Asia as well as the New World. By 1600, English investors had concluded that the wealth of the spice trade would be most secure if there were one company with a monopoly over that commerce. The crown agreed—and then stood aside.

In the early years of the seventeenth century, however, the English would not match Dutch seapower or manpower in Asia and could not muster the right mix of goods for Asian markets. In particular, they kept trying to sell English cloth, which could not compete for quality with Indian cloth or for attractiveness with Chinese silk. They established themselves in several places in Southeast Asia, including Banten in western Java, Patani on the Malay peninsula, and Ayutthaya. They recruited Chinese, Gujerati, and Malay seamen to augment their forces. In 1613, they established a trading station at Hirado, in Japan, hoping to make that a base for business with Southeast Asia, Korea—and possibly even China—but that venture failed. They could not establish direct trade relations with China and in the Malukus, had to settle for the bone that the Dutch threw them. In all, it must be said that the English got off to a poor start and in mid-century it would have been a foolhardy investor who would have bet on the future of England's empire in Asia.

Southeast Asia: Magnet for the West

It was Southeast Asia, especially island Southeast Asia, that attracted the Europeans to Asia. The region experienced an enormous expansion of trade in this period. It had begun earlier, in the fifteenth century, in the years when Ming China was its most dynamic and Zheng He and his ships were exploring and opening the sea lanes. The Chinese imported large quantities of pepper and spices, purchasing most of the region's export of those products as late as 1500. In the sixteenth century the markets for pepper and spices in Europe and the Middle East grew rapidly. Asians produced more to meet the greater demand and by 1600 more than half of this larger amount was being shipped to Europe and the Middle East. And the Europeans came. For Southeast Asia, the peak of the boom came between 1570 and 1630, fueled by silver from Japan and the Americas.[6]

And it was, of course, Southeast Asia that was changed most by the impact of both the Chinese and European-driven expansion of trade. Most striking was the emergence of multiethnic port cities, some of which came under European control. In the fifteenth century, most of the foreigners who resided in these cities were Arabs, Chinese, Indians, and Persians. In the sixteenth century, Dutch, English, Japanese, Portuguese, Spanish, and Turkish merchants and adventurers swelled the ports—and there was a smattering of others—including Jews from all over the Mediterranean, Venetians, Frenchmen, Danes, and Greeks. In each city, absent Chinese or European women, mestizo communities arose. Chinese cut off from returning to their homes by Ming restrictions on travel married local women and assimilated into local cultures in the sixteenth century. For them the process of assimilation slowed in the seventeenth century, especially after the rise of the Qing dynasty and the relaxation of obstacles to round-trip voyages. Many, probably most, of the others also formed interracial unions, which provided not only solace for the long-distance traveler, but were often of considerable commercial value as well. Local wives or concubines facilitated access to local merchants and authorities and helped bridge cultural barriers. Mestizos, here, as everywhere throughout history, were ideal intermediaries between the indigenous and foreign. Inevitably, the demands of Chinese and Europeans sojourners also stimulated the growth of prostitution in the late sixteenth century.

Whether foreign born or mestizo, these new elements in Southeast Asian society enjoyed remarkable social mobility. In several countries foreign merchants were chosen for high office, providing expertise to which the local ruler would not otherwise have had access. Some of those who assimilated eventually merged with the local aristocracy. And many held lesser posts, usually trade-related, or simply served as advisers, military and political as well as commercial. One remarkable figure was Constance Phaulkon (Constantine Hierarchy), a Greek employed initially by the English East India Company in Ayutthaya, married to a Japanese woman who had converted to Christianity, becoming the principal adviser to the Siamese king and turning to the French for help in countering Dutch and English pressures on his sovereign.[7]

In every port city, whether controlled by locals, other Asians, or Europeans, there were large numbers of Chinese. Mostly merchants and artisans, they played a critical role in the development of these emporia, providing skills otherwise in short supply. They migrated for economic reasons, seeking opportunities not found at home to employ their capital or their labor. Ayutthaya on the mainland, Banten in western Java, and Manila had the largest Chinese settlements in the last third of the sixteenth century and Hoi An, in central Vietnam, attracted Chinese as it grew in importance in the seventeenth. For a brief time, in the 1620s, the Japanese dominated trade with Ayutthaya and many Japanese resided there, but most were massacred in 1632 at the order of the Siamese king and the Chinese quickly regained control.

In the cities controlled by indigenous peoples, as for example, Ayutthaya, the Chinese seem to have mixed easily with the local population, frequently becoming officials and part of the court aristocracy. Successful Chinese merchants found it expedient to become partly Thai to obtain appointment to positions that enabled them to further their commercial interests. In Hoi An, Phnom Penh, and Banten this pattern prevailed. In cities that came under European control, such as Manila and Batavia, the Chinese were separated from the local people. Both the Spanish and the Dutch were uneasy about the large numbers of Chinese who migrated to their cities. The Spanish in particular feared them as potential agents of a hostile Chinese government, tried unsuccessfully to limit their numbers, and on several occasions conducted pogroms against Chinese resident in Manila. On one occasion, Chinese in Java suffered a similar Dutch-sponsored attack. But both the Dutch and the Spanish found the Chinese indispensable as middlemen, using them to serve their own ends against the interests of the indigenous population. The Dutch appointed Chinese tax "farmers," contracting the collection of taxes to them. This practice spread to other parts of Southeast Asia, guaranteeing tension between the Chinese and the local people from whom the taxes were exacted.

The Chinese also served both Dutch and Spanish authorities as importers of consumer goods and as skilled craftsmen who built and maintained the port cities to which they thronged.

The burgeoning trade of Southeast Asia further changed the region by bringing Islam and Christianity in its wake. More than half of Southeast Asians converted to one or the other in the sixteenth and seventeenth centuries. Muslims had been present in the region for centuries, but Islamicization accelerated in the sixteenth century as Muslim traders, mostly from India, settled in the cities along the maritime trading routes. The Portuguese perception of their activities as part crusade against Islam led them to target wealthy Muslims, many of whom they drove from Melaka when they took that port in 1511, scattering them throughout the Indonesian archipelago. Accustomed to operating under Muslim laws governing commerce, these merchants, like pebbles tossed into a pond, sent their religion rippling across the lands in which they settled. They brought teachers from Mecca, Cairo, and Istanbul, establishing centers of Islamic culture.

In 1527, once powerful Majapahit, with its Hindu and Buddhist traditions, fell to nearby Islamic states, resulting in the Islamicization of Java. By mid-century there was a substantial flow of pilgrims from Southeast Asia to Mecca and a steady flow of teachers from the Middle East to various cities of Southeast Asia. The conversion of the ruler of Makassar in 1605 stimulated Muslim missionary activity in Sulawesi and the Philippines. The rise of the Mughals in India and the successes of the Ottoman Empire against Christian Europe may have facilitated the acceptance of Islam in the region. And everywhere the Muslims prevailed, the export of slaves, a longstanding Indonesian practice, was halted. Another obvious impact of the coming of Islam, perhaps not to be applauded, was the declining status of women, many of whom had served as powerful shamans in indigenous religious practices, and a few as rulers.

Catholicism came, of course, with the Portuguese and the Spanish. But despite their hostility to Islam and their efforts to drive it out wherever they went, the Portuguese took proselytizing far less seriously than they did their quest for commercial advantage. It was the coming of the Jesuits in mid-century that inaugurated the era of substantial missionary work and it was the Spanish government that took the Pope's charge to heart, supporting missionaries to block the spread of Islam in the Philippines. The Jesuits, including some who fled Japan, had considerable success in Vietnam as well. A leading student of Southeast Asia, Anthony Reid, has suggested that Muslims were more successful in winning converts than Christians because the latter relied on Spanish and Portuguese priests who could not marry local women and who made little use of Asian colleagues before 1700. Muslims, on the other hand, married locally and many of those proselytizing were locals.[8] Where the Christians were successful, they, too, diminished the status of women.

Another reason for the spread of Islam in Indonesia was its political role in the resistance to the Portuguese and Dutch. Dutch Calvinists were less militant than their Portuguese Catholic counterparts, but the VOC yielded to no other entity in its aggressiveness. Island rulers sought and obtained aid from other Muslims as far away as India and Ottoman Turkey. Fragmentation among Southeast Asian polities allowed the Europeans and especially the Dutch to prevail, but Islam swept the archipelago, held off only by the Spanish on Luzon, the Portuguese in East Timor, and the Hindus of Bali.

The Dutch rise to dominance came quickly in the first half of the seventeenth century. The VOC, formed in 1602, became by-mid century the dominant commercial and naval power in the region. Javanese seapower, a force to be reckoned with in the sixteenth century, all but vanished in the seventeenth. Aceh, on Sumatra, aided by Turkish mercenaries and cannon, had beaten back the Europeans in the sixteenth century, but suffered a major defeat in 1629 and its resistance waned thereafter. Loss of control of the sources of pepper to the Dutch signaled its demise. Constant warfare among the people of the region facilitated European inroads. Just as the various rulers of the islanders tried to use Europeans against each other, it was easy for the Dutch and other Europeans to exploit local rivalries. Asian mercenaries provided the bulk of the forces with which the Europeans maintained their control. In general, however, the mainland states of the region proved too strong for the Dutch or other Europeans to control and, lacking spices, they were not worth the effort to sixteenth- and seventeenth-century merchant adventurers.

In 1618, the Dutch founded the city of Batavia which became the administrative center and symbol of VOC power. Mistrusting the Javanese, they kept them out of the city, relying primarily on Chinese to build and staff it. They gave the tobacco monopoly in Batavia to Japanese residents. Dutch contempt for the local people and the ruthlessness with which they pursued their ends is perhaps best illustrated by the case of the nutmeg-producing islands of Banda. Tiring of negotiations with the islanders, the Dutch governor-general at Batavia, Jan Pieterszoon Coen, sent a fleet to Banda, ordered the massacre or enslavement of nearly all fifteen thousand inhabitants, and sent Dutch planters and their slaves to take over production. Gradually, many of the peoples of Indonesia were forced into cash cropping or destroyed their spice crops in hope of escaping the Dutch.

TABLE 6.2.   Some Notable Dates of the Sixteenth
and Seventeenth Centuries
(Dates are approximate. Events in boldface are mentioned in text)

Portuguese seize Goa	**1510**
Portuguese capture Melaka	**1511**
Portuguese arrive at Guangzhou	**1517**
Luther excommunicated by Pope Leo X	1520
Hernando Cortes seizes control of Mexico	1521
Mogul Dynasty in India	1526–1761
Francisco Pizarro massacres Inca in Peru	1533
Francis Xavier, S.J. arrives in Japan	**1549**
Portuguese establish trading colony at Macao	**1557**
Coronation of Elizabeth I	1559
Spanish establish foothold in Philippines	**1565**
Battle of Lepanto	**1571**
Dutch war of independence begins	1572
Portuguese priests expelled from Japan	**1587**
Defeat of Spanish Armada	1588
Hideyoshi unites Japan	**1590**
Japan invades Korea	**1592**
Ming forces engage Japanese in Korea	**1593**
Boris Godunov seizes throne, elected Tsar of Russia	1598
Dutch reach Japan	**1600**
Spanish massacre Chinese in Manila	**1603**
Tokugawa Iseyasu named shogun	**1603**
Settlement of Jamestown (Virginia)	1607
Dutch East India Company (VOC) establishes base in Java	**1618**
Mayflower sails for America	1620
Shah Jahan builds Taj Mahal	1628–1650

Manchus proclaim Qing Dynasty	1636
Russian forces reach the Pacific	1639
Japanese restrict trade to the Dutch	1640
English civil war	1642–1646
Collapse of Ming Dynasty	**1644**
Peace of Westphalia ends Thirty Years War	1648
Oliver Cromwell becomes Lord Protector of England	1653

Obviously, the sixteenth and seventeenth centuries constituted an era in which most of the states of the region were deeply involved in trade and diplomacy, an involvement that went well beyond the traditional Asian interstate system. Southeast Asian rulers tended to be much more interested in trade, much more directly involved in profiting from trade than were their Chinese counterparts. The principal trading states at mid-seventeenth century, Aceh, Ayutthaya, Banten, and Makassar, dealt with China, India, and representatives from Spain, Portugal, England, and the Netherlands—in addition to the relations they maintained among themselves. Although Southeast Asian rulers became increasingly aware of European diplomatic practice, they were hardly willing to surrender their own, as evidenced when the sultan of Aceh requested two English women for his harem—presumably as proof of the English king's good will.

Mainland Southeast Asia was less affected by the coming of the Europeans. Polities such as Ayyutthaya, Burma, and Vietnam were more unified than those of the islands. Lacking the pepper and spices that excited greed, they were less attractive to the Europeans. There was little incentive to pay the price necessary to control them. But there was no lack of activity on the part of adventurers, merchants, and priests from Europe and the Middle East, as well as other parts of Asia. Mainland port cities were filled with Bengalis and Gujeratis from South Asia, Chinese and Japanese from East Asia, and men from all over Europe and the Middle East. They brought goods to sell, gods to worship, military technology, and political advice. Christianity and Islam were less successful against Buddhism on the mainland, but they gained footholds there as well. Also striking was the tendency toward centralization of power in Burma, Siam, Vietnam—even Cambodia and Laos—partly in response to European pressures, but also in response to conflicts among themselves.

But the middle of the seventeenth century marked the collapse of the trade boom and the beginning of a worldwide economic crisis. The weakening of Aceh meant the loss of the "Muslim" spice route, direct from Sumatra to the Red Sea. Southeast Asian contact with Arabs, Persians, and Turks dropped sharply. But the decline in the sales of pepper and spices was much broader, reflecting the collapse of the Ming dynasty in China, wars in Europe, revolution in England. The integration of the region into the world economic system meant that Southeast Asia was vulnerable to the vicissitudes of markets in Europe, the Middle East, and other parts of Asia. It was affected by the supply of silver from Japan and the Americas. Southeast Asia's share in international trade declined sharply. The port cities declined in importance. And as the crisis grew, the people of Southeast Asia had to forgo purchases of luxury items like the Indian cloth they had grown to love. Desperate for something to sell to the Javanese, the Dutch imported opium from Bengal. To attract consumers to this new and vicious product, the VOC initially sold it below market price to Chinese dealers who peddled it throughout the island. The VOC was not an eleemosynary institution.

The Last Days of the Ming

The Wanli emperor, who reigned from 1572–1620, became increasingly irresponsible as the years passed, neglecting affairs of state and hoarding state revenues for his personal use. It was an obvious formula for disaster. In 1608 the brilliant Catholic missionary Matteo Ricci, then resident in Peking, wrote wonderingly of how so powerful an empire, with such an enormous army, could seem so insecure, so fearful of the smaller states on its periphery.[9] Clearly he had not taken cognizance of the mauling of Ming troops by the Japanese earlier in his stay in China. The absence of imperial leadership, the costly battles with Japan in Korea, the loss of control of the rural bureaucracy and the revenue it should have provided, the venality and misdirection of court eunuchs to whom the operation of government had been abdicated, all left the Ming regime inadequate to the pressures that mounted during Wanli's years on the throne.

Though the Mongols were relatively quiet, the threat from the north persisted, this time from the Jurchen tribes of Manchuria, united by

Nurhaci late in the sixteenth century. As the Chinese fought the Japanese in Korea, the Jurchen moved from northeast to central Manchuria, expanding their influence along the Great Wall. Ricci may have thought their concerns exaggerated, but military men in Peking worried about the anticipated Jurchen challenge. Still the emperor's interest could not be aroused and the eunuchs who controlled the state's administrative apparatus were focused on issues other than national security. In 1603 Ming authorities negotiated a boundary agreement with the Jurchen, agreeing to close Jurchen lands to Chinese emigrants. As late as 1615, the Jurchen sent tribute to the Ming emperor. And then in 1618, the Jurchen attacked a Chinese town, beginning a series of strikes that did not end until by mid-century they had driven the Ming out of China, leaving them with a tiny remnant of their army in Burma and the famed Koxinga (Zheng Chenggung) mounting a futile resistance from Taiwan.

The Jurchen march across China was greatly facilitated by Chinese rebels who weakened the government and drove it out of Peking in 1644. By the late 1620s, insurrections had errupted across the country. In 1635 an extraordinary conference of disparate rebel groups occurred in Henan, achieving at least nominal coordination of their activities. Within a few years the rebels were in control of northwestern China while the Jurchen, renaming themselves Manchus, launched incessant attacks in the northeast. In April 1644 one rebel force marched into Peking, driving the Ming emperor to suicide. Two months later the Manchus took control of the city as Ming forces fled southward. The new Qing dynasty, proclaimed earlier by the Manchu leader, moved into the Forbidden City.

As the Ming battled with the familiar scourges of insurrection and nomadic hordes, China was also caught up in a world economic system that its leaders could not understand and could not control. A massive influx of silver from Japan and America in the late sixteenth and early seventeenth centuries disrupted Ming finances, in part as new wealth brought inflation in its wake. Dutch marauders, harassing trade in the 1620s, interrupted the flow of silver from Manila and Japan, at least until they were driven out of the Pescadores to Taiwan, reducing the scale of the problems they posed. But fluctuations in the flow of silver, dictated by the output of American mines, the policies of Spanish authorities in the New World, the expulsion of the Portuguese from Japan, buffeted the Chinese economy. Under the best of circumstances, Chinese leaders would have had difficulty coping with this new phenomenon. Lacking direction from the top, fighting off the Manchus and rebellious peasants, the Ming were overwhelmed.

Ming pleas for foreign assistance went unanswered. The Koreans attempted to help in some of the early skirmishes with the Manchus, but the Manchus responded by invading Korea and forcing its surrender in 1636. Increasingly desperate, the Ming turned to Japan. The Tokugawa were sympathetic, but concluded that the Manchus were too strong, that the Ming were beyond rescue. Ming leaders even petitioned the Pope and the Portuguese for help. The Pope sent his blessings, but they were no match for the Manchu banners that drove Ming forces into Burma in 1659 and eliminated them in 1662. It took the Manchus, aided greatly by defecting Chinese generals and officials, another two decades to complete the conquest of China.

Conclusion

The sixteenth and seventeenth centuries constituted an era of enormous change in East Asia. Much of that change—the centralization of power in Japan and the aggressiveness of Hideyoshi, the rise of Manchu power and the fall of the Ming—would have occurred without the intrusion of the West. But the rapid integration of the West into the economy of Asia, into the Asia-centered world economy, derived from the West's lust for Asian goods, the silks and porcelains of China and, most of all, the pepper and spices of island Southeast Asia. Christianity, which established an enduring hold over the Philippines and parts of Indonesia, came with the Spanish and Portuguese traders and warships. Even Islam, long present in the region, spread more rapidly through Southeast Asia as Muslims traders were dispersed by the aggressive Europeans and as local people turned to Islam and Islamic states for help against the intruders.

The rise of Japanese power had its greatest impact on its neighbors: the devastation of Korea, the subordination of the Ryukyus, the weakening of the Ming. The European impact was greatest on the politically fragmented island societies of Southeast Asia—modern Indonesia and the Philippines. The Portuguese who came first were ruthless enough, but they lacked the power to hold much of the region. Nonetheless, their enclaves at Goa in India and Macao in China endured nearly to the twenty-first century. Their impact as traders and missionaries in Japan was enormous, however transient. The Spanish held the Philippines for more than three centuries and left a permanent mark on the culture of the islands. But it was the Dutch in Indonesia who dominated Southeast Asian waters, who came close to monopolizing the spice trade, who transformed the islands that came under their control, not hesitating to massacre the inhabitants who were slow to accept their direction.

The Chinese, who had been drifting into the various port cities of East Asia at least since the time of Zheng He's voyages, came in large numbers to the cities the Europeans controlled, especially Manila and Batavia, but also to Ayutthaya and Hoi An on the mainland where the Thai and Vietnamese people retained control. Whether they maintained their separate identity as Chinese or assimilated into the local populations, their capital and their skills were essential to the development of those cities. In far smaller numbers the Japanese could also be found in some of these enclaves, sometimes as traders, often as mercenaries fighting under European command.

Beyond the great political and economic changes of the era, there were also exchanges of material culture of considerable long-term significance. East Asian cuisine was changed radically by the introduction of the chili pepper from South America. The potato, too, was introduced into Japan, a useful hedge against famine in the years that followed. Sweet potatoes and maize, both of which grew on marginal land unsuited for rice, facilitated Chinese expansion into the highlands and led to a demographic explosion in China. Less benign was the introduction of tobacco, one addiction to which Asians had not previously been subjected.

In the art world, the most striking cultural transfers came in ceramics. The Japanese turned out magnificent pottery in the seventeenth and eighteenth centuries, in large part due to the techniques learned from Korean artists who either followed or were kidnapped by Hideyoshi's returning armies. All along the trade routes Chinese ceramics, especially Ming blue and white porcelains, were sold in large quantities. At minimum, inexpensive ceramics constituted salable dunnage, wonderful for filling the bottoms of holds and keeping the silks and spices dry. At their finest, these porcelains were sought by collectors all over Asia, the Middle East, and Europe. Indeed, the Dutch capitalized on the craving for Ming blue and whites by producing copies at home, the still renowned Delft ware.

East Asia had been in contact with the West for more than a millennium, largely through overland migrations and trade routes, but occasionally, indirectly, by sea. Nothing in the previous experience of the peoples of the region prepared them, however, for the infinitely more intensive interaction of the sixteenth and seventeenth centuries. Still, the Koreans were minimally involved and the Chinese and Japanese had little difficulty maintaining control of the terms of contact. So, for the most part, did the mainland polities of Southeast Asia. Only Spain in the Philippines and the Dutch in Indonesia foreshadowed the role the West would play in the future.

SEVEN

The Great Qing Empire

Rebuilding of the "Chinese" Empire

From the middle of the seventeenth century to the close of the eighteenth, the Qing empire, of which China was the center, was the dominant force in East Asia. Europeans, wracked by war and civil strife at home, in the Americas, and in South Asia, had few resources left with which to do much damage in East Asia. Certainly the Dutch exploited the weakness of the political entities of the Indonesian archipelago and Spain extended its dominance of the Philippines, but the remainder of the region was beyond the means of the Europeans. The rulers of Ayutthaya, Burma, and Vietnam strengthened their control over their territory and people, partly in response to threats from heavily armed Europeans in the region. Korea remained distant and without attraction. Japan was too powerful to be challenged and the Dutch accepted the crumbs the Tokugawa allowed them to gather at Deshima. And Qing China, subjected to constant tugging from the world's traders, continued to intimidate their governments and was left free to rebuild its empire and establish its authority over large areas of Central Asia. Not until the last days of the mighty Qianlong emperor did any European nation dare to question China's primacy—and then without success.

Qing leaders were forced to concern themselves with maritime affairs in the early years of the dynasty because of the threat from naval forces loyal to the Ming, especially those under the control of the Zheng family. Although wary of the European presence on the south China coast, the Qing allied with the Dutch, who had lost their base on Taiwan to Zheng (Koxinga), to drive Ming marauders out of their strongholds on the mainland. The Dutch were offered special trading privileges in return, but these were rescinded because of Manchu dissatisfaction with Dutch performance. Unable to dislodge the Zhengs and their supporters from Taiwan, the Qing took the drastic steps of banning coastal trade and forcing the coastal population of China to move inland. Qing strategists hoped to cut Taiwan off from access to food, manpower, and trading goods. The collapse of the Zheng satrapy on Taiwan in 1683 came only months after a massive Qing naval assault destroyed Zheng forces in the Pescadores. Taiwan was then incorporated into the empire as a prefecture of Fujian province.

The end of the restrictions on coastal activities in 1684 led to a boom in Chinese trade with Southeast Asia. Chinese merchants pushed the Europeans and West Asians out of mainland markets and dominated those of Ayutthaya, Burma, Cambodia, and a divided Vietnam throughout the century that followed. Chinese successes resulted in part because of existing networks established through the migrations of the Ming era and in part because of the mistrust Asians had come to have of heavily armed European merchantmen. The one group of Europeans who continued to prosper throughout Asia were the Armenians, who came without the blessings—or the stigma—of a powerful state behind them and were forced to practice nonviolent means of obtaining the goods they sought. For a brief period, beginning in 1717, the Qing attempted once more to restrict trade, fearing contact between their subjects and the potentially subversive Chinese diaspora. The effort failed and was abandoned by 1727.

Probably because of their origins, Qing leaders worried mostly about their northern and western frontiers. Apart from their concerns about subversion, they had little interest in seaborne trade or in maritime southeastern China. They allowed the Portuguese to keep their base at Macao. Moreover, attacks across their land frontiers were far more likely. Central Asia in particular posed many problems. The largely Muslim peoples of the Tarim Basin region were unsettled by economic problems resulting from political fragmentation and the weakening of the caravan trade when the collapse of the Timurid empire left Central and West Asian land routes vulnerable to nomadic raiders. It is also likely that the rise of European maritime trade reduced the movement of goods overland. Discontent had led to rebellions against the Ming. The change of dynasties in mid-century did not satisfy the rebels and they had to be subdued by Qing troops in 1650. The Mongols persisted in stirring trouble throughout the seventeenth century and on into the eighteenth. The Qing integrated Outer Mongolia into their empire late in the seventeenth century and continued to fight their principal rivals, the western Mongols (Zunghars), in Chinese Turkestan. A new source of concern arose as Russians moving across Siberia in search of furs began to press against territories the Qing perceived as part of the Qing empire.

Russian explorations in Central Asia and Siberia had aroused the apprehension of the late Ming rulers, but they were not in a position to do much about it. In 1651, Russians built a fortified outpost at Albazin, a point on the Amur River, due north of Peking. The Qing were troubled, sparred with the Russians, but as they were in the process of establishing their authority over China proper, they were unable to respond effectively. First, they had to deal with Koxinga and other Ming loyalists. Before that assignment could be completed, they had to put down a major rebellion in the southeast, led by Chinese generals who had initially facilitated their victory over the Ming. But in 1685 they were ready and a major land and river operation was ordered against the Russian base at Albazin. Overcoming stiff Russian resistance, Qing troops razed the fort and drove the Russian settlers out. Before long, however, the Russians returned, necessitating a second offensive by Chinese forces. Again, the Russians fought hard to hold their ground, but back in Moscow their leaders decided they could not defend the disputed territory. Wisely, they decided to seek a negotiated settlement. At the Russian town of Nerchinsk, just west of Albazin, Russian and Manchu negotiators, aided by Jesuit interpreters, agreed to the Treaty of Nerchinsk in 1689. The treaty was unusual, in that the Qing, eager to be rid of a distraction in order to focus on the Zunghars, treated the Russians as equals. It was also enormously important, as it established a border between China and Russia that has endured with little modification ever since.

The Qing emperor Kangxi perceived as the greatest danger the threat posed by the Zunghar confederation of western Mongols, who had adopted Tibetan Buddhism, found a gifted leader, dominated Chinese Turkestan, and threatened Outer Mongolia. The Zunghars were expanding their influence in Central Asia, driving refugees in hordes across China's frontiers. They threatened the stability of China's northwest and they gained control of the caravan routes, China's overland links to the West. They could easily stir trouble in Tibet and there was always a danger that they might join forces with the Russians. They had to be eliminated.

In 1696 Kangxi himself led Qing troops into battle and drove the Zunghars out of Outer Mongolia. The death of their leader a year later led him to believe his problems were over, but they remained a threat in Turkestan and Tibet. The problem festered well into the eighteenth century and much of the remainder of Kangxi's life. In 1717 the Zunghars dug in at Lhasa, capital of Tibet, and annihilated a Qing relief column that arrived in 1718. In 1720, however, a Qing pincer movement aimed at Lhasa drove the Zunghars out and enabled Kangxi to impose his choice as Dalai Lama. He proved to be acceptable to the Tibetans, who were confronted with a Qing garrison and had little opportunity to resist. The Qing also detached eastern Tibet, redesignating it as part of Sichuan province.

Tibet did not disturb Kangxi's last days, but, like so much of world affairs, there could not be a final resolution of the problem. Both the Tibetans and Zunghars would bring further grief to his descendants. Kangxi did have to face a revolt against Qing authority on Taiwan in 1621, a year before his death, but it was quickly suppressed. During his last days, despite his grief over the instability of his one-time heir apparent, Kangxi might have taken solace from his foreign policy accomplishments. He had kept the Dutch and Portuguese at arms length, dealt successfully with the Russians, incorporated Taiwan into the empire, gained control over Outer Mongolia and part of Central Asia, and established a protectorate over Tibet. And his failure to deal adequately with taxation and revenue collection for the state was mitigated, at least for the court, by its exactions from trade.

One other international complication, resolved peacefully but with mutual unhappiness, was forced upon Kangxi by the Pope. Jesuit priests had resided in Peking almost constantly since Ricci had gained the privilege in 1601. Kangxi had shown particular interest in them, valued their scientific knowledge and frequently turned to them for advice. Their religion had no appeal to him, but he allowed them to practice it and in 1692 had issued an edict of toleration. Accepting a distinction drawn by Ricci, he and the Jesuits in China perceived ancestor worship and Confucian rituals to be civil affairs in which Christian converts would participate. The Pope had other ideas. He, like most Dominicans and Franciscans, mistrusted the Jesuits and suspected them of courting favor with the Chinese at the cost of undermining the authority of the church to determine acceptable religious practice. Negotiations between the Pope's emissary and the emperor broke down and the missionaries in China were ordered to disregard the Ricci/Kangxi distinction. Kangxi refused to allow the Pope to undermine his authority and expelled those missionaries who rejected his position. Jesuit hopes for bringing Christianity to China foundered on the arrogance of Rome. As Jonathan Spence has noted, the

Chinese, too, paid a price, losing access to the vital scientific knowledge the priests had provided.[1]

Kangxi's son and successor, Yongzheng, spent his relatively brief reign in constant conflict with the Zunghars, coping with new complications with the Russians and Tibetans, old complications with the Miao, and completing the pacification of Taiwan. It was also during his reign that the opium that the Dutch had brought into the region began to pose a problem for Chinese society. By all accounts, he was a capable and conscientious administrator, whose efforts advanced the cause of the Qing empire.

Yongzheng had long been involved in imperial affairs and did not doubt that the Zunghars posed the major external threat to China. He paid little heed to maritime affairs and they gave him little cause for anxiety. The problems with Taiwan were not caused by Europeans and were managed easily with adjustments to emigration policies that allowed more Chinese to move to the island and to landholding policies that facilitated rentals by Chinese while reserving lands for the indigenous people. The opium problem was treated as an internal matter with sensible efforts to punish users and dealers. It did not become a major issue in his lifetime.

Eliminating the Zunghars was Yongzheng's principal strategic goal and toward that end he reconfigured the bureaucracy, providing himself with the equivalent of a small national security council which reported only to him. He was thus able to maintain maximum secrecy in his preparations for a major campaign in the northwest. But as he carried out a massive military buildup in what is now Xinjiang province, other issues vied for his attention. Yongzhen had attempted to trim costs in Tibet, reducing China's administrative and military presence there, but a rebellion in 1727 necessitated dispatch of a Qing army to assure control by pro-Chinese forces. Tibet had become a Qing protectorate. The Miao peoples of the southwest continued to resist Chinese migrations and exploitation of their homelands. Skirmishes increased in intensity in the late 1720s and required the use of substantial force in Yunnan and Guizhou and the region was not pacified until 1732.

In addition, the Russians were pouring into Siberia in search of gold as well as furs, colluding with various Central Asian peoples, threatening China with new border problems. In 1719 Peter the Great sent an officer to Peking to discuss commercial relations and the right to build a church there. After he performed the required kowtow, the Russian representative's credentials were received and he met several times with the emperor. In 1728 a new treaty was signed at Kiakhta, resolving a range of issues including borders, trading privileges, and rights of residence in Peking. By 1730 the Russians had a de facto diplomatic mission operating there. In 1731 and again in 1732, Qing embassies arrived at Moscow and St. Petersburg where, in an act of reciprocation, they genuflected before the tsarina in conformity with Russian ceremonial requirements. The Russian problem did not go away—indeed it would never go away—but Qing diplomats had reason to be pleased with themselves. For the moment, at least, they had pacified a major European power.

After all these other fronts were reasonably quiet, the great offensive against the Zunghars was finally launched in 1732. Unhappily for the Qing generals who led it, the Zunghars outmaneuvered Chinese forces, suffering a blow at their capital, but retaliating with great success. One Qing army was ambushed and decimated. Both Qing generals were executed by order of a very dissatisfied emperor. The Zunghar threat festered on and Yongzheng died in 1736.

Fortunately for the Qing, the Qianlong emperor who ruled from 1736 to 1799, the longest reign in Chinese history, also proved to be exceptionally able. Under his leadership the Zunghars were finally crushed, the Tibetan protectorate strengthened, and the Europeans, Russians as well as those who came by sea, kept at bay. To the south, Burma, although unvanquished, accepted vassalage and the Ghurkas of Nepal were similarly forced to accept tributary status. Internally, Muslim unrest in the northwest and Miao disturbances in the southwest were repressed. But there were also disquieting signs.

Qing armies had not been able to crush the Burmese, Russian strength in Asia was growing, and the British were becoming fretful and dissatisfied with their place in the world order as perceived from Peking. Equally as troubling was the beginning of a reversal in the terms of trade, long favorable to China, as the impact of opium imports, exacerbated by the declining demand for Chinese silk, hit in the 1770s and 1780s. Qianlong's accomplishments were great, but his last years were troubled by portents of disagreeable change.

Qianlong inherited the Zunghar problem and was determined to succeed where his father had failed. He enlarged Yongzheng's security council, creating what came to be called the "Grand Council," and was in fact the dominant policy office in the government. Slowly they devised military responses to problems on the Tibetan borders where difficult campaigns were fought in the late 1740s. All semblance of Tibetan independence evaporated after attacks on Qing representatives at Lhasa in 1750 provoked a Qing invasion in 1751. Thereafter the selection of the Dalai Lama and his civil authority were brought under Qing control. Finally, in the late 1750s, after years of horrific fighting and misery endured by both sides, the Qing succeeded in conquering the Zunghars. Seeking a final solution to the threat, Qing forces massacred the remnants of the troops they defeated. There would continue to be battles along the Tibetan borders, but the Zunghars were eliminated forever as a political entity. The territory now known as Xinjiang was under Qing control, a vast expansion of the Qing empire. With it, of course, came a large and frequently discontented Muslim population, which necessitated the permanent posting of a substantial part of the Qing army in the region.

By mid-century, the demands of Europeans seeking to trade with China became bothersome. Qianlong and his advisers understood that international commerce was important to the people of China's southern coast, that there would be trouble in Guangdong and Fujian if they attempted to resume the restrictive policies of the seventeenth century. Kangxi's efforts to stop coastal trade in the last years of his reign had failed and been abandoned by Yongzheng. Qianlong was satisfied with what came to be known in the West as the "Canton system," a means of regulating and controlling maritime trade that kept Chinese merchants content, squeezed them for valuable income, and prevented foreigners from becoming a threat to the stability and security of the empire. Under the Canton system all European—and later American—sea borne trade was limited to the port of Canton (Guangzhou). The Westerners were allowed to deal only with the Cohong, a merchant guild that was in turn held responsible for their good behavior. The foreigners were denied any direct access to Chinese government officials. None of the Western traders were happy with the conditions under which they were forced to operate, but they lacked the means to persuade the court to change its policies. Verbal and written protests proved to be of no avail. Qing China could not be challenged in East Asia: all who came to China's shores would live by Qianlong's rules. But in Europe, Great Britain had built a mighty fleet and the British, despite their problems in Europe and America, concluded that they were worthy of and would insist upon being treated with greater respect by the Chinese. Their East India Company, having demonstrated its power in Bengal, was focusing increasingly on China.

Initially, the Qing court seemed oblivious to the potential danger from the West. Chinese scholars and foreign affairs specialists of the eighteenth century did not concern themselves with the European threat. If China maintained domestic tranquillity and controlled foreigners to preclude subversion, it need not fear the West. When the Zunghars were crushed, those Qing forces not needed on the western frontiers were used not for coastal defense but rather for four campaigns against Burma. Burmese attempts to dominate much of Southeast Asia and successful campaigns against Laos and Ayutthaya provoked Chinese military responses between 1765 and 1769. As with past Chinese invasions of Southeast Asia, the results were decidedly mixed. The Burmese were forced to retreat, as they likely would have in any event once they had sacked Ayutthaya, but in four tries, Chinese troops could not reach the Burmese capital at Ava. Wisely, the Burmese offered homage to Qianlong, and the Chinese went home.

The campaigns in Burma may have prompted China's historic memory of the problems of campaigns in Southeast Asia—the logistical difficulties to be sure, but also the unfamiliar climate and strange diseases to be endured. When a deposed Vietnamese ruler appealed to his Qing suzerain for assistance, the Grand Council reluctantly approved the dispatch of forces, attempting to use them only as a gesture of support, rather than as combat troops. The local Qing commander, however, had visions of extending the empire and, contrary to his instructions, remained in Hanoi after the king had been restored to power. When rebel forces approached the city, the king fled again and Qing forces beat a hasty and clumsy retreat, suffering major casualties when a bridge collapsed under them. Additional Qing troops were massed at the border, but never invaded; nor did they come under attack by the Vietnamese. The erstwhile rebel leader became the new king of Vietnam, offered tribute to Qianlong, and a peaceful settlement was arranged. Vietnam continued to be a Qing tributary, while sacrificing none of its independence. Both sides were satisfied.[2]

But when the Gurkhas of Nepal infringed on the Qing's Tibetan protectorate, Qianlong's advisers, wrongly suspecting British complicity, ordered an attack. In 1792 Qing armies invaded Nepal and defeated the

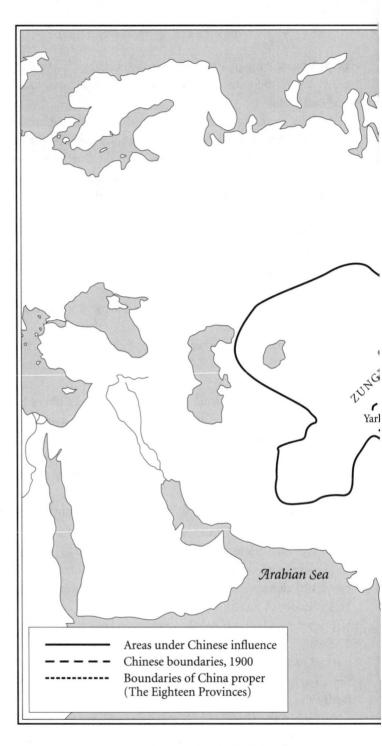

ZUNG

Yarl

Arabian Sea

————	Areas under Chinese influence
– – – – –	Chinese boundaries, 1900
··············	Boundaries of China proper (The Eighteen Provinces)

MAP 20.   QING EMPIRE, C. 1800.
After Dun J. Li, *Ageless Chinese*, p. 317.

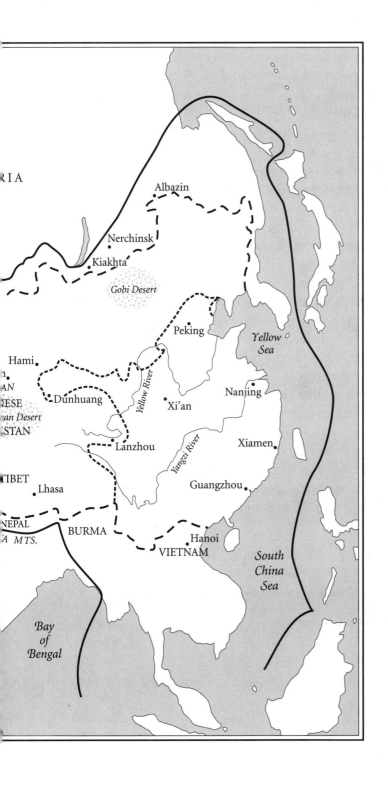

Gurhkas, winning their nominal obeisance to Qianlong. Nonetheless, the British *were* coming and Qing strategists, however grudgingly, had to prepare to deal with them.

After a century and a half of Qing empire-building and more than a half century of Qianlong's rule, the way in which Qing leaders viewed the world and their empire was readily apparent. They had no desire to isolate themselves from the rest of the world: they were clearly intrigued with Western science and quite ready to adopt Western technology.[3] Nonetheless, they had no use for alien ideologies and were suspicious of their subversive potential. Certainly their suspicions were aggravated by the conflict with Rome.

The early Qing emperors and their advisers appear to have shared the ancient idea of universal rulership, but their vision was less assimilationist than that of most of their predecessors. As Jurchen or Manchus, however sinicized they became, they anticipated that all subordinate people, all subordinate rulers, would remain separate people. They would be submissive to the emperor of China, but they would retain their own identities, whether Korean, Vietnamese, Mongol, or British. With few illusions of being invincible, they understood when it was necessary to treat others as equals. They considered all foreigners who came within their territory to be subject to their power and abandoned all Chinese who went abroad to the mercies of their hosts. The rites may have been very different, but the Qing concept of imperial power does not, in retrospect seem so very different from that of European empires.[4]

TABLE 7.1.   Some Notable Figures of the Late Seventeenth
and Eighteenth Centuries
(Names in boldface are mentioned in the text)

Koxinga (Zheng Chenggong)	**1624–1662**
Baruch Spinoza	1632–1672
John Locke	1632–1704
Louis XIV of France	1638–1715
Isaac Newton	1642–1727
Kangxi	**1654–1722**
Peter the Great of Russia	1672–1725
Tokugawa Yoshimune	**1683–1751**
Benjamin Franklin	1706–1790

Alaungpaya of Burma	**1710–1763**
Qianlong	**1711–1799**
Jean Jacques Rousseau	1712–1778
Frederick the Great of Prussia	1712–1786
George Washington	1732–1799
Rama I of Siam	**1740–1809**
Thomas Jefferson	1743–1826
Napoleon Bonaparte	1769–1821

Japan and Korea

Early Qing strategists focused on Central Asia when they could and dealt with the annoyance of seafarers along China's coast when they had to. With Japan they had little cause for anxiety. The Tokugawa evidenced no hostile intent toward China and were clearly much more concerned with the political and economic development of their homeland. In the seventeenth century they had succeeded in putting an end to the subversive intrusions of European priests and gained substantial control over foreign trade, especially that with Europe. The Tokugawa had also demonstrated to the Europeans that Japan was not to be taken lightly; that it had the power and the will to protect its interests and avenge the mistreatment of Japanese abroad.

Like the Qing, the Japanese perceived Europeans to be peripheral. There was much to be learned from the West and the Dutch provided them with sufficient access to Western knowledge. Having established control over all contact with the Europeans, the Japanese had no reason to fear them. The West no longer posed a threat to Japan's security. They had no need for Western goods or for Western markets. Japan in the late seventeenth century and throughout the eighteenth century met all its needs in Asia.

Although Japan remained outside the Qing tributary system, rejecting China's claims to overlordship, rejecting Peking's China-centered world order, there continued to be extensive trade between the two countries. Many Chinese resided at Nagasaki, but they represented only a small part of the commercial links. The Ryukyu Islanders, who managed to maneuver between the rival claims to their homage of both Chinese and Japanese, provided an additional entrepot. Much of Japan's extensive trade with Korea, mostly through Tsushima, also involved Japanese exports destined for China and Chinese goods that found their way to Japan.

In the seventeenth century, the rapid urbanization that had characterized the last years of the sixteenth continued. Along with the movement to the cities came a striking expansion of commercial activity. By 1650, the Tokugawa shogunate was well-established as a strong central authority in a secure, prosperous country. It functioned much the same way through the eighteenth century, with minimal opposition from rival daimyo.

The so-called policy of "seclusion," of isolating Japan from the rest of the world, was also well-established by mid-seventeenth century, although Japan was hardly isolated. What had vanished under the Tokugawa was the free-wheeling exchange of goods and ideas, the relatively free movement of Japanese to other parts of East Asia and the accessibility of Japan to men from all over the world. The timing was unfortunate because the internal economy was growing so rapidly and Japan had been positioned nicely for a significant expansion of its foreign trade, in the Philippines as well as mainland Southeast Asia, China, and Korea. Certainly Japan's economic development was retarded by Tokugawa restrictions on trade and travel. But this was a price Japan's rulers were prepared to pay for national security—and the preservation of Tokugawa control. Trade restrictions were aimed in large part at eliminating the economic power of the western daimyo, as well as keeping out potentially subversive foreigners and foreign ideas.

In fact, foreign trade grew in the seventeenth century, doubtless less than it would have without the Tokugawa restrictions, but enough to cause concern about the outflow of precious metals, especially copper carried off by Chinese and Dutch vessels. In the 1680s, hundreds of Chinese junks arrived at Nagasaki every year—and there appears to have been a substantial amount of smuggling as well. In 1685 the bakufu attempted to put a limit on total foreign trade. By 1687 the Chinese were limited to 73 ships a year and the Chinese merchant community in Nagasaki reduced, but smuggling increased and was virtually impossible to stop, since the local daimyo were among the beneficiaries.

Arai Hakuseki, a historian of note and adviser to the bakufu, issued a report in 1714 that suggested the need for further restrictions on trade to stop the hemorrhaging of specie. For a brief period, his ideas were implemented. The amount of copper the Dutch could carry out was reduced and efforts were made to limit Japanese imports to avoid balance of trade problems. Arai's argument, heard often from Confucian officials in China and Japan, was that most imports were unnecessary luxuries. And, like trade officials throughout recorded history, when confronted with an unfavorable balance of trade, he called for a program of import substitution—of replacing foreign imports with Japanese products.

Yoshimune, who became shogun in 1715, was unimpressed by Arai's program and unenthusiastic about the implicit call for austerity. Gradually he reversed course, determined to solve the balance of trade problem by finding new commodities to export to China. Given the traditional Chinese elite's craving for exotic foods, the Japanese harvested and marketed large quantities of shark's fin, sea slugs, and seaweed. These sales helped enormously, although copper remained Japan's most valuable export.

Yoshimune was also interested in the West and encouraged the study of Western achievements. Chinese translations of Western books were allowed into the country after 1720 as Yoshimune and his advisers were persuaded that the gains from the study of Western science and technology greatly outweighed the danger from subversive ideologies like Christianity. His approach flagged in mid-century after his death, but was resumed by Tanuma Okitsugu, the grand chamberlain who dominated policy from 1760 to 1786. Tanuma, too, believed in a vigorous export policy, targeting the market in China. And in the second half of the century, interest in "Dutch learning" swept the country.

By the 1770s, Russian goods began appearing in the markets of Osaka. The Russians had reached the shores of the Pacific, were established in Kamchatka, and in contact with Japanese on what is now Hokkaido, Sakhalin, and various smaller islands of the region. A Russian request for trading privileges was denied in 1777, but the exchange of goods continued. In 1792, a Russian officer sailed into a harbor on Hokkaido and asked to establish diplomatic and trade relations. The Japanese were not ready to accede to Russian wishes, but they understood that pressures would increase. As they pondered their response, they simultaneously strengthened their coastal defenses.

The Russian approach came after a century in which the Tokugawa shoguns had devised an essentially Japan-centered conception of diplomatic relations.[5] Japanese leaders had never liked the Chinese claim that their emperor was the son of heaven and all other rulers were subordinate to him. The shogun who accepted that role for pragmatic reasons, to profit from trade, was viewed with contempt by many of his contemporaries and those who followed him. The Japanese endured two invasions by the Mongols because of their refusal to accept Khubilai as their overlord. Despite their profound respect for Chinese culture, they had followed Hideyoshi in his challenge to the Ming. And the rise of the Tokugawa coincided with the decline of the Ming. The Tokugawa were hardly likely to pay homage to the barbarian Manchus who overran China in the seventeenth century.

Despite the hostilities of the late sixteenth century, the Ming were not too proud to seek Japanese assistance against the Manchus in the mid-seventeenth century. The Japanese were tempted: the Manchus were only too reminiscent of the Mongols. But after debate, the shogun's advisers decided against intervention. Nonetheless, the Japanese preference for the Ming was clear. Chinese merchants who accepted the Qing and wore the queue were discriminated against. The revolt in southeast China in the 1670s stimulated Japanese hopes for a Ming revival. But the Qing retained control of China's empire and the Japanese paid increasingly less heed to the Chinese conception of world order. They would construct their own.

As the Tokugawa bakufu established its authority over the country it also developed practices for governing contacts with foreign entities. With China under barbarian control, the Japanese could claim centrality for themselves. They could perceive themselves as at least equal to the Chinese and arguably superior. They could imagine a Japan-centered order in East Asia. By mid-seventeenth century the Koreans, who had been manipulated into restoring relations early in the century, were no longer using the Chinese calendar in their correspondence with the Japanese. In 1674, after numerous pleas from the king of Siam, the Japanese restored relations that had been broken in the 1630s because of the mistreatment of Japanese resident there. Formal diplomatic relations between China and Japan proved impossible in the eighteenth century as in the seventeenth, since neither would accept an inferior position. Trade and other informal contacts continued, but after 1715 Chinese who wanted to trade in Japan had to have credentials dated by the Japanese calendar. Ryukyu sent regular tribute missions to the Shogun in the eighteenth century. Even the mighty VOC had to accept Japanese terms of contact. The Dutch could

not exchange state-to-state correspondence; messages from Dutch officials were unacceptable. On the other hand, the Dutch were "allowed" to
present greetings to the shogun at Edo and to perform for his entertainment. They also were given assignments to carry out: to provide the
Japanese with books on Western science and technology and intelligence
about events in China and the rest of the world.

By the end of the eighteenth century it was evident that the Tokugawa,
although troubled by rebellion and riot at home, had created an international posture that worked for them. They had established their independence from the Chinese world order and perceived their nation as second to none. They were in control of all contacts with external forces and
were successful in keeping their country safe from potential foreign
invaders and pirates. Trade flowed and provided them with the few products they required from abroad. They were content with the international
system as they imagined it. But now, ominously, there were Western
ships sailing in their coastal waters and Russians to be fit into the Japanese
order. The Tokugawa prepared to meet these new challenges.

The Koreans, too, were feeling Russian pressures. After failing to exe-
cute their planned attack on the Manchus in mid-seventeenth century,
the Koreans joined forces with them from time to time to repel Russian
adventurers. Their only other contact with Westerners involved shipwrecked Dutch sailors whom they detained and employed and Catholic
priests encountered by diplomatic missions in Peking. Although the court
was disdainful of any foreign learning other than Chinese, Korean intellectuals *were* responsive to Western ideas. In Peking they were able to
pick up Chinese translations of Western books on subjects like astron-
omy and cartography—and Christianity. The maps taught them that
there was more to the world than Asia and gave them a new and not
entirely welcome view of Korea's place in it. From the priests and their
teachings they found a religion that they and lower class Koreans found
attractive. Catholicism spread in Korea in the late eighteenth century,
entirely on the basis of information brought back from Peking. There
were no Catholic missionaries in Korea until 1795, when one Chinese
priest slipped across the border. But Catholicism was banned in 1785 and
persecutions began before the end of the century.

It was clear that new ideas in Korea continued to be filtered through
China and contacts between Korea and Qing China were extensive, both
in the form of diplomatic missions to pay tribute to the Qing and in the

substantial exchange of goods. A considerable amount of trade occurred around the Yalu border where Korean merchants acted as middlemen between China and Japan, obtaining Chinese goods for resale to Japanese at Pusan or Tsushima and selling Japanese goods provided for the Chinese market. Korea was at the center of this triangular trade, but on the periphery of most other activity in the region at this time.

Southeast Asia in Flux

The Dutch East India Company, the VOC, had become the dominant naval power in Southeast Asia by the beginning of the seventeenth century and by the end of the century had established its supremacy on Java. It was the envy of every European merchant fleet and the scourge of local producers and traders. But the proverbial handwriting was on the wall. From the late seventeenth century through the eighteenth century, piracy surged in the region and Buginese pirate fleets, most likely operating out of Celebes (Sulawesi), targeted the VOC. By mid-eighteenth century the Dutch had lost control of the sea. Their interventions in various succession crises on Java, their interference in the internal affairs of Javanese polities, brought vast territory under their control, but at great cost, both financially and in increased administrative burden. On the mainland, Chinese merchants pushed them aside. They were slow to get into the tea trade that boomed in the eighteenth century, far surpassing trade in spices and pepper, and were unable to control it. Wars in Europe and America afflicted their homeland, and left them vulnerable to British raids. By the second half of the eighteenth century, the British had pushed them aside as the leading traders in Asia and even briefly taken Melaka. In 1799, in the midst of the Napoleanic Wars, the VOC was dissolved by the revolutionary authorities of the Napoleanic Republic of Batavia. What remained, however, was the Dutch presence in Indonesia.

In the mid-seventeenth century, the two most powerful indigenous kingdoms of the archipelago were Mataram on Java and Aceh on Sumatra. The Dutch relationship with Mataram changed after they intervened in a succession struggle in 1677. The once mighty ruler of Mataram thereafter depended on Dutch protection. Aceh was tougher, a formidable naval power that controlled the pepper trade on Sumatra and extended its authority to several tin-producing districts on the Malay peninsula.

But Aceh came under weak leadership in the latter half of the century, enabling the Dutch to break its hold on both the pepper trade and the tin country. In both instances, however, Dutch control was more apparent than real. On Java, the Dutch remained an "alien body on the fringe,"[6] in actual control of little more than the coastal districts and their effort to replace the Acehnese monopoly on the pepper trade of Sumatra was thwarted by Chinese merchants, who competed successfully everywhere but Java.

By 1700 pepper and spices were no longer the most valuable cargoes the VOC carried back to Europe. First, Indian textiles and silks from China, Bengal, and Persia were more profitable—and then came the extraordinary rise in the demand for coffee and tea. Although the Dutch failed to obtain a significant share of the tea trade, they had better luck with coffee. Responding to Turkish interference with shipments from Mocha on the Red Sea, the VOC introduced coffee production in Java— but it was not enough to sustain the company.

Despite constant hostile pressure from the Bugis, the Dutch managed to find a way to become involved in several more disastrous wars in Java. In general it is fair to say that they exploited existing antagonisms among the Indonesians rather than pursuing a conscious policy of divide and rule over peoples too numerous to conquer. Early in the eighteenth century they intervened in the second war of succession and by mid-century they were in a third that lasted from 1749 to 1757. The Mataram empire was disintegrating and all the Dutch forces couldn't put it back together again. In the midst of all this, from 1740 to 1743, the Dutch and their Javanese allies fought a war against the island's Chinese residents, including a massacre of almost all Chinese resident in Batavia. A Dutch effort to control the influx of impoverished Chinese from Fujian, presumably a very different class from the skilled craftsmen, merchants, and agricultural workers they had once recruited, led to Chinese resistance. Fearing insurrection, the Dutch and Javanese, resentful of the Chinese role as middlemen, attacked and butchered most of the Chinese. Survivors allied with Javanese eager to be rid of the Dutch fought a guerrilla war that lasted several years. And in the midst of the third Javanese war of succession, in 1756, the Bugis attacked Melaka and were just barely beaten off. A second Buginese assault on Melaka in the 1780s might well have succeeded had not the Dutch government sent a squadron that arrived in time to lift the siege.

Ultimately it was the British who undermined the VOC and left the Dutch government little recourse but to terminate its charter. VOC bet wrong on the battle for Bengal, opposing the victorious British who consequently restricted their access both to the silks and the opium to be found there. In the war for American independence, the Dutch, insisting on freedom of the seas, opposed the British in the Atlantic. In retaliation, the British overran Dutch posts in both the East and West Indies. Most were recovered by the terms of the ensuing peace treaty, but the British were back to take Melaka in 1795—although they returned the city to the Dutch in 1802. It was not military action that destroyed the VOC, however. On the contrary it was the success of the rival British East India Company, armed with superior capital resources, in control of Bengal, and virtually monopolizing the tea trade, that finished the VOC on the eve of the nineteenth century.

The Indonesian archipelago seemed a shambles with the decline of Aceh and Mataram and the apparent weakening of the Dutch position there. The Bugis had succeeded in conquering a number of political entities on the islands and the Malay peninsula, but did not appear to be creating a cohesive empire. The British were passing through and had picked up a potential emporium at Penang in 1786. For the moment the resources of the region seemed less important than the products of India and China. The islands that had first attracted the Europeans to the region had lost much of their allure.

Similarly, the Malay peninsula was more the object of competing mainland forces than a coherent polity. Burma and Siam were the principal contestants, but by the seventeenth century there was substantial European activity, English and French as well as Dutch. For most of the seventeenth century, Burma, too, was fragmented. Both the VOC and the English East India Company had looked for trade opportunities early in the century but had been disappointed. Siam, centered around its capital at Ayutthaya, was stronger and wealthier, but not immune to European intrigue. Japanese influence, very substantial in the early years of the century, evaporated after a massacre of Japanese residents in 1632. The English played their hand poorly, but the Dutch were able to force a commercial treaty on the Thai ruler, gaining monopoly privileges in 1664. Then came the French, whose success in establishing themselves as a force with which to be reckoned led to anti-French violence and civil war. The Vietnamese, divided north and south, spent much of their time fighting each other, including an indecisive struggle that lasted from 1620–1674. When periods of relative calm occurred, the southern Annamite regime pushed southward against the scattered Cham people and on into Cambodia, where it frequently encountered Thai forces with competing goals. The Cambodians were the constant victims of their more powerful neighbors. The southern Vietnamese regime, unable to mobilize an army equal to that of its northern antagonist, frequently sought European support. It cannot be said that life was more placid on the continent than on the islands of Southeast Asia.

Burma suddenly reemerged as a powerful force in the region in the 1750s under the leadership of Alaungpaya, who, with minor assistance from the British East India Company, led a Burmese revival against the Mon of southern Burma. But the ambitions of Alaungpaya and his successors transcended mere unification of the country and could not be satisfied by defeating the Mon and Shan minorities. They struck out in all directions, targeting China's Yunnan province, the kingdom of Arakan, separating Burma from Bengal, and, most of all, Ayutthaya and its pretensions to the Malay peninsula and the region around Chiengmai.

Caravan trade between Burma and Yunnan had increased significantly in the seventeenth century and the Burmese-Chinese border was more imagined than real. Fleeing Ming forces had been pursued by Qing armies in the 1660s and Chinese worked tin mines in northern Burma. In the 1760s Burmese troops operated in areas considered by Peking to be part of its empire. Inevitably the Qing decided to teach the Burmese manners and launched a series of invasions in the mid-1760s. The Burmese fell back each time, but a combination of Burmese tenacity and Qing ineptitude saved the Burmese capital. The Qing were forced to retreat and eventually peaceful trade was resumed. The Burmese were justly proud of their successful resistance, but little had been accomplished by either side.

The principal Burmese victim was Ayutthaya. The preponderance of Burmese forces in the 1760s were engaged against the Thai and in 1765 they destroyed Ayutthaya and established Burmese rule over the region. The Thai city never recovered, but the Burmese ultimately withdrew, unable simultaneously to suppress the Thai and defend themselves against the Qing. In the 1770s, the Thai succeeded in pushing the Burmese out of their land, recovering most of the disputed territory including Chiengmai. Again, the peoples of both countries suffered during these lengthy hostilities. To be sure, the misery inflicted on the Thai was greater, but the Burmese had nothing to show for their aggression.

The attack on Arakan may well be considered a fatal mistake for the Burmese, in large part because of their success. Arakan had been in a virtual state of anarchy for much of the eighteenth century and in 1784 the Burmese decided to add it to their territory. A well-planned campaign succeeded quickly and Arakan became a Burmese province—instead of a buffer between Burma and British India. Tensions between the British and the Burmese were not avoided, ultimately with unfortunate results for the Burmese. But initially, encouraged by the ease of their conquest, the Burmese decided to attack Siam again. This time the results were disastrous as the Thai repelled several major offensives . At the close of the century, Burma was on the defensive against Thai armies and had managed to arouse the apprehensions of the British East India Company.

The Thai approach to the outside world was markedly less confrontational. Ayutthaya was probably the most cosmopolitan city in seventeenth-century Southeast Asia. The Thai opened their capital to foreigners from everywhere and the Dutch, English, and French as well as the Japanese and Chinese were active there. Most of Ayutthaya's trade was with China and the court recognized the value of Chinese middlemen by appointing them to royal offices to facilitate the movement of goods. Indian Muslims, also present in large numbers, served as bankers and were the wealthiest of the foreign communities. A woman of Mon descent monopolized Dutch-Thai trade in the 1640s through her relationships with successive Dutch factors who needed her services to gain access to the ruling elite. King Narai (r. 1657–1688) had an Indian cook and imported his clothes from Persia. Ethnicity did not seem to matter to the Thai and men of part Chinese ancestry ascended to the throne before the end of the eighteenth century.

In the 1660s the VOC became uneasy about King Narai's warm reception of English and French potential competitors. His unwillingness to grant the Dutch special privileges displeased them and they dispatched a fleet to which he proved more amenable. In 1664, under duress, he signed a treaty that gave the Dutch control of the trade between Ayutthaya and China and other privileges. In the 1680s, however, working with his adviser Constantine Phaulkon, the erstwhile employee of the English East India Company, King Narai invited French assistance, hoping to play the French off against the Dutch. But the arrival and garrisoning of French troops threatened the independence of the country and provoked a rebellion by Thai forces. In the course of the revolt, King Narai died, Phaulkon was executed, and the French departed. European influence in Siam declined sharply.

In the first half of the eighteenth century, the Thai sparred with the Khmer of Cambodia with mixed results. Their principal interest appears to have been to preempt Annam's dominance of Cambodia, but in that effort they failed. By the end of the century the Thai determined that their interests were better served by an arrangement to divide Cambodia with the Vietnamese. The people of Cambodia, who had routed Thai forces in 1622 and dealt them one of the greatest defeats in their history in 1717, could not overcome the avarice of their two more powerful neighbors.

It was, of course, the Burmese who hurt the Thai most severely when they sacked Ayutthaya in 1765. Most of the people in the vicinity of that great city were killed and it was not until the third decade of the twentieth century that the population again reached the level of the mid-seventeenth. It took the anti-Burmese resistance movement six years to drive the Burmese out—and twenty-two more years before the conflict was brought to an official halt in 1793. Laos and Cambodia did not escape the war's devastation. The Thai hero who drove the Burmese out and had the wisdom not to pursue them was the man who became King Rama I (r. 1782–1809).

It was Rama I who chose to support the Annamese leader who eventually reunified Vietnam and worked out the division of Cambodia with him. From 1788 to 1801, the ruler of Annam regularly acknowledged his vassalage to the Thai king. It was also Rama I who consolidated Thai power at home and gave Siam the foundations of a modern centralized administration. And finally, it was Rama I who set his people firmly on the course of accommodation and adaptation of Western ideas and technology. The Thai continued to be the people of Southeast Asia most responsive to the changing international setting in which they functioned.

The Vietnamese, on the other hand, were more cautious in their dealings with the outside world. After centuries of resisting Chinese domination, they seem to have developed a stronger sense of national identity than most other Southeast Asians, a stronger sense of being part of a nation-state than the Chinese whose culture had so influenced them. Nonetheless as civil strife rent the country in the seventeenth century, both sides, the Nguyen and the Trinh, were constantly enlisting European assistance. Indeed, the Nguyen persecution of Christians in the 1660s may have been prompted by anger at not receiving anticipated aid from the Portuguese. But in the expulsion of French missionaries in the years that followed there was also fear that the Catholic priests were forerunners of soldiers who would do to Vietnam what the Spanish had done to the Philippines. Awareness of events in the Philippines and in Japan reinforced Vietnamese caution.

Similarly, the Vietnamese of Tongking in the north seemed singularly uninterested in foreign trade. Thang-long, modern Hanoi, was a heavily populated domestic market city, one of the world's largest, but goods from Europe or Japan or island Southeast Asia were relatively rare. Unlike most Southeast Asian capitals, it was not an international emporium. The Annamese, on the other hand maintained a major international port at Hoi An, where the Chinese remained after the Japanese left in mid-seventeenth century. There they handled junk trade that continued to come from Japan, China, and most of the rest of the region. Indeed whatever international commerce there was in Vietnam was dominated by Chinese merchants.

After Annam defeated Tongking in 1673, the Vietnamese enjoyed a long period of relative peace. Annam pressed into Cambodia and had confrontations with Thai forces there, but between north and south Vietnamese there was a century of respite. In 1773, however, a rebellion in the south gave Tongking leaders an excuse to invade and their forces seized Hue in 1775. Elsewhere in the south the so-called "Tayson" rebels prevailed and eventually marched north. In 1786 they retook Hue and two years later had conquered all of Tongking, uniting all of Vietnam under their control. But the Tayson triumph was short-lived. They were immediately confronted in the north by Qing armies determined to restore Qianlong's defeated vassal to his throne and in the south by the sole survivor of the Nguyen family they had overthrown in Annam. The long peace of 1673 to 1773 seems to have been an aberration in the historic experience of the Vietnamese people.

The Tayson had better luck against the Qing, easily rallying their people against the invaders. After the Qing took Hanoi, a counterattack sent them fleeing home at great cost as the Tayson deployed mines along their escape routes. It was the Tayson emperor who Qianlong recognized as the legitimate ruler of his Vietnamese tributary. But the Nguyen, aided by the French, the Thais, Chinese pirates, and Cambodian merce-naries, slowly fought their way north, eventually seizing control of the entire country in 1802. This time Peking looked aside. Prudently, the new emperor requested investiture by the Qing, duly granted in 1803.

At the close of the eighteenth century, the Philippines remained firmly under Spanish control and the Dutch had acquired territory that included most of Java. Elsewhere the European presence was minor. Much of the region's international trade was controlled by expatriate Chinese, most evidently in Siam, Vietnam, and in the cities of Batavia and Manila. Unlike the Europeans, the Chinese came without government support and posed no political or strategic danger. But continental Southeast Asia faced no threat from Europe either. Burma, Siam, and Vietnam had strong central governments and were very much in control of their own affairs. Indeed, declining interest in the products of Southeast Asia, how-ever unfortunate economically, suggested that outside predators like the Portuguese, Spanish, and Dutch might cease to be a problem for the region.

The Approach of the British Empire

The English East India Company, chartered in 1600, had begun looking for commercial opportunities in East Asia almost immediately, with rel-atively little luck. The Dutch squeezed it out of most of the spice and pepper trade, killing Englishmen who challenged them. Hostile Spaniards controlled Manila. Efforts to set up shop in Japan failed. Approaches to China were sporadic and of limited value. Eventually the Company estab-lished itself in India, depending largely on Indian cotton textiles and what-ever pepper and spices it could obtain for shipment back to Europe. In 1639, the great Mughal emperor, Shah Jahan, granted the English a site at Madras and in 1661 England acquired Bombay from Portugal and gave it to the East India Company. The Company's promise was enhanced by early involvement in the Guangzhou tea trade in the 1660s and 70s—long before tea threatened to surpass spirits as the drink of choice in Europe.

But the assumption that India would provide a haven for English trade with Asia did not go unchallenged. In addition to frequent collisions with native forces, the English were confronted by a new European contest-ant for the riches of the Orient. In 1664 the French created their own government-controlled trading company and in the mid-1670s they were established at Pondichery, not far from the main English commercial center at Madras. The Anglo-French rivalry that ensued was part of a competition for world power that spread over five continents, afflicting Africa and the Americas as well as Asia and Europe.

In India the crucial decades of the struggle between England and France came in the mid-eighteenth century, during the two upheavals known in the West as the War of the Austrian Succession (1740–1748) and the Seven Years War of 1756–1763. In both wars the French took the offensive in India, attempting to drive the English out. As the Mogul empire disintegrated, the French in India, as in North America, conspired with Indians, to attempt to eliminate English influence. In 1746, when they learned that war had been declared between France and England, the French, employing native troops they had been training for years, captured Madras. For better or worse, they returned the city to English control as part of the Treaty of Aix-la-Chapelle in 1748, but French authorities at Pondichery continued to seek hegemony over all of central and southern India. They very nearly succeeded in 1751.

And then Clive came to the rescue. The key to French success had been the manipulation of Indian regional leaders, supporting them with French-trained, highly disciplined native troops. Robert Clive, who had survived the attack on Madras, used the same methods against the French and won a brilliant victory in 1751, reversing the momentum of the struggle. In 1754, to protect British interests against France, the government in London sent royal troops to India for the first time. Undeterred, when war broke out again in Europe in 1756, the French and their Indian allies struck at Calcutta. The infamous Black Hole of Calcutta was where the surviving residents were interred by the victors, the more fortunate of them to be rescued by Clive in January 1757. Over the next two and a half years, he battered French-led forces in Bengal and withstood the efforts of a seaborne French relief expedition. Dutch intervention against Clive in 1759 failed and in 1761, the French surrendered at Pondichery. Bengal was completely under English control. The great English historian G. M. Trevelyan wrote that the acquisition of Bengal "converted the East India company from an armed trading corporation into an Asiatic Power."[7]

And it was in Bengal that the British found the answer to their need for a product to exchange for Chinese tea. The tea drinking habit had boomed in Europe and the market in England alone had soared from 54,600 pounds imported in 1706 to 2,235,000 pounds by 1750—and going up.[8] In the eighteenth century China was the world's only source of tea—and Bengal was the world's premier source of opium. As the East India Company acquired territory and the administrative responsibilities that went with it, its leadership concluded that opium consumption in Bengal was having deleterious effects on the local peasantry and its productivity. It had to be exported. Similarly, as tea became a larger and larger percentage of the Company's net profit, approximately 25 percent before the end of the century, the sale of opium to China solved two problems: the opium problem in Bengal and the balance of trade problem with China. Of course, the impact on China was quite the reverse, creating both a serious drug problem and a hemorrhaging of silver—but that was of little concern to London as Chinese silver became one of the principal sources of support for the British administration in India.

TABLE 7.2. Some Notable Dates of the Late Seventeenth
and Eighteenth Centuries
(Events in boldface are mentioned in the text)

Treaty of Nerchinsk	**1689**
Rise of Asante state in West Africa	1700–1750
Massacre of Chinese in Batavia	**1740–1743**
Chinese invasion of Tibet, control of Dalai Lama	**1751**
Seven Years War (French and Indian War in America	1756–1763
Burmese destroy Ayutthaya	**1765**
American Revolution	1775–1783
French Revolution	1789
Macartney mission	**1792**
Reign of Terror begins in France	1793

Despite the loss of part of its North American empire in the course of the War for American Independence, England in the closing decades of the eighteenth century perceived itself to be the most powerful state in the world. In India, it took up what came to be called the White Man's Burden: it accepted the mission an omniscient God had given it to civilize the heathen of India—and any other non-European peoples that came under their sway. The East India Company and the British government became increasingly impatient with the failure of China to recognize the glory of the British Empire and with the petty restrictions the Chinese imposed on traders. Toward the end of the eighteenth century the Enlightenment admiration for Chinese civilization, for Confucius and chinoiserie, was fading. China evoked irritation rather than affection. In 1792, the British concluded that the time had come to act.

Although the merchants were a little uneasy about the possibility of alienating the Chinese, the British government decided to send a high-level embassy to Peking. It was tasked to impress the Qing with the importance of Great Britain, to establish official diplomatic relations, and to gain new commercial privileges. London's chosen instrument was Lord George Macartney, an experienced diplomat who had served recently in India. He carried with him a letter from King George III and gifts the British hoped would fill the Qing with awe.

The Qing were not overjoyed with the British initiative. They were quite content with the existing state of relations between China and the West. They had chosen to focus their energies elsewhere, content with the maritime customs collected at Guangzhou that helped finance their empire-building efforts in Central Asia. Their policy toward the coastal regions was defensive, designed to protect the country against pirates, subversion by Ming supporters among the overseas Chinese, and any complications that might be posed by foreign merchants. They were satisfied with the results and had not asked for direct contact with London.

On the other hand, Qianlong and his advisers were very much aware of growing British naval and commercial strength. They understood that the British were now the strongest of the European powers pressing against the floodgates. They perceived the British as potential troublemakers, both at Guangzhou and in Tibet. There was no point in insulting them gratuitously: Macartney would be received. Nonetheless, the court was uneasy about the embassy, uncertain of British intentions. Would the British envoy understand and accept Qing protocol or might he do something to embarrass his hosts? He claimed to have come to honor Qianlong on his eightieth birthday: what did he really want?

As the historian James Hevia has explained, the Macartney embassy constituted an encounter between two "imperial formations."[9] The two most powerful empires of the day were meeting and each was attempting to impose its vision, its sense of the appropriate nature of the relationship between them. The British were determined to establish their sovereign equality and the Qing were equally determined to maintain their emperor's claim to supreme lordship, a status superior to that of George III. In the closing days of the eighteenth century, China could still dictate the terms of contact. Macartney failed.

Arguably, the British made three mistakes that guaranteed what was almost certainly the mission's preordained failure. First, they mixed diplomacy with trade: the emperor and the court would not deign to deal with commercial matters and were contemptuous of the British king for doing so. If Macartney's business was trade, he was less worthy of the emperor's attention and hospitality. Second, they underestimated the state of Chinese technology and scientific sophistication: the Qing were underwhelmed by the gifts Macartney brought them—and he was humiliated when they showed much finer and more advanced objects in their existing collections. Finally, Macartney refused to play his part in the Qing ritual for guests: he would not perform the *kowtow*. Graciously, Qianlong permitted him to bow on one knee, as an Englishman would before his own ruler, but instructed Qing officials to reduce the level of hospitality for the embassy. In terms of the specific requests for the right of diplomatic residence in Peking and the improvement of trade arrangements, the Qing yielded nothing. And Macartney went home.

Conclusion

The first 150 years of Qing rule over China were marked by the greatest extension of empire since the days of the Mongol domination of the Eurasian land mass. Burmese, Koreans, Mongols, Tibetans, Vietnamese, and Europeans, whether they came by land or by sea, were forced to follow Qing dictates. Although the Russian empire was pressing to the north and British strength in Asia had increased significantly by the end of the eighteenth century, the Qing remained dominant.

In general, Qing strategists recognized the emerging new power structure and responded pragmatically. They entered into diplomatic relations with Russia when that seemed the prudent response to a potential threat in the northwest. Similarly, they accepted the Macartney embassy and treated it with the utmost respect. With lesser powers, when they perceived force to be effective, as with the Zungaris and Nepalese, they did not refrain from applying it as ruthlessly as circumstances required. When their estimates were wrong, as in Burma and Vietnam, they did not hesitate to accept face-saving solutions and cut their losses. The Japanese were left alone. Minor European powers—the Dutch, Portuguese, and Spanish—quickly learned not to challenge China, which did not impose particularly onerous conditions on their intercourse. The essential point, of course, is that the terms were imposed by the Qing. The Americans, too, when they arrived in 1784, were channeled easily into the Canton system.

Elsewhere in the region, the European thrust that had disrupted the international system of the sixteenth century had been blunted. The obvious exceptions were the Spanish in the Philippines and the Dutch in Indonesia. Although a handful of Russian adventurers were roaming close to the Yalu, the Koreans were untouched by Europeans. Japan had things well under control, obtaining what it wanted from the annual Dutch voyage to Deshima, alert to Russian probes among its northern islands. In Southeast Asia, the continental states varied in their receptivity to the West, with Siam the most open, but the Thais and the Vietnamese had easily contained presumptuous Europeans. The islanders were, of course, more vulnerable to European seapower, less organized politically—and they paid the price of losing control of land. And throughout Southeast Asia, a flood of Chinese migrants could be found in every seaport, wherever foreign goods might be exchanged—and, with increasing frequency, in the hinterlands, in the service of the local rulers, indigenous or foreign.

Unlike the legendary King Canute of eleventh-century England, Denmark, and Norway, the Qing emperors, the Japanese shoguns, and the various rulers of continental Southeast Asia had held back the tide. But it was gathering force and their nineteenth-century heirs were not equal to the task. The days in which East Asians could control the terms of contact with Europe and the United States were about to be interrupted. In particular, the demand for expanded commercial opportunities—and especially for Chinese tea, proved irresistible to the West. And a revolution in military procedures and technology in Europe overwhelmed the natural advantage of Asians who were numerically superior and fighting on their own territory.

EIGHT

Triumph of the West

By the onset of the nineteenth century, seaborne Europeans had been penetrating the coastal waters of Asia for three hundred years. The sixteenth-century fleets, Portuguese, Spanish, and Dutch, came as heavily armed marauders, forcing their way into existing trade routes and emporia. They came initially in search of pepper and spices and attempted to monopolize trade, to extract wealth from the region. The Portuguese and Spanish carried the cross with them and attempted, with considerable success, to plant Christianity in Asia. With the notable exception of the Spanish in the Philippines, they did not seek to occupy Asian lands, satisfied to control cities such as Melaka, Macao, and Batavia. They took advantage of the relatively docile peoples they found along the coast of the Indian subcontinent and the fragmented polities of island Southeast Asia. At no time, however, did they have the power to challenge China or Japan or to overcome the resistance of the more organized societies of Burma, Siam, and Vietnam—or the fierce Acehnese and Bugis.

But time ran out on the peoples of Asia in the course of the nineteenth century. Technological advances in the West, specifically steamships that could overcome adverse currents and wind conditions, and steel artillery, gave the Europeans an enormous advantage in maneuverability and firepower. William McNeill argues that equally as important was the ability of the British and the Dutch to transfer European techniques for creating highly disciplined armies to India and Indonesia where they trained local troops and used them to overcome the poorly organized forces of native rulers.[1] Advanced military technology and dependable local forces enabled a handful of Europeans to control a vast amount of Asian territory—and to threaten the region's two greatest powers, China and Japan.

The British Are Coming

As the power of the East India Company grew in Bengal, as the British "Raj" took root, the exigencies of defending its interests caused its leaders to think like those of any great state. England and France had been at war for much of the eighteenth century and the French had very nearly driven the Company out of India. France was the most obvious threat to the Raj and its naval successes in mid-century had taught the English an important lesson. They needed port facilities on the eastern coast of the Bay of Bengal to enable their sailing vessels to cope with the shifting monsoon winds, to hide from the autumnal hurricanes, and to provide ship repairs. In 1786 they took control of the island of Penang in the Strait of Melaka, just off the Malay peninsula. Although the island's location gave it the added attraction of facilitating the Company's burgeoning trade with China and of providing improved access to the products of the Indonesian islands, strategic considerations appear to have been paramount. But, in the course of the Napoleonic Wars, it became apparent that Penang would not be satisfactory for any of the purposes for which it had been acquired.

In 1781, while fighting the French and the Dutch in the War for American Independence, the British had attacked and taken over Dutch holdings in Sumatra. They withdrew in 1783 in accordance with the terms of the Treaty of Paris. They captured Sumatra again in 1795 and in 1811 added Java to their conquests. Once more, however, when peace was restored in Europe, the British returned control of the islands to the Dutch, retaining just a corner of Sumatra—which they surrendered in 1824 in exchange for Melaka.

British generosity toward the Dutch was hardly altruistic. Fear of the revival of French power in Asia suggested the value of the Dutch as allies. The East India Company, still the principal source of British strength in Asia, was concerned primarily with maintaining its dominance over India and trade with China. And in 1819, the British had added Singapore to their holdings—an island that provided all they had hoped to find in Penang. By 1824, with Penang, Singapore, and Melaka under their control, British naval forces could easily protect the sea routes between India and China.

Peace in Europe allowed the British to focus their attention again on the obstacles to expanding trade with China—and upon their failure to get the Qing court to accept their overtures for formal and regular diplomatic relations, beginning with a permanent British mission in Peking. Once again the East India Company prevailed upon London to send an embassy to the Qing emperor. In 1793, Qianlong had replied famously to George III's letter to him, explaining that China had not "the slightest need of your country's manufactures." Nonetheless, the Qing had received Macartney graciously, as befitted one who had come from so far. In 1816, Lord Amherst fared less well. Qianlong was long dead and in his place was an emperor less wise, less sensitive, less understanding of the rapid pace at which the world was changing. Perhaps because Great Britain was simultaneously at war with Nepal, at the time a Qing tributary, but more likely because the Chinese ascertained that he had had no intention of performing the necessary ritual, Amherst was treated brusquely and expelled from the country without an audience with the emperor. British officials, while outraged, were not yet ready for a vigorous response. The Company decided against further efforts, fearful of endangering the tea trade, which accounted for all of its profits.

The Company also had other problems, closer at hand: Burmese expansion toward India was creating chaos in the border regions. The Burmese king, determined to build a great empire, had conquered Arakan in 1784 and soon afterward launched an unsuccessful invasion of Siam. Burmese activities in Siam concerned the British far less than events in Arakan and the hovering of French warships in Burmese ports. In the 1790s, Arakanese refugees, including rebels against Burmese rule, were crossing the frontier into India. They were pursued by a large Burmese force which set up camp on the British side. The incident was settled peacefully when the British seized the rebel leaders and turned them over to the Burmese. Fearful of further, less manageable incidents, and apprehensive about the possibility of French naval forces operating out of Burma against India, the British Raj tried a diplomatic approach to the Burmese court in 1795. Diplomacy brought modest results. Although the Burmese king indicated his contempt for the lowly governor-general of India, he did grant the British the right to post a resident in Rangoon to supervise trade. He rejected the request to close his ports to French warships, but the issue, which had been serious during the War for American Independence, did not reemerge during the Napoleonic Wars.

Border incidents continued to abrade Anglo-Burmese relations for a few years and diplomatic efforts proved frustrating, often disagreeable for the British envoys. Then came a brief respite which lasted only until the next major Arakanese rebellion that began in 1811 and continued until 1814, despite efforts by both Burmese and Company forces to suppress it. The inability of the British to capture the rebel leader appears to have been viewed by Burmese leaders as evidence of either British weakness or hostile intent—or both. Diplomatic contact ended.

At the end of the decade, the setting for Anglo-Burmese conflict had shifted to Assam, which the Burmese invaded in 1819, and spread to several other small border states in the early 1820s. In 1823 the Burmese launched a major invasion of Kachar, which, although beaten back, left no further doubt of their intent to invade Bengal. In 1824, Lord Amherst, now governor-general of India, declared war on Burma. Although the British-led forces suffered heavy losses, mostly from disease, and the fighting lasted for nearly two years, the Burmese army was destroyed and Burma was forced to surrender Arakan and Assam. In addition, the British exacted an enormous indemnity and forced Burma to agree to accept a British resident diplomat and to post a Burmese envoy at Calcutta. The British empire in India had expanded, despite a lack of enthusiasm in London, where additional responsibilities and expenses raised concerns, and British seapower had gained hegemony over the Indian Ocean.

Burmese hostility to the British was hardly likely to dissipate in the aftermath of so harsh a peace—and it did not. Preoccupied by more pressing matters in Afghanistan and China, the British tolerated considerable friction in their relations with Burma until mid-century. Simply stated, Burmese leaders did all they could to avoid compliance with the peace terms that had been forced upon them. They ignored demonstrations of British power elsewhere and, ultimately, they pushed the British too far.

Before resuming the struggle with Burma, the British focused their attention on China. Private British merchants in China were demanding an equitable commercial treaty that would put an end to arbitrary Chinese restrictions and the persistent uncertainties of doing business in Guangzhou. They called for a permanent diplomatic presence in Peking and suggested that an island beyond the reach of Chinese authorities, Taiwan perhaps, be seized as an entrepot. Criticism of the East India Company came from British textile manufacturers, confronted by German and American competition and eager for access to the Chinese market. Unlike the Company, they were unwilling to settle for whatever profits the Chinese allowed. They perceived the Company as an obstacle and demanded its elimination. In 1834, after the Company's monopoly over trade with China was terminated, Lord Napier, named first superintendent of trade in China, arrived in Guangzhou.

By all accounts, Napier's efforts were disastrous. He was ill-prepared for the assignment, having had no diplomatic or Asian experience and having been briefed inadequately as to conditions at Guangzhou. Upon arrival he demanded direct access to the provincial governor-general, attempting to bypass the Cohong—the merchant guild to which the Qing had delegated responsibility for managing foreign trade. His presumption of equality with a senior Chinese official was rejected, and when he persisted in his demand the Chinese first halted trade with the British and then cut off supplies to the British trading post in Guangzhou. Unwilling to yield to the Chinese tactic, Napier had two British warships force their way up river where they exchanged fire with Chinese defenses. The Chinese were not cowed and blocked the ships from reaching the city. Napier sent to India for reinforcements and retired to Macao to await them as British and Chinese merchants urgently pursued a compromise. In October, three months after his arrival, Napier died of malaria and the crisis ended. Trade was resumed and both sides were clearly relieved.

For several years thereafter, leading British merchants in Guangzhou petitioned their government to send warships, a force sufficient to intimidate the Chinese. They demanded redress for losses incurred during the 1834 trade stoppage, the opening of northern ports, and abolition of the Chinese merchant guild, the Cohong. London ignored their pleas. Conditions in Guangzhou became chaotic as the number of British firms there more than doubled between 1834 and 1837 and several important Chinese merchants were driven into bankruptcy by sharp increases in what they had to pay middlemen for tea. Pressure on the British government to obtain more equitable and dependable conditions of trade mounted.

The first die was cast by the Daoguang emperor (r. 1821–1850) when he decided in 1838 to enforce the ban on opium sales and usage. For years he and his advisers had been wrestling with the financial and moral problems posed by drug addiction. Imports of Indian opium drained silver from the country and had resulted in an unfavorable balance of trade. Smuggling of the illegal drug had led to corruption of officials and widespread contempt for the ban, a threat to respect for the nation's legal institutions and social dislocation. Arguments for legalizing and taxing the sale of opium and driving out the Indian import with better quality Chinese opium had been given serious consideration. Ultimately the emperor was swayed by moral arguments against drug use. In March 1839, Lin Zexu, appointed imperial commissioner and ordered to suppress opium trafficking, arrived in Guangzhou.

The second die was cast in London when the truculent Lord Palmerston was appointed to serve his second tour as foreign minister. Palmerston had been partly responsible for the Napier fiasco, having sent a man of questionable qualifications to Guangzhou with carelessly framed instructions. Ever sensitive to his nation's honor, he would not tolerate a second insult by the Chinese, of whom he was utterly contemptuous. Palmerston was a man with a perennial chip on his shoulder—and Lin Zexu was about to knock it off. Napier would be avenged.

Commissioner Lin cleaned up Guangzhou with astonishing speed, battling successfully against users and dealers. Simultaneously, he turned to the foreign merchants in the city and demanded that they hand over their opium stocks without compensation. They refused. Lin weighed his options carefully. The naval forces available to him were not adequate for a quick strike against the foreign ships. His hasty study of international law led him to appeal to Queen Victoria, citing a nation's right to control its international trade and arguing that the British would not allow foreign merchants to flood their country with opium. That approach was to no avail, nor were his other efforts at persuasion or at dividing the merchants by ordering the arrest of just one of the leading opium dealers.

In the past, threats to stop trade had usually sufficed to bring foreign merchants into line and Lin was prepared to resort to that tactic. Overlooking British control of India as a source of supplies and reinforcements, he calculated that Great Britain was too far away to mount an offensive against China. In the last days of March, he ordered the cessation of all trade and blocked the escape of all foreigners in their factories at Guangzhou. For six weeks, the foreign merchants held out, enduring sleepless nights during which Chinese troops blew horns and banged gongs incessantly. Finally, they turned 20,000 pounds of opium over to the British superintendent of trade who promised compensation, then delivered the drugs to Commissioner Lin—who washed them into the sea. Lin allowed the British to flee Guangzhou for Macao. He then pressed the Portuguese to chase them out of Macao. Eventually they took refuge in deserted Hong Kong harbor where they were harassed by Chinese war junks and the handful of Chinese living on the island.

Lin was too wise merely to exult in his success. He anticipated that the British would attempt a military response and he prepared for it. He fortified the waterways leading to Guangzhou and suspended huge chains across the channel. Let the British come. What little chance remained for a peaceful outcome to the confrontation probably vanished after small-scale battles between the British and Chinese war junks occurred in the waters between Guangzhou and Hong Kong. Blood was shed on both sides.

In London, merchants with interests in China led the charge, lobbying intensely to win parliamentary support for a punitive expedition. Parliament proved responsive, authorizing the dispatch of a large fleet and the mobilization of troops in India. The armada headed for Guangzhou included sixteen heavily armed ships of the line and four newly designed armed steamships. An army of four thousand men was carried on twenty or more transports. Parliament directed the force commander to obtain "satisfaction and reparations." Palmerston wanted nothing less than the humiliation of the Qing. Britain would suffer no more indignities at Chinese hands.

The British fleet reached the Pearl River estuary leading to Guangzhou in June 1840. To Commissioner Lin's dismay, it made no effort to proceed to Guangzhou where Chinese militias had been aroused against it. Instead, the British left four ships to blockade the river and proceeded north. They then blockaded the Zhejiang port of Ningbo and seized the island of Zhoushan from which they could harass shipping in and out of the Yangzi River. A few weeks later they rounded Shandong peninsula and appeared at the approaches to Tianjin. At this point the Qing emperor and his advisers concluded it was time to negotiate. British forces were much too close to Peking.

The British were persuaded to return to Guangzhou to complete the negotiations, much to the relief of the Qing court. The British superintendent of trade at Guangzhou and the Manchu official with whom the emperor replaced Commissioner Lin reached agreement in January 1841. The Qing diplomatist agreed to allow the British to resume trade at Guangzhou and committed his government to payment of an indemnity that would presumably cover the cost of the lost opium. He further acquiesced to the British demand for direct contacts with Qing officials and ceded the island of Hong Kong to them.

Unfortunately for both negotiators, their principals were outraged by the agreement. Palmerston did not think his man had obtained nearly enough, berated him for not using sufficient force, and fired him. The Qing emperor thought his man had yielded too much and ordered him executed. He was fortunate to have his sentence reduced to mere banishment. As unreasonable as Palmerston may have been, it was clearly better to work for him than for the Daoguang emperor.

Palmerston's dissatisfaction with the January 1841 agreement led to a year of additional warfare, from August 1841 through August 1842. Despite frequent fierce resistance, the British fleet took Xiamen in Fujian province, Ningbo, and, with reinforcements from India, Shanghai as well. As they reached the city of Nanjing, the Qing surrendered and accepted British terms. By this time Palmerston was out of office, but even he may have been pleased with the results. In the Treaty of Nanjing, the Chinese were forced to open five ports to British trade, residents, and consulates. The despised Cohong was abolished and a "fair and regular" tariff was promised. Diplomatic correspondence as between equals was to be allowed and, as before, Hong Kong was ceded to the British. The emperor perceived that he had no choice but to accept the treaty. China's "one hundred years of humiliation" had begun.

Britain's triumph in the "Opium War," as the Anglo-Chinese hostilities of 1839 to 1842 are known, was possible because the military organization of the Manchus had decayed, because the Manchus had never been sufficiently attentive to coastal defense, and because Chinese military technology had lagged. The British, on the other hand, had honed their skills in constant continental warfare, had built the world's most powerful navy, had developed military assets in India that could be brought to bear in East Asia, and benefited from the most advanced technology, especially, by most accounts, the steam-powered warship. The war proved to be a turning point in the history of East Asia. It began an irrevocable change in the structure of the East Asian international order.

Great Britain was now the dominant power in East Asia as well as in the Indian Ocean. In mid-century and afterward, the Chinese, the Burmese, and the Thai peoples would see evidence of British might. But perhaps more ominous was the example the British had set, the evidence they had revealed of the vulnerability of the great Qing empire. Other Europeans and the Americans would soon follow in Britain's wake and no state in the region could ignore the threat of the West.

The expansion of British interests and influence in East Asia did not end with the Treaty of Nanjing. Within a year they exacted a supplementary treaty from China that fixed tariff rates on the goods most important to British traders, with the extraordinary exception of opium which continued to be sold illegally. Of yet greater importance was the British insistence on "most-favored-nation treatment," a treaty-based guarantee that any privileges China granted to any other foreigners would automatically accrue to the British. This meant that in the years that followed, when the Americans or the French or any other foreigners wrung further rights or privileges from their hard-pressed Chinese counterparts, British citizens would share in these new concessions.

The most-favored-nation provision paid off almost immediately, when the American treaty was signed in 1844. The Americans obtained the right to acquire land on which to build churches and hospitals—the goal of one Peter Parker, a medical missionary who served as the interpreter for the American negotiator—and extraterritoriality, a clause that declared that Americans who committed crimes in China were subject only to the jurisdiction of American officials in accordance with American law. In other words, wherever an American stood in China was the equivalent of (extra) American territory. Without any additional negotiations, the British enjoyed the same privileges and immunities. A notable exception to this exemption of Americans from Chinese law applied to opium traders who would be left to the none too tender mercies of the Chinese legal system. The historian Akira Iriye has labeled this use of the most-favored-nation clause "multilateral imperialism," describing a practice that emerged in the course of the nineteenth century wherein no foreign power absorbed China into its empire, but all of the great powers shared in the infringements on Chinese sovereignty, the "unequal treaties" against which later Chinese patriots would rail.[2]

The Daoguang emperor and his advisers had been forced by British military superiority to accept an opening to the West they did not want, treaty relationships they found objectionable, and treaty provisions they hoped to evade. Unfortunately for the Qing, internal affairs of state were also drifting out of their control. In mid-century rebellion after rebellion wracked the Chinese polity. The White Lotus rebels had arisen in north central China in the late eighteenth century and continued to be a problem in the nineteenth century—a problem quickly overshadowed by the Nian and then the Taiping uprisings. In mid-century Peking lost control of much of the country. China was fortunate not to disintegrate or to be carved up by the Europeans and Americans. But neither the court nor local officials had the strength to escape additional foreign demands and the failure to comply with these led to renewed foreign intervention.

Fortunately for the Qing, their British tormentors were otherwise occupied for much of the 1850s. In 1852, war broke out anew in Burma. Tensions between the Burmese and the British had mounted in the 1830s

MAP 21. TREATY PORTS, C. 1842.

After Warren I. Cohen, *America's Response to China*, 3rd ed., p. 14; see also Spence, *Modern China*, p. 159.

as the Burmese court rebounded from its defeat and aspired to regain its lost provinces. British diplomats and merchants were harassed, but British resources were strained first in India and then in China. No additional military encounters were desired. But by 1852, the governor-general of India was able to focus on the Burmese situation. He had adequate military resources at his disposal and was irritated sufficiently to use them. His warships and troops easily eliminated Burmese land and sea opposition and annexed yet another Burmese province. Although the Burmese court refused to recognize the annexation, peace was restored in 1853. Eventually the annexed provinces were redesignated British Burma, with its capital at Rangoon. For one more generation, Upper Burma remained under Burmese control.

Over the next few years the British were preoccupied with a major conflict in Europe and the Middle East, the Crimean War, in which the Russians were their principal opponents. And in 1857 the Sepoy Mutiny in India disrupted their forces in Asia. All this time, China was being torn apart by the Taiping Rebellion, notable not only for the extraordinary suffering of the Chinese people, among whom as many as forty million died between 1851 and the defeat of the rebels in 1864, but also because its titular leader had been inspired by Christian teachings and imagined himself the younger brother of Jesus. His alleged Christianity aroused brief interest in the West, but his doctrinal differences with established Christian practices soon cost him any support that might have come from that quarter.

As millions of Chinese died in internal strife, the British in China pressed their advantage, insisting on revising the treaties to expand foreign privileges, open as much of the country as possible to foreign trade, and legalize the sale of opium. Fearful of losing whatever pretensions to power and legitimacy they still retained, the Qing refused to yield. The Europeans and Americans found the governor-general at Guangzhou especially recalcitrant. Hampered initially by their participation in the Crimean War and then by the great mutiny in India, it was late 1857 before the British were prepared to act decisively, with French and at least nominal American military assistance. Anglo-French forces stormed Guangzhou, took the city, and shipped the offending official off to Calcutta where he remained until his death. An Anglo-French fleet, accompanied by American and Russian diplomats, sailed once more for the approaches to the northern city of Tianjin, and quickly positioned themselves for an attack on Peking itself. To forestall the attack, the emperor agreed to accept a new treaty.

The treaty dictated by the British at Tianjin was designed to strip the Chinese of all protection against foreign exploitation. They were forced to open eleven new treaty ports and to allow foreign vessels to sail up the Yangzi, into the heart of China. Foreigners were granted the right to travel in the interior; missionaries and their converts had to be tolerated everywhere. The Chinese tariff was fixed at a minimal five percent and the import of opium was legalized by including the drug on the tariff schedule, despite Chinese laws precluding its sale or use. The Chinese government's control of its national economy was further limited, as was its ability to keep out what it considered to be subversive Western ideas.

Foreigners could go where they pleased, do as they pleased, independent of Chinese law, with foreign troops and gunboats never far behind. British and French guns forced the Chinese to accept these terms, but the American and Russian diplomats present at Tianjin were quick to demand equal rights for their own countrymen.

One further provision, especially repugnant to the court, required the Qing to accept foreign ambassadors resident in Peking. If a Chinese emperor was required to treat foreigners in his capital as the representatives of his equals, his stature among his own people would be diminished, the legitimacy of his rule brought into question. Desperately the emperor and his advisers looked for a way to evade this humiliation. They revived illusions of using Americans to mediate, but quickly realized it was too late. They dared to hope that the foreigners would be satisfied with the commercial opportunities they had gained. Finally, the emperor ordered the repair and strengthening of Tianjin's defenses as soon as the Anglo-French fleet departed. The Qing would be ready when they returned.

When the Western diplomats arrived in 1859 to exchange ratifications of their treaties, they found the Chinese evasive. Once again they attacked the approaches to Tianjin—and were rudely surprised. This time they were beaten back in heavy fighting, during which Chinese gunners wounded the British admiral, prompting the Americans to come to the rescue. Four British gunboats sank in the battle. Outraged, the British and French returned in 1860 with an enormous fleet and nearly 20,000 men, many of them Indians. Overcoming the opposition of imperial forces, they entered Peking in October. Further angered by Chinese tactics, the chief British negotiator ordered the destruction of the emperor's magnificent summer palace. There could be doubt no longer that the Qing emperor had lost the ability to protect the Chinese people from foreign exploitation, as indeed he had thus far been unable to cope with domestic challenges to his rule. To the extent that the Chinese had imposed their conception of world order on the region, the West would now impose its own, a treaty-based system imposed first on the Chinese and subsequently on much of the rest of East Asia.

One example of Asian accommodation to the changing structure of the international relations of the region was Siam's decision to open itself to the West without waiting to be coerced. Thai rulers had been very uneasy about European intentions since their experience in the seventeenth century with France. In the eighteenth and early nineteenth century, Americans as well as various Europeans indicated interest in trade and missionary activity. Individuals met with occasional success, but no Western state foisted itself upon Siam. In mid-nineteenth century, a new Thai king, Rama IV—upon whose life the popular entertainment "The King and I" was based—reached out to the West. He studied Western science, and English, taught by American missionaries, became his second language. Appreciative of British power, suspicious of French intentions, he was eager for friendly relations with Great Britain. In 1855 he agreed to a treaty with Queen Victoria's envoy that provided for a fixed and very low tariff, legalized the sale of opium, duty-free, provided for a resident British consul at Bangkok and gave the British extraterritorial legal privileges. These treaty privileges and rights were rapidly extended to other Western nations over the next few years, but British capital and British influence remained dominant as Siam maneuvered to spare itself the fate of its Burmese, Chinese, Malay, and Vietnamese neighbors.

TABLE 8.1.   Some Notable Events in the Years 1800–1866
(Events in boldface are mentioned in text)

British burn Washington, D.C.	1814
Congress of Vienna	1814–1815
Napoleon defeated at Waterloo	1815
Amherst mission to China	**1816**
Latin American states achieve independence	1816–1825
British take Singapore	**1819**
Terranova Case	**1821**
First Anglo-Burmese War	**1824–1826**
First Anglo-Ashanti (modern Ghana) War	1824–1827
Great Trek of the Boers in southern Africa	1835–1837
Coronation of Queen Victoria	1838
Opium War	**1839–1842**
Taiping Rebellion	**1850–1864**
Commodore Perry at Edo	**1853–1854**
Crimean War	1854–1856
Sepoy (Indian) Mutiny	1857
American Civil War	1861–1865

| Bismarck becomes prime minister of Prussia | 1862 |
| **French driven off by Koreans** | **1866** |

The Yanks Are Coming

Students of American history will recall that one stimulus toward revolution in the late eighteenth century had been discontent among New England merchants with the monopoly the East India Company enjoyed over trade with China. They will also remember history's most famous tea party, when in December 1773 a group of "patriots" dumped a Company cargo of Chinese tea into Boston harbor. Almost as soon as word reached New York that independence had been won and a treaty of peace signed with Great Britain, the *Empress of China* set sail for Guangzhou, arriving in 1784.

In the years that followed, individual American entrepreneurs swarmed over East Asia, searching for opportunities to trade. They appeared in the Indian Ocean and on the islands and mainland of Southeast Asia. During the Napoleanic Wars in Europe, Americans replaced the Dutch for the annual run to Japan. And, of course, they elbowed their way into the Canton system, peddling opium—usually Turkish—in competition with the British. In the early years of the republic, however, the government of the United States played a minimal role, primarily stimulating trade with tariffs favorable to American shipping. There was no contact between it and any of the governments of Asia. Some Americans chafed at the restrictions with which the Chinese and other Asian peoples obstructed their opportunities, but their government lacked both the will and the power to intervene on their behalf.

The initial attempt by the United States to regularize its relations with East Asian countries came in the early 1830s. As early as 1800 a few of its warships, the East India Squadron, had sailed into Asian waters in search of pirates and to offer a modicum of protection to merchant vessels. In 1815 American merchants in Guangzhou had petitioned Congress for a consul, but to no avail. A U.S. naval vessel appeared at the entrance to the Pearl River in 1819, but was denied provisions and sent away by Chinese officials—much to the relief of American merchants who feared it would attempt to force its way up river to Guangzhou and jeopardize their trade. In 1832, several American warships sailed to East Asia, primarily to punish Sumatrans who had despoiled an American merchantman. On board one of these was an emissary of the president of the United States, empowered to seek treaties with Siam and Vietnam. He later received instructions to proceed to Japan as well. He succeeded in obtaining a modest treaty with Siam that facilitated trade on a basis comparable to what the British already enjoyed, but failed in Vietnam. He chose not to try Japan on this voyage, but did plan to make that effort when he returned to Asia in 1836. He became ill in Siam, however, and died shortly afterward in Macao. At the outset of the Opium War, the only government to government relations the United States enjoyed with an Asian state were those with Siam.

In the 1830s, the first American missionaries also arrived in Guangzhou in the guise of merchants and physicians. Propagating Christianity was illegal in China, punishable by death, but those who heard the call went anyway, adding a new and increasingly important dimension to the interests of the United States in China. In their quest to find a place for the Chinese in the Kingdom of God, the American Protestant missionaries learned their language, studied their culture, and for many years were the principal interpreters of China for the American people. It was in the churches that many Americans absorbed what little they knew about China.

As the Opium War unfolded, American merchants took advantage of the distress of their British colleagues to extend their own share of the market. Uncertain as to how the war would develop, they asked their government to send a commissioner to negotiate a commercial treaty and for some warships to protect them if things got out of hand. The East India Squadron was dispatched to Guangzhou where its commander found the Americans in no danger and refrained from interfering in the Anglo-Chinese war. In due course, he made contact with Qing officials who had visions of using the American barbarians against the English barbarians.[3] The American persistently urged the Manchus and Chinese he met to extend trade privileges to his wards and the Qing kept holding out the promise of such privileges in an effort to win the relatively well-behaved Americans over to their side. When the war ended, the Qing court decided it would be to its advantage to give the Americans the same privileges exacted from China by the British. In November 1843, the emperor declared that since the British had been allowed to trade, "the United States and others should naturally be permitted to trade without discrimination, in order to show Our tranquilizing purpose."[4]

In general, American merchants in China were content to enjoy the rights and privileges for which the British had fought, but their government was not. If Great Britain had formal treaty relations with China, the United States would settle for no less. Moreover, the United States had concerns that had not been addressed by the British: American missionaries wanted the right to build churches and proselytize in China and the United States was not satisfied with the workings of the Chinese criminal justice system. An American envoy, Caleb Cushing, was sent to China to get an American treaty.

In the negotiations that followed, the principal Qing goal was to keep the Americans from going to Peking and embarrassing the emperor. Once it was clear that Cushing's demand to travel to Peking was a bluff, agreement on the real issues was obtained with relative ease. The Chinese were quick to agree to trading privileges they had already offered. The right to build churches in ports opened by the treaties with the West was gained perhaps largely because of the ties between the Qing negotiator and Dr. Peter Parker, Cushing's interpreter, who had treated the official's parents in his clinic. At least as important, and ultimately more offensive to the Chinese, was the grant of extraterritoriality in the American treaty, a right other foreigners would acquire through the most-favored-nation clause in their treaties.

The first American minister to China told the U.S. Senate in 1858 that the insistence on extraterritoriality was as evil as the opium trade. This was largely because, until the mid-1850s, the American consul charged with holding Americans who committed crimes in China accountable to U.S. laws was selected from among the ranks of merchants in each port and was often involved in criminal activities, such as the selling of opium. Even if he had been more inclined to enforce the law, the failure of the U.S. government to provide any jails, would have posed an insurmountable obstacle.

Extraterritoriality was unquestionably an affront to Chinese sovereignty and in the early years a disgrace in implementation—or lack thereof. There was, however, a record of terrifying encounters with Chinese legal customs that drove the Americans and other foreigners to demand it. The two most notorious cases involved accidental homicides committed by sailors, one on a British ship and one on an American. Both were executed despite assurances to the contrary by the Chinese and despite the fact that the death penalty was not the Chinese custom in such cases. In both instances, Chinese officials at Guangzhou seemed intent upon demonstrating to the foreigners that they dictated the terms of contact.

The American case, in 1821, involved a sailor named Terranova on the *Emily*, out of Baltimore. He was alleged to be responsible for the death of a boatwoman struck by debris swept off the deck of the *Emily*. When the Chinese pronounced Terranova guilty and demanded that he be turned over to them, the Americans initially refused. Chinese officials responded by stopping trade and arresting the Chinese security merchant who was deeply in debt to the American traders. Faced with financial disaster, the Americans agreed to allow Terranova to be taken by the local authorities, who promptly executed him and commended the Americans for their submissiveness. In 1821, Americans at Guangzhou feared the capriciousness of Chinese legal practice, but deemed themselves powerless to resist. In 1844, when Cushing was negotiating his treaty, the balance of power in East Asia was shifting and Americans no longer felt compelled to tolerate a legal system they considered arbitrary and unjust. In substituting extraterritoriality for the Chinese courts, however, they created a legal structure that in practice was at least as unfair to China as Chinese authorities had been to them. And, of course, the privilege of extraterritoriality was extended to all other nations whose treaties included most-favored-nation clauses.

In the years between the founding of the treaty system in the early 1840s and the conclusion of the American civil war in 1865, Americans in China and their government in Washington generally followed the British lead. From time to time various Chinese noted that the Americans were less belligerent, but they eventually understood that it was a relative lack of power—not greater goodwill—that accounted for American behavior. Whatever the British and other foreigners gained by force, the Americans quickly claimed by virtue of the most-favored-nation clause in their first treaty, a practice some historians have labeled "jackal diplomacy." In 1851 a shrewd Qing official warned that the Americans "do no more than follow in England's wake and utilize her strength."[5]

In the opening of Japan to the West, however, the Americans took the lead. As American whalers and merchant ships roamed the Pacific, interest mounted in establishing some level of formal contact, perhaps some sort of arrangement for the treatment and repatriation of ship-wrecked sailors. The Protestant church also began to look toward Japan as a potential field for missionary activity. In 1837, an American merchant in Guangzhou sent a ship to Edo to return Japanese castaways, hoping to gain entry through this humanitarian act, but the Japanese opened fire, driving the ship away. By the mid-1840s, the United States had expanded to the Pacific, and the bumptious republic was threatening all who got in its way, such as the British in the northwest territories it claimed, and the Mexicans whose lands north of the Rio Grande Yankee settlers were overrunning. It was prepared to be more assertive in East Asia as well, as demonstrated in 1846 at the port of Tourane (now Danang) in central Vietnam when the *U.S.S. Constitution* shelled the city in an effort to win release of a missionary imprisoned there.[6]

In 1846, Commodore James Biddle led the first official U.S. naval expedition to Japan. Efforts to negotiate with Japanese authorities failed and Biddle's attempts to ingratiate himself with the Japanese were apparently perceived as weakness. Biddle was himself treated rudely, jostled quite possibly by intention, and sent away with nothing to show for the adventure. It was evident that the Japanese had no interest in providing new trading opportunities or in allowing foreigners to think they could be intimidated. They were fully aware of events in China and determined not to give foreigners an opportunity to repeat the process in Japan. Japan would control the terms of contact with the West and it was quite content with the existing arrangements with the Dutch at Deshima.

A second American naval force sailed into Edo Bay in 1849, determined to avoid humiliation by behaving belligerently. Designed primarily to rescue shipwrecked American sailors, this mission succeeded. The lesson drawn by the U.S. Navy was that the Japanese were more responsive to demonstrations of power than to polite efforts at diplomacy. By 1852, the United States was ready to press the issue. The Americans had acquired ports on the west coast of North America and Japan lay athwart the Great Circle route to the coast of China. Japanese ports could provide useful waystations for shipping between the west coast of the United States and all parts of East Asia. In addition, having surrendered the dominance the great American sailing vessels, the clipper ships, had enjoyed in the 1840s to the steamships of mid-century, the voyagers were also interested in coaling facilities. Commodore Matthew Perry accepted the assignment to open Japan, by diplomatic effort if possible, with cannon if necessary.

Perry arrived at Edo Bay in July 1853 after a display of force in the Ryukyus and a voyage to the Bonin Islands, south of Japan, which he claimed for the United States. He had four ships, two of them steamers, under his command and the Japanese, forewarned by the Dutch and by word of his behavior in the Ryukyus, quickly perceived that he was not to be trifled with. They had no choice but to accede to his insistence that they accept a letter from the president of the United States to the emperor, whereupon he sailed off, promising to return the following year for the response.

In February 1854, Perry's squadron, now doubled in size, returned to Edo. In his absence the shogun had died and the dominant figure in the shogunate had taken the unprecedented step of consulting all the daimyo. With varying degrees of understanding of events in the outside world and varying estimates of the nation's ability to resist foreign pressure, the daimyo were divided in their advice. Some advocated the use of force to drive Perry away, a substantial minority were willing to offer some trade concessions, and the remainder, while opposed to trade, thought it necessary to make some concessions to postpone a military showdown until Japan's defenses had been strengthened. The Japanese negotiators tried to rid themselves of Perry with a polite refusal of the president's request. Perry left no doubt in their minds that he would not be put off. Finally, after a month of sparring and veiled threats by Perry, the Japanese signed the Treaty of Kanagawa. It was not a commercial treaty, but rather a modestly enhanced shipwreck convention. Nonetheless, it began the process of forcing Japan into the new, Western-dominated international order in East Asia.

Perry's treaty won for the United States access to two minor ports where its ships might stop briefly for provisioning and the exchange of goods. A consular official was to be allowed to reside in one of these, Shimoda, and the Japanese promised not to mistreat any Americans shipwrecked on their shores. Most important for the future was the provision for most-favored-nation treatment. And then, one after another, the Europeans came—the British, the Russians, and the Dutch, adding extraterritoriality and opening additional ports. Slowly, but inexorably, change was being imposed upon a reluctant Japan.

It was another American, Townsend Harris, who succeeded in getting the Japanese to take the next great step, opening the country to trade, to foreign residence in the treaty ports, and providing for the exchange of diplomatic missions. Harris arrived in Shimoda in 1856 as the first foreign consul to take up residence on Japanese soil. Without any military support, he endured a year of isolation and physical threats before he made any progress, another six months before he won an audience with the shogun, and seven further months—a total of more than two years—before he persuaded the Japanese to sign his treaty. It was only a matter of weeks before the Europeans, the British, Dutch, French, and Russians, had their treaties also. Japanese leaders had concluded, the Great Elder Ii Naosuke foremost among them, that conciliation was the wisest course available to them. In February 1860, a large Japanese diplomatic mission left for Washington.[7]

A few weeks after the Japanese embassy sailed off, Ii Naosuke was assassinated, at least in part for his role in opening Japan to increased foreign influence and presence. A weak government was unable to cope with economic dislocation and intense antiforeignism that swept the country, even among those most familiar with western science and military technology. Foreign residents were endangered, the secretary of the American consul murdered, the British legation attacked, and in 1863 the daimyo of Choshu had his forts open fire on foreign shipping, in effect closing the Strait of Shimoneseki between the principal islands of Honshu and Kyushu. Although the Americans were in the midst of their devastating civil war, fighting for the survival of their nation, they sent a warship to join the Western squadron that reopened the strait in 1864.

As the shogunate unraveled and Japan struggled to put its house in order, the United States ceased to play a major role in its affairs, resuming its place as a minor power in the region. Individual American merchants and adventurers could be found everywhere, missionaries proliferated in China and in smaller numbers elsewhere, and a scattering of American diplomats and naval officers could be found in all the treaty ports. An American naval force even attempted to force open Korea in 1871, but was too small to overcome Korean resistance. Washington, however, was preoccupied with the demands of civil war and reconstruction. Nonetheless, the country's need for labor to develop its western precincts resulted in new and unimagined links to East Asia as Chinese coolies crossed the Pacific by the thousands.

TABLE 8.2.   Some Notable Figures of the Period 1800–1865
(Names in boldface are mentioned in text)

Andrew Jackson	1767–1845
Prince Metternich of Austria	1773–1859
Simon Bolivar	1783–1830
Lin Zexu	**1784–1851**
Lord Palmerston	**1784–1865**
Shaka, King of the Zulus	1787–1828
Rama IV of Siam	**1804–1868**
Guiseppe Garibaldi	1807–1882
Abraham Lincoln	1809–1865
Charles Darwin	1809–1882
Ii Naosuke	**1815–1860**
Karl Marx	1818–1883
Victoria, Queen of England	1819–1901

France's Quest for Glory

France had faired poorly in its struggle with Great Britain in America and in India. But before the eighteenth century had ended, Napoleon had emerged to lead the nation to the near conquest of all of Europe. His defeat at Waterloo in 1815 ended that dream, but France remained a great power, determined to play that role in world affairs. East Asia was marginal among French concerns; nonetheless France sought and obtained influence there, sometimes in cooperation with the British, as in China, sometimes in competition, as in Southeast Asia.

French overtures to Vietnam in the 1820s were rejected rudely. Vietnamese leaders refused to sign a commercial treaty and in 1826 terminated formal relations with France. The emperor who had ascended to the throne in 1820 was hostile to Christianity and began the systematic persecution of missionaries and their Vietnamese converts. The outbreak of the Opium War in 1839 appears to have led him to reconsider, but he died in 1841 and his successor, oblivious to the evidence of Western power, continued to mistreat foreign missionaries and frustrate traders. In addition to the action of the *U.S.S. Constitution*, a number of

French warships threatened Vietnam and two of them were attacked in 1847.

In the 1850s, tensions between Vietnam and France intensified. In 1856 a French missionary was tortured and executed by the Vietnamese and in 1857 the emperor had the leading Spanish missionary killed. Neither the French nor the Spanish were willing to tolerate such abuses any longer. Both had forces nearby, but the Vietnamese court was undeterred. French demands for religious freedom, commercial opportunity, and a diplomatic resident at Hue were brushed aside—as the French had anticipated. Late in the summer of 1858, French forces that had completed their mission against China joined Spanish forces from Manila and landed at Tourane. Hindered by disease and short of supplies, the Europeans moved on to Saigon. Renewed fighting in China drew away a substantial part of the French contingent, but a small garrison held the city for a year until reinforcements arrived and seized control of a large part of southern Vietnam before the end of 1861.

The Vietnamese were forced to cede several southern provinces to France, in addition to paying a large indemnity, promising religious toleration, and opening several ports to French trade. France had a new colony, over which it maintained a tenuous hold in the face of Vietnamese rebellions and reservations in Paris about the wisdom of an East Asian empire. In a few years, the French posted to Vietnam expanded their responsibilities greatly. In 1864 they forced a French protectorate on the king of Cambodia and bought off their Thai rivals for control of that country by giving them two Cambodian provinces, including Angkor with its extraordinary ruins. In 1866 they annexed three more provinces in southern Vietnam and began to look northward for a river route to the trade of western China. Only the outbreak of the Franco-Prussian War in 1870 preserved a semblance of Vietnamese independence for a few more years.

Mistreatment of Catholic priests had provided the rationale for French action against both China and Vietnam. Apparently perceiving themselves to be the military arm of the Vatican, French forces attacked Korea in 1866 to avenge the execution of priests. Lacking a substantial landing force, it is unlikely that they began with great expectations, but had the Koreans cowered before them, they very likely would have demanded at least the opening of trade. In the event, after emptying their cannon on Korean fortifications at the entrance to the Han River, they were driven off, failing to establish contact with authorities at the capital.

Russia as a Pacific Power

To the north, the Russians had been nibbling away at the borders of the Qing empire, seeking contacts with Japan, and reaching across to America. In the eighteenth century, when seaborne trade was restricted to Guangzhou, the Russians did comparatively well trading overland. At mid-century, they were exporting goods to China probably worth twice what the British were able to sell there.[8] And Russian adventurers and officials pushed eastward across the Bering Straits to Kodiak Island and Alaska. In 1799, Russia formed the Russian-American Company, modeled after the British East India Company. As Russia joined the ranks of great powers in Europe, Russian leaders were determined to extend their influence to the Pacific as well.

A series of efforts to establish relations with Japan failed in the late eighteenth and early nineteenth centuries. One envoy who sailed into Nagasaki harbor in 1804 was detained for about eight months and sent off with the admonition never to return. A senior naval officer captured while exploring the Kurile Islands in 1811 was imprisoned for two years. Russian attempts to enter the seaborne trade at Guangzhou were similarly rebuffed by the Chinese who reminded them that their treaties allowed only for overland commerce.

The Opium War, in which the Russians did not participate, nonetheless marked an important turning point in their relations with China. On the one hand, it revealed that China was vulnerable, that the balance of power had shifted; on the other, it left Russians at a disadvantage in trade opportunities. The treaty system imposed on the Chinese by the British and Americans conveyed access to ports and granted privileges that were not extended to the Russians, whose treaties with China did not provide for most-favored-nation treatment. Moreover, the sea routes used by the British were more economical than the overland routes to which the Russians were limited. Initially, all the Russians could do was to press for more overland trade concessions—some of which were granted by the Chinese in 1851. The Russians remained determined to gain entry to the treaty ports and privileges like that of extraterritoriality, but the Chinese chased them off when they sailed into Shanghai in 1853 and continued to deny them access to other open ports.

The outbreak of war in the Crimea briefly stalled the Russian advance in East Asia. Indeed Russian forces in Siberia were attacked by an Anglo-French force in 1854—an obvious indication that the so-called Crimean War was not limited to the Crimea. Seeking to open up still another front, the Russians appealed to the Qing to attack British India. In the midst of the Taiping Rebellion, however, the Qing were not looking for foreign adventure. On the other hand, the war did not prevent the Russians from sailing into Edo Bay in the wake of the Americans and British to get their own treaty with Japan in 1855.

After the Crimean War, the Russians, like the British and French, were ready to give the Chinese some unwanted attention. As the Anglo-French force attacked Guangzhou, the Russians hoped to take advantage of the Chinese practice of playing "barbarians" off against each other, of divide and rule. Distinguishing themselves from China's tormentors, the Russians tried to gain favorable boundary agreements, new trade privileges, and rights of residence in the treaty ports. Finding the Chinese unyielding, they switched tactics, joining the British, French, and Americans demanding treaty revisions at Tianjin in 1858. At this point the Qing returned to form and agreed to negotiate boundaries with the Russians in an unsuccessful effort to divide the offending powers. In May 1858 the Russians and the Qing negotiators signed the Treaty of Aigun settling the boundary question, but that did not deter the Russians from rejoining the other powers, and acquiring a treaty with a most-favored-nation clause that gained them equal access to Chinese ports. A couple of months later, the Russian envoy crossed over to Japan where he obtained a treaty roughly equivalent to that of Townsend Harris—and the Russians were full participants in the new international order in East Asia.

And Then There Were the Dutch

By the conclusion of the Napoleanic Wars, the Dutch had no pretensions to being a major power or a major player anywhere. Only British concern for a revived France allowed the Dutch to recover their empire in Indonesia. This geopolitical stratagem outweighed the efforts to the contrary of Sir Thomas Raffles—the famed Raffles of Singapore—who was appalled by the brutality of Dutch colonial practices. With Raffles stalling, it was 1819 before the Dutch had regained their prewar position in the islands.

Once back at Batavia, the Dutch found that the trade of the region was largely in the hands of British and American merchants. The colonial administration was underfinanced, and had only a small army and no navy to support it. It faced widespread unrest not easily suppressed. The new Dutch officials attempted to improve conditions, to protect the natives from local rulers as well as from foreign predators, but succeeded only in banning the slave trade. In 1825 an insurrection exploded on Java as a result of discontent with land policies, taxes, and hatred of the Chinese who were employed as tax farmers. Europeans and Chinese were massacred in central Java and it took the Dutch five years to pacify the rebels. To prevent recurrence, the Dutch annexed additional lands around the island. To meet their expenses, they turned their backs on the enlightened vision of free peasant cultivators and introduced a new practice, the "culture system," designed to force peasants to grow export crops, to be monopolized by the Dutch. In addition, the Dutch closed the areas they controlled to British, American, and other foreign imports: the market would be open only to the products of Dutch industry.

In 1830, as the war in Java wound down, the Dutch-dominated kingdom of the Netherlands came apart. Union with Belgium, an arrangement that followed the Napoleanic wars, collapsed as the Belgians revolted and, with French assistance, gained their independence. The cost of the struggle further impoverished Holland, resulting in efforts to squeeze as much out of Java as possible, to exploit the peasantry of Java for the benefit of its colonial masters in Europe. Events totally outside the Asian context brought extraordinary misery to the people of Java. Profit-bearing export crops multiplied over intense native opposition and far too often at the expense of rice cultivation, resulting in frequent famine. The peasants could not live on indigo, sugar, coffee, tea, tobacco, and spices and too often were denied the opportunity to grow enough to eat.

In mid-century Holland, there was no shortage of liberal intellectuals and reformers willing to demand an end to the misery being inflicted on the people of Java, but they had little impact on events in the colony. In 1860, an extraordinary novel, *Max Havelaar*, contained the barely veiled story of a minor official's encounters with the horror of the culture system and briefly stirred the consciences of the Dutch people. But they

MAP 22. Western colonies in East Asia, c. 1880.
After Fairbank and Reischauer, *East Asia*, p. 410; see also Cohen,
America's Response, p. 40.

never came up with a satisfactory solution to their conflicting desires to improve the lot of the native peoples of Java *and* maintain and profit from their empire. Indeed, fearful of intrusion by the British or other foreign elements, the Dutch gradually extended their power over the whole of Indonesia.

Conclusion

Clearly the mid-nineteenth century was a watershed in the history of international relations. The East Asian international order over which China had been at least nominally dominant for thousands of years had been shattered. Western power had proved itself superior to that of Asia and had enabled a relative handful of Europeans and Americans to overcome the resistance of hundreds of millions of Asians. Advanced military technology, improvements in military discipline and supply, the coopting of native forces, especially from the Indian subcontinent, contributed mightily to Western success. Obviously, the erosion of central power in China and Japan also facilitated Western inroads. By 1870, most of East Asia had been opened to Western goods and the influence of Western ideas.

Some of the peoples of the region, most obviously those of Southeast Asia, had lost control of their territory, even of their lives. On the other hand, resistance to the Western-organized international system remained strong. Korea, into which Western influence dribbled indirectly from China, had repelled all efforts to force open its doors to trade with the Europeans and Americans. Japanese central authorities had concluded that a conciliatory—and dilatory—policy was the wisest response to evidence of Western might, but powerful provincial forces were determined to fight, to "expel the barbarians." China, crippled by internal strife, the Qing dynasty arguably dependent on Western support for its survival, retained its territorial integrity. Chinese students of statecraft and many Chinese officials were already laying the groundwork for a movement to strengthen the country and enable it to stand up to its foreign tormentors. For Siam, appeasement had worked, and skillful leadership gave its people reason to hope for their continued independence. The Vietnamese continued to resist French imperialism vigorously and everywhere else in Southeast Asia there were pockets of rebellion against the dominant Europeans.

In sum, the West had triumphed in its confrontation with East Asia. In some parts of the region, the position of Asians would continue to deteriorate. But the victory of the West was not final.

NINE

The Ascendance of Japan

In the last three decades of the nineteenth century, the West continued to rearrange the structure of the East Asian international order. All of the states of the region came under pressure. Indonesians, Burmese, and Vietnamese lost whatever semblance of independence they had managed to retain in their struggles against the Dutch, the British, and the French. The Filipino revolt against Spanish rule was swept up in the torrents of the war between Spain and the United States: the Filipinos rid themselves of a colonial power in a state of terminal decline only to become subjects of the rising American empire. All of the Western powers squeezed additional privileges out of China. In addition, the Russians took advantage of China's internal strife to avail themselves of more Chinese territory in the northwest and the French and Chinese fought a brief war that ended Chinese claims to suzerainty over Vietnam. Even Korea was drawn involuntarily into the new order, despite its successful resistance to French and American threats between 1866 and 1871.

The most striking story of the era, however, was the rapid recovery of Japan from the doldrums of the late Tokugawa years. It was Japan, in fact, that forced Korea to open its doors and came to dominate that country before the end of the century. It was Japan that became China's greatest tormentor. And it was Japan that rose to challenge the West's design for East Asia, repelling the Russian thrust into Korea and Manchuria in the early years of the twentieth century. In the fifty years that followed Perry's successful mission to Edo, the Japanese created a state powerful enough not only to stop the Russians, but also to win an alliance with Great Britain and to threaten the interests of the United States in the Pacific.

Restoration and Self-strengthening in China

The incredible chaos that ravaged China in mid-century, the cumulative impact of the Taiping, Nian, and Muslim rebellions, suggested the imminent collapse of the Qing dynasty. Although any diviner worth his or her upkeep would have surmised that the Qing had lost the mandate of heaven, the Qing held on through the first decade of the twentieth century.

Slowly the rebels were beaten back and destroyed and order restored. The Taipings were crushed in 1864 after the death of their leader and the loss of their capital at Nanjing. The Nian fought on until they were overrun in 1868. Muslim unrest, spreading from Yunnan in the southwest to Shensi, Gansu, and Chinese Turkestan in the northwest, never disappeared, but the organized rebellions were crushed by 1873.

The Qing court contributed little to its own survival. The heroes were provincial officials, Zeng Guofan, the most famous of them, and his lieutenants, Li Hongzhang and Zuo Zongtang—none of them Manchus. They received a little help from the West against the Taipings after Western diplomats concluded that their interests would be served best by a Qing government strong enough to meet its treaty obligations. The Western-officered Ever Victorious Army, for example, played a valuable role against the Taipings. The foreign-managed Inspectorate of Customs established in 1854 preserved customs revenues for the Qing when the Qing lost control of Shanghai. But Zeng and the scores of other Chinese officials who saw their way of life threatened by the Taipings were the pillars of success—the men who raised the armies and the money essential to beat back the rebels. Indeed, the Muslim rebels benefited from British support which extended their ability to hold out against Zuo's forces.

Zeng and most of his supporters perceived themselves to be Confucian traditionalists, determined to restore the preeminence of Confucian values in an orderly society. But they were not blind to the need for change if China was to preserve its independence and culture against foreign pressures. Cooperating with like-minded Manchus, they began the unending search for a way to adapt the sources of Western wealth and power to Chinese society. They wished to preserve the core of their civilization while selecting those elements of Western learning and technology essential to survival in the modern world. They were steering a course to be followed eventually by every Asian society confronted with nineteenth-century Western might. Along the way, the Confucian concern for government by virtue lost primacy.

The most obvious deficiency to be remedied was in military technology. China needed state-of-the-art warships and cannon. In the short run—and especially for use against the Taipings—these weapons and men with the skill to use them could be hired. On one occasion Prince Gong, the court's representative in foreign affairs, actually persuaded the British to provide him with a fleet of manned gunships, but a misunderstanding about command and control aborted this venture. The Chinese did succeed, however, in using mercenaries on a smaller scale.

For the future, China would have to be able to build ships and manufacture all necessary weapons itself. It would also require the capacity to train those who would make and those who would use the weapons. Again, China would have to begin by looking to foreigners for the machinery and the teachers. In 1864 Zeng Guofan sent Yung Wing, an extraordinary young Chinese who had been educated by missionaries and graduated from Yale University in 1854, back to the United States to purchase the machine tools needed for a modern arsenal. By 1868 the Chinese were able to build their own steamships. Several years later, Li Hongzhang endorsed Yung Wing's idea of sending young Chinese to the United States to prepare to attend the U.S. Military Academy at West Point and the Naval Academy at Annapolis. When the Americans denied the Chinese admission to their military academies, Li simply diverted his efforts to France and Germany, countries quite willing to train the next generation of Chinese military leaders. These were all elements of what came to be called the "self-strengthening" movement.

However grudgingly, the Qing court took steps to bring itself into line with Western diplomatic practices. In 1861 the Qing established the *Zongli Yamen*, a primitive foreign office, with Prince Gong, the emperor's brother, as de facto foreign minister. Within three years he and his staff were able to digest Wheaton's *Elements of International Law*, translated for them by an American missionary, and use it to win a case against Prussia, which had violated China's territorial waters by seizing Danish ships anchored near Tianjin. Of still greater importance was the gradual acceptance by the court of the value of sending officials abroad to gain a clear sense of the outside world. Qing diplomats had already been to Moscow and St. Petersburg, and in 1866 Prince Gong sent a senior Manchu official on a tour of Europe from which he returned prematurely, allegedly appalled by European customs.

A more successful effort to establish communications with those who controlled policy in the imperialist world came in 1868 when the retiring American minister to Peking, Anson Burlingame, led a Chinese mission to Washington, London, Paris, and Berlin. Prince Gong was realistic enough to understand that he could not hope to rid China of the treaty system the powers had imposed on it, but he hoped to persuade the West to ease the pace at which it was forcing change in China. Burlingame won the desired promises from British, German, and American leaders. Exceeding his instructions he even signed a treaty with the American secretary of state in which he obtained a promise that the United States would not interfere in the internal affairs of China.

Prince Gong was pushed aside in 1869 after a confrontation, unrelated to foreign affairs, with the Empress Dowager, the formidable Cixi. But China's engagement in international diplomacy never flagged. In 1871, the Qing government sent diplomatic representatives to London and Paris. In 1873, the court decided to end the perennial fuss Westerners raised over the requirement for performing the kowtow as a condition for gaining an audience with the Son of Heaven. The Qing agreed to allow foreign diplomats to follow the customs of their own countries when paying homage to the emperor. Macartney would have felt vindicated. In 1878, the Qing posted its first minister to Washington.

International trade, the underlying goal of the Western assault on China, increased as order was restored in the country. The treaty tariff, fixed at 5 percent, brought in revenue averaging four million ounces of silver annually in 1850 and more than twice that much by the 1870s. Tariff revenues doubled again in the 1880s indicating the rapid growth in Chinese consumption of foreign goods, but the market failed nonetheless to meet the expectations of foreign merchants. In an era of worldwide trade expansion, China's imports and exports were not commensurate with its size or population. Although foreigners in the treaty ports suspected official obstruction as the cause, the reality was that China after the dislocations of mid-century was relatively poor, that access to internal markets was hampered by a primitive transportation infrastructure, that foreign goods were still perceived as exotic to many Chinese—and opium still drained a substantial part of the monies available for imports.

Nonetheless, China had been drawn deeper into the world economy as the opening of the Suez Canal in 1869 halved the distance to European ports and the laying of cables connected Shanghai to the rest of the world telegraphically. Economic growth in the treaty ports was providing the country with both the entrepreneurial skills and the investment capital that were prerequisites to China playing a major role in international commerce.

One other element of the treaty system, the privileges granted missionaries to preach and build churches anywhere in China, proved exceptionally important, both a blessing and a curse for China.[1] Missionaries became the principal bridge between China and the West, interpreting China for audiences back home and explaining Western culture to the Chinese. Although their ultimate concern was the salvation of the heathen Chinese through conversion to Christianity, they came also as teachers and doctors. And they came in huge numbers, building thousands of churches, hospitals, schools, and orphanages in the last half of the nineteenth century. As teachers they provided access to Western knowledge, to languages and history as well as mathematics and science. They translated textbooks in a wide range of subjects. And as the Chinese began to create their own schools for Western learning, missionaries often served as faculty. As doctors, they added new lore to the wonders accomplished by practioners of Chinese medicine. In brief, their contribution to China was enormous.

On the other hand, their efforts to bring Christianity to China threatened the existing social order. To the extent that missionaries insisted that their converts renounce ancestor worship, they were isolating them from one of the fundamental elements of Chinese culture. Their attacks on other traditional Chinese practices, such as footbinding of women, were subversive, as was their insistence on educating women and generally encouraging feminism. They interfered in local politics and judicial proceedings to protect the interests of their parishioners. Their actions constituted a challenge to the local gentry, accustomed to presiding over their communities. And perhaps worst of all, when tensions between missionaries and the local people erupted into violence, foreign gunboats and foreign troops often intervened—or forced Qing officials to exact retribution. Despite their great contribution to China's goal of self-strengthening, the missionaries were in China as beneficiaries of the hated "unequal treaties."

Perhaps the most brutal reminder of the tensions the missionaries created was the "Tianjin massacre" of 1870. As in many other locales, hostile Chinese in Tianjin spread scurrilous rumors about the missionaries' perverse practices and unfriendly crowds frequently harassed and unnerved those in the churches. Unlike cities and towns of the interior, Tianjin had a French consul in residence, a man who considered himself responsible for protecting the Catholic community. Unable to gain satisfaction from the local magistrate, he attempted to shoot him, killing a bystander instead. An outraged mob killed the consul and went on a rampage. They also killed several French families, burned Tianjin's new Catholic church, and raided a convent where they murdered the nuns they found inside. Obviously, the French government could not tolerate this treatment of its nationals; nor could the Qing government fail to meet French demands. A putative investigation led to the execution of Chinese equal in number to the foreigners killed, the exile of senior officials, and payment by China of a huge indemnity. On this occasion, China's involvement in world affairs worked to her advantage: the outbreak of the Franco-Prussian war in 1870 prevented France from humiliating China further. Nothing about the incident or its resolution was likely to result in a warmer welcome for the missionaries.

In one other striking way the Chinese became involved intimately with the outside world—through large-scale emigration across the Pacific, as well as to more accessible destinations in Southeast Asia. By the time Burlingame undertook his mission to Washington in 1868, there were already more than 100,000 Chinese in the United States. Within a few years there were as many in Peru—and tens of thousands more working on the sugar plantations of Cuba and Hawaii. Almost all of these were men, almost all of them were indentured laborers, and many of them died in foreign lands, fatalities added to the numbers lost in the transoceanic voyages which often equaled the horrors of the notorious "middle passage" of African slaves being transported across the Atlantic a century or more before.

Like the Western missionaries who came to China, the Chinese who migrated to the West served as cultural interpreters and icons. They provided the only link to China most people in the West ever had. In the United States in particular, the results of the interaction between the Chinese and the Americans of European ancestry were unfortunate. The Chinese were perceived by those who preceded them as sojourners, men who came to make their fortune and return to China, who had no intention of becoming Americans. In the "Chinatowns" that sprang up in various cities, they clung together and continued to speak Chinese, eat Chinese food, and join lineage and work associations imported from China.

Far from their ancestral tablets and their women, they developed a sub-culture in which opium smoking, gambling, and prostitution were more widely practiced than they would have been at home. In addition to appearing so exotic, to deviating from community norms of behavior, they were alleged to be willing to work for wages lower than those demanded by immigrants from Europe. By the time Burlingame had reached Washington with his mission in 1868, the American image of the Chinese was not attractive.

Nor, given the way in which they were mistreated in the West, did the Chinese have particularly favorable impressions of their hosts. Violence against the Chinese was all too common. Beyond what they endured in transit and the subhuman conditions in which they were often forced to work, individual Chinese were subjected to beatings and humiliations—and occasionally murdered. They kept coming because their native villages had nothing to offer them, because they were deceived as to the opportunities and working conditions that awaited them, and not a few because they had been kidnapped by labor contractors. "Coolie" labor became a substitute for slavery in the post-Civil War United States and elsewhere in the Western Hemisphere.

The Qing government, as it stepped gingerly into the world of Western diplomacy, was forced to put the oversight of emigrants on its agenda. Westerners had come to China in violation of its wishes and its laws. When these foreigners were treated as barbarians, contemptuously, the Western powers demanded that they be treated as equals and used force to impose Western values on China. Most Chinese who went to the Americas had been recruited and played an important role in the industrialization of the United States and in the development of several Latin American states. And in the West, where Westerners controlled the terms of contact, the Chinese were treated brutally—and the Chinese had no gunboats to send across the Pacific. Once the Qing became aware of these conditions—and once they understood that to tolerate the mistreatment of Chinese overseas was to invite contempt—they attempted to regulate the coolie trade at home and to use diplomacy to win better treatment for Chinese abroad. But a weak government had limited success on both counts.

Whether Qing statesmen focused on national defense, on issues of trade and industry, or the interaction of Chinese and foreigners at home or abroad, it was clear to all that self-strengthening was essential. Only a strong China could be assured of its security, its independence, its territorial integrity, and its ability to win equitable treatment in its economic affairs, and its contacts with other peoples. Confucian virtue would not be enough, nor would the outside world tremble any longer in the shadow of the once mighty Qing empire. The critical question was whether China could act soon enough to protect its interests. Much would depend on the quality of its leadership in the last quarter of the nineteenth century—and, sadly, it was found wanting.

The Meiji Restoration

The arrival of the Western warships, followed by diplomats and merchants, served as the catalyst for the destruction of the Tokugawa shogunate. The bakufu had confronted the Western challenge and, in the minds of most Japanese, it had failed. Its tactics of conciliation and delay had prevented the disaster that had overtaken China, but that was not good enough: Americans and Europeans had posted themselves on Japanese soil. And the newcomers were not nearly as docile, as subservient as the Dutch. What was happening in China could still occur in Japan unless the Japanese pulled themselves together and expelled them. This perception of an external threat to the Japanese polity, to the Japanese way of life, was the most powerful influence on Japanese society in the first fifteen or twenty years after Perry sailed into Edo Bay.

Fortunately, Japan's internal divisions never evolved into a conflict on the scale of the Taiping Rebellion to dissipate the energies of its people and distract the minds of its leaders. Perhaps equally as fortunate was the fact that the Western powers were preoccupied with events in China in the late 1850s and early 1860s. But after the assassination of Ii Naosuke in 1860, it was apparent that the bakufu lacked the leadership to cope with the foreign crisis. Increasingly, the daimyo looked to the imperial court, to the emperor, as an alternative, as a symbol around which they could rally. Eager to be rid of both the shogunate and the foreign presence, their rallying cry became "revere the emperor, expel the barbarian." Roving samurai attacked foreigners and proponents of conciliation. As foreign trade and financial practices began to disrupt the Japanese economy, unrest mounted and civil war was not inconceivable.

The early 1860s were marked by the rivalry between the Choshu and Satsuma hans, both distant from the sources of Tokugawa strength. Each of these was a relatively wealthy, major military force, blessed with strong leadership. Each sought to undermine the bakufu, win the favor of the imperial court, and rally the nation behind efforts to drive Americans and Europeans out of the country. As they maneuvered against the shogunate and each other, their leaders came to realize that their antagonism was an obstacle to achievement of their goals, that they were playing into the hands of the shogunate. Divided, neither could win. In 1866, they allied secretly and Satsuma allowed Choshu to defeat the shogunate's forces later that year.

Choshu and Satsuma attacks on foreign ships had led to devastating reprisals by Western naval units in 1863 and 1864 and all but the most rabid xenophobes were prepared to moderate their foreign policy goals. Aware that France was arming and training the shogun's forces, Satsuma, whose castle town of Kagoshima had been bombarded by the British in 1863, turned to the British in the mid-1860s for arms and advice. Choshu also found the British helpful in procuring modern weapons. Both han sent young samurai abroad to gain knowledge of the West and both employed Western military technology and discipline in their drive to national power. Years before they overthrew the shogunate, the leaders of Choshu and Satsuma had surrendered any hope of expelling the Westerners and adopted a more pragmatic policy. They were nothing if not realists.

French efforts to the contrary notwithstanding, the shogun's forces were defeated by "imperial" forces led by the Choshu-Satsuma alliance in 1868 and his representatives surrendered Edo in May 1868. Resistance continued in Hokkaido for another year, but the "imperial restoration" was underway and the fourteen-year-old Meiji emperor was put forward as the symbol of national unity. Actual power rested in the hands of the young samurai who had been responsible for the destruction of the bakufu, although for several years they maneuvered discreetly behind elder statesmen who served as glorified figureheads.

The leaders of the new Japanese polity were motivated primarily by their concern for Japan's security and their determination to rid Japan of the unequal treaties the West had imposed upon them, especially the treaty tariff and extraterritoriality. Aware that they were in no position to make significant progress toward these goals in 1868, they vowed to "seek

knowledge throughout the world to strengthen the foundations of imperial rule."² In the interim they attempted to put an end to attacks on foreigners in Japan, punishing those who persisted. As a signal to the West of
their intent, they invited the representatives of foreign governments to an
audience with the young emperor, even before the shogunate had fallen.

Domestically, the Meiji leaders were determined to create a strong
central government and a strong military. They moved the emperor and
his court to Edo, renamed Tokyo (eastern capital), and moved with deliberate speed first to eliminate han autonomy and then, in 1871, to eliminate the han entirely, buying off the daimyo with generous stipends.
Throughout the decade they instituted economic and social reforms
designed both to modernize the society and to put the central government on a strong financial footing. In 1870 the thirty-two year old samurai Yamagata Aritomo returned from his studies in Europe to take charge
of the new government's army. In 1871, Yamagata's Imperial Army, modeled after the French army, was formally created. Two years later, Japan
adopted universal military conscription, requiring all men to serve on
active duty for three years—a dramatic step that eliminated the division
between armed samurai and unarmed peasants. It was a move of great
social as well as military significance. And not least, the Tokyo government took over han as well as shogunate warships to create the Imperial Japanese Navy, for which the British navy was the obvious model.

Having concluded that conciliation was the appropriate course for
Japan's immediate relations with the West, the Japanese sent a major
embassy abroad in 1871, a venture that involved more than a hundred
Japanese officials and students. The mission traveled to the United States
and the several European powers over a period of almost two years, seeking to demonstrate Japan's acceptance of its place in the new international order and ultimately to win revision of the unequal treaties.
Tokyo's representatives succeeded in persuading all with whom they met
that Japan's resistance to Western diplomatic and trade initiatives was a
thing of the past. They failed, however, to gain any relief from imposi-
tions of the treaty system.

The embassy, led by Prince Iwakura, a court noble with ties to
Choshu, and including many of the most important members of the new
regime, had to rush back to Tokyo in September 1873, to cope with one
manifestation of the greatest domestic threat the imperial government
faced: samurai discontent. Lesser eruptions of dissatisfaction with the

declining status of the samurai had been suppressed, but the conscription law of 1873, ostensibly depriving them of their remaining superiority over mere peasants, had been too much for many of them.

Fearful of an explosion that would undermine the government, some Japanese leaders advocated a foreign war as a safety valve. Korea seemed to be the most attractive target. Most obviously, it was close by, offering minimal logistical complications. But the Koreans also had offended the Japanese gratuitously by refusing to recognize the political changes that occurred since the fall of the shogunate. They disparaged what they perceived as Japan's willingness to surrender its Confucian heritage for Western ways. They were no more willing to open diplomatic and trade relations with Japan than they were with the Western nations that kept importuning them. Moreover, having driven off the French and the Americans, they had little fear of the Japanese.

Agitation for war with Korea mounted in Japan during the winter and spring of 1873. That summer the government, minus Iwakura and his colleagues, decided to attack. Racing back, Iwakura reached Tokyo in September, in time to reverse the decision. Korea was safe for the moment, but the Meiji government was in very serious trouble. Several of those who favored war resigned from the government and aligned themselves with disgruntled samurai. Something had to be done to mollify them. Iwakura, who dominated foreign policy in the 1870s, decided on a smaller scale military operation: a punitive expedition against Taiwan.

Taiwan was, of course, part of China, but Qing control over the island was imperfect. The aborigines who had roamed the island before the arrival of any Chinese fought all who infringed on their lands. They also happened to be headhunters. In 1871 they fell upon fifty-odd shipwrecked mariners from the Ryukyus, with disagreeable results for the latter. Searching for an excuse to go into action, the Japanese focused on this incident. In 1872, they had forced the king of the Ryukyus, formerly a vassal of Satsuma as well as the Qing emperor, to come to Japan to offer homage to the Meiji emperor. As Japanese vassals, the Ryukuyu islanders were entitled to Japan's protection—at least in the minds of the Japanese. In 1874, approximately three years after the murders occurred, the Japanese sent an expedition to Taiwan, and occupied the eastern part of the island, remote from the areas administered by the Qing.

Although some Japanese leaders very likely were eager to emulate the Western powers and seize territories for an imagined Japanese empire, the 1874 attack on Taiwan appears to have been merely an effort to deflect samurai rage. The ensuing diplomatic crisis with China was brief, as the Japanese indicated their willingness to remove their forces from Taiwan and the Chinese, involved in a conflict with France over Vietnam, appeased the Japanese with an indemnity to pay for the cost of the expedition and for the families of the murdered Ryukyuans.

Samurai discontent was not eliminated by the Taiwan operation or any other actions the government took to win them over. Tensions finally led to a major rebellion in Satsuma in 1877 which pitted 60,000 of Yamagata's conscripts against a samurai force of 40,000 warriors. Better equipped and more mobile, Yamagata's peasants prevailed after nearly nine months of bloody fighting. It was the last domestic military challenge the Meiji government had to face, although samurai opposition was slow to disappear.

Between the Taiwan expedition and the Satsuma Rebellion, Prince Iwakura and other Japanese leaders concerned with foreign affairs focused on two issues: a perceived Russian threat to Japanese interests in Sakhalin, the Kuriles, and Hokkaido and the continued obstinacy of the Koreans. In confronting the Russians in 1875, the Japanese knew they were dealing with a major power and used diplomacy. The Koreans, on the other hand, received a reprise of the treatment that the Japanese had received from Perry: naval demonstrations in successive years. Negotiations with the Russians resulted in trading Japanese interests in Sakhalin for Russian interests in the Kuriles. Hokkaido would be protected by other means, including improved defensive capabilities and American assistance in developing the island. A brief military encounter in 1876 persuaded the Koreans to negotiate and the Japanese succeeded in getting them to open two more ports to Japanese trade and included an assertion of Korean independence in the treaty they signed. Fearing Russian intervention in Korea, they did not press their obvious advantage over the Koreans.

The Japanese had learned a great deal about international relations from the West and they were determined to join the ranks of great powers. When they were strong enough to defend themselves against the Americans and Europeans, they would rid themselves of the unequal treaties and establish themselves as the dominant power in East Asia. They had tried in 1871 to force an unequal treaty on the Chinese, but had failed to obtain either a most-favored-nation clause or extraterritoriality. But it was still early.

TABLE 9.1.   Some Notable Figures of the Years 1867–1905
(Names in boldface are discussed in text)

Benjamin Disraeli	1804–1881
William Gladstone	1809–1898
Zeng Guofan	**1811–1872**
Taewon'gun	**1821–1898**
Li Hongzhang	**1823–1901**
Cixi	**1835–1908**
Sitting Bull	1837–1890
Yamagata Aritomo	**1838–1922**
Ito Hirobumi	**1841–1909**
Sergei Witte	1849–1915
Cecil Rhodes	1853–1902
Nicholas II of Russia	1856–1917
Theodore Roosevelt	**1858–1919**
Kang Youwei	**1858–1927**

Japan Ascendant

Qing leaders and their Chinese associates understood that China was not confronting another in the series of disunited tribesmen that had plagued it for thousands of years. Their tormentors were not simply another breed of barbarians coming from another direction. To meet this new threat, China had undertaken self-strengthening. It began the process of industrializing and it moved quickly to modernize its military technology. But the modernizers did not go unchallenged in Peking. Strong conservative opposition slowed China's progress and the traditional scholar-gentry bureaucracy remained in place, minimizing the rewards for change. As a result, the most rapid and successful strengthening occurred in the provinces, under the direction and control of provincial governors, most notably Li Hongzhang.

The absence of central direction proved to be the fatal flaw in the Qing modernization program. Li Hongzhang built an arsenal, an army and a navy, a steamship company and a railroad, a textile plant and a coal mine, but he rather than the nation was the principal beneficiary of his efforts. These assets increased his personal wealth and power greatly; they were not necessarily available when needed elsewhere in China. The best example of the shortcomings of provincial control of self-strengthening was Li's refusal to use his forces against the French in 1884.

France's continuing imperialist drive through Vietnam led the court at Hanoi to appeal to its nominal suzerain in Peking for help. Reluctantly, the Qing sent imperial troops to deter further French advances, but France sent additional forces to the region, attacked Taiwan and the new Chinese naval base at Fuzhou. Li Hongzhang was not ready to test his strength against a major European power. Preserving his own men and ships, he failed to come to the aid of southern provincial leaders whom he perceived as rivals rather than as countrymen threatened by foreigners. Unopposed by Li, the French prevailed easily, destroying the base at Fuzhou and the southern fleet. Then, as de facto foreign minister after Prince Gong ran afoul of the empress dowager, Li negotiated a settlement with the French wherein China surrendered its status as overlord of Vietnam.

China began a major ship-building program after 1885, but its new navy remained handicapped by the absence of central command. The four largest fleets, operating out of four separate ports, under four separate commands, could not be deployed in one national effort. Just as Li was unmoved by the plight of the southerners in 1884, they remained on the sidelines as he struggled with the Japanese in the decade that followed. Although Cixi was an extraordinarily gifted manipulator of men and power, she lacked the ability to coordinate the activities of her regional military leaders. Neither foreign affairs nor military strategy were her forte. No one provided national leadership.

By contrast, Meiji Japan was strikingly successful in creating a strong central authority dedicated to developing the nation's military power. The ultimate concern of Japanese leaders was the preservation of Japan's independence. If that required undermining traditional Japanese values, so be it. They were extraordinarily receptive to Westernization, occasionally to absurd extremes. They adopted Western dress and Western hairstyles, Western architecture and painting techniques, as well as Western technology and diplomacy. A modern financial system, including a European style central bank, was created. Rapid industrialization followed. By 1889 a modern, Western style constitution had been promulgated and a bicameral parliament, the Diet, was convened in 1890. Perhaps equally as impressive was the ease and speed with which most Japanese surrendered their regional loyalties and commitments to tradition and rallied around their new modern state.

Korea provided the principal arena in which the contest between China and Japan for primacy in East Asia was staged. Much of Korea's misfortune was geographically derived. Its territory was easily accessible to its larger and more powerful Asian neighbors and, with Russian expansion to the Pacific, of interest to the Tsar's minions as well. But Korea's internal affairs had much to do with its inability to organize itself for effective resistance against those who would deny it its independence.

The Korean court knew what was happening to China in the nineteenth century and concluded that isolation was its best defense. It dreaded the spread of Western ideas, especially of Catholicism, which had proved both popular and subversive early in the century. Foreign priests and their many converts questioned the legitimacy of *yangban* rule, of the dominance of Korean society by a hereditary aristocracy. In 1864, the man known as the Taewon'gun came to power as regent. He crushed a major peasant rebellion in the southeast and then began the systematic persecution of Catholics, executing several French priests and thousands of Korean converts. He instituted reforms intended to strengthen the central government and enhance its military power. It was at his direction that French and American efforts to open Korea were repulsed forcefully. Korean successes confirmed the wisdom of his approach, at least in his own mind.

The Taewon'gun was no longer in power when the Japanese came to demand a treaty modeled on the unequal treaties the West had imposed on other Asian states. He opposed the treaty and left no doubt that were he still running the country, he would have resisted the Japanese by all available means. But a faction had emerged in Seoul that favored modernization and looked to Japan as an example of how Korea might proceed. In 1880 a Korean official returned from a mission to Japan with a seminal treatise written by Huang Zunxian, a Chinese diplomat posted in Tokyo.[3] Huang argued that the principal threat to Korea's independence was Russia and that Korea could fend off the Russians only if it adopted Western technology and institutions, as had the Japanese. He argued also for Korean ties to both China and Japan—and to the United States, probably because of the role of American educators in Meiji Japan. The reformers needed little encouragement to proceed along the course

Huang urged. They sent students to Tianjin to study subjects of military value at Li Hongzhang's schools and moved with deliberate speed to adopt Western technology. In 1881 they reorganized and modernized the Korean government, filling key positions with reformers. They sent cultural missions to China, Japan, and the United States.

But the predominant influence in Korea in the 1880s remained Chinese. It was Li Hongzhang who negotiated Korea's first treaty with the United States and persuaded the Koreans to accept it in 1882. The Qing still perceived Korea as their vassal and Li hoped that a Western stake in Korea would forestall the expansion of Japanese influence. The Korean queen and her family looked to China for support and were unsympathetic to the Japanese approach to change. A failed coup attempt by the Taewon'gun in 1882 also appears to have been aimed at the reformers and their Japanese supporters. His men did succeed in burning down the Japanese legation.

Frustrated, the reformers attempted a coup of their own in December 1884. With the connivance of Japanese diplomats in Seoul, they assassinated several of their opponents in the government and kidnapped the king. The Japanese may have assumed that China was too involved in war with France to respond, but Li and his protégé, Yuan Shikai, posted as "resident" in Seoul, were much more interested in Korea than in Vietnam. China responded quickly and with greater force than the Japanese were prepared to overcome. The coup failed and there was little doubt that Yuan was the most powerful man in Korea. The Japanese settled for an 1885 agreement between Li Hongzhang and the great Japanese statesman, Ito Hirabumi, in which China and Japan each promised not to intervene in Korean affairs without the permission of the other.

The two principal factions in Korean politics in the 1880s had each compromised their country's independence by seeking foreign support. The Korean economy was also being disrupted by the rapid penetration of Chinese and Japanese merchants. At this point, the Russians made their bid for influence in Korea. An able Russian minister, abetted by Western advisers to the Korean government, urged the Koreans to look to Russia for protection, primarily as a means of shaking loose from Chinese control. When the king and queen appeared responsive to Russian overtures, the British, ever alert to Russian expansion, sent a naval expedition to occupy Komun island, off the southwestern coast of Korea, where they remained for more than a year, until certain the Russians would back off.

Some Korean political figures even turned to the United States, hoping the Americans would intervene to preserve their independence. Clearly, a weak Korean government had lost its ability to protect its people, economically or politically. Korean leaders looked frantically first to one and then another of the available foreign contenders in their efforts to gain or maintain power—"not by winning the support of the Korean people."[4]

In 1894, a resumption of the rebellion that had wracked the south in the early 1860s panicked the government. The king petitioned Li Hongzhang for help in suppressing the rebels and he responded favorably. But the Japanese, perceiving Chinese military operations in Korea as a threat, also sent troops and they reached Seoul first. They seized the king in late July, held him captive, and appointed the Taewon'gun as regent to carry out their wishes, including a Korean declaration of war against China. On the same day that Japanese troops took the palace, a Japanese warship sank a British transport carrying Chinese reinforcements. A few days later China and Japan formally declared war on each other. Japan, increasingly inclined to resist foreign pressures, brushed aside European and American efforts to mediate the dispute.

At last Li Hongzhang's modern navy sailed into action and met its Japanese equivalent at the mouth of the Yalu River. The two fleets were equal in size, but in nothing else. The Japanese fleet proved to be better trained, equipped, and commanded. The battle was over quickly and only a handful of Chinese ships survived and escaped. It was later determined that the ordnance of the Chinese warships had been defective; that corrupt associates of Li Hongzhang had substituted sand and scrap iron for explosives and that the shells fired against the Japanese had hollow rather than explosive warheads.[5] The Chinese never had a chance. An effort to save the rest of the fleet by hiding it in a protected harbor failed when the Japanese attacked from the landward side in January 1895.

With Japan in control of the seas, it was able to reinforce its troops easily and in two months time they drove the Chinese out of Korea. To the dismay of the Qing court, the Japanese army did not stop at the Yalu, but continued on into Manchuria and seized Weihaiwei on the Shandong peninsula in China proper. There was little to stop it from marching on to Peking. The Qing had no choice but to sue for peace and Li Hongzhang was forced to go to Japan to negotiate once more with Ito.

The Japanese public was consumed with war fever and exhilarated by Japan's successes in the field, partial compensation for the humiliations imposed by the West since Perry's ships sailed into Edo Bay. Expectations regarding the spoils of victory were great and Ito did not dare hold back. He demanded Chinese recognition of the independence of Korea, the ceding of Taiwan, the Pescadores, and the Liaodong peninsula to Japan, a huge indemnity and new commercial concessions, including the opening of four new ports. Only a failed assassination attempt on Li, embarrassing to his Japanese hosts, precluded more outrageous demands. The Qing had no recourse but to accept the terms of the Treaty of Shimonoseki.

Most frightening to the Qing court was the loss of the Liaodong peninsula which would put the shadow of Japanese troops over Peking. Foreign intervention was China's only hope. Fortunately for China, Russia had its own aspirations in Korea and Manchuria and was eager to contain Japan. It manipulated its French ally and a German government desirous of Russian support in Europe into joining it in a diplomatic intervention against Japan. Threatening military action if thwarted, the three European powers demanded that Japan return Liaodong to China. The Japanese leaders were not ready to challenge the Europeans and accepted an additional indemnity in place of the peninsula. The Japanese public was outraged, charging Ito and his foreign minister with having lost the peace. The Japanese would not forget.

The debacle in Korea, the failure of China's modern military forces, the harshness of Japanese peace terms, the indignity of defeat at the hands of the "dwarf bandits," devastated the Qing court and the Chinese officials who maintained it. Intellectuals across the country mobilized public opinion in opposition to the Treaty of Shimonoseki and in favor of genuine reforms. It was apparent that self-strengthening had failed. Li Hongzhang's forces had been undermined by corruption—not least his own and that of his relatives—and a lack of commitment to change by the tradition-bound Confucian scholars who staffed his bureaucracy and filled the ranks of his officer corps.

The nation's defense had been compromised by regionalism, by the failure of the southern fleet to support Li's navy against Japan, pay-back for his unwillingness to risk his ships against France ten years before. The dynasty would have to respond rapidly or confront doubts about its continued mandate.

China had even less time than most informed Manchus or Chinese realized. Japan had exposed China's weakness. The Europeans, especially the Russians, were eager for further territorial and commercial concessions. The Russians expected to be rewarded for forcing the Japanese to disgorge Liaodong. Others would demand comparable concessions. The empire was on the verge of being threatened by dismemberment, the "slicing of the Chinese melon."

The French, with Russian support, came first, obtaining railroad and mining concessions in the south, adjacent to their empire in Indochina. The Russians, determined to play the leading role in East Asia, pressed the Qing for concessions in Manchuria. In 1896 a weary Li Hongzhang traveled to St. Petersburg to negotiate a secret Sino-Russian alliance aimed at Japan. The Russians extorted an 80-year railroad concession allowing them to run the Trans-Siberian Railway across Manchuria. Eager to play a role, the Germans looked to Shandong and used the murder of two German missionaries in 1897 as a rationale for seizing control of the harbor of Qingdao, following it up with a 99-year lease of the port city and railroad and mining concessions throughout Shandong. German actions seem to have relieved the other powers of any sense of restraint they might have had. Over the next few months the Russians took Port Arthur and Dalien and the right to connect their holdings by railroad, giving them effective control of Manchuria. Unnerved by Russian expansion, realizing the Chinese could do little to stop the Russians, the British took the naval base at Weihaiwei, across from Port Arthur and Dalien, where the Gulf of Chihli flows into the Yellow Sea. The French demanded more and the Italians came and by the end of 1898 much of China was divided into spheres of influence, controlled by foreigners, filled with foreign officials, merchants, investors, and troops. Annexation of these spheres, and the end of China's existence as an independent state was only a step away.

The United States as an East Asian Power

Americans—merchants, seamen, and missionaries—had been poking around East Asia almost from the moment of their nation's conception. While America's role was never as important as that of Great Britain or France or Holland, Americans had nonetheless made their presence known in every port city of the region. Their speedy clipper ships had dominated the carrying trade to China in the 1840s, the last days of the great sailing vessels. Americans led the way in the opening and modernizing of Japan and were the first Westerners to win a treaty with

Korea. They were everywhere, and their Asiatic Fleet indicated their government's intention to protect its citizens and their interests; but the United States had claimed no territory as its colony, had no sphere of interest in East Asia at the time of the Sino-Japanese War.

Early in 1898, two unrelated events ultimately led to a striking increase in American involvement in the affairs of East Asia. The first, in January, was the formation of the American Asiatic Association, an organization of businessmen dedicated to stimulating public interest in China as a means of bringing pressure to bear on their government to do more to protect commercial interests and opportunities there. The second, in February, was the explosion that sank the *U.S.S. Maine* in Havana harbor, leading to war between the United States and Spain two months later.

In the course of the American crusade to liberate Cuba, an order was sent to the commander of the Asiatic Fleet to proceed to the Philippines and destroy Spanish naval forces in the Pacific. He carried out his orders and a few months later, with the assistance of Filipinos in rebellion against Spanish imperialism, the Americans had defeated Spain in the Philippines as well as in Cuba. Spain surrendered and the United States had two choices: it could hand the islands over to the Filipino independence movement or it could replace Spain as the imperial power in the Philippines. It chose empire. The Philippines became an American colony.

Historically, Americans had prided themselves in their antiimperialism, in their commitment to self-determination for all peoples, rationalizing their expansion by offering statehood to the territories they conquered. But they knew the Philippines would be different. Racism in the United States was a powerful force that had extended beyond enslavement of Africans and the mistreatment of free African-Americans, beyond the betrayal of native American Indians, to the exclusion of Asian immigrants and the denial of citizenship to those already in the country. The Philippines would never be considered for statehood; Filipinos were not considered suitable for citizenship in the United States. America would rule the Philippines, as Britain ruled India, France ruled Indochina, and Holland ruled Indonesia. The United States had become an imperialist power in Asia.

The Filipinos had not assisted the Americans against Spain in order to extend their subservient position, least of all to surrender the realizable dream of winning their freedom from a fading Spanish empire in order to become the hapless subjects of a rising power. They refocused their effort against the United States. For the next two years they fought a ferocious guerrilla war against the overwhelming power of the United States, to which they ultimately succumbed. It was not one of the finer hours of the American people as their troops committed atrocities against Asians whose humanity they did not respect.

There were a number of reasons for the American decision to take the Philippines, as there usually are when a nation undertakes to build an empire. One of these was a shift in the attitudes prevailing in the American business community toward colonies. In general there was fear that the domestic demand was not adequate to sustain growth. Some businessmen were apprehensive about European reprisals against the high tariffs the United States had imposed to protect its industries; others feared that European and Japanese imperialists, as they carved their spheres of influence in China, would deny opportunities for Americans. The victory of U.S. naval forces at Manila was perceived as an opportunity for the United States to establish a foothold in the region, to seize a position from which Americans could compete with others for the resources and markets of Asia. As the historian Richard Leopold contended, "the desire for the Philippines and a concern for China became mutually supporting."[6]

Businessmen concerned with China remained uneasy, demanding more vigorous action by their government. In addition, the acquisition of the Philippines and the war that followed against the Filipinos stimulated the U.S. Navy's interest in a coaling station in China. The war in particular focused public attention on East Asia beyond the hopes of the lobbyists and publicists of the American Asiatic Association. Leading commentators on foreign affairs, including the navalist Alfred Thayer Mahan and the future president, Theodore Roosevelt, wrote and spoke about the importance of East Asia in the world balance of power and the opportunity for the United States to shape that balance. Pressures on the government mounted and in 1899, Washington made an important gesture to appease its critics, in and out of the government.

John Hay, the American secretary of state, was unwilling to risk a major involvement in Chinese affairs. He was not persuaded that a serious threat to American interests, economic or political, existed. The situation warranted no more than a diplomatic effort to gain assurance from those powers with spheres of influence in China that they would not discriminate against American trade within those spheres. At the urging of his principal adviser on Chinese affairs, he also was willing to ask the powers not to interfere with the work of the Chinese Imperial Maritime Customs Service, to assure the Chinese government an essential source of income. In September 1899, he sent off the first of the requests that have come to be known as the "Open Door Notes," a modest initiative designed to satisfy both businessmen who sought the expansion of American economic interests and romantic nationalists eager to see the United States playing a larger role in world affairs.

The United States was asking the other powers with interests in China to pursue a policy of self-denial in the areas under their control. In return for equal treatment for their exports, the Americans offered nothing. On the other hand, the United States was not challenging the existing spheres of influence, nor seeking to compete in railroad and mining development, crucial to the Russians and Japanese. There was nothing to be gained by rejecting the American request outright and little to be lost by endorsing it with qualifications that protected the particular interests dearest to each nation. The responses Hay received were evasive, but he was nonetheless satisfied and declared that American interests in China had been safeguarded. He achieved all he could have hoped to accomplish with six pieces of paper.

Hay also appears to have believed that he had contributed meaningfully to the preservation of the Chinese empire. No expressions of gratitude came from Peking, however. It is worth noting that at the time the Open Door notes were formulated and delivered, relations between China and the United States were very tense as a result of the extension of discriminatory practices against Chinese immigrants to the new American territories of Hawaii and the Philippines. Benevolent feelings toward China did not motivate Hay, nor did the Chinese have any illusions.

TABLE 9.2.   Some Major Events of the Period 1867–1905
(Events in boldface are discussed in text)

Russia sells Alaska to the United States	1867
Meiji Restoration	**1868**
Opening of Suez Canal	1869
Franco-Prussian War	1870–1871
Alexander Graham Bell invents the telephone	1876
Korea opened to trade by treaty with the United States	**1882**

Sino-French War over Vietnam	1884
Sino-Japanese War	1894–1895
Dreyfus Affair in France	1894–1906
China's 100 days of reform	1898
Spanish-American War	1898
Filipino Insurrection against American imperialism	1898–1900
Boer War	1899–1902
Boxer War	1900
Anglo-Japanese alliance signed	1902
Russo-Japanese War	1904–1905

The Boxer War

The terms of the Treaty of Shimonoseki and the aggressive actions of the Western powers in the years immediately following the war between China and Japan had a strikingly disruptive impact on coastal China. The foreigners seemed to be everywhere, digging mines, building railroads and factories, treating the Chinese with contempt in their own land. Educated Chinese and others in the port cities could not escape the knowledge that China was but one nation among many—and that it was not faring well in the world competition for wealth, power, and status. The situation was intolerable: something had to be done.

The years between 1895 and 1900 were years of intellectual and political ferment in China as scholars, officials, and many Chinese who had experienced the West or Westerners directly or recognized the accomplishments of Meiji Japan struggled to find a means to preserve their country's independence and restore its historic grandeur. In 1895, 1,200 leading young scholars, in Peking to take the examinations for the highest degree in the imperial system, signed a memorial urging continued resistance to Japan and comprehensive reform. They feared that unless China changed course quickly, the imperialists would take over their country, as they had India. Led by Kang Youwei, a 37-year-old Cantonese scholar, they called for the creation of a modern army, a revamping of the financial system, the application of modern technology to agriculture, the construction of railroads, and all the other accouterments of a modern industrial infrastructure. There was no response from the court.

Other, more radical efforts to change China, such as that led by the Western-educated revolutionary Sun Yat-sen, were easily crushed by the Qing. Sun himself barely escaped kidnapping by Qing diplomats in London in 1896.

As conditions worsened in China, as the threat to its survival as a sovereign entity grew, the young emperor asserted himself. In 1898 he called Kang Youwei to Peking and began what historians call the "Hundred Days of Reform," a program of sweeping economic, political, military, and educational changes, including a streamlining of the bureaucracy. Officials who thought the reforms mistaken or hasty, or who felt threatened by the emperor's plan, rallied around his aunt, the empress dowager Cixi, who was herself uneasy about the impact of the changes on the future of the dynasty. Rumors that Cixi was planning to seize power prompted the reformers to preemptive action, an attempt to have Yuan Shikai, the powerful leader of the modern Beiyang army, neutralize military forces presumed loyal to Cixi. The move backfired when Yuan betrayed the reformers. Informed of the plot, Cixi responded ruthlessly. She resumed power, placed the emperor under house arrest, and had several of his advisers executed. Kang Youwei escaped to Hong Kong and traveled widely thereafter, but his subsequent efforts, like those of most political exiles, had no impact on his native land.

Cixi held the reins of power firmly and nearly all of the emperor's reform edicts were repudiated. But the problems that had prompted the efforts of Kang and the emperor still festered. The Chinese government could not devise the means to check foreign intrusions and unrest intensified, especially in North China. Apparently arising first in Shandong in 1898, a crypto-nationalist movement, whose members were known as the Boxers, a loose amalgam of martial arts and invulnerability ritual societies, began to harass foreigners, especially missionaries, and native converts to Christianity. The court was ambivalent about the Boxers, obviously conscious of their possible usefulness in efforts to expel foreign influence, but also fearful that they might turn against the dynasty as other secret societies had throughout Chinese history. Increasingly, as all else failed, Cixi inclined toward supporting the Boxers.

The Europeans and the Americans demanded that the court protect the missionaries and their converts, but to no avail. Occasionally the court yielded to pressures and transferred officials offensive to the West, but Cixi became determined to take the offensive. The success of the

Boxers in Shandong and Shanxi brought the hope that China could be purged of foreign influence. China had endured too much—all foreigners in the country would die and there would be an end to imperialist encroachments and subversion. To the magic powers allegedly possessed by the Boxers, Cixi added the modern arms of the imperial army. In June 1900, the Boxers stepped up their activities in Tianjin and Peking and many points between those two cities. Some local officials attempted to control them; others encouraged them. An attempt by several Western powers to send troops to reinforce the legation quarter in Peking was routed by the Boxers, who tore up the railroad tracks and decimated the troops who tried to march on. Before the month was over, Cixi ordered the massacre of all foreigners, including the diplomatic community, and the court declared war on all the foreign powers.

Suddenly, the legation quarter became an embattled fortress, subjected to incessant attack, cut off from outside contacts. Fortunately for those trapped within, most of the best trained and equipped Qing troops held back and allowed Boxer irregulars to lead the offensive. Foreigners elsewhere in North China were less fortunate. The governor of Shanxi province offered protection to the missionary families in his capital and when they accepted, had them all executed. The Boxers attacked mission compounds and any other foreigners they could lay hands on. Many were brutally murdered, as were Christian converts. For almost two months, public attention throughout much of the world focused on the progress of Western and Japanese troops fighting their way in from the coast, seeking to reach Peking in time to save some of the men, women, and children surrounded by the Boxers.

As the war between China and the powers began, it was evident that American hopes for averting the dismemberment of China were in jeopardy. The possibility of voluntary restraint by the Europeans and Japanese suddenly seemed very remote. Given the war and the need for an expedition to rescue the foreigners in Peking, it was likely that the powers generally and the Russians in particular would find sufficient pretext for further encroachments on Chinese sovereignty. Once the foreign armies marched on Chinese soil, it might well prove difficult to remove them—and in Washington there was concern lest American interests in China be injured.

In July 1900, Secretary of State Hay sent off a circular message stressing the importance of preserving Chinese sovereignty, "the territorial and administrative entity" of China. Employing the myth that the Boxers were acting spontaneously, without the collusion of the Qing court, he defined the situation in China as one of "virtual anarchy." Power and responsibility rested with local authorities who were attempting to keep the peace in areas under their control. Washington then developed contacts with high-ranking Chinese officials who controlled the southern and central provinces and provided diplomatic support for their efforts to limit the war to North China. Several powerful Chinese officials suppressed the Boxers and provided protection for foreigners and their property. In return the United States deflected proposals from the powers to extend operations against the Boxers to other parts of the country. Limiting the war in area and intensity decreased the likelihood of China being partitioned.

The United States, in pursuit of its own interests, opposed the further dismemberment of China and recommended self-denial to the other powers involved in the expedition to relieve Peking. In 1900, as in 1899, the great powers acceded, for the moment, to American wishes—not out of fear of the United States, but because of the essential wisdom of the course proposed and the mutual mistrust of several of the participating states. In particular, the Americans, British, and Japanese were highly suspicious of Russian intentions. The satisfaction of further imperialistic ambitions could await a more propitious moment.

In August 1900, the international expeditionary force lifted the siege of Peking. Cixi and her entourage fled from the city, taking refuge in Xian. As in 1860, the foreign troops looted the city, providing fine Chinese art—and not so fine Chinese art—for collectors all over the world.[7] In due course, a protocol ending the war was signed in September 1901, after a delay occasioned by disputes over the size and distribution of the indemnity to be exacted from China. The Chinese were forced to take on an enormous financial burden that impeded the dynasty's ability to rule and retarded the country's efforts to industrialize. In addition, they were required to grant their conquerors the right to station troops between Peking and the sea—new protection for foreigners in North China and new monuments to China's weakness. China's borders, however, remained intact.

By this time, even Cixi was convinced of the need for radical reform if she was to save the dynasty. In the remaining years of her life her commitment to modernization, even obvious Westernization, appears to have been sincere. China's educational system was reorganized from top to bottom, introducing Western mathematics and science into the curriculum. More significantly, the traditional examination system, based on Confucian learning and calligraphy, was abolished, ultimately privileging Western studies. Thousands of Chinese students went abroad, especially to Japan, for modern educations. The army was reorganized, the men dressed and drilled like Western and Japanese troops. The people were promised a constitution and a national assembly. The Qing court's primary concern was the preservation of the dynasty and Cixi and her advisers were prepared to swallow strong medicine to achieve their purpose. The question that remained, both for the dynasty and for all Chinese, was whether there was time to recover before the dynasty was challenged by another great rebellion or the whole country victimized by renewed imperialist attacks.

In The Light of the Rising Sun

Russia posed the principal threat to China and to the shaky balance of power that had emerged in East Asia in the last years of the nineteenth century. The Russians had exploited the unrest in China to move their forces into Manchuria. There was little to indicate that they had any intention of withdrawing when order was restored—or that they would permit other nations to retain commercial privileges in the territory they controlled. They were deeply involved in the internal affairs of Korea. In 1896, they provided the Korean monarch with a place of refuge from his enemies in their legation in Seoul where he stayed for a year. They pressed aggressively for timber concessions in the north. In general, the Russians left no doubt that they intended to be the dominant power in northeast Asia.

Neither the Chinese nor the Koreans had the means to deny the Russians their objectives. The Americans and the British were troubled by Russian actions, opposed them diplomatically, but were not prepared to fight. Neither Great Britain nor the United States had vital interests in Korea or Manchuria. The Japanese, however, did perceive a threat to their security, as well as to their economic interests in the region. Japan's aspiration to join the great powers, to be treated as an equal, was also being challenged by Russian intransigence.

The Japanese, especially Ito Hirobumi, tried very hard to reach an accommodation with the Russians, but the Russians yielded no ground on Manchuria and rejected a Japanese request for a free hand in Korea in exchange for acceptance of the Russian position on Manchuria. The Russians would pursue their interests in Korea as well. Neither tensions in Europe nor unrest at home shook the confidence of the men in St. Petersburg who perceived no threat from Japan. Only Count Sergei Witte, the finance minister, revealed any apprehension as he argued against what he believed to be imperial overreach. The tsar brushed aside his objections.

In 1901 the Japanese approached the United States, suggesting joint action against Russia, but the American response was unequivocal: the United States was not prepared to use force to achieve its goals in Asia. At approximately the same time, Great Britain had concluded that an alliance with Japan would protect British interests in East Asia. The rise of German power in Europe worried the British and the possibility of German collusion with the Franco-Russian allies against London's interests in China was also troublesome. The British offered the Japanese an alliance in July 1901 and in January 1902, after exhausting all possibility of accommodation with the Russians, the Japanese accepted the offer. Japan's leverage in negotiations with the Russians increased significantly, as did its standing among the nations of the world.

The Russians initially became more conciliatory, agreeing to withdraw some of their troops from Manchuria, but they failed to keep to the schedule for withdrawal. They continued to reject Japanese overtures for a division of spheres of influence, the offer of Manchuria for Korea. Japanese military leaders and foreign ministry officials concluded war was their only option and that the alliance with Great Britain precluded any other European state from joining forces with Russia. Efforts by the Meiji elder statesmen, the *genro* Ito and Yamagata, to continue negotiations failed and they reluctantly approved the preparations for war. Despite Japanese fear that their military power was not adequate to challenge a great power, the unwillingness of the Russians to yield any ground appeared to leave no alternative but war. The Japanese broke off diplomatic relations early in February 1904 and two days later attacked the Russian fleet at Port Arthur.

Having negotiated ineptly, the Russians proceeded to suffer a disastrous military defeat. Their forces in East Asia were outnumbered and outgunned and their logistical problems—of moving reinforcements from Europe to the Pacific—were overwhelming. If the battlefield situation in Manchuria was not bad enough, the beginnings of the 1905 revolution further weakened the Russian cause.

The Japanese were having problems of their own, particularly a shortage of funds, mitigated but not solved by loans from American bankers. They were also confronting a shortage of manpower. Wisely they turned to the United States, asking the American president Theodore Roosevelt to provide his good offices in bringing about peace talks. Roosevelt was happy to oblige. His initial delight over Japan's military success in 1904, his contention that Japan was serving America's ends, had given way to recognition that Japan might prove to be an even more formidable opponent of American interests in East Asia than Russia. The Western powers operating in the region would have important interests in Europe, the Middle East, South Asia, and Africa—"divided interests, divided cares." Japan would focus on East Asia and have "but one care, one interest, one burden." It would be good to end the war while Russian power remained sufficient to maintain a semblance of a balance of power in the region.

Roosevelt proved to be a little more even-handed than the Japanese had anticipated, but he succeeded in pushing the two sides toward a peace they both desperately needed. The Japanese gained control of southern Manchuria, including the railway and both Port Arthur and Dalien. In addition they won Russian acceptance of their "paramount" interests in Korea. The Russians held on to northern Sakhalin while ceding the southern part of the island to the Japanese. On one issue, the Russians remained adamant: they would not pay an indemnity—and it was the failure to win on this issue that infuriated the Japanese public, unaware of the precariousness of Japan's position. Ultimately, some of the blame for the failure was deflected on Roosevelt.

Although the Treaty of Portsmouth that ended the Russo-Japanese War left many Japanese feeling cheated of the fruits of victory, in fact Japan's gains had been enormous. Its navy dominated the shores of northeast Asia. It had gained a de facto protectorate over Korea and an extraordinarily valuable sphere of influence in Manchuria. Allied with Great Britain, conqueror of Russia, it had greatly increased its status in the world. Japan had become a great power.

Conclusion

Japan's rise to primacy among the imperial powers in East Asia had come with incredible speed. In less than forty years it had carried out extensive reforms, modernizing its government and its society. It built an army and navy superior to any other force in the region. It moved from being the victim of Western imperialism to victimizer of its neighbors. It easily defeated China, long the dominant political force in the international system of the region. It won a powerful European ally in Great Britain and defeated a European enemy. There was little reason to doubt that Japan would play the leading role in the international relations of East Asia for some time to come.

Korea and China were the big losers over that same period, the closing decades of the nineteenth century and the first few years of the twentieth. Korea seemed stagnant through the nineteenth century and then became the prize in a struggle among three powerful empires as the Chinese, Japanese, and Russians vied for control of the peninsula. In the end, Korea lost its independence, becoming a Japanese protectorate in 1905—before matters became even worse.

China retained its existence as an independent political entity, but just barely. It lost the Ryukyus, Taiwan, and the Pescadores to Japan. The British, French, Germans, Japanese, and Russians held de facto control over huge tracts of Chinese territory. Foreign troops were stationed on its soil and foreign ships plied its inland waters. It lost wars to France and Japan, demonstrating its inability to defend countries—Vietnam and Korea—over which it had claimed overlordship. The Qianlong emperor's mighty empire was reduced to a shell. Only a veneer of sovereignty remained. No one in China could imagine that China was the center of the universe. The tributary system was gone in theory as well as practice. And, as the historian Immanuel Hsu as written, these years marked "the total disintegration of the imperial tradition of foreign intercourse."[8]

TEN

Challenge to the West

Japan's defeat of Russia in 1905 was a clear indication to Asia and the West that Western domination of East Asia would not endure forever. The Japanese, struggling frantically to rid themselves of the capitulations forced upon them by the European powers and the United States, so as to achieve equal standing in the international order, had succeeded. Their art had won the admiration of the world at the Chicago Columbian Exposition of 1893. In 1899 they had won revision of the so-called unequal treaties, ended the extraterritorial privileges Westerners had enjoyed in Japan, and also gained important concessions on the road to tariff autonomy, fully achieved in 1911. In 1902 they had been wooed by the strongest power in the world, Great Britain, and had entered into an alliance with that nation. And now, in 1905, they had defeated a European state and found themselves with the strongest army in East Asia and the most powerful navy in the Pacific. In the age of imperialism, in the era in which Darwinian thought influenced the foreign policies of the world's leaders, the Japanese had proven themselves to be competitive. They were the only Asian imperialists.

The Japanese victory in 1905 also galvanized nationalist movements elsewhere in Asia, as the fallibility of the Westerner was revealed. The most striking act of nationalism, following immediately on the heels of the Russo-Japanese War, was the anti-American boycott, organized in China, and there were comparable activities in Indochina and Indonesia as well. But Chinese nationalism was quickly rechannelled into opposition to *Japanese* imperialism and the Koreans proved no more receptive to Japanese colonization than other Asians did to that of the West.

The expansion of the Japanese empire and the growth of Chinese nationalism were the dominant motifs in Asia during the quarter of a century that followed the signing of the Treaty of Portsmouth. These were also years in which the European powers, through their self-destructive wars, lost further stature among Asian intellectuals, in which the Russian Revolution and the activities of the Comintern inspired some of those intellectuals, and in which the locus of power in the world shifted from Europe to the United States.

Development of the Japanese Empire

At the outset of the Russo-Japanese War, Korea tried desperately to stand aside, declaring its neutrality. The Japanese ignored the Korean declaration and sent troops to Seoul. They forced the Korean government to grant them the right to station troops at strategic points across the country and they quickly eliminated all traces of Russian influence. But they did not stop there: they also insisted that Korea recall its overseas diplomatic missions. It was evident that Japan had no intention of respecting Korean independence, that Korea had become a Japanese protectorate. The primary goal of the Japanese government was to prevent any other power from gaining control of Korea and thus constituting a threat to Japan's security.

Once the war was over, Korea increased in importance to Japan as the essential path between Japan and its new sphere of interest in southern Manchuria. The Russians had conceded Japanese hegemony and the British posed no challenge. China was helpless. The American minister to Korea, Horace Allen, left no doubt that he wanted the United States to intervene on behalf of Korean independence, but he aroused little interest in Washington. President Roosevelt, who perceived the American colony in the Philippines to be his country's Achilles' heel, solicited and received assurances that Tokyo would not challenge the role of the United States in those islands. The 1905 Taft-Katsura meeting between the American secretary of war and the Japanese prime minister resulted in American acquiescence in Japan's position in Korea as well as an expression of support for the Anglo-Japanese alliance. No country would come to Korea's rescue. A treaty forced on the Koreans in 1905 gave Japan control of Korea's foreign affairs and provided for a Japanese resident-general who would be de facto ruler of the country.

In March 1906 Ito Hirobumi arrived in Seoul to serve as resident-general and all foreign legations were closed. Japanese police took control of the king's palace guard. The Japanese instituted a series of well-intentioned reforms designed to remake Korea in their image, presumably to advance the level of Korean civilization. They had a well-founded sense of cultural affinity with the Korean people, from whom much of their own culture was derived, but they also had a strong sense of superiority. Japan had modernized quickly and thrown off the shackles of Western imperialism: the Japanese would drag the Koreans into the twentieth century. Japanese political institutions would be substituted for indigenous ones. The underlying plan was that Koreans would be transformed into loyal Japanese subjects and equipped with the skills required for modern life, but not, of course, for control of their society. In fact, the Koreans were to be second-class citizens in their own land.

Thousands of Japanese entrepreneurs poured into Korea in the years that followed. Many Japanese, after all, were less interested in high politics and military strategy than in making money. They built a modern industrial infrastructure designed to serve Japanese interests. They took over railroad and telegraph construction, sometimes using forced Korean labor, reformed the currency, took control of Korea's finances, and began to buy up the land.

The Japanese appear to have been genuinely surprised by the Korean lack of gratitude, by the resistance movement that grew rapidly. Intellectuals and businessmen, Confucianists and Christians, shared the desire to have Japan expelled. In 1907, the Koreans appealed to the Second Hague Peace Conference, but were denied the right to participate in the proceedings. Acts of violence were committed against Japanese in Korea and the Japanese responded harshly. The police force, Japanese-directed, but including many Koreans, brutally crushed the resistance movement. Hundreds of Koreans were killed. Censorship, resisted by the bilingual *Korea Daily News*, became more effective when the English journalist who had controlled it was forced out of the country. Private schools, many run by American missionaries, came under pressure.

To Japanese leaders in Tokyo, it appeared necessary to take stronger action against the Korean nationalists, to force them into submission. As they debated the modalities, a Korean patriot assassinated Ito, who was in Harbin to forewarn the Russians of Japan's intentions. To bring the Korean people "into a completely satisfactory relationship with us," the Japanese decided to annex Korea. The Minister of War was sent over with forces adequate to coerce the Korean government into signing a secret treaty of annexation in August 1910. Soon afterward he was named governor-general of Japan's new territory. The pace of economic exploitation accelerated and the whole country was organized to serve Japan's interests, economic as well as strategic.

The Japanese could proceed quickly and ruthlessly in Korea in large part because of their confidence that the rest of the world would not interfere. Initially there had been some fear that the Russians would seek revenge at the earliest possible moment, but by 1907 a rapprochement with Russia had been concluded. In a secret convention they recognized each other's sphere of influence in Manchuria. The Russians formally accepted Japanese control of Korea in exchange for Japanese recognition of their special interests in Outer Mongolia.

The likelihood of a vengeful Russia attacking Japan or its interests on the continent had declined, but not sufficiently to allay the concerns of the Japanese army. From the outset of its movement into Manchuria, the army brushed aside directives from civilian officials in Tokyo and acted as it deemed necessary. Army leaders insisted that Japanese interests in Manchuria were principally strategic and that the army, not the foreign ministry, would determine how those interests would be protected. The army was determined to wrest southern Manchuria from Chinese control: it was not satisfied with the mission assigned to it by Tokyo which would have preserved Chinese sovereignty. The Japanese military obstructed the operations of Western commercial enterprises and encouraged Japanese carpet-baggers to take over from American and British as well as Chinese merchants. Customs operations were skewed to favor Japanese imports and Western investment opportunities were threatened.[1]

Great Britain and the United States were troubled far more by Japanese actions in Manchuria than they were by events in Korea where their economic interests were trivial. Manchuria was more important to both countries and it was also perceived as a test case of adherence to the Open Door policies both Western countries endorsed: equal opportunity for commercial enterprise and respect for the sovereignty and territorial integrity of China. In 1906 London and Washington protested against the discriminatory practices of Japanese authorities in Manchuria. The protests included implications that British and American support might not be forthcoming in the event of renewed Russo-Japanese hostilities.

The Japanese government was responsive to Western concerns. Japanese diplomats, as well as Japanese businessmen, understood the importance of good relations with the Americans and the British. Bankers in

London and New York provided the loans with which Japan paid the bills for the war with Russia—and Western capital and markets would be important to the development of the Japanese empire for years to come.

What emerged in Japan were competing visions of empire. The foreign ministry and financial sector approach focused on the wealth Japan might accumulate in China through cooperation with the West and a benign paternalism toward the Chinese. To this end, the Japanese government gave assurances to the Americans and the British of their adherence to the Open Door in their sphere of interest and attempted to leave administrative control over the region to the Chinese government. The army, however, was less interested in commercial and financial affairs or in propitiating the Chinese or any of the Western powers. Charged with defense of the empire, it was determined to maximize Japan's position, running roughshod over all who stood in its way—and it was the army that controlled the situation in the field.

Given the limited resistance to Japanese activity in Manchuria, the army position prevailed. The Qing government could do no more than protest. The British made their displeasure known, but apprehension about conditions in Europe, especially the rise of German naval power, left the British in no position to alienate their Japanese allies. The Americans, however, worried the Japanese government. American naval power was also growing and there was no doubt that American businessmen, journalists, and missionaries in China were eager for their government to restrain Japan. Moreover, another issue, that of the mistreatment of Japanese who migrated to the United States, was generating tension in the relationship. Public anger directed against the United States for its racism narrowed the options of the Tokyo government to the advantage of the army's inclination to ignore the Americans. By 1907, Japanese naval war plans portrayed the United States as a potential enemy.

Japan was fortunate in the early years of the twentieth century to find Theodore Roosevelt in the White House. Roosevelt was apathetic toward American business interests in East Asia. He recognized the growth of Japanese power and was eager to direct it toward continental expansion, away from the Philippines, Hawaii, and the west coast of the United States. He worried about anti-Japanese outbursts in California. It was one thing to mistreat Chinese immigrants whose government could do little to protect them; it was quite another to mistreat the Japanese. Central to Roosevelt's policy toward East Asia was his determination to avoid conflict with Japan. Nothing the Japanese did in Korea or Manchuria affected any vital American interest. He was willing to protest against Japanese violations of the rights of Americans on the Asian continent. He was not willing to force a confrontation.

A "Gentlemen's Agreement" on the immigration issue early in 1907 bought Roosevelt some time. Roosevelt persuaded the authorities in San Francisco to retreat from their decision to segregate Japanese in the schools and the Japanese government undertook to limit the emigration of laborers to the United States. Anti-Japanese sentiment in California ran too high, however, and a sense of crisis with Japan intensified in Washington.

Roosevelt, long a disciple of Mahan, had been very successful in winning appropriations for shipbuilding. As early as 1906, the U.S. Navy had begun developing plans for the possibility of war with Japan. The crisis of 1907, coming soon after the British launching of the *H.M.S. Dreadnought*, the most powerful warship the world had ever seen, prompted Roosevelt to ask Congress for additional battleships. To generate support for his request, he decided to send the battlefleet on a round-the-world cruise. He hoped simultaneously to intimidate the Japanese with a display of American power and to persuade his critics that he was not merely appeasing Japan.

The Japanese were not intimidated, but were nonetheless eager to put the immigration issue behind them. Even before the American fleet crossed the Pacific, Japanese leaders had concluded that the flow of excess labor was best directed toward Manchuria; that protecting the right of Japanese to emigrate to the United States was an unnecessary irritant in an important relationship. Determined to ease tensions, they welcomed the fleet to Yokohama and ordered their ambassador in Washington, Takahira Kogoro, to convey their reassurances and to negotiate an agreement with the American secretary of state, Elihu Root. To Root and to a friend of Roosevelt who met with the Japanese foreign minister in Tokyo at approximately the same time, the Japanese affirmed their intention to restrict emigration across the Pacific and to respect both American possessions in the Pacific and the Open Door in China.[2] At the same time they left the Americans with no doubt that they no longer considered Manchuria part of China; that they would redirect emigration to the continent and that southern Manchuria was the defensive bulwark of their continental empire.

The Americans gave reciprocal assurances of their desire for friendly relations and acquiesced in Japan's intentions. The Japanese would have liked an unequivocal statement of American support for their position in Manchuria, but with the Root-Takahira agreement of 1908 they settled for passive acceptance. Mistreatment of Japanese immigrants in the United States continued to plague the relationship, but the war scare evaporated.

Unfortunately, from Japan's perspective, Roosevelt's successor in the White House had a decidedly different approach to foreign affairs and a threat to Japan's position in Manchuria quickly reappeared. William Howard Taft had served as governor of the Philippines and had toured East Asia as secretary of war. He had grown apprehensive about Japan's intentions and had concluded that Roosevelt was wrong to appease Japan. As president he was determined to promote the economic interests of the United States aggressively all over the world. In particular, he was persuaded that the markets of China proper and Manchuria held great potential for American exporters. He also believed that the political ends of the United States in East Asia, a stable balance of power resting on a sovereign China, could be attained by economic means, by "dollar diplomacy."

Central to the Taft administration's policy toward East Asia was recognition of the extent to which trade success was related to the volume of investments. By forcing American capital into China, Taft and his advisers hoped to undermine Japan's position there and facilitate the expansion of American trade. Although the Open Door policy was understood by the powers to relate exclusively to trade, the Taft administration insisted that it assured Americans equal opportunity for investment throughout China, without regard to spheres of interest.

The American effort to penetrate the investment market in China began in the summer of 1909. Taft personally pressed the Qing court to grant American bankers a share of a loan China was floating for the construction of a railroad between Hunan and Guangdong. The Qing government was eager to draw the Americans into China, especially into Manchuria, but Taft's pressures were misdirected. The Qing could not grant the American request until the United States gained the acquiescence of the British, French, and German banking groups.

In their desperate efforts to retain sovereignty over Manchuria, the Qing resorted to the time-honored policy of using barbarians to manage barbarians. Their principal defense was a plan to bring in American and possibly British investors, to give them a stake in the area, in the hope of using the strength of the other powers to prevent the Japanese and Russians from annexing their northeastern provinces. The opportunity to finance railroad development seemed like the most attractive bait.

The Americans surprised everyone by proposing the internationalization of all railroads in Manchuria. They apparently expected the Russians to agree to have other nations underwrite some of their losses with the Chinese Eastern Railroad and hoped to get British, French, and German support with which to isolate Japan. If the plan worked, Japan would be forced to surrender control of the South Manchuria Railroad, ending its domination of southern Manchuria and reducing the threat to China's sovereignty. The infusion of American capital into the area would enhance opportunities for trade, increasing profits for investors and merchants.

The American plan failed. Japan's position in Manchuria was too strong, its place in the world balance of power too secure, and its determination to resist the American scheme was unrelenting. Rather than separating the Russians from the Japanese, the Americans drove them closer together. Both rejected the plan in markedly similar terms and formalized the division of Manchuria between them. The British support which the Americans anticipated was never forthcoming. British commercial interests were unhappy about Japanese practices in Manchuria, but the Foreign Office treasured the alliance with Japan far more than the potential advantages to be derived from internationalizing the railroads there—and far more than it valued the good will of the Americans. Similarly, the French stood by their Russian allies and the Germans, sufficiently worried about encirclement in Europe, were not prepared to challenge the world on behalf of Chinese sovereignty or American investment opportunities. The Americans were getting a lesson in the workings of international politics: unwilling to concede Japan's position in Manchuria, they lacked the power to do anything about it. On the other hand, Japanese apprehension about American intentions intensified.

The Rise of Chinese Nationalism

Some historians have perceived nationalism in the inchoate ideology of the Boxer movement. Certainly the Boxers were antiforeign; almost certainly they were patriots as they fought for their land against foreign intruders. Few, however, seem to have had a sense of nation, such as that which infused educated Chinese at the turn of the century. In 1905, buoyed by Japanese success against Russia and angered by American mistreatment of Chinese immigrants, Chinese students, some returned from study in Japan, organized an anti-American boycott, arguably the first sustained nationalist movement in Chinese history.

Unquestionably, the Chinese had ample reason to be outraged by American racism. A Chinese translation of Harriet Beecher Stowe's classic *Uncle Tom's Cabin* included a preface and an afterward that drew parallels between the enslavement of African-Americans and the oppression of Chinese by Americans and China by the West.[3] The organizers of the boycott, however, were not particularly anti-American. They indicated their awareness that the immigration policy of the United States reflected the demands of American labor and not of Americans generally—and hoped to gain the support of other Americans. Moreover, the boycotters were concerned with issues larger than American racism, which, although hateful, merely provided a convenient target at which to direct their resentment. They sought to strike a blow for Chinese prestige. Unable to match Japan's performance at Port Arthur, they sought a more modest victory. Lacking the military power necessary to strike at the imperialists, they harnessed the energies available, using an organized public opinion against that power least likely to respond with force.

The boycott never received the official support of the Qing government, which feared provoking foreign intervention and a new round of humiliations. The American Asiatic Fleet lay at anchor off of Shanghai and the Americans had not refrained from gunboat diplomacy in the past. Nonetheless, many Chinese, especially those in the Foreign Ministry, recognized the value of such a popular movement as a diplomatic weapon. Once reasonably certain that the Americans would not retaliate, the Qing acquiesced in and unofficially supported the boycott. Had it not, there was always the risk that public indignation would be directed against the dynasty. Similarly, as agitation for the cancellation of a railroad concession to an American company mounted, the government estimated correctly that it could yield to popular demand without serious risk.

The Americans demanded that the Qing government suppress the boycott, but by President Roosevelt's efforts to improve treatment of Chinese in the United States acknowledged the justice of their complaints. The American minister in Peking protested frequently, demanded the punishment of the leaders of the boycott, and warned the Qing that they would be held accountable for losses sustained by his countrymen. Although the Qing refused to accept responsibility for the boycott and rejected demands that it be suppressed, the United States refrained from using or threatening to use the force available.

In the fall of 1905, after the boycott had been sustained in the coastal cities for about five months, it lost its vitality. The Qing began to fear it would turn violent and ultimately ordered its suppression. Probably of greater importance was the fact that Chinese businessmen, who were sacrificing the most, lost interest. Nonetheless, some Americans understood the message of the movement: that a modern nationalist movement was emerging in China and that China could no longer be treated with contempt. In December 1905, in his annual message to Congress, Roosevelt placed responsibility for the boycott on the American people. He insisted that "grave injustice and wrong have been done by this nation to the people of China." A few years later he wrote of "the growth of a real and intelligent spirit of patriotism in all parts of China."[4]

One other major sign of burgeoning Chinese nationalism was the "rights recovery" movement, an effort to wrest control over the construction and operation of railroads from foreigners. The movement spread across the country between 1904 and 1907 and generated mass support. Efforts were made to raise capital among overseas Chinese and to put Western-trained Chinese engineers in charge of construction. In terms of capturing control of railroad development, the movement failed, but as a school for nationalist organizers, it played an important role.

The awakening of China to which Roosevelt had referred and the demand for change continued at a quickening pace. New forces in China raced along several tracks, each pointing toward the creation of a modern nation-state, exercising sovereignty within its borders. The Qing court might hope to lead the race; it could not pull back on the reins. It was forced to move toward constitutional government as its only hope of preserving the dynasty. But the court could not move quickly enough and the promise of a constitutional monarchy was no longer sufficient to satisfy its critics. Led by Sun Yat-sen, the revolutionary movement had grown. Sun and his allies were determined to drive out the Manchus, establish a republican form of government, and carry out a land reform program borrowed in large part from the single-tax ideas of Henry George, an American economist. These forces of unrest, together with the "rights recovery" movement, further undermined the shaky Qing regime.

Sun and his friends made a series of abortive attempts to spark the revolution, including a spectacular failure at Guangzhou in April 1911. At approximately the same time, the international banking consortium, to which the Americans had finally gained entry, pressured the Qing into accepting a loan for construction of the Hunan–Guangdong railroad, galvanizing the "rights recovery" movement. Widespread disorders began in Sichuan, the center of Chinese financial interest in the railroad. In October, as the Qing attempted to pacify Sichuan, a military revolt erupted. It spread quickly through south China and within a few months the era of Manchu rule had ended.

Recognizing the danger, the Qing reacted quickly to the revolution in the south. The court recalled Yuan Shikai, whom it had forced into involuntary retirement only a year previously, to serve as commander of its military forces. Yuan chose this opportunity to rebuild and solidify his own power, becoming simultaneously premier of a new cabinet government. Using the modern Beiyang Army, largely his own creation, he defeated the rebel forces around Wuhan, then paused north of the Yangzi, allowing the rebels to destroy the Manchu garrisons in the south. Meanwhile, Sun, who had been in the United States when the critical revolt at Wuchang occurred, returned to China to join the provisional government his forces had established at Nanjing. Sun was elected president of that government, but he and his colleagues understood that Yuan was the only man with the power to unite China. A disunited China would invite foreign intervention and possibly dismemberment. Sun offered Yuan the presidency of the republic and agreement between the two sides was reached quickly. Yuan negotiated the abdication of the Qing emperor and was duly elected president of the Republic of China early in 1912.

The major powers with interests in China—Great Britain, France, Germany, Japan, Russia, and the United States—were all caught by surprise. The Japanese, in particular, had flirted with various revolutionary groups, but they were no more prepared than the others for the sudden collapse of the Qing. Japanese leaders were sympathetic to the possibility of a constitutional monarchy emerging; they were not pleased by the establishment of a republic, especially one led by their long-time nemesis, Yuan Shikai. Although the Japanese were divided as to what they wanted to do and see in China, none of them favored a strong China—and they feared Yuan as a capable and unfriendly leader. The Kwantung army in Manchuria immediately devised schemes for separating Manchuria and Mongolia from the rest of China, perhaps under a puppet Manchu regime. The Foreign Ministry and important business interests perceived opportunities for economic advantage in all of China by pursuing less overtly aggressive policies. Other Japanese imagined a revivified China assisting Japan in ridding Asia of Western imperialism.

The Americans, British, French, and Germans were concerned primarily with maintaining their existing privileges in China. They were willing to work with Sun or Yuan or anyone else who would honor the treaty system. Their bankers wanted to be sure that any new government in China would repay foreign loans. The Russians seem to have discerned an opportunity to weaken Chinese control over Outer Mongolia.

Clearly surrounded by predators, the Republic of China nonetheless fared reasonably well under the circumstances. The Russians succeeded in undermining Chinese authority in Outer Mongolia, but the Japanese Kwantung army plan for Manchuria and Inner Mongolia was aborted. Yuan was acceptable to the Western powers and he was willing to give them the assurances they demanded. Nonetheless they withheld recognition until he concluded an agreement for a large loan by the foreign banking consortium—a loan designed to enable him to operate his government efficiently enough to service and repay the preexisting Manchu obligations to the bankers.

Only the new American administration of Woodrow Wilson broke ranks, withdrawing support to the American participants in the banking consortium and unilaterally recognizing Yuan's government in April 1913. Wilson was suspicious of the bankers and of his predecessor's dollar diplomacy. He mistrusted the other great powers, questioning their intentions toward China. Ignorant of world affairs generally, certainly of Asian affairs, he was determined to help China and to find higher moral ground for American policy. Efforts by the Japanese to call his attention to the fact that the Chinese republic was on the verge of civil war, that Yuan had usurped power, that Sun and his Guomindang Party were disputing Yuan's exercise of authority and preparing to fight, that recognition was tantamount to interference on the side of Yuan, were all brushed aside. Even the assassination of the Guomindang leader of the republic's parliament at the behest of Yuan did not alter Wilson's desire to extend his blessings to the new republic. A month later, civil war broke out in China as the Guomindang, unable to check Yuan by parliamentary means, was forced to the battlefield.

Yuan crushed the Guomindang revolt, but he was not able to check the political aspirations of his military subordinates. No democrat, Yuan decided he would rather be emperor than president. He certainly did not want to be bothered by a parliament. But confronted by the opposition of the Guomindang in the south—with some support from Japan—and the defection of key lieutenants, Yuan was forced to surrender his dream and most of his power. He died in June 1916, and with him went the last semblance of national government. The age of the warlords had dawned; regionalism triumphed. And once again, China was fortunate to survive as a sovereign entity.

In the first few years after Yuan's collapse, the main stage was dominated by a succession of military men, each seeking to build a coalition that would give him supreme power in China. While one group of warlords struggled to dominate the Peking government, another vied with Sun Yat-sen for control of the rival regime established at Guangzhou. Frequently there was simultaneous fighting between North and South for control of the entire country. Amidst the resulting chaos, the Japanese consolidated their position.

TABLE 10.1. Some Major Figures of the Period 1915–1931
(Names in boldface are discussed in text)

John D. Rockefeller	1839–1937
Georges Clemenceau	1841–1929
Booker T. Washington	1856–1924
Woodrow Wilson	**1856–1924**
Yuan Shikai	**1859–1916**
William II of Germany	1859–1941
David Lloyd George	1863–1945
Sun Yat-sen	**1866–1925**
V. I. Lenin	**1870–1924**

In August 1914, a great war had begun in Europe with dramatic consequences for China. Suddenly the European powers were too busy to interfere in Chinese affairs. Unfortunately for China, Japan was not. On the other hand, neither were the Americans, who perceived themselves as China's champions.

In accordance with the terms of their alliance with Great Britain, the Japanese promptly overran German possessions in East Asia, including the German concession in Shandong. The Chinese were not unhappy to see the Germans go, but were not pleased by the presence of additional Japanese forces in North China. Nor did these gains satisfy the Japanese. A month later, in January 1915, the Japanese minister to China presented Yuan with twenty-one demands, divided into five groups. The Japanese sought to have the Chinese confirm and legitimize their gains in Shandong and their existing encroachments on Chinese sovereignty in Manchuria. They demanded new concessions in Manchuria and central China. The Chinese were required to commit themselves not to allow any other power to acquire or lease any harbor, bay, or island along their coast. In the fifth group, the Japanese demanded that they be consulted before any foreign capital was allowed into Fujian, that they be granted new railroad concessions, that China purchase at least half her armaments from Japan. Of still greater danger to China's sovereignty, the fifth group required the Chinese to accept Japanese "advisers" in China's political, military, and economic affairs and to share with the Japanese responsibility for police activities at key points throughout China. In sum, China was to become a Japanese protectorate, to be exploited much as Japan was exploiting Korea just before annexation. Even their British ally's interests in the Yangzi valley would not go unchallenged. Clearly the Japanese assumed that the war in Europe had left them with a free hand and they were moving rapidly to capitalize on the opportunity.

Despite Japanese warnings to keep their demands secret, Yuan leaked the necessary information to sympathetic American diplomats and missionaries and to the foreign press generally. The American missionaries telegraphed Washington, asking the American government to demand to be represented at the negotiations between China and Japan—and to guarantee justice for China. The Chinese government paid for the telegram and United Press releases publicizing it. The initial response of the Department of State was to avoid involvement, but it soon shifted toward offering to acquiesce in Japanese imperialism in Shandong and Manchuria in exchange for an end to Japanese complaints about California legislation denying Japanese immigrants the right to own land: let the Japanese send their emigrants to Manchuria. Eventually, President Wilson took control of American policy and insisted that the United States demonstrate its intention to support China. He insisted that the United States would surrender no rights in China nor would it ask the Chinese to accept any infringement of their sovereignty.

The Japanese recognized that they now faced American opposition. At least as important were British protests. But the Japanese were well aware that the Europeans could not oppose them in any meaningful way and the Americans, given their more limited interests in the region, were hardly likely to do more than express their displeasure as the Japanese tightened their grip on China. For the moment, the fifth and most obnoxious group of demands was dropped, but the Chinese were given an ultimatum threatening force if the first four groups were not acceded to immediately. With no help in sight, Yuan yielded on the next day.

In April 1917, the United States intervened in the war in Europe. The American minister in China urged the Chinese to associate themselves with the United States in the fight against Germany so as to enable them to receive direct aid from the American government. He and others also argued that a Chinese declaration of war would win China a place at the peace conference and an opportunity to challenge Japanese claims to the German concession in Shandong. The Chinese, for similar reasons, were eager to join the fray. In August 1917, China entered the war and approximately 100, 000 Chinese laborers assisted British, French, and American forces in France. They suffered several thousand casualties, including those lost at sea when a German submarine torpedoed the ship that carried them. When the war ended in November 1918, Chinese diplomats went to the peace conference at Versailles with great hopes based on their country's role in the war, the increasingly prominent place of the United States in the international system, and the anti-imperialism explicit in Woodrow Wilson's Fourteen Points.

The Chinese dream was of ridding themselves of all of the symbols of their semicolonial status, but they were especially interested in regaining control of the former German concession in Shandong. Having allied with the victors for just such a purpose, they put forth restoration of complete Chinese sovereignty over Shandong as their minimal demand. At Versailles, however, the Chinese representatives learned that Japan had signed secret treaties with her European allies that bound them to support Tokyo's claims to the German concessions. In addition, in the treaty by which China had accepted Japan's Twenty-one Demands of 1915, Yuan Shikai had also bound the country to accept any German-Japanese decision as to the disposition of German concessions. Wilson was China's only hope—and he failed them. Persuaded that Japan's claim had merit under international law and troubled by a Japanese threat to quit the peace conference rather than yield, Wilson abandoned his support for the Chinese position.

In China—and among Chinese everywhere—the decision at the peace conference to transfer control of Shandong to Japan generated outrage. Beginning with a demonstration in Peking on May 4, hundreds of thousands of students took to the streets in cities throughout China, committing acts of violence against allegedly pro-Japanese members of the government and organizing an effective boycott against Japanese goods. The students won widespread support from business groups and workers. They had become the ingredient necessary for the cementing of what Sun Yat-sen called China's "loose sands" into a powerful nationalist force.

The leaders of what came to be known as the May Fourth movement were angry about the verdict at Versailles, but they were also disgusted by internal disorder, with the disunity that prevented the nation from mobilizing its energies against foreign pressures. To the aroused public, they expressed the need for a complete transformation of Chinese civilization. They concluded that the modernization of China required destruction of the traditional society and called for many of the same kinds of social and intellectual changes sympathetic Westerners had argued would result in the "civilizing" of China. Spurred by Chen Duxiu, dean of Peking University, they called for "Mr. Science" and "Mr. Democracy" as antidotes to Confucian traditionalism. The student activism triggered by China's failure at Versailles was propelling China toward a great nationalist revolution.

Nationalism Elsewhere in East Asia

Korean intellectuals were confronted with a situation far worse than semicolonialism. The Japanese had annexed their country and exercised total control of it, exploiting it for the benefit of their home islands. With the Japanese serving as unwitting tutors, traditional xenophobia evolved into modern nationalism. Deliberately, American mission schools promoted Korean nationalism—as long as it was directed against Japan. The Korean historian Han Woo-keun contends that "the progressive, democratic spirit of American Protestantism made the institutions founded by missionaries the natural breeding places for leaders of the resistance."[5] Protestant hymns were converted into *Ch'angga*, patriotic songs sung to Western melodies. But their experience of resisting the Japanese was by far the most important teacher for Korean patriots.

Many Korean nationalists went into voluntary exile, both in China and the West. Some tried to organize independence groups; others attempted to win foreign support, especially American. A Korean Youth Army School was established in Nebraska in 1909. But the activities of the exiles had little impact on Korea or Japanese imperialism. Only slightly more effective were the freedom fighters operating out of Manchuria and the Russian Maritime provinces. Not until March 1919, two months before the May 4 demonstrations in Peking, did Korean nationalists achieve their first major success.

The catalyst, as for much of the nationalist fervor in East Asia, was Woodrow Wilson's call for self-determination, presumably for all the world's people. A demonstration was planned for March 3, coinciding with funeral rites for the late king. Various religious organizations mobilized hundreds of thousands of Koreans. On March 1, thirty-three of the movement's leaders signed a declaration of independence and were arrested by the Japanese authorities. Nonetheless, the demonstration went forward and by some estimates more than two million people around the country took part. The demonstrations were met with military force. Japanese troops opened fire on the participants and torched the schools and churches to which they fled for refuge. They killed approximately 7,500 people. Scores of thousands were injured or arrested.

In April 1919, the provisional government of the Republic of Korea was established in Shanghai and in May it sent a representative to Versailles to plead Korea's case at the peace conference. American and European newspapers, alerted to the events by missionaries, were highly critical of the Japanese response, but no Western government stepped forward to champion Korean independence. The Japanese government realized it had a public relations problem and for much of the next decade found more subtle ways to contain Korean nationalism. Armed resistance to Japanese rule from bases in Manchuria and Siberia was an irritant, but never a threat to Japanese domination of the peninsula.

Korean nationalism was further stimulated in the 1920s by Soviet Russia. In 1920 a Korean Communist Party was formed in Shanghai with modest Soviet support. Koreans in the Maritime Provinces and Soviet troops there, united by opposition to Japanese imperialism, joined in operations against Japanese forces in Manchuria. Unfortunately, the Korean nationalist movement, like others around the world, was ultimately riven by tensions between communist and noncommunist members, to the detriment of the Korean people.

All of Southeast Asia, except, arguably, Thailand, had been absorbed into Western empires, but as Carl Trocki has noted, "nothing was more deceptive than the illusion of total European control, for, in learning from the West, the most ardent collaborators prepared themselves to throw off foreign rule."[6] The late nineteenth century was marked by prolonged anticolonial movements in the region, often involving religious movements—the unwillingness of one or another religious group to accept the rule of nonbelievers.

The Filipinos fought the Spanish, led in part by Filipino priests rebelling against domination by Spanish priests, only to find themselves being subjugated by the far more powerful Americans. The Moros, Muslims in the southern Philippine Islands, fought both the Spanish and the Americans, attempting to protect their culture against Christian intrusions. The long war between Aceh and the Dutch in Sumatra took on elements of a *jihad*, a holy war of Muslims against infidels. In Indochina and in Burma, Buddhist temples were active in opposing European rule and Christian proselytizing. But backed by vastly superior firepower, supported by Asian troops uninfected by nationalism, the Americans and Europeans consistently prevailed.

One major obstacle to the development of nationalism in Southeast Asia was the multiplicity of ethnic groups in several of the countries. Chinese could be found everywhere and constituted as much as 40 percent of the population of British Malaya. Indians could be found in large numbers wherever the British were in control. The British and the Dutch were masterful in their ability to divide their subject people by ethnicity, generally sharing power with wealthy Chinese. The Dutch succeeded in winning the support of the Ambonese and exploiting the indifference of the Acehnese of Sumatra to nationalist movements on Java. In the Philippines, the Moros concluded that the Americans offered them greater protection for their religious freedom than did native Filipino Christians.

Nonetheless, nationalism spread in the region during the early years of the twentieth century—and the Western colonial powers facilitated its growth. For some peoples, the territorial basis of their nationalism was provided by borders drawn by the West. For almost all, contacts with European administrators, Western education, either at home or in the colonial metropole, the teachings of Western missionaries and the lessons provided by Western merchants, and foreign travel, including pilgrimages to Mecca, stimulated the desire to create a modern nation state, free of foreign rulers, regardless of how benign.

Between 1905 and 1910, Japan appears to have served as the model of what could be. The Japanese had created a modern state, defeated a major European power, and won a place for their country among the great powers. In the Philippines and Vietnam, in particular, intellectuals striving to win independence for their people were excited by Japan's accomplishments. But Japanese imperialism in Korea and China reduced Japan's appeal among Southeast Asians, especially ethnic Chinese. In 1911, the revolution in China and the creation of a republic won the attention of many. Vietnamese who had been influenced by the thought of Kang Youwei and other Chinese reformers as well as by Japan's successes and American and French liberal ideas, now thought in terms of a nationalist revolution to create a Vietnamese republic. The overseas Chinese complicated matters throughout the region by their strong support of the Chinese revolution and the anti-Japanese movements to which they were drawn in 1905 and by news of Japan's Twenty-one demands in 1915.

The years 1914–1918 provided a major stimulus to nationalism in Southeast Asia. The slaughter the Europeans were inflicting on each other eroded whatever sense of Western superiority remained among Asians. Many Vietnamese served in France as laborers. Siam went to war on the side of its British protectors. Wilson's Fourteen Points, specifically his call for self-determination, inspired politically mobile peoples of the region. Ho Chi Minh, who later led the fight for Vietnamese independence against both France and the United States, went to Versailles to gain Wilson's support for his efforts. Last, but obviously not least, was the Bolshevik Revolution in Russia. Initially it provided evidence that a handful of determined revolutionaries could overthrow a powerful state. Subsequently, Lenin's critique of imperialism and the activities of the Communist International (Comintern) in Asia provided hope, guidance, and material support for those who would free their lands from colonial oppressors.

The anti-imperialism espoused by Wilson and Lenin won freedom for no colonial people. After the world war ended, the colonial powers reasserted their authority, occasionally substituting the rule of one of the war's victors for that of Germany. But ideas have consequences and the legitimacy of colonial rule, of nineteenth-century imperialism, was being questioned in the West as well as among the victims of colonialism. Even the Japanese, irritated by having the rules changed before they had won the share of the spoils to which they felt entitled, understood that more subtle methods of extending their empire were required. Suppressing nationalist movements in the decades that followed would be an unending and ultimately futile task.

Washington and Moscow Look to East Asia

Tensions building between Japan and the United States troubled leaders of both countries. They had succeeded in finessing the immigration issue and other problems caused by racism in America. The Japanese had easily outmaneuvered the Americans when the Taft administration attempted to use "dollar diplomacy" to reduce Russian and Japanese influence in Manchuria, but the Americans swallowed their pride and settled for membership in an international banking consortium that in 1912 included Japan. In the absence of support from the Wilson administration, the American bankers withdrew in 1913, and the consortium came to be perceived by Americans, Chinese, and Japanese as an instrument of Japanese policy. Japan's Twenty-one demands had alerted Wilson to Japan's intentions in China and the threat of Japanese domination of China to American interests there and he began to grope ineffectually for a response.

Wilson's apparent unfriendliness created anxiety in Tokyo, especially after the United States intervened in the European war in April 1917. The Japanese sent Ishii Kikujiro, probably their most experienced diplomat, to Washington, where he and the American secretary of state, Robert

Lansing, managed to paper over the differences of their respective countries in the ambiguous language of their profession. Ishii left no doubt that the Japanese considered Manchuria to be under their exclusive control and assured Lansing that Americans would not be denied economic opportunities in the rest of China. At the peace conference, tensions arose again as the United States opposed Japan's retention of the German concession in Shandong. Soon Washington and Tokyo were arguing over the meaning of the Ishii-Lansing agreement and the question of whether the island of Yap, a potentially important cable station, was included among the mandated territories awarded to Japan by the Treaty of Versailles. Before the end of 1919, these disagreements and new immigration problems generated a war scare. If that was not enough, both governments had intervened in Siberia in 1918, ostensibly to rescue Czech forces trapped by the Russian civil war. The Japanese military had more ambitious plans for extending its influence permanently. American apprehensions about the insatiability of Japanese imperialism mounted when Japanese force levels far exceeded the numbers agreed upon and the Japanese showed no sign of going home when the war ended.

The Americans had another idea for defending China and their interests in China that ultimately eased the crisis. They would create a new international banking consortium that would be used to restrain Japan. The British liked the idea enormously. They had become increasingly apprehensive about the intentions of their Japanese ally and hoped that Anglo-American cooperation would protect their interests in China, something London no longer believed it could do on its own. Negotiations began in 1919 during the peace conference, only to have the Japanese insist on excluding Manchuria and Mongolia from the scope of the consortium. Although the American and British governments found the Japanese exception objectionable, their bankers were less troubled. Neither American nor British bankers had any interest in competing with the Japanese in areas in which the Japanese were entrenched and under circumstances that would jeopardize their bilateral endeavors with Japan. They were more attracted to opportunities in stable Japan than to risky ventures in chaotic China.

Ultimately, the American and British bankers reached agreement with their Japanese counterparts. Japan did not insist upon explicit assurances that its sphere of interest in Manchuria would be respected, but the Japanese government declared, for the record, that it understood American assurances of concern for its right of self-preservation to mean just that. The American government was not pleased with the arrangements, but accepted them grudgingly—and the war scare passed as the new consortium came into being in 1920.

Both American and Japanese war planners recognized that their countries had many issues that divided them and might lead to military confrontation. In particular, the navies of the two Pacific powers watched each other very carefully. The Japanese were deeply troubled by the enormous growth of the U.S. Navy during the world war. The United States had suddenly emerged as the greatest naval power in the world and its capacity to outstrip Japan in an arms race was all too obvious. Japanese leaders were also aware that their British allies could not be counted on against the Americans. The security of the empire was at stake.

Japanese naval building worried strategic analysts in Washington. American security, including that of Hawaii and the Philippines, seemed to require a massive ship-building program. But in the immediate postwar years, agitation for disarmament was very strong in the United States, mingling with the desire of Americans, who had failed to join the League of Nations established by the Treaty of Versailles, to find some other means to lead the world toward an enduring peace. American leaders realized that the only way to both provide for their nation's security *and* satisfy the public clamor for disarmament was to negotiate an agreement with Japan to halt the incipient arms race. They understood that the arms race could not be separated from a host of other problems, including the Anglo-Japanese alliance, Japanese imperialism in China, and the balance of power in East Asia. They were receptive, therefore, to British overtures for an American-initiated conference that would include all nations with interests in the western Pacific, including China, but not Soviet Russia. In 1921, the British, Chinese, Japanese, and five other states joined the Americans at a major meeting in Washington.

The invitation to participate in the Washington Conference was exhilarating to many politically aware Chinese. The Chinese press reflected hopes of ridding China of foreign spheres of influence, of extraterritoriality, and of restrictions on tariff autonomy—of the many humiliations China had suffered since the Opium War. But in 1921 the country was still in chaos. Sun Yat-sen's fortunes rose and, buoyed by the new swell of nationalism, he planned for the military reunification of the country. In July, the Chinese Communist Party was formally established with the help of Soviet agents—who also had discussions with Sun and other potential powers in China. While Sun's Guomindang or Nationalist Party and the Communists plotted and the warlords fought each other, the rest of the world communicated with China through whoever controlled the regime in Peking. The invitation to Washington struck all factions as an opportunity to reverse the failure at Versailles.

By the eve of the conference, however, thoughtful Chinese realized that their nation's disunity, chaotic conditions, and empty treasury would force its delegates to negotiate from weakness. Sun's Guangzhou regime refused to participate in a joint mission and finally declared that it would not recognize any decisions made in Washington. Fear that China would be betrayed by its own representatives or victimized by the other participants deflated earlier expectations.

From the American vantage point, the conference was a tremendous success. Rejecting an invitation to join the Anglo-Japanese alliance, they succeeded in replacing it with a harmless four-power nonaggression pact, in which they and the French joined the British and Japanese. Infinitely more satisfying to the American people was a five-power treaty in which Italy joined the other four in an agreement to limit the size of their respective navies, thus checking the arms race. The naval agreement left Japan secure in its home isles while limiting the ability of the Japanese navy to conduct offensive operations in the eastern Pacific. As an indication of the growing might of the United States, Great Britain conceded parity to the American fleet, surrendering its historic determination to maintain a fleet strong enough to defeat a combination of the second and third strongest naval powers.

As a result of the equilibrium achieved via the Four Power and Five Power treaties, the conference then turned to the matter of China—of great power competition in the western Pacific and of Chinese aspirations. Sentiment in the United States favored Chinese challenges to Japan and European infringements on their sovereignty and the Chinese and American delegations worked closely together, but the principal concern of the Americans, like the Japanese and the Europeans, was protection of their interests in China. The Americans pressed for a broad interpretation of the Open Door, extending beyond economic opportunity to include preservation of China's territorial integrity. The Japanese delegates sought acceptance of their claim to special interests in Manchuria and Inner Mongolia.

American insistence on equal opportunity for trade and investment did not trouble the Japanese. They were confident of their ability to compete successfully against the United States or any other country that challenged their economic position in China. American insistence on China's territorial integrity, however, continued to disturb them. But as they had in the consortium negotiations, the Japanese persuaded their American counterparts to exclude their existing holdings, allowing them to conclude that their interests in Manchuria and Inner Mongolia would not be compromised. The Europeans were easily reconciled to the Japanese-American agreement. Only Chinese dreams were shattered.

Ultimately, in the Nine Power Treaty, the participants in the conference agreed not to interfere in the internal affairs of China, to allow the Chinese to unify and modernize their country in their own way and at their own pace. This was the "internationalization" of the American Open Door policy, the contracting parties agreeing "to respect the sovereignty, the independence, and the territorial and administrative integrity of China." To the Americans, this was the solution to coexisting with Japanese power in East Asia. All the powers with significant interests in the region—except for Soviet Russia—were committed to peaceful competition without prejudice to the future of China.

For the Chinese the outcome of the conference was far less satisfying. At best the Nine Power Treaty promised no *further* encroachments on Chinese sovereignty. Most of those attributes of sovereignty that China had been forced to surrender over the previous eighty years were unretrieved. In response to China's demand for the freedom to set its own tariff rates, the powers offered a five percent increase on imports and a promise of further discussion. The Chinese demand for extraterritoriality was met with the promise of a commission to study the problem. China's demand for the withdrawal of foreign troops from its soil went unanswered.

The United States did help the Chinese obtain British and Japanese promises to evacuate leaseholds, including substantial concessions on Shandong, but the Americans were unwilling to jeopardize the larger settlement by challenging Japan's position in Manchuria. In supporting the Chinese campaign against spheres of influence the Americans, having no

sphere of their own, sacrificed nothing. Toward those privileges of imperialism in which Americans shared, the United States was less forthright.
The United States was no more willing than any of the other powers to
end extraterritoriality or grant the Chinese tariff autonomy.

Several members of the Chinese delegation resigned in protest in the
midst of the negotiations. Dissatisfaction with the results of the conference led to protest marches in China and by Chinese in the United States.
In Shanghai, 20,000 demonstrators indicated their displeasure. As far as
politically involved Chinese were concerned, the conference had served
the ends of the imperialists, but had done little for China. The point was
underscored in Moscow, where representatives of Sun's Guomindang
and of the Chinese Communist Party attended a Comintern-sponsored
"Congress of the Toilers of the Far East."

The failure of communist revolutions in Europe had led Lenin and
some of his colleagues to look to Asia and the Middle East as prospec-
tive arenas in which their vision might succeed. The first congress of the
Comintern in March 1919 had included the Chinese struggle against
Japanese imperialism among those efforts by colonial peoples worthy of
support. In July 1920, the Comintern had emphasized the need to support risings and revolts in oppressed nations, again including China. Lenin
sent Soviet agents to China to gather information and to find worthy collaborators. Under pressure from Chinese, Japanese, and Korean radicals,
and in the context of the Washington Conference, the Comintern convened its own meeting of "Toilers of the Far East" in January, 1922. It
was a way of asserting Soviet interest in any Pacific settlement—of reminding the powers that Russia also had interests in East Asia—and of
offering Chinese nationalists an alternative to American guidance. Specifically, the Comintern attacked the Washington Conference and claimed
to speak for the exploited Asian masses while their masters divided the
spoils in Washington.

The Chinese representatives at the Moscow conference endured some
awkward moments when Mongolian delegates complained of Chinese
imperialism and the Russians reminded them of the Golden Rule. But it
was the Guomindang delegates who were forced to fend off criticism
from several speakers, including the head of the Comintern, who complained about Sun Yat-sen's alleged pro-American sympathies. After
Trotsky had called American capitalism the stronghold of world imperialism, the charge was indeed grave. For most Chinese, however, the bat-

tle against very apparent Japanese and British infringements was far too important to justify diverting energy into an anti-American campaign. The Chinese were not yet ready to follow the line emanating from Moscow. Nonetheless, the Soviets had served notice that they would not accept a settlement to which they had not been a party and in the years that followed a growing number of Chinese nationalists surrendered their hopes of American assistance and turned to Moscow.

Nationalist Revolution in China

In March 1920, politically engaged Chinese were excited by reports that Soviet Russia had renounced the concessions in Manchuria that Tsarist Russia had extorted from China. In the "Karakhan manifesto" of July 1919 the Soviet government denounced imperialism and expressed solidarity with the Chinese people in their struggle against foreign oppression: it would surrender railway, mining, and forestry rights without requiring compensation. The statement had been issued during a dark moment in the Russian civil war and by the time the Chinese saw it, Lenin and his colleagues were feeling hardly more generous than their Tsarist predecessors. But Soviet denials of the authenticity of the Chinese text received little publicity and popular gratitude for the manifesto went unabated. The Russian Revolution might indeed lead to a new world order, one in which China would be freed from the imperialist yoke.

From 1920 to 1922, Comintern agents established contacts with important Chinese intellectuals and political figures. Most significant were those that led to the formation of the Chinese Communist Party and to ties with Sun Yat-sen. Sun's political fortunes had reached another low point in 1922 when he was forced to flee from Guangzhou after a disagreement with the local warlord. His dream of uniting China seemed hopeless. Over the years, Sun had looked to Japan, to the West, and especially to the United States for guidance and material assistance. In general, he had been disappointed by the response. When the Soviets reached out to him in 1922, he had little to lose by accepting their help.

The Soviet government had much to fear from a powerful anticommunist Japan on its border and much to gain if a China strong enough to confront Japan emerged from the turmoil that had followed Yuan

Shikai's death. Recognizing the reality that the nascent Chinese Communist Party had no power and little influence, the Russians approached the Peking government and various warlords as well as Sun. Ultimately, it was the alliance with Sun that served the ends of both parties. In a joint declaration of 1923, Sun and the Soviet representative with whom he had negotiated announced that Russia would provide Sun's Guomindang with aid while accepting Sun's contention that conditions in China were inappropriate for the development of communism. Arrangements were made to have the Guomindang reorganized along the lines of the Soviet Communist Party and Sun agreed to a coalition with the Chinese Communists.

As part of the cooperation between Sun and the Russians, a mission led by Jiang Jieshi (Chiang Kai-shek) went to Moscow and the Comintern sent Michael Borodin to Guangzhou. In Moscow, Jiang studied the organization of the Red Army and then returned to become superintendent of the newly created Whampoa Academy where the officers of the Guomindang army were to be trained and indoctrinated. Borodin, in Guangzhou, became Sun's adviser, helping with the reorganization of the party and training political cadres in the art of mobilizing the masses. And in 1924, the Soviet Union further ingratiated itself with Chinese nationalists by surrendering some of the privileges of the "unequal treaties."

Despite all these developments and evidence of the increasing success of the Guomindang-Communist effort to build a mass base for a new Chinese revolution, despite evidence that Sun was preparing to march north to unite China by force, the other great powers clung to their privileges, to all of the hated symbols of imperialism. There was little to indicate that they recognized that Sun's operations were something other than warlordism. Late in 1923, when he claimed a share of the customs duty surplus for his southern regime, American, British, and Japanese warships joined in a naval demonstration to thwart him.

Lenin died early in 1924 and Sun's death followed a year later, but the Guomindang-Soviet alliance held. Russian arms and military advisers enabled Jiang Jieshi and his students to beat back attacks by nearby warlord armies. Well-equipped, well-led, and most of all highly motivated, Jiang's forces began to extend their control over south China. And then, in May 1925, their cause received an unintended boost from the foreign community in Shanghai.

A strike by Chinese workers against a Japanese-owned textile mill in the city turned violent, resulting in the death of one of the strikers. Demonstrations against Japanese imperialism followed, and on May 30 thousands of Chinese marched into the International Settlement chanting anti-foreign slogans. The British police officer in charge of the municipal constabulary ordered the crowd to disperse and then ordered his men to fire: an estimated dozen demonstrators were killed and a score more wounded.

The incident led to a spontaneous outburst of anti-imperialist, antiforeign sentiment that spread from Shanghai through China's cities and ultimately even to the countryside—the "May 30th Movement." A few weeks later, as Guomindang and Communist organizers mobilized thousands of workers, peasants, students, and soldiers in antiforeign demonstrations and strikes in Guangzhou, British troops fired on a march that passed close to their position protecting the foreign concession. Fifty-two Chinese were killed and many more wounded. A fifteen-month strike in Hong Kong and a boycott against British goods greatly strengthened the Guomindang-Communist alliance, winning enormous support for its cause throughout the nation.

For the next year, the Guomindang's newly formed government fought to consolidate its position in the south while devising plans to realize Sun's vision of a Northern Expedition to unite the country. The prospects were not terribly promising: warlord armies outnumbering Guomindang troops by a ratio of at least 5:1 stood before them. Probably the most dangerous of the warlords was Zhang Zuolin, operating out of Manchuria with apparent Japanese support. And there was always the possibility of direct foreign intervention, given Japanese and Western hostility to communism and the Guomindang's Soviet ally.

In addition to facing overwhelming military odds, the Guomindang was beset by internal divisions as well. Without Sun to impose his will on the party, opposition to his policy of allying with Soviet Russia mounted and split the party. One faction saw no difference between Russia and other foreign powers that tried to control China and mistrusted the Chinese Communists. Jiang Jieshi and his allies pushed the anti-Soviet faction aside in January 1926, expelling its members from the party. Then, in March, Jiang, contending that the Communists were plotting to gain control of the army, deprived them of all positions of military authority, arrested several of them and all of the Russian advisers in Guangzhou. He now had effective control of Guomindang military power and had established himself at the political center of the nationalist movement.

The Chinese Communists were eager to rise in opposition to Jiang's coup, but the Comintern decided that the time was not right. Borodin was instructed to offer approval for commencement of the drive north, continued Soviet aid, and restraints on Communist agitation in return for Jiang's agreement to contain anticommunist pressures within the Guomindang. In July, 1926 Jiang launched the Northern Expedition. With surprising ease his armies marched through central China, driving warlord troops out of the Yangzi valley. A Communist-led uprising in Shanghai eased Jiang's task in capturing that city in March 1927 and a few days later Guomindang forces occupied Nanjing.

As Jiang's forces fought their way toward the Yangzi, they met with little foreign interference. The British, whose interests were greatest in the region and who had been the targets of much of the antiforeign agitation, chose to come to terms with the Guomindang. In December 1926 they indicated a willingness to revise the unequal treaties. A month later, the Americans, eager to seize the lead, followed suit. The Japanese, concerned primarily with protecting their interests in Manchuria, also acted with restraint.

Nonetheless, when Guomindang troops occupied Nanjing a grave crisis suddenly arose. Whereas Shanghai was taken without serious incident, in Nanjing Chinese troops attacked foreigners and foreigner property, including the American, British, and Japanese consulates. The attacks did not stop until after American and British warships appeared and fired on the offending troops. With more than a hundred Western and Japanese warships in the region and thousands of foreign troops on hand, the threat of a major intervention to stop the Guomindang advance loomed large.

Jiang claimed that the violence in Nanjing was the work of agents provocateurs, but the powers insisted on holding the Guomindang responsible. In concert they demanded punishment of those responsible for the murders and looting, reparations for damages and loss of life, and assurances that foreigners henceforth would be protected. Although pressure from the various foreign nations affected was great, a British effort to declare a time limit within which the demands would have to be met and to threaten sanctions was blocked by Japan and the United States, providing Jiang and his advisers with time desperately needed to cope with a power struggle that had erupted within the Guomindang.

On the same day that he received the demands from the foreign powers, Jiang ordered the arrest and massacre of hundreds of Communists and labor leaders in Shanghai. At a critical moment in his relations with Japan and the West, he perceived an urgent need to initiate a series of political and military maneuvers that ultimately enabled him to best Stalin and squeeze out the Communists before they could eliminate him. Because of the timing, the foreign policy issue and the internal political issue became intertwined: too recalcitrant a response to the foreign powers might provoke intervention and too conciliatory a response surely would result in charges that he had sold out to the imperialists.

The Japanese had the clearest understanding of the turmoil within the Guomindang and counseled patience to the other imperial powers. They perceived Jiang as a man with whom they could work, a man who would respond reasonably to their determination to preserve their interests in China. Less enamored of Jiang, but lacking a viable alternative, the Americans and British followed suit. The American minister in China was convinced that tensions between Jiang and his Communist allies were a sham and that Jiang, in any event, was just as hostile to American interests as were the allegedly more radical elements in his coalition. Washington nonetheless ordered him to negotiate with Jiang.

In the late spring and early summer, tensions arose between Guomindang leftists, already alienated from Jiang, and both the Communists and their Soviet advisors. In July the Guomindang left turned on the Communists and the "White Terror" swept China as both Jiang and his rivals within the Guomindang pursued and massacred Communists and their supporters. The Soviet advisers fled the country and most of the surviving Chinese Communists took to the hills, ultimately regrouping in a remote area of Jiangxi. A few months later, as various factions within the Guomindang vied for control of the party apparatus and its army, the Comintern ordered an abortive uprising in Guangzhou. After the ill-fated "Canton Commune" was crushed, it was apparent that real power within the Chinese revolution rested with the army, controlled by Jiang.

Confident of Japanese support, Jiang concluded he could reach an understanding with the Americans, leaving the British no choice but to follow along. In March 1928 he accepted American terms for settling the

Nanjing incident and won an expression of regret from the Americans for the naval bombardment in which they had participated. But formal recognition of his regime as the government of China remained out of reach. The powers were awaiting the outcome of the resumed Northern Expedition against Zhang Zuolin and the warlord regime in Peking.

Suddenly, in May, Japanese troops, undermining the efforts of Japanese statesmen to work with Jiang, clashed with Guomindang forces in Shandong. When the government in Tokyo attempted to retrieve the situation by forcing Zhang Zuolin to return to Manchuria, the Japanese army assassinated him in a vain effort to take complete control of that region of China. Neither military nor civilian authorities in Japan supported the efforts of the army in the field, but no Japanese leader was willing to accept Chinese sovereignty over Manchuria, precluding a new understanding with Jiang.

With Zhang Zuolin eliminated, Guomindang forces soon took over the major cities of Shandong and Peking. Jiang and his allies were in control of most of China and diplomatic recognition soon followed. In July 1928 the United States negotiated a treaty granting tariff autonomy to China and constituting recognition of Jiang's Nanjing regime. By the end of the year, all of the major powers had recognized the new government and negotiated new treaties granting it tariff autonomy. On October 10, 1928 the Guomindang government was formally proclaimed, basking in its military and diplomatic successes. When Zhang Zuolin's son, Zhang Xueliang, raised the Guomindang flag over Manchuria a few months later, China was at least nominally reunited under the leadership of Jiang Jieshi. The revolutionary vision of Sun Yat-sen had been realized. Treaty revision had begun. The era of imperialist domination of China had ended—or had it?

TABLE 10.2. Some Notable Events of the Period 1905–1931
(Events in boldface are discussed in text)

Anti-American boycott in China	**1905**
Gentlemen's Agreement between Japan	
and the United States	**1907**
Union of South Africa established	1908
Japan annexes Korea	**1910**
W.E.B. Dubois founds NAACP	1911

Revolution in Mexico	1911
Revolution in China, collapse of Qing,	
proclamation of republic	**1911**
Titanic sinks	1912
World War I begins in Europe	**1914**
Panama Canal opens	1914
Einstein formulates theory of relativity	1915
China and the United States intervene in world war	**1917**
Russian Revolution	1917
Paris Peace Conference	1918–1919
May Fourth Movement erupts in China	**1919**
Boston Red Sox sell Babe Ruth to New York Yankees	1920
Washington Naval Conference	**1921–1922**
T.S. Eliot publishes *The Waste Land;*	
James Joyce publishes *Ulysses*	1922
Jiang Jieshi launches Northern Expedition	**1926**
Lindbergh flies non-stop from New York to Paris	1927
Kellogg-Briand Pact outlaws war	1928
Black Friday, crash of U.S. stock market	1929
Coronation of Haile Selassie I of Ethiopia	1930
Mukden incident	**1931**

Crisis in Manchuria

Defeating the various warlords and reunifying China turned out be easy relative to the task of resuming the modernization of the country. In foreign affairs, relations with China's two closest neighbors, Soviet Russia and Japan, were strained. The quest for the restoration of China's sovereign rights proceeded slowly. Tariff autonomy was gained by 1930 and a number of European concessions were returned to Chinese control. A few smaller states surrendered extraterritoriality, as had the states defeated in the world war, but Great Britain, Japan, and the United States refused to yield that privilege for their citizens. Foreign troops were still quartered on Chinese soil and foreign ships continued to cruise China's inland waters. Most of the symbols of China's humiliation remained.

Moreover, Jiang's government had little with which to work: the treasury was nearly empty and existing sources of income were inadequate. A host of economic, social, political, and military obstacles blocked the collection of taxes. China's credit rating among world bankers was low and the Guomindang's aggressive nationalism was not likely to attract new foreign investment. Politically, party unity was but a facade. The government was a one-party dictatorship organized along Leninist lines and while all the generals joined the party, few surrendered their taste for power. A host of Guomindang politicians was constantly maneuvering to replace Jiang and the Communists were mobilizing peasants in Jiangxi in preparation for guerrilla warfare.

Despite these formidable problems, the Nanjing government made considerable progress toward its goals between October 1928 and September 1931. Tariff autonomy brought greatly increased customs revenues. Loans came from American banks, encouraged by improved relations between China and the United States. Technical advisers were provided by the League of Nations and others came from the United States. American corporations undertook the essential task of developing Chinese transportation and communication facilities—the network through which Jiang could aspire to exercise actual control over all of China. There was far more British and Japanese capital invested in China, but little of it for projects conceived by the Chinese government.

In the coastal cities evidence of change was striking. In some ways, these cities were reminiscent of Meiji Japan as Western clothing styles and practices spread. Roads and automobiles proliferated, as did universities and hospitals. Major initiatives in adult literacy and public health were undertaken, reaching into rural China. There was a semblance of order, there was reform, and there was hope. Europe and the United States appeared ready to come to terms with Chinese nationalism, to assist rather than obstruct the creation of a modern state in China.

It was in Manchuria that Chinese hopes for an end to imperialism were dashed and it was, of course, the Japanese who were responsible. Jiang was determined to force the Soviets and Japanese out of what he perceived as China's northeastern provinces. Zhang Xueliang proved surprisingly amenable to Jiang's overtures and surprisingly resistant to Japanese demands. An initial effort to seize the Soviet-controlled Chinese Eastern Railroad provoked a strong military response and the Chinese

MAP 23.   JAPANESE EMPIRE, C. 1931.

After Fairbank and Reischauer, *East Asia*, p. 564,

were forced to back off. The two Chinese leaders then focused their efforts against the Japanese.

No Japanese leader—and few knowledgeable Japanese—were willing to countenance the loss of privileges in Manchuria. Moreover, 1931 was a particularly bad time to challenge Japan. The country had been hurt badly by the Great Depression and the loss of markets around the world, including those in China. The military had been outraged by the government's concessions at the London Naval Conference of 1930. Patriotic societies were increasing the level of domestic violence including the assassination of the prime minister in late 1930. Tokyo had neither the will nor the ability to control its troops in Manchuria.

Fearful that Manchuria was slipping from its grasp, contemptuous of the weak responses from Tokyo, Japan's Kwantung army offered its own response to Chinese nationalism. On September 18, 1931, after setting off an explosion on the Japanese-owned and operated South Manchuria Railroad in order to allege Chinese provocation, thousands of Japanese troops executed a well-organized plan to begin the conquest of Manchuria. The age of Japanese militarism had dawned and with it a new threat to Western interests in East Asia. As it crushed nationalism in Korea and fought it in China, Japan asserted its claim to lead nationalist movements throughout the rest of Asia, promising to preserve the continent for Asians, to free it from Western influence.

War and Decolonization, 1932–1949

Japan was, of course, the dominant power in East Asia in the 1930s, as it had been, arguably, since the World War. Japanese military power, resorted to increasingly by Tokyo and its men in the field, dictated the international affairs of the region. After they consolidated their hold on Manchuria in 1931 and 1932, the Japanese gradually edged into a full-scale war with China. Although they punished the Chinese brutally and forced Jiang's regime to retreat to Chongqing (Chungking) in the southwestern province of Sichuan, the war proved unwinnable. First the Soviets and then the Americans sent materiel aid to China and the war dragged on. On December 7, 1941, it exploded across the Pacific as the Japanese took a desperate gamble and attacked the American fleet at Pearl Harbor in the Hawaiian Islands.

Determined to control the resources and territory they deemed essential to their nation's security, Japanese leaders concluded that Western imperialism had to be expelled from Asia. In the course of World War II Japanese forces drove the Americans out of the Philippines, the British out of Burma, Malaya, and Singapore, the Dutch out of Indonesia, and the French out of Indochina. The day when Asia would be ruled once again by Asians, free of European or American colonialism, had arrived, at least for the people of East Asia. Regrettably, the Japanese conception of a New Order in East Asia proved in practice to be no less exploitative than the order that had been imposed by the West. Nonetheless, the Japanese succeeded in setting in motion a process of decolonization that proved unstoppable, continuing even after their crushing defeat.

In The Beginning It Was Manchuria

When Japanese military operations in Manchuria began, Jiang's government was unable to respond effectively. The forces that had held together in the 1920s, long enough to unite the country, had fragmented badly by 1931. A dissident Guomindang faction had established a rival government in Guangzhou and the Communists had eluded the trap Jiang had set for them in Jiangxi. He chose not to resist the Japanese in Manchuria, in part to deny them an excuse for further attacks and largely because he gave priority to his struggle against the Communists. He perceived his erst-while allies of the Northern Expedition as a cancer that had to be destroyed before China could fight an external enemy. In addition to his own efforts to localize the Manchurian incident, he hoped that appeals to the League of Nations, Great Britain, and the United States would result in sufficient international pressure to give pause to the Japanese. His hopes were not fulfilled.

The Japanese Kwantung Army had no intention of limiting its efforts to one city in Manchuria. The Japanese intended to drive all Chinese authority, civilian as well as military, out of the northeastern provinces—and to substitute their own. Wishful thinking would not prevent their conquest of Manchuria; nor would international diplomatic pleas absent the will to employ force. The major Western states—France, Great Britain, and the United States—were struggling in the depths of the Great Depression, desperately eager for the crisis to pass without need for their involvement. The League of Nations, to which the United States did not belong, could not act without strong British leadership, which was not forthcoming. From the United States came admonishments, first gentle, then increasingly stiff, to no avail. Words rarely stop aggressors, but the international community had nothing more to offer. The dream of col-lective security evaporated when each of the great powers determined its interests in Manchuria were not sufficient to justify the risk of war with Japan.

Early in 1932 the Japanese army completed its conquest of Manchuria and the Japanese navy made its bid for glory by attacking Shanghai. The bombing of that city, with the largest international settlement in China, stirred considerably more concern abroad. Even Americans, generally indifferent to the affairs of Asia, were outraged by Japanese actions, but not enough to move them to effective opposition. American forces in Shanghai were reinforced, but Washington had no intention of using them—and the Japanese were not intimidated. Once they overcame the tenacious resistance of local Chinese troops, forced back by superior fire-power and inadequate support from their own government, the Japanese withdrew from Shanghai. For the moment they were satisfied with Manchuria, where in March 1932, they proclaimed the puppet state of

"Manchukuo"—country of the Manchus—to be ruled nominally by Puyi, the last emperor of Qing China.

In May, a League of Nations appointed commission arrived in Manchuria to investigate conflicting Chinese and Japanese versions of the events following the explosion in September 1931, but it came too late. The Japanese army had already accomplished its purpose. Although the commission's report was critical of Chinese as well as Japanese actions, Japan withdrew from the League when the League Assembly adopted the report early in 1933. Japan had become a pariah nation, but its military leaders, firmly in control of Manchuria, cared little about world public opinion. Its civilian leaders were somewhat more troubled, but confident of their ability to persuade those nations that mattered that their best interests required accommodation with Japanese power. Their judgment proved to be correct as none of the great powers was prepared to alienate Japan. The American secretary of state at the time of the Manchurian crisis, Henry Stimson, tried hard to indict Japan for its aggression, but succeeded only in angering the Japanese without gain to China or his own country. The subsequent administration of Franklin D. Roosevelt initially chose to avoid any policy that might lead to confrontation, bringing the United States into line with Britain and France.

For Japan, after the conquest of Manchuria, the next question was what to do about the rest of China. The Kwantung Army was eager to apply its Manchurian tactics to neighboring provinces of northern China. However reluctantly, the civilian government conceded the value of attempting to undermine the loyalty of Chinese officials to the central government. Gradually the Japanese army pushed into Chinese provinces adjacent to Manchuria to provide a protective buffer for Manchukuo. By 1935 it had forced the Chinese government to accept a semiautonomous regional government for north China, subordinate to Japanese interests. Month after month the areas under Jiang's control receded and Chinese patriots once more had reason to fear the dismemberment of their country. The rest of the world hardly took notice and the Nanjing government feared the Communists more than it feared the Japanese.

Japanese aspirations were not limited to China. Japanese industry and especially the Japanese navy needed assured access to oil. Dependence on an increasingly unfriendly United States was not acceptable. Navy leaders looked southward to the Dutch East Indies, eager for an arrangement to give Japan control of that source of oil. It obviously would be useful to encourage the independence movement in the Philippines, to deprive the Americans of their principal bases in the Western Pacific. A few Japanese, more often intellectuals and publicists than officials, kept returning to the idea of an Asia under Japanese leadership. Japan, they hoped, would liberate the backward peoples of the region from Western imperialism and bring them into the twentieth century, as they had the people of Korea and Taiwan. There was no official blueprint for Japanese expansion over all of East Asia, but the vision was there and more worldly military men were pushing against the existing limits of the Japanese empire.

China Imperiled

In Nanjing, Jiang and his colleagues struggled to hold their government together, challenged from within by faction leaders and generals who thought they could run the country better—or merely sought more power for themselves. An armed Communist force operated out of the mountains of Jiangxi and in 1934 escaped Jiang's encirclement and extermination campaign to begin its historic Long March to Shaanxi province in northwest China. And in the northeast, like the plague, Japanese authority spread and infected local government, leaving Jiang with at best nominal control of the region.

For a brief time Jiang could find solace in the relationship he was developing with Germany. He had been pleased with several German economic and military advisers with whom he had worked in the late 1920s and in 1933 new ties were established with the Germany of Adolf Hitler. Several senior German military officers provided Jiang with valuable advice and before long all of the major German corporations were operating in China, helping to modernize its infrastructure and industry. The Chinese navy and air force were remodeled along German lines, but the promised U-boats and Messerschmitt and Stuka aircraft never arrived. The new self-strengthening movement was interrupted when Hitler decided to ally with Japan instead.[1]

Efforts by Jiang and Japanese diplomats to reach a rapprochement were undermined by the Japanese Army's operations in north China in 1935. Dissatisfaction mounted with Jiang's insistence on appeasing Japan until he had suppressed the Communists and other internal opponents. In December, student demonstrations demanding unified resistance to

Japan instead of civil war broke out in Peking. Before the month was over, the demonstrations spread to other cities throughout the country and anti-Japanese activities proliferated. Jiang's government could not contain what came to be known as the national salvation movement.

The outburst of patriotic fervor in China, exacerbated by Japanese troop deployments and evident preparations for further military expansion in China, threatened to draw support away from Jiang to his domestic rivals, including the Communists. In 1932, from the safety of their mountain stronghold thousands of miles from the Japanese, the Communists had declared war on Japan. Before the end of 1935, responding to Moscow's call for a worldwide united front against fascism, the Chinese Communists issued a call for all Chinese to join in a united front against Japanese imperialism. Generals nominally loyal to the Nanjing regime were attracted by the arguments of the Communists and the national salvation movement. Zhang Xueliang, having been driven out of Manchuria by the Japanese, had served Jiang faithfully in the anti-communist extermination campaigns. By 1936, however, he and his troops longed to return home and began to wonder why they were fighting other Chinese instead of the Japanese. In the southwest, old-style warlords, who had found it expedient to join the victorious Guomindang in the 1920s, were growing restive and perceived a patriotic duty to overthrow Jiang, ostensibly to allow them to fight Japan.

Jiang outmaneuvered and suppressed the southwestern rebels with remarkably little bloodshed, drawing them once again into uneasy collaboration with his regime. The Communist threat, which he remained determined to eliminate, persisted. Mao Zedong and his forces had survived the Long March and were entrenched in the northwest, near Xi'an. Overtures from Mao to Zhang Xueliang found fertile ground and, ignoring Jiang's exhortations, Zhang lost interest in fighting the Communists. Indeed, he began meeting secretly with Zhou Enlai, Mao's highly persuasive diplomatist, while simultaneously sounding out other Guomindang generals about means to focus China's military effort against the Japanese.

In the fall of 1936, two events electrified China. In November, troops from Manchukuo, bolstered by Mongolian units of the Kwantung Army, and supported by Japanese planes and tanks, were repulsed by Chinese troops when they launched an invasion of Suiyuan province. It was the first major victory of Chinese forces since the Kwantung Army had begun its rampage in September 1931. The Nanjing government announced that the time had passed when foreigners could encroach on China's periphery. But the news of December 1936 was even more dramatic: Zhang Xueliang had taken Jiang prisoner and was insisting on an end to civil war and increased resistance to Japan.

Rumors of fraternization between Zhang's forces and the Communists had been circulating in Nanjing throughout the year. Jiang had flown to Xi'an in October in an unsuccessful effort to revitalize the anticommunist campaign. Frustrated again when he returned in December, he decided to relieve Zhang of his command. Zhang responded by staging a coup. Despite some sentiment in Xi'an for executing Jiang and in Nanjing for bombing Xi'an despite Jiang's presence there, calmer views prevailed and, with the help of a directive from Stalin to the Chinese Communists, Jiang survived. The Soviet Union was eager to strengthen China against Japan and Stalin had concluded that no man had a better chance of unifying the country than the man who had outmaneuvered him in 1927, Jiang Jieshi. Once freed, Jiang grudgingly moved toward rapprochement with the Communists in a united front against Japan.

On New Year's Day, 1937, China's leading newspaper prophesied the dawn of a new age: "From today China will have only the united front , and never again will there be internal hostility."[2] The willingness of Jiang and Mao and disparate warlords to submerge the past and abandon their future intentions toward each other was minimal, but they could not stem the tide of popular enthusiasm, of patriotic fervor. Jiang clearly was perceived by politically aware Chinese as the symbol of national unity, as the great national leader who would join the nation in battle against the Japanese. Americans in China were caught up in the general euphoria and diplomats and missionaries alike began to portray Jiang more favorably, sometimes in Christlike terms. The Christian bible that he had allegedly read while imprisoned was put on display and doubtless would have become a great Christian relic had Heaven ordained a different future for China.

Obviously, these events in the fall of 1936 were viewed differently by the Japanese Army and by less militant forces in Tokyo as well. Few Japanese imagined that a united China was in their interest and the Communists were viewed by most Japanese with more loathing than the Guomindang. Indeed, several Japanese leaders, military as well as civilian, had long favored reaching a settlement with Jiang to preclude a Communist victory in China and to keep Soviet influence out of Asia. The possibility of a Guomindang-Communist united front generated new anxieties. The Japanese Army was a powder keg, awaiting a spark to set it off. That came in July 1937.

War Comes to Asia

Certainly the Japanese government was not seeking war with China in 1937. Even the Army General Staff hoped to avoid any major confrontation with the Chinese. But in July, Japanese forces on maneuvers in the vicinity of Peking came under fire from nearby Chinese positions. Mistakenly believing that a missing man had been killed or taken prisoner by the Chinese, the Japanese commander ordered an attack. A series of skirmishes followed by unsuccessful negotiations and threats from both sides soon escalated into fullscale warfare. Japanese officers in China were eager to strike and the mood in China precluded further appeasement by Jiang. Seeking a rapid victory, a "final solution" to their problems with the recalcitrant Chinese, the Japanese poured troops into China. World War II had begun in Asia.

An August attack by the Chinese on Japanese positions in Shanghai and Japanese ships in the harbor misfired. Japanese reinforcements rushed to the region, supported by carrier and Taiwan-based bombers as well as a naval bombardment. They punished Chinese troops severely. The battle for control of the Yangzi valley, from Shanghai to Nanjing, lasted nearly five months and cost the Chinese approximately 250,000 casualties, 60 percent of the men they had put into the field. In December, the Japanese took Nanjing where officers unleashed their troops for a two-month orgy of looting, rape, and murder-atrocities unsurpassed in the history of modern warfare—subsequently referred to as the Rape of Nanjing. China's best trained and equipped forces had been decimated and its capital lost to the enemy. By its actions at Nanjing, the Japanese Army wrecked mediation efforts by Hitler, aimed at preventing the spread of communism in China.

The Chinese government retreated into the interior, pursued hesitantly by Japanese troops. Chinese defenders won several battles, most significantly in April 1938, when they smashed two Japanese columns advancing toward a major railway junction at Xuzhou. The Japanese could not be stopped, but they could be delayed and a heavy price exacted for their progress. Nonetheless, before the end of 1938, they controlled the eastern seaboard, from Tianjin in the north to Guangzhou in the south. To their surprise, however, the Chinese kept fighting—and as the battle moved westward, the terrain became increasingly favorable to the defenders. Jiang finally set up his last wartime capital at Chongqing (Chungking), a city frequently bombed by Japanese planes, but beyond the reach of Japanese troops. Japan had started a war that it could not finish.

Jiang had hoped that the League of Nations or the Americans might come to his rescue, but as in 1931, little but words of comfort came from those quarters. Both the League Council and the United States condemned Japanese aggression, but neither took action to stop it. The Europeans were focused on the activities of Hitler and Mussolini, much closer to home, and the Americans were still dominated by the profound neutralist and pacifist mood that had captured the country after the failure of the world to stop Japan in Manchuria. Indeed, when the war began in China, the United States *recalled* a shipment of bombers enroute to China on a U.S. government-owned vessel. Initially, only the Soviets, fearful of a Japanese attack on their Asian lands, provided significant aid. Soviet planes and pilots harassed the Japanese airforce, providing the Chinese with vital air cover, and small quantities of munitions were trucked across the Silk Road, ultimately reaching both Guomindang and Communist forces. Soviet military advisers, including Stalin's most brilliant soldier, Georgi Zhukov, came to offer assistance. O. Edmund Clubb has noted that while "Britain and the United States were continuing their profitable trade with the Japanese, the Soviet aid to China was substantial and critical."[3] Over 200 Soviet pilots were killed in action flying planes with Chinese insignia.

There was no doubt, however, where American sentiments lay and it was apparent that American leaders were groping toward some way to stop Japan. President Franklin Roosevelt had taken advantage of Japan's decision not to declare war and refused to apply his country's mandatory neutrality law. It was a vain effort to enable the Chinese, as victims of aggression, to purchase war materials in the United States. Unfortunately the Chinese lacked both the necessary funds and the means to transport supplies. In October 1937, Roosevelt made a widely publicized speech calling for a "quarantine" of aggressors. In November, the British initiated a meeting of the signatories of the 1922 Nine Power Pact signed in Washington to discuss the implications of Japanese action, but accomplished nothing. Throughout 1938, well into 1939, the Japanese pushed on, bombing civilians, brutalizing those who did not flee before them, and the United States held back. American property was destroyed by the Japanese, an American warship deliberately sunk by Japanese planes, American commerce ravaged, and American citizens killed, but the United States was unwilling to risk being drawn into the war. Unlike Stalin, Roosevelt was not ready to send his countrymen to fight and die for China.

A poll taken in January 1939, reported that by a margin of 48 to 32 percent, Americans had responded negatively to the question: "Would you favor changing our neutrality so as to give more aid to China but no aid to Japan?"[4] But a month earlier, Roosevelt and his aides had come up with an idea for helping China in a way that they believed would provoke neither an American public overwhelmingly opposed to being drawn into the war—nor the Japanese. They gave China a $25 million credit to buy trucks in the United States. The Japanese were outraged, not least because the loan came precisely at the moment they had gained the defection of a prominent Guomindang leader and were hoping a demoralized Jiang would be forced to come to terms. The Chinese were buoyed by the loan, trivial in and of itself, but perceived correctly as a harbinger of a shift in American policy, a promise of greater support in the future.

Friends of China in the United States and advocates of collective security eager to see the United States act to stop aggression combined forces in 1938 and 1939 in a highly successful public relations campaign to win support for economic sanctions against Japan. By the spring of 1939, polls showed overwhelming support for an embargo on war supplies to the Japanese. But Roosevelt held back, fearful of precipitating a crisis with Japan at a time when the situation in Europe was growing increasingly ominous.

In August 1939, the Soviet Union signed a nonaggression pact with Hitler's Germany, facilitating the Nazi attack on Poland, and also leaving Stalin less concerned about having to fight a two-front war. During the week the pact was signed, Soviet and Mongolian troops repelled a Japanese attack at Nomonhan on the border between Manchukuo and Mongolia. In a counteroffensive directed by Zhukov they destroyed the Japanese force, inflicting an estimated 55,000 casualties. Stalin concluded that he needed China less, and Soviet support to China dropped off sharply.

The Nazi-Soviet nonaggression pact took Tokyo by surprise, as did the defeat of Japanese forces on the Mongolian border. The Japanese had hoped for an alliance with Germany against the Soviet Union and many Japanese leaders had been eager for war with the Soviets. Suddenly, that idea did not look very promising. Its proponents were discredited, leaving the field open to those who argued for expansion to the south and were prepared to risk confrontation with Western seapower. Indeed, in April 1941, the Japanese signed their own nonaggression pact with the Soviets.

The coming of war in Europe in September 1939 left the Chinese in desperate straits. Moscow had turned its back on China's plight and the Americans now focused their attention on events across the Atlantic. Britain was fighting for its life. China stood virtually alone and there were questions in China as well as in Western capitals as to how long morale could be sustained, how long it would be before Jiang was forced to succumb to Japan's relentless pressure. Bereft of Soviet aircover, China could muster few planes to counter systematic Japanese bombing, especially of Chongqing. And in March 1940, Wang Jingwei, one of Jiang's rivals for leadership of the Guomindang, accepted Japanese terms for heading a puppet government in Nanjing. Against overwhelming odds, Jiang and his Guomindang government in Chongqing and Mao and his Communist forces in and around Yan'an, held out.

The Japanese increasingly were looking southward, eager to exploit opportunities created by Hitler's pressures on Britain, France, and the Netherlands. In September they forced the French to allow their forces to move into Indochina. And a few days later, September 27, 1940, they concluded the Tripartite Pact, the Axis Alliance, with Germany and Italy, intended to intimidate the United States by threatening a two-ocean war if it went to war across either the Atlantic or the Pacific. It was an event of enormous importance for Japan's relations with the United States—and, indirectly, of tremendous benefit to China. No words, no act, could have been more effective in convincing Americans of their stake in the outcome of the Sino-Japanese war than Japan's decision to ally with Nazi Germany.

For several years, the only assistance the United States offered China came in the form of purchases of Chinese silver and relatively small credits to buy American agricultural and manufactured goods—a fraction of the aid China was obtaining from the Soviet Union. In the six months following the Tripartite Pact, however, the United States extended credits totaling $95 million. Of greater importance was the decision to send the Chinese one hundred fighter planes and to allow them to recruit American pilots, the mercenaries who would become the famed "Flying

Tigers." By fall 1941, these planes were inflicting significant losses on attacking Japanese aircraft. Also in 1941, China became eligible for lend-lease, the aid program initially designed to provide Great Britain with the means to defend itself, and many millions of dollars worth of military equipment were allocated for China.

At the same time, and primarily in response to Japanese pressures on the European empires of Southeast Asia, the United States began to apply economic sanctions against Japan. On the day before the Tripartite Pact was signed, Washington announced an embargo on the sale of iron and steel scrap, except to its neighbors in the Western hemisphere—and to Great Britain. Scrap metal constituted one of the most important Japanese imports from the United States and the Japanese understood the embargo to be an "unfriendly act." Ignoring American warnings in 1941, the Japanese stepped up their occupation of Indochina. The Americans responded by freezing Japanese assets in the United States in July 1941.

The Japanese military had long since concluded that it needed control of the resources of Southeast Asia to avoid dependence on the United States and European powers for vital materials such as oil, iron ore, tin, and rubber. Discussions throughout the 1930s had left no doubt that to achieve its aims in Southeast Asia Japan would have to go to war against the British and the Dutch, quite possibly the French and Americans as well. When war began in Europe, reducing customary imports from that continent and the United States, the importance to Japan of the Dutch East Indies, Indochina, and Malaya was underscored—and the war provided an opportunity to act.

The determination to move south was not merely an expression of the will of officers in the field, as Japanese aggression in China had been so often. It unquestionably reflected the policies of the central government—although it is fair to conclude that civilian leaders were not always aware of military plans. Foreign Minister Matsuoka Yosuke, principal Japanese negotiator of the Tripartite Pact, imagined extending Japanese control even beyond Southeast Asia, to India, Australia, and New Zealand. After the Nazi blitzkrieg against Western Europe in the spring of 1940, the Japanese increased their pressure on Indochina and Indonesia. They sent troops into northern Indochina in September and demanded fixed supplies of oil and other essential raw materials from the Dutch in Indonesia. The Dutch stalled and the Japanese prepared to seize the archipelago, seeking some way to do so without provoking the United States.

Once having decided to advance southward and to take the strategic defensive in the north, the Japanese responded favorably to Stalin's overtures for a nonaggression pact. Nonetheless, when the Germans invaded the Soviet Union in June 1941, only two months after he had signed the promise to remain neutral if the Soviets were attacked, Matsuoka urged his colleagues to seize the opportunity to attack the Soviet Far East. But on July 2, 1941, an Imperial Conference brushed aside Matsuoka's arguments and confirmed the decision to go south. Out of the meeting came orders for expanded military operations in Indochina. The participants were well aware that their chosen course might lead to collision with the United States.

American economic sanctions did not appear to be having the desired effect on Japan. Advocates of sanctions in Washington demanded an increase in pressure on the Japanese and they won a partial oil embargo in August. American military leaders, as yet unready for war and desperately anxious to avoid a showdown with Japan, succeeded in getting Roosevelt to authorize the licensing of some Japanese oil purchases. Although Roosevelt had rejected an appeal for a meeting from Japanese prime minister Konoe Fumimaro in June, the United States agreed to negotiations in Washington aimed at achieving a *modus vivendi*. Most American leaders were interested in reaching an understanding that would prevent war with Japan and allow them to concentrate on the war they considered more dangerous to the United States, in Europe.

Throughout the autumn of 1941 Japanese and American diplomats met in Washington seeking to avert war between their countries. But time was running against Japan and the Japanese military planners understood that fact. The historian and one-time senior State Department official, Herbert Feis, wrote that "the oil gauge influenced the time of decision."[5] As Japan's oil reserves ran down, its time ran out. If the Americans would not provide the oil essential to Japan's war machine, it would have to be found elsewhere—and soon, before spring. The American Pacific fleet at Pearl Harbor would have to be destroyed to preempt American interference in Japan's conquest of Southeast Asia and its control of the oil reserves of Indonesia. Weather—the horrendous seas of the North Pacific in winter—precluded waiting beyond early December. The failure of diplomacy would necessitate war—and diplomacy failed to resolve Japanese-American differences.

Fear that Jiang would surrender if the United States appeased Japan stiffened the American negotiators. The British, too, were apprehensive and Winston Churchill, the British prime minister, warned Roosevelt that a Chinese collapse would increase the danger to British and American interests in East Asia. In Washington and in London, there was also concern that a Japan freed from Chinese resistance would attack the Soviets, facilitating a Nazi victory as Hitler's armies pounded Leningrad (St. Petersburg) and Moscow.[6]

Until the Japanese added to Great Britain's distress by their maneuvers in Southeast Asia and then joined the Rome-Berlin Axis, appeasement of Japan had been relatively easy for the United States. Afterward, even when the Tripartite pact became virtually expendable to Japan, the American commitment to the British cause and China's status as an ally prevented a *modus vivendi* between Japan and the United States.

And so, to the great relief of Jiang and the people of China, war came to America in the form of a brilliantly executed Japanese attack on Pearl Harbor on the morning of December 7, 1941, "a date," Roosevelt told his countrymen, "which will live in infamy." Japanese leaders had little expectation of defeating America, but they saw no alternative to war if Japan was to maintain the momentum of its imperial expansion. They did believe they could deal a blow to American naval power sufficient to buy the time to build an impregnable position in East Asia. And when they had constructed their Greater East Asia Co-Prosperity Sphere, they hoped the Americans would not be willing to pay the price of trying to take it away from them. It was a gamble they were willing to take.

TABLE II.I.   Some Notable Events of the Period 1932–1949
(Events in boldface are mentioned in text)

Japan proclaims state of "Manchukuo"	**1932**
Franklin D. Roosevelt elected president of the United States	1932
Adolf Hitler appointed chancellor of Germany	1933
Japan withdraws from the League of Nations	**1933**
German plebiscite approves Hitler as Fuhrer	1934
Germany institutes Nuremberg laws against Jews	1934
Chinese Communist "Long March" to Yan'an	**1934–1935**
Spanish Civil War begins	1936
Xi'an incident	**1936**

George VI crowned king of England	1937
Marco Polo Bridge incident	**1937**
Munich Conference	1938
Nazi-Soviet nonaggression pact	**1939**
Germany invades Poland	1939
Germany, Italy, and Japan sign tripartite pact	**1940**
Battle of Britain	1940
Roosevelt elected to third term as president	1940
Germany invades Soviet Union	1941
Japanese bomb Pearl Harbor	**1941**
U.S. "relocates" Japanese-Americans	1942
Battle of Midway	**1942**
Soviets defeat Germans at Stalingrad	1943
Germans massacre Jews in Warsaw Ghetto	1943
D-Day	1944
Battle of Leyte Gulf	**1944**
Germans attack Britain with V-2 rockets	1944–1945
Germany surrenders	1945
U.S. drops atomic bombs on Hiroshima and Nagasaki	**1945**
Japan surrenders ending World War II	**1945**
Philippines granted independence	**1946**
India granted independence, partitioned	1947
Communist coup in Czechoslovakia	1948
Palestine partitioned, state of Israel proclaimed	1948
Berlin blockade	1948–1949
Indonesia gains independence	**1949**

Japan's Greater East Asia Co-Prosperity Sphere

The idea of liberating Asia from Western imperialism was a strong current in Japanese thought from Meiji times through World War II. For many Japanese the vision was altruistic, but for most it was hardly distinguishable from the paternalistic sense of mission that had dominated the discourse of late-nineteenth-century European and American imperialists. To be sure, no Japanese argued for taking up the "white man's burden," but the need for the Yamato race to take control, to lead its fellow Asians, was no less pressing.

As the Japanese government looked toward Asia in the late nineteenth century and in the years leading up to the Pacific War, its policy planners developed a more Japan-centered, more self-interested conception of their nation's role. When Japan seized control of virtually all of East Asia in the course of the war, it was inevitable that the military would implement policy. In practice, control of a territory by the Japanese Army meant ruthless exploitation on the grounds of military necessity, aggravated by racist insensitivity to the culture or even survival of the local people.

Although proclamation of the Greater East Asian Co-Prosperity Sphere came only in August 1940, its foundations date back to the Meiji era, to the seizure of Taiwan and the annexation of Korea. To those parts of the empire, Japan added Manchukuo and North China in the 1930s. These lands were to be integrated with Japan, to provide the heavy industrial base for the empire. As it became apparent that this industry required assured access to raw materials, Japan's economic planners pointed to Southeast Asia. There was never a blueprint or schedule for expansion, but the general outlines were clear to policymakers by 1940—and the German occupation of Western Europe that spring provided the impetus.

Initially many Southeast Asian nationalists, especially those in Burma and Thailand, were responsive to the Japanese and collaborated with them in hope of freeing themselves from Western domination or of gaining some advantage over their neighbors. They quickly learned that the realization of their aspirations was not a high Japanese priority. Japanese liberators rapidly became Japanese occupiers, diverting important resources to Japan, forcing indigenous peoples to support its war effort. Japan could neither absorb traditional Southeast exports nor provide the consumer goods the region customarily imported. Conditions worsened as the American navy attacked the sea lanes, severing the links between Japan and Southeast Asia. Economic dislocation, unemployment, and famine, combined with mounting evidence that Japanese dominance might prove less bearable than Western, drove collaborators into the resistance movement. Most of all, it was the brutal behavior of the Japanese military police, the *kempeitai*, bordering on genocide against ethnic Chinese, that turned the people of Southeast Asia against their erstwhile liberators.

The Vietnamese were the first to realize they could expect nothing from Japan. The Japanese negotiated their entry into Indochina with a

Vichy government itself dominated by Nazi Germany. Ignoring their promise of an Asia for Asians, they found it expedient to work through the existing French colonial apparatus to take what they wanted. They gave parts of Cambodia and Laos to Thailand as a reward for Thai accept-ance of alliance with Japan. Vietnamese nationalists turned to China and found modest support from both Jiang's Guomindang regime and Mao's Communists for their resistance. The Viet Minh, led by Ho Chi Minh, and increasingly Communist-dominated, cooperated with the Americans as well as the Chinese, using American-provided arms to drive Japanese troops out of several northern provinces in the closing months of the war. As defeat loomed, the Japanese created a puppet government under the Emperor Bao Dai, but it lasted only a few weeks after the war's end. On September 2, 1945, Ho declared Vietnam's independence.

Thailand fared a little better, both in terms of the spoils the alliance forced on it by Japan provided and in the conditions of the Japanese occu-pation. Here, too, the Japanese left the existing government in place and there was less of the brutality exhibited by Japanese troops elsewhere in Southeast Asia. But the economic benefits the Thais expected never came and as the war progressed, Thai resources were diverted increasingly to Japan. An anti-Japanese underground movement grew as the likelihood of Japan's defeat became evident. Japan's surrender spared the Thais the need for combat operations to demonstrate their realignment with the victors.

Burma, on the other hand, was managed more like Manchukuo. Real power rested with the Japanese army and Japanese advisers, but a native Burmese government, headed by a nationalist leader who had been imprisoned by the British, was formed in the summer of 1942. Burmese leaders were promised independence, presumably at war's end. A Bur-mese Independence Army, led by Japanese-trained Aung San and Ne Win, assisted Japanese troops in driving British and Chinese forces out of the country. Despite this initial support for the Japanese, despite being labeled traitors by the British, Burmese leaders were quickly disillusioned with Japan. The brutality of the *kempeitai* appears to have been decisive. By mid-1943, resistance to the Japanese was mounting and even a formal grant of independence by Tokyo could not prevent Burmese nationalist leaders from looking anew to the British. In March 1945, the Burmese army turned against the Japanese and contributed significantly to their defeat in Southeast Asia.

MAP 24.   JAPAN DOMINATES EAST ASIA, C. 1943.

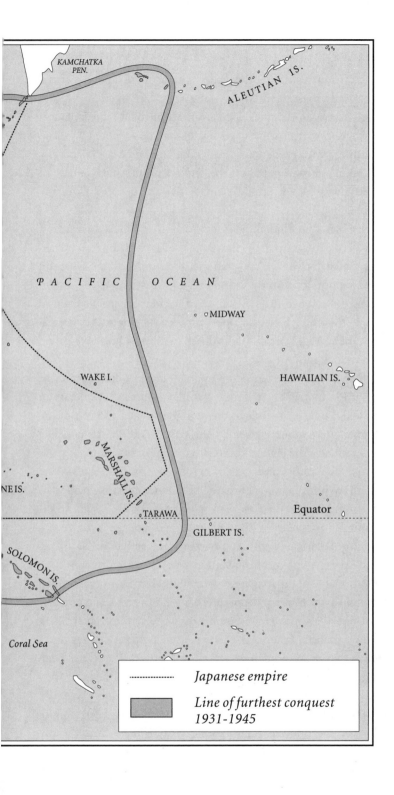

Malaya, like Burma, was under the direct control of the Japanese army, which systematically massacred ethnic Chinese, especially in Singapore, driving survivors into active resistance. A program of forced Japanization, derived vaguely from policies previously applied in Korea and Taiwan, was attempted with predictable results. Indians and Malays, initially attracted by Japan's anti-imperialist, anti-British propaganda—and not unhappy to be favored over ethnic Chinese—were alienated from the occupying force.

On the other hand, an "Indian National Army," composed largely of British Indian troops captured by the Japanese at Singapore, and led *against* British India by the radical nationalist leader Subhas Chandra Bose, received support from the local Indian community. As the tide of war shifted against Japan in 1943, Tokyo tried to win the cooperation of the local people by offering greater opportunities for political participation, but critical shortages of food and other consumer goods doomed the effort. Resistance mounted.

Island Southeast Asia experienced comparable misery under Japanese occupation. The Philippines and the main islands of Indonesia came under army control and the lesser islands of the archipelago and the rest of the southwest Pacific were administered by the navy. The Philippines, like Burma, were intended to be incorporated into the empire as a puppet state, run by Filipino collaborators under the watchful eyes of the *kempeitai* and Japanese civilian advisers. Java and Sumatra, site of the economic resources the Japanese war machine craved, were to be Japanized and exploited mercilessly, without thought of even nominal independence.

After crushing American and Filipino resistance at Bataan and Corregidor in the spring of 1942, the Japanese worked with collaborators from the traditional Filipino oligarchy—families that had collaborated earlier with Spanish and American conquerors. Few of these had any particular antipathy toward the United States or sympathy for Japan. Few were radical nationalists. Independence was their preference, but not a cause for which they were prepared to die. For them, U.S. rule had been relatively painless. Had the Japanese occupation been as benign, they doubtless would have been equally content to run their country under the Japanese flag. But once again, the *kempeitai* brutalized the local population and Japan's economic exploitation of the islands hurt the oligarchy. The result was widespread hatred of the Japanese and resistance to their rule. Guerrilla movements, most notably that of the Communist-led *Hukbalahap* or "Huks," harassed the Japanese and contributed substantially to their eventual defeat. The granting by the Japanese of nominal independence in 1943 did nothing to change the situation. In October 1944, the greatest naval battle in the history of East Asia was fought at Leyte Gulf in the Philippine Sea, resulting in the near total destruction of Japanese naval power and facilitating the return of American forces to the islands.

In Indonesia, finding no Dutch collaborators, mistrustful of the Eurasian and Chinese minorities in the islands, the Japanese relied heavily on Javanese, Sumatrans, and the indigenous population of the various other islands they occupied. Indonesian nationalist leaders sought to outmaneuver the Japanese by agreeing among themselves both to collaborate *and* to organize a resistance movement. Their only goal was Indonesian independence and they understood from the outset that they could expect no assistance from the Japanese. Japan's economic exploitation of the islands proved even more ruthless than that of the Dutch. The *kempeitai* performed as viciously as they did everywhere else they were stationed. Nonetheless, thousands of Indonesians gained valuable administrative experience under Japanese rule. As the Japanese war effort flagged, the Indonesian resistance grew in strength and preparations for a mass rising against the Japanese, to be followed by a declaration of independence were cut short by Japan's surrender in August 1945.

Japan had conquered Southeast Asia with incredible speed in the six months following the attack on Pearl Harbor. But defeat in the naval battle of Midway in June 1942 eliminated Japan's capacity to carry the war to the eastern Pacific, to remain on the offensive. By the summer of 1943, Japanese troubles were sufficient to prompt them to offer more concessions to local nationalists in the vain hope of gaining greater cooperation. Ultimately, Southeast Asia contributed far less to the Japanese war effort than Japanese military planners had anticipated.

In the months and years that followed, Japan fought tenaciously to hold on to every inch of territory it had seized, but slowly the Americans brought their superior wealth and industrial power to bear and pushed the Japanese back, island by island. American submarines conducted a ruthless war against Japanese shipping, gradually cutting the home islands off from the empire Japan had carved out with such grim determination. And then came American bombers, relentlessly pounding Japanese positions at home and abroad. Tokyo was firebombed in

March, 1945 and, nearly defenseless, the Japanese islands endured the onslaught of American B-29 "Superfortresses." The Greater East Asia Co-Prosperity Sphere had long since disintegrated into total disorder and it was only a matter of time before the Japanese military would be forced to admit defeat.

The War Ends in East Asia

For Japan, the warning bell had sounded at Midway in June 1942. A few days later, however, Japanese troops landed on two of the American Aleutian islands. Perhaps the gods of war were still with them. But in the months that followed, the Americans and their allies pushed the Japanese out of one island stronghold after another. The Japanese navy lost scores of ships that could not be replaced easily. The Japanese army suffered a rare but major defeat at the hands of Chinese government troops. Some Japanese strategists concluded by mid-1943 that the tide of battle had shifted and that Japan's wisest course was to seek a negotiated settlement before matters worsened. The Americans might still be willing to concede some Japanese gains rather than pursue a costly fight to the finish. Fear of assassination by the Japanese army muted these men. American calls for Japan's "unconditional surrender" hampered their cause. The cabinet never debated the issue.

The war went on amidst terrible suffering throughout East Asia. Casualty rates among combatants were high, but noncombatants also endured extraordinary misery. Many were killed and maimed as battles ranged nearby or as shells and bombs rained on soldier and civilian alike. Others died as the Japanese conscripted them for forced labor or starved closer to home. And the war went on.

As the vise closed on Japan in 1944 tensions between army leaders determined to fight to the death and the men who favored peace, military as well as civilian, mounted. The "moderates" won a victory in July 1944 when they forced the resignation of General Tojo, who served as both prime minister and army minister, but months passed, Japan suffered one bloody defeat after another, and still the word "surrender" could not be uttered.

In April 1945, the Japanese suffered more than three hundred thousand casualties in Southeast Asia where the British, with American and

Chinese assistance, completed the destruction of Japanese forces on the mainland. At approximately the same time, at enormous cost, the Americans won the battle for Iwo Jima, a mere 750 air miles from Tokyo. A few weeks later they landed on Okinawa, where Japanese resistance was even fiercer, but when the battle was over, the distance to major Japanese cities was less than 400 miles. In May, Germany surrendered, Japan was alone, and the greatest bombing offensive in world history began as U.S. planes finished off Japan's navy and industrial base. And still the Japanese gave no indication of their willingness to surrender.

American leaders knew that victory over Japan was in reach. The questions that remained were when and at what cost. As Washington looked for a strategy with which to end the war, it concluded that Jiang Jieshi's China would not be much help. In 1944, Washington concluded that Jiang was husbanding his resources to fight the Chinese Communists and was leaving the war against Japan to the Americans. Of course, Jiang and other Chinese leaders, long angered by their allies' "Europe First" strategy, had concluded the Americans and Europeans wanted to leave the war against Japan to the Chinese while they concentrated their efforts against Germany. A confrontation between Jiang and General Joseph Stilwell, his American military adviser and commander of American forces in China, led to Jiang's demand for Stilwell's recall in October 1944. President Roosevelt appeased Jiang by recalling Stilwell and then turned to the Soviet Union for the assistance American forces could no longer anticipate from China. At Yalta in February 1945, Roosevelt elicited a pledge from Stalin to abrogate the Soviet-Japanese nonaggression pact and attack Japanese forces within three months after the surrender of Germany. In return he promised to gain Jiang's agreement to the restoration of Tsarist privileges in Manchuria—a small price for the United States to pay.

In the aftermath of Yalta, Japanese leaders anticipated Soviet intervention in the war in Asia. They chose, nonetheless, in their desperate effort to avoid unconditional surrender, to look to Moscow as a mediator between Tokyo and Washington. Calls from mid-level officials for a direct approach to the United States went unheeded. Japanese intelligence had determined that the surrender terms were in fact negotiable, but the appeal to Washington was never attempted. In April 1945, Roosevelt died, to be succeeded by Harry S Truman. In May, Germany surrendered. In July, at Potsdam, amidst the ruins of the defeated Nazi empire, Churchill, Stalin, and Truman issued the Potsdam declaration, calling upon Japan to surrender, and spelling out their terms. They warned that Japan faced "utter destruction" if it failed to accept the offer. Akira Iriye, the leading historian of Japanese-American relations, has argued that "the Potsdam declaration should have been accepted immediately and unequivocally by the Japanese government, for it gave them just what they were seeking, 'a peace on the basis of something other than unconditional surrender.'"[7]

Committing possibly the greatest mistake in recorded history, the Japanese government chose to delay its decision in order to win over the military and prepare the people for surrender. Unintentionally, the prime minister indicated to the press and the world that Tokyo did not take the Potsdam declaration seriously. Assuming continued Japanese resistance comparable to that encountered at Iwo Jima and Okinawa, determined to end the war quickly and at minimal cost in American lives, Truman ordered the air force to drop the first atomic bomb. On August 6, 1945, the people of Hiroshima were struck by the most horrible weapon mankind had ever devised. The world would never be the same.

As the great mushroom cloud cleared, Japanese military officials inspected the carnage at Hiroshima, noted they were dealing with a weapon of extraordinary destructive power, and remained unwilling to surrender. Two days later, Soviet troops invaded Manchuria and rapidly overran the depleted Kwantung army. On August 9, a second atomic bomb obliterated Nagasaki—and still the Japanese military opposed surrender. It took five more days and the intervention of the emperor to move the Japanese government to acceptance of the American terms for peace. The war in Asia was over.

And the stage was set for the next great confrontation in East Asia. Despite the Japanese surrender, Soviet forces continued their drive through Manchuria, pouring 300,000 men into the territory in less than two weeks, and exacting heavy casualties from the remnant Japanese units. Simultaneously, the Red Army liberated much of Korea, pushing across the 38th parallel long before the first American troops arrived. In Washington—and particularly among American military leaders—apprehension about Soviet intentions emerged. Frustrations generated by Soviet differences with their Anglo-American allies over Eastern Europe had led some American leaders to seek to end the war in Asia *before* the Soviets intervened, before they established a military presence in the region. Stalin clearly was determined to reassert Soviet power in East

Asia and at Yalta Roosevelt had conceded Soviet influence in Manchuria and claims to territories the Japanese had wrested from the Tsar in 1905. But Roosevelt was dead and among his advisers were many who thought he had conceded too much. The men who had crafted the victory over the Axis powers were not about to tolerate a Soviet challenge to their perception of the security of the United States and its interests across the Pacific.

The disposition of forces at the end of the war allowed the United States to deny the Soviets—or any other nation—a meaningful role in the occupation of Japan. Similarly without significant challenge, the U.S. Navy occupied island after island in the Pacific. On the mainland, however, the situation was quite different. Soviet troops were dominant in the northeast and Stalin's diplomats drove a hard bargain in their negotiations with the Chinese. Although the Soviets had been China's principal supporters in the early stages of the war, arguably providing the aid that staved off defeat, Jiang had not hesitated to take advantage of them when Hitler's Wehrmacht was pounding at the gates of Leningrad and Moscow. Edmund Clubb has referred to China's elimination of Soviet influence in Xinjiang in 1942–43 as "Chungking's excessive profit-taking in time of Soviet military distress."[8] Certainly Stalin had not forgotten a few years later when the war ended and, with his troops in control of most of Manchuria, the balance had shifted in his favor. Jiang was forced to accept the "independence" of Outer Mongolia, ratifying the long-standing fact that Mongolia had been in the Soviet orbit since the 1920s. The Chinese negotiators also accepted Soviet demands for control of Manchurian railways and ports, receiving in return recognition of at least nominal Chinese sovereignty over Manchuria and Stalin's acceptance of the status quo—Chinese control—in Xinjiang.

In Korea, Soviet troops did not take advantage of the opportunity provided by the delayed arrival of the Americans and withdrew north of the 38th parallel, the point at which Soviet and American leaders had agreed to divide their zones of occupation. The Japanese were disarmed and expelled from north and south, but the Koreans, initially hailing their liberation, anticipating independence, were appalled to find their country divided and occupied, the freedom and independence promised in the victors' Cairo Declaration postponed. Led by Yo Un-hyuong, the Koreans had formed the Korean People's Republic, but it was brushed aside by the Americans. The provisional government formed by Korean exiles in Chongqing fared no better as Moscow and Washington worked out plans for a United Nations trusteeship for Korea. The resulting political vacuum was exploited by rightists in the south and communists in the north. Throughout the country demonstrations were staged by Koreans of all political persuasions, almost unanimously outraged by the denial of their independence.

Increasingly, in the months following Japan's surrender, the Soviet Union and the United States perceived each other as potential adversaries, with enormous ramifications for the peoples of East Asia. Koreans and Chinese began to look to one or another of those great powers to achieve their own political ends, linking their own civil strife to the growing enmity between the Americans and the Soviets. Questions of freedom, independence, and power for the peoples of the region became enmeshed in the emerging Cold War. Not even the states of Southeast Asia, long subject to other masters, could avoid these new shadows.

Decolonization in Southeast Asia

To Churchill's chagrin, Roosevelt and Stalin shared one important value: anti-imperialism. The restoration of European empires in Asia was not an objective of either American or Soviet policy during World War II. The Japanese had granted nominal independence to Burma and the Philippines in 1943. Sukarno and Ho Chi Minh declared the independence of Indonesia and Vietnam almost immediately after the Japanese surrender. The Americans planned to end Filipino tutelage in 1946 and give the islanders their freedom, but the Europeans had no intention of abandoning their empires.

Leadership changes in Britain and the United States in the course of 1945 had significant outcomes for Southeast Asia. Most important was the decision of the British people to turn to the Labour Party in July 1945, replacing a Conservative government committed to preservation of the empire with one that was ideologically hostile to imperialism. The death of Roosevelt, on the other hand, left behind an American government less interested in Southeast Asia and less troubled by the imperial aspirations of its friends in Europe.

Initially, the British role in Southeast Asia was detrimental to the aspirations of the region's nationalists. British troops had primary responsibility for disarming and repatriating Japanese forces there. In their own colonies, Burma and Malaya, they returned with every expectation of picking up where they had left off before the Japanese drove them out. In Indonesia they brought back Dutch officials and used Japanese troops to help them regain control of cities seized by Sukarno's forces. In southern Vietnam they brushed aside Viet Minh administrators and reinstalled the French—in striking contrast to the Chinese who liberated northern Vietnam and left Ho Chi Minh's officials in place. But the determination of the Europeans to restore the *status quo ante* underestimated the determination of the nationalist leaders to maintain their independence.

In Burma, Aung San and his followers continued to press their cause and the Labour Party proved sympathetic. Once the British government had reconciled itself to the independence of India, "the jewel in the crown," fighting to hang on to Burma made little sense. In January, 1947, Aung San and British prime minister Clement Atlee agreed on the steps to Burmese independence. A year later, despite the assassination of Aung San by Burmese political rivals, independence was formally declared. Burma rejected the British offer of membership in the British Commonwealth and turned inward. The years that followed were rife with rebellion, communist-inspired and separatist. Before the end of the decade the Burmese, despite all their efforts to isolate themselves from external currents, found their lives further complicated by an infusion of Chinese Nationalist troops who fled across the border after their defeat by the Chinese Communists. Unwelcome under any circumstances, these troops became deeply involved in drug-trafficking in the years that followed. But Burma was independent.

The situation in Malaya was considerably more complicated, primarily because of tensions between the Malay and Chinese communities. Before the war, there had been little sense of nation in either community, but the Japanese had stimulated anti-Chinese feelings among the Malays—who now demanded a "Malaya for the Malays." The large Indian community was also targeted. Efforts to put together a viable state out of the several sultanates—Penang, Melaka, and Singapore—proved difficult—and ultimately impossible—because of Malay fears of Chinese dominance. The separation of the largely Chinese city of Singapore was probably inevitable and was first arranged with the formation in February 1948 of a federation of Malay states, in which the special position of Malays was to be preserved by the British High Commissioner. In the same year a major Communist revolt exploded which, although contained in little more than a year, festered on for many more. The insurgency appears to have been part of a coordinated Soviet effort to stir trouble throughout the region, but given the fact that the rebels were almost exclusively Chinese, their grievances against discrimination by British and Malays alike may also have fed their hostility to the new regime. It was 1957 before Malaya actually became independent. Singapore became a self-governing city state in 1959.

The British acclimated themselves to second-class status in the international system much more easily than did the Dutch, partly because Indonesia was so very important to the economy of the Netherlands as well as to Dutch memories of the days when they had one of the world's great empires. Despite their efforts to help the Dutch return, the British concluded that negotiations with the Indonesians were essential. As soon as the Japanese had been repatriated, the British left. The Dutch simply did not have the power to suppress Indonesian independence. But they tried.

An agreement negotiated between Indonesian authorities and the Dutch in November 1946 gave Sukarno and his colleagues de facto control over Java and Sumatra, the principal islands of the archipelago. In July 1947, however, the Dutch, despairing of concluding an arrangement that would meet their needs, launched a full-scale military attack against the Indonesian regime, forcing Indonesian leaders to seek refuge in the hills. Almost immediately, the United Nations Security Council called for a cease-fire which both sides accepted, but the war raged on and off for two more years. The Indonesians anticipated support from the United States, but it was not forthcoming. Washington was far more concerned with European affairs and its relations with the Netherlands.

During one hiatus in the fighting, the Soviet Union, apparently the last bastion of anti-imperialism, entered the fray. Moscow sent a veteran Indonesian Communist home to attempt a coup in September 1948, but the Indonesian government succeeded in crushing it. Having demonstrated its anticommunist credentials, Sukarno's government was now viewed more favorably by the Americans. When the Dutch resumed their offensive in December, capturing Sukarno and most other senior Indonesian leaders, the Americans shifted sides. The UN Security Council demanded an immediate end to the fighting, the release of the imprisoned Indonesian leaders, and the transfer of sovereignty to the Indonesians no later than July 1, 1950. Under pressure from the United States, which feared that continued strife would work to the advantage of the communists, in Europe as well as Indonesia, the Dutch eventually caved in. The independence of the United States of Indonesia was proclaimed and recognized in December 1949.

The people of Indochina were less fortunate. Charles de Gaulle, leader of the Free French, had indicated in January 1944 that Indochina would not be granted independence although his remarks allowed for greater autonomy *within* the French empire. The French were as determined as the Dutch to reassert their authority and they had greater manpower and resources to bring to bear. And again, any hopes that Ho Chi Minh or other nationalists in the territory had of American support were not realized. With Roosevelt dead, the insistence of military planners that the restoration of French control would serve the strategic interests of the United States went unchallenged. Similarly, in 1945 and 1946, with Jiang Jieshi's intensely anticommunist regime still dominant in China, Ho could not expect any help from his northern neighbor.

The French returned in 1945 and by the end of the year they had forcibly retaken control of much of southern Vietnam and reached agreements with the kings of Cambodia and Laos to accept the supervision of a French governor in return for a bit more autonomy. In March 1946, Ho opted for a negotiated settlement in which the French appeared to recognize Vietnamese independence, but placed Vietnam in an Indochinese federation which was to be part of a larger French "union," presumably a euphemism for the French empire. The Viet Minh then allowed French troops to return to Hanoi unopposed. In the ensuing months, however, France's intent to maintain imperial control over Indochina became increasingly apparent and by December 1946, fullscale war erupted between French forces and the Viet Minh.

France's intransigence was fed by the desire of French leaders, humiliated by Hitler during the war, to restore France to its former glory, by fear of setting a precedent in Indochina that would undermine the empire in Africa, and by the determination of French colonial families in Indochina to retain their holdings and their status. The fact that Ho was a Communist who had worked many years for Moscow—and the prominence of Communists among Viet Minh leaders—enabled those in Europe and the United States who abhorred colonialism but feared the Soviet Union more to refrain from demanding an end to French suppression of the Vietnamese revolution. As Communist activity in East Asia increased in the late 1940s, the Vietnamese struggle for independence was caught up in the Cold War—a price for which the Vietnamese people paid dearly. The war with France went on and in 1949 the French established a puppet government in Saigon under Bao Dai, the former emperor. By this time the Chinese Communists had driven Jiang off the mainland and were willing and able to provide assistance to their comrades in Vietnam. The internationalization of the conflict in Vietnam was imminent.

Nominally, the Philippines had the easiest time gaining independence. The Americans had promised the Filipinos that they would be granted their freedom in 1946 and they kept their promise. On July 4, 1946, the Republic of the Philippines was formally inaugurated. But the Americans did not go home. Devastated by the war, dependent on the United States for their security as well as for market access and other forms of economic assistance, the Filipinos had little recourse but to grant the Americans a 99-year lease of more than a score of military bases, the retention of which Washington deemed essential to its control of the western Pacific. They were also forced to give American citizens equal opportunity to exploit the natural resources of the islands. If the concept of neocolonialism ever had any substance, the relationship between the Philippines and the United States might have provided a model. For the Filipino oligarchy, that relationship may well have been essential to survival. Without American military assistance, the Filipino elite would not likely have been able to contain and ultimately defeat the Communist-led Huk rebellion.

Thailand, of course, had retained its independence, at least in theory, throughout the age of western imperialism. In fact, European influence had been very powerful and Great Britain had dominated the Thai economy on the eve of the war. Under pressure from the Japanese, the Thai government had declared war on the British and the United States in January 1942, but the Thais were quick to change sides when Japan's defeat became apparent. In September 1945, a man who had spent the war years in the United States as a leader of the Free Thai Movement was named prime minister. Quickly, the Americans moved in to protect the Thais from the British, who intended to treat them as a defeated enemy, and American influence easily replaced that of the war-weakened British.

As communist insurgencies raged across mainland Southeast Asia and sputtered in the adjacent islands, Thai leaders perceived a threat to their own power and Thailand voluntarily became an American protectorate. At minimum, the imperialist powers—the Americans, British, Dutch, and French—had learned that the cost of empire had increased greatly. The Congress of the United States had determined in the 1930s, in the midst of the Great Depression, that the Philippines were not worth the price. The American military thought otherwise. In 1946 and 1947 the Americans demonstrated to their own satisfaction that they could have it both ways. They reduced their responsibilities by granting the Philippines independence—and retained by "mutual" agreement the strategic and economic benefits that empire had previously provided. The British surrendered their imperium in Southeast Asia with astonishing grace, recognizing soon after the war that they could no longer afford to pretend to be a great power. Nonetheless, they paid the price for the sins of their elders by standing by the Malays until they could manage their own affairs. The Dutch and the French were tragically slow to accept the new state of affairs. Fortunately for the Dutch, their adversaries in Indonesia were anticommunist, precluding the American support that allowed the French to bleed themselves and the Vietnamese until 1954. The colonial era was over in East Asia, regardless of whether the Europeans were ready to concede the fact.

Conclusion

The 1930s and 1940s were years of enormous turmoil in East Asia, with Japan rather than some outside force serving as the principal catalyst. Japan's reaction to the Chinese Nationalist revolution of the 1920s triggered a series of cataclysmic events. The Japanese army's campaigns in Manchuria and North China destabilized the Chinese government, facilitated the survival of the Chinese Communists, and led to full-scale war between Japan and China. The Sino-Japanese War exacerbated tensions between the United States and Japan, ultimately provoking the Japanese to attack the American fleet at Pearl Harbor. Once the Americans were sidelined in the Pacific, the Japanese drove the European imperialists out of East Asia and created their Greater East Asia Co-Prosperity Sphere. Although the ravages of war precluded prosperity for any of the Sphere's participants, willing or otherwise, the Europeans were discredited by their defeat and their erstwhile colonial subjects mobilized for independence.

The United States recovered quickly, of course, and battered the Japanese empire mercilessly in 1943, 1944, and 1945. Perhaps the greatest tragedy of all came when the Japanese government, by its failure to acknowledge defeat, unwittingly invited the beginning of the Atomic Age. But perhaps it was too much to expect greater wisdom from the men who gave the world the Manchurian crisis and condoned the rape of Nanjing, the Bataan death march, and countless lesser atrocities committed by the *kempeitai* all over East Asia. When the war ended, Japan was in ruins and the shadow of American power loomed over East Asia, the Pacific an American lake.

Not least of the war's outcomes was the heightened struggle for independence among every East Asian people who had suffered under imperial rule. Many had been granted nominal independence by a Japanese government hoping to stave off defeat by winning their cooperation. As in World War I, American leaders had encouraged expectations of self-determination everywhere. Soviet leaders also had been tireless in their verbal attacks on imperialism. Had Soviet-American relations not deteriorated, decolonization might have gone more smoothly.

The Burmese were probably the most fortunate, gaining their freedom from British rule quickly and at little cost. Their subsequent problems were largely of their own making, beginning with the assassination of Aung San. The Filipinos were the first to gain their independence, but remained in a state of near total dependence on the United States. Malays had to wait for ten years after the war's end, but largely because of the Communist insurrection rather than British recalcitrance.

The principal villains of the decolonization effort were the Dutch and the French—and the emerging Cold War. The Dutch and the French were determined to regain control of their valuable colonies and did not hesitate to inflict great misery on the people of Indonesia and Indochina in pursuit of their ends. Absent a Communist threat in Indonesia, fearful that the Dutch would stimulate one, the United States forced the Dutch to back down. In Indochina, where the leading nationalist was also the leading Communist, the Americans first muted their criticism of French imperialism, then supported it, and ultimately replaced it.

If any country in East Asia might have seemed assured of regaining its independence with the defeat of Japan, it was Korea. The Koreans had been victimized by Japan for forty years, endured various efforts at forced Japanization, but never surrendered their sense of national identity. Their liberators were the Soviets and the Americans, two countries dedicated to the anti-imperialist cause. From the outset, the liberators deferred independence, insisting on a period of trusteeship. But as the relationship between Moscow and Washington became increasing adversarial, increasingly confrontational, each attempted to re-create the area it controlled in its own image. Neither succeeded, but they did manage to divide Korea into two antagonistic states, so that when independence came, it brought little joy to the Korean people.

The era began with Japan dominant in East Asia. It ended with the United States dominant in the Pacific and Soviet-backed communist revolution sweeping over the mainland.

The Cold War In East Asia

Gar Alperovitz has argued that the atomic bomb dropped on Hiroshima on August 6, 1945, was the first shot of the Cold War.[1] Although most scholars continue to insist that the decision to drop the bomb was motivated by military considerations related to the war against Japan, few would disagree with Alperovitz's conviction that Truman hoped the bomb would intimidate the Soviets. Evidence that American leaders were increasingly concerned about the role the Soviet Union would play in postwar Asia is abundant. Planning to counter a Soviet challenge to American hegemony in the region had begun before the defeat of Japan, even as the Americans urged Soviet intervention in the Asian war.

Soviet troops had raced down the Korean peninsula weeks before the first American liberators arrived, but withdrew north of the 38th parallel, the mutually agreed upon line of demarcation between their zones of responsibility. They swept through Manchuria and, although they promised the Chinese government that they would withdraw ninety days after the surrender, they were perceived as a threat to North China, comparable to that posed by the Japanese when they dominated Manchuria. Stalin's determination to control Manchuria's railroads and major ports was apparent in the treaty he had negotiated with the Chinese in August 1945. There remained the critical question of the relationship between Moscow and the powerful indigenous communist forces of China and mainland Southeast Asia. Would Stalin support them in their drive for local power? Would he attempt to use them for the ends of the Soviet state? Did he or could he control them?

At war's end the Americans seemed unconcerned with Southeast Asia. They sought economic opportunities for their citizens, but perceived most of the region as a British or European sphere of interest. Their involvement in Korea was treated as a temporary nuisance, to be terminated as soon as possible. China and Japan were unquestionably the foci of American attention. China had long been a magnet for American missionary and business interests, neither meeting with striking success. With Japan crushed and Europe gravely weakened by war, the United States anticipated the opportunity to assert paramount influence in China. American leaders were suspicious of Soviet intentions and increasingly apprehensive about the growing strength of the Chinese Communists, whose subservience to Moscow was suspected. Japan was viewed primarily as a potential threat, to be occupied with the purpose of eliminating that danger. Japan would be demilitarized and, if possible, democratized. There would be no Soviet complication such as the Americans had experienced in Europe. The occupation of Japan would be an American operation.

East Asia did not prove responsive to the vision from Washington. In Southeast Asia, only the British performed admirably. The Dutch and the French botched their recovery efforts. The Americans, trying to cope with major issues in Europe, were forced to push the Dutch aside in order to deny Indonesian Communists or the Soviet Union an opportunity for advantage. In Indochina, where the French persuaded Americans they were combating international communism rather than Vietnamese nationalists, the French proved unable to win on their own or with substantial American help. Ultimately, the Americans decided, with disastrous consequences for all concerned, to undertake the assignment themselves, to send American boys to do what French boys had lacked the will to do. In China, Jiang Jieshi was not amenable to American advice and his demoralized forces were defeated by the Chinese Communists, whose fear of and hostility toward the United States were quickly manifested. The effort to withdraw from Korea was so blatant as to suggest utter indifference to events in that country, inviting an invasion of the south by the communist-controlled north. Only from Japan could the Americans draw much solace. From one end of the country to the other, the people embraced pacifism and democracy as warmly as they had recently embraced militarism and imperial rule. Wartime hatreds evaporated rapidly and the enemy of World War II became the most loyal ally the United States had in Asia.

And then one day an American president arrived in Peking to pay homage to Mao Zedong and soon the Cold War was over in East Asia. Washington courted China once more, brought its boys home from Vietnam, and began to suspect the Japanese of economic warfare, of using trade policy to accomplish what its military power failed to accomplish during World War II.

The Occupation of Japan

The Japanese people had been called upon to fight to the finish. At the moment the emperor announced his decision to surrender, they were training to drive the expected American invaders off their beaches with bamboo spears. To most Japanese, the thought of an occupation by alien troops was unimaginable. Nothing in their nation's history had prepared them for it. When it became clear that they would have to endure an American military occupation, they anticipated the worst. They expected the Americans to rape and pillage as Japanese soldiers had in China and elsewhere in East Asia. The authorities began to recruit Japanese women to provide sex for the Americans to minimize the ravishing of innocents,[2] arguably a more benign process than the conscription of Korean "comfort women" to service Japanese troops during the war. They were astonished and delighted by the disciplined and extraordinarily generous behavior of the victors, who used candy bars, chewing gum, and other long-forgotten consumer goods—rather than bayonets—to win the favor of the Japanese people.

Nominally an international operation directed by an eleven- (later thirteen) nation Far Eastern Commission and a four-power Allied Council, control of the occupation was in fact monopolized by the Americans. They placed a charismatic celebrity general, Douglas MacArthur, in the role of Supreme Commander Allied Powers (SCAP) and he dominated the process of demilitarizing and democratizing Japan. MacArthur and his staff administered the country through the existing bureaucracy, presumably purged of the men responsible for Japan's aggression in the 1930s and 1940s.

The principal concern of the Americans, widely shared by their allies and Asians generally, was to eliminate Japan as a military threat. The men responsible for atrocities or believed responsible for starting the war were tried as war criminals. Japan was stripped of its empire and its military and civilian population overseas repatriated. Its armed forces were demobilized, although the Imperial Japanese Navy, in collusion with officers of the U.S. Navy and contrary to the intentions of the U.S. government, kept part of its organization intact against the perception of a Soviet menace shared by the admirals of both nations.[3] The *kempeitai* was disbanded and the Japanese were denied a centralized police force that might take on a paramilitary character. Japan's arms industry was dismantled. Even shintoism came under attack as the spiritual source of Japanese aggression. Committed to freedom of religion, the Americans refrained from destroying the shrines, but insisted on cutting off state support.

A second important American objective was the democratization of Japan. In practice that meant remaking Japan in America's image or, in the context of the Roosevelt era in the United States, a New Deal for Japan. In 1946 the Japanese were forced to accept a new constitution drafted primarily by MacArthur's staff. It eliminated the emperor system whereby the emperor was presumed to rule and placed sovereignty in the people to be exercised through their elected representatives in the Diet, Japan's parliament. The emperor, having renounced his divinity at the beginning of the year, was reduced to being a powerless symbol of the state.

The constitution, put into effect in 1947, created a new form of government along British lines, with the prime minister and cabinet drawn from the dominant parliamentary party and responsible to the Diet. The right to vote was granted to all men *and* women twenty and over. As in the American system, the judiciary was made independent of the legislative branch and the Supreme Court was granted the right of judicial review, to pass on the constitutionality of legislative acts. Basic human rights were protected by the constitution, including a right to collective bargaining. Most striking, and in accord with the highest American priority, article 9 required the Japanese to renounce war as an instrument of national policy and consequently the right to maintain military forces. None of these changes would have been made voluntarily by Japanese officials, but they accepted what they lacked the power to reject and adapted to the new system quickly and quietly, if not always to SCAP's satisfaction.

But the American reformers were not finished. Key members of SCAP were determined to bring economic and social democracy as well as political democracy to Japan. To this end, they challenged concentrations of wealth and power both in agriculture and in industry. They forced a program of land reform on rural Japan, ending centuries of peasant exploitation by absentee landlords, and they sought to bring about the dissolution of the *zaibatsu*, the huge monopolies that dominated the Japanese economy and were believed to have underwritten Japanese aggression. They pushed through laws to encourage the labor movement and a Labor Standards Law to improve working conditions. They even stipulated that men and women would receive equal pay for equal work, a vision yet to be realized in Japan or the United States. Japanese bureaucrats and more conservative members of SCAP undermined some of these reforms, but there can be no doubt that postwar Japan gradually became more democratic and more egalitarian than it had ever been before.

The Japanese elites, the bureaucrats and businessmen upon whose cooperation the occupation authorities became dependent, were unsympathetic to most of these reforms. In general these men welcomed demilitarization—which eliminated troublesome competitors in the society. However grudgingly, they accepted the need for land reform, in part because they feared peasant revolt. On the other hand, they resisted changes in the status of the emperor, until he intervened to declare them acceptable. They were outraged by the support given to the labor movement and fought an ultimately successful battle to undermine labor reforms. Similarly, they were unsympathetic to SCAP's efforts to break up the *zaibatsu* and succeeded in preventing antitrust activity from achieving more than minimal success. And ultimately they succeeded in rehabilitating and returning to public life most of the men purged by SCAP because of their wartime activities.

Yoshida Shigeru was the dominant Japanese political figure during the years of the occupation, serving as prime minister for most of them. A retired career diplomat, untainted by wartime service, considered a "moderate" by Anglo-American specialists on Japan, he developed an excellent working relationship with MacArthur, especially after American pressures for social and economic reform eased. He perceived his role as one of containing American zeal, preventing SCAP from doing irreparable harm to the elite's vision for the nation before the end of the occupation, at which time Japan would restore its traditional polity. He was successful, on the whole, but when the occupation ended, he and his fellow conservatives found that some of the reforms could not be reversed, that the Japanese people embraced the pacifism of Article 9 of the American-imposed constitution, and that land reform had created a powerful class of small landholders whose interests could not be challenged. The historian John Dower has written that the legacy of the occupation was "a new conservatism, but within a restructured state in which progressive and reformist ideals, and laws, retained a substantial constituency among the Japanese people themselves."[4]

A considerable part of Yoshida's success came from the skill with which he exploited the fear of communism that he and MacArthur shared and that gradually shaped Washington's agenda. Yoshida and his colleagues complained constantly that leftists in SCAP were trying to communize Japan by strengthening the labor movement and weakening the police power of the state. These charges resonated with MacArthur, the more conservative members of his staff, and an American Congress hostile to labor and prone to finding communists behind every event its members disliked. By 1948, with support for the New Deal ebbing in the United States, American pressure on Japan to reform had eased.

In Washington, the men responsible for America's foreign relations and national security were changing their priorities, especially with regard to the vanquished states of Germany and Japan. As tensions between the United States and the Soviet Union increased and the leadership in both countries came to perceive their differences as irreconcilable, the Americans concluded that containing Soviet power and influence was more important than suppressing Germany and Japan. They chose to strengthen their erstwhile enemies and to integrate them with other nations that chose to align themselves with the United States in its confrontation with the Soviets.

In Japan, to the despair of American and Japanese reformers, SCAP responded to the new directions in American policy by appeasing Yoshida and the Japanese traditionalists he epitomized. George Kennan, principal architect of America's policy of "containing" the Soviet Union, argued that the occupation policy had achieved its goals in Japan by early 1948, that the stability of Japanese society was now critical. He was contemptuous of the purges and of the efforts to break up the *zaibatsu*, both of which he considered disruptive. It was time, he insisted, to give the Japanese a greater sense of responsibility, of control over policy. MacArthur agreed and implemented Kennan's proposals. To all those who dreamt of a new Japan, a social democratic Japan, it seemed clear that the United States had abandoned them, that their vision had fallen victim to the exigencies of the Cold War.

From 1948 to 1950, the Americans looked for a way to end the occupation, to return control of the country to the Japanese before the Japanese became hostile to the American presence. American leaders were confident that the Japanese could be relied on to oppose communism at home and abroad, to work with the United States and its allies against the spread of Soviet influence. SCAP and the Japanese authorities cooperated in the purging of communists in the labor movement and in undermining the Japanese left generally. Washington was also eager to have the Japanese economy recover so that it would cease to be a drain on American resources. American policy planners saw Japan as central to an integrated regional economy, the "workshop" of Asia, the engine of Asian economic growth. A few went further and wanted to see Japan rearm so that it could defend itself and support the containment policy of the United States.

Fully aware of the role in which the United States had cast Japan, the Soviet Union was in no hurry to see a free and independent Japan resume its place in the world order. A resurgence of Japanese power might be acceptable to the Americans, but it held no joy for the Soviets or their allies in East Asia. Japan alone had been a terrible threat to the region for nearly half a century. The prospect of a powerful Japan allied with the United States, could only produce nightmares in the capitals of the Soviets and their friends. Indeed, there were few Asians—or Australians and New Zealanders for that matter—eager to see Japan unfettered. Consequently, the Soviets refused to sign a peace treaty with Japan to end the occupation and, lacking strong support from any direction, the Americans chose not to proceed unilaterally. Nominally, the occupation continued. In fact, Yoshida and his colleagues were in control of domestic affairs.

Revolution in China

The Chinese government was ill-prepared for the sudden Japanese surrender, but the Americans provided transportation to move more than 100,000 of Jiang's best trained and equipped troops from the interior to the major coastal cities, most of which had been liberated by U.S. forces. There were millions of Japanese, civilian as well as military, in eastern China and it would take months to ship them all back to Japan. For this task, Jiang could count on American assistance, both financial and logistical. But Jiang confronted a much more serious problem at war's end:

the challenge of the Chinese Communists. He was determined to rid the country of the menace posed by Mao's adherents and he realized that external forces, Soviet and American, might pose obstacles. He had out-maneuvered Stalin once, in the 1920s, and might succeed a second time. The Americans, his wartime allies, were almost as troublesome. Relations had soured in the course of the war and, although optimistic, Jiang was uncertain about the directions that might be taken by the post-Roosevelt leadership in Washington. He would proceed cautiously.

Chinese government and Communist forces had cooperated briefly in the aftermath of the euphoria that followed Jiang's return from captivity in Xian in 1936. Both sides had wooed popular support by publicly agreeing to a united front against Japan. Of course, neither Jiang nor Mao ever surrendered the goal of achieving one-party control of the country by eliminating the other. The Guomindang and the Communists had united uneasily before, each trying to manipulate the other to its own advantage. Nothing had changed between them. In January 1941, government troops attacked and decimated a Communist army attempting to establish itself in central China. From that time on, there was little pretense of unity and Jiang deployed 500,000 men to prevent the Communists from expanding from their base areas in the Northwest. Efforts by American military leaders to focus Jiang's energies on the fight against Japan failed. There was little doubt that civil war would erupt in China after the defeat of the Japanese.

Although the victors directed the Japanese in China to surrender to Jiang's forces and Japanese troops in China tried to comply, the Communists insisted on their right to liberate enemy-held territory. Rejecting Jiang's order to remain in place, they raced eastward and, in Manchuria in particular, were able to arrive in advance of government troops. In those areas where the Soviet Red Army had disarmed the Japanese, Chinese Communist forces obtained vital stocks of arms and ammunition. It was only a matter of time before government and Communist troops would clash as both sides attempted to extend the areas under their control.

Neither Moscow nor Washington had a clear plan for coping with the situation in China. Mao had not been Stalin's choice to lead the Chinese Communists and in a "rectification" campaign in 1942 he had purged the Party of those most likely to be subservient to the Soviets. He had demonstrated during the war that he would not sacrifice the interests of his followers to serve those of the Soviet Union. Jiang, on the other hand, had conceded to Stalin virtually all that Stalin had demanded regarding Mongolia and Manchuria. Ideologically, Stalin preferred to work with the Communists. The vision of a communist revolution sweeping Asia remained attractive to the Soviet ruler, but he was not prepared to sacrifice the gains he had won from Jiang on behalf of the prickly, uncontrollable Mao. A weak China, ruled by the Guomindang and threatened by Communist rebels, was an appealing prospect. Stalin's ambivalence was reflected in Soviet actions in the months immediately following Japan's surrender. Soviet authorities in Manchuria vacillated between arming the Chinese Communists and pushing them aside, between being responsive to Jiang's requests and ignoring them. Very early, Mao confessed to party cadres that "Soviet policy cannot be understood."[5]

American policy was similarly muddled, partly because China was not initially a high-priority issue, partly because American officials were sharply divided in their evaluation of the competing forces. Some American leaders were convinced that the Chinese Communists were servants of Moscow and that their victory over Jiang would tip the balance in Asia in Stalin's favor. They called for continued support to Jiang. Others stressed the evidence of nationalism in the Chinese Communist movement, contended that a Maoist China would not necessarily be hostile to the United States, and argued that Jiang was doomed in any event. They urged the administration not to take sides. Leaning toward support of Jiang, despite wartime criticism of his government, the Americans tried to mediate between the competing parties, trying to prevent a civil war. They hoped "moderates" in both parties would create a centrist government, unsullied by the fascist tendencies they saw in Jiang's Guomindang or the threat of communist totalitarianism they perceived in a Maoist regime.

Deeply suspicious of the United States, but outgunned and uncertain of Soviet support, Mao welcomed American mediation. The Communists were not ready for an all-out confrontation. The first postwar American effort led to six weeks of direct talks between Jiang and Mao shortly after the Japanese surrender. On the surface, the meetings went well and the rivals issued a promising joint declaration on October 10, the national holiday of the Chinese Republic. Their troops, however, pushed on. In November, Jiang launched a major offensive against the Communists and the negotiations ended. The failure of this effort and the acrimonious resignation of the American mediator forced Washington to focus on China's problems. General George C. Marshall, the principal architect of the American victory in the war against Germany and Japan, came out of retirement to undertake a mission to China.

Marshall's mission lasted virtually all of 1946, but its failure was apparent by mid-year. His early successes in winning a truce and gaining the confidence of the Communists provided a few months of hope, but it was soon obvious to both sides that however fair Marshall may have been, the United States was not neutral. Jiang concluded that American fear of the Soviet Union assured him of Washington's support no matter what he did. He decided on all-out war and his armies went on the offensive in late May. Similarly, Mao concluded that the United States was committed to the Guomindang cause. On July 1, 1946, he ordered an anti-American propaganda campaign, accusing the United States of trying to colonize China, discrediting Jiang as the "running dog" of the American imperialists.

A full-scale civil war raged in China from mid-1946 through mid-1949. The Americans and Soviets watched each other carefully, but neither intervened. The Americans disengaged gradually, but continued to provide Jiang's government with a modicum of support. The Soviets held back until it was apparent that the Chinese Communists would win with or without their support. In effect, the two great powers deterred each other and neither considered the outcome of the battle of vital importance to its own security—as long as the other stayed out. In the context of the emerging Cold War, the Americans were relieved to see Soviet forces withdraw from China and gambled on Chinese nationalism to keep a Maoist China from becoming an "adjunct of Soviet power." The Soviets would do nothing to hinder a Communist victory in China, but remained apprehensive almost to the end about possible military intervention by the United States. When, in late 1948, Jiang's forces suffered a series of major defeats and the end was in sight, *both* Washington and Moscow sought ways to reach accommodation with the incoming regime, which was beholden to neither of them.

The Communist victory in the Chinese civil war was by no means foreordained. At the outset, government troops outnumbered the Communists by a ratio of 3:1, were supported by a monopoly of airpower, and possessed vastly superior quantities of tanks and heavy artillery. Mao and his colleagues proved able military strategists, but they were helped enormously by the incompetence of Jiang and his generals. They were aided also by the decline in support for the Guomindang regime among the Chinese people. The return of Jiang's troops and officials to regions vacated by the Japanese was accompanied by looting, corruption, and debilitating inflation. Areas liberated by the Communists were far better governed, Communist troops were better disciplined, and Communist land reform programs won broad support in rural areas. In 1949, Jiang fled to Taiwan, to which, in his wisdom, he had previously dispatched 300,000 troops, much of the military equipment provided by the Americans, the government's gold supplies, and many of China's greatest art treasures. On October 1, 1949, Mao Zedong stood in Tiananmen Square and proclaimed the establishment of the People's Republic of China.

As a committed Marxist-Leninist, Mao had no reservations about aligning his country with the Soviet Union in its Cold War with the Americans. In June 1949, he publicly denounced the United States and declared that China would lean to the side of the Soviets. But Mao and Zhou Enlai, his principal aide and diplomatist, recognized the potential value of an accommodation with the United States. They were very much aware that the Americans were more able than the Soviets to provide the assistance they needed for the reconstruction and modernization of China. As Chinese patriots, they were unwilling to become dependent on Stalin. Assuming, as they did, that American capitalists desperately needed markets, mutually beneficial economic relations with the United States might be possible. If the Americans would refrain from further interference in China's internal affairs and treat China with respect, as an equal, Mao and Zhou might be receptive to overtures from Washington.

Although American leaders remained divided over the possibility of a useful working relationship with the People's Republic, Secretary of State Dean Acheson, , who dominated the policy process, was interested. He despised communism and led his country's preparations for conflict with the Soviet Union, but he also despised Jiang. He was intrigued by the idea that China's communists might be kept from becoming an instrument of Soviet policy. Domestic political considerations—the opposition party's charge that the Truman administration had "lost" China to the communists—handicapped his efforts, but he kept the door open until catastrophe in Korea slammed it shut late in 1950.

Stalin was very conscious of the attraction of American wealth and power to some Chinese leaders. He had no intention of supporting a regime in Peking that might play him off against the Americans. Unable to install a leader more malleable than Mao, he held Mao at arm's length until assured that he could count on Chinese support in any confrontation with the United States. Mao and his colleagues had a simple choice: commit themselves to the Soviet Union and gain Soviet support against any external threat or gamble on the good will of the avowedly anti-communist government in Washington.

The choice was an easy one for Mao. Despite his mistrust of Stalin, he was ideologically opposed to everything the United States represented, the bourgeois capitalist democracy that it epitomized. He was profoundly troubled by the high esteem in which many Chinese intellectuals and urbanites, even some members of the Communist Party, held the United States. Increasingly, he was convinced that good relations with the Americans would prove inimical to his own agenda for China. A hostile relationship with the United States, on the other hand, might facilitate his efforts to root out bourgeois democratic tendencies at home. He would sacrifice any benefits that the Americans could provide, allow his people to pay that cost, if he could obtain an alliance with the Soviets at a reasonable price.

Stalin did little to smooth the path for Mao. Although his aides traveled to Peking for discussions, he kept Mao at arm's length until December 1949, when the Chinese leader was allowed to meet Comrade Stalin in Moscow. The negotiations were difficult, sometimes demeaning for Mao, but after two arduous months he gained the alliance that would protect him from the Americans and their new friends, the resurgent Japanese, without surrendering China's independence. Stalin also granted a $300 million credit, to be spread over five years. On the other hand, he yielded little of the concessions he had exacted from Jiang. Mao won a Soviet promise to return Manchurian ports to Chinese sovereignty in 1952, but was forced to concede the "independence" from China of the Soviet-dominated Mongolian People's Republic. Ideology bound the two men and their nations, but there was little warmth in the relationship.

The Sino-Soviet alliance was a setback to Acheson's plans for accommodation with the People's Republic, but he persuaded Truman to remain on course. In particular, the Americans intended to extricate themselves from involvement in the Chinese civil war by abandoning Jiang's rump regime on Taiwan. Once the Communists took Taiwan, an event the American intelligence community expected in the summer of

1950, and there was only one claimant to authority over China, partisan opposition could be overcome and Mao's government recognized. No one in Washington anticipated friendly relations, but Acheson was persuaded that a working relationship useful in pursuit of American interests in Asia *was* possible. Eventually, he predicted, Soviet imperialism would drive the two communist states apart. The United States wanted to be close in order to drive home the wedge.

One signal the Americans sent to Mao came in their announcement of their "defensive perimeter" in the Pacific. It excluded the island of Taiwan. Truman and other American leaders indicated publicly that Taiwan was not essential to the security of the United States. But the defensive perimeter proclaimed by the Americans also excluded the entire Asian mainland, raising questions about how the United States might respond if the communists, Soviet, Chinese, or Korean, attacked the noncommunist, indeed intensely anticommunist, Republic of Korea which had been established south of the 38th parallel. Acheson replied that the South Koreans would have to defend themselves, a possibility American military assistance had made conceivable, and that their next line of defense was the United Nations. The Yanks were not coming. It was a fascinating message for Stalin to consider.

As of June 1950, Acheson still had hopes of reaching an accommodation with Mao's China—although opposition to the administration plan to abandon Jiang on Taiwan was mounting, within the administration as well as among its domestic enemies. Mao had concluded that the invasion of Taiwan would have to be delayed until 1951 to be assured of success. In Korea, the mutually hostile regimes that had emerged on the peninsula were at each other's throats, each eager to launch an attack on the other, to unify the country under its own control. The Americans still denied the southern regime they supported the offensive capability it desired. In the spring of 1950, Stalin decided to give the northern communist regime the supplies and military advisers it needed to overrun the south. The gun was loaded.

TABLE 12.1.   Some Notable Events of the Period 1947–1953

(Events in boldface are mentioned in text)

Japanese "accept" American-imposed constitution	**1947**
Truman Doctrine proclaimed	1947

Jackie Robinson plays for Brooklyn Dodgers	1947
Mahatma Gandhi assassinated	1948
Mao proclaims establishment of People's Republic of China	**1949**
Treaty creating NATO signed	1949
Rise of Joe McCarthy	1950
Sino-Soviet alliance signed	**1950**
Korean War	**1950–1953**
Death of Stalin	1953
Anti-Mosaddeq coup in Iran; restoration of Shah	1953

War in Korea

The people of Korea had endured nearly a half century of Japanese domination. No nation had suffered more during World War II. The Japanese took away their food to feed their own people. They took every metal object they could find for their war effort. They conscripted Korean men to work in their factories and to fight in their armies. They conscripted Korean women to provide sex for their troops. After decades under Japanese colonial rule, Korean society was a shambles.

For most Koreans, the expectation of freedom and independence regained, as promised by the Americans and their allies in the Cairo Declaration of December 1943, was exhilarating, carrying with it almost millennial hopes. The announcement, in October, 1945, that their liberators planned to impose a trusteeship on them, an indefinite delay of their independence, shattered Korean euphoria. It was one issue, perhaps the only issue, on which the Korean people were united: they wanted independence *now*! Widespread demonstrations broke out across the nation, lasting months, but the great powers that controlled Korea's fate could not be deterred. In December 1945, at a conference in Moscow, the Americans, British, and Soviets decided on a four-power trusteeship, to include China, and to last for five years.

As the days passed, the 38th parallel, intended as a line for the temporary division of the country into Soviet and American zones of liberation, came to divide the Korean people. In the north, the Soviets facilitated control by Korean communists, led by Kim Il Sung, a one-time guerrilla leader in Manchuria, who had spent the last few years in Soviet training camps. Kim's followers suddenly defected from the national consensus and endorsed the trusteeship arrangement. In the south, the Americans continued their pursuit of the Holy Grail, a liberal democratic regime in the image of their own government. They hoped to create, through democratic political processes that they would introduce into Korea, a government of moderate rightists and leftists—much as they tried to do in China and everywhere else they went. To this end they rejected the best chance for a united, democratic regime, Yo Un-hyong's popular left-leaning Korean People's Republic, *and* the more conservative provisional government in exile in Chongqing. The result was chaos, exploited by the rightists, led by Syngman Rhee, who continued to oppose the trusteeship arrangement and demanded immediate independence.

As the Soviet-American relationship deteriorated, the chances for reunifying their zones into one Korea vanished. In the south, Rhee, with strong support with those who had collaborated with the Japanese and were eager to retain their wealth and power, terrorized intellectuals, peasants, and workers determined to punish collaborators and create a more egalitarian society. Indeed, Carter Eckert has argued that long before the 38th parallel divided Koreans, "Korea was already an ideologically bifurcated society, held together by the power of the colonial state."[6] The Americans found Rhee unappealing, but preferred a southern Korea ruled by right wing thugs to a united Korea under Kim Il Sung and the communists. With the support of American troops, the Korean National Police, a remnant of Japanese colonialism, and a constabulary created by the Americans, killed tens of thousands of supporters of the leftist Korean People's Government, few of whom had any connection to the Communist Party. Rhee had competing national leaders, including Yo Un-hyong, assassinated, facilitating his own election as president in May 1948. The Republic of Korea (ROK) was proclaimed in August, with its capital in Seoul. North of the 38th parallel, elections brought the communists to power and in September they proclaimed the establishment of the Democratic People's Republic of Korea (DPRK), with its capital in Pyongyang.

There were now two Korean states, one communist-controlled and supported by the Soviet Union and one intensely anticommunist, however undemocratic, and backed by the United States. Neither Korean entity accepted the division of the country. Kim and Rhee were each determined to unite it under his own leadership. From the end of 1948 to June 1950 there were constant cross border skirmishes initiated by both sides, and in the south a bloody civil war was under way as Rhee brushed aside the democratic processes the Americans had attempted to impose on his government and tried to exterminate all opposition to his rule. Thousands more were killed. Disgusted, the Americans withdrew their armed forces from Korea and denied Rhee the means to launch a full-scale attack against his communist rivals.

The consolidation of Rhee's power in the south troubled Kim Il Sung greatly. The communist apparatus in the south to which he had looked to undermine the Seoul regime had been eliminated. From the vantage point of Pyongyang, an aggressive anticommunist dictator in the south was clearing the obstacles to his plans to attack the north. Several times in 1949, Kim implored Stalin to give him the means to strike the south first. Stalin was sympathetic, but apprehensive about sparking a confrontation with the United States. He did not expect the Soviet Union to be ready for war with the United States before the mid-1950s and had backed away from a confrontation over the far more important question of Germany. Kim's importuning did not cease and as the months passed Stalin noted the American acquiescence in the communist victory in China, the with-drawal of American troops from Korea, and the fact that Korea was out-side the announced defensive perimeter of the United States. An oppor-tunity to strengthen his strategic position against the United States and its new Japanese friends was apparent. With the approval of Mao Zedong, he sent Kim the arms and materiel he required—and Soviet advisers to plan the attack.

As the weeks passed and preparations for the attack went unnoticed, the Soviets were heartened by the unwillingness of the American Con-gress to provide funding for significant military assistance to Rhee's forces. Stalin threw caution to the winds and gave the insistent Kim the green light to invade the south. Kim was confident that he could gain control of all of Korea quickly, before the Americans could muster a response. Stalin, with so many signals of American lack of interest in Korea, was betting that there would be no American response. They were wrong and the world, most especially the Korean people, paid a terrible price for their miscalculation.

On June 25, 1950, Korean communist forces swept across the 38th par-allel, rapidly throwing back Rhee's outnumbered and less well-equipped army. But to the dismay of Kim, Stalin—and Mao—American troops from Japan arrived before Kim's men could secure the peninsula. They, too, fell back before the well-planned and well-executed offensive, but combined U.S. and ROK troops were able to hold the line around the port city of Pusan in the southeast while reinforcements and supplies poured in under the auspices of the United Nations, responding to the first apparent act of aggression since the organization had been created in 1945 to succeed the moribund League of Nations.

Despite its decision to place Korea outside its defensive perimeter, the United States chose to come to the aid of the ROK when its survival was threatened. American leaders were fearful of the repercussions of inaction at home and abroad. Domestically they were still under fire for the "loss" of China and could not afford to appear indifferent to further communist gains in Asia. Abroad they perceived a direct threat to Japan and to the credibility of the United States as a defender of its friends. Finally, they drew on the lessons of the past. Japanese aggressors had tested the collective security guarantees of the League of Nations in 1931 and the League had been found wanting. Further aggression and World War II followed. The Americans were determined to see the UN succeed—and to send a message to Stalin. If Stalin was testing the will of the United States to resist Soviet expansion, the Americans accepted the challenge.

Most of those who fought against Kim's armies were Koreans or Americans, but fifteen other members of the United Nations also sent troops, most notably the British and the Turks. General MacArthur was named commander of UN forces in Korea. Fighting under the flag of the UN, his men beat back a series of major North Korean attacks on the Pusan perimeter and by mid-September were strong enough to launch their first counteroffensive. Simultaneously fighting their way out of Pusan and successfully executing a risky amphibious operation at Inchon, far behind communist lines, they quickly destroyed the North Korean forces. Mao Zedong had foreseen the Inchon landing, but his warning was ignored by Kim and his Soviet advisers. It took MacArthur's troops less than a month to drive the northerners out of the south and back across the 38th parallel.

Kim and Stalin had guessed wrong and Kim's government was confronted with the possibility of complete destruction. The Chinese were apprehensive. If the Americans rolled back the North Koreans and eliminated the communist state on China's border, would they continue their offensive into Manchuria? Would they attempt to overthrow the communist government of China and return Jiang Jieshi to the mainland? The Americans had already ordered ships to the Taiwan Strait to prevent Mao's men from attacking Taiwan and mopping up the remnants of Jiang's army there. Frantically, Chinese leaders warned the Americans that if UN forces crossed the 38th parallel into north Korea, China would intervene against them.

Contemptuous of Chinese power, eager for an opportunity to show their critics that they could and would reverse the "Red tide" that once seemed to threaten all of Asia, that the United States would contain communism in the East as in the West, American leaders authorized MacArthur to send his men across the 38th parallel. The plan was to annihilate North Korean forces, and prepare to unite all of Korea under a noncommunist government.

If Kim and Stalin were panicky, Mao was not. By the end of September 1950, he was convinced that China would have to fight the United States eventually and he preferred to fight the Americans in Korea rather than on his own soil. A grateful Stalin offered air support, then withdrew the offer, fearful of provoking the United States. Mao hesitated and then against the advice of the rest of the Chinese leadership, he sent Chinese "volunteers" across the Yalu into Korea. Eventually, Soviet air support, planes and pilots, did enter the war surreptitiously. Several hundred thousand Chinese soldiers managed to slip into Korea undetected until they attacked MacArthur's forces briefly in October and then, in a series of massive attacks in November, drove them back down the peninsula, across the 38th parallel—and reeling in disarray back to Pusan. China had taught the United States an important lesson.

But the Americans and their allies were not finished. Once again they were able to hold the line at Pusan and once again their superior firepower took an enormous toll on their enemies. Slowly UN forces drove back the overextended Chinese in bitter fighting and eventually pushed them back across the 38th parallel. Mao was determined to throw the Americans out of Korea, but subsequent Chinese offensives failed and in July 1951, both sides reluctantly accepted a truce that brought the border between northern and southern regimes close to where it had been before the carnage started. It took two years of acrimonious negotiations and sporadic fighting before an armistice agreement was reached in 1953.

The Chinese had succeeded in demonstrating to the world that they could not be ignored. Their intervention prevented the unification of

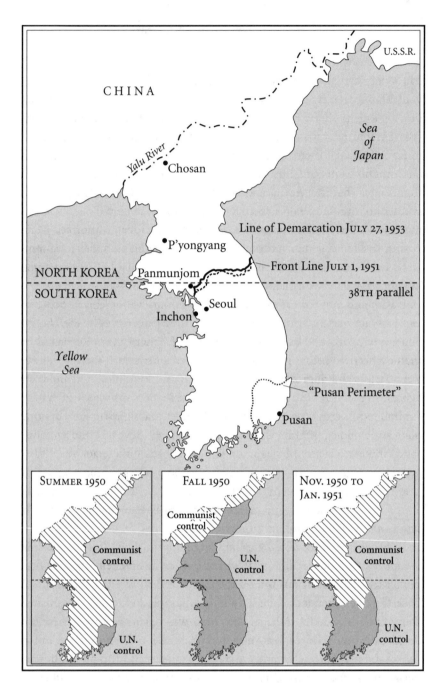

MAP 25.   STAGES OF KOREAN WAR, 1950–1953.
After William Stueck, *The Korean War*, pp. 49, 87, 129, 226.

Korea under a government likely to be hostile to them. It also denied the Americans a successful march north that might have tempted them to continue into China. But the price of China's intervention was very high. Chinese casualties are estimated at over 800,000. Mao's son was one of those who died in battle. For decades the Chinese and the Soviets argued bitterly over the $2 billion bill the Soviets presented Peking for the aid they gave to China's military. And the Americans reentered the Chinese civil war, reenlisting on the side of Jiang Jieshi's rump regime, and preventing Peking from sending its forces to conquer Taiwan. But the United States was not likely to underestimate China again.

American leaders consoled themselves with the fact that they had preserved the southern half of Korea as a bastion of anticommunism and they had helped the United Nations demonstrate its ability to punish acts of aggression, to succeed where the League had failed. All of this, of course, could have been accomplished with minimal American casualties had MacArthur been ordered to halt at the 38th parallel in September or October 1950. Washington's opportunism, the decision to expand its war aims and those of the UN, cost the Americans, British, Turks and other UN forces in Korea many thousands of lives. It was responsible for a good part of the nearly three million Korean deaths in the war. And at home, the war hysteria nurtured the anticommunist crusade called "McCarthyism," after a senator who built a career fanning his countrymen's fears.

The direct confrontation between China and the United States ended American efforts to reach an accommodation with Peking. As Chinese killed Americans in Korea, a hostile American public perceived China as a rogue state, a dangerous aggressor for whom there was no place in the United Nations and with whom the United States should not have diplomatic relations. The domestic political context in the United States required continued recognition of Jiang's government on Taiwan as the legitimate government of all China and a commitment to the overthrow of Mao's communist regime. Jiang was clearly the principal beneficiary of the American and Chinese interventions in the war between the rival Korean states.

The Japanese also made striking gains as a result of the war. Most of the goods and services required by UN forces in Korea were procured in Japan, providing a $4 billion stimulus to the Japanese economy. Japanese minesweepers, part of a growing "defense" establishment of dubious constitutionality, cleared Korean harbors of mines that baffled the U.S. Navy, facilitating the landing of UN troops. And in 1951, ignoring the objections of China and the Soviet Union, the United States and forty-seven other states signed a treaty of peace with Japan, leading to the end of occupation. On the same day, the Japanese were forced to sign a security treaty that allowed the Americans to maintain bases, troops, and ships on Japanese soil and in Japanese waters. In return, of course, the Japanese were to be shielded by the American "nuclear umbrella." A number of sovereignty issues remained, but the Japanese had regained their freedom.

The war in Northeast Asia also had important ramifications for Southeast Asia. The United States and its friends were determined to contain communism in Asia as in Europe. Indochina became the next battlefield in the Cold War. French efforts to justify their attempt to restore imperial control by insisting that Indochina was another theater in the Cold War gained credence as Mao's government began to aid the Viet Minh. American assistance to the French began in May 1950, on the eve of the Korean War, and increased substantially over the next few years. As in Korea, the war in Indochina became internationalized, bringing incredible misery to its people.

And finally, the Korean War became a critical turning point in the Soviet-American confrontation. Once Americans died on the battlefield, their leaders lost interest in diplomatic solutions. The war became the catalyst for a terrifying arms race, the results of which could hardly have been more unfortunate for the world or more disastrous for the Soviet Union. Stalin's opportunism in Korea had produced a nightmare for the Soviet people, mitigated only by the coincidence of his death before it was over. Although the struggle to control Europe was the highest priority of both Washington and Moscow, East Asia continued to provide most of the Cold War's casualties.

Southeast Asia and the Cold War

No country in Southeast Asia was free of communist insurgents, but the region was remote from Soviet concerns and geography prevented Moscow from sending substantial supplies even if Stalin had been so inclined. Two major changes, coinciding with the Korean War, altered the situation. First, and probably most significant, was the communist victory in the Chinese civil war. By the time the Korean War began, the People's Liberation Army (PLA) had cleaned out most remaining Guomindang forces in south China and was sending arms and munitions across the border to Indochina. Second, a few months before the armistice Stalin died. His successors were much more interested in supporting friends in Southeast Asia and the "Third World" of developing nations generally. Nonetheless, Indochina was the only part of the region in which support from the Chinese and Soviets proved important. And it was Indochina that suffered the most from the Cold War.

Boosted by aid from China, the Viet Minh had seized the initiative in 1950 and the French were on the brink of disaster, from which they were rescued as usual by the Americans. Initially, American aid to the French in Indochina was conceived as a clever device for diverting funds the Congress had intended for Jiang Jieshi. Seeking accommodation with Peking, the Truman administration was attempting to extract itself from the Chinese civil war, but was forced to accept funds earmarked for the "general area of China," meaning wherever Jiang happened to be, e.g. Taiwan. The administration argued ingenuously that Indochina was in the general area of China and sent aid there instead. But once the Chinese intervened in the Korean War, and after the Chinese and Soviets recognized Ho Chi Minh's government in 1950, Washington opened its coffers and wholeheartedly supported the French fight against the Viet Minh, providing 80 percent of the funds and materiel needed to sustain the French imperial vision. And even when the French knew they were beaten, in 1954, the Americans urged them onward.

In Moscow and in Peking fears grew that the United States would intervene in Indochina, denying Ho the victory his forces seemed certain to achieve on the battlefield and posing a threat to China's southern borders. The Soviets and Chinese proposed an international conference to seek a negotiated peace in Indochina, less humiliating than outright defeat to the French and, they hoped, in time to prevent complications by the Americans. The Americans and British, as well as the French, agreed to meet in Geneva in May 1954. In the months leading up to the conference, both the French and the Viet Minh attempted to strengthen the hands of their negotiators by improving their military positions on the ground, the Viet Minh by seizing control of additional territory, the French by throwing back the attackers. The critical battle came at Dienbienphu, an important strategic location west of Hanoi, where the French had massed their forces to block the Viet Minh advance. There the Viet Minh astonished their enemy by the extraordinary feat of carrying cannon up the mountains surrounding the French base and inflicted the decisive defeat on French forces. A new French government committed itself to end the war and it did so at Geneva in the weeks that followed.

At Geneva the French extricated themselves from Indochina with uncharacteristic grace. The Americans looked on unhappily, refusing to sign the final accord that assured Ho Chi Minh and his followers control of Vietnam north of the 17th parallel immediately and the remainder of Vietnam after a nationwide election scheduled for 1956. It was, from Washington's perspective, no way to contain communism. In fact, however, Ho had settled for less than he had won on the battlefield, urged none too gently by the Soviets and Chinese who rightly still feared intervention by the United States. He was assured, however, that in two years he would have it all and without further suffering by his people. It was an offer he couldn't refuse.

Unfortunately for the people of Indochina, the Americans were confident that they could do what the French could not: draw the line at the 17th parallel and create a viable nationalist regime south of it that would stop the spread of communism. They perceived their country as the beacon of democratic revolution, untainted by a history of colonialism. They would provide protection and assistance to those Vietnamese who wanted independence not only from France but from international communism as well. Indochina would be the site of the next round in the contest with the Sino-Soviet bloc. A few weeks after the Geneva Conference, in September 1954, the United States supervised creation of the Southeast Asian Treaty Organization (SEATO) to provide for the region's security. The Americans joined Britain, France, Australia, New Zealand, the Philippines, Thailand, and Pakistan to deter further communist expansion, with specific reference to southern Vietnam, Cambodia, and Laos.

Working with Ngo Dinh Diem, a prominent Catholic nationalist, the United States poured millions of dollars and hundreds of advisers, civilian as well as military, into southern Vietnam in support of an anticommunist regime. The election scheduled for 1956 was blocked because American intelligence agencies estimated that Ho would win 80 percent of the vote. The principle of free elections lost its attractiveness in Washington when the likely victor was a communist.

Initially, Diem succeeded in suppressing potential rivals and consolidating his power, but in the process he alienated much of rural Vietnam, Buddhist activists, and local intellectuals. His American-designed land reform program was less attractive than the more radical version of the Viet Minh, his officials seemed more sympathetic to landlords than to peasants, and his "strategic-hamlet" program drove villagers away from their homes and burial grounds into fortified camps. Buddhists were troubled by the preference accorded Catholics in government postings. Intellectuals and much of the rest of the Vietnamese elite, repressed by Diem's secret police, turned against him. By 1960 there was an insurrection underway in the countryside and minimal support for Diem beyond the urban Catholic minority. The Viet Minh were again active in the south and receiving support from Ho's government in Hanoi. The American vision for Vietnam was imperiled.

In a classic example of imperial arrogance, reminiscent of Khubilai Khan's persistent efforts against Japan, the Americans determined to prevail in Vietnam. They tried counterinsurgency techniques, they employed the most advanced military technology available, they replaced Diem and several of his successors, to no avail. They tried napalm and chemical defoliants, the one a jellied petroleum product that clung to the skin while it burned and the other chemicals that denuded forests and destroyed the productivity of the soil. But the Vietnamese forces they oversaw kept losing ground to the communists, to the "Viet Cong." Desperate, they sent troops, first by the thousands and then by the hundreds of thousands. They bombed presumed rebel positions in the south and they bombed the north with extraordinary firepower. Supported by the Soviet Union and China, Ho's government sent more and more regular troops into action against the Americans. Soviet surface-to-air missiles and Chinese antiaircraft crews brought down scores of U.S. planes. American as well as Vietnamese casualties mounted rapidly. The greatest power the world had ever known could not achieve its objective in Vietnam: it could not create a viable nationalist regime. It could not prevent the communists from uniting all of Vietnam and eventually bringing all of Indochina under communist control.

On the morning of January 30, 1968, while most Vietnamese relaxed during the Tet or lunar new year, the Americans received a rude shock. Viet Cong guerrillas penetrated the American embassy compound in the southern capital of Saigon and besieged it for six hours before they were overcome. The attack on the embassy was symbolic of what was happening across the length and breadth of southern Vietnam. Simultaneously, the rebels hit four of the other five major cities and scores of provincial and district capitals. A force the Americans imagined they were on the verge of liquidating launched a brilliantly conceived attack that demonstrated that no one was beyond its reach.

Vietnamese Communist troops suffered very heavy losses in their Tet offensive and all the territory seized in the attacks was regained by the American troops and the Vietnamese they supported. The primary target of the North Vietnamese planners, however, was American public opinion and with that audience they were strikingly successful. The will to continue the war drained out of the American people and their leaders. Peace remained, however, a long way off. Thousands of Americans and hundreds of thousands more Vietnamese would die before the Americans went home, but negotiations between Hanoi and Washington began in May 1968. An agreement reached in October, with Soviet assistance, was rejected by a Saigon regime that had been promised a better deal by the political opposition in the United States. The war went on.

Slowly American troops began withdrawing from Vietnam and reliance on air power increased, as the new administration of Richard Nixon tried to reduce American casualties in order to relieve antiwar pressure at home. In support of South Vietnamese troops, the air war was extended to staging areas in Laos and infiltration routes in neutral Cambodia. Early in 1970, the neutralist government of Cambodia was overthrown in a military coup led by officers friendly to the United States. In May, American troops invaded neutral Cambodia, seeking to eradicate Vietnamese Communist sanctuaries there. Caught between the Americans and the Vietnamese, hundreds of thousands of Cambodians died. Their country was devastated and control ultimately passed to a murderous group of communist insurgents, the Khmer Rouge, who subsequently, in an act of extraordinary depravity, slaughtered perhaps as many as two million more of their countrymen. A February 1971 attack on Vietnamese Communist sanctuaries in Laos also proved disastrous for the Americans and their Vietnamese allies. Time was running out on the American government.

Nixon ultimately succeeded in gaining Soviet and Chinese support for his efforts to end the war on terms acceptable to Saigon. After a North

Vietnamese invasion was stopped in March 1972, Hanoi succumbed once more to the pressures of its allies, each with its own interest in improving relations with the United States. In October, it accepted a diplomatic arrangement short of victory. Still more killing ensued, as the Americans demanded additional concessions to pacify angry authorities in Saigon, and supported their demands with the heaviest bombing campaign of the war. Finally, in February 1973, the war ended for the Americans.

For the Vietnamese, the fighting continued for two more years. American support for the Saigon regime diminished rapidly after Nixon was driven from office in disgrace. By mid-1974 its armies were hampered by inadequate supplies and the morale of its troops declined precipitously. Enormous numbers of government troops deserted. When Hanoi's forces struck in March 1975, in the first of what was supposed to be a two-year series of major attacks, the South Vietnamese army panicked and disintegrated. The Americans did not ride to the rescue. A few weeks later, it was over. The communists controlled all of Vietnam and Saigon was renamed Ho Chi Minh City. After a war of thirty years, the Vietnamese revolution had triumphed over the French, the Americans, and all internal opposition. Shortly before the fall of Saigon the Khmer Rouge triumphed in Cambodia and not long afterward the communist Pathet Lao seized control of Laos. Where once the French tricolor had flown, three independent states now stood, united by their leaders' shared allegiance to the doctrines of Marx and Lenin.

One leading student of the affairs of Southeast Asia, R. B. Smith, has argued that the United States intervened in Vietnam to save Indonesia.[7] Although there is little evidence to support his contention, it is consistent with the claims of successive American presidents that they were fighting to prevent the "dominoes" from falling, to prevent the entire region from falling to the communists. Surely resource rich Indonesia was the most valuable domino—and the Americans did maneuver ceaselessly to keep the Indonesian Communist Party (PKI) from seizing power.

Once Indonesia had gained its independence, there was little to replace the opposition to Dutch imperialism that had held its people together in the 1940s. Sumatrans chafed at Javanese dominance of the government and the outlying islands demanded greater autonomy. Sukarno and his followers in Jakarta chose the opposite path. In 1950, in a step toward strengthening central authority, they replaced the federal United States of Indonesia with the unitary Republic of Indonesia. Over the next decade, there was frequent unrest in much of Sumatra and in other islands, exploding in the late 1950s into open civil war.

In addition to the difficult task of bringing together disparate people with little sense of nation, there was also the more common problem faced by those who liberated themselves from colonial powers. Having won home rule, the successful revolutionaries had to decide *who* would rule at home. Religious and ideological rivalries as well as mere contests for personal or institutional power complicated the political scene. Only continued assaults on the Dutch legacy seemed to transcend these myriad differences and Sukarno exploited these. In 1954 he dissolved the Dutch Indonesian Union. In 1956 he repudiated the debt his government had assumed in 1949. In 1957 he began the expulsion of Dutch nationals—nearly 50,000 of them—and expropriated Dutch shipping and air lines. He also found it useful to demand that the Dutch hand over West New Guinea, called West Irian by the Indonesians, a territory populated by a people ethnically different from the majority of Indonesians and connected to them only by the fact of having come under Dutch imperial control.

Sukarno proved to be a master politician and popular leader. Throughout the 1950s and early 1960s, he succeeded in manipulating and balancing alternative sources of power such as the PKI, the army, Muslim parties both large and small, and those long affiliated with him in his nationalist party. In foreign affairs, he pursued an analogous course, keeping Indonesia neutral in the Cold War and emerging as one of the leaders of the "nonaligned" camp. In acknowledgment of his stature, in 1955 Indonesia was chosen to host the first major meeting, at Bandung, of African and Asian countries seeking to expand their influence in a world Moscow and Washington imagined to be bipolar. Like Egypt's Nasser and India's Nehru, Sukarno had considerable success playing the superpowers off against each other and gaining assistance from both.

The greatest threat to the Jakarta government in the 1950s came from separatist movements led by military commanders in Sumatra and Celebes. The danger intensified when the United States decided to aid the rebels in 1957 and the possibility of overt American military intervention loomed in 1958. Sukarno's maneuvers, at home and abroad, clearly unnerved Washington. He was perceived by the Eisenhower administration as moving leftward, flirting with the Soviets and the Chinese, both of whom he visited in 1956. Sukarno was unquestionably impressed by the apparent success of China's economic development and spoke glowingly of what he had seen there. Equally as troubling to the Americans was Sukarno's acquiescence in the growing influence of the Indonesian Communist Party. PKI gains in local elections in Java in 1957 sounded alarms in Washington.

American intelligence analysts suggested that the breakup of Indonesia was possible and urged support for anticommunist separatist movements that could be used as counters to Sukarno and the PKI. In November 1957, the United States began to supply arms and training to rebel forces. Air drops from planes taking off from Malaya (facilitated by British authorities), the Philippines, Taiwan, and Thailand began early in 1958. Before the brief civil war ended in the spring of 1958, the Americans sent bombers and pilots to the aid of the insurgents. The source of the arms and attacks was no secret to the Indonesian government, especially after one of the bombers was shot down and its American pilot captured. Moreover, the proclamation of a new revolutionary anticommunist government by the rebels was greeted in Washington with public expressions of interest in the growth of noncommunist influence in Indonesia. The U.S. Seventh Fleet, the world's most powerful naval force began to move into position to intervene.

Contrary to American expectations, the Indonesian military moved quickly to crush the rebellion. Its leader, General Abdul Haris Nasution, emerged as the new powerbroker in Indonesian politics and the military as a whole functioned independently of civilian authority. Sukarno continued to balance contending forces adroitly, staying a step ahead of both the military and the PKI, moving toward a form of authoritarian government he called "guided democracy." Nasution's role was welcomed by the Americans who saw him—and the military—as able to contain communist influence. By the end of 1958, the United States, erstwhile supplier of the rebels, was competing with the Soviet bloc to supply the Indonesian army with modern weapons. In Washington and in Jakarta, the leaders, with perhaps unseemly haste, seemed content to mute past differences.

On two major issues of foreign relations, Sukarno, Nasution, and the PKI were united. They all demanded that the Dutch hand over West Irian and were irritated by the initial American support for the Dutch position. Similarly, they were all angered by the British plan to unite Malaya, Singapore, and several of its territories in the region into one Malaysian federation. Both of these external affairs peaked in the early 1960s.

In 1960, Indonesia tired of Dutch recalcitrance, broke off diplomatic relations with the Netherlands, and threatened military action to seize the disputed territory. In the 1950s the United States had insisted that no weapons it supplied could be used against its Dutch ally, to the delight of the PKI which could point to American support of the imperialists. But the Kennedy administration that took office in 1961 was eager to woo Sukarno and other leaders of the nonaligned states. In 1962, Indonesian military probes began. The Americans persuaded the Dutch to back off and won their reluctant agreement to turn the territory over to the UN which in turn would pass control to Indonesia, a face-saving device for the Dutch. Sukarno had promised the people of the territory the right of self-determination, but to no one's surprise, reneged immediately after Indonesian forces moved in. The world looked the other way.

In 1962, in the midst of the crisis over West Irian, the Indonesians—and the Filipinos—responded unfavorably to a joint British-Malayan statement of their intent to create the Malaysian federation by uniting Malaya, Singapore, and three British protectorates on the island of Borneo. Both Indonesia and the Philippines supported insurgents on Borneo and had interests of their own in the lands protected by the British. Moreover, the Indonesians were still smarting from British and Malayan assistance to the Sumatran rebels a few years earlier. In the spring of 1963, however, the foreign ministers of Indonesia, Malaya, and the Philippines met in Manila and reached an agreement on the creation of Malaysia, provided the UN ascertained that the plan was supported by the people of the Borneo territories.

Shortly afterward, the British and Malay governments tactlessly announced they would proceed with creation of the new state regardless of the outcome of the UN inquiry, provoking both Indonesia and the Philippines to break relations with Malaysia, despite the UN report indicating that the majority of the people of Sarawak and Sabah favored the arrangement (Brunei had opted to stay out). An Indonesian mob sacked the British embassy in Jakarta. Before long, Sukarno escalated the crisis into a military confrontation. Threats quickly gave way to the use of force as Indonesian troops crossed into Sarawak and even more dramatically when Indonesian paratroopers were dropped on the Malay peninsula. The British perceived no need to succumb to Sukarno's tactics and sent troops, planes, and ships to defend Malaysia. A major war was in the offing.

Sukarno may have been willing to risk a war with Great Britain, but his army was not. Clearly the British would control the air and sea lanes. A war would be disastrous for the Indonesian army and, in the minds of its leaders, it would open the door for a takeover by the PKI. Acting independently, army leaders assured the British that they did not want war and were eager to find a way out of the confrontation.

Aware of the lack of support from his army, Sukarno turned increasingly to the PKI. Angered by the refusal of the United States to support him in his demand for a plebiscite in British Borneo, he rejected further American economic assistance to his country and taunted the Americans by recognizing the Hanoi government in Vietnam. Finally, in December 1964, after Malaysia won a seat on the UN Security Council, he withdrew Indonesia from the United Nations, reminding American leaders of Japan's withdrawal from the League in 1933. As if he had not been sufficiently provocative, he proposed the establishment of a counterinstitution in which he would join forces with China and North Korea, states viewed by Washington as pariahs.

Relations between Indonesia and the United States deteriorated rapidly in 1965 and then, suddenly, one of the commanders of Sukarno's palace guard launched a coup. He alleged that his intention was to protect Sukarno, presumably against an attempt by the army to overthrow the Indonesian leader. Most of the leading generals were murdered, although Nasution escaped. Also spared was General Suharto, commander of the Strategic Reserve. His troops crushed the coup in less than twenty-four hours and then, blaming the PKI for the attempt, he ordered the massacre of PKI members, and any workers, peasants, or students suspected of supporting the communists. As many as 500,000 men, women, and children were killed. An American intelligence report called the purge "one of the worst mass murders of the 20th Century."[8] Sukarno was helpless and yielded power to Suharto in April 1966. Suspicions of American involvement in the coup have never been verified, but American support for Suharto's actions was unrestrained. The communist threat in Indonesia had been eliminated and Indonesia's relations with the United States improved rapidly.

The Philippines decision to side with Indonesia in opposition to the creation of Malaysia was one of the few occasions when its government diverged from the main outlines of American policy in East Asia. Although the islands had gained their independence from the United

States in 1946, dependence on American economic assistance and military protection persisted. Filipino elites were quite content to support American anticommunism in their own land and elsewhere in the region. In 1951 the Philippines signed a mutual defense treaty with the United States and in 1954 hosted the conference that led to the creation of the Southeast Asian Treaty Organization (SEATO). The Filipinos were widely perceived by their neighbors as American surrogates.

The United States continue to interfere in the internal affairs of the Philippines. The American Central Intelligence Agency played a major role in the new nation's politics throughout the 1950s and 1960s. Ramon Magsaysay, probably the most successful leader the Philippines ever had, achieved prominence with the close support and advice of the Americans. Together they eliminated the Huk threat in the 1950s. His concern for social justice and efforts to carry out land reform, modeled on the successful Taiwan program, separated him from the traditional political elite and satisfied the American craving to find foreign leaders who were democrats as well as anticommunists. His untimely death in 1957 ended social reform for years to come.

The Philippines remained a key American base in East Asia throughout the Cold War. There, as everywhere, tensions between the local people and culturally insensitive foreign troops arose. The issue of whether to allow the American bases to remain and to what the Filipinos were entitled in return was constantly debated. The desire for greater respect internationally as well as from the United States also roiled the political scene from time to time. Nonetheless, a generally uncomplicated relationship existed until 1972, when Ferdinand Marcos, rather than surrender the presidency after two terms, as mandated by the constitution, declared martial law. Supported by the previously apolitical military, he remained in power as de facto dictator. However egregious his rule, however contrary to the democratic principles the Americans prided themselves on having taught the Filipinos, the United States continued to see him as an ally.

Thailand proved to be a valuable American ally in the Cold War, rewarding American success in limiting British demands on the Thais at the end of World War II. It was also one of the dominoes the United States was determined to prevent from falling by its actions in Vietnam. The Thai government was dominated by a succession of generals in the 1950s and 1960s, most of whom found cooperation with the Americans personally profitable. The Thais joined SEATO and their leaders were outspoken in their demand that it become more active in defending the region against the communist threat. In 1962, they elicited a promise from the United States to defend Thailand without waiting for SEATO approval.

The United States began to station troops in Thailand, largely to deter border raids and to train Thai troops in counterinsurgency tactics. By late 1966 there were at least 35,000 American military men and women stationed in Thailand, but more important to the war in Vietnam were the air bases from which U.S. planes bombed Laos and North Vietnam. The Thai government also sent token naval and air units to fight alongside the Americans in Vietnam. When the United States lost the war and withdrew its forces from Vietnam, there was apprehension in Bangkok, but the Vietnamese were too exhausted for reprisals. The domino did not fall. A popular revolution in October 1973 led to a brief period of parliamentary democracy during which Thailand made overtures to China and the American military presence in the country was greatly reduced.

The early years of Burmese independence had been wracked by internal struggles, ideological, ethnic, and political. Two separate communist groups rebelled, the Karens demanded independence from Burma, and various leaders vied for dominance after the assassination of Aung San in 1947. There were other lesser rebellions and the problems caused by the fleeing Guomindang troops who had occupied Burmese territory as they came across the border from Yunnan province.

Domestic chaos dictated extreme prudence in foreign affairs. Tenuous links to the British remained. The Burmese had promised to respect British economic interests and, presumably for the purpose of defending Burma, the British retained until 1954 the right to use airbases there. But with China on their border, Burmese leaders wanted no part of the Cold War. They recognized Mao's government in 1950, but problems with domestic communists left them wary of communism generally. They chose to support UN action against North Korea in June 1950, but carefully refrained from supporting the subsequent resolution condemning Chinese intervention. The Chinese occupation of Burmese territory in 1956 led Rangoon to accept American aid for the first time. The border problem was finally resolved in 1960 with China and Burma dividing the disputed area.

General Ne Win, a colleague of Aung San, emerged in the 1950s as the dominant figure in Burma. It was Ne Win who drove back the rebels in the late 1940s and Ne Win who asked the British to surrender their right to maintain airbases in 1954. And it was Ne Win who pacified the Burmese Communist rebels and the Guomindang Chinese troops in the late 1950s. For about a year and a half, from late 1958 to early 1960, he and his colleagues ran the country at civilian request. By 1962 he had tired of weak and fractious civilian government and abolished it. He had the constitution rewritten to establish the army's Revolutionary Council as the sole repository of government power and ruled thereafter by decree.

Unhappy with the lack of progress in economic development, Ne Win nationalized much of the economy, expropriating foreign holdings and driving most foreign corporations out of the country. Army officers took control with generally disastrous results. Most foreign nongovernmental organizations were also forced out. Gradually Burma withdrew from all but official contacts with the outside world. The regime became increasingly repressive, army officers ran almost everything, and Burma fell behind the rest of the region, competing with the states of wartorn Indochina for the lowest standard of living in East Asia.

Clearly, Indochina was Southeast Asia's greatest victim of the Cold War. Vietnam, winner of its revolutionary war against French imperialism and America's misguided attempt at nation-building, suffered terribly at foreign hands. Those Cambodians who avoided being caught in the cross-fire between the Vietnamese and the Americans had to face the genocidal mania of Pol Pot's Khmer Rouge—massacres which dwarfed Suharto's. The Laotians fared much better, but their country, too, was bombed by the Americans and had the lives of its citizens squandered as pawns of Americans, Chinese, Soviets or Vietnamese operatives. By the mid-1970s, they were all free of foreign intervention, but their countries lay in ruins and their leaders had little idea of how to bring about recovery and development. As Cold War tensions ebbed in the region, ancient quarrels were resumed.

Although the Americans and—to a lesser extent because of their more limited capabilities—the Soviets attempted to influence affairs in the rest of Southeast Asia, the Cold War was by no means central to local concerns. Burmese, Filipino, Indonesian, Malayan, and Thai communists all received some outside advice and assistance, but would surely have pressed their agendas without the urging of Chinese or Soviet agents. Elites in all of these states except Burma attempted to manipulate the superpowers toward their own ends, often gaining support that in the case of Indonesia and the Philippines may have been decisive in thwarting the left. British aid to Malaya was certainly essential to the defeat of the communist insurgency there.

And finally, for many of the countries of the region, the Chinese diaspora posed problems. In some countries, like Indonesia. the Chinese were perceived as the capitalists who dominated the economies. In others, like Malaya, they were the backbone of the communist insurrection. In Burma, there was the additional problem of displaced Guomindang troops. In Singapore, they were a left-leaning majority who worried Indonesian and Malay elites. After the establishment of the People's Republic of China new questions arose, both of their loyalty to the states in which they resided and of the possibility of China intervening to protect them against the pogroms to which they were occasionally subject. And in every Chinese community, Mao's agents and Jiang's agents vied for support.

TABLE I2.2.   Some Notable Events in the Period 1954–1969
(Events in boldface are mentioned in text)

Geneva Conference on Indochina	**1954**
Creation of SEATO	**1954**
U.S. Supreme Court rules against school segregation	1954
First crisis in Taiwan Strait	**1954–1955**
Bandung Conference	**1955**
Brooklyn Dodgers win their first world series	1955
Khrushchev denounces Stalin	1956
Anti-Soviet uprisings in Poland and Hungary	1956
Grace Kelly marries Prince Rainier of Monaco	1956
Suez crisis	1956
Soviets launch first satellites, Sputniks I and II	1957
Cardinal Roncalli becomes Pope John XXIII	1958
Second crisis in Taiwan Strait	**1958**
American U-2 shot down over Soviet Union	1960
Belgian Congo granted independence	1960
Berlin crisis	1961
Cuban missile crisis	1962
John F. Kennedy assassinated	1963
Martin Luther King awarded Nobel Peace prize	1964

Cassius Clay (Muhammad Ali) wins world heavyweight boxing title	1964
Jomo Kenyatta becomes president of Republic of Kenya	1964
Suharto orders massacres in Indonesia	**1965**
Cultural Revolution begins in China	**1966**
Israel wins Six Day War	1967
Tet offensive in Vietnam	**1968**
Robert Kennedy and Martin Luther King assassinated	1968
Prague Spring crushed by Warsaw pact forces	1968
Yasir Arafat elected chairman of executive committee of PLO	1969

China, Taiwan, and the United States

After the Korean War, the central tension in the Cold War in East Asia was between the United States and China. Having bloodied the Americans in Korea, the Chinese gained great status on the world scene, but they also embittered a powerful enemy, the one country that could prevent Mao's legions from invading Taiwan and concluding the civil war. When the war ended in Korea in the summer of 1953, the Truman administration and those in it who were working toward accommodation with the People's Republic of China were gone. In their places were leaders determined to isolate and eventually destroy Mao's regime, and to protect Taiwan until Jiang's forces were ready to regain control of the mainland. American military leaders were eager to avenge their losses in Korea by taking the war to China. They hoped Truman's successor would release them from the restraints of limited war and allow them to use nuclear weapons.

The principal flash points of the 1950s were the 38th parallel in Korea, the 17th parallel in Vietnam, and probably the most dangerous of all, the Taiwan Strait. In the course of the war in Korea, the United States stationed warships in the strait to prevent an invasion from the mainland and it continued to maintain a naval presence there for nearly two decades. American aid to the Guomindang regime on Taiwan resumed, much of it military. Jiang pressed the United States for an alliance and negotiations for a mutual defense treaty began in 1953, shortly after the

Americans signed such a treaty with the Republic of Korea. By 1954 it was clear that Washington was reluctant, fearful of irritating its European allies who were less supportive of Jiang, and troubled by the possibility of Jiang dragging the United States into a war. Instead the Americans looked for other ways to contain China, creating SEATO, from which they excluded Jiang's government. At that point Mao chose to initiate a crisis in the Taiwan Strait.

In September 1954, shore-based batteries of the PLA opened fire on Guomindang-held islands off the coast of China. Mao's intent was to intimidate the United States, to prevent a Taibei-Washington alliance, by warning the Americans that it could lead to war. China's actions were counter-productive. When Mao's forces attacked and occupied several lesser islands, American leaders decided to give Jiang the alliance he wanted as a means of deterring an attack on Taiwan. American military capabilities in the region were increased. As a result, the Guomindang remained in control of several islands, most significantly Jinmen, Mazu, and the Penghus, perceived by the Eisenhower administration as important to the morale of the people on Taiwan—if not to their defense. Concluding that they had underestimated American resolve, the Chinese backed off in the spring of 1955 and offered to negotiate with the United States.

Pressed by its European allies, the United States accepted the offer and ambassadorial level talks began in August. The two sides quickly reached agreement on the repatriation of Americans in China and Chinese in America, civilians who had been stranded when their counties became enemies in 1950. And then the talks broke down over the critical issue of Taiwan. The United States demanded that China renounce the use of force against Taiwan as a prerequisite to any larger agreement. The Chinese insisted that Taiwan was part of China and that they had the right to use force to conclude their civil war by eliminating Jiang's rump regime. Chinese leaders offered their view that force would not prove necessary, that peaceful liberation of the island was increasingly likely, but the Americans were not appeased. It was soon evident that the Eisenhower administration was not interested in reaching an accommodation on the basis of anything less than Peking's acceptance of Taiwan's independence, of two Chinas or, one China, one Taiwan. China's efforts to continue the dialogue were rejected and the United States broke off the talks at the end of 1957.

Mao tired of American tactics, especially when the United States was facilitating small-scale Guomindang raids on the mainland. He perceived little reason for continued efforts to woo the Americans. By 1957, the Soviet military buildup had neutralized American power and Soviet successes in the space race suggested that the East wind was prevailing over the West. In August 1958, assuming the Americans were preoccupied with their intervention in the Lebanonese civil war, Mao was ready to take the offensive. China resumed the bombardment of Jinmen and harassed shipping to other Guomindang-held islands on the mainland coast. Quickly another crisis developed, deliberately provoked by China.

Once again Mao had underestimated American support for Taiwan. The United States hastily sent supplies and naval forces to convoy them to the off-shore islands. Guomindang planes equipped with American air-to-air missiles dominated the skies over the strait. Reports that the Americans were preparing to use nuclear weapons against China surfaced. Absent any indications of support from his Soviet ally, Mao had no choice but to back down again. His efforts, however, were not unrewarded. In the United States and in the capitals of *its* allies, there was widespread unease with the prospect of a major war developing over a handful of tiny islands of no strategic value, within reach of shore batteries. American leaders were compelled to mute their belligerent rhetoric and they in turn insisted that Jiang announce that his mission of ending Communist rule of the mainland would not require the use of force. Chinese provocations succeeded in creating tension in the relationship between Taibei and Washington and in increasing doubts about American policy toward China among its Western allies. Making the best of a bad situation, Mao claimed victory. He declared that he would not seize the off-shore islands because he did not want to facilitate America's two China policy by severing the links between Taiwan and the mainland.

A major additional side effect of the strait crisis of 1958 was an intensification of discontent that had been growing in the Sino-Soviet relationship. Although the Chinese had regained full control of Manchuria after Stalin's death, they still smarted over Soviet looting of the region after World War II, Soviet denial of Chinese claims to Mongolia, and the terms of Soviet economic and technical assistance generally—not least the charges for supplies during the Korean War. A Soviet offer of military advisers and requests for submarine basing rights and a radio station on Chinese soil to broadcast to Soviet submarines aroused Chinese sus-

MAP 26.   COLD WAR IN ASIA, C. 1960.

picions. In the late 1950s Soviet foreign policy struck Chinese leaders as excessively cautious. Unlike the states the Soviets dominated in Eastern Europe, the Chinese were also displeased by Soviet domestic policies, especially de-Stalinization. From the perspective of Peking, the Soviets seem to be losing their revolutionary fervor.

Worst of all, Soviet advice to moderate Chinese policy, to avoid provoking the United States, irritated Mao. When, in 1958, the Soviets failed to provide what the Chinese considered adequate support for their operations against Taiwan, Peking suspected the Soviets of indifference to China's interests. Perhaps the final indignity was the suggestion by Nikita Khrushchev, the Soviet leader, that Mao accept the two Chinas policy toward which the United States had moved—in other words, to forget about Taiwan. Mao was profoundly offended and this episode may have precipitated the break between the two countries. Angry exchanges, focused primarily on differences over ideological matters, led to the recall of Soviet technicians from China in 1959 and an unsuccessful attempt by the Soviets to sabotage China's nuclear weapons program. In the years that followed, the relationship became increasingly hostile.

At approximately the same time, relations between China and India began to deteriorate rapidly. The two countries had never agreed to the demarcation of the borders between them, drawn differently on their respective maps. Most of the disputed territory was high in the Himalayas, virtually uninhabitable. In the late 1950s, however, China built a highway from Xinjiang to Tibet through a plateau claimed by India, outraging New Delhi. Disagreements over border issues were exacerbated in 1959 when, after a revolt in Tibet, India granted asylum to the Dalai Lama and thousands of his followers—an ostensibly humanitarian act perceived by the Chinese as interference in their internal affairs.

The shooting started in August 1959, and continued sporadically along the border until mid-1962 when the Indian army attempted to establish its presence in the contested frontier area. In October, after ignoring demands from Peking that they withdraw, Indian forces crossed into undisputed Tibetan lands. They shouldn't have. The Chinese attacked almost immediately and launched a second offensive in November. The PLA humiliated the Indian army, easily driving it out of all disputed territory. The Chinese had prevailed and retained control of the land they considered their own, but they forced India to turn to the United States and the Soviet Union for support. Khrushchev, competing with the

Americans for influence in India, challenged Peking's version of the events, further alienating his Chinese comrades.

As Mao and Khrushchev drove each other and their countries apart with their harsh rhetoric, China was rent internally by divisions within the Communist Party. The Party leaders, of whom Mao was clearly paramount, had reached a consensus on several key domestic policy decisions over the first few years after their victory over the Guomindang. Land reform had been essential to maintain the support of the peasantry that had brought them to power. The attack on the business community, launched with less certainty, seemed essential to undermine a likely source of opposition to the Party's rule. Closely connected was the decision to follow the Soviet model of economic development. But as the PRC struggled to reorganize Chinese society, differences arose over the pace of change and the value of intellectuals to the state. In 1957, with Mao's influence ebbing, he launched the "Hundred Flowers" campaign, offering intellectuals an opportunity to criticize the Party's efforts. For several weeks, they did—and whether Party members or outsiders, they paid a heavy price for coming forward. Horrified, those Party leaders who had little use for intellectuals, who prized party discipline most highly, reacted strongly against the campaign, carrying Mao with them. Several hundred thousand intellectuals were labeled "rightists," many severely punished, all suffering major disruptions in their lives.

Next came the "Great Leap," Mao's vision of mobilizing the masses to achieve rapid progress in agricultural and industrial production. It included the abolition of private plots and the creation of huge agricultural communes. It involved the diversion of resources into more than a million backyard steel furnaces. And it led to enormous disappointment when it became evident that agricultural production had fallen and that locally produced steel was generally of poor quality. The country was wracked by a famine that took as many as 20 million lives between 1959 and 1962. Tensions between Mao and other Party leaders increased sharply. His primacy was in question.

Among Party leaders there were serious policy differences that had become apparent during the Hundred Flowers and Great Leap campaigns. Mao's infallibility could no longer be taken seriously. Others were eager to take the reins of power, either because they wanted to redirect the course of the nation or because they lusted after power—or both. By 1966 the country had recovered from the Great Leap and economic progress had resumed, but the strains within the Party could no longer be contained. That summer the Cultural Revolution exploded and images of Mao at Tiananmen facing tens of thousands of youngsters, "Red Guards," waving their little red books, their *Quotations from Chairman Mao*, became the symbol of China.

The cult of personality transcended anything even Josef Stalin had enjoyed. Within months Mao's supporters, most notably his wife, Jiang Qing, had succeeded in wrecking the Party hierarchy, humiliating and purging the head of state and the secretary-general of the Party, as well as thousands of lesser officials. China's young, goaded by Mao and his allies, attacked their parents, their teachers, and Party officials, beating thousands to death and driving thousands more to suicide. Intellectuals, cultural artifacts, and anyone or anything remotely related to the West were worthy targets of the rampage. And despite the tenuous position of China in an international system in which it had succeeded in antagonizing both of the superpowers, the country's foreign policy apparatus was destroyed and all but one of China's ambassadors was recalled from abroad. The Cultural Revolution brought China's economic development to a halt and damaged the reputation it had won in world affairs since 1949.

By mid-1967 China was in chaos, with pitched battles between various revolutionary factions, battles in which the PLA occasionally became involved, slaughtering thousands of its own people. Hundreds of thousands of intellectuals and Party cadres were sent to the countryside for labor and reeducation. Until the summer of 1968, there was little semblance of order in the country.

In 1968, a warning bell sounded for any Chinese leader sensible enough, and secure enough to pay attention to foreign affairs, to be concerned about national security. Soviet military intervention crushed an heretical reform movement in the Communist Party of Czechoslovakia. Shortly afterward, the Soviet leader, Leonid Brezhnev, pronounced the "Brezhnev Doctrine," claiming the right to use force in the defense of Moscow's conception of socialism. But most Chinese, especially those directing the Cultural Revolution, could not be distracted or intimidated by this external threat. As the Soviets massed troops along their borders with China in Xinjiang and Manchuria, tensions increased.

In March 1969, fighting errupted in the vicinity of Chenbao Island in the Ussuri River. Clashes between Chinese and Soviet patrols resulted in heavy casualties on both sides. In Washington and elsewhere in the world apprehensions mounted. In some quarters there was doubtless delight in the prospect of the two great communist states at each other's throat, but China had become a nuclear power and the prospect of nuclear war in which fallout respected no one's neutrality was frightening.

Moscow demanded negotiations to settle the disagreements, but still driven by the fervor of the Cultural Revolution, the Chinese were unyielding. After several ultimatums were ignored by China, Soviet forces, supported by helicopters, marched into Xinjiang in August. Fearful of a preemptive strike against their nuclear installations in the region, the Chinese agreed to meet with the Soviets, defusing the immediate crisis, but doing little to improve Sino-Soviet relations.

By 1970, Mao was persuaded that the Cultural Revolution had to be restrained, that the governing bureaucracy and the Party had to be strengthened. Some of his advisers were also troubled by the increased power and influence of the PLA. He was also persuaded that the Soviet threat was serious and that it might be wise to seek accommodation with the United States as a counterweight to Soviet pressures. Jiang Qing and those closest to her did not agree with efforts to moderate the Cultural Revolution or the idea of improving relations with the Americans. As a result of strong differences within the leadership, progress on both fronts was slow and uncertain.

Their war in Vietnam had taken a toll on the willingness of the American people to continue to support policies aimed at containing and isolating China. American leaders began to perceive the Chinese as potential allies against the Soviets and as a source of support for their efforts to extricate themselves from Vietnam. In the late 1960s the United States made several quiet overtures to Peking, but found the Chinese unresponsive. In 1969 the American president in several ways signaled his desire to ease tensions in the relationship. Travel and trade restrictions that had existed since the Korean War were eased. U.S. navy patrols in the Taiwan Strait ceased. The American ambassador to Poland courted the senior Chinese diplomat in that country. And then, early in 1970, ambassadorial level conversations were resumed. The Chinese had concluded that the United States was less of a threat to them than was the Soviet Union.

Each side moved cautiously, aware of opposition to rapprochement in both countries. As had been the case in the 1950s, Taiwan was the irresolvable issue. Unlike the 1950s, in 1971 the Americans and Chinese found compelling reasons to compromise. Peking still insisted that there was only one China and that Taiwan was one of its provinces. To protect Taiwan, whose forces few people anywhere imagined could retake the mainland, the Americans had tried to gain acceptance of the idea of two Chinas, one with its capital in Peking, the other with its capital in Taibei. Both Mao and Jiang, however, rejected the idea. The winning formula was "one China, but not now." The United States acknowledged the fact that Chinese on both sides of the strait insisted on one China and expressed its expectation that the future of Taiwan would be determined peacefully, by the Chinese themselves, at some later time. In July 1971, much of the world was astonished to learn that the American president's national security adviser had been to Peking and that the president himself would visit China early the following year. In the summer of 1971, the United States supported the seating of representatives of the People's Republic of China in the United Nations. Gradually the Americans moved to disengage themselves from Taiwan, to which they were bound by the mutual defense treaty of 1954.

Succession crises in both China and the United States precluded major conciliatory steps for several years. The American president, Richard Nixon, was forced to resign after being implicated in the cover-up of criminal acts by his aides. During his last days in office he proved to be too weak to overcome opposition to abrogating the commitment to Jiang. In China, there was dissatisfaction with American inaction on that front and with Nixon's success at achieving détente with the Soviet Union, which Peking now viewed as its principal antagonist. The failing health of both Mao and Zhou Enlai provided an opportunity for radicals led by Jiang Qing to attack the moderate policies both men had pursued in the early 1970s, including allegedly unnecessary overtures toward the United States. For both countries, the struggle for power at home took precedence in 1976.

By 1976, China and the United States had ceased to be adversaries. The meetings in 1971 and 1972, and the establishment in 1973 of liaison offices, tantamount to embassies by each country in the other's capital, signaled the beginning of a new era in their relationship. The leaders of both countries had concluded that cooperation against the Soviet Union was of greater immediate importance than the many issues that still divided them. There remained, however, many powerful figures in each country opposed to rapprochement and the future of the relationship depended on the outcome of domestic political struggles in both.

TABLE 12.3.   Some Notable Events of the Period 1972–1975

(Events in boldface are mentioned in text)

U.S. and China issue Shanghai Communiqué	**1972**
Government of Salvador Allende overthrown by Chilean military	1973
Americans accept defeat, withdraw from Vietnam	**1973**
Yom Kippur War	1973
Dictatorship ended in Portugal; democracy begins	1974
Richard Nixon resigns presidency of the United States	1974
Franco dies; democracy restored in Spain	1975

Conclusion

The Cold War in East Asia was virtually over by the mid-1970s. The United States had withdrawn its forces from Vietnam in 1973 and stood aside as communist forces from the north routed America's friends in the south and united the country in 1975. All of Indochina came under communist control. Defeat of the United States was exhilarating to the victors, but the reconstruction of wartorn countries unquestionably would be a slow and painful process. The Cambodians in particular gained no respite as Pol Pot's murderous regime devastated their country. But despite the profound suffering of the people of Indochina, the Chinese-American rapprochement, depriving the United States of the principal rationale for its aggressive posture in East Asia, provided the region with the hope of peace.

There was, of course, continued tension on the 38th parallel, and Kim Il Sung's regime showed no evidence of softening its hostility toward its brethren south of that line or toward the United States. American troops remained at the border between the two Korean states, a deterrent to a repeat of Kim's 1950 offensive. But elsewhere, there was no serious threat of communist expansion or evidence of any danger to American strategic interests in the region.

Although the United States was in the process of pulling back from the peak of its military involvement in East Asia, it remained the dominant power there. It retained overwhelming naval superiority in the Western Pacific and maintained bases in Japan and the Philippines, as well as in Korea. The cost of its military presence was a tremendous burden to the American people, but perhaps surprisingly, that presence was welcomed by most East Asian leaders as a source of stability, a means both of containing communism and of preventing a resurgence of Japanese military power. And while the Americans bore the burden of maintaining peace and stability, regional leaders could concentrate on the rapid economic development of their nations.

The Resurgence of East Asian Economic Power

The Cold War was not the only activity in East Asia in the years between the Chinese Communist victory in their civil war and the moment in which the Americans finally reached an accommodation with Mao's regime. These were also years of extraordinary economic activity. Japan led the way with an incredible burst of growth that took it from dependency on the largesse of the United States to becoming one of the world's largest economies and Washington's most feared commercial rival. But the Japanese were not alone. There were also the "Four Little Dragons."[1] South Korea, however reluctantly, came to terms with its former tormentor and used both Japanese capital and the Japanese model to launch its own highly successful industrialization. Singapore, Hong Kong, and Taiwan, all primarily ethnic Chinese entities, outpaced many larger states, including the People's Republic of China. Long before the end of the Cold War, several Southeast Asian nations, including Indonesia, Malaysia, and Thailand saw their economies boom. By 1980, American trade across the Pacific surpassed that with its traditional trading partners across the Atlantic. The economic importance of East Asia had increased incredibly. If mainland China recovered from the Cultural Revolution and mimicked the economic growth of its neighbors, East Asia once again would be central to the international economic system.

Japan as Number 1

In the spring of 1950, Japan was in a deep recession resulting in large part from the austerity program imposed on it by the Americans in 1949. The enormous boost from American expenditures in Japan during the Korean War brought economic recovery and enabled the Japanese to recover their pre-World War II standard of living. The Korean War also brought the peace treaty signed at San Francisco and an end to the occupation. Japan had regained its independence. When the war in Korea ended in 1953, however, the inflow of dollars dropped sharply and the country slid into another recession. A deeply ingrained sense of vulnerability quickly resurfaced. Virtually all Japanese were aware of the extent to which their nation's prosperity depended on access to energy sources and many other raw materials from abroad. Many remembered the quest for economic autonomy, for control of all necessary resources, that had prompted their country to act aggressively, resulting in the Pacific War. Could Japan find a peaceful means to meet the requirements for strong economic growth?

Japan's leaders had little trouble reaching a consensus on the nation's goals, but short-term dependence on the United States complicated the process of achieving them. Across the political spectrum, Japanese were eager for *complete* independence, to be rid of American troops and bases, to regain lost territories such as Okinawa occupied by the Americans and the small islands north of Hokkaido occupied by the Soviets, to be able to trade freely with China, to regain access to the markets and raw materials they had controlled in the 1930s and early 1940s. But Yoshida and his successors recognized the limits of their power. They could beg, but they could not demand; they could manipulate the Americans, but they could not dictate to them. To prosper in an unfriendly world, they required economic assistance and protection only the United States could provide.

Yoshida had been remarkably successful in managing Japan's relationship with the United States. He had been forced to accept peace terms he abhorred, including continued American military presence in the home islands, but he turned that reversal into an asset. With Japan's security assured by the United States, he saw no need to expend scarce resources on its defensive capabilities and he persistently resisted Washington's pressure to rearm against the communist threat. Rebuilding Japan's economic power became his highest priority. He would push against the Americans on all fronts, whittling away at their hold on Japan, utilizing their fear of losing his country to the communists to gain access to their market and their technology. Few of his successors were as adept, but all played variations on his theme.

Yoshida was himself intensely anticommunist and apprehensive about Soviet intentions, but like most Japanese, he had trouble taking seriously the American perception of the threat posed by China. Japanese contempt for Chinese military prowess was boundless. Nothing in their experience enabled them to imagine a powerful China that might pose a danger to Japan. On the other hand, China had been an important source of raw materials for Japanese industry and, communist or not, it might become a valuable trading partner. The efforts of the United States in the 1950s to isolate China posed an undesirable restraint on Japan's commercial relationship with Mao's regime and became a frequent source of friction between Tokyo and Washington. Again, Japanese leaders found this tension useful in prying open American markets for their goods. American Cold War strategists needed little reminder of the direction in which Japan might be forced to turn if denied access to the markets and resources of the "free world." Their Japanese counterparts were always very quick to call attention to "neutralist' or "leftist" sentiment among their people.

The Japanese had some success exploiting China's desire to drive a wedge between Tokyo and Washington, but their efforts to regain territory from the Soviet Union or win access to the riches of the Soviet Far East met with more resistance. Always the Americans were looking over their shoulders, offering vague threats of unpleasantness to follow if Japan moved too close to either of the communist giants. Japan's eagerness for trade with China was tempered also by its desire to maintain good relations with Jiang's regime on Taiwan and by Peking's declared opposition to the separation of politics from commerce.

Yoshida had signed a peace treaty with the Taiwan government in 1952, but quickly reached out to the People's Republic in search of economic opportunities. His successors followed his policy of maintaining diplomatic relations with Taibei while trading with both Taiwan and the mainland. Their efforts were facilitated by Eisenhower's conviction that trade sanctions against the Peking government were misguided, however necessary they might be for the United States in a time of anticommunist hysteria. He argued, moreover, that if restrictions imposed on Japan's right to trade with China were not eased, the American taxpayer would be forced to subsidize the Japanese economy. The Japanese shrewdly based their case on the apparently desperate condition of their economy. Textile interests in the United States, eager to avoid competition with Japanese exports, were also receptive to Japan's desire to trade with China, as were America's British allies for much the same reason.

Japanese businessmen found themselves welcome in China and several "nongovernmental" commercial agreements were reached in the mid-1950s. In 1955, China held trade fairs in Tokyo and Osaka, and in 1956 Japan reciprocated with fairs in Peking and Shanghai. Trade between the two countries expanded rapidly, only to collapse in 1958 when the Japanese government fell off the tightrope it walked between Taibei and Peking. In 1957 Jiang threatened to cut off trade if the Japanese persisted in expanding their trade with the mainland. An effort by the Japanese to appease Jiang angered Mao and, in 1958, he responded to a minor incident by canceling all trade contracts. The linkage Peking insisted on between politics and business could not have been made clearer.

Negotiations with the Soviets failed to reach agreement on a peace treaty, but accomplished Japan's minimum objective of a resumption of diplomatic relations. Territorial issues continued to fester, however, and commercial gains were inconsequential. In particular the Japanese asked for the return of four islands, the "northern territories," occupied by the Soviets in 1945. The Soviets offered to return two of them as part of a comprehensive settlement, but domestic political considerations and American pressure delayed acceptance of the compromise. By the time the Japanese were ready to act, Moscow was offering less agreeable terms. Nonetheless, in October 1956, relations between the two countries were restored and the Soviets dropped their objections to Japan's membership in the United Nations, clearing the way for admission.

Coping with the United States, however, remained Japan's most important and most difficult challenge. No other country could equal American military power or provide a comparable market for Japanese exports. No other country occupied as much Japanese territory. The Americans had come to regret their efforts to prevent the rearmament of Japan and pressed constantly for the Japanese to rebuild their military for integration into the forces defending the " Free World" against the "International Communist Conspiracy." The Japanese parried these thrusts easily, pointing to the limitations imposed by the constitution the Americans had written for them and to intense domestic political opposition to amending its relevant provision. Yoshida and his equally conservative successors also constantly noted strong public opposition to the Japanese-American security treaty, heightening American fears of a leftist victory at the polls. The Japanese had the weaker hand, but they played it very well.

Two incidents in the mid-1950s fanned anti-American sentiments in Japan. In the first of these, in 1954, a Japanese fishing boat sailing downwind of an American nuclear test at Bikini Atoll was struck by radioactive ash. One crew member eventually died and several others suffered the effects of radiation poisoning. The American response was shockingly slow, insensitive, and inadequate, jeopardizing the relationship. An apology and compensation eventually came from Washington, but it took the better part of a year to ease the tension and opposition to the security treaty mounted among the Japanese people. Resentment grew in 1957 when an American soldier stationed in Japan shot and killed a woman who was collecting scrap metal on a firing range. The testimony of both Japanese and American witnesses suggested that he acted maliciously. Under the status of forces agreement that governed jurisdiction over American troops in Japan, however, an American accused of a crime while on duty was to be tried by a U.S. military court. The Japanese, noting that the act occurred while the soldier was on a rest break, claimed that their courts had jurisdiction. Public opinion in both countries was inflamed as Japanese saw the American as a murderer to be tried in their courts and many Americans saw him as a potential victim of Washington's desire to keep the Japanese friendly. On this occasion, both governments acted shrewdly. The Americans turned the soldier over to the Japanese who charged him with a relatively minor crime, suspended his sentence, and deported him.

It was clear, nonetheless, that the security treaty had to be revised if it was to be viable. The Americans would have to be less overbearing in the relationship, and manifest greater respect for Japan's independence. They would have to surrender the right to intervene militarily in Japanese affairs. The Japanese government had to be given a voice in the deployment of American troops stationed in Japan. To counter the readily appreciated Japanese allergy to nuclear weapons, Tokyo would have to be granted the right to deny their deployment on Japanese territory. The Americans would retain bases, presumably essential to the defense of Japan as well as the interests of the United States in the region, but the new status of forces agreement was comparable to that between the Americans and their NATO allies.

All these concessions, however, did not satisfy Japanese opponents of the security treaty. When an unpopular prime minister, propped up in part by covert American contributions to his party, forced the revised treaty through the Diet in 1960, tens of thousands of Japanese took to the streets to demonstrate against it. Although the revised treaty survived the unrest, a planned visit by the American president to Japan had to be canceled and the despised prime minister was driven from office.

Ultimately, Japan's leaders understood the American connection was at least as important to Japan as it was to the United States. The bureaucrats and politicians who ran the country were no more sympathetic to communism than were their American counterparts. Much as they would have preferred complete freedom of action, they were not so naive as to believe it attainable. In the context of the Cold War, it was sensible to be aligned with the United States, to gain its protection, to prosper under the American nuclear umbrella, to let Americans fight Japan's battles.

Equally as important as the security provided by the Americans was the market for Japanese goods provided by the United States and the easy access Americans gave them to the world's most advanced technology, agricultural as well as industrial. In 1955 the Japanese economy began an extraordinary growth spurt that was halted only briefly by the world-wide recession of 1958. It was an era in which the economy of the United States and its support to its friends provided an extremely high rate of world economic growth, a climate favorable to Japanese exports. The Japanese also benefited from a decline in crude oil prices and in the cost of raw materials generally in the 1950s and 60s. These external conditions provided an opportunity that Japan skillfully exploited. As a result of shrewd industrial policy, Japan's growth rate averaged an incredibly high 10 percent annually.

By the 1960s, American concern about Japan becoming a financial burden to the American taxpayer gave way to worldwide concern over Japan as a commercial threat, an economic giant. In 1965, for the first time, Japan gained a favorable balance of goods and services with the world, exporting more than it imported. In 1968, debts to Japan exceeded Japan's foreign debt. Japan had become a creditor nation and its foreign currency reserves grew rapidly. More gratifying to the Japanese was the fact that in that same year, Japan's gross national product surpassed that of West Germany. Japan now had the second largest economy in the world and could dream of overtaking the United States, of Japan as number 1. It was not an outcome Americans were prepared to countenance. Nor was Japan's economic power a source of comfort to its neighbors, who remembered only too well Japanese efforts to dominate East Asia earlier in the century.

Initially, the Americans welcomed Japan's dependence on the U.S. market, delighted by the links thus forged between the two countries which were perceived as strengthening their alliance. To most American leaders, the political-military considerations of the Cold War greatly outweighed trade issues. In the 1960s, however, the complaints of domestic industries hurt by Japanese competition could no longer be ignored. In

1968, despite its preoccupation with Vietnam, the U.S. government demanded that Japan restrict its steel exports. Friction over trade issues began to trouble relations between Washington and a Japanese government that supported America's war in Vietnam despite the intense opposition of the Japanese public.

Japanese dissatisfaction with the United States increased during America's war in Vietnam. Particularly irritating was the use of Okinawa as a staging ground for the American military assault on North Vietnam in the late 1960s. Once again, the Japanese asked for the return of Okinawa and other islands still held by the Americans. In 1968 the Americans returned the Bonins, tiny islands of little strategic value but of symbolic importance to the United States because of the bitter battle fought there on one of them, Iwo Jima, in the spring of 1945. The American military would not consider surrendering its bases on Okinawa, however. The territorial question soon became enmeshed in frictions over trade issues.

In fact, the continued rapid growth of the Japanese economy owed a great deal to the war in Vietnam. As part of their effort, the Americans spent billions of dollars in Korea, Taiwan, and Southeast Asia, as well as Japan. These American expenditures created a regional boom from which the Japanese benefited greatly. As American industry geared itself increasingly for war production, the United States was forced to import consumer goods to keep its own population from rebelling against the war. Again, Japanese exporters were among the principal beneficiaries. But when Washington asked the Japanese to restrict their shipments of synthetic fiber textiles to the United States, the Japanese refused.

American leaders found that Japan showed no more gratitude for American economic assistance than it did for America's nuclear umbrella. About the only concession they received from Japan was a muting of Japanese demands for more contact with China—a relatively easy gesture for Japan to make in the midst of the chaos of China's Cultural Revolution. On the other hand, agitation for the return of Okinawa worried Washington and it became apparent that it would be best to agree to reversion and attempt to hold on to bases there. The alternative might be to reinforce burgeoning nationalism and anti-Americanism in Japan, resulting in an explosion comparable to that of 1960. In 1969 negotiations began between the two countries in which the Okinawa and textile issues were joined. If the Japanese would acquiesce to American demands that they limit their synthetic textile exports to the United States, the Americans would agree to return Okinawa to Japan under conditions that would be politically acceptable to the Japanese.

In November 1969, the Japanese prime minister, Sato Eisaku, met in Washington with the American president, Richard Nixon. Sato accepted Nixon's offer to return Okinawa to Japan in 1972 and agreed to allow the United States to maintain bases there. Secretly, he consented to the reintroduction of nuclear weapons on Okinawa in an emergency. Nixon thought he also had obtained Sato's promise to limit Japan's textile exports. Both sides were enormously pleased with the handling of the Okinawa reversion issue. The textile settlement, however, quickly collapsed. Sato could not deliver on his promise.

The next few years were extraordinarily difficult for a Japanese government caught between powerful domestic interests and the wrath of the American president, himself indebted to domestic textile manufacturers and under pressure from their advocates in the Congress. For over a year, tense negotiations between the two countries embittered their relations and the possibility of a trade war loomed large. And then, in the summer of 1971, came what the Japanese called the "Nixon shocks."

In July 1971, Nixon dramatically informed the world that his national security adviser had visited Peking secretly and that he himself would visit China early in 1972. The United States was proceeding toward rapprochement with the People's Republic. The Japanese were given less than one hour's notice of this remarkable shift in American policy, although virtually every advocate of rapprochement in the American government had underscored the importance of keeping Tokyo informed.[2] Nixon had taken his revenge on Sato, who, faithful to his American ally, had long resisted popular demands for improving relations with China. This was shock number one.

In August, Nixon struck again. The American economy was in trouble, largely the result of mismanagement at home, an effort to defer the financial pain caused by the war in Vietnam. Inflation increased. The economic growth rate slowed. The balance of payments deficit was roaring out of control. Nixon announced a temporary freeze on wages and prices in an effort to control inflation, imposed a 10 percent surcharge on all U.S. tariffs in an effort to improve the trade balance, and began a process that ultimately forced a revaluation of the Japanese yen and the German mark upward against the dollar—a de facto devaluation of the U.S. dollar to make American goods more competitive. Washington had sent Tokyo a clear message: it would no longer subordinate its economic interests to its foreign policy objectives. Given Japanese dependence on the American market, the threat was profoundly troubling.

The Nixon shocks changed the nature of the Japanese-American relationship. The Japanese could no longer count on benign neglect in Washington's response to Japan's commercial expansion. And if anger over trade issues frayed the alliance, could Americans newly enamored of China be relied upon to provide for Japan's security? To some Japanese leaders, it was evident that the United States was turning to China for insurance against the growing power of Japan. Japan would have to fend for itself in the international arena.

In fact, Japanese-American relations, although frequently troubled by economic issues, remained reasonably constant. The Japanese could not easily find replacements for the American market or a cheaper source of protection. Few Americans were prepared to contemplate a hostile Japan, however useful rapprochement with China was to the American Cold War contest with the Soviet Union. And in 1972, despite Chinese propaganda decrying the rise of Japanese militarism, China and Japan established diplomatic relations, nearly a decade before the United States and China could surmount the obstacles that prevented normalization of relations between Washington and Peking. The triangular relationship proved satisfactory in the 1970s.

The Japanese economy was in for more shocks in the 1970s, not all of which could be attributed to U.S. commercial or fiscal policies. Amidst a worldwide inflationary cycle, to which the Americans had contributed significantly, war broke out in the Middle East in October, 1973—the so-called Yom Kippur War between Israel and its Arab neighbors. Israel's military success was countered by an Arab decision to use oil as a weapon, to force's Israel's foreign supporters to back off by denying them access to oil. Most of Japan's oil came from the Middle East. When the United States could not assure Japan of an adequate supply, Tokyo perceived no alternative to abandoning its support for America's pro-Israel policies and courting the Arabs. But the Arabs and non-Arab members of OPEC (Organization of Petroleum Exporting Countries) were able to quadruple crude oil prices, disrupting the international economic system and exacting a terrible toll on Japan. Inflation soared, retrenchment followed, and Japan's era of rapid economic growth ended. In 1974 Japan's economy began its severest recession since World War II. The only road to economic recovery seemed to be increased exports.

In 1975 Japan was in the midst of a serious recession, but its troubles could not disguise the fact that over the previous two decades, Japan's economic power had grown rapidly. It was now one of the world's wealthiest countries. Its people enjoyed a standard of living comparable to that of Americans or Western Europeans. Its industrialists had demonstrated that they could produce products of the highest quality, creating a worldwide demand for Japanese goods. The resurrection of Japan's economy after its devastating defeat in World War II had come with unimagined speed. It remained to be seen whether that economic power and particularly Japan's export capacity could be integrated into the existing international economic system.

Little Dragons

The Japanese model was followed with relative ease by South Korea. In the colonial era, Japan had viewed Korea as an integral part of its economic system and had laid the foundations for a modern industrial infrastructure on the peninsula—although most of the industry was in the northern half of the peninsula. The Japanese had also created institutions in Korea, similar to their own, approximating what Chalmers Johnson and others have called the developmental state,[3] a bureaucratically run regime focused on economic growth. Virtually all Korean officials and businessmen spoke Japanese and most were quite comfortable working with them. Indeed, many were viewed as collaborators by Korean workers and intellectuals.

Were it not for the Cold War and American intervention in Korean affairs, those perceived by their countrymen as collaborators would have been purged after World War II, as they were in the areas under communist control. The Americans as occupiers and subsequently as protectors placed their highest priority on anticommunism. A history of collaboration with the Japanese was not necessarily a handicap. A knowledge of Japanese and contacts in Japan proved enormously valuable after 1965, when Park Chung Hee's military dictatorship forced the people of South Korea to swallow a treaty of normalization with Japan.

South Korea was ravaged by its civil war with the north and the division of the country left the people of the south without an industrial base upon which to build their economy. Generous American aid and technological assistance helped but was not sufficient to overcome the incompetence of the Rhee regime that survived until 1960. Beyond patriotism and anticommunism, Rhee had few noticeable virtues and an understanding of economic development was not one of them. His government, relying on a broadsweeping National Security Law and the support of the national police, became increasingly oppressive. Finally, in 1960, attacks on student dissidents provoked riots and resulted in the withdrawal of American support. When his troops refused to fire on demonstrators, Rhee was forced to resign. Elections followed and Korea finally had a government freely chosen by its people.

Democracy in Korea lasted less than one year. In May 1961, the Korean army, trained and equipped by the United States, seized power. General Park Chung Hee, who had served as an officer in the Japanese army in World War II, quickly became the dominant figure. His troops brought unruly students and workers, perceived as leftists, under control. American aid continued. Korea continued to receive American advisers who helped revive its textile industry. It also received special access to markets in the United States. Clearly, what mattered most to the United States was the ability of South Korea to defend itself against the communist north and to contribute more broadly to the defense of the "free world." On the other hand, Washington was eager to be relieved of the burden of supporting its Korean protectorate and hoped to see Korean-Japanese cooperation serve its ends. Park overrode intense public opposition and reached a settlement with Tokyo. East Asian specialists in the American government estimated that Korean-Japanese rapprochement would save the United States a billion dollars between 1965 and 1975.

Park showed his gratitude to the Americans for their acceptance of his dictatorship by sending two divisions of combat troops, ultimately a total of 300,000 men, to support their war in Vietnam. Korea in turn received massive compensation, billions of dollars, both in cash and in contracts to Korean companies. The war in Vietnam, between 1966 and 1973, provided Korea with an exceptional opportunity to speed its economic development. Like the Japanese during the Korean War, they made the most of it.

Beyond retaining power, which he exercised for eighteen years before he was assassinated, Park was determined to build a wealthy and powerful nation. Economic development was his mission and his advisers, both foreign-educated Korean technocrats and Americans, helped him refine and implement his ideas. Korean development would have to be export-driven, given the relatively small size of the domestic market. Its comparative advantage lay with its well-disciplined, low-wage work force. Park's troops and his dreaded KCIA prevented labor demands from getting out of hand and his planners took initial aim at light industries—textiles, footwear, small appliances—that were being abandoned by Japan and the United States. In the 1960s, the United States provided few obstacles to Korean exports of cheap goods. Korean exports soared from $42 million in 1962 to $1 *billion*, primarily manufactured goods, in 1970. Although the new wealth was distributed poorly, concentrated in relatively few hands, the standard of living for most Koreans rose, gaining acceptance and legitimacy for the Park regime.

Although a considerable amount of Japanese money came into Korea after 1965, Park and his advisers were uneasy about the reduction of American aid. They were also discomforted by indications in the early 1970s that the United States was decreasing its strategic involvement in East Asia, seeking détente with China and the Soviet Union. Chinese-American tensions, the overall Cold War international system, had served South Korea well in the 1960s. A drawdown of American power in the region posed a threat to South Korea, specifically as it confronted an implacably hostile regime in the north. These anxieties gave Park a rationale for declaring a state of emergency, throwing out the constitution that limited his term of office and substituting a new one that provided for a "legal" dictatorship.

Assured of continued control of the country, Park eagerly pushed on to the next step on his economic agenda: the development of heavy industries such as steel, automobile manufacturing, and ship building. Persuaded that Korea needed large companies to compete internationally, he pushed the development of large highly diversified industrial conglomerates, the *chaebol*. His government won the support of wealthy businessmen by giving them tax incentives and inexpensive credit, as well as by keeping labor docile. Large-scale foreign borrowing turned Korea into one of the world's leading debtor nations in the 1970s, but Korea succeeded in developing its heavy industry and moving into high-tech electronics as well. In 1981, its exports totaled $20 billion, twenty times the figure that had seemed a miraculous leap in 1970. And its construction industry, having demonstrated its excellence in Vietnam, won most of the contracts for projects Middle East oil-producing countries conjured up to dispose of their new-found wealth from 1973–1979. Park had driven Korea into the front ranks of the world's economic powers.

Park's assassination in 1979 was soon followed by another military coup, headed by a general who lacked Park's intelligence and reputation for rectitude. He and the general who succeeded him continued the emphasis on economic development, but both succumbed to corruption and neither could carry out the adjustments required by a changing international economic climate. A bailout by the Japanese in 1983 facilitated recovery from the doldrums that struck immediately after Park's death, but Korea was forced to open its markets as a price for Japanese and other foreign assistance. Brutal repression of an uprising in the less prosperous southern city of Kwangju by Korean troops with close ties to the American military radicalized students and workers, many of whom believed the United States was complicit in the death of thousands of demonstrators. The vicissitudes of the 1980s allowed many Koreans to look back to the days of Park Chung Hee with nostalgia.

It became increasingly apparent in the 1980s and 1990s that Korean prosperity had been built in part on the backs of its underpaid workers and that it was threatened by their growing demands for job security and a fair wage. But most of all, it was the corrupt relationship that developed between the ruling military elite and the *chaebol* that boded ill for the future. Middle-class anger, American pressure, and the example of People's Power overthrowing dictatorship in the Philippines in 1986, led the military to accept political reform and elections in the late 1980s, but Korea seemed unlikely to move beyond a *chaebol*-friendly one-party democracy on the Japanese model. The nation was unquestionably an important force in the world economic system, but its core problems, economic and political remained—as did the security threat across the 38th parallel.

Taiwan was arguably the greatest beneficiary of the Korean War—and especially of Chinese intervention in that war. The movement of mainland Chinese to Taiwan after World War II had begun disastrously. Guomindang troops, greeted as liberators, plundered the island, dismantling and shipping back to the mainland much of the Japanese-installed equipment they found there. In February 1947 they slaughtered thousands of islanders who rose in protest against Guomindang oppression. Taiwan's economy had been integrated with Japan's for nearly fifty years, but the Japanese market for its goods evaporated in 1945. In 1949, with the communist conquest of mainland China, markets there were lost as well.

In 1950, the communists were preparing to invade Taiwan and complete their victory by mopping up the remnants of the Guomindang army. The Americans had decided to seek accommodation with Peking and to stand aside when the invasion occurred. But Mao's troops were not ready for so ambitious an amphibious operation in 1950 and hoped to attack in 1951. Once war broke out in Korea, however, the United States reintervened in the Chinese civil war, eliminating the possibility that the People's Liberation Army could cross the Taiwan Strait. Again, in the Strait crises of later years, American naval forces dominated the waters of the region. And in 1955, Jiang's government succeeded in obtaining a mutual defense agreement from the United States.

Taiwan's economy benefited similarly. The Truman administration had been determined to cut off all aid to Taiwan, convinced that it would be a poor use of limited American resources to support a corrupt and defeated regime. After Chinese troops entered the war in Korea, economic and military assistance to Taiwan was resumed. American industrial goods, factories, and equipment flowed to the island in the 1950s and early 1960s, producing an enormous percentage of its gross national product. The United States facilitated land reform and working through the Joint Sino-American Commission on Rural Reconstruction (JCRR) stimulated agricultural production. Taiwan's political leaders and government technocrats received training in American universities. Many Chinese scientists and engineers trained in the United States during World War II went to Taiwan in the 1950s and played important roles in its economic development, as did several of those who stayed in America and enriched that society. And once it seemed clear that Taiwan had become an American protectorate, Japanese and American companies seeking low-priced goods arrived to buy what Taiwan could produce.

By the late 1950s, the economy had stabilized, but it was evident that the domestic market had been saturated and that stagnation threatened. Jiang's technocrats, aware of Japan's export strategy, concluded that export promotion was the answer to Taiwan's needs. They required foreign exchange with which to purchase new machinery and the most advanced technology. Like the Japanese, they concentrated their efforts on achieving rapid economic growth, adjusting the island's productive structure in relation to the opportunities they saw in the international economy. Step by step they were able to shift the focus of planning from Jiang's dream of recovering the mainland to creating a solid economic base for a *de facto* independent Taiwan. Between 1959 and 1965, when American economic assistance began to be phased out, Taiwan's foreign trade increased at the phenomenal rate of 22 percent a year—admittedly from a very low base.

In the mid-1960s, partly in response to American pressures, Taiwan moved increasingly away from state-owned enterprises to private enterprise and allowed direct foreign investment. Multinational corporations seeking cheap labor flocked to the island, producing goods there for export. Taiwan created the world's first export processing zone in the southern city of Kaohsiung in 1966. An enormous flow of private foreign investment followed with funds coming from the United States, overseas Chinese everywhere, Japan, and western Europe. From 1965 to 1973, Taiwan's trade increased at a rate of 33 percent per year, financing very rapid industrial expansion. To ease Jiang's anxieties, more broadly felt after the American rapprochement with China in 1971–72, the heavy industry needed for defense was built, specifically steel and chemicals. Taiwan also invested wisely in the electronics industry, both for defense and for export goods.

The 1970s required some painful readjustments, but Taiwan's leaders proved equal to the task. First came the shock of Chinese-American rapprochement and the fear of abandonment and isolation that accompanied it. Then came the oil embargo and huge increase in oil prices in 1973. Taiwan could not escape the worldwide recession and its rate of growth slowed precipitously. Soon afterward, several major U.S. corporations, forced by Peking to choose between doing business on the mainland or on Taiwan, chose the larger potential of continental China. And finally came trade tensions with the United States beginning in 1977. A trade war with the Americans was inconceivable, both for political reasons and because the United States provided a market for 40 percent of Taiwan's exports.

Shrewdly, Taiwan invited some of the world's leading multinationals to operate on the island under favorable conditions, giving other countries and influential companies a stake in its future. Its lobbyists in Washington, second only to the Israelis in sophistication and accomplishment, protected Taiwan's interests, working primarily through the American legislature. It sent purchasing missions all over the United States to advertise its willingness to "buy American." And to cut production costs, its industries began to move to Southeast Asia to take advantage of cheaper labor costs. By 1979 tiny Taiwan was the twenty-first largest trading country in the world and it soon was second only to Japan in the amassing of foreign reserves.

There were more blows in the years that followed. The United States recognized the Peking regime as the government of China and abrogated its mutual defense pact with Taiwan. Taiwan was expelled from the United Nations and eventually from several other international organizations important to its commercial operations. There were more oil crises from which the economy of no oil importing country could escape adverse effects. But generally Taiwan continued to thrive, the result of excellent leadership, skillful lobbying and diplomacy, and a buoyant world economy to which it was an important contributor. One important indication of its promise was the return of thousands of students who had studied in the United States, remained there to work, and conjured up fears of a brain drain in the 1950s and 1960s. By the 1980s, they found ample scope for their skills on Taiwan. And with prosperity, political conditions improved as the Guomindang confounded its critics by moving toward democracy.

A third "little dragon," Hong Kong, has never been a country in any sense. Arguably, it might be perceived as a city-state, such as Singapore became, but the reality is that since the Opium War it has been merely a tiny British colony, at its largest hardly bigger than New York City. At various times it has served, however, as a regional center, an entrepot for the trade of south China and for the world's trade with China. More recently it has played a similar role for neighboring parts of Southeast Asia.

Hong Kong, which had fallen quickly to the Japanese in the opening weeks of the Pacific War, was liberated by the British in August 1945. Throughout the war the Americans had pressed the British to return the territory to China, but were soon grateful for this vestige of the old imperial order. After Mao's forces swept across mainland China, the Americans put comparable pressure on Great Britain to defend its Hong Kong colony. In the two years preceding Chinese intervention in the Korean War, Hong Kong prospered as the essential conduit for trade between China and the noncommunist world. It also gained, as had Japan, from

U.S. procurement needs during the war. But China's intervention provoked first an American and then a UN embargo on the sale of "strategic" goods to China. When Hong Kong complied, Peking responded by reducing its purchases of nonrestricted products. Hong Kong was caught in the middle and the resulting drop in trade was nearly catastrophic for its economy.

Hong Kong was saved primarily by refugees from the Chinese civil war, especially the Shanghai industrialists who fled from the communists and were able to divert to Hong Kong both the capital they had sent abroad and the equipment they had purchased abroad. Other refugees provided a huge supply of cheap labor that enabled the city to be competitive internationally, especially with textile exports. The colony's extraordinary civil service had no need for a Japanese model. Those concerned with trade and finance needed no one to tell them their local market was too small for economies of scale; that they had to export to survive and that they could only be competitive in a small number of sectors. Early planning facilitated industrialization and Hong Kong progressed rapidly in the 1950s. By 1962, 70 percent of its exports were manufactured goods of local origin—for which the United States proved to be the leading buyer. The Hong Kong government was never as intrusive as that of Japan or Korea or Taiwan, but it was dedicated to maintaining a social order and political conditions that would serve the needs of its entrepreneurial class—and it performed superbly. Labor fared less well and housing conditions for workers remained appalling for decades to come.

Hong Kong ran into problems with protectionist pressures in the United States in the early 1960s and was forced to reduce its exports to that country, but there was ample compensation. American consumers continued to buy enormous quantities of the city's products and the United States supplanted Britain as its most important trading partner. American corporations were second to none in their appreciation of cheap skilled labor and began moving production facilities to Hong Kong. As the war heated up in Vietnam, Hong Kong businessmen profited significantly from procurement contracts and the city's tourist industry boomed both from recreational visits by U.S. servicemen and women and a great influx of American civilians in search of shopping bargains as well as exotica.

Despite problems with a torrent of refugees (the "boat people," from Vietnam), despite the worldwide recession of 1974, Hong Kong had another burst of rapid growth between 1969 and 1982. Manufacturing moved slowly from textiles to high technology electronic appliances, but gradually declined in importance. In the course of the 1970s, the service sector, providing financial services such as banking, insurance, and investment management for the region became increasingly central. By 1980 it was contributing more to the local economy than was manufacturing. Foreign, especially western companies with interests in China, found the business services they required in Hong Kong. Per capita income in the city was also rising and it was apparent that it would soon be higher than in Great Britain. Moreover, in the 1980s, Hong Kong investment in Great Britain exceeded British investment in Hong Kong.

The 1980s brought new and serious problems. Hong Kong exporters were again threatened by protectionism in the United States as Americans sought scapegoats for their unfavorable balance of trade and mounting budget deficits. Another oil crisis and another worldwide recession hurt. But worst of all were the questions about the colony's political future. The British lease on the New Territories, an area essential to the viability of the island of Hong Kong and adjacent Kowloon, was to expire in 1997. China was likely to reclaim its lost land. Doubt that the British would succeed in protecting the colony's capitalist system contributed to a fall in the value of the Hong Kong dollar in 1983.

Once again, the city bounced back. Hong Kong entrepreneurs moved production across the border into an increasingly receptive China, utilizing that country's abundant supply of low paid workers. The opening of China to foreign trade and investment brought new opportunities for the service sector, better able to function in China than any potential competitors. Once again, Hong Kong became the critical entrepot between China and the rest of the world. Anxiety about reunification with China remained high, but the city was prosperous and playing an enormously important role in the international economic system.

The fourth of the "little dragons," Singapore, had a history comparable in some ways to Hong Kong. The British took it over early in the nineteenth century at the insistence of the famed colonial administrator Sir Stamford Raffles. Like Hong Kong, perhaps more like Melaka which it superseded, it became an important entrepot, serving Malaya and Indonesia in particular, transshipping their goods to South Asia, the Middle East, and Europe, and goods from those regions to Southeast Asia. Its population included Malays from both the peninsula and the archipelago, Indians who followed the British, and, increasingly, Chinese from a wide range of southern Chinese origins, part of the great Chinese diaspora of the early Qing era. There was also the usual scattering of Arab and Jewish merchants and expatriate Europeans.

The British built a major base at Singapore, an anchor for the empire in Southeast Asia. Early in 1942, the Japanese raced down the Malay peninsula and, with relative ease, overran defenses designed to protect against an attack from the sea. There were few complaints, not even from the Americans, when the British returned in 1945. But the British-educated Singaporean elite, politically Left, resumed its demand for independence. In the context of the emerging Cold War and the communist insurgency in Malaya, composed largely of ethnic Chinese, the British feared communist subversion in the city in the late 1940s and early 1950s. In 1959, however, Great Britain, eager to reduce its commitments in the region, granted Singapore self-rule in its internal affairs, while reserving control over foreign affairs.

Singapore's population was by this time overwhelmingly (75%) Chinese. Lee Kuan Yew, a British-educated ethnic Chinese, emerged as the city's dominant political figure. As he split with the left wing of his party, seizing the political center, he was able to win London's confidence and negotiate an arrangement that would grant Singapore complete independence in 1963 as a member of a larger Malaysian Federation. Not without cause, the Chinese Left opposed the arrangement, fearful of being dominated by more conservative Malays. Lee eliminated the opposition and Singapore became part of Malaysia.

Lee's plan was to develop Singapore's economy by expanding domestic industry and selling to the larger market provided by membership in the federation. His intent was to overcome dependence on the transshipment of international trade and the limitations of the tiny local market of his city. But Lee underestimated Malay antipathy toward the Chinese and Malay fear that he would become the dominant political leader in the whole federation, and that his city would upset the rural-urban balance. In 1965 Singapore was expelled from the federation. Bereft of most of their anticipated domestic market, Lee and his planners had to change course. The difficulty of their assignment increased significantly when the British decided in 1968 to abandon their naval base in Singapore, employer of 20 percent of the city's work force.

Singapore's leaders were equal to the task. They realized they had little recourse but to undertake an export-oriented development strategy—and they knew they had come to the international market relatively late. Japan, Hong Kong, and Taiwan were already provoking protectionist outcries in the United States and Europe. Without the influx of Shanghai industrialists who had been the catalyst for Hong Kong's industrial development, Singapore was also handicapped by a lack of both entrepreneurial skills and capital. It would require considerable foreign assistance, particularly foreign investment. Lee and his colleagues planned with extraordinary care, controlling the choice of sectors in which to concentrate their efforts—electronics, shipbuilding and repair, petroleum processing, and telecommunications—and attracting overseas capital. Their disciplined, virtually incorruptible, authoritarian government provided the perfect environment for foreign investors: political stability and a docile, low-wage labor force.

From 1965 until the world recession of the early 1980s, Singapore's economy grew by at least 10 percent annually. The developmental state transformed the country into a manufacturing and service industry giant. Foreign firms flocked to the city, producing their goods there for reexport to the rest of the world—and particularly the United States. Domestic industry all but atrophied. By 1975 foreign companies absorbed more than 75 percent of total industrial input and produced nearly as large a percentage of total output. By the late 1970s they were producing 70 percent of the manufactured goods exported by Singapore and that percentage was still going up. One scholar has noted that foreign capital "dominates the economy of Singapore more than that of any other Third World nation"—although few would dare to call Lee Kuan Yew's domain "Third World."[4]

Whereas Hong Kong is often praised for its "laissez-faire" political economy, receiving the highest grades for its free market capitalism, Singapore has succeeded in avoiding obstacles to foreign investment in a much more controlled society. The people of Hong Kong, natives or sojourners, have enjoyed greater personal liberty and freedom of expression than the residents of Singapore, but Singapore has been far more successful in providing social services, especially adequate housing. Both cities did what they could over the years to keep wages down by undermining labor movements and utilizing immigrants to avoid labor shortages and upward pressure on salaries. Ultimately, neither succeeded, as companies moved their factories from Hong Kong to China and from

Singapore to Malaysia, Thailand, and Indonesia in pursuit of lower labor costs. Singapore adjusted to these losses and American trade restrictions by expanding its construction industry and its service sector. In particular, it succeeded in exploiting its superb telecommunications to persuade multinational corporations to set up regional headquarters. Singapore became increasingly attractive as the moment for reversion of Hong Kong to Chinese rule approached.

By the 1970s, the four "little dragons" had all become important parts of the international economic system. South Korea and Taiwan were major industrial centers and Hong Kong and Singapore moved gradually from dependence on exports to the provision of financial and communication services. All were subject to disruptions far from home, such as the world recession of the 1980s, currency fluctuations, and protectionist pressures in markets vital to them, such as the United States. All were subject to competition from newly industrializing states, both in East Asia and elsewhere in the world. But all had prospered, raised the standard of living of their people remarkably, and were now themselves providing markets and investment opportunities for the advanced industrial states of Europe, Japan, and the United States. Moreover, the capitalists of Taiwan and Hong Kong were providing substantial funding for the development of China and parts of Southeast Asia. There were more "dragons" in the making.

Southeast Asia

The Korean War had stimulated many of the economies of East Asia and much of Southeast Asia benefited from the regional boom. The recovery of Western Europe and the consumerism of the West generally also contributed to economic growth over much of the area in the 1950s—as did American efforts to redirect Japan's interest in China toward the resources and markets of Southeast Asia. From 1965 to 1973, the United States poured billions of dollars into Vietnam and Thailand in particular, but neighboring states also picked up some of the procurement contracts and some of the money spent by the Saigon regime and by American servicemen and civilians who passed through.

Burma, determined to develop in isolation from the world economy, ridding itself of European, Chinese, and Indian entrepreneurs, was least affected by these events. Its economy stagnated throughout the years after it won its independence and it fared no better when it changed its name to Myanmar. The Philippines suffered the misfortune of falling under the dictatorial and corrupt rule of Ferdinand Marcos. Hundreds of millions of dollars that might have been spent on economic development ended up in his various foreign accounts. Recovery from his depredations came slowly and began only after he was overthrown by a popular rebellion, "People Power," in 1986, facilitated by the belated withdrawal of American support for his rule.

North Vietnam, and after its unification of the country in 1975, all of Vietnam, suffered not only from the devastation of nearly thirty years of warfare, but also from ideological obstacles to any effective strategy for development. After the communist takeover of 1975, Laos suffered the same fate. Cambodia, of course, suffered more horribly than any other state in the region, its people the victims of Pol Pot's genocidal policies.

Three Southeast Asian states, Indonesia, Malaysia, and Thailand, exploited opportunities in the late 1960s, 1970s, and 1980s to develop their economies and accelerate economic growth. Indonesia and, to a lesser extent, Malaysia benefited from the sharp rise in oil prices in the 1970s. All three succeeded in attracting large-scale foreign aid or investment. All three attracted multinational corporations seeking lower labor costs as wages rose in Hong Kong, Korea, Singapore, and Taiwan. And all three struggled with the fact that their domestic commercial life was dominated by ethnic Chinese.

In 1967, leery of developments in Indochina, Indonesia, Malaysia, the Philippines, Singapore, and Thailand met to form the Association of South East Asian Nations (ASEAN). The expectation was that they would arrive at a plan for regional economic and security policies. The central conceit was that they would cooperate against the threat of communism, but they could not reach agreement about Indochina—or whether Vietnam or China posed the greater threat to their security. Little was accomplished over the next decade and each member pursued its interests independently.

Indonesia's economic development was hampered by a lack of domestic capital, difficulty disengaging from the structure put in place by the Dutch, and policies that alienated potential foreign investors. Without capital, plans for industrialization failed and manufacturing actually declined between 1953 and 1958. Until 1958, more than two thirds of the plantations in Java and Sumatra were still Dutch-owned—and most of the rest belonged to ethnic Chinese. In the late 1950s, the government decided to expropriate foreign-owned property and attempt state-directed development comparable to that of Japan. Indonesian leaders understood that expropriation would preclude foreign investment, but nationalist passions prevailed and they were confident that they could finance their program through commodity sales, especially of oil and rubber. Unfortunately, commodity prices fell and funds available for development were not adequate. Indonesia's economy was in serious trouble when the Sukarno government collapsed in the mid-1960s.

When foreign ownership declined, it was the Chinese-Indonesians who were most likely to enhance their holdings. These ethnic Chinese may have thought of themselves as Indonesians after the long struggle against the Dutch, but to their less well-off Javanese and Sumatran neighbors, they remained a source of envy and suspicion and, too frequently, they became targets of communal violence. In the chaos of 1965, tens of thousands of them were among those massacred—simply because of their Chinese ancestry.

After Suharto came to power in 1966, Indonesia charted a very different course. His quest for stability required ending Sukarno's confrontation with Malaysia and muting his hostility toward the West, especially the United States. He turned the economy over to a group of young U.S. trained technocrats who immediately began to integrate the country into the world economy. To attract foreign investment they returned expropriated foreign assets and invited multinational corporations to operate in Indonesia. They appealed to the United States, Europe, and Japan for financial aid and were enormously successful. An Inter-Governmental Group on Indonesia was formed and it supplied Suharto's aides with a steady and generous flow of assistance. Japan and the West were weary of the mercurial Sukarno and eager to have a friendly Indonesia. Suharto seemed an answer to their dreams.

Suharto's power came to rest on the military, foreign investment, and a handful of Chinese-Indonesian businessmen. Economic growth was the glue that bound them. To keep the officer class reliable, large sums of money were necessary. Senior officers became "sleeping partners" in the operations of foreign companies skimming a large but generally tolerable share of the profits.[5] The Chinese businessmen were encouraged to build large conglomerates with Suharto, or members of his family, or senior officers as partners. All involved became very rich and were, of course, very loyal to each other.

And the nation prospered. Between 1967 and 1975 the manufacturing sector grew rapidly, quickly meeting domestic consumer demands and, in the 1970s, beginning to export. The increase in oil prices in the mid-1970s was a great boon to the economy, which grew at an average annual rate of 8 percent. Urban prosperity was striking and the emerging middle class had every reason to be supportive of the Suharto regime.

On the other hand, there were some problems evident. There were complaints that the economy was controlled by Japan and the United States. Indeed, between 1967 and 1985, more than half of investment in the oil industry was American and nearly two-thirds in manufacturing was Japanese. It was obvious that the multinational corporations were depleting Indonesia's natural resources, not only oil but mineral wealth and timber as well. Enhanced revenues from the rise in oil prices enabled the government to counter those concerns by closing off some sectors to foreign investment and resuming state-led development. But oil prices declined eventually, requiring an increase in overseas borrowing in the 1980s. Indebtedness, corruption, and the maldistribution of wealth began to cast a shadow on Suharto's rule.

For all the problems that manifested themselves in the 1980s, the Indonesian economy had soared since the end of Sukarno's "Guided Democracy." The country was very much a part of the world economy. Not only was it increasingly vulnerable to fluctuations in distant commodity and capital markets, but also some foreign investors and lenders were increasingly dependent on Indonesia's continued development. But these were dangers common to all in the era of "globalization."

Neighboring Malaysia had a more difficult time finding an identity and creating a nation. In the second half of the twentieth century, Malays were probably never more than a bare majority in the territory the British had cobbled together. In the brief period when Singapore was included in the federation, they were a minority. A coalition of Malay, Chinese, and Indian parties persuaded the British, eager to be rid of their colonies in the region, that they could live together in peace—and protect existing British investments on the Malay peninsula, The British granted independence in 1957, and plans for a federation with British Borneo and Singapore came to fruition in 1963, with only Brunei opting out. But the prospect of Chinese domination, depriving Malays of a land of their own, soon led to the expulsion of Singapore.

Before independence, the country's economy was dependent on the export of rubber and tin. Immediately afterward, Malaya's leaders began the process of diversification and industrialization, supported by the usual developing nation practice of import substitution. Manufacturing increased, as did timber exports, and, most strikingly, by 1966, Malaysia was the world's largest producer of palm oil. By 1968 it was ready to commence an aggressive export program.

As elsewhere in the region, the ethnic Chinese community profited most from the growth of the Malaysian economy, a point that was not lost on most Malays. When, in 1969, Chinese political parties gained strength in the elections, the spectre of Chinese political dominance loomed again, provoking communal rioting, especially in the capital city of Kuala Lumpur. Malay politicians recognized the need for action and devised a series of plans designed to undermine Chinese dominance of the domestic economy. One of these, put forward in 1971, was the New Economic Plan, which included the establishment of free trade zones. The planners hoped to shift equity from local Chinese and foreign to Malay hands, but instead increased the Chinese share as foreigners were squeezed out.

Nonetheless the New Economic Plan, export driven, stimulated growth in the 1970s and the country prospered. Then, like much of the rest of the world, Malaysia was hurt by the world recession of the early 1980s, spared possible collapse by surging palm oil sales. At this point, the leadership promoted a "Look East" policy, touting "Asian values" of hard work and high rates of savings, while pointing to Japanese and Korean models of development. It called for a program of heavy industrialization that met with minimal success. The country suffered another recession in the mid-1980s and its leaders recognized the need to attract more foreign investment. At this they succeeded and in the late 1980s, the economy grew at a rate of nearly ten percent, stimulated by investments primarily from Taiwan and Japan, but also from the United States and Korea. In most instances these investments came from electronics and textile concerns moving in search of cheaper labor. Apparently much of the Taiwan money was actually Malaysian Chinese money moved overseas and back to take advantage of the incentives to foreign capital. In 1989, the real income of ethnic Chinese in Malaya was estimated at 65 percent higher than that of Malays.

In the late 1980s Malaysia was becoming urbanized. Although most of its income still came from commodity sales, the industrial sector was growing, reaching nearly 25% of gross domestic product. It was certainly more prosperous than most of its neighbors, but it was not without its problems. Petroleum products had replaced rubber as the main source of revenue—and petroleum prices were declining. Markets for its goods were expanding, especially in southern Africa, but its focus on electronics and textiles exports, produced largely by multinationals, left it vulnerable to the vagaries of the international marketplace. The companies that came to Malaysia for cheap labor yesterday could easily move somewhere else tomorrow. And the country's external debt was notably large. Nonetheless, Malaysia, too, was clearly a part of the world economic system and of great importance in its region—not least as a source of employment for surplus Indonesian labor.

Finally, there was Thailand, a poor country that transformed its economy between 1950 and 1990, but with the most impressive gains coming only in the last four years of the period. The country was handicapped by political instability, largely the result of frequent military coups. The development bureaucracy, however, managed to function despite the political situation. As in Indonesia and Malaysia, ethnic Chinese dominated domestic commerce, especially the financial sector. Unlike those two countries, there was little ethnic tension in Thailand.

It was not until 1961 that the first of seven development plans was implemented. Following the advice of the World Bank, the Thai government concentrated its meager resources on creating an infrastructure to stimulate growth in the private sector. From a very low base, gross domestic product grew at an average annual rate of better than eight percent from 1961 to 1966, falling to about seven and a half percent from 1966–1971. But it was America's war in Vietnam rather than Thai planning that accounted for this accomplishment. The United States spent hundreds of millions of dollars in Thailand and Thailand hosted 40,000 American troops. As American spending fell off, so too did Thailand's rate of growth.

While the Americans were there, the population of Bangkok nearly doubled to meet the their needs. Rail service and roads improved for military movements, especially to bases in the north, helped farmers market their products. There was a marked increase in the export of agricultural commodities, especially rice, a major source of export revenues. The American contribution to the Thai economy enabled the government in Bangkok to buy political acceptance with economic and social improvements.

Unlike Indonesia and Malaysia, Thailand lacked oil to sell and was hurt by the crisis of 1973 and the rise in petroleum prices that followed. In 1977 the government borrowed abroad for the first time. A poorly regulated stock market crashed in 1979 and then came the world recession of the early 1980s. At this point government became more active in economic affairs and agencies created for industrial planning met with remarkable success. Administration of the stock market improved and in 1985 the manufacturing share of gross domestic product overtook that of agriculture. The value of manufactured exports soared and there was a dramatic increase in domestic and foreign investment in Thai industry.

According to the agricultural economist Peter Warr, the Thai economy was the fastest growing in the world between 1986 and 1990.[6] The export boom appears to have had two basic sources: the depreciation of the Thai currency, which was pegged to a depreciating U.S. dollar, and the influx of capital from Japan and the four little dragons. The industrialists of Japan, Hong Kong, Korea, Singapore, and Taiwan were relocating their factories wherever labor was cheap and docile—to South China, Indonesia, Malaysia, and Thailand as opposed to the Philippines, where the overthrow of Marcos presaged labor unrest. And American investors were not far behind.

As the last decade of the twentieth century approached, Indonesia, Malaysia, and Thailand could be described as newly industrialized nations. Together with Japan and the four little dragons, they produced a major share of the world's wealth and played an enormously important role in international trade. What happened in these countries would have an effect on the world's economy—and what happened elsewhere in the world might well contribute to the rise—or fall—of their individual economies.

China Joins the World Market Economy

Potentially the greatest impact on the world economy was the decision of China's leaders, in the late 1970s, to abandon self-reliance and to seek the rapid modernization of their industry through increased contact with the outside world. China had not been an important member of the world trading community since the Great Depression and many of its communist leaders opposed contact with the West, fearing dependence on outside, ideologically hostile forces. On the eve of Mao's death, as the Cultural Revolution petered out, there was a great struggle within the Party leadership between those still committed to isolating China from foreign influence and those who believed that China's progress required greater openness and reintegration in the international system. Those who argued that China could be strengthened by importing foreign technology and expertise without sacrificing its political principles prevailed, but the tension persisted for more than a decade after Mao and Zhou Enlai were gone.

The leading advocate of opening China to the world was Deng Xiaoping, one of the party leaders who had been purged early in the Cultural Revolution. Restored to a position of power by Zhou in 1973, he survived a second purge and then elbowed aside Mao's chosen successor, Hua Guofeng. Before the close of 1978, Deng emerged as China's paramount leader.

Deng and his allies moved quickly to reform the political economy that Mao and the Cultural Revolution had left in a shambles. They were supported by party leaders less receptive to integration in the world economy, less comfortable abandoning the Soviet-style planned economy, but equally as convinced that Mao's utopian visions had brought the country to ruin. This second group frequently forced Deng to move more cautiously, more slowly than he might have wished—and sometimes necessitated a step backward before reform could proceed again. But all China's leaders appear to have agreed that some reform, some opening to the rest of the world was essential to the goal of a strong and prosperous China. All were committed to the "Four Modernizations"—of agriculture, industry, science and technology, and defense.

Their first obvious success came in agricultural reform. Appalled to realize how poorly peasants lived, how many of them lived in abject poverty, Deng and his colleagues gradually moved away from collectivized farming toward a family-based system. Peasants regained control over what they grew, were paid more by the state for their assigned quotas, and were allowed to lease land from the collectives. They were permitted to sell surplus produce in legal free markets, keeping the profits. This restoration of some incentives of the family farm led to extraordinary growth in agricultural production and to a striking improvement in the peasant standard of living. Equally significant was increased peasant demand for consumer goods, providing a market for increased industrial output.

Although the results manifested themselves more slowly, the leadership's decisions to accept foreign loans, foreign aid, and foreign direct investment were no less important. They allowed a private enterprise sector to emerge and compete with state-owned operations. Billions of dollars poured into the country, more than could be readily absorbed. American, European, and Japanese businessmen were eager to explore China's vast market and to invest in industries that would benefit from the country's enormous supply of low-wage, nonunionized labor. Technology that China might have required another generation to develop on its own was immediately available. Deng expected no less, having noted the gains other East Asian states had achieved when they entered the world economy.

Deng also moved quickly to cement rapprochement with the United States, a process that had slowed in the mid-1970s. He and the American negotiators put aside continuing differences over Taiwan and established formal diplomatic relations early in 1979, opening the floodgates for investment in China—and providing China with an important friend as it attacked the Soviet Union's Vietnamese ally at about the same time. China's Vietnam adventure, provoked by Vietnam's invasion of Cambodia, demonstrated the need for modernizing the PLA. China had great difficulty moving supplies and troops to the combat zone and suffered heavy casualties. After a few weeks. Chinese troops withdrew, having accomplished little. But the Soviets did not intervene and Deng may have assumed that he deterred them by playing his American card.

Although the usefulness of the Americans for tilting the balance of power in China's favor may be questioned, there is no doubt that the contribution of the United States to China's modernization was enormously important. Over the next decade, American universities trained thousands of Chinese scientists, competing with American businessmen in the transference of technology to a country so recently their nation's enemy. As China's export industry grew, the United States became its principal market, absorbing as much as a third of the manufactured goods the Chinese shipped abroad. Although political tensions, related primarily to the unresolved differences over Taiwan, recurred in the 1980s, the cultural and economic links between the two countries multiplied.

China's economic growth and the speed with which it became a major trading country and an important participant in international capital markets was extraordinary. Its 9 percent rate of growth in gross national product for the years 1978–1993 was the fastest of any country in the world (not excepting Thailand whose GNP grew faster for the late 1980s). Despite continued low per capita income, the gross national product of China's billion people overtook that of Germany, placing China third in the world behind the United States and Japan. Many analysts predicted it would have the world's largest economy by the middle of the twenty-first century. Its international two-way trade soared from less than $15 billion in 1977 to more than 115 billion in 1990 and nearly $200 billion by 1993. China joined the World Bank, the International Monetary Fund, and the Asian Development Bank to become eligible for low-interest loans and economic and technical advisers. In the late 1980s it became the largest recipient of United Nations Development Programme funding. Its exports were three times that of India's and it was obtaining a hundred times as much foreign direct investment. And its people were eating far better than they had in Mao's day.

There were problems to be sure. Corruption was rampant. Income inequality was striking, worse than in most developing countries, especially between the urban and rural populations. Some reform policies threatened the social safety net as market considerations became paramount. China's exports were encountering protectionist complaints in the developed world. Although the Americans complained that the Chinese sold more than they bought, adding significantly to the deficit in the U.S. balance of trade, China was in fact importing more than it was exporting, running a deficit world-wide despite its advantage in bilateral trade with the United States. Some of these problems stirred discontent within the Communist Party leadership and elsewhere in the country. Time and again they were forced to slow down or step backward, but Deng and his allies pushed on toward a vaguely defined "socialist market economy."

The Japan That Can Say No

The Japanese economy recovered from the recession of 1975 and Japan's trade surplus continued to mount rapidly. It might have used that surplus to improve the quality of life in Japan, but both government and corporate leaders seemed obsessed with gaining market share, with exporting more and more. It might have acceded to American demands that Japan increase its defense spending, but it preferred not to. Inevitably, its relations with its trading partners, the United States especially, but Western European and other East Asian states as well, were strained. In much of the rest of the world the suspicion grew that Japan was using unfair business practices, such as "dumping," the selling of goods abroad at a price below that charged at home, to increase its exports. And Japan's low level of imports led to allegations of unreasonable barriers to the entry of foreign goods.

When exports surged again in the early 1980s, Japanese leaders realized they were in danger of provoking a series of trade wars, that protectionist pressures were rising in the United States and Europe. Although there was virtually no internal demand for increasing imports or reducing exports, Tokyo responded to external pressures and began to take steps to open its markets to the goods of its trading partners. The Japanese could not afford to risk being shut out of foreign markets, certainly not the essential American market where it sold nearly a third of its exports. The results, however, were not dramatic, and their partners remained unsatisfied.

To circumvent barriers to their goods, Japanese corporations followed a practice at which the Americans had excelled when they dominated world markets in the 1920s. They became multinational corporations, building segments of their industrial empires abroad, especially in the United States. If American automobile workers demanded protection of their jobs against automobiles manufactured in Japan, Honda, Mazda, and Toyota would build plants in the United States, employing Americans. Restrictions on the imports of Japanese cars would not apply to those manufactured in the United States. Japanese multinationals soon became an important part of the internal economy.

Shrewd, aggressive, efficient business practices, supported by a producer-friendly government, brought Japan more capital than could be utilized wisely in Japan. As American domestic economic policies, the "Reagonomics" of the 1980s, transformed the United States from being the world's leading creditor nation to becoming the leading debtor nation, Tokyo became the world's most important capital exporter. Between 1981 and 1985, the Japanese government and Japanese private investors bought billions of dollars worth of U.S. Treasury notes, approximately 35 percent of those sold to cover the nation's budget deficit. By the mid-1980s Japan held 20 percent of the total debt of the U.S. government. With money left over the Japanese bought major American icons such as New York's famed Rockefeller Center, CBS Records, and Hollywood motion picture studios. American financial dependence on Japan could not have been more evident—and the Americans did not like it.

The U.S. government blamed Japan and Germany for its problems and demanded that they stimulate their economies to generate more domestic consumption, presumably leading to fewer exports and more imports. Fearing inflation, convinced that America's financial troubles were self-inflicted, both countries refused. In 1985 steps were taken to cope with an apparently overvalued U.S. dollar, but the currency realignment that followed proved insufficient. Americans bought fewer costly Japanese goods and Japanese imports increased, but American exports did not increase enough to redress the balance. American leaders remained convinced that Japan was competing unfairly and continued to demand that the Japanese import more American goods.

Japanese leaders grew increasingly irritated by American demands and increasingly contemptuous of a superpower that was not managing its decline with grace. Before the end of the decade, analysts in much of the developed world, including the United States, had concluded that American industry had ceased to be competitive, that Japan had become and would remain the dominant power in the international economy. Japan had supplanted the United States as the leading contributor of foreign aid in the world and its capital outflow was providing jobs for Europeans as well as Americans. It was in 1989 that a minor Japanese political figure created a sensation with a book entitled *The Japan That Can Say No*, arguing for an end to concessions to the United States, an end to dependence on the United States, and blaming American racism for Washington's criticism of Japanese business practices.

But the Americans were not alone in their dissatisfaction with the relatively low level of Japanese imports. Other Asians, Europeans, and Latin Americans encountered the same difficulties in their efforts to export to Japan. And American goods that could not penetrate the Japanese market were successful in other developed countries. However grudgingly, Tokyo was forced to promise internal changes to pacify its trading partners. In 1990, the Japanese and American governments negotiated an agreement on "structural impediments," constituting the first serious attempt to modify its domestic business practices that served as barriers to imports. Progress was slow and inconsequential, at least partly because of serious problems that developed in Japan's domestic economy.

Japan's enormous cash reserves in the 1980s led to widespread speculation in real estate and stocks. Prices rose astronomically. In 1989 the Bank of Japan concluded that it was essential to raise interest rates. The speculative "bubble" burst and very quickly, the assumption that Japan would remain the dominant force in the world's economy came into question. Before long Japan's financial stability was in question as stock and real estate prices declined sharply, growth slowed, banks were unable to collect on loans, and unemployment rose. Japan was in serious trouble. However different capitalism in Japan may have been from capitalism elsewhere in the world, it was not immune from the business cycle. Japanese corporate managers may have been the best in the world, but they were not infallible. Hubris, long associated with the United States, had blinded the Japanese to the dangers of their compulsive exporting.

Japan's troubles in the 1990s were severe, but they did not diminish the extraordinary accomplishments of the Japanese in the four decades since they had regained their independence. Japan still managed the second largest economy in the world and its people enjoyed a standard of living comparable to that of Americans or West Europeans. Its wealth and importance internationally had not vanished, as evidenced by Japan's contribution, however reluctant, of $11 billion to underwrite some American expenses in the Gulf War of 1991, a war the United States could not afford on its own. With Germany and the United States, it remained one of the three engines that drove the global economy. The sources of its wealth—its skilled and highly motivated work force and superb corporate management—were still available, ready to achieve new heights when the next turn of the business cycle occurred. What was not clear was how long it would take for a weak government to take the steps necessary to clear away the debris and permit Japan to rise again.

Conclusion

As the world entered the last decade of the twentieth century, the economies of East Asia had regained an importance lost centuries before, when the West industrialized and they did not. Militarily, China alone seemed likely to emerge as a great power in the foreseeable future—although Japan certainly had the necessary wealth and industrial base. But in an era when some analysts[7] argued that economic prowess would prevail over brute force, that the age of the trading state was upon us, Japan, the four little dragons, Indonesia, Malaysia, Thailand, and China all seemed assured of being major players. Their share of the world's exports had more than doubled since 1960. The rate of increase was likely to decline in the 1990s, but some of the region's countries were just getting started. Before the twenty-first century was over, East Asia was poised to regain its place as the locus of the world's economic power. Only Japan's troubles hinted of other possibilities.

On the Eve of the Twenty-first Century

The men and women who lived through the last years of the twentieth century witnessed one of the major events in the history of the world, the collapse and disintegration of the Soviet Union. They were also witnesses to one of the great triumphs of the human will, the election of Nelson Mandela as president of South Africa, marking an end to the apartheid regime that had shamed that nation. Only one event in East Asia was of comparable iconic import—the Tiananmen massacre, the brutal suppression of the democracy movement in China.

For the peoples of East Asia, there were other events of unusual, even extraordinary significance. South Korea and Taiwan both emerged as stable democracies. A war between an impoverished but nuclear North Korea and the United States was narrowly averted. Attempting to intimidate Taiwan, China provoked a confrontation with the United States. The people of Hong Kong, many profoundly troubled by the events at Tiananmen, watched as the PLA marched into their city and China resumed sovereignty over it. And before the century ended, the economic miracles of East Asia began to unravel as currencies tumbled, banks failed, stock and real estate values fell, and unemployment rose. The stability of some of the region's regimes seemed less certain as the legitimacy that came with prosperity was undermined. The most striking change came in Indonesia, where Suharto was driven from office after dominating his country for more than thirty years. Of gravest concern was the possibility of East Asia's economic troubles resulting in a worldwide depression. The price of globalization could prove to be very high for all concerned.

Disaster at Tiananmen

In the 1980s, the reformers to whom Deng Xiaoping had turned over the day-to-day operations of the Chinese government were enormously successful. Great progress was made in agriculture and industry. The standard of living of the Chinese people rose. China's stature in the world grew commensurably and its representatives performed ably and responsibly in a host of international settings. Foreign businessmen flocked to China and scores of thousands of Chinese traveled abroad to learn what they could from the developed world. Relations with Japan and the West were occasionally difficult, but Deng had great cause for satisfaction with his handiwork. Even the American president, Ronald Reagan, a longtime supporter of the Taiwan regime and passionate enemy of communism, traveled to Peking and applauded what he was shown.

Western approval of China's reforms provided little comfort for more conservative Communist Party members who were appalled at the deviations from the teachings of Marx, Lenin, and Mao. Many party cadres and their families stood to lose power and opportunity as expertise was given precedence over ideological fervor or class, as control over universities and factories began to slip out of cadre hands and back to the academic and managerial classes from which the revolution had stripped them. On several occasions, the reformers stumbled and their opponents succeeded in launching campaigns against "bourgeois liberalism" and "spiritual pollution"—euphemisms for the Western values many Chinese found seductive. But Deng and his aides pushed on.

Although Chinese society in the 1980s was unquestionably more open, the hand of the state applied more lightly than in the 1960s and 1970s, Deng was not interested in what one young Chinese called the "fifth modernization"—*political* modernization and eventual democracy. None of Deng's policies were intended to weaken the Communist Party's grip on the government. He had no more affection for political pluralism, multiparty elections, and the other trappings of Western democracy than had Mao or Josef Stalin. As the Chinese people became better informed about the outside world, however, many among them, especially intellectuals, wanted more than better food and clothing. They wanted freedom from the arbitrary exercise of governmental power—freedom to criticize incompetent and corrupt officials, freedom to express their own views, perhaps even to choose their own leaders.

Chinese leaders and educated Chinese across the country were aware that "People Power" had overthrown the dictatorship of Ferdinand Marcos in the Philippines in 1986. In the late 1980s they were conscious of Mikhail Gorbachev's effort to reform the Soviet Union with *glasnost* and *perestroika*. Some Chinese leaders were sympathetic to the idea of greater intellectual freedom for their people, convinced that it would accelerate the modernization of the country and provide a safety valve against political explosion. Others feared the emergence of dangerous ideas, were appalled by Gorbachev's reforms, and feared that the level of criticism already tolerated posed a threat to the Communist Party and the beliefs for which it stood. In 1987, the conservatives persuaded Deng to remove his heir apparent, Hu Yaobang, from his post as the party's secretary general, allegedly because of his support for students demanding political reform.

Hu's departure may have slowed but it did not end the intellectual ferment in the country. On university campuses preparations went forward for massive demonstrations to be held on May 4, 1989, the seventieth anniversary of the outbreak of the historic student-led May Fourth Movement. Moreover, Gorbachev, the symbol of a liberalizing Soviet Union, was coming to China in May to signal the success of his efforts to end the Sino-Soviet conflict. Suddenly, in April 1989, Hu Yaobang died. His death triggered demonstrations and, in a few days, Tiananmen Square, Peking's huge central square, was filled with tens of thousands of Chinese protesting corruption and calling for democracy.

The Chinese government responded with remarkable restraint. For weeks it allowed the growing numbers of demonstrators to control the square, through Hu's funeral and even during Gorbachev's visit. Hundreds of journalists and photographers from all over the world, who had come to Peking to cover Gorbachev's meetings with Chinese leaders, sent back stories and film footage of the extraordinary activities of the students and the workers, teachers, journalists, policemen, soldiers, and party cadres who supported their demands. As in 1919, Chinese students abroad demonstrated on college campuses and in front of Chinese embassies.

But Deng was growing impatient. The unruly students were reminders of the noxious Red Guards of the Cultural Revolution, who had inflicted misery on him and his family as well as disrupting China's economic development. He wanted the square cleared, the democracy movement crushed, and its leaders bloodied. He wanted no one to doubt the determination and ability of the Communist Party to retain control of the country. When the party general secretary resisted the call to use force against the demonstrators, Deng pushed him aside. In late May, troops were sent toward the square, but the citizens of Peking blocked their movements and begged them not to attack the students. A group of retired military leaders circulated a letter urging the government to refrain from using the PLA against the people. Deng was not swayed and student demands that he retire proved counterproductive.

On June 4, 1989, a day that the Chinese people will never forget, Chinese troops, supported by tanks, massacred hundreds, perhaps thousands of demonstrators, mostly young students, in Tiananmen Square and vicinity. Savage attacks on student protesters were carried out in other cities, such as Chengdu, capital of Sichuan province, as well. In the days that followed, security forces began rounding up student leaders and their supporters, and the most prominent of those caught received long prison sentences.

The brutal suppression of these Chinese, many of them members of the Communist Party, shattered the dreams of those who imagined they could move China toward democracy through nonviolent means. Television viewers worldwide had seen footage of the demonstrations and now of its violent suppression. The actions of the Chinese government were quickly condemned by the United States and most European countries. Japan and the Soviet Union were also critical. There were massive protest demonstrations in Hong Kong. The United States suspended the sale of weapons to China, canceled scheduled high-level visits, and blocked loans to the Chinese government from the international financial organizations it dominated. Other nations took comparable steps. Suddenly, China was again a pariah state, its treatment of its own people earning it the contempt of free peoples everywhere.

Deng was undeterred. China's foreign relations had suffered a severe setback. New foreign investment and foreign loans declined sharply. His modernization program was in jeopardy, threatened by the loss of intellectual capital as well when many students sent abroad now refused to return. But he and his closest comrades were convinced that their highest priority was to maintain order in the society. All victims of the Cultural Revolution, they were determined to prevent renewed chaos from threatening them or the Party's grasp on power. A wealthy and powerful state in the wrong hands was of no interest to them, but they were also persuaded that without the discipline they were determined to enforce, China could not go forward.

China's economic growth faltered slightly, but as the months passed, one nation after another rescinded sanctions against China and resumed efforts to profit from Deng's continuing economic reform program. Before the end of 1990, the United States was the only major industrial state that still maintained economic sanctions, and even the Americans had backed off, ending their opposition to World Bank loans to China. Deng's choices had been vindicated. China was too big, too powerful, too promising a market for goods and capital, to be isolated. The growth of its economy resumed at an exceptionally high rate, its people grew more prosperous, and many of them, too, seemed prepared to accept the contract the state offered: forget politics and enjoy the good life.

In the early 1990s, the principal remaining irritant to the Chinese leadership came in its relations with the United States. If the Americans chose to withhold technology from the Chinese, China could get much of what it wanted elsewhere—from France, Israel, Japan, or Russia. But if the Americans denied China "most-favored-nation" trading status (MFN)—placed higher than normal tariffs on Chinese exports—then the impact on China's development might be severe. No other country or combination of countries in the world would provide a market equivalent to what would be lost. Many Americans and their representatives in the Congress, memories of scenes at Tiananmen etched in their memories, wanted to punish China—and denial of MFN treatment to Chinese goods became their weapon of choice. In the 1992 presidential campaign, Bill Clinton, the challenger, criticized the incumbent president's policy toward China and promised to be much tougher if elected. Tying the granting of MFN treatment to China's progress in human rights—the release of prisoners of conscience, especially those arrested after Tiananmen—was one prominent idea voiced by American critics of China.

Clinton was elected president by the American people, primarily because of domestic economic problems his predecessor had presumably neglected. He and his principal advisers on policy toward China threatened to intensify sanctions, but the Chinese were unyielding. They offered no concessions on issues they considered their internal affairs. American corporations eager to sell aircraft and other high-technology goods to China, fearful of being closed out of the market in China in retaliation for U.S. sanctions, joined China specialists convinced of China's continuing strategic importance and the value of good relations to persuade the president to back down. Again, Deng outmaneuvered the Americans.

With internal dissent stifled and the economy on track, Deng and the party leaders looked to 1997 for the recovery of Hong Kong from Great

Britain. They would regain Macao from the Portuguese in 1999. Increasingly their thoughts turned to Taiwan and the reunification of which they—and Jiang Jieshi—had long dreamt. But Jiang was dead and his son and his son's successor were succumbing to a new and very different vision of the future.

Democracy Comes to Taiwan

Taiwan, in the 1950s and 1960s, was a protectorate of the United States. Without American military assistance and the presence of the U.S. Seventh Fleet, Taiwan very likely would have been assaulted by and conquered by the PLA. As protectors are wont to do, the Americans attempted from time to time to push their client in directions dictated by the interests of Washington. In general, Jiang Jieshi was quite successful in resisting these pressures. In the 1960s, he received a little outside help when the American candidate to succeed him died of cancer, thwarting Washington's hope of keeping Jiang's son, Jingguo, from replacing his father and maintaining the Jiang dynasty.

Jiang Jingguo, by virtue of his parentage alone, but also by his actions, was presumed to be hostile to the liberal democracy Americans hoped to see evolve in all their client states. He was known to be loyal to his father's visions of a one-party state and the reconquest of the mainland. He was perceived to be ruthless and intolerant of dissent. But the United States could not prevent him from becoming the dominant figure in Taiwan as age forced his father to loosen his grip.

Of course, Jiang Jingguo surprised most American officials in the 1970s and 1980s—and he surprised many residents of Taiwan as well. He became premier in 1972, after Taiwan had lost its seat in the United Nations to the Peking government and when it was clear that the United States was planning to recognize the People's Republic and abrogate its mutual defense treaty with the Guomindang regime on Taiwan. One after another, nations that had recognized Taibei as the capital of China moved their embassies to Peking. The legitimacy of Guomindang rule, opposed by the indigenous majority on Taiwan, and recognized by fewer and fewer countries, had all but evaporated. It was Jiang Jingguo's task to reestablish it and he was equal to the assignment.

The younger Jiang's support for the technocrats who had provided the intellectual drive behind Taiwan's economic success was expected, but nonetheless gratifying to local entrepreneurs and foreign investors. His attack on corruption, even when men close to his father were involved, was more worthy of note. And then he released some political prisoners, critics of the Guomindang. Close observers were also struck by the fact that he was replacing old mainland Chinese with Taiwanese, gradually moving toward a Guomindang Party and a government that were predominantly Taiwanese. When he became president in 1978, he had a Taiwanese politician, Lee Teng-hui, named as vice president. It was readily apparent that the political and intellectual ambiance on the island was changing, that there was more scope for criticism of the Guomindang, even the possibility of political pluralism.

As with the reforms in the People's Republic, there were some striking setbacks in the years that followed. In 1979, an anti-Guomindang rally in a southern city ended in violence and the leaders were tried, convicted, and sent to prison by the government. But the opposition persevered, won heavily in local elections, and in 1986 announced formation of the Democratic Progressive Party (DPP). Jiang resisted demands from Guomindang conservatives that the new political movement be crushed and the DPP, although illegal, continued to function, winning more than 20 percent of the vote in the elections of 1986. In 1987, Jiang had martial law lifted and allowed political and social organizations to proliferate. Taiwan was moving toward democracy.

When Jiang died in January 1988, Taiwan suddenly had a native-born president. Efforts by mainland Chinese on the Guomindang Central Committee to push Lee aside failed. Later that year he consolidated his hold on both party and government. Under his leadership, Taiwan's economic development continued and progress toward democracy accelerated. Opposition political parties were legalized and the DPP increased its support to 35 percent in multiparty elections in December 1989. Although it was illegal to do so, several DPP candidates ran on platforms advocating independence for Taiwan. The events at Tiananmen earlier that year further eroded already diminished interest in reunification with the mainland.

The issue of Taiwan's relationship to the mainland had been extremely sensitive ever since the Guomindang defeat in the Chinese civil war. Jiang Jieshi was committed to reconquering the mainland and initially viewed Taiwan as nothing more than a temporary base of operations. He and his comrades from the mainland justified their rule on the grounds that they constituted the national government of China, of which Taiwan was merely one province. Although it soon became evident that the Guomindang government in Taibei was but a rump regime that would not likely rule China again, it was essential to maintain the fiction of Jiang as the *national* leader to allow the minority mainlanders to continue to dominate the indigenous Taiwanese. Advocacy of an independent Taiwan, presumably to be ruled by Taiwanese, was prohibited on the island and the nascent independence movement persecuted ruthlessly.

Similarly, Jiang, no less than his antagonists in Peking, resisted the concept of two Chinas or one China, one Taiwan, that became popular in the United States in the late 1950s—and reflected reality. When American and Chinese Communist leaders achieved their rapprochement in the 1972 Shanghai Communiqué, the Americans finessed the issue by acknowledging that Chinese on both sides of the Taiwan Strait insisted there was only one China. The Americans had no objection to reunification, provided it was achieved peacefully. On the other hand, when a president of the United States finally recognized the Peking government in 1979, severing diplomatic relations with Taiwan, the American Congress passed a Taiwan Relations Act to indicate its determination to assure Taiwan the arms it needed to defend itself and treatment equivalent to that of a nation. It warned the People's Republic that it would view the use of force against Taiwan as a matter of "grave concern."

Deng Xiaoping was displeased by the American Congress's support for Taiwan, and increasingly troubled by pro-Taiwan sentiments expressed by Ronald Reagan, victor in the American presidential election campaign of 1980. In 1981 Deng reached out to Taiwan, calling for economic and cultural exchanges and talks on reunification. He later elaborated with his conception of "one country, two systems,' a vague plan for reunification under which Taiwan would enjoy considerable autonomy. Taibei rejected the overture: there would be no contact, no negotiation, no compromise with the communists.

The reality was quite different. In the 1980s, unofficial trade between Taiwan and the mainland, filtered through Hong Kong, boomed and was condoned by Jiang Jingguo. In 1987, Jiang's rigid stance vanished as he authorized visits to the mainland, ostensibly for family reunions. Within months, hundreds of thousands of mainland-born residents of Taiwan traveled to the People's Republic. Over the next six years more than six million people crossed the strait. Business ties exploded, and phone and mail service provided new links between the two societies. Before long, a cross-strait dialogue began between the two governments. The horrors of the Tiananmen massacre interrupted these contacts only briefly.

But Tiananmen and the relatively poor conditions the visitors from Taiwan found on the mainland cooled what remaining ardor there was on the island for reunification. The People's Republic consistently threatened to attack if Taiwan declared independence—and that was a risk few were willing to take. There was some renewed agitation for independence, especially among supporters of the DPP, but polls showed that most people were content with de facto independence. Nonetheless, there was a growing demand for Taiwan to be more assertive internationally, to reclaim its role in international organizations, and to have its economic power and emergent democracy given the recognition they had earned. And in a democratic political system, politicians are usually driven by their constituents.

Lee Teng-hui had been remarkably successful in rising to the top of the Guomindang in its pre-democratic guise. In the early 1990s, he was being pushed by public opinion to move more rapidly toward de facto independence than Guomindang mainlanders found agreeable—and perhaps faster than he desired to move himself. But he was determined to be the first democratically elected president of Taiwan. To hold the votes of young Taiwanese eager to have their country play a larger role in world affairs—and to deflate pressure for a declaration of independence— Lee lobbied successfully for an opportunity to visit the United States in June 1995, ostensibly returning as a distinguished alumnus to speak at the university from which he had received his doctorate. American policy had precluded visits by senior officials from Taiwan, but Congressional pressure forced the administration to issue the necessary visa. Lee used the occasion well to promote himself and to publicize Taiwan's successes and aspirations. He accomplished his purpose, but the Peking government exploded with rage, creating a new and serious crisis in the Taiwan Strait.

In the course of the next year, as Lee campaigned for the presidency, the Chinese military conducted a series of increasingly threatening military maneuvers in the strait. Demonstrating its power, the PLA fired missiles into the strait and over Taiwan, bracketing the island and leaving no doubt of its capabilities. Taiwan's trade was disrupted and its economy shaken. As the tension mounted, fears grew in Washington that if

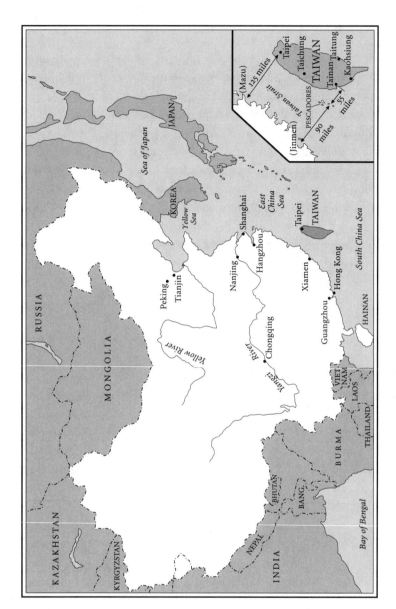

MAP 27. TAIWAN, TAIWAN STRAIT.
After Cohen, *America's Response*, p. 182.

the United States did nothing, Peking might be emboldened to attack Taiwan. In March 1996, two U.S. carrier groups were ordered to the area, a demonstration of American concern and resolve. Lee won his election and the crisis passed, but the Chinese government remained intensely suspicious of Lee's intentions. It also perceived the American role as evidence of a renewed effort by the United States to "contain" China, to deny China its place as the rising power in East Asia.

In July 1999, while Chinese-American relations were strained by the accidental bombing of the Chinese embassy in Belgrade by aircraft engaged in NATO's effort to stop ethnic cleansing in Kosovo, Lee stirred the pot again. This time he announced that henceforth Taiwan would insist that relations with the People's Republic be conducted on a "special state-to-state basis." Chinese leaders perceived another step in the direction of independence and their concerns were intensified by the "clarifications" of Lee's remarks issued by his aides. From China came renewed threats to use force against Taiwan and rumors of military preparations. Desperately eager to prevent violence in the strait, the American government assured Peking of its continued commitment to a one China policy and attempted to persuade Lee to soften his remarks. As the century came to a close, it was evident that the Taiwan issue had lost none of its volatility.

The Korean Peninsula: Democracy and Nuclear Weapons

1987 proved to be an extraordinary year in Korean history. The general who seized power and had himself declared president in 1980 announced that he would step aside at the end of his seven-year term of office. His designated successor, former general and military academy classmate Roh Tae Woo, averted civil strife and astonished the world by accepting the opposition's demand for a direct election of the next president. Given the widespread public hostility toward his party, Roh was undertaking a daring gamble. Fortunately for him, the opposition majority split between two candidates, Kim Young Sam and Kim Dae Jung, neither of whom would stand aside for the other, allowing Roh to win with only 36 percent of the votes cast. Korea was beginning another experiment with electoral democracy.

As president, Roh initiated a remarkable diplomatic offensive, reaching out to most of the world's communist states, including North Korea. Discussions with Pyongyang were difficult, but some potentially important agreements were reached. The results of Seoul's efforts with Eastern European states, the Soviet Union, and finally China, were stunning. Trade relations, especially with China, grew quickly. South Korea had industrialized rapidly and had much to offer countries in the process of moving from command to market economies. Advisers to the Soviet leadership even offered the Korean model as an approach to economic reform. Diplomatic relations were more troublesome for both Moscow and Peking, given their alliances with North Korea. By 1990, after their empire began to disintegrate, the Soviets' need for cash and development assistance was so great that they were willing to abandon Kim Il Sung as the price for South Korean aid. The Chinese were driven less by economic considerations than by the opportunity to undermine Taiwan's status in the world by getting Seoul to move its embassy from Taibei to Peking. They recognized Roh's government in 1992. In 1991, both North and South Korea were admitted to the United Nations, a step long resisted by the North, but to which it agreed when it became apparent that neither the Soviets nor the Chinese would veto the admission of the South.

The increased isolation of Kim Il Sung's regime, its loss of Soviet support, and concerns about potential limits on further Chinese assistance probably contributed to its willingness to enter into a dialogue with the South in 1990. Its efforts to reach out to Japan and the United States that year proved fruitless. Muting its hostility toward Seoul was not easy for a regime that had twice in the 1980s resorted to major acts of terrorism against its antagonist across the 38th parallel. In 1983, in Burma, the North Koreans had attempted to assassinate the visiting South Korean president, killing four cabinet ministers and several other senior officials. In 1987, North Korean agents planted a bomb that destroyed a South Korean airliner over Southeast Asia, killing all 115 persons on board. But in the mid-1980s, Pyongyang had also entered into both public and secret talks with Seoul, although a summit meeting between heads of state, proposed by the South, did not materialize.

The North-South meetings in the early 1990s resulted in two promising agreements. In 1991 the two governments issued a Joint Declaration on the Denuclearization of the Korean Peninsula. Under pressure from the United States, Seoul had earlier halted its effort to develop nuclear weapons. Kim Il Sung's flirtation with such weapons had long troubled leaders in the South, as well as the Americans. It was difficult for the Americans to deny the logic of Kim's argument that the United States had nuclear weapons in Korea with which it attempted to intimidate his country. But in 1991, with the collapse of the Soviet Union, and confident that it could provide a nuclear umbrella for the South without storing weapons in Korea, the United States removed the last of these from the peninsula. The North Koreans then accepted the Joint Declaration and agreed to verification through outside inspection of its suspected nuclear reprocessing plant at Yongbyon.

The second, the "Basic Agreement," was designed to attempt some level of reconciliation between North and South and ultimately included a nonaggression protocol. The two Korean entities set up liaison offices and committees to facilitate exchanges and to implement political and military cooperation. Pyongyang and Seoul agreed to respect each other's political system. It was a promising moment, but it lasted only a few months.

What little momentum had been gained toward a North-South rapprochement was lost as a result of widespread fear that the North was developing nuclear weapons. In 1985, as a Soviet condition for supplying nuclear power reactors, the North Koreans had signed the Nuclear Nonproliferation Treaty (NPT), requiring them to permit inspections by the International Atomic Energy Agency (IAEA). By 1992, satellite intelligence led American officials to conclude that Pyongyang was close to having nuclear weapons capability. IAEA inspectors were denied access to suspicious sites and they found North Korean answers to their questions inconsistent with their observations. The UN Security Council, without opposition from Russia or China, warned that it might take punitive action if inspection requests were ignored. In March 1993, the world was shocked by Pyongyang's announcement of its intent to withdraw from the NPT, presumably because it was determined to produce nuclear weapons. A new crisis was looming on the Korean peninsula.

The nuclear issue was complicated by South Korean and American provocations of the North. Joint Korean and American military exercises, obviously designed to prepare for war with the North, had been dropped in 1992 to contribute to the easing of tensions. In October 1992, the American and South Korean defense ministers announced the exercises would be resumed in 1993. At the same time, the domestic politics of South Korea, a presidential election campaign, undermined efforts toward rapprochement. Former opposition leader Kim Young Sam had become the ruling party's candidate and he feared that improved relations with the North would lead to the election of his rival, Kim Dae Jung. Others in Seoul's national security bureaucracy were determined to slow the pace of rapid progress in North-South relations. Together, Kim Young Sam's campaign and the national security bureaucrats generated a new "red scare," designed to discredit Kim Dae Jung, a staunch supporter of reconciliation, and to retard North-South cooperation.[1]

Pyongyang's nuclear weapons program forced the world to pay attention. North Korea was a desperately poor country, of no account in the international economic system. Its gross national product was probably one-sixteenth that of the south. The Cold War was over and few cared that it remained a Stalinist dictatorship, albeit with Korean characteristics. But the possibility that it had nuclear weapons and might sell these to various Middle Eastern states, like Iraq, to which it had previously sold missiles, sounded an alarm in many world capitals, not least in Washington. When the North Koreans approached the Americans in May, 1993 the Americans did not dare rebuff them.

Talks between Pyongyang and Washington in the spring of 1993 averted North Korean withdrawal from the NPT. It was evident that the North Koreans were practicing a form of nuclear blackmail, seeking to obtain diplomatic recognition, security assurances, and economic assistance in return for dropping their weapons program. The Americans were determined to concede as little as possible, but readily acknowledged that negotiations were preferable to war. A North Korean proposal that the United States provide it with a different kind of nuclear reactor, a light-water reactor from which weapons-grade material was not easily produced, suggested to the Americans that Pyongyang was looking for a way out of the impasse. These reactors were expensive, however, and the Americans were unwilling to commit themselves to support anything more than the concept. In addition, they insisted that the North resume its discussions with the South and with the IAEA.

Although direct talks between the United States and North Korea had relieved tensions in mid-1993, the danger remained. Before the year was out, it was apparent that war was on the horizon. Seoul was angered by the contacts between Pyongyang and Washington and feared accommodation between its bitter enemy and its most important ally. American acquiescence in South Korean demands, particularly Seoul's insistence on the exchange of North-South special envoys prior to the next meeting between U.S. and North Korean officials, infuriated Pyongyang, increasing the difficulty of negotiation. But the most serious problems emerged between the North Koreans and IAEA. IAEA inspection demands were not met and the UN General Assembly urged Pyongyang's immediate cooperation. Pressure mounted on the American government to apply sanctions against North Korea.

In 1994 the United States began lobbying in the UN for sanctions against Pyongyang and the North Koreans warned that they would consider sanctions a declaration of war. In May, the North began procedures at Yongbyon that were designed to produce plutonium for nuclear weapons. The Americans began to strengthen their military posture in the area and readied themselves for war: they would not permit North Korea to go further in the development of a nuclear arsenal. Diplomacy would give way to force.

At this point, Jimmy Carter, a former American president who had devoted his post-presidential years to conflict resolution, stepped forward. Disregarding protests from Seoul and the national security apparatus in Washington, he decided to go to Pyongyang to meet with Kim Il Sung. Prominent American leaders were demanding a military strike against Yongbyon, but Carter's mission met with success. He persuaded the North Korean ruler to allow IAEA inspectors to remain at Yongbyon and to freeze his country's nuclear program until after the next round of talks with the United States. In return he promised to recommend U.S. support for Pyongyang's request for light-water reactors. American officials insisted on an increased level of inspection and the North Koreans accepted. Carter had contributed enormously to the avoidance of a military confrontation that likely would have cost millions of lives. And, before he left, Kim Il Sung accepted his proposal for a summit meeting with the South Korean president, Kim Young Sam.

Carter and Kim Il Sung had defused the crisis and Kim's apparent willingness to negotiate on all fronts provided a moment of great promise. And then, a few weeks later, suddenly, Kim Il Sung was dead of a heart attack. Fortunately, the negotiations with the Americans over North Korea's nuclear program went forward and an "Agreed Framework" was signed in October. Pyongyang was promised two light-water reactors, a lifting of some of the economic sanctions the United States had imposed on it, and agreed to move toward "normalization" of relations. Until the reactors were functional, the Korean Peninsula Energy Development Organization (KEDO) formed by the United States, Japan, and South Korea, promised to supply fuel oil. In return, the Americans and the rest of the world were promised that North Korea would proceed no further with its nuclear program.

On the other hand, Kim Il Sung's death and the refusal of the South Korean president to send condolences to Pyongyang eliminated the possibility of a summit meeting between the leaders of the two Korean states. The leadership in Seoul was convinced that the North was on the verge of collapse. It was unwilling to seek accommodation. North and South, hostile propaganda machines resumed their attacks across the 38th parallel.

Over the next several years, as outsiders wondered if Kim Il Sung had succeeded in passing power on to his son, it became increasingly evident that North Korea was in desperate economic straits. Food shortages were obvious and soon the government had to admit the danger of famine. Only large shipments from China, on a barter basis, and humanitarian aid from abroad through a United Nations appeal prevented widespread starvation. But there was no relief in sight as the millennium approached. The miseries of the people of the North intensified, some of the elite defected, some peasants fled across to China and Russia, but there was no sign of an imminent collapse of the regime. And it retained its most powerful weapon: the threat of resuming its nuclear program if its needs were not met.

The last years of the 1990s were not good for the South either. In 1995, the most appalling evidence of the corruption that linked the political leaders, the *chaebol*, and the country's banking system was exposed. It was discovered that former president Roh Tae Woo and his predecessor had taken the equivalent of nearly three *billion* U.S. dollars in bribes, largely from *chaebol* heads, much of it hidden in other people's bank accounts, some of it in boxes in a warehouse. Both men were then tried, found guilty, and imprisoned for their corruption and for their roles in the military coup of 1979 and the Kwangju massacre of civilians in 1980.

The larger society was hit harder by the decline in economic growth that was apparent in 1997. Several *chaebol* collapsed, the Korean currency lost nearly half its value against the U.S. dollar and the stock market plunged. Once wealthy South Korea was suddenly dependent on the International Monetary Fund (IMF)—on outside assistance—to halt the decline. Although the economy improved in 1999, there was little chance of a full recovery before the end of the century. Viewing their plight, few South Koreans still hoped for the rapid collapse of North Korea. Having witnessed the cost to West Germany of absorbing East Germany when its communist government fell, most people in the South realized they could ill afford the burden of reviving the destitute North.

There remained two glimmers of hope for the South in particular, but with possible redemptive power for the North as well. Kim Dae Jung, the opposition leader most feared by Korean elites, long victimized by the Korean military and security apparatus, narrowly won the presidential election in December 1997. His election in the midst of economic crisis was most important as a symbol of his nation's dedication to democracy, to which he himself was profoundly committed. Also significant was his reputation as the South Korean leader most eager for reconciliation with the North. In addition to Kim Dae Jung's election, December 1997 was also the occasion for the first session of four-party talks involving representatives of China and the United States as well as those of North and South Korea. These meetings were aimed at moving from the armistice that ended the Korean War to a formal peace treaty and they had the potential to resolve some of the issues dividing North and South. Little progress was made in 1997 or 1998, but at least until 1999 the Chinese were working well with the Americans to keep the Koreans at the table. Although Pyongyang continued to be unpredictable and capable of seemingly self-defeating actions, such as ordering spying missions into the South, firing missiles in the direction of Japan, and constructing facilities that brought them close to violation of the Agreed Framework, Kim Dae Jung and the Americans refrained from ratcheting up the tension. The 38th parallel remained the most volatile border in East Asia, the odds were not great, but a negotiated peace was a little more imaginable than it had been for some long time.

Red Star Over Hong Kong

In the course of World War II, Great Britain had ceased to be a great power and it gradually divested itself of colonies it could no longer control or defend. The British knew that they lacked the strength to contest rising Chinese power in East Asia. They knew that China could seize the British colony of Hong Kong almost at will. Britain's lease over the New Territories, constituting more than 90 percent of the colony, was scheduled to expire in 1997 and Peking left no doubt that it intended to reclaim its land. By the late 1970s it was apparent to the authorities in London that Hong Kong island and Kowloon, the areas known best to foreign tourists, could not be maintained alone. In 1979 they initiated talks with Deng Xiaoping about Hong Kong's future. Active negotiations followed in 1982.

Some British officials, convinced that Peking did not understand the importance of rule of law to the colony's political and economic success, fantasized about retaining administrative control over Hong Kong even after Chinese sovereignty was restored. The Chinese, fearful that the British would find a way to run off with Hong Kong's wealth, quickly disabused them of that notion and left no doubt that they were the ones who were negotiating from strength. But both sides thought it important to keep Hong Kong stable and prosperous and in 1984 they reached agreement, setting forth a Sino-British Joint Declaration that came to have the force of a treaty.

The critical point of the Joint Declaration was the Chinese promise to allow Hong Kong to retain its existing political and economic institutions for fifty years. Hong Kong would become part of China on July 1, 1997, but as a Special Administrative Region (SAR). China and Hong Kong would be "one country, [with] two systems." Responsibility for the defense of the SAR and its foreign relations would pass to Peking. Responsibility for preparing the Basic Law or constitution under which Hong Kong would be governed would also reside with China.

In Hong Kong, the United States, and at home, the British government was criticized for yielding to Chinese pressures to halt the modest democratization of the city's political system that had it had begun only too recently. The people of Hong Kong were more highly educated, skilled, and prosperous—better prepared for self-rule than most other colonial peoples set free by European imperialists—and they were being handed over to a communist dictatorship. Any sense of guilt British leaders might have felt and the apprehensions of the people of Hong Kong and their friends abroad were greatly magnified by the Tiananmen massacre of 1989. Peking left no doubt that Chinese rule could be brutally repressive and the demand for rapid democratization as insurance against the arbitrary exercise of Chinese power accelerated, strongly supported by the United States, which had developed an enormous economic stake in the city.

In response to the massive anti-Chinese protests triggered in Hong Kong by the events at Tiananmen, Peking strengthened the clause against subversion in the Basic Law. It was an unmistakable warning to the protesters, a clear threat to the liberties they had enjoyed under British rule. In 1991, when the British allowed direct election to eighteen (of sixty) seats in the city's Legislative Council, the people of Hong Kong replied by voting in fifteen men and women openly critical of Peking. They rejected every candidate supported by China. They were not intimidated.

From China's perspective, matters worsened after the arrival of the new British-appointed colonial governor, Christopher Patten, in 1992. Patten and a newly aggressive Legislative Council, without consulting Peking, pushed through a series of reforms that broadened voting rights, giving pro-democracy forces a chance to gain a majority in the Council, and reduced the political influence of the wealthy Hong Kong businessmen who had long dominated the city. The businessmen were troubled and Chinese leaders were outraged: Marx would not have been amused by their alliance. Peking perceived an anticommunist plot, a violation of the Joint Declaration, and put all concerned on notice that they would dismantle the existing representative institutions when they took control of the city in 1997.

Patten nonetheless persisted in his plans to strengthen self-rule for the people of Hong Kong. The Hong Kong government made major—and largely successful—efforts to keep American businessmen and the American government involved in the city by awarding a series of major contracts to American firms. Tensions grew between Patten and Peking and were exacerbated in 1995 by elections to the Legislative Council in which pro-Chinese candidates again fared poorly and supporters of democracy gained additional seats. The Chinese government refused to deal with the Council, arguing that it had been elected under rules inconsistent with the Basic Law. Instead, it created its own Provisional Legislative Council, dominated by men and women sympathetic to Peking. In December 1996, China's leaders arranged to have a wealthy and respected Hong Kong businessman, whose loyalty to them seemed assured, appointed as chief executive, the man who would succeed Patten in July 1997.

Despite the surface tensions, it was clear that China wanted the transition to Chinese rule to go smoothly. A peaceful resumption of Chinese sovereignty and continued stability and prosperity in Hong Kong might even further the cause of reunification with Taiwan. Heavy-handedness would doom that prospect for at least another generation. In 1996 and 1997, Peking became far less truculent and while it never embraced Patten, it did resume cooperation with the British government. When July 1, 1997 arrived, the British bowed out gracefully and China resumed sovereignty over the city without incident, a performance that brought credit to all concerned.

In the year that followed, the Peking government demonstrated a sophistication and restraint in Hong Kong that surprised many of its critics. The Hong Kong government was allowed to exercise an extraordinary degree of autonomy. Protests against both Chinese and Hong Kong governments were permitted. The press, despite some initial self-censorship, remained free. The international business community, which had been poised to flee, functioned unfettered as before. American warships continued to make port calls, interrupted only when new tensions arose in Chinese-American relations in 1999. In May, a new election to the Legislative Council was permitted and pro-democracy forces performed extraordinarily well, winning most of the seats up for direct election. Peking did not interfere.

As the century moved toward its end, political problems seemed the least of those confronting the people of Hong Kong. On the contrary, it was the economy, its greatest strength, that was at risk, largely a result of circumstances external to the city. The collapse of one East Asian economy after another could not fail to have an impact on that of Hong Kong. The government had to intervene to prop up the Hong Kong dollar and then, in a move unprecedented by a city proud of having the world's freest market, the government intervened to bolster sliding stock prices. As the financial crisis of East Asia spread to the rest of the world, conditions promised to get worse before any recovery could be anticipated.

Crisis in Southeast Asia

At the beginning of the last decade of the twentieth century, much of Southeast Asia was prospering and there was renewed hope for several of the countries that were not. ASEAN, having amounted to little in the early years of its existence, had come to life and gave the region an illusion of unity. Through ASEAN and the broader Asia-Pacific Economic Cooperation forum created in 1989, the influence in global affairs of the rapidly developing states of Southeast Asia had grown markedly. The threat of being marginalized by the end of the Cold War did not materialize.

ASEAN had been created in 1967 in the hope of promoting regional peace and stability, initially by integrating Indonesia. It remained largely inactive until the mid-1970s, when the Vietnamese, fresh from their victory over the United States, seemed to pose a threat to their neighbors—a danger given weight in late 1978 when they invaded Cambodia. In the 1980s, the Vietnamese occupation of Cambodia provided the glue that held ASEAN together, gave it a cause for which ASEAN diplomats worked assiduously in the United Nations and with various competing forces in Cambodia. The settlement reached in October 1991 that ended the Vietnamese occupation and offered hope that the ordeal of the Cambodian people might end was a result of ASEAN diplomacy. In the 1990s, ASEAN took greater initiative in regional affairs—and it expanded. Vietnam was admitted in 1995. Burma, having renamed itself Myanmar, gained admission in 1997, despite distaste for its brutal dictatorship. Fear that a Burma excluded from the organization would become a stalking horse for Chinese penetration of Southeast Asia overcame all other concerns. Laos, too, joined in 1997, leaving only Cambodia, riven by internal strife, beyond the pale.

In the 1990s, apprehension over China's growing military power and its aggressive action in the South China Sea permeated ASEAN. The organization was never intended as an alliance or collective security arrangement. Its principal focus had been on economic modernization. It was a security community only in the sense that its members were pledged not to interfere in each other's internal affairs or to use force to settle the many territorial and other disputes among them. But after China used force in 1992 to back its claim to the Paracel islands, the ASEAN states grew increasingly fearful. At a meeting in Manila that year they agreed unanimously that although their combined navies and air forces were superior to those of the PLA, in the long run only the United States had the power to balance China—or to constrain Japan. But the Americans no longer dominated East Asia as they had in the early years of the Cold War. The United States was still the major actor in the region, but its power had declined relative to that of Japan and China—and there were doubts as to the will of the Americans to play the role in which ASEAN had cast them. Indeed they had surrendered their extensive system of bases in the Philippines in 1992 rather than meet the demands of Filipino nationalists.

The obvious solution to the security dilemma in which the ASEAN states found themselves was to engage China in multilateral discussions of the political and security issues that concerned them. In 1993 they created the ASEAN Regional Forum (ARF) bringing together all of the states with interests in the area, including Australia, Canada, the European Community, Japan, South Korea, and Russia, as well as the United States and China. ARF was intended to be the principal arena for the discussion of security issues of the Western Pacific and East Asia. Its meetings have all been held in ASEAN states and it has been these states rather than the great powers that have controlled the agenda. In addition to this official level, security discussions were also instituted among nongovernmental organizations, ostensibly independent research institutes in the ARF member states whose scholars can freely study and debate issues presumably too sensitive for their leaders. At the nongovernmental level, China was even willing to permit its researchers to work with those from Taiwan.

Although all of these ASEAN-led arrangements have made progress with confidence-building measures among the participants, they have yet to eliminate concerns about China's intentions. In 1995, the PLA seized control of Mischief Reef, a tiny, largely submerged island in the Spratlys claimed by the Philippines. Peking's claim to sovereignty over all of the Paracels and all of the Spratlys worries those Southeast Asian states with expectations of developing offshore energy resources in the South China Sea. China has become more willing to discuss the issues involved, less belligerent when its claims are challenged, but it has yielded nothing— and its power relative to that of the ASEAN states is almost certain to grow. Little help can be expected from the United States, which seeks only to keep the sea lanes open—a demand that the Chinese have promised to meet. Nonetheless, most of the states in the region are delighted by the presence of an American fleet in the Western Pacific and Singapore has led the way in assuring the United States access to naval facilities. Indonesia went a step further in December 1995, and signed a mutual defense treaty with Australia, almost certainly designed to deter China.

Ultimately, each of the ASEAN states remains responsible for its own defense arrangements.

In 1997, the surging economic power and influence of Southeast Asia came to an abrupt halt. Estimates that the combined gross national product of the East Asian states would equal or even surpass that of the United States or the European Union by 2000 had to be revised. The Asian financial crisis started with the collapse of Thailand's currency in July and spread across the region. The crisis struck hardest in Indonesia, Korea, and Thailand, whose economies shrank significantly in 1998. Malaysia and the Philippines were also hurt badly. Japan, of course, had been mired in recession for years, its leaders lacking the political will to take the steps outsiders believed essential to recovery—and Japan's revitalization was perceived as essential to that of the rest of the region.

Outside of Singapore, it quickly became apparent that the nations of Southeast Asia had moved to market economies too hastily, liberalizing their financial markets before they had the necessary regulatory institutions or the expertise to manage them. In Indonesia, which had lagged behind in opening its markets, "crony capitalism" emerged as a critical problem—a banking system that lent unwisely to unproductive enterprises favored by Suharto and his family.

There were early signs of trouble as export growth slowed and Thailand, in particular, was importing more than it was exporting. The International Monetary Fund had quietly warned the Thai government that it needed to act to reduce its balance of payments deficit. But Thailand had a weak government facing a critical election in 1996 and it could not risk the recommended austerity program. Tax increases are always unpopular and reduced spending unthinkable for a government that had to buy votes to stay in power. Thailand ignored the warnings, inviting an attack on its currency by speculators who were well aware that Bangkok lacked the reserves to defend itself. As the attacks on regional currencies spread, confidence in exchange rates fell and funds began to flow out. Ultimately there was an enormous reversal in capital flows. Foreign capital had poured into Southeast Asia in the late 1980s and early 1990s; suddenly it began to drain out, preventing even sound, profitable companies from obtaining essential working capital.

Without capital or credit, many firms went bankrupt. Unemployment soared. Hardship, especially in Indonesia, prompted attacks on ethnic Chinese, their businesses, their homes, and their families. Many fled the country, aggravating shortages of essential commodities whose distribution they had managed. Historically, in bad times, the Chinese of Southeast Asia are often victimized, as were the Jews of Europe. Chinese in Singapore, Taiwan, and the People's Republic of China expressed alarm at events in Indonesia and there was always the danger that anti-Chinese pogroms would trigger outside intervention. There were other ethnic tensions as well. Illegal laborers, Indonesians in Malaysia and Burmese in Thailand, were driven out. Malaysia, labor-short in 1996, was approaching 4 percent unemployment in 1998. Two million Thais were out of work. There were massive population movements and efforts by each country to prevent an influx of economic refugees.

The principal political change wrought by the crisis was the end of Suharto's authoritarian regime as Indonesia unraveled in 1998. The economy was shattered, the army divided, and separatist movements erupted in several parts of the archipelago. Students emulating those in China in 1989 organized massive anti-Suharto demonstrations—and met with greater success than the young men and women so brutally crushed at Tiananmen. Indeed, Indonesians in the late 1990s enjoyed more freedom of expression than at any time in the previous forty years. But conditions in the country were appalling, with unemployment estimated at 17 percent. Twenty million people were living in conditions of absolute poverty. Indonesia's territorial integrity and hopes for economic development were threatened in the last days of the twentieth century. It was not a promising backdrop for the emergence of democracy.

Many economists and officials of international financial organizations argued that the economies of most Southeast Asian countries were fundamentally sound, that they would rebound in a year or two. But the unprecedented loss of wealth and income in the region and the mass suffering inevitable in the absence of adequate social safety nets left the peoples of most of these states resistant to outside advice, and incredulous at demands for austerity. As the crisis spread to other parts of the world, there seemed little reason for optimism on the eve of the twenty-first century. Arguably the only region-wide benefit derived from the crisis was a precipitous drop in military spending.

Individually, the nations of Southeast Asia were staggering. Burma, one of the poorest, suffered further economic setbacks as a result of the forced return of thousands of Burmese employed in Thailand. As long as its military junta remained in bad odor with most of the developed

world, there was little prospect for foreign assistance. Cambodian leaders continued to lust for personal power and wealth with minimal regard
for the well-being of their people—and minimal involvement in the
global economy. Laos was still a backwater and likely to remain one for
some long time, lacking any of the attributes for rapid development and
having slipped off the horizon of the great powers in the post-Cold War
world. Filipinos, freed of the U.S. military presence that had symbolized
their islands' dependence on their former colonial ruler, found themselves without the revenue once provided by the American bases, and
unable to protect themselves.

Vietnam, still controlled by the Communist Party, opening its markets haltingly and retaining currency controls, was beginning to make
significant progress in the mid-1990s. Trade with Europe was increasing.
The United States removed obstacles to international borrowing as it
gradually normalized relations with the country that had so recently
humiliated it in battle. Amidst the crisis of the late 1990s the Vietnamese
economy stalled, but was hurt less badly than that of its neighbors more
fully integrated into the global marketplace. Taiwan, the principal investor in Vietnam's economic development, had managed its affairs well
and did not have to withdraw capital to meet domestic needs. Similarly,
Vietnam's trade relations were primarily with China, another country
whose controlled currency was safe from attacks by speculators and were
largely unimpaired. Vietnamese eagerness to become an integral part of
the world economic system may have abated.

Malaysia, on the other hand, vacillated between adherence to the
norms of the International Monetary Fund and a desire to protect itself
by withdrawing from full participation in global currency markets. The
country's volatile political leadership, a sponsor and beneficiary of crony
capitalism, struck out in all directions, alternately blaming its problems
on currency speculators, Jews, Americans, ethnic Chinese, and Singapore,
but never accepting responsibility. There was every indication that the
Malaysian people would pay the price of such folly if their leaders succeeded in isolating them from the international economy.

One interesting trend in the last years of the twentieth century was the
beginning of a retreat from faith in the free market economic model many
economists in the West, especially in the United States, had urged upon
the region. The recommendations of the International Monetary Fund
brought modest relief at best. Everywhere the need for an improved social

safety net—more government spending on the welfare of those hurt by the market economy—was recognized. Those who still looked to the West for models were less likely to emulate the Thatcherism and Reagan economics of England and the United States in the 1980s than to long for something akin to the welfare state the American president Franklin Roosevelt stumbled onto in the midst of the Great Depression of the 1930s.

Conclusion

At the close of the twentieth century, the idea so prominent a decade earlier, that the twenty-first century would belong to East Asia, that the locus of power was returning to where it had been a thousand or more years before, had to be put aside. It was, of course, entirely possible that at the next turn of the business cycle, the Asian dragons, big and little, would surge forward and dominate international trade. It was conceivable that the shaky Chinese banking system would be repaired in time to allow the continued rise of China's economic and military strength, as well as its political influence. One might even assume that eventually a strong and competent Japanese government would exist and revitalize that nation, whose well being was so critical to that of the region. But in all of these countries, the dominant emotion was fear of economic catastrophe and political instability.

A striking feature of the 1990s, of enormous importance to East Asia, was the resurgence of the American economy. It had been clear throughout the decade that all of the states that feared China—or Japan—or North Korea perceived the presence of American military power as a source of security. Before the end of the century, it became apparent that the United States was again being pressed into the role of economic hegemon, at very least as the market of last resort. Japanese and American leaders were no closer to agreement on matters of trade and finance, but now it was the Americans who were urging the Japanese to get their house in order, to have their economy serve as the engine that would drive those of the rest of the region.

Before the decade ended, the United States and China backed away from their confrontation in the Taiwan Strait, and groped toward what they called a "strategic partnership." However absurd the term, it was vastly superior to the brief period when the Chinese found it necessary to remind the Americans that the PLA had missiles that could destroy Los Angeles. In the fall of 1997, China's president visited the United States and in mid-1998, the American president traveled to China. Each man was given ample opportunity to explain and defend his country's policies toward the other. China's leader was challenged on the official version of what happened at Tiananmen and the American leader was forced on the defensive regarding the policy of the United States toward Taiwan. Neither man satisfied his critics, at home or abroad, but both acquitted themselves well, accomplishing their principal goal of easing tensions between China and the United States. The Asian financial crisis, the situation in North Korea, and the urgency of confronting the proliferation of weapons of mass destruction demanded their cooperation. Moreover, China's seat on the UN Security Council provided Peking with influence in parts of the world, such as the Middle East, where American interests were being threatened. Nonetheless, the American bombing of the Chinese embassy in Belgrade in 1999, the vehemence of the Chinese reaction, and the continuing tensions in the Taiwan Strait allow for little optimism about the future of Chinese-American relations. Assuming the eventual recovery of East Asian economies from crisis, the answer to the question of whether China will be a responsible member of the international community or attempt to use its growing power to maximize its own position, ultimately destabilizing the region, is likely to define the twenty-first century.

CLOSING THOUGHTS

After reviewing approximately 4,000 years of activity in East Asia, there are inevitably indications of continuities and discontinuities. There are lessons of the past that might be seen as guides for the future—and lessons some will draw that are likely to prove no more valuable than a record of last year's performance is for judging a stock or bond's prospects for next year.

The most obvious continuity over these several millennia has been the importance of China. For several thousand years, China was the strongest, richest, and most powerful political entity in the region. From time to time it was battered by Inner Asian nomads such as the Xiongnu and the Mongols. Occasionally it suffered defeat in battles with neighbors such as Japan, Korea, Tibet, and Vietnam. Certainly it was overshadowed throughout the twentieth century by Japan's superior military and economic power. Often it was hurt by internal weakness: poor leadership, mistaken policies, corrupt administrators, and civil strife. On several occasions, alien peoples ruled China, but were ultimately sinicized, as were most of the people the "Chinese" conquered and absorbed as they expanded their territory from the North China plain to its present boundaries. But in the nineteenth century, the Chinese were overcome by peoples from the West, who were determined to Westernize China rather than be assimilated into Chinese civilization. The interlude of Western and Japanese domination lasted but a hundred years or so, and China's "hundred years of humiliation" ended half a century ago.

China is likely to reemerge in the twenty-first century as the preeminent military power in East Asia and it is building an ocean-going navy likely to make it a major sea power for the first time since the days of the great Zheng He. By mid-century, It may have Asia's largest economy, if not the world's. It is assured of being an important player in the international economic system, although not likely to play the hegemonic role assumed by the United States after World War II. The critical question for other East Asian states and for the Europeans and Americans with important interests in the region cannot be answered with any degree of certainty: how will China use its power in the next century?

Study of the nation's past performance in international affairs provides little if any guidance. There does not appear to be a peculiarly *Chinese* foreign policy. For much of its history, China has been the regional hegemon, absorbing its neighbors, creating an empire in much the same way the Russians and Americans did. Regardless of the teachings of Confucius and other great Chinese thinkers or strategists, China has behaved in the past, as it does in the present, as do all great powers throughout recorded history: it has been aggressive when it was strong and defensive when it was weak. Despite the German words that have become part of our vocabulary, the Chinese invented the practices we call *Realpolitik* and *Machtpolitik*. Nothing in Chinese culture or tradition either demands or precludes aggressive action.

China *will* be strong in the twenty-first century, but the resurgence of American economic strength after the Cold War provides one important check on its actions. A Japan likely to remain a major economic power, with significant military potential, serves as another. On the other hand, China might well conclude that its interests are served best through partnership with its neighbors and with the United States. There can be no doubt that most of China's leaders understand that their nation's economic interests—and ultimately their own legitimacy—can only be damaged by a truculent foreign policy. China, at the close of the twentieth century, has become a major trading state. Its economic growth depends on foreign markets, capital, and technology transfers, all of which are most accessible in times of peace. Moreover, China is confronted by no threat to its security or its territorial integrity. Arguably, no rational leaders in Peking would resort to force in an effort to maximize either their economic or strategic position. But, of course, in 1941, on the eve of their attack on Pearl Harbor, it was argued that no rational Japanese leader would order an attack on the United States.

The problem, of course, is that leaders do not always act rationally—at least not according to the views of academic analysts. In 1941, the Japanese military's calculus was quite different from that of the men in Washington. Over the millennia, a host of Chinese leaders have attacked when greater wisdom called for defense, expanded when they should have solidified their empire, acted unilaterally when they should have sought allies. No one can predict what China's leaders will decide in the years to come, whether China remains a communist dictatorship or evolves into a stable democracy. Nationalism seems certain to be dominant in either case, and the voice of Chinese nationalism today demands the continued occupation and forced sinicization of Tibet, and the reabsorption of that wayward province, now de facto independent democracy, Taiwan. Tomorrow it may demand the recovery of Mongolia, as did both Mao Zedong and Jiang Jieshi.

On the other hand, China enters the twenty-first century awash in what some of its current leaders not long ago denigrated as spiritual pollution. American fast food chains—McDonalds, Kentucky Fried Chicken, and Pizza Hut—are proliferating in Chinese cities much as they have in much of the rest of the world. Blue jeans and designer clothes from Japan and the West, plus local copies, can be seen everywhere. Western music, both classical and popular, is readily available on pirated compact discs. Similarly, American movies are distributed quickly in China, as often as not on pirated video discs or tapes. Chinese television broadcasts American and other foreign sports events, allowing the great American basketball player, Michael Jordan, to become the world's most popular figure with China's youth. Across from Peking's massive new Foreign Ministry building is an upscale shopping mall, equal to that in any wealthy American suburb, featuring boutiques such as Nautica and Alfred Dunhill. And thousands of foreign merchants flood Chinese cities, buying and selling. The Communist Party still reigns, as it may well for some long time, but this is not the China of Mao Zedong.

Part of what is changing China is the globalization that has reached almost every part of East Asia—and globalization has usually meant Westernization, even Americanization. China and much of the region have been engaged in world affairs for several millennia, exchanging goods and ideas with the rest of Asia, the Middle East, Africa, Europe, and in due course, the Americas. The flow has never been in one direction. For most of recorded history, the products of East Asia—Chinese silk, porcelains, and tea, the pepper and spices of Southeast Asia—were the great treasures of world commerce, as evidenced by the many sagas of the Silk Road through Central Asia and the daring exploits of fifteenth-century Portuguese sailors. Although peoples elsewhere on the globe usually found some means to pay for what they sought from China or the islands of the Indonesian archipelago, it was not until the nineteenth century that the terms of trade shifted against East Asia—not until industrialization in the West made its products more valuable than those available from China or any of its neighbors. The realization that the science and technology of Europe and the United States were integral parts of the growing wealth and power of the West and a prerequisite to competing successfully, perhaps to surviving as independent entities, led first Japan, then China, and eventually most other states of East Asia to open their doors to Westernization.

The enormous growth of international trade and finance in the post–World War II era and the gradual integration of communist and former communist states into the global economy created a level of interdependence such as the world has never known. From the 1960s until the late 1990s, most nations of East Asia benefited enormously from their participation. Japan soared and the little dragons—Hong Kong, Singapore, South Korea, and Taiwan followed. In the 1980s, Indonesia, Malaysia, and Thailand began producing economic miracles of their own. China joined the club in the 1990s. The free flow of goods and capital bestowed wealth on all who participated. Stock and real estate values rose astronomically in most of these states. And then, in the late 1990s, it all came tumbling down. Whether it was the "bubble" that burst in Japan, leading to a decade of recession there or the collapse of the Thai baht years later, it was clear that the economic linkages that had been established could bring pain as well as benefits. As markets shrank and capital flow slowed precipitously, first all of East Asia and then much of the rest of the world's market economies felt the impact. Awareness that the collapse of the economies of East Asia could precipitate a worldwide depression was a grim way to underscore the renewed salience of the region in the international system.

The political and economic ups and downs of East Asia relative to the rest of the world are surely important, but they are only a part of the story. For these several millennia, intercultural relations have also had enormous significance. Most notably, religions originating elsewhere have developed deep roots in many of the nations of the area. Buddhism, Christianity, Hinduism, and Islam have held sway in various places at various times. Buddhism in divergent forms swept the entire region, reaching China early in the modern era, pervading Chinese society by the sixth century. It remains a part of religious life in contemporary China, Japan, and Korea and remains dominant in much of mainland Southeast Asia. Catholicism, forced upon the Filipinos by Spain in the sixteenth century, survived in the Philippines long after the Spanish were gone—the efforts of American Protestant missionaries not withstanding. Pockets of Catholicism also persisted in what had been French Indochina and Portuguese East Timor. At the conclusion of the twentieth century, one-fourth of Koreans south of the 38th parallel had embraced Protestant Christianity and evangelical Protestant missionaries were scattered across East Asia, proselytizing even in communist countries. The Hindu religion, once the principal rival to Buddhism in Java, remained vital on the Indonesian island of Bali. And Islam found adherents everywhere Arab merchants and Arab armies penetrated. In the twentieth century, Indonesia was the world's most populous Muslim country. Of the major world religions, all of which originated in the Middle East or South Asia, only Judaism, which does not seek converts, did not establish itself in Asia—although synagogues, used primarily by foreigners, exist in many major cities. Curiously, in matters of religion, the flow of ideas ran only into East Asia, although Zen Buddhism has found a small, but responsive, audience in the West.

In art the cultural transfers were more nearly equal, with the West appearing to have taken more from East Asia than it gave. East Asian art not only fills Western museums, most notably the Guimet in Paris, the Freer and Sackler in Washington, and the Asian Art Museum in San Francisco, but it also had a striking impact on eighteenth-, nineteenth- and twentieth-century art in the West. Chinoiserie was the rage in Europe in the eighteenth century and Japonisme in turn had great influence on late-nineteenth-century French and American painters, not least Monet, Manet, Degas, Gauguin, Toulouse-Lautrec, and James Whistler. From the West, Asian painters appropriated perspective, chiascuro, and oils and Asian museums in recent years have built impressive collections of Western art, especially of the twentieth century. One striking symbol of the rising wealth of East Asia in the late twentieth century was the return to Asia of art that had been collected there by Americans and Europeans in the nineteenth and early in the twentieth century. American and European museum curators could no longer compete at auction with Asian collectors. The movement of art has proven to be an excellent indicator of the flow of economic power.

Has Asia or the West benefited most from the cultural transfer of food? For every American fast food restaurant in Asia there are probably ten or twenty Chinese restaurants, Japanese sushi bars, Korean, Thai, and Vietnamese restaurants in the United States. There is probably not a major city in the West without a district in which Chinese or Indonesian restaurants abound. The impact on Western cuisine more than compensates for the peanuts, potatoes, and chilis the West introduced into Asia. And where would the British be without tea?

Of course, intercultural relations has included the realm of political and economic ideas. European and American philosophers and political theorists of the Enlightenment were fascinated by what they understood of the teachings of Confucius. Some of Thomas Jefferson's ideas came from corrupted translations of Chinese texts—just as bad translations of Darwin and Marx had their impact on Chinese and Japanese intellectuals a century or more later. More often than not, ideas lose—or gain—something in translation or mutate in alien soil, but their impact cannot be denied. In the late nineteenth and early twentieth centuries, intellectuals and political activists all over East Asia looked to Western thinkers to find the keys to wealth and power. During the May Fourth Movement demonstrations of 1919, Chinese students called for "Mr. Science and Mr. Democracy." Before Marx and Lenin, the thought of the American philosopher John Dewey and the British philosopher Bertrand Russell had attracted them. Ultimately, many young Asians put their faith in Marxist-Leninism, enthralled by the apparent success of a handful of Russian revolutionaries in ridding their country of despotism and setting it on the road to modernization. But before the century had ended, only a few old men still had confidence in the nostrums of Marx, Lenin, Stalin, or Mao. The new panacea was thought to be the market economy—free trade and the free flow of capital across international borders—as advocated and sometimes practiced by the most advanced industrial states. Hope for that remedy was also eroding in the last days of the twentieth century.

There was one big Western idea that interested Asian intellectuals but not many of their political leaders—the idea of democracy, which Churchill called the worst form of government known to man—except for all others. In China, Hong Kong, Indonesia, Malaysia, and Singapore, the men who held power insisted that Asian values were different from those of the people of the West, that in particular Asians valued order over freedom and the right of the state over that of the individual. In the years when these men presided over economies that were remarkably prosperous, they attributed their success to those Asian values. Little more was heard from them when several of their economies collapsed and the economies of the great Western democracies appeared relatively strong.

But Japan had developed a political system that might conceivably be called democratic. Taiwan and South Korea embraced political democracy in the 1990s. Thailand, too, was attempting to move in that direction. American historians have included Franklin Roosevelt among their nation's great presidents on the grounds that in the 1930s he proved that democracy could survive the Great Depression, at a time when totalitarian movements were overcoming Germany, Japan, and the Soviet Union. Perhaps the day will come when leading one's\nation to democracy will be the test of greatness in Asia.

In sum, it is apparent that every approach to international relations known to man probably was tried first in ancient China. Arguments for appeasing or attacking enemies, for and against defense spending, about who determined the national interest, who benefited from various foreign policies, and how to pay for military expenses by squeezing businessmen all appear in the annals of China, before or during the Han Dynasty. Collective security and the concept of the hegemon date back at least to the era of the Warring States. To misappropriate (and mistranslate) the title of Erich Maria Remarque's classic, *Im Western Nicht Neues*, there is nothing new in the West.

Similarly, East Asia's involvement in world affairs began thousands of years ago, many centuries before Portuguese ships found their way around the Horn of Africa, across the Indian Ocean, across the Bay of Bengal, through the Strait of Melaka, to the South China Sea and on to landings in China and Japan. East Asia has been an important part of Western Civilization since that civilization's claim to existence. The movement back and forth of goods and ideas has been constant. And since the seaborne contact between Europe and East Asia began, millions of men and women have joined the flow, often as sojourners. Increasingly, however, Asians have sought and found permanent residence in the West. Indeed, the United States is dependent on Asians to staff its hospitals and its scientific laboratories.

Few East Asians still consider their lands to be the center of the universe, but they do demand and deserve the respect due peoples whose economic success is essential to the global economy. Wealthy European nations and the United States contend that only Japan has the power to bring about recovery of international markets. Mighty China has risen again, sits on the Security Council of the UN as a permanent member, brandishes its missiles, and reminds the world it is a nuclear power. Korea remains the last state divided by the Cold War—with the North seemingly poised somewhere between exploding and imploding. The nations of East Asia have long been an important part of the international system. At the end of the twentieth century, their economic failure threatened to trigger a global depression. They are not likely to be less important in the twenty-first century.

NOTES

Chapter 1.

1. See Elizabeth Wayland Barber, *The Mummies of Urumchi* (New York: Norton, 1999).

2. Oracle bones were sometimes not bones but rather turtleshells. Whether bones or shells, they were inscribed with questions, usually posed by the king or other members of the ruling class, and then cracked with a hot metal point. The oracle or shaman would divine answers from the direction of the cracks.

3. Chinese tradition posits a Xia dynasty from 2205 to 1766 BCE. Skepticism among scholars has been diminished by recent archeological discoveries revealing the existence of organized communities in North China in that period. Doubts remain, however, as to whether these were, in fact, parts of the legendary Xia state. For a useful discussion, see Cho-yun Hsu and Kathryn M. Linduff, *Western Chou Civilization* (New Haven: Yale University Press, 1988), 9–17.

4. David N. Keightley, "The Late Shang State: When? Where, and What?," in David N. Keightley (ed.) *The Origins of Chinese Civilization* (Berkeley: University of California Press, 1983), 529.

5. Sherman E. Lee, *A History of Far Eastern Art*, 4th ed. (New York: Harry N. Abrahms, 1982), 30.

6. Li Xueqin, *Eastern Zhou and Qin Civilizations*, (New Haven: Yale University Press, 1985), 14.

7. A recent translation with commentary can be found in Ralph Sawyer, *The Seven Military Classics of Ancient China* (Boulder, Colorado: Westview Press, 1993).

8. Alastair Iain Johnston, *Cultural Realism: Strategic Culture and Grand Strategy in Chinese History* (Princeton: Princeton University Press, 1995), 93–105, 139–43.

9. Herrlee G. Creel, *The Origins of Statecraft in China*, (Chicago: University of Chicago Press, 1970), 10.

10. My discussion of ancient Chinese political thought rests heavily on the work of Benjamin I. Schwartz. See in particular his *The World of Thought in Ancient China* (Cambridge: Harvard University Press, 1985).

11. Ki-baik Lee, *A New History of Korea* (Cambridge: Harvard University Press, 1984), 13–14.

12. Thomas J. Barfield, "The Xiongnu Imperial Confederacy: Organization and Foreign Policy, *Journal of Asian Studies*, 41 (1981): 45–61. See also his *The Perilous Frontier: Nomadic Empires and China* (Cambridge: Basil Blackwell, 1989).

13. Sechin Jagchid and Van Jay Symons, *Peace, War, and Trade Along the Great Wall* (Bloomington: Indiana University Press, 1989), 36.

14. Richard White, *The Middle Ground: Indians, Empires, and Republics in the Great Lakes Region, 1650–1815* (Cambridge: Cambridge University Press, 1991).

15. Yu Ying-shih, *Trade and Expansion in Han China: A Study in the Structure of Sino-Barbarian Economic Relations* (Berkeley: University of California Press, 1967), 190.

16. Creel, *Origins of Statecraft in China*, 251.

17. K. H. J. Gardiner, *The Early History of Korea* (Honolulu: University of Hawaii Press, 1969) , 20; Han Woo-keun, *The History of Korea* (Seoul: Eul-Yoo Publishing Company, 1970), 20–21; Sherman Lee, *A History of Far Eastern Art*, 4th ed., 62.

18. Michael Loewe, *Crisis and Conflict in Han China, 104 BC to AD 9* (London: George Allen & Unwin, Ltd., 1974), 72–107 offers a useful discussion of the debate.

19. Martin J. Powers, *Art and Political Expression in Early China* (New Haven: Yale University Press, 1991), 42. See also Jonathan Chaves, "A Han Painted Tomb at Luoyang," *Artibus Asiae*, 30 (1968), 5–27.

20. Powers, *Art and Political Expression in Early China*, 106–7.

21. Hans Bielenstein, "Wang Mang, the Restoration of the Han Dynasty, and Later Han," in Denis Twitchett and Michael Loewe (ed.), *The Cambridge History of China, I: The Ch'in and Han Empires, 221 B.C.–A.D. 220*, (Cambridge: Cambridge University Press, 1986), 239.

22. Yu Ying-shih, "Han Foreign Relations," in Twitchett and Loewe, *Cambridge History of China, I*, 443.

23. The Qiang are often referred to as Tibetans or proto-Tibetans. Christopher I. Beckwith, a specialist on the Tibetan Empire, argues that the Chiang were not related to the peoples who founded the Tibetan Empire in the seventh century CE See his *The Tibetan Empire in Central Asia* (Princeton: Princeton University Press, 1987), 5–8.

24. The Chinese equivalent of the English expression "speak of the devil" is *shuo Cao Cao, Cao Cao jiu lai* [say Cao Cao and Cao Cao will come].

25. John King Fairbank and Edwin O. Reischauer, *East Asia: The Great Tradition* (Boston: Houghton Mifflin, 1960), 137.

26. For an explanation of how the Longmen friezes came to the United

States, see Warren I. Cohen, *East Asian Art and American Culture* (New York: Columbia University Press, 1992) 111–20.

27. Han, *History of Korea,* 47.

28. The name of this ancient Japanese culture derives from its primitive technique of making pottery without a wheel, creating objects out of strings or cords of clay. The American art collector Edward B. Morse appears to have been the original source of the name while he was teaching in Meiji Japan. For a brief sketch of his career, see Cohen, *East Asian Art and American Culture,* 23–29.

29. Kenneth R. Hall, "Economic History of Early Southeast Asia," in Nicholas Tarling (ed.), *The Cambridge History of Southeast Asia, I, From Early Times to c. 1800* (Cambridge: Cambridge University Press, 1992), 192–93.

30. Keith W. Taylor, "The Early Kingdoms," in Tarling, *Cambridge History of Southeast Asia I,* 153–54.

Chapter 2.

1. Arthur F. Wright, *The Sui Dynasty: The Unification of China, A.D. 581–617* (New York: Alfred A. Knopf, 1978) 184–85.

2. Howard J. Wechsler, "'T'ai-tsung (Reign 626–49) The Consolidator," in Denis Twitchett (ed.) , *The Cambridge History of China, Volume 3, Sui and T'ang China, 589–906, Part I* (Cambridge: Cambridge University Press, 1979), 228.

3. Edward H. Schafer, *The Golden Peaches of Samarkand* (Berkeley: University of California Press, 1963), 140.

4. Beckwith's *The Tibetan Empire in Central Asia* is the best source for Tibetan affairs in this era.

5. Ibid., 137.

6. Naoki Kojiro suggests that Nara was modeled after Loyang. See his "The Nara State," in Delmer M. Brown ed. *Cambridge History of Japan,* I (Cambridge: Cambridge University Press, 1993), 221–67.

7. Edwin A. Cranston, "Asuka and Nara Culture: Literacy, Literature, and Music," in Brown, *Cambridge History of Japan,* I, 498.

8. Lee, *History of Far Eastern Art,* 268–69.

Chapter 3.

1. Lee, *New History of Korea,* 96.

2. Kenneth R. Hall, "Economic History of Early Southeast Asia," in Nicholas Tarling (ed.), *The Cambridge History of Southeast Asia, I: From Early Times to c.*

1800 (Cambridge: Cambridge University Press, 1992), 183–275, is the most accessible source on the subject.

3. Tao Jing-shen, "Barbarians or Northerners: Northern Sung Images of the Khitans," in Morris Rossabi, *China Among Equals: The Middle Kingdom and its Neighbors, 10th–14th Centuries* (Berkeley: University of California Press, 1983), 80.

4. Wang Gungwu, "The Rhetoric of a Lesser Empire: Early Sung Relations with its Neighbors," in Rossabi, *China Among Equals*, 62.

5. Edwin O. Reischauer and John K. Fairbank, *East Asia: The Great Tradition* (Boston: Houghton Mifflin, 1960), 211.

6. Peter Duus, *Feudalism in Japan*, 3rd ed. (New York: McGraw-Hill, 1993), 35.

Chapter 4.

1. Jagchid, *Peace, War, and Trade Along the Great Wall*, 20.

2. Charles A. Peterson, "Old Illusions and New Realities: Sung Foreign Policy, 1217–1234, in Morris Rossabi (ed.), *China Among Equals*, 209.

3. For a discussion of this unusual woman, based on Hebrew, Latin, and Persian sources, see Morris Rossabi, *Khubilai Khan: His Life and Times* (Berkeley: University of California Press, 1988), pp. 11–14.

4. Ibid., 82–86.

5. John King Fairbank plays with this concept in his *East Asia: The Great Tradition*, 276.

6. Han, *Korea*, 176.

7. Michael C. Rogers, "National Consciousness in Medieval Korea: The Impact of Liao and Chin on Koryo," in Rossabi, *China Among Equals*, pp. 165–66.

Chapter 5.

1. Fairbank, *East Asia: The Great Tradition*, 317–19.

2. See Alastair Iain Johnston, *Cultural Realism: Strategic Culture and Grand Strategy in Chinese History*.

3. Hok-Lam Chan, "The Chien-wen, Yung-lo, Hung-hsi and Hsuan-te reigns, 1399–1435," in Frederick Mote and Denis Twitchett (eds.), *Cambridge History of China*, VII, Part I (Cambridge: Cambridge University Press, 1988), 260. I have relied heavily on Chan's essay which is the best brief account of Yongle's foreign policy.

4. Ibid. 235.

5. Kawazoe Shoji, "Japan and East Asia," in *Cambridge History of Japan*, III (Cambridge: Cambridge University Press, 1990), 443.

6. Kenneth R. Hall, "Economic History of Early Southeast Asia," in *Cambridge History of Southeast Asia, I: From Early Times to c.1800* (Cambridge: Cambridge University Press, 1992), 217–18.

7. Ibid., 229.

8. D.G.E. Hall, *A History of South-East Asia*, 4th edition (New York: St. Martin's Press, 1981), 229.

9. Frederick M. Mote, "The Ch'eng-hua and Hung-chih Reigns, 1465–1505," in Mote and Twitchett, *Cambridge History of China*, VII, 395.

10. Ibid., 396.

Chapter 6.

1. C.R. Boxer, the great chronicler of the Portuguese empire, remarked that virtually every Portuguese in Asia and Africa spent his time "alternately fighting, trading, and fornicating with the local inhabitants." See his *Four Centuries of Portuguese Expansion, 1415–1825* (Berkeley and Los Angeles: University of California Press, 1969), 35.

2. Ray Huang, The Lung-ch'ing and Wan-li Reigns, 1567–1620," *Cambridge History of China*, VII, 570.

3. Peter Duus, *Feudalism in Japan*, 3rd ed., 76.

4. Ki-baik Lee, *New History of Korea*, 215. Sherman Lee attributes the manufacture of fine porcelain in seventeenth-century Japan in part to the influence of Korean potters whom he suggests "immigrated" to Japan. Lee, *History of Far Eastern Art*, 501–2.

5. C.R. Boxer, *The Dutch Seaborne Empire, 1600–1800* (New York: Alfred A. Knopf, 1970, 24.

6. Anthony Reid's two-volume *Southeast Asia in the Age of Commerce, 1450–1680* (New Haven: Yale University Press, 1988, 1993) is essential reading on this subject.

7. Reid, *Southeast Asia in the Age of Commerce*, II, 307.

8. Ibid., 140–41.

9. Jonathan D. Spence, *The Memory Palace of Matteo Ricci* (New York: Penguin Books, 1985), 54.

Chapter 7.

1. Jonathan Spence, *The Search for Modern China* (New York: Norton, 1990), 71–72.

2. See Truong Buu Lam, "Intervention versus Tribute in Sino-Vietnamese Relations, 1788–1790," in John K. Fairbank, *The Chinese World Order* (Cam-

bridge: Harvard University Press, 1968), 165–79 for an interesting analysis of these events.

3. Joanna Waley-Cohen, "China and Western Technology in the Late 18th Century," *American Historical Review* (1993), 98: 1525–44.

4. For variant analyses, see James Hevia, *Cherishing Men from Afar: Qing Guest Ritual and the Macartney Embassy of 1793* (Durham: Duke University Press, 1995) and Evelyn Rawski, "Presidential Address: Reenvisioning the Qing: The Significance of the Qing Period in Chinese History," *Journal of Asian Studies* (1996), 55: 829–50.

5. The essential source for the study of seventeenth century Japanese statecraft is Ronald P. Toby, *State and Diplomacy in Early Modern Japan: Asia in the Development of the Tokugawa Bakufu*, (Stanford: Stanford University Press, 1991). No one has done more to dispel the notion of Tokugawa Japan as an isolated and "isolationist" state.

6. Boxer, *Dutch Seaborne Empire*, 194.

7. G.M. Trevelyan, *The History of England*, III (New York: Doubleday, 1952), 124.

8. Basil Williams, *The Whig Supremacy, 1714–1760*, 2nd ed. (Oxford, Oxford University Press, 1961), 325.

9. James L. Hevia, *Cherishing Men from Afar: Qing Guest Ritual and the Macartney Embassy of 1793* is a major and persuasive reinterpretation of Macartney's experience in China.

Chapter 8.

1. William H. McNeill, *The Pursuit of Power: Technology, Armed Force and Society Since A.D. 1000* (Chicago: University of Chicago Press, 1982), 151; see also, Geoffrey Parker, *The Military Revolution: Military Innovation and the Rise of the West, 1500–1800* (Cambridge: Cambridge University Press, 1988).

2. Akira Iriye, "Imperialism in East Asia," in James B. Crowley, *Modern East Asia: Essays in Interpretation* (New York: Harcourt, 1970), 129.

3. See, for example, the memorial from I-li-pu to the emperor, February 6, 1841, in Earl Swisher, ed., *China's Management of the American Barbarians* (New Haven: Yale University Press, 1953) 57–58.

4. Ibid., 137.

5. Memorial, Lin Kui to the emperor, March 15, 1851, Ibid., 190–91.

6. Hall, *History of South-East Asia*, 686–87.

7. For a stimulating analysis of the perceptions of this mission, see Masao Miyoshi, *As We Saw Them: The First Japanese Embassy to the United States* (Berkeley: University of California Press, 1979).

8. Edmund Clubb, *China and Russia: The "Great Game"* (New York: Columbia University Press, 1971), 71.

Chapter 9.

1. Paul A. Cohen, *China and Christianity: The Missionary Movement and the Growth of Chinese Antiforeignism, 1860–1870* (Cambridge: Harvard University Press, 1963) is the essential source on the subject for this period.

2. This was the fifth article of the so-called "Charter Oath" of April 1868.

3. For a fascinating discussion of Huang's thought and other writings, see D.R. Howland, *Borders of Chinese Civilization: Geography and History at Empire's End* (Durham: Duke University Press, 1996).

4. Lee, *New History of Korea*, 281.

5. Frederick Wakeman, Jr., *The Fall of Imperial China* (New York: The Free Press, 1975), 193.

6. Richard W. Leopold, *Growth of American Foreign Policy* (New York: Alfred A. Knopf, 1962), 212.

7. James Hevia, "Looting Beijing: 1860, 1900," unpublished paper circulated spring, 1998.

8. Immanuel C.Y. Hsu, "Late Ch'ing Foreign Relations, 1866–1905," in John K. Fairbank and Kwang-ching Liu, *Cambridge History of China, Vol 11 Late Ch'ing, 1800–1911, Part 2* (Cambridge: Cambridge University Press, 1980), 70.

Chapter 10.

1. W.G. Beasley, *Japanese Imperialism, 1894–1945,* (Oxford: Clarendon Press, 1987), 90–100.

2. For a valuable discussion of meetings between Roosevelt's emissary, John O'Laughlin, and Japanese foreign minister Komura Jutaro, see Charles E. Neu, *An Uncertain Friendship: Theodore Roosevelt and Japan, 1906–1909* (Cambridge: Harvard University Press, 1967) 272–74.

3. R. David Arkush and Leo O. Lee (eds), *Land Without Ghosts: Chinese Impressions of America from the Mid-Nineteenth Century to the Present* (Berkeley: University of California Press, 1989), 77–80.

4. Theodore Roosevelt, *State Papers as Governor and President, 1899–1909* (New York: Scribner's, 1925), 376–77; Roosevelt, "The Awakening of China," *Outlook* (1908), 90: 665–67.

5. Han, *History of Korea*, 458.

6. Carl A. Trocki, "Political Structures in the Nineteenth and Early Twentieth Centuries, in Nicholas Tarling (ed.) *Cambridge History of Southeast Asia,*

II: The Nineteenth and Twentieth Centuries (New York and Cambridge: Cambridge University Press, 1992), 83.

Chapter 11.

1. William Kirby, *Germany and Republican China* (Princeton: Princeton University Press, 1984) is the standard work on Chinese-German relations in this period. See also F.F. Liu, *A Military History of Modern China: 1924–1949* (Princeton: Princeton University Press, 1956), 90–102.

2. From the *Ta Kung Pao*, quoted in Jerome Ch'en, *Mao and the Chinese Revolution* (New York: Oxford University Press, 1967), 230.

3. Clubb, *China and Russia: The Great Game*, 310.

4. Hadley Cantril (ed.), *Public Opinion, 1935–1946* (Princeton: Princeton University Press, 1951), 1156.

5. Herbert Feis, *The Road to Pearl Harbor,* (Princeton: Princeton University Press, 1950), 269.

6. On this point, see especially Waldo Heinrichs, *Threshhold of War: Franklin D. Roosevelt and American Entry into World War II* (New York: Oxford University Press, 1988), 178–79.

7. Akira Iriye, *Power and Culture: The Japanese-American War 1941–1945* (Cambridge: Harvard University Press, 1981), 263.

8. Clubb, *China and Russia*, 343.

Chapter 12.

1. Gar Alperovitz, *Atomic Diplomacy: Hiroshima and Potsdam*, rev. ed. (New York: Penguin Books, 1985) The original edition was published in 1965 and became one of the essential pillars of the revisionist account of the origins of the Cold War. See J. Samuel Walker, "The Decision to Use the Bomb: A Historiographical Update," *Diplomatic History* (1990), 14: 97–114 for an excellent discussion of the literature.

2. Yukiko Koshiro, *Trans-Pacific Racisms and the U.S. Occupation of Japan* (New York: Columbia University Press, 1999), 69–70.

3. James E. Auer, *The Postwar Rearmament of Japanese Maritime Forces, 1945–1971* (New York: Praeger, 1973).

4. J.W. Dower, *Empire and Aftermath: Yoshida Shigeru and the Japanese Experience, 1878–1954* (Cambridge: Harvard University Press, 1979), 313.

5. Hu Xigui, *Shiju bianhua ho wode fangzhen* [The changing political situation and our policy], mimeographed transcript of lecture to cadres, August 30, 1945. Archives of the Bureau of Investigation, Republic of China.

6. Carter J. Eckert, et al., *Korea Old and New: A History* (Cambridge: Korea Institute, Harvard University, 1990), 329.

7. R.B. Smith, *An International History of the Vietnam War: The Kennedy Strategy* (New York: St. Martins Press, 1985).

8. U.S. Central Intelligence Agency, *Indonesia—1965; The Coup That Backfired*, quoted by Audrey R. Kahin and George McT. Kahin, *Subversion as Foreign Policy* (New York: The New Press, 1995), 227–28.

Chapter 13.

1. See Ezra Vogel, *The Four Little Dragons: The Spread of Industrialization in East Asia* (Cambridge: Harvard University Press, 1991).

2. In October, 1971, I reviewed the files of the Bureau of East Asian Affairs at the U.S. Department of State in an effort to understand why American actions had been kept secret from the Japanese. Every memorandum I saw argued for keeping the Japanese informed. When I asked Secretary of State William Rogers, he spoke of the need to preserve secrecy and of a Japanese government notorious for its leaks. Interviews with specialists in the department and with members of the National Security Council staff all pointed to Nixon's determination to embarrass Sato for his failure to deliver on textiles.

3. See Chalmers Johnson, *Japan: Who Governs? The Rise of the Developmental State* (New York: Norton, 1995) and Meredith Woo-Cumings (ed.) *The Developmental State* (Ithaca, New York: Cornell University Press, 1999).

4. Frederick C. Deyo, "Singapore: Developmental Paternalism," in Steven M. Goldstein (ed.), *Minidragons: Fragile Economic Miracles in the Pacific* (Boulder: Westview Press, 1991).

5. David Joel Steinberg (ed.), *In Search of Southeast Asia*, 2nd ed. (Honolulu: University of Hawaii Press, 1987), 427.

6. Peter G. Warr, "The Thai Economy," in Peter G. Warr (ed.) *The Thai Economy in Transition* (Cambridge: Cambridge University Press, 1993), 1.

7. See, for example, Richard Rosecrance, *The Rise of the Trading State* (New York: Basic Books, 1986).

Chapter 14.

1. See Dan Oberdorfer's *The Two Koreas: A Contemporary History* (Boston: Little, Brown, 1998). Most of this book is based on interviews with American and Korean participants. A documentary record of these events is not likely to become available for many years, if ever.

FURTHER READING

The most accessible and most useful references for the reader who wishes to study the place of East Asia in world affairs are the many volumes of the Cambridge histories. I have relied most heavily on them for the premodern era. The multivolume *Cambridge History of China* is incomplete but the books already published are a treasure trove of information and insights provided by the world's leading scholars. The same is true of the *Cambridge History of Japan* and the *Cambridge History of Southeast Asia*. Regrettably, the *Cambridge History of Early Inner Asia* is less helpful. In some instances, especially in the earlier volumes, the essays do not reflect the most up-to-date scholarship, but the reader rarely will be led astray. In the chapter by chapter listings below, I will include more recent works as well as the classics to which I am indebted.

Other surveys, valuable for much of the region's history, are: Sherman E. Lee *A History of Far Eastern Art*, 4th ed. (1982); Han Woo-keun, *The History of Korea* (1970); Ki-baik Lee, *A New History of Korea* (1984); D.G.E. Hall, *A History of South-East Asia*, 4th ed. (1981); John Whitney Hall, *Japan: From Prehistory to Modern Times* (1970); Charles O. Hucker, *China's Imperial Past* (1975); Jonathan D. Spence, *The Search for Modern China* (1990); Franz Michael and George Taylor, *The Far East in the Modern World*, 3rd ed. (1975); and, of course, John K. Fairbank, Edwin O. Reischauer, and Albert Craig, *A History of East Asian Civilization*, 2 vols. (1960, 1965). Although some of the essays in James B. Crowley (ed.) *Modern East Asia* (1970) are dated, most are unsurpassed in their insights into the last half of the nineteenth century and the first half of the twentieth. A successor volume edited by Merle Goldman and Andrew Gordon, *Historical Perspectives on Contemporary East Asia* (2000), reflects more recent scholarship.

I also found several "world" histories very helpful, including: Philip D. Curtin, *Cross-Cultural Trade in World History* (1984); Ferdinand Braudel, *The Perspective of the World* (1984); William H. McNeill, *The Pursuit of Power: Technology, Armed Force, and Society since AD 1000* (1983).

Chapter One.

Pre-Han China.

H. G. Creel, *The Origins of Statecraft in China* (1970); Benjamin Schwartz, *The World of Thought in Ancient China* (1985); Jessica Rawson (ed.), *Mysteries of Ancient China* (1996); Cho-yun Hsu and Katheryn M. Linduff, *Western Chou Civilization* (1988); Liu Xueqin, *Eastern Zhou and Qin Civilizations* (1985); Richard L. Walker, *The Multi-State System of Ancient China* (1953); David N. Keightley (ed.), *The Origins of Chinese Civilization* (1983); J.I. Crump, Jr. (trans.), *Chan-Kuo Ts'e* (1970); Ralph D. Sawyer (trans.), *The Seven Military Classics of Ancient China* (1993); Alastair Iain Johnston, *Cultural Realism: Strategic Culture and Grand Strategy in Chinese History* (1995).

Ancient Korea.

K.H.J. Gardiner, *The Early History of Korea* (1969); Takahashi Hatada, *A History of Korea* (1969); Peter H. Lee, et.al. (eds.), *Sourcebook of Korean Civilization*, I (1993).

Ancient Japan.

George Sansom, *A History of Japan to 1334* (1958).

Han China.

Yu Ying-shih, *Trade and Expansion in Han China* (1967); Michael Loewe, *Crisis and Conflict in Han China, 104 BC to AD 9* (1974); Hans Bielenstein, *The Bureaucracy of Han Times* (1980); Martin J. Powers, *Art and Political Expression in Early China* (1991); Sechin Jagchid and Van Jay Symons, *Peace, War, and Trade Along the Great Wall* (1989); Thomas J. Barfield, *The Perilous Frontier: Nomadic Empires and China* (1989).

Chapter Two.

Arthur F. Wright, *The Sui Dynasty: The Unification of China, A.D. 581–617* (1978); Edward H. Schafer, *The Golden Peaches of Samarkand* (1963); Arthur F. Wright and Denis Twitchett (eds.), *Perspectives on the T'ang* (1973); Christopher I. Beckwith, *The Tibetan Empire in Central Asia* (1987); Charles Backus, *The Nan-chao Kingdom and T'ang China's Western Frontier* (1981); Howard J. Wechsler, *Offerings of Jade and Silk: Ritual and Symbol in the Legitimation of the T'ang*

Dynasty (1985); George Sansom, *History of Japan to 1334* (1958); Peter Duus, *Feudalism in Japan*, 3rd ed.; Takahashi Hatada, *History of Korea*.

Chapter Three.

Morris Rossabi (ed.), *China Among Equals: The Middle Kingdom and its Neighbors, 10th–14th Centuries* (1983); George Sansom, *History of Japan to 1334*; Peter Duus, *Feudalism in Japan*, 3rd ed. (1993); Takahashi Hatada, *History of Korea*.

Chapter Four.

Sechin Jagchid and Van Jay Symons, *Peace, War, and Trade Along the Great Wall*; Morris Rossabi (ed.), *China Among Equals*; Morris Rossabi, *Khubilai Khan: His Life and Times* (1988); George Sansom, *History of Japan to 1334*.

Chapter Five.

Alastair Iain Johnston, *Cultural Realism*; D.S. Richards (ed.), *Islam and the Trade of Asia* (1970); Timothy Brook, *The Confusions of Pleasure. A History of Ming China (1368–1644)* (1998); Philip Snow, *The Star Raft: China's Encounter with Africa* (1988); Morris Rossabi, *China and Inner Asia from 1368 to the Present Day* (1975); John K. Fairbank (ed.) *The Chinese World Order* (1968); George Sansom, *A History of Japan, 1334–1615* (1961); Anthony Reid, *Southeast Asia in the Age of Commerce*, 2 vols. (1988, 1993); K.N. Chaudhuri, *Trade and Civilization in the Indian Ocean: An Economic History from the Rise of Islam to 1750* (1985).

Chapter Six.

K.N. Chaudhuri, *Trade and Civilization in the Indian Ocean*; C.R. Boxer, *Four Centuries of Portuguese Expansion, 1415–1825* (1969); C.R. Boxer, *Portuguese Merchants and Missionaries in Feudal Japan, 1543–1640* (1986); James B. Boyajian, *Portuguese Trade in Asia under the Habsburgs, 1580–1640* (1993); Timothy Brook, *The Confusions of Pleasure*; John K. Fairbank (ed.) *The Chinese World Order*; Morris Rossabi, *China and Inner Asia*; Anthony Reid, *Southeast Asia in the Age of Commerce, II*; Peter Duus, *Feudalism in Japan*; George Sansom, *History of Japan, 1334–1615*; Derek Massarella, *A World Elsewhere: Europe's Encounter with Japan in the Sixteenth and Seventeenth Centuries* (1990); C. R. Boxer, *The*

Dutch Seaborne Empire, 1600–1800 (1970); Jonathan Spence, *The Memory Palace of Matteo Ricci* (1984); Andre Gunder Frank, *Reorient: Global Economy in the Asian Age* (1998).

Chapter Seven.

Jonathan Spence and John Wills (eds.), *From Ming to Ch'ing: Conquest, Region, and Continuity in Seventeenth Century China* (1979); Frederick Wakeman, *The Great Enterprise: The Manchu Reconstruction of Imperial Order in Seventeenth-Century China*, 2 vols. (1985); Ralph Croizier, *Koxinga and Chinese Nationalism: History, Myth and the Hero* (1977); James Hevia, *Cherishing Men From Afar: Qing Guest Ritual and the Macartney Embassy of 1793* (1995); Joanna Waley-Cohen, *The Sextants of Beijing: Global Currents in Chinese History* (1999); Morris Rossabi, *China and Inner Asia*; George Sansom, *A History of Japan, 1615–1867* (1963); Ronald P. Toby, *State and Diplomacy in Early Modern Japan: Asia in the Development of the Tokugawa Bakufu* (1984); K.N. Chaudhuri, *The Trading World of Asia and the East India Company*; Immanuel Wallerstein, *The Modern World System II: Mercantilism and the Consolidation of the European World Economy, 1600–1750* (1980); Andre Gunder Frank, *Reorient*; Anthony Reid, *Southeast Asia in the Age of Commerce, II*; C. R. Boxer, *The Dutch Seaborne Empire, 1600–1800*.

Chapter Eight.

Geoffrey Parker, *The Military Revolution: Military Innovation and the Rise of the West, 1500–1800* (1988); Daniel R. Headrick, *The Tools of Empire: Technology and European Imperialism in the Nineteenth Century* (1981); K.N. Chaudhuri, *The Trading World of Asia and the East India Company*; Immanuel Wallerstein, *The Modern World-System III: The Second Era of Great Expansion of the Capitalist World-Economy, 1730–1840s* (1989); John K. Fairbank, *Trade and Diplomacy on the China Coast* (1953); Frederick Wakeman, *Strangers at the Gate: Social Disorder in South China, 1839–1861* (1966); Michael Greenberg, *British Trade and the Opening of China, 1800–1842* (1951); Warren I. Cohen, *America's Response to China*, 4th ed. (2000); Michael H. Hunt, *The Making of a Special Relationship: The United States and China to 1914* (1983); Edward V. Gulick, *Peter Parker and the Opening of China* (1973); George Sansom, *A History of Japan, 1615–1867* (1963); Arthur Walworth, *Black Ships off Japan: The Story of the Opening of Japan by Commodore Perry in 1853* (1946); Masao Miyoshi, *As We Saw Them: The First Japanese Embassy to the United States* (1979); Morris Rossabi, *China and Inner Asia*; O. Edmund Clubb, *China and Russia: The "Great Game"* (1971).

Chapter Nine.

Mary Wright, *The Last Stand of Chinese Conservatism: The T'ung-chih Restoration, 1862–1874* (1957); Jane Kate Leonard, *Wei Yuan and China's Rediscovery of the Maritime World* (1984); Immanuel Hsu, *China's Entrance into the Family of Nations: The Diplomatic Phase, 1858–1880* (1960); Albert Feuerwerker, *China's Early Industrialization: Sheng Hsuan-huai (1844–1916) and Mandarin Enterprise* (1958); John Rawlinson, *China's Struggle for Naval Development, 1839–1895* (1967); Hao Yen-p'ing, *The Commercial Revolution in Nineteenth Century China* (1986); R. Bin Wong, *China Transformed: Historical Change and the Limits of European Experience* (1997); D. R. Howland, *Borders of Chinese Civilization: Geography and History at Empire's End* (1996); Ian Nish, *Japanese Foreign Policy, 1869–1942* (1977); Albert Craig, *Choshu in the Meiji Restoration* (1961); W.G. Beasley, *The Meiji Restoration* (1973); Marius B. Jansen and Gilbert Rozman (eds.), *Japan in Transition: From Tokugawa to Meiji* (1986); Roger Hackett, *Yamagata Aritomo in the Rise of Modern Japan, 1838–1922*, (1971); W. G. Beasley, *Japanese Imperialism, 1894–1945* (1987); Paul A. Cohen, *History in Three Keys: The Boxers as Event, Experience, and Myth* (1997); Shumpei Okamoto, *The Japanese Oligarchy and the Russo-Japanese War* (1970).

Chapter Ten.

Ian Nish, *Japanese Foreign Policy, 1869–1942*; W. G. Beasley, *Japanese Imperialism, 1894–1945*; Peter Duus, et al., (eds), *The Japanese Informal Empire in China, 1895–1937* (1989); Ramon H. Myers and Mark R. Peattie, *The Japanese Colonial Empire, 1895–1945* (1984); Bruce Cumings, *Korea's Place in the Sun: A Modern History* (1997); Charles E. Neu, *An Uncertain Friendship: Theodore Roosevelt and Japan, 1906–1909* (1967); Michael H. Hunt, *The Making of a Special Relationship: The United States and China to 1914*; Michael H. Hunt, *Frontier Defense and the Open Door* (1973); Mary C. Wright (ed.), *China in Revolution, the First Phase* (1968); C. Martin Wilbur, *Sun Yat-sen, Frustrated Patriot* (1976); Ernest Young, *The Presidency of Yuan Shih-k'ai: Liberalism and Dictatorship in Early Republican China* (1977); Ch'i Hsi-sheng, *Warlord Politics in China, 1916–1928* (1976); Chow Tse-tsung, *The May Fourth Movement: Intellectual Revolution in Modern China* (1960); Arif Dirlik, *The Origins of Chinese Communism* (1989); Lloyd Eastman, *The Abortive Revolution: China under Nationalist rule, 1927–1937*

(1974); Akira Iriye, *After Imperialism: The Search for a New Order in the Far East* (1965); Dorothy Borg, *American Policy and the Chinese Revolution, 1925–1928* (1947).

Chapter Eleven.

James B. Crowley, *Japan's Quest for Autonomy: National Security and Foreign Policy, 1930–1938* (1966); Sadako Ogata, *Defiance in Manchuria: The Making of Japanese Foreign Policy, 1931–1932* (1964) W. G. Beasley, *Japanese Imperialism, 1894–1945*; Peter Duus, et.al., (eds), *The Japanese Informal Empire in China, 1895–1937*; Ramon H. Myers and Mark R. Peattie, *The Japanese Colonial Empire, 1895–1945*; William Kirby, *Germany and Republican China* (1984); John Hunter Boyle, *China and Japan at War, 1937–1945: The Politics of Collaboration* (1972); Benjamin Schwartz, *Chinese Communism and the Rise of Mao* (1958); John W. Garver, *Chinese-Soviet Relations 1937–1945: The Diplomacy of Chinese Nationalism* (1988); Bruce Cumings, *Korea's Place in the Sun*; Dorothy Borg, *The United States and the Far Eastern Crisis of 1933–1938* (1964); Dorothy Borg and Shumpei Okamoto (eds.), *Pearl Harbor as History* (1973): Waldo Heinrichs, *Threshhold of War* (1988); Xiaoyuan Liu, *A Partnership for Disorder: China, The United States, and their policies for the postwar disposition of the Japanese Empire, 1941–1945* (1996); Lloyd Eastman, *Seeds of Destruction: Nationalist China in War and Revolution, 1937–1949* (1984); Chalmers Johnson, *Peasant Nationalism and Communist Power: The Emergence of Revolutionary China, 1937–1945* (1962); Akira Iriye, *Power and Culture: The Japanese-American War, 1941–1945* (1981); John W. Dower, *War without Mercy: Race and Power in the Pacific War* (1986); Leon V. Sigal, *Fighting to a Finish: The Politics of War Termination in the United States and Japan, 1945* (1988).

Chapter Twelve.

Marc Gallicchio, *The Cold War Begins in Asia: American-East Asian Policy and the Fall of the Japanese Empire* (1988); John W. Dower, *Empire and Aftermath: Yoshida Shigeru and the Japanese Experience, 1878–1954* (1979); Michael Schaller, *The American Occupation of Japan: The Origins of the Cold War in Asia* (1985); Theodore Cohen, *Remaking Japan: The Occupation as New Deal* (1987); James Reardon Anderson, *Yenan and the Great Powers, 1944–1946* (1980); Odd Arne Westad, *Cold War and Revolution: Soviet-American Rivalry and the Origins of the Chinese Civil War* (1993); Suzanne Pepper, *Civil War in China: The Political Struggle, 1945–1949* (1978); Dorothy Borg and Waldo Heinrichs (eds.),

Uncertain Years: Chinese-American Relations, 1947–1950 (1980); Nancy Bernkopf Tucker, *Patterns in the Dust: Chinese-American Relations and the Recognition Controversy 1949–1950* (1983); Yonosuke Nagai and Akira Iriye (eds.) *The Origins of the Cold War in Asia* (1977); Carter J. Eckert, et. al. (eds.) *Korea Old and New: A History* (1990); Bruce Cumings, *The Origins of the Korean War*, 2 vols. (1981, 1990); William Stueck, *The Korean War: An International History* (1995); Sergei Goncharov, John W. Lewis, and Xue Litai, *Uncertain Partners: Stalin, Mao, and the Korean War* (1993); Chen Jian, *China's Road to the Korean War* (1994); David G. Marr, *Vietnamese Anti-Colonialism* (1971); Bernard Fall, *Street Without Joy* (1972); Gary R. Hess, *The United States Emergence as a Southeast Asian Power, 1940–1950* (1987); George McT. Kahin, *Intervention: How America Became Involved in Vietnam* (1986); Marilyn Blatt Young, *The Vietnam Wars, 1945–1990* (1991); Robert J. McMahon, *Colonialism and Cold War: The United States and the Struggle for Indonesian Independence* (1981); Nick Cullather, *Illusions of Influence: The Political Economy of United States-Philippine Relations, 1942–1960* (1994); Audrey R. Kahin and George McT. Kahin, *Subversion as Foreign Policy* (1995); Gordon Chang, *Friends and Enemies: The United States, China, and the Soviet Union, 1948–1972* (1990); Warren I. Cohen and Akira Iriye (eds.) *The Great Powers in East Asia, 1953–1960* (1990); Ralph N. Clough, *Island China* (1978); Nancy Bernkopf Tucker, *Taiwan, Hong Kong, and the United States, 1945–1992* (1994); Kenneth G. Lieberthal, *Sino-Soviet Conflict in the 1970s* (1978); Harry Harding, *A Fragile Relationship: The United States and China since 1972* (1992); James Mann, *About Face: A History of America's Curious Relationship with China, from Nixon to Clinton* (1999).

Chapter Thirteen.

Nakamura Takafusa, *Lectures on Modern Japanese Economic History, 1926–1994* (1994); Akira Iriye and Warren Cohen (eds.), *The United States and Japan in the Postwar World* (1989); Takashi Inoguchi and Daniel I. Okamoto (eds.) *The Political Economy of Japan: The Changing International Context* (1988); Stephen D. Cohen, *An Ocean Apart: Explaining Three Decades of U.S.-Japanese Trade Frictions* (1998); Ezra F. Vogel, *The Four Little Dragons: The Spread of Industrialization in East Asia* (1991); Steven M. Goldstein (ed.) *Minidragons: Fragile Economic Miracles in the Pacific* (1991); Jung-en Woo (Meredith Woo-Cumings), *Race to the Swift: State and Finance in the Industrialization of Korea* (1991); Meredith Woo-Cumings (Jung-en Woo) (ed.) *The Developmental State* (1999); David Joel Steinberg (ed.), *In Search of Southeast Asia*, 2nd ed. (1987); Peter G. Warr (ed.), *The Thai Economy in Transition* (1993); Richard

Baum (ed.), *China's Four Modernizations: The New Technological Revolution* (1980); Harry Harding, *China's Second Revolution: Reform after Mao* (1987).

Chapter Fourteen.

Timothy Brook, *Quelling the People: The Military Suppression of the Beijing Democracy Movement* (1992); Harry Harding, *A Fragile Relationship*; James Mann, *About Face*; Nicholas R. Lardy, *China in the World Economy* (1994); Warren I. Cohen, *America's Response to China*, 4th ed.; Nancy Bernkopf Tucker, *Taiwan, Hong Kong, and the United States, 1945–1992*; Tien Hung-mao, *The Great Transition* (1989); Ralph N. Clough, *Cooperation or Conflict in the Taiwan Strait?* (1999); Bruce Cumings, *Korea's Place in the Sun*; Don Oberdorfer, *The Two Koreas: A Contemporary History* (1997).

INDEX

Aceh, 184, 208, 210, 232–33, 320
Acheson, Dean, 380
Adams, Will, 198
Africa, 161
African slaves, 185
Agreed Framework, 463
agricultural reform, 442–43
Ainu, 99
Airlangga, 122
Alaungpaya, 235
Allen, Horace, 304
Allied Council, 372
Alperovitz, Gar, 370
American Asiatic Association, 292, 293
Amherst, Lord, 247, 248
An Lushan, 81–82, 84, 90–91
Angkor (state), 89, 123–24
Angkor Wat, 125
Annam, 158–59, 235, 238
Arabs, 62, 70, 72, 77, 80–81, 83, 95, 98, 114, 181
Arai Hakuseki, 228–29
Arakan (kingdom), 235, 236, 247, 248
Arigh Boke, 134–35
Armenians, 217
art, 11, 47, 71, 200, 481
Ashikaga shoguns, 168–72
Ashikaga Takauji, 168
Asia-Pacific Economic Cooperation Forum, 469
Asiatic Fleet (U.S.), 292, 311
Assam, 248

assimilation, 82; of Eastern Turks, 68; during Northern Wei, 44; during Qing dynasty, 226; and Southeast Asia, 205; during Zhou, 8; resistance to, 17, 31, 33, 102, 108
Association of South East Asian Nations, 436, 469–71
atomic bomb, 360, 370
Aung San, 353, 363, 401
Ayutthaya, 146, 173, 206, 210, 235, 236, 237

banking, 323–24
Banten, 206
Bao Dai, 353, 366
barbarians, 4, 8, 39, 110. See also assimilation; nomadic cultures
Barfield, Thomas, 21
Basic Agreement, 461
Basic Law, 467
Batavia, 206, 208–209, 232
Beckwith, Christopher I., 486
Biddle, James, 262
Bikini Atoll, 418–19
Black Death, 147
Bolshevik Revolution, 321–22, 328
Borobudur, 103
Borodin, Michael, 329, 331
Bose, Subhas Chandra, 356
Boxer War, 296–99, 310–11
boycott, 311–12
Brezhnev Doctrine, 410
Brezhnev, Leonid, 410

British East India Company, 204, 223, 234, 239, 245–48
bronze, 1, 3, 4, 11
bubonic plague, 147
Buddhism, 37, 46–47, 70, 84, 86, 97–98, 100–101, 120, 140, 480
Bugis, 232, 233, 234
bureaucracy, 16, 83
Burlingame, Anson, 275–76
Burma and Burmese, 210, 469, 472; and Britain, 247–48, 253–54; and China, 192, 221, 223; independence movement, 363, 401–402; isolation of, 435–36; and Japanese, 352, 353; nationalism in, 320; power of, 234–36; and Mongols, 145;
Burmese Independence Army, 353

Cairo Declaration, 383
Cambodia, 102–103, 235, 266, 394, 395, 402, 469, 473
Canton Commune, 332
Cao Cao, 40, 41
Carter, Jimmy, 463
Catholicism, 207, 278, 287, 480–81
Celebes, 396
Central Asia: conflict in, 93–94; during Han dynasty, 31, 38; during Ming dynasty, 155, 158, 179, 180; and Mongols, 146–47; during Qing dynasty, 217–18, 220–21; during Tang dynasty, 79–81. See also Western Regions
Central Intelligence Agency (U.S.), 400
ceramics, 214
chaebol, 426, 427, 464
Chaghadai Khanate, 132, 135, 146–47
Cham people, 64, 121–22, 123
Champa, 58, 86, 145, 173

Chan, Hok-lam, 155
Chang'an, 70, 95
Charles I, 187
Chenbao Island, 410
Chiang Kai-shek. See Jiang Jieshi
Chiengmai, 173, 235
China: beginnings of state, 1–4; disunity of, 41–43; expansion of, 16–17, 59–60; feudalism in, 8; issues in international relations of, 40–41; and Japan, 36, 51–52; and Korea, 17–18, 42, 387, 389; nationalism in, 310–18; Nationalist revolution in, 328–33; Republic established, 313; unification of, 16; at Washington Conference, 244–27. See also China, People's Republic of; China, Republic of; Chinese Communist Party; Guomindang; names of individual dynasties
China, People's Republic of: economic growth of, 441–44; established, 380; future of, 477–79; internal campaigns, 409–10; and Japan, 417–18; reform in, 440–51; and Soviet Union, 406, 408, 410–11; and Taiwan, 412; and Tibet, 408; and United States, 411–13, 422, 474–75. See also Korean War; Mao Zedong
China, Republic of, 313. See also Jiang Jieshi
Chinese Communist Party, 325, 327, 343; and Chinese Revolution, 377–80; and Guomindang, 330, 331–32, 339, 341; internal divisions in, 409–10. See also China, People's Republic of
Chinese Eastern Railroad, 335
Chinese Revolution, 376–82

Chinggis Khan, 128–30
Chongqing (Chungking), 345
Choshu han, 281
Choson (state), 18, 26
Christianity, 70, 185–86, 231, 481; and Japan, 195–96, 198–99; in Southeast Asia, 207–8. *See also* Catholicism; missionaries
Chu (state), 9–10
civil war, Chinese, 378–80
Cixi, 276, 286, 296, 297, 298–99
Clinton, Bill, 453
Clive, Robert, 240
Cloister Government, 119
Coen, Jan Pieterszoon, 209
coffee, 233
Cohong, 249, 252
coins, 120, 171
Cola, 121
Cold War, 362, 390–403. *See also* Korean War
collective security, 10
Comintern, 327, 328, 331
concessions, international, 291, 316
Confucius and Confucians, 9, 10, 28, 83, 84, 98
Congress of the Toilers of the Far East, 327
constitution, Japanese, 372
Creel, H. G., 11
Crimean War, 268
cuisine, 214, 481–82
cult of personality, 410
Cultural Revolution, 410
culture system, 269
Cushing, Caleb, 260, 261

Dai Viet, 123, 159
Dalai Lama, 219, 222, 408
Daoguang emperor, 249, 251, 253

de Gaulle, Charles, 365
decolonization, 362–67
democracy, 482–83
Democratic Progressive Party, 455, 457
demonstrations, 341–42, 451–52, 472
Deng Xiaoping, 442–43, 449–53, 456, 466
Dezong (emperor), 92
Diem, Ngo Dinh, 392–93
Dienbienphu, 391–92
disarmament, 324
dollar diplomacy, 309
Dong-san drums, 19
Dower, John, 374–75
Drake, Francis, 204
Duke Huan of Qi, 10
Dunhuang, 38–39
Dutch East India Company (VOC), 201–203, 208, 211, 230, 232–33, 236
Duus, Peter, 119

East India Squadron, 258, 259
Eastern Jin, 43–44
Eastern Zhou dynasty, 8–12
Eckert, Carter, 384
Eisenhower administration, 405, 417
Elements of International Law, 275
emigration, 278–79, 307, 403
emperor, concept of, 4
Empress Dowager. *See* Cixi
Esen, 165–66
Ever Victorious Army, 274
examination system, 83, 98, 140, 299
extraterritoriality, 253, 260–61, 267, 326, 327

Fairbank, John King, 151–52
Far Eastern Commission, 372
Feis, Herbert, 349

Ferghana, 22, 25
feudalism, 9
fifth modernization, 450
Five Power Treaty, 325
Flying Tigers, 347–48
Former Han Dynasty, 20–33
Four Power Treaty, 325
Fourteen Points, 321
France, 234, 239–40, 265–67, 286, 391–92
Franciscans, 187–88
Fu Jian, 43–44
Fujian, 191
Fujiwara clan, 84–85, 118–19
Funan, 55, 58

Gaozong (emperor), 72–74
garrisons, agricultural, 31
Gempei War, 120
Geneva Conference, 392
Gentlemen's Agreement, 308
George III, King, 246
Germany, 317–18, 341
globalization, 479–80
Goa, 202
Gong, Prince, 275–76
Gorbachev, Mikhail, 450–51
Go-Toba (emperor), 143
Grand Canal, 63
Grand Council, 221–22, 223
Great Britain: and China, 222–23; and Hong Kong, 465–66; in India, 239–41; and Japan, 198, 306–307, 310; and Qing dynasty, 242–43, 248–53, 255–56; and Southeast Asia, 246–48, 253–54, 256–57, 362–64; and White Man's Burden, 241–42; and World War II, 350. See also British East India Company
Great Leap Forward, 109

Great Wall, 12, 164
Greater East Asia Co-Prosperity Sphere, 351–58
Guan Zhong, 10
Guang Wudi, 33, 39
Guangdong, 20, 27
Guangxi, 20, 27, 180
Guangzhou (Canton), 36, 70, 91, 95, 191, 222, 248–49, 250, 255, 258
Guanyin, 47
Guifang people, 5
Guomindang, 314, 315, 327, 329–33; and civil war, 378–80; and Japan, 338–39; on Taiwan, 381–82, 405, 427–30, 455; post-World War II, 377
Gurkhas, 221, 223, 226

Hainan Island, 27, 180
Hall, D. G. E., 178
Hall, Kenneth, 55, 58, 174–75, 178
Han (state), 150
Han dynasty, 17; decline of, 31–33; establishment of, 19–21; frontier defense during, 29, 37–38; and Japan, 36; and Korea, 26–27, 32; economy of, 28–29; and South-east Asia, 27–28, 31; trade during, 25–26, 35–37; and tributary system, 25–26; and Xiongnu, 20–25, 31, 32. See also Later Han dynasty
Han Gaodi, 20–21
Han Woo-keun, 319
Han Wudi, 20, 21–22, 60
Harris, Townsend, 264
Hay, John, 293, 297–98
hegemon, 10
Heiji Monogatari, 119–20
Heiji Rising, 119–20
Heike Monogatari, 120

Hevia, James, 242
Hideyoshi Toyotomi, 186, 187–88, 192–94, 195–96
Hinduism, 480–81
Hindus, 86, 103
Hirado, 198
Hiroshima, 360
Ho Chi Minh, 321, 353, 362, 365, 391, 392–93
Hoi An, 206, 238
Hojo family, 143, 144
Hong Kong, 251, 430–32, 453–54, 465–68
Hongwu, 166–68
horses, 11
Hsu, Immanuel, 302
Hu Yaobang, 451
Hua Guofeng, 442
Huang Chao, 95–96
Huang Zunxian, 287
Huang, Ray, 193
Hua-Xia, 3
Hu-han-yeh, 24, 25
Huizong (emperor), 111
Hukbalahap. See Huks
Huks, 357, 366
human rights, 453
Hundred Days of Reform, 295–96
Hundred Flowers campaign, 409
Hungwu emperor, 148, 150

Ii Naosuke, 264
Imperial Japanese Army, 282, 306, 307
Imperial Japanese Navy, 282, 372–73
Imperial Maritime Customs Service, 294
India, 34, 55, 71, 239–40, 248, 408
Indian National Army, 356
Indochina, 348, 364–66

Indonesia: independence movement, 395–99; Islam in, 208; Japanese in, 348, 357; recent events in, 436–38. See also Java; Sukarno; Sumatra
Indonesian Communist Party (PKI), 395, 397, 399
Inner Mongolia, 24
Inspectorate of Customs, 274
intellectuals, 10
International Atomic Energy Agency, 461, 463
International Monetary Fund, 465, 471, 473
international system, 2, 10, 17, 85
Iriye, Akira, 253, 360
Iron and salt debates, 28–29, 64
Iron monopoly, 28
Ishii Kikujiro, 322–33
Ishii-Lansing agreement, 323
Iskandar Shah, 178
Islam, 178, 207, 480–81
Ito Hirabumi, 288, 300, 304
Iwakura, Prince, 282, 283, 284

Jagchid, Sechin, 128
Japan That Can Say No, The, 446
Japan: Ashikaga period, 168–72; and British, 306–307; and Dutch, 230–31; early history of, 51–54; economy of, 444–47; expansionism of, 304–10, 316–18, 339–42; future of, 478; and Han dynasty, 36; Heian period, 99–101; and Jiang Jieshi, 332–33; Jomon culture, 18, 52; and Korea, 51–54, 196, 199–200, 283, 287, 304–305; and Korean War, 389–90; in Manchuria, 338–40; Meiji Restoration, 280–84, 286–87; military in, 282;

Japan (*Continued*)
and Ming dynasty, 152, 153, 160, 213; and Mongols, 142–45; occupation of, 361, 372–76; opening of, 261–64; and PRC, 417–18; and Portuguese, 185–86; postwar importance of, 415–24; and Republic of China, 313; and Russians, 229, 284, 299–301, 306; and Soviet Union, 343, 376, 418; and Spanish, 197–98; and Sui dynasty, 65; and Tang dynasty, 84–86; in tenth-twelfth centuries, 118–21, 127; Tokugawa period, 227–31; unification of, 52–54, 194–200; and United States, 306–10, 418–23; in World War II, 344–50, 358–62; Yayoi culture, 18, 51–52. *See also* Greater East Asia Co-Prosperity Sphere
Java, 86; and British, 246; and Dutch, 232–33, 269; early history of, 103; Majapahit empire, 174; Mataram empire, 232, 233; and Mongols, 246; in World War II, 356
Jayavarman II, 102
Jayavarman VII, 125
Jesuits, 186, 188, 207–8, 219
Jews, 62, 114, 183–84
Jiang Jieshi (Chiang Kai-shek), 329–33, 341–43, 359, 376–80, 389, 404–405, 412, 454
Jiang Jingguo, 454–55, 456, 456
Jiang Qing, 410, 411, 412
Jiaqing emperor, 190, 192
Jin (Jurchen state), 116–17, 126, 128–29
Jin (people), 112, 114
Jin (state), 10
Jin dynasty, 43
Jin Wudi, 43

Jinmen, 405, 406
Johnston, Iain, 11
Joint Declaration on the Denuclearization of the Korean Peninsula, 460–62
Jordan, Michael, 479
Judaism, 481
Jurchen people, 112, 116, 159, 211–12

Kamakura bakufu, 120, 143–44, 168
Kammu, Emperor, 100
Kang Youwei, 295–96
Kangxi emperor, 218–19
Karakhan manifesto, 328
Karashahr, 32
Karen people, 401
Kawazoe Shoji, 170
Kaya (federation), 52, 54
Keightley, David, 4
kempeitai, 353, 356, 357, 373
Kennan, George, 375
Kennedy administration, 398
Kertanagara, 146
Khaidu, 146–47
Khitan people, 64, 76, 78, 81, 107, 108, 110, 115–16
Khmer people, 86, 102, 123, 125, 173, 237, 394, 395, 402
Khrushchev, Nikita, 408–409
Khubilai Khan, 131–47
Kim Dae Jung, 459, 462, 465
Kim Il Sung, 383–86, 413, 460–61, 463, 464
Kim Young Sam, 459, 463
Kipchak Khanate, 132, 135
Kirghiz peoples, 94
Koguryo, 27, 32, 38, 42, 48, 50; and Japan, 53; Later, 99; and Sui Dynasty, 63, 66; Tang Dynasty, 67, 69–70, 72, 73, 82

Kokonor, 32
Konoe Fumimaro, 349
Korea, Democratic People's Republic of, 384, 462–63
Korea, Republic of, 384, 424–27
Korea: early relations with China, 17–18; French in, 266–67; and Han dynasty, 26–27, 32; and Japan, 51–54, 199–200, 283, 287, 304–305; and Ming dynasty, 159–60, 166–68, 213; and Mongols, 130; nationalism in, 318–20; political organization of, 18; post-World War II, 361–62, 382; and Qing dynasty, 287–90; recent events in, 459–65; Republic established, 319, 384; and Russians, 231, 288, 320; and Sui dynasty, 63; and Tang dynasty, 73, 82–84; in Three Kingdoms era, 48–51; unified, 99. See also Korean War; names of individual dynasties
Korean Communist Party, 320
Korean Peninsula Energy Development Organization, 464
Korean People's Republic, 361
Korean War, 383–90
Korean Youth Army School, 319
Koryo, 99, 114–18, 131, 141–42
Kotoku, Emperor, 85
kowtow, 243, 276
Koxinga (Zheng Chenggung), 212
Kwantung Army, 339–40, 342

Labour Party (British), 363
Lansing, Robert, 322–23
Laos, 395, 469, 473
Laozi, 13, 15
Later Han Dynasty, 33–41
Le Loi, 159
League of Nations, 339, 340, 345

Lee, Ki-baik, 98
Lee Kuan Yew, 433
Lee Teng-hui, 455, 457, 459
Lee, Sherman, 4, 200
Legislative Council (Hong Kong), 467–68
lend-lease, 348
Lenin, V. I., 322, 327
Leopold, Richard, 293
Li Hongzhang, 274, 275, 285–86, 288–90, 291
Li people, 180
Li Yuan, 66
Liao (state), 107, 110, 112, 126
Liaodong Peninsula, 290
Lin Zexu, 249
Lingdi, Emperor, 40
Linyi. See Champa
literature, Chinese, 47
little dragons, 424–35
Liu Bang, 20
Liu Yue, 44
lost-wax technique, 1, 11
Luolang (commandery), 27
Ly Dynasty, 123
Ly Phat Ma, 123

Macao, 185, 454
MacArthur, Douglas, 372–75, 386
Macartney, Lord George, 242–43
Magellan, Ferdinand, 187
Magsaysay, Ramon, 400
Mahan, Alfred Thayer, 293
Majapahit (kingdom), 86–87, 174, 207
Malaya and Malays, 55, 58, 86, 356, 363–54
Malaysia, 398–99, 433, 438–40, 472, 473
Maluku, 174, 202, 203, 204
Man people, 35, 39

Manchukuo, 340

Manchuria, 289, 306, 309–10, 333, 335, 337–40

Manchus. See Qing dynasty

mandate of heaven, 5

Manila, 206

Mao Zedong, 379–82, 385, 386, 389, 397, 06, 409–10, 412, 442

Maodun, 17, 20, 21

Marcos, Ferdinand, 400, 436

Marshall, General George C., 379

Matsuoka Yosuke, 348, 349

Max Havelaar, 269

May 30th Movement, 330

May Fourth movement, 318

Mazu, 405

McNeill, William, 245

Meiji Restoration, 280–84

Melaka, 161, 174, 175, 178, 182, 184, 190, 201–202, 233, 234, 246

Mencius, 13, 15

metallurgy, 51

Miao people, 180, 192, 220

Michinaga, 118–19

Middle Ground, 24

military technology, 274–75

Minamoto family, 119–20

Ming dynasty: and Central Asia, 155, 158, 179–80; decline of, 189–94; and Japan, 153, 159, 192–94; and Koreans, 159–60, 167; and Mongols, 154–55, 164–66, 180, 190, 192; naval expeditions, 160–61; and Portuguese, 180–81; rise of, 150–66; and trade, 164; and tribute system, 151–52, 159–61; and Vietnam, 158–59

Mischief Reef, 470

missionaries: American, 259, 260; in Japan, 197–98, 262; in Korea, 319;

in Philippines, 187–89; privileges in China, 277–78; in Vietnam, 238. See also Jesuits

Mongke, 133–34

Mongols: Asian resistance to, 141–47; expansion of, 131, 140–41; and Jin, 128–29; and Koreans, 117–18; and Ming dynasty, 152, 154–55, 165–66, 180, 190, 192; navy, 136; and Qing dynasty, 217; reasons for success, 129, 130–31; rise of, 132–35; and Song dynasty, 134–35, 136–37; and succession issues, 135; Yuan dynasty, 140–47

Moros, 320–21

most-favored nation status, 252–53, 267, 453

Mote, Frederick, 180

Mozi, 13

Myanmar. See Burma

Nagasaki, 360

Nanjing, 344

Nanjing incident, 331–32, 333

Nanyue, 20

Nanzhao (state), 81, 86, 89, 90–91, 93, 94–95, 125, 131; attacked by Mongols, 133

Napier, Lord, 248–49

Nara, 85

Narai, King, 236–37

Nasution, General Abdul Haris, 397

national salvation movement, 342

nationalism, 304–305, 310–22, 479

Nationalist Revolution, 328–33

Ne Win, 353, 401–402

Nepal, 221, 223, 226

Netherlands: and Chinese, 206; and decolonization, 364–65, 398; dominance of, 208–209; establishes

trade, 201–203; and Japan, 198, 199, 230–31; and Java, 232–33, 269, 271. *See also* Dutch East India Company (VOC)
New Economic Plan, 439
Nguyen, 238–39
Nian rebellion, 253, 274
Nine Power Treaty, 326
Nixon, Richard, 394–95, 412, 422
nomads, 11, 60–61, 63. *See also* barbarians; Xianbi; Xiongnu
Northern Expedition, 331
Northern Wei dynasty, 44–45, 46–47
Northern Zhou (state), 45
Nuclear Nonproliferation Treaty, 461–62
nuclear weapons, 418–19, 461, 463–64
Nurhaci, 212

occupation, Japanese, 372–76
Oda Nobunaga, 194–95
Ogodei Khan, 130–31
oil, 438, 440
Okinawa, 41–22
Onin War, 168
Open Door, 294, 306, 307, 309, 325–26
Opium War, 251–52, 259, 267
opium, 211, 220, 221, 241, 249–52
oracle bones, 2, 3, 4, 5
Outer Mongolia, 24, 314
Overseas Chinese, 206–207, 437, 439

Paekche (kingdom), 48, 50, 53, 54, 63, 73, 82; Later, 99
Pagan, 125, 145
Palmerston, Lord, 249–52
Paramesvara (Iskandar Shah), 175, 178
Parhae, 78–79, 83–84, 99, 115

Park Chung Hee, 424–27
Parker, Peter, 253, 260
Parthians, 36, 37
Pathet Lao, 395
Patten, Christopher, 467
Pearl Harbor, 350
Pei Zhu, 64, 65
Penang, 246
Penghus, 405
People's Liberation Army, 410, 411
Pepper, 71, 174, 479
Perry, Matthew, 263
Persia Khanate, 132, 135
Persians, 62, 70–72, 114
Phaulkon, Constance (Constantine Hierarchy), 206, 236–37
Philip II, 187
Philippines, 187–89, 191–92, 207, 292–93, 320–21, 426, 473; independence of, 366, 367; U.S. influence in, 399–400; in World War II, 356–57
Phnom Penh, 206
piracy, 120–21, 143, 169, 172, 184, 191, 201, 232
Polo, Marco, 174
porcelain, 114, 126
Portuguese: enter China, 180–81, 185, 190; and Dutch, 202; and Japan, 185–86, 198; missionaries, 207; reasons for success, 183–84
Potsdam declaration, 359–60
Prambanan, 103
Provisional Legislative Council (Hong Kong), 467
Prussia, 275
Puyo people, 48

Qiang (Tibetans), 35, 39, 41, 43–44
Qianlong emperor, 221–22, 226, 238, 246

Qin (state), 9, 12, 15–16, 18, 19
Qing dynasty: border problems during, 217–22, 223, 226; and British, 242–43; emigration during, 278–79; end of, 313; established, 212–13; and European concessions, 290–91; and Japan, 227; and missionaries, 219, 277–78; and opium, 22, 241; rebellions during, 273–74; self-strengthening movement, 275–76, 279–80, 285–86, 290; trade during, 216–17, 222–23, 240–41, 276; and treaty system, 276–77
Qing people, 5
Qinshi Huangdi, 12, 16–17

racism, 311
Raffles, Sir Thomas, 268–69
railroads, 310, 312, 313
Rama I, King, 237
Rama IV, King, 257
Rape of Nanjing, 344
Reagan, Ronald, 456
Reid, Anthony, 208
Rhee, Syngman, 384–85, 425
Ricci, Matteo, 185, 211
rice, 51
rights recovery movement, 312, 313
Roh Tae Woo, 459–60, 464
Roman Empire, 36
Romance of the Three Kingdoms, 41
Rong people, 8, 12
Roosevelt, Franklin D., 340, 345, 346, 359, 361, 362
Roosevelt, Theodore, 293, 301, 304, 307–308, 311
Root, Elihu, 308, 309
Root-Takahira agreement, 308, 309
Rossabi, Morris, 136
Russia, 217–18, 220–21, 229, 267–68,

288, 299–301; Bolshevik Revolution, 321–22, 328; and China, 314; and Japan, 306. See also Soviet Union
Russian-American Company, 267
Russo-Japanese War, 300–301, 304
Ryukyu Islands, 172–73, 196, 227–28, 230, 283

salt monopoly, 28
samurai, 282–84
Sanguozhi yanyi, 42
Sapir, Edward, 82
Sato Eisaku, 422
Satsuma han, 281
Satsuma rebellion, 284
Schafer, Edward, 70
sculpture, 47, 71
seclusion policy, 228
security treaty, 410
Sejong, 167
self-strengthening movement, 275, 279–80, 285–86, 290
Sesshu, 171
Seven Years War, 240
Shan people, 153
Shandong, 317–18, 333
Shang dynasty, 3–5
Shang Yang, 15, 16
Shanghai, 329–30, 339
Shanghai Communique, 456
Shintoism, 101, 373
shipbuilding, 169, 286, 308, 324
Shu Han (kingdom), 41, 42
Siam, 234, 236–37, 247, 256–57, 259, 321
silk, 11, 36, 58
Silk Road, 36
Silla (kingdom), 50, 53, 54, 69, 73, 78, 82, 97–99

silver, 187, 205, 212, 241

Singapore, 246, 356, 363–64, 402, 432–35

Sino-British Joint Declaration, 466

Six Dynasties, 45–46

Soga clan, 54

Song dynasty, 89, 107–14, 129, 130–31, 134–37

Song Taizong, 107–108

South Manchuria Railroad, 310

Southeast Asia: early history of, 54–59; and Cold War, 390–403; decolonization in, 362–67; European interest in, 204–11; and Ming dynasty, 173–78; and Mongols, 145–46; nationalism in, 320–21; recent events in, 435–41, 468–74; relations with China, 18–19; in seventh and eighth centuries, 86–87, 101–106; in tenth and eleventh centuries, 121–23, 125, 127; and tribute system, 152; in World War II, 348–49. *See also individual countries*

Southeast Asian Treaty Organization (SEATO), 392, 400, 405

Soviet Union: and Chinese Communists, 377–80, 410–11; and Germany, 346–47; and Indonesia, 364; and Japan, 359, 360–61, 418; and PRC, 406, 408. *See also* Russia

Spain, 187–89, 191, 197–98, 376

Spence, Jonathan, 219

spice trade, 103, 174–75, 182. 205, 205, 211, 479

Spratlys, 470

Spring and Autumn period, 9–11

Srivijaya (kingdom), 86, 103, 106, 121, 122

Stalin, Josef, 370, 380–82, 385, 386, 391

Stilwell, General Joseph, 359

Stimson, Henry, 340

students, 83, 472

Suharto, General, 399, 472

Sui dynasty, 62–66

Sui Wendi, 62–64

Sui Yangdi, 64–65

Sukarno, 362, 364, 395–99, 437

Sukothai, 173

Sulawesi, 207

Sumatra, 86, 121, 208, 395–96; British in, 246; and China, 174–75; Islam in, 178; and Mongols, 146; in World War II, 356. *See also* Aceh

Sun Wu (Sun Zi), 10, 11

Sun Yat-sen, 296, 312–13, 324–25, 328–29

Sun Zi, 10, 11

Sun Zi's Art of War, 11

Supreme Commander Allied Powers (SCAP), 372, 373–75

Suryavarman, 125

T'aejo, King, 115, 167

Taewon'gun, 287

Taft, William Howard, 309

Tai people, 122, 125, 145–46

Taiping Rebellion, 253, 255, 274

Taira Kiyomori, 119, 120

Taiwan, 65, 202, 203, 212, 473; and Cold War, 411–12; democratization of, 454–57, 459; economic growth of, 427–30; and Japan, 417, 418; Jiang's regime on, 380, 381–82; and PRC, 404–405, 455–57, 459; during Qing dynasty, 216–17, 219, 220, 283–84

Taiwan Relations Act, 456

Taiwan Strait, 404–405, 457

Taizong (emperor), 67–70

Takahira Kogoro, 308, 309

Tang dynasty: and Arabs, 80–81; early years of, 66–67; contact with other cultures, 70–72; decline of, 81–82, 89, 90, 94–97; expansionism of, 68–70; and frontier defense, 77–78; influence of, 87–88; and Japan, 84–86; and Korea, 67, 69–70, 72, 73, 82–84; problems of empire, 74–76; and Tibet, 73–74, 76, 77, 79–81, 92–94; and Turks, 75–76

Tang Gaozu, 66–67

Tang Xianzong, 94

Tangut people, 110

Tanuma Okitsugu, 229

Taoism, 70–71

Tarim Basin, 73–74, 75, 94, 217

Tayson rebels, 238

tea, 232, 240–41

Temujin (Chinggis Khan), 128–30

Terranova (sailor), 261

Tet offensive, 393–94

textiles, 421–22

Thai people, 86

Thailand, 352, 353, 366–67, 400–401, 440–41, 471. See also Siam

Thang-long, 238

Three Dynasties, 2

Three Kingdoms, 41–43

Tiananmen, 451–52, 457, 466–67

Tianjin massacre, 277–78

Tibet and Tibetans: and Ming dynasty, 152; and Mongols, 148; and PRC, 408; during Qing dynasty, 219, 220, 221–22; during Song dynasty, 111; during Sui dynasty, 65; during Tang dynasty, 67, 68–69, 73–74, 75, 76, 77, 79–81, 92–94. See also Qiang

Timur (Tamerlane), 155, 158

Tojo, General Hideki, 358

Tokugawa Ieyasu, 196–98

Tokugawa shogunate, 227–31, 280

Tongking, 238

trade, 480; and British, 239, 240–42, 246–47; and Europeans, 189; and Funan, 55, 58; during Han dynasty, 25–26; Japanese, 120–21, 143, 168, 169–71, 227–29, 230–31, 420–21, 444–47; Korean, 168, 228, 231–32; during Ming dynasty, 164, 190–91; and Portuguese, 184–85; during Qing dynasty, 222; and Russians, 229–30 during Shang, 4; during Song dynasty, 111, 114; in Southeast Asia, 19, 55, 58, 103, 122–23, 125, 210–11, 232–33, 234, 238, 239; during Spring and Autumn period, 11; during Tang dynasty, 83, 85, 87, 98; and tributary system, 35; during Yuan dynasty, 141. See also British East India Company; Dutch East India Company

Tran Dynasty, 123

Treaty of Aigun, 268

Treaty of Kanagawa, 263

Treaty of Nanjing, 252

Treaty of Nerchnisk, 218

Treaty of Portsmouth, 301

Treaty of Sargasso, 187

Treaty of Shimonoseki, 290, 295

Treaty of Tianjin, 255–56

treaty system, 251–52, 255–56, 260, 267, 276–77

tributary system: beginnings of, 4, 25–26, 60; and Japan, 53, 170–71; and Korea, 110, 167; during Ming, 151–52, 155, 159–60, 167; and trade, 35; and Vietnam, 55, 110

Trinh, 238

Tripartite Pact, 347

Trocki, Carl, 320

Truman, Harry S, 359–60, 370, 391–92, 428

Tu Yuehun, 65

Tuoba people, 44, 63

Turfan, 190

Turks, 63, 64–65; Eastern, 67, 68, 75–76; Northern, 75; Western, 68, 72, 75, 76, 96

twenty-one demands, 316–18

two Chinas, 456

Uncle Tom's Cabin, 311

united front, 342

United Nations, 364, 386, 399, 475

United States: and Japan, 261–64, 322–24, 348, 349. 372–76, 418–23; and Korea, 264, 385–90; and Philippines, 292–93; and postwar China, 378–81; and PRC, 443, 453, 474–75; and Qing dynasty, 253, 258–62, 293–94, 297–98; and Vietnam, 392–95; at Washington Conference, 324–27; in World War II, 347–49

United States Navy, 308, 324

universal kingship, 15, 226

universal state, 5, 12

Uyghurs, 91, 93, 94, 155

Versailles peace conference, 317–18

Viet Minh, 353, 365, 391–92

Vietnam, 55, 86, 121, 443, 473; and decolonization, 365–66; French in, 265–66, 286, 365–66; and Han dynasty, 26, 27, 33; and Ming dynasty, 173; and Mongols, 145; nationalism in, 320; post-World War II, 391–92; and Qing dynasty, 223, 238–39; rebellion in, 94–95; during Tang dynasty, 64, 101–102; and trade, 55, 122–23; unrest in, 234–35, 237–38; war in, 393–95, 421; and World War II, 352–53

Vietnam, North, 436

Vijaya, 174

VOC. See Dutch East India Company

Wa people, 48

Wang Gungwu, 110

Wang Jingwei, 347

Wang Mang, 20–33, 31–33

Wanli emperor, 211

War of the Austrian Succession, 240

warlords, 315

Warr, Peter, 441

Warring States period, 11–16

Washington Conference, 324–27

Wechsler, Howard, 68

Wei (kingdom), 41–43

Wei dynasty, 52

Wei Man (Wiman), 26

West Irian, 396, 398

Western Regions, 22, 25, 30, 32, 33; challenges in, 38–39; trade with, 35. See also Central Asia

Western Zhou dynasty, 5, 8

Whampoa Academy, 329

White Lotus rebellion, 253

White Man's Burden, 241

White Terror, 332

White, Richard, 24

Wilson, Woodrow, 314–15, 317, 319, 322

Witte, Count Sergei, 300

women, 208

World War I, 317

World War II, 344–50, 358–62
Wright, Arthur, 65
Wu (kingdom), 41, 42
Wu (state), 150
Wu Yue (state), 107
Wu Zhao. *See* Wu, Empress
Wu, Empress, 74–76
Wuhuan people, 34, 35, 38, 39

Xavier, Francis, 185
Xia dynasty (Tanguts), 110
Xia, 3
Xianbi people, 34, 35, 38, 39, 41,
    43–44, 48, 60–61
Xiao Wendi, 44–45
Xiao Yan, 44
Xinjiang, 222
Xiongnu, 11, 12, 17, 32, 33, 35, 42, 43–
    44; and Han Dynasty, 20–25, 60–
    61
Xizong (emperor), 95–96
Xuan Zang, 70
Xuanzong (emperor), 77–81, 80

Yalta, 359, 361
Yamagata Aritomo, 282, 284, 300
Yamato (state), 52–54
Yang Guifei, 81, 82, 90
Yang Jian (Sui Wendi), 62–64
Yang Qian, 45
Yao people, 180
Yellow Turban rebellion, 40
Yen (kingdom), 17–18, 42
Yi dynasty, 159–60, 167–68
Yi Song-gye, 167
Yi Sunsin, Admiral, 200

yi yi zhi yi, 39
Yizing, 103
Yo Un-hyong, 384, 361
Yongle emperor, 153–55, 158–61
Yongzheng emperor, 220–21
Yoritomo, 120, 143
Yoshida Shigeru, 374–75, 416–17, 418
Yoshimitsu, 159, 170
Yoshimune (shogun), 229
Yu Ying-shih, 25
Yuan dynasty, 140–47
Yuan Shikai, 288, 296, 318
Yung Wing, 275
Yunnan, 27, 31, 153

zaibatsu, 374
Zeng Guofan, 274–75
Zhang Boha, 98
Zhang Qian, 22–108
Zhang Xueliang, 333, 335, 342, 343
Zhang Zuolin, 330, 333
Zheng Chenggung (Koxinga), 212
Zheng He (voyages), 160, 161,
    162–65, 174, 178, 477
Zhenla, 102
Zhou dynasty, 5, 8–12; Later, 197
Zhou Enlai, 380, 412
Zhu Wen, 96
Zhu Yuanzhang (Hungwu
    emperor), 148, 150
Zhukov, Georgi, 345
Zongli Yamen, 275
zoo, 4
Zunghar confederation, 218–19, 220,
    221, 222
Zuo Zongtang, 274